V. T. Mitchell
1975

Louis Morton, *General Editor*
DARTMOUTH COLLEGE

VOLUMES PUBLISHED

HISTORY OF THE UNITED STATES ARMY
Russell F. Weigley
TEMPLE UNIVERSITY

FRONTIERSMEN IN BLUE
The United States Army and the Indian, 1848–1865
Robert M. Utley
NATIONAL PARK SERVICE

PRESIDENT WILSON FIGHTS HIS WAR
World War I and the American Intervention
Harvey A. DeWeerd
THE RAND CORPORATION

THE SWORD OF THE REPUBLIC
The United States Army on the Frontier, 1783–1846
Francis Paul Prucha
MARQUETTE UNIVERSITY

BLOOD ON THE BORDER
The United States Army and the Mexican Irregulars
Clarence C. Clendenen
HOOVER INSTITUTION ON WAR, REVOLUTION, AND PEACE

THE WAR OF AMERICAN INDEPENDENCE
Military Attitudes, Policies, and Practice, 1763–1789
Don Higginbotham
UNIVERSITY OF NORTH CAROLINA

VOLUMES IN PREPARATION

THE COLONIAL WARS
Douglas E. Leach
VANDERBILT UNIVERSITY

THE WAR OF 1812
R. A. Preston
ROYAL MILITARY COLLEGE OF CANADA
S. F. Wise
QUEENS UNIVERSITY (CANADA)

THE INDIAN WARS 1865–1890
Robert M. Utley
NATIONAL PARK SERVICE

THE MEXICAN WAR
K. J. Bauer
RENSSELAER POLYTECHNIC INSTITUTE

THE CIVIL WAR
Jay Luvaas
ALLEGHENY COLLEGE

WORLD WAR II (PACIFIC)
Louis Morton
DARTMOUTH COLLEGE

HISTORY OF AMERICAN MILITARY DOCTRINE
Fred Greene
WILLIAMS COLLEGE

HISTORY OF THE UNITED STATES AIR FORCE
Alfred F. Hurley
UNITED STATES AIR FORCE ACADEMY

AMERICAN MILITARY INTERVENTION
Annette Baker Fox
INSTITUTE OF WAR AND PEACE STUDIES, COLUMBIA UNIVERSITY

HISTORY OF THE UNITED STATES NAVY
Raymond G. O'Connor
TEMPLE UNIVERSITY

THE SPANISH–AMERICAN WAR
J. A. S. Grenville
UNIVERSITY OF LEEDS

David Trask
STATE UNIVERSITY OF NEW YORK (STONY BROOK)

WORLD WAR II (EUROPE AND AFRICA)
Hugh M. Cole
RESEARCH ANALYSIS CORPORATION

THE KOREAN WAR
Martin Blumenson

# The War of American Independence

# THE WAR
# OF AMERICAN
# INDEPENDENCE

*Military Attitudes, Policies, and*
*Practice, 1763-1789*

❧ ☆ ❧

Don Higginbotham

*The Macmillan Company, New York, New York*

*Collier-Macmillan Ltd., London*

*The Macmillan Company*
*866 Third Avenue, New York, N.Y. 10022*
*Collier-Macmillan Canada Ltd., Toronto, Ontario*

Library of Congress Catalog Card Number: 74-132454

FIRST PRINTING

Printed in the United States of America

# Contents

|  |  |  |
|---|---|---|
| | PREFACE | XV |
| *1.* | *The Colonial Tradition* | I |
| *2.* | *The Military Origins of the Revolution* | 29 |
| *3.* | *Militia versus Regulars* | 57 |
| *4.* | *Congress Takes the Helm* | 81 |
| *5.* | *Boston Gained, Canada Lost, Independence Proclaimed* | 98 |
| *6.* | *Britain at War* | 122 |
| *7.* | *Campaign of 1776* | 148 |
| *8.* | *Campaign of 1777* | 175 |
| *9.* | *Civil–Military Tensions, 1777-1778* | 204 |
| *10.* | *The International Conflict* | 226 |
| *11.* | *Loyalties and Liberties* | 257 |
| *12.* | *The Economic Front* | 288 |
| *13.* | *War on the Frontiers: The West and the High Seas* | 319 |
| *14.* | *Defeat and Victory in the South* | 352 |

*15.   The Continental Army*                                              389

*16.   The Revolutionary Impact: Europe*                                  420

*17.   The Revolutionary Impact: America*                                 438

    BIBLIOGRAPHICAL ESSAY                                                 469

    INDEX                                                                 493

# Maps

British North America following the Seven Years' War      32

Boston, Lexington, and Concord      60

The Northern Campaigns      109

New York City, New Jersey, Pennsylvania Operations      156

New York      157

The War on the Western Frontier      326

The West Indies after 1763      333

The Western European Theater      343

The Southern Campaigns      358

# *Preface*

THIS BOOK IS an attempt to trace the military history of the American people during the era of the American Revolution, 1763–1789. It is more an effort to examine military policy and attitudes toward war than it is an exercise in battles and campaigns. By enlarging upon the traditional dates of the War of Independence (1775–1783), I have sought, additionally, to examine the causes and the consequences of the Revolution as they relate to things military. I have tried to keep in mind the idea that armies are but projections of the societies from which they spring, as well as the notion that the interaction between warfare and society produces significant effects upon both civil and military institutions of a country. Although I have not been unmindful of the British side of the story and of the international aspects of the struggle for independence, this is a book that concentrates on American history. The United States was born in war rather than in peace, a fact that has profoundly influenced our later history.

My thanks are due, first, to my family. My wife, Mary Lou, displayed a sympathetic ear and a firm will that kept me in my study when I might otherwise have spent more time with her. My children— Lea, Larry, Robbie, David, and Jimmy—all showed an interest in my project, just as they insisted that their names be mentioned here. My father and mother have been an unfailing source of inspiration to me in this undertaking as well as in other ways. I am indebted to my previous academic institution, Louisiana State University, for various forms of assistance; Dean Max Goodrich of the Graduate School and John L. Loos, chairman of the Department of History, were most helpful. My former mentor, John R. Alden, generously read the manuscript and saved me from embarrassing errors. A number of other friends read one or more chapters: Douglas E. Leach, George F. Scheer, E. James Ferguson, William S. Price, James Edmonson, David Griffiths, and James Leutze—to all of them I am grateful. Finally, I express my appreciation to Mrs. George F. Scheer, an excellent critic and typist; and to Ira D. Gruber, who kindly allowed me to read his unpublished study of the Howe brothers.

*Chapel Hill, N.C.*                                                    DON HIGGINBOTHAM

*The War of American Independence*

# 1. The Colonial Tradition

THE AMERICAN REVOLUTION was an upheaval of profound significance. It was a peoples' war for political independence, the first
successful struggle to sever an imperial relationship in modern
times. In one way or another it helped shake human society to its very
foundations—first in Europe, then in Latin America, and eventually in
Africa and Asia, where the impact continues even today. In America the
Revolution produced new social and intellectual currents that have in
some cases still to run their course. Yet, cast against the background of
the American colonial experience, the Revolution was a manifestation of
continuity as well as change. As wise old John Adams liked to point
out, Americans fought to maintain cherished ideals and institutions
rooted in a century and a half of British-American history. Moreover,
they fought largely within a military framework that had already become a living tradition.

From the earliest settlements, military considerations were important in the lives of colonial Americans. Confronted by hostile Indians,
in addition to French, Dutch, and Spanish colonial rivals in a wilderness three thousand miles away, the colonists were ever mindful of the
need to protect themselves. Just as the British Crown offered little more
to colony-founders than company charters and proprietorial grants, so
it originally expected the settlers to defend themselves. As the charter
of Massachusetts Bay made clear, the inhabitants alone were "to in-
counter, expulse, repell and resist by force of armes, as well by sea as
by lands" any attempt to invade or destroy their community.

## The Nature of American Warfare

The seventeenth and eighteenth centuries in Europe saw the growth of a vast body of military literature attempting to standardize methods of fighting and prescribe the boundaries of warfare. The library of the intellectually curious soldier or statesman might include volumes like Elton's *Compleat Body of the Art Military* (1650), de Crisse's *Essay on the Art of War* (1754), and Saxe's *Reveries* (1756), as well as Grotius' *On the Law of War and Peace* (1625–1631) and Vattel's *The Law of Nations* (1758). One of the triumphs of rationalism, with its emphasis upon a scientific approach to human problems, was in isolating and specializing the military's role in society. Historians therefore generally recognize the period of American colonial and Revolutionary history as coinciding with an Age of Limited Warfare in Europe.[1] Since armies were small and carefully trained and disciplined, the rules of warfare were well known. Generals preferred to engage an enemy on open, flat-surfaced ground. There they could properly arrange their bulky, close-order linear formations that so depended on synchronization of movement for success; there they could maneuver their machine-like battalions as though they were pawns on a chess board. Because of the reliance upon these intricate evolutions, a battle in the woods, an attack at night, or a campaign in winter was fraught with grave risks. Such wars were not pervasive; the populace often seemed scarcely aware of hostilities. "Never before or since," wrote Walter Dorn of the mid-eighteenth century, "save perhaps in Renaissance Italy, was the civilian population more secure against wanton devastation, atrocities and the systematic plunder of requisition warfare."[2] It is probable, as a recent writer claims, that in some ways European warfare was less rigid and stereotyped than is usually painted. The Old World had its flexible soldier, in the *chausseur* and the *jäger*, and its occasional forms of military obligation for those outside the ranks of the professional.[3] But in its broad hues the traditional canvas of eighteenth-century conflict is faithful to the facts.

Although Revolutionary histories frequently leave the impression that Nathanael Greene and Henry Knox were the only Americans to have studied the "scholars" on warfare, a considerable number of Americans did read European military treatises.[4] In 1756 Colonel George Washington of the Virginia militia sent to England for Humphrey Bland's *Treatise of Military Discipline* (1727 and subsequent edns.), the classic British military manual of the day, a volume Washington strongly recommended to the officers of his Virginia Regiment. But for Washington and other provincial officers, the chief value of military manuals was to teach men order and discipline through rigorous, exacting drilling.

If the English colonies produced no formal body of military thought, they were well versed in their own military history. Accounts of war-fare in the New World filled many a pamphlet and bulked large in American histories written in the eighteenth century. Mary Rowland-son's stirring *Narrative of . . . Captivity* in King Philip's War, first printed in 1682, was republished three times between 1771 and 1773. Roughly a third of Jeremy Belknap's *History of New Hampshire* to 1763 is the story of skirmishes, raids, massacres, and battles, themes that are also underlined in Thomas Hutchinson's *History of Massachu-setts Bay*. Another form of expression was the training-day sermon or artillery sermon. Benjamin Wadsworth's *A Letter . . . Directed to Christian Soldiers Going Forth to War* (1709) literally bristled with Old Testament injunctions in support of a just war, as did countless orations from the pulpit during the American Revolution. Several generations of Americans saw themselves transformed into the Biblical David, while France (and later Britain) was Goliath incarnate.

Methods of warfare, like other aspects of an emerging American culture, were a composite of the Old World and the New. The setting and the adversary gave preponderance to one or the other. Undoubt-edly the most salient European inheritance in fighting the Indian was the white man's superior social organization, which enabled the colonials to act collectively. This was virtually impossible for the Indian war party, usually little more than a body of individual warriors attracted by the prestige of the chief. The colonials not infrequently added the Indians' own tactics—ambush, hit-and-run, mobile detach-ments, and personal marksmanship. On April 29, 1756, the *Maryland Gazette* reported that "Thomas and Daniel Cresap (Sons of Col Cresap) went out about three Weeks since, with sixty People, dressed and painted like Indians, to kill the Women and Children in the In-dian Towns, and scalp them, while their Warriors are committing the like Destruction on our Frontiers." "Come and help me fight the King's regular troops," Ethan Allen begged a group of Iroquois in 1775. "You know they stand all along close together, rank and file, and my men fight as Indians do."[5] Skillful as many provincials were in the ways of the aborigines, by no means all Americans—or even a majority—were Cresaps, Allens, or Daniel Morgans. Yet they were far more at home in forest fighting than the King's regulars, who, especially after Braddock's disaster in 1755, had little stomach for woodland operations; nor would the redcoats' attitude change two decades later, when they described rebels who shot from behind cover and marked out officers for annihila-tion as white barbarians or semi-savages. Washington deliberately reinforced these notions in 1777 when he advised the commander of a ranger unit to "dress a Company or two of true Woods Men in the right Indian Style and let them make the Attack accompanied with screaming and yelling as the Indians do, it would have very good consequences."[6] The Revolution was not wholly, or even principally, a backwoods war, but the influence of the backwoods was keenly felt.

What Americans needed to withstand Britain in the Revolution was not a guerrilla army, although assuredly guerrillas had their place, especially in the hinterland. On the coastal plain Americans would need a more traditional army, trained and disciplined, capable of maneuvering *en masse* and fighting pitched battles along the lines of European engagements. In the tense months immediately prior to Lexington and Concord, Timothy Pickering of Salem, Massachusetts, brought forth his *Easy Plan of Discipline for a Militia* in order to remedy his countrymen's deficiencies in the art of *"regular* war." Although Pickering had "consulted the best authorities" including Saxe and Bland, he made clear that he had not been blinded by them. The Massachusetts militia officer sounded a theme of the Enlightenment when he inveighed against "custom and prejudice"; in military thought, as in other fields of learning, they had far too long held forth at the expense of "reason." Americans were "too much enlightened to be duped" by unworkable theories. Pickering's task was to modify European procedures in light of American experience by, among other things, prescribing a simplified version of British army drill and calling for a continuation of the American habit of individual marksmanship.[7]

If the rules of warfare were often different in America, particularly away from the cleared ground on the Eastern seaboard, so was the composition of military forces. Whereas in Europe the military obligation fell mainly upon a small, professional class of soldiers, in America it fell upon nearly all, for warfare at some time or another took place everywhere. No person was immune from a military obligation in times of crisis, warned the Reverend Ebenezer Gay—"no Exemption for Men, nor Women; for the Righteous, nor the Wicked; for the High, nor the Low; for the Rich, nor the Poor; for the Strong, nor the Weak; for the Old, nor the Young; for the most busiy; the new-married, nor the faint-hearted."[8] Even in the older settlements, where fear of armed invasion receded with the passing years, weapons continued to be prerequisites for obtaining food and protecting property. And in South Carolina, a colony ever fearful of slave uprisings, a law of 1743 required all men to carry arms to church on Sundays. Jefferson, with patriotic pride (and some exaggeration), informed a friend in Europe that "every soldier in our army" had "been intimate with his gun from his infancy."[9] In contrast, American General Charles Lee, an ex-British officer, described "the lower and middle people of England . . . almost as ignorant in the use of a musket, as they are of the ancient Catapulta."[10]

Growing American urban centers also felt the impact of war. "Let no reader assume that actual fighting was alien to the townspeople," states a historian of colonial cities. The five seaport cities of Newport, Boston, New York, Philadelphia, and Charleston were all caught up in the eighteenth-century struggle for empire involving England, France, and Spain. The imperial conflicts led to new urban profiles, for each city acquired military installations. Charlestonians erected brick barracks, a bombproof magazine, and an armory; Fort St. George at Newport was as carefully planned as any on the western shores of the Atlantic; Castle William in Boston Harbor was one of the strongest fortifications built in the colonial era. As centers of concentrated population, the cities, more than the rural areas, contributed men to seaborne military operations. In 1748 a Bostonian declared that "we have lost, in the Compass of three Years, near one fifth of our Males; and most of these in the Flower of Youth." Privateering also employed the energies of urban dwellers. During the French and Indian War, one-third of Newport's adult male population sailed forth in quest of fame and fortune.[11]

But the cities, and the colonists in general, lacked the industrial facilities for carrying on a prolonged struggle. John Blair of Virginia reported: "We do not make a Saw, Air-gun, Gimlet, File or Nails or Steel, and most Tools in the Country are imported from Britain."[12] Though enormous quantities of military stores came from abroad during the War of Independence, the colonists obviously were by no means destitute of arms; nor were they totally without the means of making them. In a predominantly rural society confronted by formidable problems of transportation, procurement and distribution were sometimes greater obstacles than that of adequate supply. In the middle colonies, skilled gunsmiths were fairly numerous; their famous Pennsylvania (later Kentucky) rifle, noted for its range and accuracy, was a uniquely American weapon, designed to meet the needs of Indian fighting and hunting in the backwoods. The American provinces at the beginning of the rebellion were producing annually a seventh—30,000 tons—of the world's crude iron.[13] During the war the output increased as American furnaces, forges, and foundries turned from the production of pig iron, bar iron, and domestic items to that of cannon, balls, shot, and muskets. Americans in the colonial wars had met their military expenses by resorting to the printing press, emitting paper money since specie was drained away in trade with Britain; and this same procedure was the chief method of financing the Revolution at home.

On economic matters colonial officials had regularly sought the advice and assistance of their local merchants, a class with the combined power of today's banking, mercantile, manufacturing, and shipping interests. Samuel Vetch, a highly influential commercial figure who had settled in Boston, directed the preparations that lay behind the capture of Port Royal in Acadia by an expedition from the Northern colonies in 1710. William Pepperrell, a merchant of wealth and prestige from Kittery in Maine, led New Englanders in the capture of the fortress of Louisbourg in 1745. Bostonian Thomas Hancock, who owed his eminence to overseas trade, singlehandedly advanced his colony nearly £20,000 in gold and military stores at the outset of the French and Indian War—the same Thomas Hancock who furnished British General James Wolfe the draught-oxen and teamsters for his artillery during the enterprise against Quebec in 1759.[14] The merchants obviously profited handsomely from the colonial wars of the eighteenth century. If some of them had at times traded with the enemy's West Indian islands in wartime, an odious practice but scarcely condemned as it would be at present,[15] the American businessmen had nonetheless afforded invaluable succor to British and provincial soldiers. Some of the prominent merchants of the Revolutionary era traced their signal beginnings to providing for Anglo-American forces in the 1750's. Two decades later their trading connections in the Caribbean were to prove exceedingly useful. For every vessel that sailed from Europe directly to America with goods for Washington's army there were dozens of rebel ships that made for the French, Dutch, and Spanish islands to load needed military cargoes in exchange for staples from the mainland. By contributing their administrative talents and by lending money, advancing supplies, and outfitting vessels, such colonial entrepreneurs as Samuel A. Otis and Thomas Cushing of Boston, Robert Morris and Thomas Willing of Philadelphia, Joseph Hewes of Edenton (North Carolina), and the Brown brothers of Providence united service to the new republic with advantage to themselves.

In the seventeenth and eighteenth centuries European military leaders longingly envisaged a perpetual training ground for troops under wartime conditions, even though one's state might be technically at peace. The Low Countries, engaged in their interminable struggle with Spain, had once been a combat school for soldiers from western and central Europe. When James I recalled regiments that had been in the Dutch provinces since 1585, he heard protests that Englishmen might lose their only chance to train for an army life. In his *Military Memoirs* (1781), William Lloyd advocated that European monarchs establish "military colonies" along their eastern borders, so that their troops could be kept in constant contact with war and therefore be prevented from ever forgetting it. In America, where war had become an institution of the citizenry, where scarcely a year passed without some conflict, where an acquaintance with firearms was more widespread than anywhere else in the world, the ideal of a military community in some ways approached reality.

## The Militia System

Few phenomena of American life have felt such devastating censure as the militia system. Washington frequently criticized the part-time soldiers in the Revolution. Professional army officers, who dominated the writing of military history in the United States until recent years, ascribed most of America's military mistakes in the Revolutionary War to our militia background and reliance upon the citizen soldier. General Emory Upton, the influential military writer, castigated eighteenth-century American militia as virtually worthless, especially in combat against regular troops.[16] Admittedly the militia heritage caused its share of headaches in the War of Independence, but it also afforded appreciable opportunities and advantages; and the study of American militia in the colonial and Revolutionary years offers some broad insights into American life.

By its very nature the militia system[17] reinforced the provincialism that was a salient characteristic of the colonial period. The county court, the town meeting, the church congregation, and the military unit consisted of local people, under local leadership, meeting local needs. "It is next to impossible," lamented General Nathanael Greene in 1775, "to unhinge the prejudices that people have for places and things they have long been connected with."[18]

Some of the obstacles to the creation of a genuine "Continental" army after Lexington and Concord are illustrated in the rejection of Benjamin Franklin's Albany Plan of Union (1754). Difficulties of bringing men together, problems of expense, and fears of leaving one's own colony bereft of adequate strength all militated against intercolonial military activity, as did suspicion that one province would be sacrificed in favor of the interests of another. After calculating the length and width of British America covered by the Plan as 1,700 miles and 1,500 miles respectively, Connecticut condemned the Albany proposal, with its provisions for a Grand Council that would have the authority to raise troops and levy taxes in all the colonies. Connecticut clearly distrusted remote authority and spoke of the Grand Council as though it were to be a foreign power. Moreover, "should officers be sent from abroad [England], we are fully satisfied . . . [our Connecticut] youth would not enlist . . . and this, we conclude, is very much the case in other [of] his Majesty's provinces and colonies on the continent."[19]

Regional jealousy pervaded the resolution of the Massachusetts legislature that the South could not be trusted to meet its obligations were the Albany Plan adopted, "the Inhabitants whereof are but little disposed to and less acquainted with affairs of war. . . ."[20] To be sure, the record of the Southern militia was less impressive than that of New England. In the seventeenth century, New England towns—the minutemen tradition became firmly established—had demonstrated a capacity to resist invasion superior to that of Virginia counties, where widely dispersed Southern farmers rallied to the standard at the risk of leaving their families exposed.[21] And as late as the middle of the next century, with scarcely an exception, the Seven Years' War witnessed an appreciably heavier contribution from the Northern Colonies, especially New England, than from the Southern provinces. It is tempting to speculate that the conduct of Massachusetts in the initial stages of the War of Independence reflected in some degree a reluctance to be saddled with the greatest military burden in the colonies, as had generally been her lot in the Anglo-French conflicts since 1689. In 1775 she turned over the responsibility for supplying and maintaining the besieging forces outside Boston to the Second Continental Congress. Simultaneously, John Adams and other New England congressmen urged the appointment of Washington, a Southerner, to command the Continental army, a step that was expected to arouse a military effort in the region below the Mason and Dixon line.[22]

One cannot necessarily assume, however, that had the British government provoked a military showdown with the South instead of New England in 1775, the Southern militia would have responded less effectively than their Yankee counterparts. The military potential of the South had greatly improved. The explanation is simple: between 1730 and the outbreak of the Revolutionary struggle approximately 250,000 immigrants occupied the back country between the Potomac and the Savannah rivers, transforming an inland wilderness into a panorama of teeming farms and hamlets.

When there was agreement between governor and assembly, and when the inhabitants themselves responded—to repel invaders (as in the Cherokee War of 1759–1761), or pre-empt Indian lands (as in Lord Dunmore's War of 1774), or end domestic disorder (as in North Carolina's War of the Regulation of 1771)—then the Carolinians and Virginians showed considerable energy and initiative.[23] Early in the Revolutionary War, they displayed their ability to take the field: swarms of North Carolina patriots from surrounding farms and towns smashed a body of 1,600 Tories at Moore's Creek Bridge; and hundreds of Virginia backwoodsmen collected at Fredericksburg on hearing of Governor Dunmore's seizure of twenty kegs from the colony's powder house in Williamsburg. In the latter instance, an eye-witness declared that had they "continued there one or two days longer we should have had upwards of ten thousand men. All the frontier counties were in motion. . . . Fredericksburg never was so honour'd with so many brave hearty men . . . every man Rich and poor with their hunting Shirts [,] Belts and Tomahawks fixed . . . in the best manner."[24]

But if the South in 1775 still was under a suspicious eye because of its alleged past sins, the Northern colonies could point to instances of their own prior concerted action. Not that there existed a viable tradition of one colony sending its men to defend the settlements of another. It was, rather, that they had joined in offensive undertakings against the French in Canada. Since it was hardly feasible to call out the whole militia, technically almost the entire white male population, leaders generally gathered a body of the younger, better trained, and better equipped militamen. Frequent use was made of the bounty, most often a monetary grant the citizen received upon enlisting for a set period or for a campaign, a system both the Continental Congress and the states found necessary to continue in the struggle for independence.

At one time or another between 1690 and 1745 the colonists had assembled for blows against Port Royal in Nova Scotia, Louisbourg on Cape Breton Island, Quebec, and Montreal. In 1690 and again in 1710, Port Royal fell to the English colonists, as did Louisbourg in 1745. This last triumph was indeed an impressive American performance. To accomplish it Massachusetts had raised 3,000 men, Connecticut 500, and New Hampshire 450. Powerful incentives explain such teamwork: to Anglo-Americans, French Canada was a dagger pointed at their exposed Northern frontiers; the hated Catholic enemies, with their Indian allies, had desecrated Schenectady, Deerfield, and many another settlement. So long as a hostile power controlled Canada the Northern colonists could never rest easy. Small wonder, then, that the revolting colonists in 1775 should choose an invasion of Canada as their first significant military undertaking in the Revolution.[25]

Too much, though, can be made of intercolonial military doings. For every fruitful enterprise there are twice that number of failures—of schemes to take Montreal and Quebec that foundered in 1690; of plans to take Port Royal that went awry on three occasions between 1704 and 1707; of abortive offensives against the French strongholds on the St. Lawrence in 1709, 1711, and 1746; of an expedition against Crown Point in 1747 that never reached its destination. Any composite explanation for these dismal showings is perhaps impossible, but certain

factors occurred with almost predictable regularity: bickering between
colonial leaders, accusations of non-support directed at this or that
province, epidemics of small pox and "bloody fluxes" (dysentery),
shortages of provisions, ill-discipline, and desertion. Even the brightest
spot in the colonial military record, the reduction of Louisbourg,
illustrates that provincial armies could not be held together for long
periods. Once the élan of victory had subsided, the troops complained
of orders against plundering and of Connecticut men receiving higher
pay than men from the other colonies; of hard labor, cold weather,
illness, and the need to return home to protect their own frontiers from
Indian incursions. Hundreds of these New England soldiers died; at
one point 1,500 were reported to be incapable of regular duty.[26] Still,
New England could take pride in the seizure of Louisbourg, the
Gibraltar of the New World, but that pride turned to bitterness in 1748
when the ministry handed the fortress on Cape Breton back to France.

For the most part, Britain's own example did nothing to inspire cooperation among the colonists or with the mother country before the
Seven Years' War. The opposite was true. In 1709 and 1746 the government in London reneged on promises to contribute substantially to
colonial military expeditions against Canada. In 1711, when Whitehall
dispatched sixty ships and an army of over 6,000 regulars for a campaign to take Quebec, part of the fleet was wrecked on the north shore
of the St. Lawrence. The fault was largely that of Admiral Sir Hovenden Walker, a timid commander, who, despite the protests of the
provincials, subsequently crowded sail for England, leaving to its own
devices a colonial force at Lake Champlain. Later, in 1741, when
3,500 Americans accompanied the British armada that hit Cartagena
and Havana, the results were disastrous. Repulsed at both places, partly
owing to mediocre British leadership, partly because of outbreaks of
yellow fever, the invasionary force suffered frightful losses; six hundred
Americans at most survived!

Whatever their traditions and inadequacies, the Americans in 1775,
unlike most other popular revolutionary movements in modern history,
began their War of Independence in control of a large military organization, the militia. The laws requiring periodic training, relaxed if not
forgotten in times of peace,[27] were revitalized: for instance, in the
spring of 1775 the patriot committee of Frederick County, Virginia, resolved that "every Member of this County, between sixteen, & sixty
years of Age, shall appear once every Month, at least, in the Field
under Arms; & it is recommended to all to muster weekly for their
Improvement."[28]

Just as in the colonial wars the militia's chief inclination had been to
protect their communities under men they trusted like Benjamin

Church, Andrew Lewis, and Richard Richardson, so the War of Independence was for Americans mainly a defensive type of struggle waged on the patriots' soil. Though militiamen evinced a reluctance to travel to distant parts of America to serve in the Continental army, they were more willing to bear arms with the regulars for a limited period if the brunt of the conflict engulfed their own region or state. (The composition of any one of the Revolutionary armies was almost invariably a reflection of the area in which it performed.) But generally when the militia turned out, they preferred to fight under their own leadership: commanded by a John Stark, a Seth Warner, a Nicholas Herkimer, an Andrew Pickens, or an Elijah Clarke. And they chose to give battle in their own way; their proficiency with firearms and their familiarity with the terrain not infrequently counterbalancing their lack of formal training—King's Mountain and Cowpens are classic examples.

Regular American army units were too thinly ranked and the theater of war too vast to avoid a heavy reliance upon the militia. As Walter Millis has brilliantly stated:

. . . repeatedly it was the militia which met the critical emergency or, in less formal operations, kept control of the country, cut off foragers, captured British agents, intimidated the war-weary and disaffected or tarred and feathered the notorious Tories. The patriots' success in infiltrating and capturing the old militia organizations by expelling and replacing officers of Tory sympathies, was perhaps as important to the outcome as any of their purely political achievements. While the regular armies marched and fought more or less ineffectually, it was the militia which presented the greatest single impediment to Britain's only practicable weapon, that of counter-revolution. The militia were often much less than ideal combat troops and they have come in for many hard words ever since. But their true military and political significance may have been underrated.[29]

What was the political significance of the militia? An examination of the militia has something to offer the fundamental revision of eighteenth-century American history now underway. Historians writing in the early decades of this century—the progressive era—depicted the political climate of colonial America as essentially like that of England and, to some extent, the continent. A ruling class of home-grown aristocrats, sanctioning European ideas of privilege and hierarchy, faced a rebellion from within on the eve of the War of Independence.

This "conflict" interpretation of colonial and Revolutionary history, with its image of an ancient regime in America, has been under steady assault in recent years. Detailed studies of colonial laws and land records indicate that progressive historians posited undue assumptions as to the degree of internal change in the American Revolution. They omitted or underestimated dynamic forces already at work in the late colonial era. The absorption of nearly the entire population into the militia system is also exceedingly significant. For in continental monarchies, where legally unequal social classes were structured upon one another, an obligation of military service could not practicably be imposed on all citizens alike. Hence, limited military participation in Europe was due to more than the expense of maintaining professional soldiers and to mercantilist principles that called for disturbing industry and agriculture as little as possible in time of war. The explanation also lies in the European social structure. Legal inequities in the American colonies, though never comparable to those on the eastern side of the Atlantic, gradually eroded and disappeared. Bernard Bailyn has observed that the "great goal of European revolutions of the late eighteenth century, equality of status before the law—the abolition of legal privilege—had been reached almost everywhere in the American colonies at least by the early years of the eighteenth century."[30]

Although a look at the colonial militia helps us see that the sharp distinctions in European society were absent in America, too much could be claimed for the political importance of the militia; it was not a manifestation of equalitarian democracy. If class lines were relatively fluid, social stratification did exist and count. At the lowest levels of society Indians, Negroes,[31] white servants, and apprentices usually fell outside the militia. At the highest echelons men could find means of avoiding military service, especially through the hiring of substitutes. Prominent young men might join elite units like the Ancient and Honorable Artillery Company in Massachusetts, the First Troop of Philadelphia City Cavalry, or the Charleston Artillery. High ranking militia officers were almost invariably planters, merchants, or lawyers. On the other hand, the preponderance of militia officers came from the vast free-holding middle class. As the Connecticut assembly phrased it, "we consider that our officers generally are chosen out of the best yeomen of this colony, who live on their own lands in peace and plenty. . . ."[32] (British officials at Quebec in 1776 were amazed that captured American officers who had been part of Benedict Arnold's army were mainly farmers, blacksmiths, tanners, and artisans, who nevertheless demanded that they be treated as gentlemen!) The lack of social cleavage between most officers and their men made for a familiarity that more than occasionally bred ill-discipline and disobedience; but the independence—or stubbornness—of the American footsoldier was also indicative of something else. He was a free man, a property owner, and a voter, not a military hireling accustomed to obeying commands. "Men must see the reason and the use of any action or movement," declared Timothy Pickering. "'Tis the boast" of European commanders "that their men are mere machines. . . . God forbid that my countrymen should be thus degraded. . . . But standing armies are composed of very different men. These serve only for their pay. . . ."[33]

The militia in the colonies was uniquely American. John Adams called it one of the cornerstones of New England society—along with towns, schools, and congregations—from which the virtues and talents of the people were formed.[34] In America the military system came close to being the nation in microcosm.

To European illuminati and to the Founding Fathers, the growth of freedom—political, social, and economic—in colonial America, as institutionalized in the great documents of the Revolutionary and Constitutional era, in numerous ways seemed to be the realization of Enlightenment ideals. American military ideas and practices likewise were seen in the Old World as a confirmation of the immutable laws of nature. For the vision of a nation in arms to maintain its liberties had become before 1776 part of the intellectual paraphernalia of the age. The American militiaman symbolized the "natural" way to fight by responding to a challenge instead of honor or reward. A militia, declared the Virginia Bill of Rights, was a "noble palladium of safety" and "the proper, natural, and safe defense of a free state." That was likewise the sentiment of Voltaire, Turgot, Quesnay, and Herder, as well as Rousseau, who maintained that every citizen should be a soldier from duty but "none by profession." In 1771 the military theorist, Comte de Guibert, described the citizen soldier as

. . . terrible when angered, he will carry flame and fire to the enemy. He will terrify, with his vengeance, any people who may be tempted to trouble his repose. And let no one call barbarous these reprisals based on the laws of nature, [though] they may be violations of so-called laws of war. Some one has come to insult this happy and pacific people. He arises, leaves his fireside, he will perish, in the end, if necessary; but he will obtain satisfaction, he will avenge himself, he will assure himself, by the magnificence of this vengeance, of his future tranquillity.[35]

The American Revolution and the upheavals of the French Revolutionary era were to demonstrate the validity of what was then, in 1771, only a theory.


## Civil Control

While most colonists looked upon warfare as a necessary recourse, Spartanism held no virtues. To Americans, the subordination of the military to civilian control was one of the major strands of British constitutionalism, which also included balanced government, limited

monarchy, free elections, annual Parliaments, jury trial, and habeas
corpus.

Many colonial Americans of the eighteenth century, steeped in the
history of England as expostulated by Paul Rapin, Algernon Sidney,
and Catherine Macaulay adhered to a mythical image of an Anglo-
Saxon utopia.[36] One feature of this "golden age" was a militia system
composed of allodial landholders (freeholders) who were the guardians
of English liberties against enemies from within and without. Josiah
Quincy, Jr., a Boston lawyer, depicted the Saxon militia as the "orna-
ment of the realm in peace, and for ages continued the only sure defence in war."[37] After 1066, according to this interpretation, the
Anglo-Norman militia was not the free, healthy institution of the past;
it was encumbered with feudalistic features and later dominated by the
country gentlemen. Endeavors to recover the pre-Norman blessings
were only partially attained prior to the accession of the Stuarts, who,
discarding the moribund militia and hiring soldiers, represented a threat
to emerging liberty and a return to Norman despotism.

Americans were well versed on Parliament's confrontations with the
Stuarts over military matters. English soldiers returning from Charles
I's wars with Spain and France in 1625 and 1626, instead of being discharged, were billeted on the citizens. Subsequently Parliament compelled Charles to sign the Petition of Right, containing provisions
against martial law, billeting, arbitrary arrest and imprisonment. In the
English civil war the "New Model" army intervened in Parliamentary
politics, and under Cromwell England felt the full impact of military
rule. With the restoration of the monarchy in 1660, Charles II retained
regiments—eventually 7,000 to 9,000 men—ostensibly only to protect
his person and the fortresses; but more than enough to arouse suspicions among his countrymen. Consequently, his reign witnessed the
birth of the classic English ideological opposition to militarism. The
obsession was not to be simply a distrust of armies in general (perhaps
composed of praetorians and janissaries) but especially of "standing
armies," permanent establishments maintained by government and
regularly supplied by the public treasury in peace as well as war. Lord
Shaftesbury, one of the fathers of the philosophical argument against
standing armies, asserted in 1675 that such forces were potential instruments in the systematic corruption of Parliament and the death of the
balanced constitution of Commons, Lords, and king. It is this type of
army closely controlled by the monarch rather than the New Model
that pervades the anti-standing army literature at this time and later:
the Cromwellian experience was deemed an aberration not to be repeated, while the crown was once again a permanent fixture.[38] The
short-lived reign of James II fortified the budding concept of militarism
as defined by Shaftesbury and others. James, swelling the army to

30,000 during Monmouth's rebellion, was accused of recruiting Irish-
men and Catholics and of threatening Parliament and the city of
London.

The Glorious Revolution removed any martial threat from James;
and Parliament, to guarantee its jurisdiction in the military sphere as
well as elsewhere, produced the Bill of Rights—stating "That the raising or keeping of a standing army within the kingdom in time of peace,
unless it be with the consent of parliament, is against the law." As a
further safeguard, the famous document declared "That the subjects
which are Protestants may have arms for their defense suitable to their
conditions. . . ." The resolution of the constitutional position of Parliament vis-à-vis the army was demonstrated by the Mutiny Act, an
annual law first enacted in 1689, which legalized the army's existence
and regulated its discipline. Without this yearly legislation, and the
monetary appropriation normally accompanying it, the army would
cease to exist.

That there occurred a happy solution to the issue is the verdict of
historians. Was it equally evident to all Englishmen in the 1690's and in
the following half century? Not so to those essayists and pamphleteers
whom Carolyn Robbins has termed "the commonwealthmen." Occupying the radical wing of the whig tradition, they mined a rich vein of
republican and nonconformist thought. The standing army question
may well have been a bogey after 1689, ignoring the exigencies of
contemporary warfare and Parliamentary safeguards. But to the commonwealthmen—Robert Molesworth, John Trenchard, Walter Moyle,
Andrew Fletcher, Moses Lowman, and Edward Montagu, and their
compatriots—the continued presence of a regular military establishment
posed a threat to English freedoms. They saw most poignantly a warning in the experience of Denmark, where in 1660 a revolution had
destroyed liberty because a corrupted nobility, enamored of privilege
instead of service, had relaxed its vigil and permitted a standing army
that destroyed the constitution and the rights it guaranteed. Not all
emphasized the same remedies for England. Arguments ranged variously from improving and relying on the militia, to employing productive citizens in a token army, arming the nobles and gentry, and
entrusting defense entirely to the navy.

Only once, from 1697 to 1700, in the aftermath of the War of the
League of Augsburg, did the anti-military issue bubble to the surface in
a bitter and protracted public debate that echoed through Parliament
and the press. For the commonwealthmen, for certain politicians led by
Robert Harley, and for other antagonists of William III, the question
was no longer who should control the army; it was whether England
should have an army at all, notwithstanding the restrictions imposed in
1689. In the end, William won the right to have a small military estab-

lishment; but his victory was hardly an easy one. Not for over half a century would an English monarch dare ask for a really substantial armed force when the empire was at peace.

Much of the standing army literature made its way to America, where the colonists were exceedingly well informed on contemporary British social and political thought, a reflection of the existence of an "Atlantic civilization" in the eighteenth century. And it was principally through this nonconformist thought that English theories reached the American provinces. An authority on early American political attitudes has observed that in the pamphlet literature of colonial politics, Locke was not the most frequently cited authority, but rather *Cato's Letters* (1720–1723), the joint product of two libertarian theorists, Thomas Gordon and John Trenchard. They agreed with James Burgh, another American favorite, that a nation with a standing army would in time lose its liberty; "a free parliament and standing army are absolutely incompatible."[39]

To British-Americans educated in the classical tradition, the likelihood of attempts at military despotism seemed greatest in colonies remote from the mother country. The point was made repeatedly—in 1764 by James Otis, who cautioned that "Rome found the truth of this assertion in her Sullas, her Pompeys, and Caesars"; in 1772 by Joseph Warren, who maintained that Caesar's legions had "perpetrated the most cruel murders" upon her dependent peoples and thus had contributed to the alienation of her dominions; and in 1774 by Josiah Quincy, Jr., who proclaimed that Roman armies were sometimes "more terrible to the Roman colonies than an 'enemy's army'"—at the very time Americans were seeing British redcoats as a more dangerous threat than the soldiers of their former French antagonists had ever been.[40]

Before the mid-eighteenth century the English colonials seldom glimpsed Britain's professional soldiers. Though regulars garrisoned the valuable sugar islands of the West Indies, where the local inhabitants, fearful of slave revolts, contributed to their upkeep, New York was the only one of the thirteen colonies to have redcoats present—usually four independent companies—during most of the era of British control. Generally forgotten or ignored by the home authorities, as were occasional small units in South Carolina and Georgia, these troops experienced "a series of horrors, miseries, frauds, stupidities and sheer neglects . . . rare in either colonial or military annals."[41] Officers had small chance for advancement, and there were no provisions for rotating enlisted men in American service. In a sense, they were sent to rot and die in a strange land. Men sickened, mutinied, and deserted, their ranks replenished with vagabonds and criminals. Small wonder that British regulars dreaded American duty; but their numbers were too sparse to arouse constitutional controversies before the French and Indian War.

Defense, of course, rested primarily with the colonial militias, and the king traditionally conferred all military power in the royal colonies upon the governors. A royal governor was an impressive figure. Arriving in the colony to assume his new post, the chief executive, escorted by militia companies, passed through the various towns to the colonial capital. There the local militia, usually the best dressed and best drilled in the province, formed double lines along the route of march to the statehouse. Receiving the salutes of the colonial officers, the governor proceeded along streets crowded with onlookers displaying colored bunting and other impromptu decorations. In the council chamber the governor took the oaths of office and performed the ceremonial duties connected with his station. Volleys of musketry, booming cannon, ringing church bells, and huzzas from the assembled populace climaxed the occasion. It seemed highly appropriate for the militia to play a full role in the day's events. The governor's commission, received directly from the king, proclaimed him "Captain-General" or "Commander-in-Chief." He was empowered to appoint all officers of the colony's military establishment, and they were subject to his authority alone. He could arm and employ all residents of the colony in repelling invasions, carrying out the king's commands, and suppressing internal rebellion.[42] In theory, the royal governor of Massachusetts need not have dispatched British regulars to seize the patriots' stores at Concord; he could have called upon the militia. In theory, royal governors could have put down the budding American Revolution with the American militia.

An indication of what the militia would really do in the event of an Anglo-American rupture was revealed during King George's War. When in 1747 Bostonians became thoroughly outraged by continued illegal impressment of seamen into the royal navy, a mob assaulted a sheriff's deputy and seized hostages to bargain for the release of the sailors. Governor William Shirley of Massachusetts, a skillful and generally popular man, reported that the Boston militia "refus'd and neglected to obey my Orders . . . to appear in Arms for quelling the Tumult, and to keep a Military watch at night. . . ." Shirley himself fled to Castle William in Boston Harbor, where he sought to free the impressed Bostonians and calm the "Outrageous Mob."[43] Another royal governor, Benning Wentworth of New Hampshire, encountered a similar problem during the Stamp Act crisis. In fact, no colonial governor, he confessed, could call out his militia, who were "the very People on the other Side of the question."[44]

Without support from the colonial legislatures, the governors' military authority was virtually nonexistent. The colonial executives needed money to establish and maintain even a meager military force. Since the governors had few monetary resources at their immediate disposal, they looked to the assemblies. As the years passed, new governors soon discovered that the maturing American legislatures appropriated monies only upon their own terms, stipulating the size of the force, the pay of the men, and the length of their service. Further legislative measures eroded the governors' authority by stating where men would serve, by naming commissioners to oversee militia expenditures, and by demanding a voice in the selection of officers. Still another check upon the executive in several colonies was an annual piece of legislation, somewhat like the British Mutiny Act, giving the militia legal existence as well as organizational structure.

In their struggles with the governors, the colonial assemblies pursued a course set by the English House of Commons. As we have seen, army affairs was one of the principal subjects of controversy between Crown and Parliament in the seventeenth century. Not only did the assemblies imitate the Commons in using the purse to limit executive dominance; the New World political bodies went beyond it. The Commons, following the Glorious Revolution, never encroached upon the king's right to appoint military officers, nor did it endeavor to supervise fighting operations. For colonial Americans it was not enough to believe that military power should rest with the civil authority; ultimately they placed colonial military power in *American* hands. Civil control came to mean *legislative* control.

The outcome of this successful American quest for military domination was to be a mixed blessing. The colonists embarked upon the Revolutionary War under the mature leadership of legislative bodies that for all practical purposes were already in command of the local military establishments. Yet the reluctance of the Revolutionary legislatures to share a full measure of military power with the Continental Congress and, indeed, with the governors of the newly created states often resulted in problems of the first magnitude. Against this background, the historians' charges against Jefferson while governor of Virginia—weak, lethargic, vacillating—appear less severe. For the American state constitutions of 1776 revealed all the old colonial fears of arbitrary executives, so that Jefferson and most of the other "war governors" of the Revolution had little more actual military authority than the royal governors had possessed on the eve of conflict.


## Rehearsal for Revolution

American attitudes concerning things military were crystallized by the Seven Years' War. Problems of recruitment, discipline, supply, and intercolonial cooperation during these years bore a striking similiarity to Washington's manifold difficulties in the War of Independence. Who better than the ex-colonel of Virginia militia knew the inability of un-trained irregulars to withstand an open-field engagement against Euro-pean regulars? Who better than the former Tidewater planter under-stood the uphill task of gathering recruits in July and August, when men on the land were needed in their fields? Or who better fathomed the legislative mind than the long-time member of the House of Burgesses? Aware of Congress' weakness as an extralegal body and cognizant of the states' jealousies, Washington saw that the Revolution, like the final conflict with France, was a peculiar kind of coalition war. Only a man nurtured in the American military experience could write as Washington did in January, 1777: "a people unused to restraint must be led, they will not be drove, even those who are ingaged for the War, must be disciplind by degrees. . . ."[45]

If the French and Indian War served Washington and his fellow colonial officers with a preview of the obstacles in the Revolution, the Anglo-French clash offered lessons for Britain as well. But the principal lesson escaped the king, the ministry, and the army: attempts to regi-ment or coerce the colonists would lead to explosive results. For even the order and control that Britain considered essential to win the Seven Years' War stirred resentment among colonials accustomed to man-aging their own affairs. Colonial militia officers balked at knuckling under to regular officers their inferior in rank. A protest prepared in 1757 by Washington for the officers in the Virginia Regiment indicates how sensitive colonials sometimes became: "there can be no sufficient reason given why we who spend our blood and treasure in defence of the country are not entitled to equal preferment" with His Majesty's officers.[46]

To the consternation of Lord Loudoun, British commander in chief in America, 1756–1757, the assemblies dallied over raising troops and held fast to their purse strings. The legislatures viewed Loudoun, the Crown's supreme military authority in the colonies, as much a threat to their constitutional position as the governors had been. Noting the impotence of the colonial executives, whose "Predecessors sold the whole of the Kings *Prerogative*, to get their Sallaries," Loudoun urged the ministry to furnish the governors with funds independent of the assemblies; "if You delay it till a Peace, You will not have force to Exert any Brittish Acts of Parliament here. . . ."[47]

The quartering of British troops in the colonies revived an old con-stitutional issue of the Stuart period. Since the Bill of Rights forbade billeting of troops upon citizens without Parliamentary approval, the House of Commons had provided sections on quartering in the British Mutiny Act. While on the march or otherwise lacking permanent barracks, the troops were to be lodged by local officials in public buildings and unoccupied dwellings, in addition to receiving candles, vinegar, salt, bedding, beer, and other essentials. But Parliament had never formally extended these sections of the Mutiny Act to America. After considerable wrangling, the colonial assemblies usually granted most of the army's demands, without following the literal provisions of the Mutiny Act. In so doing American legislatures raised the question of whether these sections of the act and, indeed, any Parliamentary legislation applied to the colonies without Parliament's expressly saying so.

The Mutiny Act prohibited the quartering of troops in private homes against the will of the citizenry. But in the colonies public buildings and unoccupied houses were exceedingly few. British officers sometimes insisted on quartering their men in private dwellings. Several colonies protested, including South Carolina, where Loudoun threatened to forcibly place redcoats in colonial homes if necessary accommodations were not extended. Undaunted, the South Carolina Commons House of Assembly declared *"that Officers and Soldiers cannot legally or constitutionally, be quarter'd in private Houses, without the special Consent of the Owners or Possessors of such Houses."*[48] In South Carolina as well as elsewhere, reasonable men on both sides compromised their differences. Nevertheless, the Carolinians' protest underscored the fact that colonials were sensitive to their rights as Englishmen. In later years they would repeatedly assert those rights, regardless of the consequences.

The removal of Loudoun seemed to end the likelihood of military domination and the threat to colonial liberties. The tall, spare, hawk-nosed William Pitt, master orator and brilliant statesman, assumed full direction of the contest for North America. Rather than waste time bickering with provincial assemblies, Pitt dipped into the treasury with a lavish hand, offering monetary compensation—instead of coercion—to the Americans for men, supplies, and equipment. Spurred on by the realization they would receive from Pitt sums proportional to the amounts they spent, colonial governments—Massachusetts, Connecticut, and New York in particular—contributed impressive numbers of men for service in the final stages of the war in the New World. (All told, Americans raised five times as many men as they had furnished in any other colonial war, to say nothing of 18,000 American seamen who swelled the royal navy.) Moreover, the spirits of provincial officers improved, for Pitt acknowledged their past complaints by according them deserved recognition.

In the triumphant years with Pitt at the helm, Americans thought less about their earlier sparring with Loudoun and the army. They cheered as, one by one, French citadels of power in the New World fell

—Louisbourg, Frontenac, Duquesne, Niagara, Quebec, and Montreal. A new cluster of military heroes like Amherst, Bradstreet, Forbes, Prideaux, and Wolfe emerged, their names and accomplishments on the lips of colonials from New Hampshire to Georgia.[49] Americans were never prouder of the empire, which by the Treaty of Paris in 1763 seemed the equal of ancient Rome in its vast territorial expansiveness; an empire which offered its subjects, in America as well as England, the many rights and liberties collectively embodied in the British constitution.

Americans felt they had contributed substantially to the victory in North America. Certain politicians in England, men who dominated the government in the years to follow, did not share that view. They remembered the controversies over rank, requisitions, and quartering, and they remembered little else. In spite of the colonials, the war had been won! Of course few if any of these Englishmen had ever visited America and seen for themselves what the colonies were like. They knew little of the rural isolation, the traditions of localism, and the course of American political development, which included a well-ingrained belief that Englishmen should govern themselves whether they lived in England, or Virginia, or New York. Nor did the British politicians realize that the colonists, living in a predominantly agrarian society, lacked huge sums of ready cash for carrying on warfare; and that the colonists lacked the administrative machinery of government comparable to the growing bureaucratic state in England. "Without a general constitution for warlike operations," admitted an unknown American writer, "we can neither plan nor execute. We must have a common council; *one head and one purse.*"[50]

British military men, like the London officials, found serious fault with colonial participation. James Wolfe, conqueror of Quebec, condemned provincial soldiers as "the dirtiest, most contemptible, cowardly dogs you can conceive. There is no depending on them in action."[51] Wolfe's superior, Jeffery Amherst, castigated the colonials thusly: "if left to themselves [they] would eat fryed Pork and lay in their tents all day long."[52] John Forbes, who chased the French from Fort Duquesne, complained that his Pennsylvania and Virginia officers were a "bad Collection of broken Innkeepers, Horse Jockeys & Indian traders" while the "Men under them, are a direct copy of their Officers."[53] A bloodless duel between British Lieutenant Colonel James Grant and Colonel Henry Middleton of the South Carolina militia enlivened public argument over the merits of regulars compared to provincial troops.[54]

The charges contained elements of truth. Americans, steeped in individualism, localism, and fighting on their own, generally performed poorly whether as enlistees in the British army or as militia units acting in conjunction with regulars.[55] The colonial farmer or artisan appeared out of place in a war that ever more became, in Lawrence H. Gipson's phrase, "a European conflict in a New World setting."[56] Both French and English pursued the canons of traditional military science, employing geometric formations and using siege operations (although British experiments with light infantry represented an effort to adopt linear maneuvers to the American terrain). As British forces pressed forward against the French clustered in forts and other fixed positions, backwoods warfare, except for reconnaissance and occasional raiding expeditions, took a back seat to European tactical doctrines. If veteran French troops could be bested in America by European methods, certainly a colonial uprising could be handled with relative ease, should one ever occur—or so it seemed to the king's officers. The New Englanders, who comprised the bulk of American troops in the conquest of French Canada, were especially deemed a mediocre species. In taking coercive measures against Massachusetts in 1774 and 1775, Britons doubted that Massachusetts would offer armed resistance. Or in the unlikely event the colony did, it could be easily subdued. Something unknown or forgotten by British leaders in the early 1770's was that many of the unimpressive Yankees of the Seven Years' War were servants, apprentices, and transients who had been drafted from outside the militia system. In fact, the Massachusetts militia on the eve of the Revolution was probably better prepared for war than any other militia in the colonies.

If Americans exaggerated their contributions to the victory over France, then Britons unduly minimized the participation of the provinces. The chief American accomplishments were in logistics, an area that would plague Britain in the War of Independence. In the colonies the troops of Loudoun and Amherst procured huge quantities of foodstuffs, making it unnecessary to transport many provisions the 3,000 miles from Britain to America. Moreover, American irregulars and workmen provided much of the muscle power to construct roads and boats, and to carry the supplies and equipment over those roads.[57] The famous "romantic" historian Francis Parkman, in his volumes on the Seven Years' War in America, emphasized the colorful, the dramatic, and the spectacular—witness his title: *Montcalm and Wolfe*. The war, however, was more than a series of heroic episodes. It took herculean efforts, advancing men and wagon trains through countless miles of forested country, for British forces to perform the feats that Parkman described so graphically. The foremost necessity of British commanders was to get their forces into contact with the French; as the war wore on, the French, like the Americans in the Revolution, increasingly waged a defensive contest. Fortunately, British generals were able to land their troops in English colonies where they were generally welcomed (despite quartering disturbances) and where colonial manpower and colonial supplies were ultimately available (despite more than a little sluggishness on the part of the assemblies).

Even so, Britain had encountered problems enough in stationing regulars among the colonists during the Seven Years' War. That relationship had created tensions and uncovered differences between the mother country and her provinces. To leave thousands of troops in America following the peace of 1763 when the colonists would see little if any need for their presence might well lead to more serious difficulties, especially if the soldiers were ever used to coerce the inhabitants. In Britain the anti-redcoat tradition was not forgotten, but its vitality had been sapped—owing to the achievement of Parliamentary safeguards, the Jacobite threats, the rivalry with France, and, in 1763, the demands for administering a far-flung empire. This change of sentiment was not of a piece with American thinking, where the militia experience, the general absence of regulars, and the commonwealth writers—exceedingly more popular in the colonies than in England—kept the fear of professional armies alive, buttressed by the colonists' reading of ancient and modern history. A large, politically minded civilian population in arms, diffused over thousands of miles—forested, ravined, interlaced by innumerable waterways—would pose unparalleled problems for Britain's eighteenth-century army.

## NOTES

1. For up-to-date discussions of the Age of Limited Warfare, see Walter Dorn, *Competition for Empire, 1740–1763* (New York, 1940); Alfred Vagts, *A History of Militarism* (rev. edn., New York, 1959); M. S. Anderson, *Europe in the Eighteenth Century, 1713–1783* (New York, 1961); Richard A. Preston, Sydney F. Wise, and Herman O. Werner, *Men in Arms* (rev. edn., New York, 1962); Theodore Ropp, *War in the Modern World* (rev. edn., New York, 1962). Some of the social and economic dimensions of eighteenth-century warfare are analyzed in John U. Nef, *War and Human Progress* (London, 1950).

2. Dorn, *Competition for Empire*, 82.

3. Peter Paret, "Colonial Experience and European Military Reform at the End of the Eighteenth Century," *Bulletin of the Institute of Historical Research*, XXXVII (1964), 49–56.

4. English military writings, beginning in 1690, were reprinted in the colonies, often soon after their first appearance. Charles Evans and Clifford K. Shipton, comps., *American Bibliography*, 14 vols. (Chicago and Worcester, Mass., 1903–1959), nos. 508, 971, 1914, 3633, 3634, 4225, 5133, 5344, 5742, 7153, 7154, 7360, 7361, 7621, 8142, 8300, 8355, 8518, 10330, 11121, 11288, 12290, 12622, 12623, 12624, 12807 (through the year 1773).

5. Ernest A. Cruikshank, *The Story of Butler's Rangers and the Settlement of Niagara* (Welland, Ont., 1893), 23.

6. John C. Fitzpatrick, ed., *The Writings of George Washington* (Washington, 1931–1944), VIII, 236–237. Complaints of British soldiers against New World conditions during the Revolutionary War are described in Eric Robson, *The American Revolution in its Political and Military Aspects, 1763–1783* (London, 1955), 93–101, 129–131. See also Fred J. Hinkhouse, *The Preliminaries of the American Revolution as seen in the English Press, 1763–1775* (New York, 1926), 183.

7. Timothy Pickering, *Easy Plan of Discipline for a Militia* (Salem, 1775), preface, 93–94. The next year Pickering's *Easy Plan* was in its second edition, which "all the Militia of this Colony are directed and enjoined to practice. . . ." Boston *Continental Journal and Weekly Advertiser*, July 4, 1776.

8. Ebenezer Gay, *Well-Accomplished Soldiers . . .* (Boston, 1738), 28.

9. Julian P. Boyd, ed., *The Papers of Thomas Jefferson* (Princeton, 1950—), II, 195. The same view in Pickering, *Easy Plan*, 1.

10. *The Lee Papers* (New York Historical Society, *Collections*, vols. 4–7 [1871–1874]), I, 162.

11. Carl Bridenbaugh, *Cities in Revolt* (New York, 1955), 58–63. In Boston, a city of approximately 15,000 people in 1775, British General Thomas Gage is said to have collected from the inhabitants 1,800 muskets privately owned and not part of the colony's military stores. John R. Alden, *General Gage in America* (Baton Rouge, 1948), 255.

12. Quoted in David John Mays, *Edmund Pendleton* (Cambridge, Mass., 1952), II, 47.

13. Curtis P. Nettels, *The Emergence of a National Economy, 1775–1815* (New York, 1962), 42. It was reported that cannons were occasionally manufactured in America before the Revolution. "Achenwall's Observations on North America, 1767," *Pennsylvania Magazine of History and Biography*, XXVII (1903), 14; *Massachusetts Gazette*, Dec. 19, 1774).

14. G. M. Waller, *Samuel Vetch: Colonial Enterpriser* (Chapel Hill, 1960), chaps. vii–ix; Byron Fairchild, *Messrs. William Pepperrell: Merchants at Piscataqua* (Ithaca, N.Y., 1954), 172–177; W. T. Baxter, *The House of Hancock: Business in Boston, 1724–1775* (Cambridge, Mass., 1945), 129–132, 139.

15. Richard Pares, *War and Trade in the West Indies, 1739–1769* (Oxford, Eng., 1936), chap. ix. For an overview, consult Pares, *Yankees and Creoles: The Trade between North America and the West Indies before the American Revolution* (Cambridge, Mass., 1956). Trading with the enemy was criticized by the *Connecticut Gazette*, June 14, Sept, 13, 1755.

16. Emory Upton, *The Military Policy of the United States* (Washington, 1904), 66–67.

17. A convenient summary of the colonists' English military background is Allen French, "Arms and Military Training of our Colonizing Ancestors," Massachusetts Historical Society, *Proceedings*, LXVII (1945), 3–21. Many of the colonial legislative acts pertaining to military institutions are conveniently found in Arthur Vollmer, *Background of Selective Service*, Mon. No. 1, Vol. II, entitled *Military Obligations: The American Tradition* (Washington, 1947). Louis Morton, "The Origins of American Military Policy," *Military Affairs*, XXII (1958), 75–83, discusses the general growth and evolution of the seventeenth-century militia and offers a useful bibliography of secondary sources. A study stressing the transmission of military institutions from Europe to America is Darrett B. Rutman, "A Militant New World, 1607–1640" (unpubl. Ph.D. diss., University of Virginia, 1959).

   That the militia as an institution was far more complicated than has usually been recognized is the theme of John W. Shy, "A New Look at Colonial Militia," *William and Mary Quarterly*, 3d. ser., XX (1963), 175–185; Shy, *Toward Lexington: The Role of the British Army in the Coming of the American Revo-*

*lution* (Princeton, 1965), 6–19. An interpretation at variance with this one is by Daniel Boorstin, "A Nation of Minute Men," in his *The Americans: The Colonial Experience* (New York, 1958), 341–372.

18. Peter Force, ed., *American Archives* . . ., 4th ser. (Washington, D.C., 1837–1846), III, 1077.

19. *The Fitch Papers* (Connecticut Historical Society, *Collections*, vols. 17–18 [1918–1920]), I, 34–36.

20. Quoted in Albert B. Hart, ed., *Commonwealth History of Massachusetts* . . . (New York, 1927–1930), II, 461. Twelve years later John Adams revealed the persistence of this opinion of the South: "Military characters in the southern colonies are few. They have never known much of war, and it is not easy to make a people warlike who have never been so." C. F. Adams, ed., *The Works of John Adams* (Boston, 1850–1856), I, 252.

21. Shy, "Colonial Militia," 177–179; Shy, *Toward Lexington*, 8–9.

22. There is abundant evidence that the New England delegates were eager to draw the South more directly into the war. A few Southerners appear to have been suspicious of New England's designs. See Edmund C. Burnett, ed., *Letters of Members of the Continental Congress* (Washington, 1921–1936), I, 112–113, 127–128; Lyman H. Butterfield, ed., *The Adams Papers: Diary and Autobiography of John Adams* (Cambridge, Mass., 1961), III, 321, 322–323; James T. Austin, *Life of Elbridge Gerry* (Boston, 1828–1829), I, 79; Force, ed., *American Archives*, 4th ser., III, 1077; John R. Alden, *The First South* (Baton Rouge, 1961), 25 n5.

23. This interpretation of the Cherokee War is not universally accepted. My account follows Robert L. Meriwether, *The Expansion of South Carolina, 1729–1765* (Kingsport, Tenn., 1940), 213–240, which is reinforced somewhat by Richard M. Brown, *The South Carolina Regulators* (Cambridge, Mass., 1963), 1–12. The opinion that British regulars were chiefly responsible for bringing the Indians to heel is expressed in Lawrence H. Gipson, *The British Empire before the American Revolution* (Caldwell, Idaho, and New York, 1936–1969), IX, 55–86.

A careful student of colonial Georgia states that British troops were no longer needed in that province by 1767, "when the increase in population allowed Georgia to defend herself against sudden attack" (W. W. Abbot, *The Royal Governors of Georgia, 1754–1775* [Chapel Hill, 1959], 13).

24. Michael Wallace to Gustavius Wallace, May 14, 1775, Wallace Family Papers, Alderman Library, University of Virginia.

25. "The importance of Canada," warned John Adams, was that in "the Hands of our Enemies it would enable them to inflame all the Indians upon the Continent . . . as well as to pour down Regulars, Canadians, and Indians, together upon the Borders of the Northern [provinces]" (Burnett, ed., *Letters of Congress*, I, 355).

26. The soldiers' complaints and sufferings are graphically chronicled in Louis E. deForest, ed., *Louisbourg Journals 1745* (New York, 1932). At one time colonial officers feared a wholesale mutiny. *The Pepperrell Papers* (Massachusetts Historical Society, *Collections*, vol. 60 [1899]), 7th ser., X, 45–46. See also G. A. Rawlyk, *Yankees at Louisbourg* (Orono, Maine, 1967).

27. The anonymous Frenchman who recorded Patrick Henry's Caesar-Brutus speech also took cognizance of the Virginia militia: "the white men amount to 60,000 which is the militia body. they are mustered four times yearly. those that are absent from the generall musters without a leagal cause are fined 10 shs., from private musters 5 shs. these are the laws but seldom put in Execution." "Journal of a French Traveller in the Colonies, 1765," *American Historical Review*, XXVI (1921), 742.

28. R. G. Albion and L. Dodson, eds., *Journal of Philip Vickers Fithian, 1775–1776* (Princeton, 1924), 24–25.

29. Walter Millis, *Arms and Men* (New York, 1956), 34–35.

30. Bernard Bailyn, "Political Experience and Enlightenment Ideas in Eighteenth-Century America," *American Historical Review*, LXVII (1962), 348.

31. In practice, however, Negroes were pressed into service in emergencies, usually to perform as laborers but occasionally to bear arms as well. Benjamin Quarles, "The Colonial Militia and Negro Manpower," *Mississippi Valley Historical Review*, XLV (1958), 643–652; Quarles, *The Negro in the American Revolution* (Chapel Hill, 1961), 8–9.

32. *Fitch Papers*, I, 35. Apparently there was never a property-holding qualification for militia officers in any of the thirteen colonies, as was the case in Britain's Barbados colony. *An Abridgement of the Laws in Force in Her Majesties Plantations* (London, 1704), 233, cited in David W. Cole, "Organization and Administration of the South Carolina Militia System" (unpubl. Ph.D. diss., University of South Carolina, 1953), 17. In the English continental colonies militia officers were not the recipients of a favored status with regard to taxes, fines, and other exactions, as was true of the home defense in New Spain. There developed in the Spanish dominions a tendency to create a distinct military class excused from public responsibility. Lyle N. McAlister, "The Reorganization of the Army of New Spain, 1763–1767," *Hispanic American Historical Review*, XXXIII (1953), 26–27, 32.

33. Pickering, *Easy Plan*, 4, 10–11.

34. Butterfield, ed., *Adams Diary and Autobiography*, III, 195; C. F. Adams, ed., *Works of John Adams*, V, 495–496. While conceding that it would be desirable to mold an army from the most stable elements in society, the Comte de Saint-Germain, a great French war minister, wrote: "But in order to make an army we must not destroy the nation; it would be destruction to a nation if it were deprived of its best elements. As things are, the army must inevitably consist of the scum of the people and of all those for whom society has no use." Quoted in Nef, *War and Human Progress*, 306. And Frederick the Great declared that "useful hardworking people should be guarded as the apple of one's eye, and in wartime recruits should be levied in one's own country only when the bitterest necessity compels." Quoted in Gordon Craig, *The Politics of the Prussian Army, 1640–1945* (Oxford, Eng., 1955), 23.

35. Comte de Guibert, *Essais General de Tactique* (Liege, 1771), xxii, quoted in Orville T. Murphy, "The American Revolutionary Army and the Concept of Levee En Masse," *Military Affairs*, XXIII (1959), 14; Vagts, *History of Militarism*, 75–78. For Guibert, who, incidentally, later renounced the opinion given above, see R. R. Palmer's sketch in *Makers of Modern Strategy: Military Thought from Machiavelli to Hitler*, ed. E. M. Earle (Princeton, 1941), 62–68.

36. H. Trevor Colbourn, *The Lamp of Experience: Whig History and the Intellectual Origins of the American Revolution* (Chapel Hill, 1965), chap. ii, and *passim*.

37. Josiah Quincy, *Memoir of the Life of Josiah Quincy, Jun., of Massachusetts* (Boston, 1825), 413–414.

38. This paragraph draws heavily upon J. G. A. Pocock, "Machiavelli, Harrington, and English Political Ideologies in the Eighteenth Century," *William and Mary Quarterly*, 3d. ser., XXII (1965), 558–564. It is possible that Pocock exaggerates the singular role of Shaftesbury in originating the intellectual rationale against standing regiments. See Caroline Robbins, "Five Speeches . . .," *Bulletin of the Institute of Historical Research*, XXVII (1955), 192, 201–202; and especially Lois G. Schwoerer, "The Standing Army Controversy in England, 1697–1700" (unpubl. Ph.D. diss., Byrn Mawr, 1956), 1–18.

39. Bailyn, "Political Experience and Enlightenment Ideas," 344; David L. Jacobson, ed., *The English Libertarian Heritage: From the Writings of John Trenchard and Thomas Gordon in 'The Independent Whig' and 'Cato's Letters'* (Indianapolis, 1965), 152–161, 215–230; James Burgh, *Political Disquisitions . . .* (London, 1774–1775), II, 348, and Book III, *passim*. The first American printing of Burgh's work, at Philadelphia in 1775, had an imposing array of sponsors headed by George Washington and including John Dickinson, Silas Deane, Christopher Gadsden, John Hancock, Thomas Jefferson, and James Wilson. Burgh presented an autographed copy of his work to John Adams, who may well have had a greater knowledge of the history of militarism than any of his American con-

temporaries. Burgh inscribed his gift to a "true friend of civil and religious liberty." Zoltan Haraszti, *John Adams and the Prophets of Progress* (Universal Library edn., New York, 1964), 302. Adams, on Dec. 28, 1774, informed Burgh of the redcoat threat, describing British General Thomas Gage as another Duke of Alva. C. F. Adams, ed., *Works of John Adams*, IX, 350–352. A thoughtful analysis is by Oscar and Mary Handlin, "James Burgh and American Revolutionary Theory," Massachusetts Historical Society, *Proceedings*, LXXIII (1961), 38–57.

My discussion of English writers owes much to Caroline Robbins, *The Eighteenth-Century Commonwealthman* (Cambridge, Mass., 1959), *passim*; Schwoerer, "The Standing Army Controversy," *passim*; Schwoerer, "The Literature of the Standing Army Controversy, 1697–1699," *Huntington Library Quarterly*, XXVIII (1965), 187–212. See also Z. S. Fink, *The Classical Republicans* (2nd edn., Evanston, 1962), 69, 70, 80–81, 185. That the colonists were aware of a sizeable portion of this anti-military literature is demonstrated in Bernard Bailyn, ed., *Pamphlets of the American Revolution, 1750–1776* (Cambridge, Mass., 1965), I, 40–44, and notes.

40. James Otis, *The Rights of the British Colonies Asserted and Proved* (Boston, 1764), in Bailyn, ed., *Pamphlets of the American Revolution*, I, 458–459; Hezekiah Niles, *Principles and Acts of the Revolution in America* (Baltimore, 1882), 20–21; Quincy, *Memoir*, 443–444.

41. Stanley M. Pargellis, "The Four Independent Companies of New York," *Essays in Colonial History Presented to Charles McLean Andrews by His Students* (New Haven, 1931), 121–122.

42. The military powers and responsibilities of royal governors are set forth in Evarts B. Greene, *The Provincial Governor* (New York, 1898); Leonard W. Labaree, *Royal Government in America* (New Haven, 1930); Jack P. Greene, *The Quest for Power* (Chapel Hill, 1964). There are excellent contemporary descriptions of the militia's part in welcoming Governor Henry Ellis to Georgia and Governor Thomas Boone to South Carolina. *South Carolina Gazette*, March 24, 1759, Dec. 26, 1761.

43. Charles H. Lincoln, ed., *Correspondence of William Shirley, Governor of Massachusetts and Military Commander in America, 1731–1760* (New York, 1912), I, 406–407. John A. Schutz, *William Shirley* (Chapel Hill, 1961), 127–130; John F. Burns, *Controversies Between Royal Governors and Their Assemblies in the Northern American Colonies* (Boston, 1923), 130–131; Bridenbaugh, *Cities in Revolt*, 116.

44. Quoted in Edmund S. and Helen M. Morgan, *The Stamp Act Crisis: Prologue to Revolution* (Chapel Hill, 1953), 197–198. Simultaneously, Governor James Wright of Georgia wrote that if he assembled the militia, they would only serve his enemies. *Georgia Historical Quarterly*, XIII (1929), 148.

45. Fitzpatrick, ed., *Writings of Washington*, VII, 33.

46. Quoted in Douglas Southall Freeman, *George Washington: A Biography* (New York, 1948–1954), II, 236. See also Frederick B. Wiener, *Civilians under Military Justice: The British Practice Since 1689* . . . (Chicago, 1967), 30.

47. Stanley M. Pargellis, ed., *Military Affairs in North America, 1748–1765: Selected Documents from the Cumberland Papers in Windsor Castle* (New York and London, 1936), 273; Pargellis, *Lord Loudoun in America* (New Haven, 1933), 186. A catalogue of the colonists' sins of commission and omission throughout the war appears in Gipson, *British Empire before the American Revolution*, VI, 44–47, 53–54, 64–75, 143–147, 185–192; VII, 27–61, 69–70, 140–143, 146–148, 157–158, 164–165, 232, 239, 253–254, 260, 290–298, 328, 333–334, 445–456.

48. Jack P. Greene, "The South Carolina Quartering Dispute, 1757–1758," *South Carolina Historical Magazine*, L (1959), 193–204. An anonymous pamphlet echoed the same complaint in Pennsylvania. *A Letter to the People of Pennsylvania* (1760), in Bailyn, ed., *Pamphlets of the American Revolution*, I, 269, 702 n11. See also *Pennsylvania Gazette*, Aug. 3, 10, Dec. 23, 1756, March 15, 1759, Jan. 31, Feb. 7, 14, 1760; *Connecticut Gazette*, March 3, 1759.

49. On September 1, 1759, the *South Carolina Gazette* vividly portrayed the citizens'

reaction to the "glorious Advices . . . on the Success of His Majesty's Fleet and Armies in *North-America* . . . Monday was observed and spent here in the usual Way of public Rejoicing: But in the Evening, the Illuminations and Fireworks exceeded any that had been exhibited before. Near one Half of the Houses in town were illuminated.

We hear from Georgia (where they received the same agreeable news before we did) that the Rejoicings there upon the same Occasion, were very remarkable; as, we since learn, they have also been at *Port-Royal, Jacksonburgh,* &c in this Province." See also *Pennsylvania Gazette,* July 6, 28, 1758, Jan. 11, March 15, 1759, Aug. 21, Nov. 13, 1762; *Connecticut Gazette,* March 31, 1759.

50. "A Review of the Military Operations in North America . . .," Massachusetts Historical Society, *Collections,* 1st ser., VII (1801), 162.

51. Quoted in Christopher Hibbert, *Wolfe at Quebec* (London, 1959), 25.

52. *The Journal of Jeffery Amherst,* ed. J. C. Webster (Toronto, 1930), 167.

53. Alfred P. James, ed., *Writings of General John Forbes* (Menasha, Wis., 1938), 205.

54. For the colonial point of view, see *South Carolina Gazette,* Aug. 1, 1761, Dec. 18, 1762; [Christopher Gadsden], *Some Observations of the Two Campaigns against the Cherokee Indians . . .* (Charles Town, 1762).

55. According to a Canadian historian, the militia of New France displayed some of the characteristics of their counterparts in British America. To the Canadians, "war was a succession of raids and attacks from ambush, 'Indian war.' They resisted the European idea of war in the open field to which their French officers tried to convert them." Gustave Lanctot, *A History of Canada from the Treaty of Utrecht to the Treaty of Paris, 1713–1763,* trans. Margaret M. Cameron (Cambridge, Mass., 1965), 209, 298 n16.

56. Gipson, *British Empire before the American Revolution,* VII, x. Gipson contends that Britain fought largely to protect her colonists from French aggression. Hence, he describes the conflict as "The Great War for the Empire." This interpretation of British motives is not universally accepted; certainly Pitt saw the contest as one of expanding British territory and influence. Two recent short studies are Edward P. Hamilton, *The French and Indian Wars* (New York, 1962), and Howard H. Peckham, *The Colonial Wars, 1689–1762* (Chicago, 1964). There are several excellent chapters on the Anglo-French wars in Douglas E. Leach, *The Northern Colonial Frontier, 1607–1763* (New York, 1966). That American frontier tactics were occasionally useful is demonstrated in John R. Cuneo, *Robert Rogers of the Rangers* (New York, 1959). Eugene I. McCormac, *Colonial Opposition to Imperial Authority during the French and Indian War* (Berkeley, 1911), the only monograph of its kind, is based entirely on printed sources and should be superseded.

57. The importance of communications, supply, and colonial manpower has received more attention of late than was previously the case. See Ropp, *War in the Modern World,* 84–85; Shy, *Toward Lexington,* 84–89. Pargellis, *Loudoun,* 228–252, 270–336; Pargellis, ed., *Military Affairs,* xiv–xxi. Gipson, *British Empire before the American Revolution,* VII, viii, and *passim,* acknowledges the contribution of "British colonial agriculture" to the final victory.

# 2. The Military Origins
# of the Revolution

**M**ILITARY POLICY HAS attracted little public attention in America save in time of war or when the country faced the possibility of conflict. There are of course exceptions. During the Cold War, Americans weighed the merits of conventional ground forces, missiles, and a host of other subjects related to preparedness and its cost to the taxpayers. Much earlier, in the dozen years before Lexington and Concord, the first serious discussions of military policy occurred. They too involved the size and type of military establishments and the means of supporting them. Americans argued with Englishmen, and Englishmen sometimes divided among themselves. Few if any developments had a more direct bearing on the coming of the American Revolution than the British decision to tax the colonists for the upkeep of a royal army in America.

### A Standing Army and Its Upkeep

At the end of the Seven Years' War the British army stood at slightly more than one hundred formal regiments. Instead of cutting the number in half, characteristic of earlier postwar reductions, the government retained seventy-five regiments in service. The greatest portion of this unprecedented increase—fifteen regiments totaling about six thousand troops—was stretched across a thousand-mile rim of the North American wilderness: cantoned at such posts as St. Augustine, Pensacola, and Mobile; Fort Pitt on the Ohio; Crown Point and Ticonderoga along the Hudson-Lake Champlain waterway; and Niagara, Detroit, and Michilimackinac on the Great Lakes. In these and other stations resided a British

military force vastly larger than any known in the colonies before the
French and Indian War.

British ministers claimed publicly the troops were sent to protect the
colonists, while Americans subsequently maintained the redcoats had
been dispatched to oppress them. Neither claim has substantial supporting evidence. To be sure, garrisons in Canada initially offered a
modicum of protection to British-American interests, for the French
settlers in the St. Lawrence Valley only gradually relinquished their
loyalties to the fleur-de-lis in favor of the crosses of St. George and St.
Andrew. The British units on the lower Mississippi, in the Floridas, and
the West Indies stood guard against the Bourbon monarchies of France
and Spain ever erasing the drastic consequences of the Treaty of Paris
in 1763. With no real friends in Europe except the weak satellites of
Hanover and Portugal, Britain stood alone, respected and feared but
not admired. Yet she had no cause for alarm so long as her navy remained strong and she avoided difficulties with her colonies and the
rest of Europe. And with the bulk of her new American military establishment deep in the interior, it could scarcely have been a useful factor
in the event of hostilities in the Old World.

The preponderance of troops in the "Indian country" prompted
George Louis Beer, an influential scholar two generations ago, to describe the redcoats' primary responsibility as that of protecting the
colonists from the tribes. In Beer's opinion, Pontiac's Rebellion, a most
destructive Indian uprising in 1763–1764, confirmed the government's
resolution to maintain several thousand troops in the West.[1] Today
Beer's thesis is less tenable. Even before 1763, possibly by 1760, a consensus was forming among politicians responsible for American affairs
in favor of retaining military forces in the interior, principally for purposes other than colonial protection. Both Benjamin Franklin in London and Indian Superintendent Sir William Johnson in America agreed
that regulars were largely ineffectual fighters when operating from
wilderness outposts. Were defense the prime reason for augmenting
the army in the West, contends a present historian,[2] ranger and light
infantry units—created expressly for their frontier skills—would have
been continued on active service after France's defeat.

It is true that some Englishmen had entertained the thought of redcoats holding the colonists in check. Between 1754 and 1763 a royal
governor, an advisor to the Earl of Bute, a customs official resident in
America, two army officers, and an anonymous pamphleteer advocated the presence of troops to keep Americans in proper subjection to
king and Parliament. The importance of such random bits of opinion
can easily be exaggerated since no American in 1763 desired independence. Although the Seven Years' War bred tensions within the Anglo-

American community, Americans looked forward to a restoration of the hitherto pleasant imperial relationship marked by its freedom from restraints.

Most Americans passed a lifetime without seeing a royal official from England. Parliament's Navigation Acts, controlling the external trade of the empire, worked relatively few hardships on colonial merchants and planters. Other Parliamentary measures designed to regulate rather than prohibit provincial manufactures appear to have been unenforced. Nor was the Molasses Act obeyed, the one navigation law capable of causing severe colonial discomfort. The duty on foreign molasses was high, and the British West Indian islands were incapable of exporting this product in quantities sufficient for the New England rum trade and distilling industry. Consequently, Yankee shippers bribed greedy customs collectors in order to land cargoes of French molasses. The existence of smuggling points up the fact that the empire was not administered with maximum efficiency and system. In spite of this administrative lag (or perhaps because of it), the colonists were happy and the empire as a whole was prosperous.

This lack of cohesion disturbed British politicians in the 1760's. But they did not envisage a reorganization for the enlarged empire resting upon abstract mercantile principles. British ministers were primarily administrators who sought solutions to specific problems as they arose. Thus the army decision as well as the famous Proclamation of 1763— prohibiting any new white settlement "for the present" beyond the Allegheny divide—were primarily the outgrowth of British experience with the West during the Seven Years' War.

As these hostilities drew to a close (and in the years immediately thereafter), the North American interior loomed uppermost in British imperial thinking. Throughout the war the various Indian tribes complained to royal officials about being cheated in land and in trade. With the French removal, the Indians were expected to be increasingly sensitive, facing the prospect of being wholly at the mercy of Britain and her colonists. Indian Superintendent Sir William Johnson, highly influential with the Six Nations, repeatedly laid the Indians' fears and grievances before the Board of Trade in London. British General John Stanwix reported that Western settlements would undoubtedly anger and provoke the Indians and lead to dire consequences. Another officer spoke of white traders as "a Shame to Humanity, and the Disgrace of Christianity. . . . The Savages daily saw themselves cheated in Weight and Measure; their Women debauched, and their young Men corrupted." Clearly the need existed for regulation and organization in the transmontane region to avoid conflicts with the aborigines. As Johnson pointed out, British forts, though of minimal worth in backwoods war-

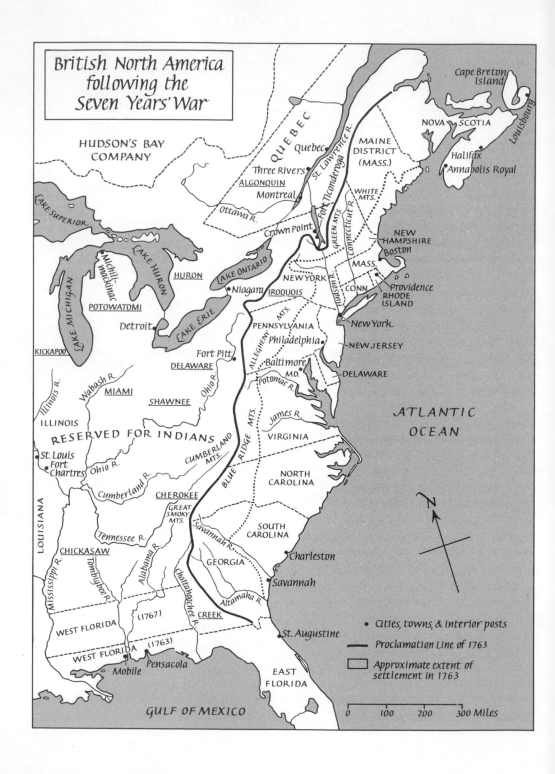

# British North America following the Seven Years' War

HUDSON'S BAY
COMPANY

LAKE SUPERIOR

QUEBEC

Quebec

Three Rivers

ALGONQUIN

Montreal

Ottawa R.

St. Lawrence R.

Fort Ticonderoga

Crown Point

MAINE
DISTRICT
(MASS.)

WHITE
MTS.

GREEN MTS.

Connecticut R.

NOVA SCOTIA

Cape Breton
Island

Louisbourg

Halifax

Annapolis Royal

NEW
HAMPSHIRE

Boston

MASS.

CONN

Providence

RHODE
ISLAND

LAKE HURON

Michili-
mackinac

HURON

LAKE ONTARIO

Niagara

IROQUOIS

MTS.

Hudson R.

LAKE MICHIGAN

POTOWATOMI

Detroit

LAKE ERIE

NEW YORK

PENNSYLVANIA

Philadelphia

ALLEGHENY MTS.

NEW YORK

NEW JERSEY

KICKAPOO

Fort Pitt

DELAWARE

Ohio R.

Baltimore

MD.

DELAWARE

Potomac R.

Illinois R.

Wabash R.

MIAMI

SHAWNEE

James R.

ATLANTIC
OCEAN

ILLINOIS

RESERVED FOR INDIANS

VIRGINIA

St. Louis
Fort
Chartres

Ohio R.

CUMBERLAND
MTS.

BLUE RIDGE MTS.

NORTH
CAROLINA

Cumberland R.

LOUISIANA

CHEROKEE

GREAT
SMOKY
MTS.

Tennessee R.

Savannah R.

SOUTH
CAROLINA

N

CHICKASAW

Tombigbee R.

Mississippi R.

Alabama R.

GEORGIA

Chattahoochee R.

Charleston

Savannah

CREEK

Altamaha R.

(1767)

WEST FLORIDA

(1763)

WEST FLORIDA

Mobile

Pensacola

St. Augustine

EAST
FLORIDA

GULF OF MEXICO

• Cities, towns, & interior posts

— Proclamation Line of 1763

☐ Approximate extent of
settlement in 1763

0    100    200    300 Miles

fare, might prove exceedingly advantageous as bases from which regulars could police the frontier by upholding tribal land claims and overseeing the fur trade. While defense against the Indians or a resurgence of Bourbon ambitions figured implicitly in the decision to keep an army in North America, the chief function of the redcoats was actually to prevent war, not to wage it.

In spite of its historic aversion to substantial standing forces, Parliament accepted the ministry's new military policy without open debate. What had happened to the English anti-redcoat tradition? Why was the response so different in 1763, hard on the heels of the decisive victory over the Bourbons, from the attitude of 1697–1700, following William III's less spectacular win over Louis XIV in the War of the League of Augsburg? William had had to fight in Parliament with all his political skill to retain a small army, one so unprepossessing that England's apparent military weakness was a factor in prompting Louis XIV (as William had predicted) to renew his expansionist ventures. The seventeenth-century heritage was not forgotten; but in the years since the opposition of Harley, Molesworth, and Trenchard it had lost much of its vitality—owing to the success of Parliamentary safeguards, the Jacobite threats of 1715 and 1745, the unremitting rivalry with France, and, in 1763, the requirements for administering a far-flung empire.

Furthermore, several additional things helped make the army's enlargement palatable. Few British army colonels in the eighteenth century passively witnessed a peacetime reduction eliminating their regiments and placing themselves on half-pay. Colonels normally acquired their commands through political connections, and they exercised those ties to remain on the regular establishment. Hence, a typical member of the House of Commons, wholly uninformed on American affairs but himself possibly a colonel, or a regimental business agent, or a member of a political faction with some ax to grind in regard to army patronage, could easily justify the new scheme on grounds having nothing to do with imperial commitments.[3] Should dissidents in the Commons raise constitutional questions about the larger standing army, as indeed some of the country gentlemen threatened to do, the ministry could point out that the augmentation would take place in the colonies rather than in the British Isles. Most important, taxpayers at home would be offered relief: after the initial year the Americans would be liable for meeting part of the army's support.

The policy of American taxation, like that of bolstering military forces in the colonies, seemingly evolved during the final years of Anglo-French conflict. From London in 1760 Cecilius Calvert confided to Governor Horatio Sharpe of Maryland: "'tis hinted . . . [an] Act of

Parliament will be moved for . . . a Standing Force in America and that the Colonies must bear at least the greatest share of Charge . . . this will occasion a Tax."[4]

Although both the army expansion and the accompanying idea of American taxation became a formal part of ministerial policy in the short-lived Bute administration of 1761–1763, the details of implementing taxation fell to Bute's successor, George Grenville, a practical, tough-minded politician specializing in finance. And the new chief minister bristled with facts and figures to support his case in the House of Commons. The British national debt rose to £122,603,336 in 1763; the colonists carried light taxation; and they had benefited from the efforts of redcoats in the late war. Grenville seemed indifferent to still other facts: the trough of depression into which the colonies had fallen after the Seven Years' War, and the American contributions to that glorious victory. Keeping American legislative disputes over requisitions foremost in mind, he judged the colonists none too responsible in financial matters. Though an American tax would be a novelty, he deemed it far more efficient and practical than the requisition system of the Seven Years' War. To produce an American revenue of £200,000 a year toward the maintenance of the army in the colonies, Grenville won Parliamentary passage of the Sugar Act in 1764 and the more far-reaching Stamp Act in 1765.

If most Americans were probably indifferent in the beginning to the presence of royal regiments on the frontiers, there were nevertheless both logical and historical reasons for looking upon this *"standing army,"* as Massachusetts lawyer James Otis called it, with apprehension, regardless of the original intentions of the ministry. Power, though essential to the basic, constituted functions of government, possessed the natural tendency to encroach beyond its legal bounds. It was man, vulnerable to seduction and vice, more than power itself that made it so—the species' almost congenital inability to avoid abusing authority when acquired.

And the greatest potential for the abuse of power lay with those "who," in Josiah Quincy's later words, "have arms in their hands and are disciplined to the use of them." Equally disturbed by the decision to station regiments in the colonies were Eliphalet Dyer of Connecticut, John Dickinson of Pennsylvania, and Richard Henry Lee of Virginia, all fearing that in future years Whitehall might be tempted to employ the redcoats in enforcing unpopular acts of Parliament. But it was Daniel Dulany, Maryland planter and author of the most influential pamphlet attack on the Stamp Act, who may well have planted a question that was to receive an affirmative answer after 1768: was the purpose of this standing army to oppress America? Was it really necessary, he asked, "to defend the colonies against *themselves* (for it can hardly be imagined that troops are necessary for their protection against any foreign enemy) . . . or [were they] to be employed in the national service of cropping the ears and slitting the nostrils of the civil magistrates?"[5]

Fear of conspiracy was another heritage of British-Americans, extending back to the days of James II. It was kept alive by the Jacobite maneuvers in the early eighteenth century and by rumors of diabolical designs on the part of the "King's Friends" under George III to monopolize positions of preferment. A favorite topic with colonial journalists was the evil of "faction" and "cabal." Grenville himself said nothing to diminish Dulany's suspicions. Indeed, by speaking of the need to protect the colonies, Grenville falsified (or misunderstood?) the reasons for the army's presence in the West; and by resorting to unprecedented taxes he slashed across a century and a half of British-American constitutional development.

Although Americans might be steeped in localism and provincialism, they could all agree that British subjects could be taxed only by their elected representatives. Scarcely a trickle of stamp money entered the coffers of the deputy paymaster of the forces in the colonies, the official who was to receive the tax monies for use in sustaining the British garrisons.[6] Not only did the colonists refuse to buy the stamps that were to accompany dice, playing cards, newspapers, and almost all legal documents; they were even prepared to fight rather than submit. In villages and towns from Georgia to New Hampshire, Americans formed associations called the Sons of Liberty. The Wallingford, Connecticut, Sons declared they would oppose the Stamp Act "to the last extremity, even to take the field." South Carolinians offered 500 men to help rid Georgia of the hated stamps. The American Revolutionary War, according to His Majesty's commander in chief in North America, General Thomas Gage, came within an eyelash of beginning on October 31, 1765, when a milling throng of several thousand New Yorkers threatened to storm Fort George, where the colony's supply of stamps had been hastily stored. Major Thomas James, the garrison's ranking officer, subsequently assured Parliament that had he opened fire on the mob, the insurgents would have assembled 50,000 armed men from the colonies of New York and New Jersey alone. Throughout the colonies in the winter of 1765–1766 government ground to a halt as governors reported the helplessness of their situations to London.[7]

The Stamp Act resistance exemplifies Britain's problems in dealing with an aroused citizenry too far from England to be coerced short of full-scale war. The folly of military reprisals in the 1770's might well have been avoided had British politicians profited by the experience of the Stamp Act controversy. But the Rockingham ministry, succeeding Grenville's in 1766, endeavored to suppress news of colonial rioting and resistance, and instead secured repeal of the Stamp Act on the justification that American economic boycotts were harmful to the trade of the empire. Thus the Americans' determination to fight if pushed, as well as their concern for constitutional issues, was submerged, only to reappear in later controversies.

## The Quartering Act

Parliament saddled no new direct taxes upon the colonists immediately following the Stamp Act repeal. But there remained to confront Americans a form of indirect taxation embodied in the Quartering Act of 1765. This law represents another instance of British concern for efficiency and economy, a statute resulting from specific problems instead of some theoretical scheme of imperial organization. Although skirting the literal terms of the British Mutiny Act, the assemblies had generally proffered considerable assistance to redcoats in the provinces during the French and Indian War. Now Gage in 1765 importuned the London officialdom to extend the Mutiny Act's billeting sections to the colonies. Since public houses were small and few in number, he sought to include permission to place soldiers in private homes without the owners' consent. Was further Parliamentary legislation essential, particularly at a time when a whole series of British measures were making Americans sensitive and suspicious? Gage's deputy quartermaster general, Lieutenant Colonel James Robertson, in a memorandum on billeting and impressment, admitted the new proposals were not based on hardships currently experienced but were in anticipation of difficulty. Gage was looking for trouble, and in time he found it.[8]

Neither George III nor George Grenville, tyrants in the eyes of nineteenth-century historians, evinced enthusiasm for Gage's idea of imposing soldiers upon colonial householders. Their attitude was likely crucial to the colonial agents' well-executed campaign that saw the controversial lodging section deleted from the proposed legislation. As finally passed, the Quartering Act proclaimed that when barracks were full or unavailable, troops were to be placed in inns and other public houses and, if necessary, empty homes or barns—at provincial expense. Other clauses ranging from furnishing firewood, candles, and beer to providing wagons and drivers at fixed rates rounded out the Quartering Act for the colonies.[9]

The new law did not enhance the army's well being in America. Previously colonial legislatures in emergencies had temporarily placed troops in private dwellings. Now, with no mention of private homes in the Quartering legislation, such an arrangement was patently illegal. The act required implementation by the colonial assemblies. If they neglected to make appropriations, the law would be inoperative; town and county officials would scarcely succor the army without reimbursement from the colony treasury. But what would be the constitutional implications if the assemblies did vote funds as the act of Parliament stipulated? In flouting the Stamp Act, Americans had denied Parliament authority to empty their pocketbooks. Could that lawmaking body indirectly divest them of their cash by forcing the assemblies to take it? The American reaction to the Quartering Act upholds the revisionist interpretations of Edmund S. Morgan and others that Americans in the years 1765–1766 displayed a high degree of unity in opposing all forms of Parliamentary taxation, internal or external, directly or indirectly applied. At the same time, they frequently demonstrated a reasonable attitude toward the British army's needs that squarely conflicts with stereotype notions of American waywardness in accepting responsibilities within the greater British community.

The wording of the Quartering Act—compelling an assembly to offer up pounds and pence—disturbed the conservative-minded John Dickinson as much as it did the fiery Samuel Adams of Massachusetts. Adams asked Christopher Gadsden of South Carolina whether the Quartering Act was "not taxing the Colonys as effectually as the Stamp Act and if so, either we have complained without Reason, or we still have reason to complain." Yet even Adams conceded that should British troops stand in need while in the Bay colony, it would be a "Disgrace" to "humanity, or in regard to our Sovereign as to refuse to grant the aid with out free consent." The New Jersey assembly, after branding the quartering law "as much an Act for laying Taxes as the Stamp Act," proceeded to meet an army request for support—without conforming precisely to the language of the law. The New Jersey response set the pattern for colonial compliance. Aid would usually be forthcoming, but by avoiding mention of the Quartering Act and presenting supplies as a free gift, the assemblies' response resembled the requisition system of the French and Indian War. By 1767 Connecticut, Massachusetts, New York, New Jersey, Pennsylvania, and South Carolina had extended goods and services to troops stationed within their borders or on the march. Though conditions and circumstances varied, a number of colonies had provided substantially for Gage's regiments; and Pennsylvania had treaded near the letter of the Quartering Act. Only Georgia balked at any military authorization as a matter of principle. Georgia, though, was somewhat unique. Only recently a royal colony, its assembly new, Georgia was involved in a quest for power like the older colonies had experienced earlier in the century. With its position less secure, the Georgia Commons House was possibly more sensitive to compromise, with less self-assurance and political maturity. Yet in time Georgia, ever influenced by her powerful neighbor South Carolina, issued nearly £200 for royal troops, twice the sum requested by Governor James Wright.[10]

Although no assembly in sustaining Gage's forces had precisely acknowledged Parliament's right to pass the Quartering Act, the degree of American cooperation seems striking in light of the ill-will engendered by the Stamp Act. British politicians might well have left the situation alone, for a kind of modus vivendi existed: American assemblies gave reasonable assistance to the troops, and the touchy constitutional issue was held in abeyance. That was not to be the course of the Chatham administration. William Pitt, now Lord Chatham, had initially castigated the pending quartering bill as harsh and excessive. As head of the ministry (1766–1768) he saw the matter differently. In May, 1766, Gage called upon New York for aid under the terms of the Quartering Act. In the past because of its location New York was the province most often asked to provide for regulars on the move. Consequently, the New York assembly justifiably feared an eventual drain on its resources equaled by no other province. Acknowledging that it, along with the other colonies, should bear some expenses, the assembly pointed to a fund of £3,999 in the treasury (created earlier for recruiting) available for the military's use. Even so, New York subsequently enacted quartering legislation—limited to a year—that omitted beer, salt, and other incidentals, and in still other ways circumvented a precise compliance with the British Quartering Act.

The Privy Council promptly disallowed the New York law. The Earl of Shelburne, secretary of state for the Southern Department (in charge of colonial affairs), had no wish to inflame all the colonies. Hence, New York was singled out: the Restraining Act of 1767 suspended the legislative authority of the New York assembly until it bowed to the terms of the Quartering Act. Chatham and Shelburne, usually pictured as sympathetic to the colonies in the 1760's, had brooked no denial of Parliamentary supremacy; and momentarily at least Shelburne had contemplated even severer forms of retaliation.[11]

The growth of the colonial assemblies was the most important political development in the history of the thirteen American colonies, and now Parliament's punishment of New York threatened the very existence of the assemblies. By what right could Parliament disturb a legislative body representing property-owning Englishmen? Would other American legislatures suffer New York's fate if they challenged —even indirectly like New York—the constitutionality of a Parliamentary measure? "[T]hough the billeting act is not yet enforced upon *us* [in Virginia]," wrote Richard Henry Lee, "we are equally with New York in the view of that oppressive measure, *for I cannot agree to call it a law.* An act for suspending the legislature of that province *hangs, like a flaming sword,* over our heads, and requires, *by all means, to be removed.*"[12]

Heatedly entertained throughout the colonies, these questions were also raised in far-off London by Benjamin Franklin, a veteran colonial agent, whose opinions on the relationship between the American colonies and the parent country ultimately foreshadowed the modern British Commonwealth. Franklin informed Londoners that, whatever the government's original intent in sanctioning representative assemblies in the New World, the American legislatures were no longer subordinate political bodies with only limited lawmaking authority:

> an assembly is a kind of little parliament in America, not an *executive* officer of government. . . . If they were oblig'd to make laws right or wrong in obedience to a law made by a superior legislature, they would be of no use as a parliament, their nature would be changed, their constitution destroyed. . . . It [the Quartering Act] was therefore look'd upon in America merely as a requisition, which the assemblies were to consider, and comply with or decline, in the whole or in part, as it might happen to suit the different circumstances and abilities of different colonies.

Though "coffee-house orators" in London screamed "REBELLION," Franklin assured his readers that nothing could be farther from the truth.[13]

The Quartering Act, though seriously straining relations between Britain and her American appendages, engendered no drastic opposition like the Stamp Act riots. When the New York assembly appropriated an additional £4,500 for Gage's men, Shelburne hastily accepted the colony's response as adequate compliance with the Quartering Act. On the constitutional issue New York had stood firm, but Shelburne, anxious to calm the storm, wisely secured the Privy Council's suspension of the New York Restraining Act. Two years later Parliament amended the Quartering Act to permit the provinces to enact any quartering laws that adequately guaranteed the army's needs. Parliament had taken prudent steps to provide for the troops on terms more palatable to Americans. But the good will one might have expected from these events was partly vitiated by a new factor: the transferal of royal regiments from the frontier to the Eastern seaboard, where they became involved in upholding unpopular customs officials and enforcing obnoxious laws of Parliament.

## The Army on the Seaboard

The new imperial programs connected with the decision to keep an army in America had spawned colonial resistance. But what of the army itself? How effective was it as a frontier police force? Land-hungry settlers, indisposed to heed the Proclamation of 1763, were spilling over the Allegheny divide as the Virginia and Pennsylvania back country became thickly populated with hordes of English, Germans, and Scotch-Irish. Gage's troops could not guard every gap and pass in the western mountains. Nor could they successfully regulate the Indian trade. Traders found it relatively easy to avoid compliance with orders requiring all exchanges with the redmen to take place at military posts. Even when garrison commanders made arrests, there was only a dubious chance of convicting offenders, who, with witnesses, had to be sent eastward to appear before civil courts, an impracticable if not an impossible task in most instances.

Maintenance of the interior garrisons was expensive, especially when the army was not accomplishing its task and when the intended Stamp Act revenue did not materialize. Gage, accordingly, favored marching a substantial part of the army to the coastal cities, where it could be provisioned more economically. Another factor also colored Gage's thinking, one that indirectly, at least, led toward Lexington and Concord: the possible employment of the army to hold the Eastern colonists in check. During the Stamp Act disturbances Gage had complained of the remoteness of the army in the West and the hesitancy of civil authorities to seek aid in combating colonial resistance. Several colonial governors would have gladly accepted bayonet support, but they were reluctant to ask for it, just as Gage, ever mindful of whiggish fears of militarism, refused to act independently of civil authority.[14] A prudent man, the General seldom went beyond the letter of his instructions, but his thinking influenced Viscount Barrington, the secretary at war. Barrington, however, would have gone beyond Gage's proposal by removing the troops from the older colonies as well as from the West, concentrating the forces at Quebec, Halifax, and St. Augustine. The troops would not be in a position to antagonize the long-established settlements, although they would be near enough in case of emergency. Differences over future control of the interior, plus the political instability of the ministry headed by the gout-ridden Chatham, left the question of troop dispositions unresolved in 1766.

Ministerial indecision led in no small part to the Townshend duties, the second major round in Britain's effort to prime the American pump. For the redcoats continued in the West, and the subject of their upkeep would not down. Early in 1767 George Grenville moved in the House of Commons that either the Americans be taxed to maintain the garrisons or the army should be withdrawn from the back country. The ministry, unwilling to credit proposals from the opposition, corralled ample votes to beat down Grenville's schemes. Then to the amazement of most of his ministerial colleagues, Chancellor of the Exchequer

Charles Townshend, "Champagne Charlie," always unpredictable, introduced taxes. Chatham's illness, confusion within the nonparty ministry, and resentment against New York on the quartering issue help explain the cabinet's acquiescence and the easy passage of the Townshend Revenue Act—levying external taxes on tea, lead, paper, paint, and glass to produce £40,000 per annum for the American military establishment and for other expenses connected with colonial government.[15] Americans reacted to Townshend's endeavors to tap their pockets in much the same way they had spurned Grenville. Petitions and pamphlets denied the constitutionality of any form of British taxation, although there was less violence and less likelihood of open warfare.

Townshend was dead in 1768 when the reassessment of British Western policy finally came to a head. Lord Hillsborough, occupying the recently created post of secretary of state for the colonies, was in general agreement with Gage and Secretary Barrington on colonial and military policy, and Hillsborough had the ear of the Crown. In March, 1768, partly for reasons of economy, Gage was given authorization to cut the number of frontier garrisons. Simultaneously, the Indian superintendents were to negotiate with the redmen for limited colonial expansion; and the provincial governments were to resume control of commercial relations with the tribes, while diplomatic relations were to stay in the hands of the superintendents.

The interior no longer stood paramount in imperial thinking. A desire for peace and order on the frontier did not wane from 1763 to 1776, but after 1765 the West slowly receded in importance as the American challenge to royal authority became the primary problem for British officials responsible for colonial affairs. Thus Hillsborough and the ministry were as much concerned with the presence of the army in the East to insure Parliamentary supremacy over the colonies as they were with military administration and saving expenses by reducing the inland posts. As Barrington confided to Gage, "Nothing can make Great Britain obey'd and respected in North America, but a proper force collected together."[16] But the disposition of regiments reflected the thinking of Gage and not Barrington. In the next four years the General abandoned no fewer than twenty-two forts in America and the West Indies. Afterward, three regiments were stationed continuously in the settled parts of the middle colonies, in addition to strong contingents at St. Augustine, Halifax, and Quebec, close enough to the older settlements to employ as the occasion warranted.

Earlier, London officials had assured Americans the army was present for their protection. But in view of these changes, could the same argument be made? Clearly Governor William Pitkin of Connecticut evinced no eagerness to see soldiers in New England during "this time of profound peace"; their presence would be an "unnecessary expense, and have an unhappy tendency to produce uneasiness among the people."[17] Pitkin was not to have his wish. Hillsborough had scarcely notified Gage of the decision to shift the army eastward before he wrote the General again to dispatch one or two regiments to Boston. There the customs commissioners complained of intimidation by Boston mobs and urged military support to enable them to collect the king's revenue. Hillsborough wanted decisive action, and Gage, who had advocated as early as 1766 the quartering of units in Massachusetts on a *permanent* basis, wholeheartedly agreed.

Massachusetts had offered spirited opposition to the stamp, quartering, and Townshend measures. Therefore the troops would likely be exceedingly unpopular in Boston, a city with genuine grievances against the customs collectors. They were, in O. M. Dickerson's epithet, "customs racketeers," a rapacious band who played fast and loose with the complicated provisions of the Sugar Act in order to collect fines which helped line their own pockets.[18] Governor Wentworth of New Hampshire, a visitor in Boston, observed that more trouble was due to servants of the administration than to local citizens. In time Gage implicitly admitted this to Hillsborough, as well as the fact that the mistreatment of the commissioners had been exaggerated.

Although Gage found, too, that his troops landed without incident, despite earlier rumors of planned armed resistance, Bostonians did not react gracefully to the sight of scarlet coats or the tread of marching feet. Steeped in the literature of English whiggery, the Boston Town Meeting read into the presence of the soldiers in their midst the great historical indicator of the way men lost their "Liberties, Privileges, and Immunities." The point was sharpened by the fact that almost simultaneously part of this same British army appeared to be subverting English freedoms in the mother country. When on May 10, 1768, a crowd assembled outside King's Bench Prison in London hoping to glimpse John Wilkes, a vigorous opponent of—among other things—Whitehall's American policy, panicky magistrates called for a regiment of Scottish Foot Guards. The soldiers opened fire, killing several persons. Bostonians wondered whether a conspiracy existed everywhere, especially since Gage's regulars remained idly in their city: there was no violence against the soldiers, no mob activity, and no harassment of the customs commissioners.[19]

What then were the troops to do? Or what was to be the administration's position vis-à-vis Massachusetts, the most refractory of all colonies in Hillsborough's opinion? Had the Colonial Secretary achieved his way, Parliament would have wrought changes in Massachusetts equally as severe as certain of the Coercive Acts of 1774, and one would have been even more repressive by providing for the quartering of troops in private homes. Most politicians in England favored a firm hand in dealing with the colonies, and it is doubtful that a majority in Parliament would normally have opposed Hillsborough.

Perhaps a degree of luck saved Massachusetts—and postponed the War of Independence. The cabinet showed alarm over the opposition's campaign to dissolve Parliament because Wilkes, editor of the *North Briton* and recently in exile, had been denied a Commons' seat though duly elected by the Middlesex freeholders. Simultaneously there were other storm warnings. In Ireland riots broke out in response to efforts to increase the Irish army. There were new tensions in the international atmosphere over French intervention in Corsica and alleged Spanish machinations in the American Southwest and elsewhere. All these developments, along with the colonial boycott of British goods in protest against the Townshend Revenue Act, go far toward illuminating Whitehall's willingness to accept a kind of *détente*: not only a rejection of Hillsborough's harsh proposals but also eventual repeal of all the Townshend duties except the tax on tea.

Any evaluation of Hillsborough's failure, however, should not neglect the constitutional implications of using troops, possibly quartered in private dwellings, to enforce a wholesale reorganization of the Bay colony. That would be "a point of such delicacy in our constitution that I doubt much of its being properly executed," wrote Lord George Sackville. It was another George, the King, a strict constitutionalist by his own definition, who may have been a sizeable factor in thwarting the Colonial Secretary. For in after years Colonial Undersecretary William Knox recalled: "I always understood from Lord Hillsborough that the King was particularly averse to the detaching his troops" against civilians in the colonies "as it serves to make the army odious to the public."[20]

So ended the threat of military coercion, not to be seriously contemplated again until 1774. Logically the troops should have been withdrawn from Boston now that force had been discredited; Gage admitted he could do nothing without authorization from civil authority. Although two regiments returned to Halifax, two remained at the insistence of Massachusetts-born Thomas Hutchinson, the new governor, who continued to give ear to the fears of the customs commissioners. As weeks and months passed, tension slowly built up, particularly after it was learned that the redcoats would stay indefinitely. The patriot press printed stories of insults to city officials, assault, theft, and rape committed by redcoats; while Gage's officers collected affidavits narrating mistreatment of the soldiers at the hands of the townspeople. The culmination, foreseen by the army and the citizens alike, was the

"Boston Massacre" of March 5, 1770, an event hopelessly clouded by controversy. Only then were the regiments pulled out of the city, leaving behind a legacy of fear and suspicion.[21]

## Rebellion in Massachusetts

Opposition to standing armies was nowhere espoused more fervently than in Boston after 1770. It was refurbished every March 5—"Massacre Day." Bells tolled, pictures of dead and dying patriots hung from windows, and a prominent citizen delivered an oration, the day's crowning event. Some historians have termed these orations buffoonery at best but more often sheer demagoguery. One pictures a fiery declamation before a turbulent crowd of men and boys, the very stuff mobs are made of. (In the shadows lurks Samuel Adams, an eighteenth-century cloak and dagger man, guilty of stirring up an otherwise complacent people.) But the facts belie the etching, for they attest to the deep and abiding fear of militarism that was now more than a seventeenth-century heritage. Josiah Quincy, Jr., a young lawyer, proposed what he hoped would be "an annual and solemn remembrance of the 5th of March." The orations, at least in the early years, were just that. Schoolmaster James Lovell in 1771 and Dr. Joseph Warren in 1772 penned learned, legalistic addresses that would have largely escaped the rabble, had they attended. They contain few if any of the wild exclamations against the soldiers so repeatedly quoted from John Hancock's oration (presumably the work of Samuel Adams) in tension-filled 1774.

To fit fighting forces into the body politic has always been an uphill task. Lovell and Warren, both educated in the classical tradition, pointed out that in Rome the military, lacking adequate civil control, had contributed to the demise of the republic. Parliament in England, by means of the Bill of Rights and the Mutiny Act, had jurisdiction over the army. But "what check have *we* upon a British army?" asked Lovell; "can *we* disband it? can *we* stop its pay?" The two orators cited Trenchard, Blackstone, and other writers to bolster their argument that excessive military establishments inevitably had resulted in engaging those forces in harmful purposes, none more so than "placing standing forces in the midst of populous communities," declared Lovell. Dr. Warren drew an implicit analogy to Boston when he averred that soldiers of imperial Rome had "perpetuated the most cruel murders upon her dependent peoples and thus had contributed to the alienation of her dominions." English colonials found it an easy matter to believe that soldiers, individually or *en masse*, were capable of such crimes.

According to mercantile theory, only the surplus nobility (forming the officer class) and the scum of society (composing the rank and file) could be released for long-term military service.[22]

Of course not every officer was a genuine aristocrat, nor was every private in the foot regiments a human derelict. And since 1763 this same army, prior to the explosion at Boston, had generally behaved itself in dealings with the colonists, who had been glad enough for the sterling of officers and redcoats spent in American stores and taverns. But one can gather from the aforementioned outpouring of anti-military sentiment in Massachusetts, to say nothing of what was to follow, that old, submerged notions—part of the intellectual equipment of Englishmen—had surfaced with a vengeance.

Such men in arms, besides posing a direct danger to the people's safety and liberty, offered an even greater threat to the morals of the community, vowed Warren. For men seduced from their virtues and responsibilities were the easiest type of prey. A friend of the distinguished Rhode Island clergyman Ezra Stiles informed him that Britons were wont to say, "Damn those Fellows [in New England], we shall never do any Thing with Them till we root out that cursed puritanick Spirit—How is this to be done?—keep Soldiers amongst Them, not so much to awe Them, as to debauch their Morals." Against such a widely held image of redcoats—"a dissolute sett of Men" exclaimed Massachusetts colonial agent Dennys De Berdt—Samuel Adams' rantings in the *Boston Gazette* and Hancock's bloodcurdling oration in 1774 struck a responsive chord among the citizenry.[23]

As Americans expounded upon the evils of standing armies, they were reminded of their own militias' shortcomings: of inadequate quantities of powder and lead, of unfilled regimental offices, of infrequent muster days, where light talk and heavy drink took precedence over drill field evolutions. The New England press launched a campaign to foster colonial preparedness. For too long the colonists had failed to see, as commonwealthman Andrew Fletcher phrased it, that he who "is armed is always master of the purse of him that is unarmed." Captain William Heath of Roxbury, a "Military Countryman," counseled readers of the *Boston Gazette*, in a series of essays beginning in 1772, to "Be wise in time" and master "the art of war." A sixty-two-year-old veteran, in the *Connecticut Courant*, swore his readiness to leave his wife and children, as he had "in times past" to engage the Bourbon enemies, to "fly with double Fury" against the "Miscreants" who now threatened his liberty. Just as "Ranger" declared in the same journal his willingness to "fight the Enemies from Britain" as he had previously fought "Indians from Canada."[24]

The "Boston Massacre," a spontaneous disturbance, had signaled the need for military readiness. But only the reverberations in London from the Boston Tea Party, a preconcerted riot, produced a wholesale military effort in Massachusetts. The British ministry, by encouraging the hard pressed East India Company to ship its taxed tea directly to the colonies in 1773, had blown up ominous clouds of resentment. The storm broke when Adams' "Mohawk Indians" consigned the dutied tea to the fish in Boston Harbor. Only the long-standing bad blood between Boston and the parent country can explain the studied harshness of Parliament's retaliation—closing the port of Boston, altering town and provincial government in Massachusetts, permitting accused royal governmental officials (including soldiers) to be tried in Britain, and providing for the billeting of troops within the city of Boston. Although this quartering legislation, authorizing British forces to use unoccupied buildings when barracks were not conveniently located, applied to all of North America, it was obviously designed to facilitate the presence of troops in the city, since the barracks on Castle Island in the harbor were scarcely adequate for additional regiments.[25]

The Coercive Acts foreshadowed the reappearance of General Gage's redcoats in Boston, 3,500 by early 1775, and they were accompanied by Gage himself, who now held a commission as governor of Massachusetts. In the torrent of opposition aroused by these so-called "Intolerable Acts," Americans did not neglect the linking of civil and military authority in Massachusetts resulting from Gage's appointment. The First Continental Congress, a mark of growing American unity, condemned the presence of regulars and deplored the naming of Gage as chief executive of Massachusetts. Calling upon the colonies to strengthen their militias, the delegates at Philadelphia advised the Massachusetts whigs to resist military aggression, in which case "all America ought to support them in their opposition."[26]

Even at this time, when Congress thought of fighting only as a last recourse, that body had inadvertently acquired one "of the greatest Military Characters of the present Age" as its unofficial advisor. A retired British officer, Captain Charles Lee fought in the colonies against France, later served in the Polish army of Stanislas Poniatowski, and in 1773 returned to America, aligning himself with the patriot cause. Witty, charming, and intelligent, Lee was a genuine child of the Enlightenment who impressed many congressmen as much by his familiarity with Locke and Rousseau as by his fund of military knowledge. Before Congress adjourned, Lee began to compose a plan of organization for a future American army, should the need arise for one. Lee discussed some of his ideas with John Adams, Thomas Mifflin of Pennsylvania, and possibly Washington, who subsequently requested a copy of the completed manuscript.

Lee had witnessed civil war in Poland, where rebel bands made it hazardous "to stir ten yards without an escort" of Russian troops. Lee's American experience, reinforced by his adventures in Eastern Europe, led him to a hearty contempt for conventional ("Hyde Park") tactics and strategy. In an influential pamphlet, *Strictures* . . . (1774), Lee at once attempted to uncover the weaknesses of British regulars in wilderness warfare and to convince Americans of the need for a well-trained, well-organized militia: "to keep the swords of your enemies in their scabbards, you must whet your own."[27]

Massachusetts, with an army of "brutal banditti" unleashed upon its "Wives, Daughters, and Grandmothers," had already taken the lead. The assembly, calling itself the Provincial Congress and sitting as an extralegal body, destroyed Governor Gage's theoretical control of the militia by securing the resignation of the colony's military officers, who, though elected, had been commissioned to serve at the governor's pleasure. The bulk of the officers were afterward re-elected, now responsible solely to the Provincial Congress. That body established a supervisory committee of safety; appointed Jedediah Preble, Artemas Ward, and Seth Pomeroy, all French and Indian War veterans, officers of general grade; and directed the field officers to recruit one-fourth of all the militia into companies of "fifty privates, at the least, who shall equip and hold themselves in readiness, on the shortest notice, to march." History remembers them as the famous minutemen.[28]

Throughout the Bay colony men from sixteen to sixty paraded and practiced maneuvers on their village greens. Few companies were uniformed and fewer still had the same firearms for all their members. Muskets of sundry types, some dating from Queen Anne's War, were evident. So were fowling pieces, blunderbusses, and virtually anything that would shoot, save the rifle, a weapon largely foreign to New England as late as 1775. When the militiamen drilled in the winter and spring of 1775, many followed the procedures outlined in Captain Timothy Pickering's *Easy Plan of Discipline for a Militia* (1775). Pickering, a tall, spare man who served as register of deeds in Salem, was, like Heath, a militia reformer; as early as 1769 he had inveighed against the carnival atmosphere of training days. His *Easy Plan*, one of the first significant military pieces by an American, was an outgrowth of generations of colonial warfare. Pickering's officers gave but one order enabling men to prime and load their weapons in only ten motions, whereas Humphrey Bland's prominent British treatise called for sixteen orders, followed in a series of forty-nine motions. British drillmasters continued to put relatively little emphasis upon the aim of the individual soldier; synchronized volleys in line combat militated against that. In contrast, Pickering stated: "Lean the cheek against the

butt of the firelock, shut the left eye, and look with the right along the
barrel . . . at the object you would hit; or, in other words (to use the
well-known phrase) *take good sight.*"[29]

Massachusetts found that its martial activities were being repeated
by the other colonies. Americans everywhere could now see—what
some had long proclaimed—that there was a *standing army* in the colonies, its aim to coerce the people into complying with tyrannical laws.
The reason for stationing regiments in the New World in 1763, never
really explained to the colonists by Whitehall, now seemed abundantly
clear to patriot penmen: this "MONSTER of a standing ARMY" was
born of "a Plan . . . systematically laid and pursued by the British ministry near twelve years [ago] for enslaving America."[30]

In Rhode Island, Connecticut, and New Hampshire, as well as in the
middle colonies, southward in Maryland, and in far-off Virginia and
the Carolinas, the appeal to Mars filled the air. On March 9, 1775, at
St. Johns Church outside Richmond, the Virginia provincial convention sat transfixed by Patrick Henry's eloquence: "The war is inevitable.
. . . The war is actually begun. . . . Our brethren are already in the
field! Why stand here idle?" Virginia did not stand idle. Like the other
colonies, and like America on the eve of all its wars, the Virginians
discovered their defenses "much neglected" and then proceeded to
accelerate the preparations already underway in many counties. The
convention, sharing with Massachusetts a belief in a "well regulated
militia" as the "only security of a free government," copied the New
England procedure of electing lower ranking militia officers and, a few
weeks later, of establishing minutemen companies. Should the shaky
peace end in New England, the Northern patriots would find the support of populous Virginia invaluable, not only because of Virginia's
resources but also because the Old Dominion would influence the conduct of her Southern neighbors.[31]

## Violence and Mob Activity

One of the fascinating mysteries about the American Revolution is
whether it was truly a revolution at all. Were not Americans primarily
enlightened conservatives striving to preserve their English liberties,
enriched and diffused in the leaven of the New World? Whatever this
interpretation has to offer (and it seemed attractive to scholars in the
1960's), one can agree with Robert R. Palmer that Americans prepared
to uphold their rights by methods revolutionaries have often found necessary and expedient. Despite the outcries of royal governors and
others in constituted authority, extralegal congresses, conventions,

associations, and committees—at the colony, city, town, and county levels—seized control of affairs. Thousands drilled in readiness for possible hostilities. The Continental Congress created machinery—the Continental Association—for enforcing a boycott of British goods, to be extended in September, 1775, to include nonexportation of American products, except rice, to Britain or her West Indian islands. (Crane Brinton sees a rough parallel between this American economic weapon and the strikes forming part of the revolutionary prelude in France and Russia.)[32]

Violence, hardly limited to France in 1789 or Russia in 1917, was likewise a factor in American whigs' solidifying their hold. At times they went so far as to lavish tar and feathers upon their fellow citizens who refused militia duty, purchased London clothing, or in other ways derided the patriots' insubordination to Crown and Parliament.

Americans joined in such crowd activities all the more readily because throughout society there were grievances against the mother country. No longer can we take at face value the loyalists' descriptions of the Revolutionary mob as a throng of wild men manipulated by their social superiors. The urban "mechanics," really a catchall term, who participated in the destruction of British control were quite likely to be holders of the franchise and possessed of a stake in the welfare of the community. Even the lowest orders, the "rabble" in the tory view, often had their own peculiar complaints. Having few channels through which to sound their distress, such inarticulate groups—laborers who found that off-duty redcoats in Boston would work for less than half their own wages—and merchant seamen who lived in steady fear of the royal navy's impressment gangs—expressed their sentiments in popular demonstrations.[33]

If the composition of the mob and the motives of its members were complex, it is equally a fact that mob violence in the pre-independence decade hardly represented an innovation in American behavior. Popular disturbances had occurred frequently since the late seventeenth century, sparing neither city nor countryside. These eruptions were not irrational outbursts but were directed at specific objectives and reflected concerns of the moment. The same pattern of relative moderation was characteristic of the whig-inspired disturbances of the 1760's and 1770's. Although there was violence and physical intimidation, it was generally restricted to specific targets and accomplished without bloodshed. "No royal governor was hanged or shot by a drumhead courtmartial," observes Howard Mumford Jones. "No stamp collector or customs official was summarily executed. . . . No 'tyrant' was decapitated, and nobody's head was borne about the streets of Philadelphia or Boston on a pole."[34]

Perhaps the restraint of the American mobs, in the Revolutionary era at least, can be explained in part by the desire of patriot leaders—law-abiding men with limited goals—to keep their cause from veering in the direction of social and political anarchy. But one cannot push such an interpretation too far when we have noted that the Revolution was more than an élitist undertaking. It may be equally or more important, as Gordon Wood suggests, to mention that only a fairly small dosage of violence was actually required to insure the breakdown of royal authority, to reduce the Crown's governors and other administrators to a state of impotence.[35] Even in Massachusetts, where Thomas Gage had an army behind him, British control scarcely extended beyond the city of Boston.

A case in point is the struggle over gunpowder, which the patriots were smuggling from both Britain and the European continent. At a meeting of the Privy Council in October, 1774, the King issued an order in council forbidding any further exportations of arms and gunpowder to the colonies except for the use of Gage's army, and the royal navy received instructions to cooperate with the customs commissioners to halt all subsequent colonial arms traffic. Such efforts were largely unavailing. New York's Lieutenant Governor Cadwallader Colden reported that "the contraband trade carried on between this place and Holland . . . prevails to an enormous degree"; his son, a customs officer, had been offered a handsome bribe "if he would not be officious in his duty." In March, 1775, Ezra Stiles learned on good authority that the Virginians had dispatched a vessel to France which had returned with powder, arms, and field pieces.[36]

Even so, the patriots were critically short of military stores. In December, 1774, the Rhode Island assembly gathered the munitions from Fort George at Newport during the temporary absence of the British warship stationed there. Almost simultaneously New Hampshire patriots seized the armaments from Fort William and Mary at Portsmouth as the six-man British garrison looked on helplessly. A little later the secret committee of the South Carolina Provincial Congress carried away powder, flints, muskets, and cutlasses from the magazine and armory in Charleston. In Virginia, however, the raiders were seamen of the royal navy, who made off with twenty kegs of powder from the provincial magazine in Williamsburg.[37] At Cambridge and Salem in Massachusetts, friction over munitions took place between whigs and Gage's soldiers, but Gage and his soldiers prudently avoided bloodshed. Much more important were the powder and other stores at Concord belonging to the Provincial Congress. The capture or destruction of those supplies was the assignment of British Lieutenant Colonel Francis Smith as he marched down the silent country road that ran through Lexington and on to Concord the night of April 18, 1775.

### The Cause of Hostilities

How do we account for the hostilities that began the following morning on Lexington green? The answer is at once simple and complex. Simple, in that the control of munitions was crucial to both sides—to the Americans for making war, to the British for avoiding it; hundreds of redcoats advancing inland to confiscate the only quantity of supplies large enough to be termed a military depot would predictably bring bloodshed. Complex, in that the ultimate responsibility for the march to Concord did not rest upon the normally cautious Gage. To be sure, Gage had done his best to prepare for conflict by fortifying Boston Neck, erecting barracks within the city, gathering information about roads and terrain, and placing spies among the Massachusetts patriots. Yet Gage drew back from a major display of force. In letter after letter, commencing in the fall of 1774, he had informed the ministry that New England, backed by Americans to the south, would fight if pressed; that New England alone would take one, possibly two, years to subdue, and only then if substantial reinforcements were forthcoming.[38]

Gage's caution elicited faint respect in London. The cabinet and Parliament, having brought the Coercive Acts, intended their enforcement with every available means, and they doubted Gage's contention that his 3,500 men were insufficient to bring Massachusetts to heel.

This is not to say that most of the cabinet wanted war; but they were averse to overtures to the colonies that might be interpreted as a sign of weakness. For this reason they looked askance at the suggestion of sending Franklin and Admiral Richard Lord Howe on a fact-finding mission to America, which would buy time and cool the heated atmosphere on both sides of the Atlantic. Even the most forthright advocates of mediation or conciliation could not quite bring themselves to deal directly with the Continental Congress, an extralegal body. Chatham and Franklin stood virtually alone in arguing that a first step toward compromise should be the withdrawal of the redcoats from Boston. Franklin warned prophetically that no settlement could be reached so long as the regulars remained, that indeed their presence would likely lead hotheads on both sides to acts that would involve the army against the civilian population, producing a "Breach that can never afterwards be healed."[39]

On this crucial point concerning the troops the attitude of the King was the key. His earlier constitutional qualms about unleashing redcoats against his American subjects had evaporated in the din and fury resulting from the Boston Tea Party and Massachusetts' defiant reaction to the Coercive Acts. Significantly, he was supported and encouraged in altering his position by his closest legal advisors, Attorney General

Thurlow and Solicitor General Alexander Wedderburn, both hard-
liners on American questions. In fact, the King seems to have assumed
that force was imperative to uphold the army's prestige before the
Yankee incendiaries, who, for all practical purposes, had confined the
soldiers to the city of Boston.

No longer did political opposition at home stand in the way of bringing the might of the army to bear. No longer was the constitutional
issue a barrier. What, if any, were the physical limits to the employment of muscle against the colonists? Although the question never received an airing in official circles, one can readily concede the magnitude of arriving at a comprehensive assessment. For a full-scale revolutionary war involving an insurgent, armed population transcended the
memory of the eighteenth century. Yet clairvoyant observers were not
wholly absent. Gage, veteran of twenty years' American service, had
uttered truths unpalatable to his countrymen. In London, Chatham,
Lord Camden, Edmund Burke, Charles James Fox, and John Luttrell
spoke prophetic warnings of staggering expenses, suffering in England,
and a weakening of British power redounding to the advantage of
France and Spain, all bitter fruits of an exhaustive American war.

Moreover, even if Britain won such a war, could she govern what
remained after the bloodshed and destruction ended? What would be
the value of a burned-out empire? These thoughts crossed the minds
of the learned Scotsman David Hume and Lord Howe. George III,
turning a deaf ear to ministerial critics, listened instead to the soldiers
at court who harbored memories of poorly trained, ill-disciplined
American fighting men in the French and Indian War. Sir Jeffery
Amherst, paying deference neither to the colonists' military abilities
nor to the tangled forests of North America, boasted that with 5,000
men he could sweep from one end of the colonies to the other. The
Americans, exclaimed Lord Sandwich of the Admiralty, would run at
"the very sound of cannon . . . as fast as their feet could carry them."[40]

The King's attitude was likely to prevail in a period when the monarch played the stabilizing role in Parliamentary politics in the absence of a party system; and within a decade after assuming the throne
George III had crushed his Parliamentary opponents and acquired a
commanding position unknown to the earlier Hanoverians. The King's
letter to his first minister Lord North, on November 18, 1774, indicates
not only his strength at home but also his feeling toward America: "the
New England Governments are in a state of rebellion, blows must
decide whether they are to be subject to this Country or independent."
It was therefore with the wholehearted approval of the King that Colonial Secretary Dartmouth wrote a "Secret" missive to Gage precipitat-
ing the War of Independence. Reaching the General in Boston on April

14, 1775, the dispatch called for military action to restore royal authority throughout Massachusetts.[41]

## NOTES

1. George Louis Beer, *British Colonial Policy, 1754-1765* (New York, 1907), 261–262. For many years most writers either followed the line of Beer or merely noted the army increase without significant comment. For examples, see Clarence W. Alvord, *The Mississippi Valley in British Politics* (Cleveland, 1917), I, 129–130; Gipson, *British Empire*, IX, 41–54. But a note of skepticism concerning several aspects of the Beer thesis was sounded in John R. Alden, *The South in the Revolution, 1763-1789* (Baton Rouge, 1957), 53–55.

2. Bernhard Knollenberg (*Origin of the American Revolution, 1759-1766* [New York, 1960], 87–98), was the first historian to demonstrate convincingly that the creation of an American military establishment could hardly have resulted simply from the government's desire to protect the colonists. But in general I have followed closely an excellent study that appears to prove beyond doubt that the army's mission was primarily that of a frontier police force. Shy, *Toward Lexington*, chap. iii, especially 52–56.

3. Rex Whitworth, *Field Marshal Lord Ligonier* (Oxford, Eng., 1958), 373–374; Knollenberg, *Origin of the Revolution*, 94–95; Shy, *Toward Lexington*, 68–79. In 1761, eighty-five Commons' seats were held by members of the armed services. Lewis B. Namier, *England in the Age of the American Revolution* (London, 1930), 254–255. The principal lobbyist for the interests of regimental colonels was John Calcraft, who, in 1762, served fifty-seven colonels as business agent, seventeen of whom were members of Parliament. "In short, he was parliamentary whip of an army group." See the excellent sketch in Lewis B. Namier and John Brooke, *The House of Commons, 1754-1790* (New York, 1964), III, 170–174.

4. William H. Browne and others, eds., *Archives of Maryland* (Baltimore, 1883—), XXXI, 527–528. Franklin sensed the changing mood in official quarters toward the colonies as early as March 1759: "The prevailing opinion, as far as I am able to collect it, among the ministers and great men here, is, that the colonies have too many and too great privileges; and that it is not only the interest of the crown but of the nation to reduce them." Leonard W. Labaree, ed., *The Papers of Benjamin Franklin* (New Haven, 1959—) VIII, 293.

5. Quincy, *Memoir*, 372–373; James C. Ballagh, ed., *Letters of Richard Henry Lee* (New York, 1911–1914), 5; Otis, *The Rights of the British Colonies Asserted and Proved*, [Daniel Dulany], *Considerations on the Propriety of Imposing Taxes in the British Colonies for the Purpose of Raising a Revenue . . .*, in Bailyn, ed., *Pamphlets of the American Revolution*, I, 458–459, 463, 469, 645; Knollenberg, *Origin of the Revolution*, 91, 318 n115; Shy, *Toward Lexington*, 140–148.

6. One authority believes that the colonists exaggerated the likely ill effects of the new British taxes since the monies collected were to remain in America: stamp collectors and customs officials were to transmit their cash for the payment of soldiers' salaries (Jack M. Sosin, "A Postscript to the Stamp Act. George Grenville's Revenue Measures. A Drain on Colonial Specie?" *American Historical Review*, LXIII [1958], 918–923). On the other hand, Americans everywhere were subject to the stamp tax, while the troops would be confined to certain areas, mainly on the frontier. Or as Franklin phrased it, the money "will be spent in the conquered Colonies, where the soldiers are, not in the Colonies that pay it." Albert H. Smyth, ed., *The Writings of Benjamin Franklin* (New York, 1905–1907), IV, 415.

7. Roger Champagne, "The Military Association of the Sons of Liberty," *New*

*York Historical Society Quarterly,* XLI (1957), 338–350; Morgan and Morgan, *Stamp Act Crisis,* 197–204; Lawrence H. Gipson, "The Great Debate in the Committee of the Whole House of Commons on the Stamp Act, 1766, as Reported by Nathaniel Ryder," *Pennsylvania Magazine of History and Biography,* LXXXVI (1962), 40; Samuel Johnston to Thomas Barker, Oct. 2, 1765, Hayes Papers, Southern Historical Collection, University of North Carolina Library.

8. Shy, *Toward Lexington,* 163–181, contains an extended discussion of the American background of the Quartering Act.

9. "I think I may Value myself on having a considerable Place in getting this clause struck out," boasted Franklin on the defeat of the objectionable billeting provision (Smyth, ed., *Writings of Franklin,* IV, 388). London merchants, who were to assist Rockingham in his drive to repeal the Stamp Act, also played no small part in aiding the colonial agents. David Barclay, a merchant in London, stated that the quartering of soldiers upon *"private* families is, in the opinion of every well-wisher to America, and every friend to liberty . . . an innovation upon the privileges of those who justly claim the natural rights of this country." Frank A. Mumby, *George III and the American Revolution: The Beginnings* (Boston, 1923), 103–104. Rhode Island agent Joseph Sherwood declared that without the merchants, "I do believe the [billeting] measure would have been carried." G. S. Kimball, ed., *The Correspondence of the Colonial Governors of Rhode Island, 1723–1775* (New York, 1926), 47. The Quartering Act is in Danby Pickering, ed., *The Statutes at Large . . .* (Cambridge, Eng., 1762–1807), XXVI, 305–318.

10. H. A. Cushing, ed., *The Writings of Samuel Adams* (New York, 1904–1908), I, 110–111; William A. Whitehead and others, eds., *Archives of the State of New Jersey* (Newark, 1880–1928), 1st. ser., IX, 577; Abbott, *Royal Governors of Georgia,* 126–144.

11. Shy, *Toward Lexington,* 188–190, 232, 245, 248–258, for the fullest treatment of the colonial reaction. See also Nicholas Varga, "The New York Restraining Act: Its Passage and Some Effects, 1766–1768," *New York History,* XXXVII (1956), 233–258; Charles R. Ritcheson, *British Politics and the American Revolution* (Norman, Okla., 1954), 85–92.

12. Ballagh, ed., *Letters of Richard Henry Lee,* I, 26. For other protests, see Cushing, ed., *Writings of Samuel Adams,* I, 134–152; Paul L. Ford, ed., *The Writings of John Dickinson* (Philadelphia, 1895), I, 143–150.

13. Verner W. Crane, ed., *Benjamin Franklin's Letters to the Press, 1758–1775* (Chapel Hill, 1950), 83–87.

14. Alden, *Gage,* 113–150.

15. Shy, *Toward Lexington,* 239–248; Jack M. Sosin, *Whitehall and the Wilderness: The Middle West in British Colonial Policy, 1760–1775* (Lincoln, Neb., 1961), 126–127, 130–135; John Brooke, *The Chatham Administration, 1766–1768* (London, 1956), 93–99, 135–138; Ritcheson, *British Politics,* 93–101.

16. Sosin, *Whitehall in the Wilderness,* 166–167; Lee E. Olm, "The Chatham Ministry and the American Colonies" (unpubl. Ph.D. diss., University of Michigan, 1960), 40–41, 254–255.

17. Massachusetts Historical Society, *Collections,* 5th ser., IX (1885), 288.

18. In his *Navigation Acts and the American Revolution,* Dickerson presents a lengthy indictment of these revenue officers of the Crown. A more sympathetic view of the customs men appears in Thomas C. Barrow, *Trade and Empire: The British Customs Service in Colonial America, 1660–1775* (Cambridge, Mass., 1967).

19. *Boston Town Records, 1758–1769* (Boston, 1886), 258–259, 261–264; George Rudé, *Wilkes and Liberty* (Oxford, Eng., 1962), 49–52; Pauline Maier, "John Wilkes and American Disillusionment with Britain," *William and Mary Quarterly,* 3d ser., XX (1963), 382–385, Mercy Otis Warren, *History of the Rise, Progress, and Termination of the American Revolution* (Boston, 1805), I, 65.

20. Historical Manuscript Commission, *Stopford-Sackville MSS* (London, 1904–1910), I, 128; Historical Manuscripts Commission, *Dartmouth MSS* (London,

1887–1896), I, 339. This account of the government's failure to resort to coercion relies heavily upon Shy, *Toward Lexington*, 297–302, 321–323.

21. The Bostonians' newspaper charges against the soldiers have been edited by Oliver M. Dickerson, who believes they are substantially true. *Boston under Military Rule* (Boston, 1936). For the trials of the soldiers involved in the Boston Massacre, see L. Kinvin Wroth and Hiller B. Zobel, eds., *The Legal Papers of John Adams* (Cambridge, Mass., 1965), III; Hiller B. Zobel, *The Boston Massacre*, (New York, 1970). Pamphlets bearing on the subject are listed in Thomas R. Adams, *American Independence: The Growth of an Idea. A Bibliographic Study of the American Political Pamphlets between 1764 and 1776 . . .* (Providence, 1965), 57–62, 64–65, 66, 67, 71, 88, 148.

22. Blackstone's remarks are in Sir William Blackstone, *Commentaries on the Laws of England*, ed. William D. Lewis (Philadelphia, 1902), I, 368, 371, 374. The "Massacre Day" orations, which continued through the Revolutionary War, are in Niles, *Principles and Acts of the Revolution in America*, 15–79.

23. Edmund S. Morgan, *The Gentle Puritan: A Life of Ezra Stiles, 1727–1795* (New Haven, 1962), 265; Albert Mathews, ed., "Letters of Dennys De Berdt, 1757–1770," Colonial Society of Massachusetts, *Transactions*, XIII (1910–1911), 435. In writing of the arrival of the redcoats in Boston, Mrs. Mercy Warren declared that the presence of such an army "introduces a revolution in manners, corrupts the morals, propagates every species of vice, and degrades the human character." Warren, *American Revolution*, I, 75–76.

24. Fletcher quoted in Robbins, *Eighteenth Century Commonwealthman*, 105; Rufus R. Wilson, ed., *Memoirs of Major-General William Heath* (New York, 1904), 15–17; *Boston Gazette*, Jan. 27, Feb. 24, Sept. 21, 1772, Nov. 15, 1773, Oct. 10, 1774; *Connecticut Courant*, Jan. 19, Dec. 14, 1773. Even before the appearance of redcoats in Boston, Worcester authorities, in 1767, expressed concern over the "General Neglect of the Militia." Lee N. Newcomer, *The Embattled Farmers: A Massachusetts Countryside in the American Revolution* (New York, 1953), 51. See also *Boston Gazette*, Feb. 24, 1772, Jan. 27, Oct. 25, Nov. 15, 22, Dec. 20, 1773, Jan. 3, 1774; *Newport Mercury*, Oct. 4, 1773, Jan. 10, 1774; Jonas Clark, *The Importance of Military Skill . . .* (Boston, 1768); Jeremy Belknap, *A Sermon on Military Duty* (Salem, 1773).

25. The Quartering Act of 1774 is in Pickering, ed., *Statutes at Large*, XXX, 410. Don R. Gerlach, "A Note on the Quartering Act of 1774," *New England Quarterly*, XXXIX (1966), 80–88, points out that many historians have erroneously stated that the Quartering Act allowed military authorities to place troops in private homes. Lord Chatham described the law as clapping a "naval and military extinguisher" over Boston. Claude H. Van Tyne, *The Causes of the War of Independence* (Boston and New York, 1922), 400–401.

26. Worthington C. Ford, ed., *Journals of the Continental Congress* (Washington, 1904–1937), I, 58, 116, 119. Thus, wrote loyalist Joseph Galloway, "the foundation of military resistance throughout America was effectually laid." *Historical and Political Reflections on the Rise and Progress of the American Rebellion* (London, 1780), 68–69. That was also the opinion of Congressional delegate Charles Carroll of Maryland. "Extracts from the Carroll Papers," *Maryland History Magazine*, XVI (1921), 31–32.

27. *Boston Gazette*, Aug. 22, 1774; John R. Alden, *General Charles Lee: Traitor or Patriot?* (Baton Rouge, 1951), 53–65.

28. *The Journals of Each Provincial Congress of Massachusetts in 1774 and 1775* (Boston, 1838), 33–34; Allen French, *The First Year of the American Revolution* (Boston, 1934), 32–43; William Brattle to Thomas Gage, Aug. 29, 1774, Artemas Ward Papers, Massachusetts Historical Society.

29. Pickering, *Easy Plan of Discipline for a Militia*, 21; Octavius Pickering, *The Life of Timothy Pickering* (Boston, 1867), I, 16–20; *Boston Gazette*, Oct. 10, 24, Nov. 28, Dec. 12, 26, 1774, Jan. 2, 9, 30, Feb. 13, March 6, 13, 27, April 3, 1775.

30. Quoted in Bailyn, ed., *Pamphlets of the American Revolution*, I, 74.

31. The Henry quotation, which contains the spirit if not the letter of his remarks, is in William Wirt, *The Life of Patrick Henry*, ed. Henry Ketcham (New York, 1903), 122–123. See also *Proceedings of the Virginia Convention of Delegates* (Williamsburg, 1775), 5. The best treatment of early military preparations in Virginia is Mays, *Pendleton*, II, 3–18, a splendid life and times study. Activities elsewhere are described in *Pennsylvania Packet*, Feb. 20, 1775; *Newport Mercury*, Jan. 30, 1775; *New York Journal*, Jan. 12, 1775; *Maryland Gazette*, Dec. 15, 1774; *South Carolina and American General Gazette*, May 5, 1775.

32. Robert R. Palmer, *The Age of Democratic Revolution* (Princeton, 1959–1964), I, *passim*; Crane Brinton, *The Anatomy of Revolution* (Vintage edn., New York, 1956), chap. iii.

33. The grievances of the inarticulate, along with their responses, are catalogued perceptively by Jesse Lemisch, "The American Revolution from the Bottom Up," in *Towards a New Past: Dissenting Essays in American History*, ed. Barton J. Bernstein (New York, 1968), 3–45; Lemisch, "Jack Tar in the Streets: Merchant Seamen in the Politics of Revolutionary America," *William and Mary Quarterly*, 3d ser., XXV (1968), 381–400. The status of seamen will be discussed more fully in a later chapter.

34. Howard Mumford Jones, *O Strange New World: American Culture in the Formative Years* (Compass edn., New York, 1967), 290, and generally chap. viii, "The Radical Republic." See also A. M. Schlesinger, "Political Mobs and the American Revolution, 1765–1776," American Philosophical Society, *Proceedings*, XCIX (1955), 244–250; Bailyn, ed., *Pamphlets of the American Revolution*, I, 581–584.

35. Gordon Wood, "A Note on Mobs in the American Revolution," *William and Mary Quarterly*, 3d ser., XXIII (1966), 635–642. See also Wood, *Creation of the American Republic, 1776–1787* (Chapel Hill, 1969), 319–328; Hugh D. Graham and Ted R. Gurr, *Violence in America: Historical and Comparative Perspectives* (New York, 1969).

36. Clarence E. Carter, ed., *The Correspondence of General Thomas Gage . . .* (New Haven, 1931–1933), II, 176; *Letters and Papers of Cadwallader Colden* (New-York Historical Society, *Collections*, vols. 49–56 [1889–1896]), VII, 249–254; Franklin B. Dexter, ed., *The Literary Diary of Ezra Stiles* (New York, 1901), I, 527; Bernard Donoughue, *British Politics and the American Revolution: The Path to War, 1773–1775* (London, 1964), 207–208.

37. Elwyn L. Page, "The King's Powder, 1774," *New England Quarterly*, XVII (1945), 83–92; John Drayton, *Memoirs of the American Revolution* (Charleston, 1821), I, 221–226; William Moultrie, *Memoirs of the American Revolution* (New York, 1802), I, 78–79, 86–90; Mays, *Pendleton*, II, 13–15; William B. Clark, ed., *Naval Documents of the American Revolution* (Washington, 1964), I, 4–60, *passim*, 208, 214–217, 257–261, 265–266, 293–294.

38. Alden, *Gage*, 218–232; John Shy, "Thomas Gage: Weak Link of Empire," in *George Washington's Opponents: British Generals and Admirals in the American Revolution*, ed. George A. Billias (New York, 1969), 24–27.

39. Ira D. Gruber, "Illusions of Mastery: The Howe Brothers, the North Ministry, and the American Revolution" (manuscript in press), chaps. i–iii; Smyth, ed., *Writings of Franklin*, VI, 250–251, 262.

40. Gruber, "Illusions of Mastery," chap. iii; J. Y. T. Greig, ed., *The Letters of David Hume* (Oxford, Eng., 1932), II, 300–301; Force, ed., *American Archives*, 4th ser., I, 1682–1683; Benjamin Labaree, *The Boston Tea Party* (New York, 1964), 208–209.

41. Sir John Fortescue. ed., *The Correspondence of King George the Third* (London, 1928), III, no. 1556.

# 3. Militia versus Regulars

WHEN THE WAR OF INDEPENDENCE began, there was no American army. During the early hostilities only the colonial militias, especially that of Massachusetts, occupied the field against Britain's regulars. At least two things stand out about the American military effort in these opening days of a war that was destined to last eight long years, twice the length of any subsequent American war before Vietnam. First, Britain was confronted by an aroused countryside, thousands of irate citizens in arms who ushered in not only a political revolution but a military revolution as well. Here the eighteenth-century military system, with its small, highly trained armies led by officers of the upper class, faced a new and unusual challenge, one that would be repeated in the wars of the French Revolution and the Napoleonic era. Second, the "embattled farmers" acquitted themselves surprisingly well against George III's professional army in the early contests at Concord and Bunker Hill. One witnesses the anomaly of people fighting for their liberties at the same time protesting they did not seek independence. In the long run, the war for Americans was a defensive struggle; initially, however, they displayed marked aggressiveness in bottling the redcoats up in Boston and in seizing the British post at Ticonderoga. In fact, the vigor and extent of American resistance, from the very beginning, pose arresting questions concerning the depths of Anglo-American antipathy by 1775 and concerning the unlikelihood of reconciliation short of independence.

## The Embattled Farmers

All these developments, in a sense, sprang from Dartmouth's letter to Gage:

> The only Consideration that remains is, in what manner the Force under your Command may be exerted. . . . the first essential step to be taken towards re-establishing Government, would be to arrest and imprison the principal actors & abettors in the Provincial Congress. . . . any efforts of the People, unprepared to encounter with a regular force, cannot be very formidable; and though such a proceeding should be, according to your idea of it, a Signal for Hostilities yet . . . it will surely be better that the Conflict should be brought on, upon such ground, than in a riper state of Rebellion.[1]

Though Gage declined to arrest the patriot leaders, who, except for Dr. Joseph Warren, were out of the city, he could not ignore the entire dispatch. What forceful measure should he take? To Gage the obvious answer was the seizure of the stores at Concord, about which he had obtained detailed intelligence, apparently from Dr. Benjamin Church, member of the Massachusetts Provincial Congress and a man who stood high in patriot circles. So well informed was Gage that he could present obese, slow-minded Lieutenant Colonel Francis Smith, commander of the expedition, with a detailed map showing the houses and buildings in Concord containing flour, powder, and equipment.[2] The patriots, however, had no more trouble keeping their secrets than the British; any army among a hostile people has difficulty in concealing its plans and movements. The Boston Port Bill had thrown hundreds of seamen out of work. Loafing about the once-bustling wharves, they were eager to report gossip from the soldiers and whatever came to their own eyes to men like Paul Revere who worked for Dr. Joseph Warren of the committee of safety. By April 16, at least, Gage's secret was out, and the sole question remaining for Revere and Warren was *when*. The assembling of 700 men, grenadiers and light infantry, at the foot of Boston Common on the night of April 18 gave the answer.

The problem for the patriots was how to get the alarm to Lexington (where Samuel Adams and Hancock were staying) and Concord, eleven and sixteen miles away respectively. Legend to the contrary, the lighting of two lanterns from the spire of Christ Church had little to do with spreading the word that the British were crossing the Charles River in boats instead of marching over Boston Neck. For both William Dawes, traversing the neck with the aid of a friendly redcoat, and Revere, rowing silently across to Charlestown, escaped the city and spurred toward Lexington. Arriving at midnight, Revere routed Adams and Hancock from their beds. Presently Dawes appeared, and the two riders set out for Concord, arousing the country people along the road. Fortunately for the patriots, Revere and Dawes were accompanied on this part of their mission by Dr. Samuel Prescott, a Concord physician, who was returning home after visiting a lady friend in Lexington. The three were still several miles from Concord when a dozen or so British officers attempted to surround them and take them into custody. Only Dr. Prescott, now largely forgotten, made his escape by turning sharply and sending his mount over a low stone wall; it was he, rather than the famous silversmith-engraver Revere, who carried the warning to Concord.

Meanwhile, Smith's expedition was slow in starting. The grenadiers and light infantry, wet and sticky from wading ashore through water over their knees, were kept waiting until after one o'clock in the morning while their supplies and equipment were ferried across from Boston. From the time the troops had gathered on the common to the moment the order to march finally rang out, between three and four hours had elapsed; even without incident they could not enter Concord until well after daylight. The expedition was hardly off to an auspicious beginning. And as the marchers trudged along through Menatomy and toward Lexington, they began to hear the pealing of church bells and the echoing of signal guns and to see patches of light from far-off farmhouse windows. Smith must have known, as Gage did, that on March 30 the Provincial Congress, sitting at Concord, had resolved: "That whenever the Army under command of General Gage, or any part thereof to the Number of Five Hundred, shall march out of the Town of Boston, with Artillery and Baggage, it ought to be . . . opposed; and therefore the Military Force of the Province ought to be assembled."[3] Anticipating trouble, Smith sent Major John Pitcairn forward with six light infantry companies to secure the two bridges just beyond Concord. Then, in his wisest decision of the day, Smith dispatched a messenger back to Boston to obtain reinforcements from Gage.

For Captain John Parker, forty-five-year-old veteran of Roger's Rangers in the last French war, there would be no reinforcements. Only his single company of minutemen stood on Lexington Green. The company had gathered there a little after Revere's midnight appearance. Most of Parker's men had spent a hard day in the fields. Spring had come early that year. Ploughing was already underway, and some of the Lexington men had already seeded their fields. Tired and sleepy, they shivered in the cold night air for an hour or so. The older men in particular (several were in their sixties) looked longingly at the candlelights flickering in Buckman's Tavern across the road.

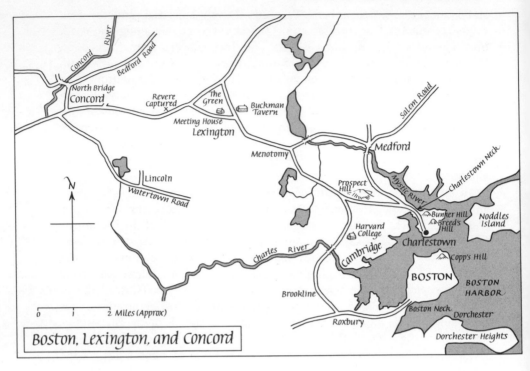

Boston, Lexington, and Concord

Finally, as no word came to confirm Revere's warning, the minutemen who lived nearby went home and the rest entered the tavern, talking, drinking a bit to cut the chill, and waiting—hopefully for a messenger to tell of a false alarm, fearfully for the massive, muffled tread of a scarlet column followed by the sharp, piercing commands of British officers. They had not liked what Revere told them. Seven years earlier, in town meeting, these men and their neighbors had declared that the presence of a British army in their province infringed upon their "natural, constitutional and chartered rights." Under the leadership of their minister of many years, the Reverend Jonas Clarke, a man steeped in political theory and its articulation, they had pledged their "estates and every thing dear in life, yea and life itself" if necessary in opposing the Coercive Acts.[4]

In time all that might be required. But not on this early morning of April 19, 1775. Captain Parker's company would be hopelessly outnumbered. They would merely draw themselves up on the common, displaying by their formal appearance their detestation for what the British were doing.[5] Then, just after sunrise, Lexington scout Thaddeus Bowman galloped up. The British were coming, and they were almost upon them! There were shouts of alarm, sixteen-year-old William

Diamond beat furiously on his drum, and Captain Parker assembled seventy or so men in two ranks as the first redcoats swung into view. A little less than half the adult male population, they ranged in age from sixty-five to sixteen or younger. Eight father and son combinations stood together in the misty haze; aging Jonas Parker was accompanied by a son and a teenage nephew. A beloved Negro—Prince Estabrook—was there, too. As a military unit, the Lexington men left much to be desired; but their very diversity illustrates the solidarity of rural New England society.

The sight of the two straggling lines must have only confirmed Major John Pitcairn's opinion of American militiamen. A warm-hearted man who personally liked Americans, Pitcairn nonetheless was disdainful of their military abilities. Barely a month before he had vowed "that one active campaign, a smart action, and burning two or three of their towns, will set everything to rights."[6] Though the Americans on the green were well out of the British line of march on the road leading to Concord, Pitcairn cantered across the grass toward the minutemen, calling upon them to throw down their arms and disperse. The regulars, coming up behind him, broke into a run and cheered wildly as they approached the Americans. Parker, sensing a serious situation, told his men to withdraw and not to fire. Colonial militia were scarcely noted for being well trained and well disciplined. (Parker's own minute company was only a few weeks old.) Consequently, they did not disperse in an orderly or prompt manner, and no one discarded his weapon. Some retired hastily; others drifted slowly back to the edge of the common.

In the midst of the confusion Pitcairn ordered his troops to move in among the Americans and disarm them. Almost immediately someone's musket flashed in the pan, followed by several scattered shots (on one side or both sides?) and, then, a resounding volley from one of the British platoons. Though Pitcairn tried strenuously to end the firing, the regulars were, as Lieutenant John Barker said, "so wild they cou'd hear no orders."[7] Stouthearted Jonas Parker was wounded by a musketball and then bayoneted to death. Only after eight Americans lay dead and ten were wounded was Pitcairn, disturbed and embarrassed, able to recover control. British casualties totaled one man wounded and Pitcairn's horse grazed. Lexington was hardly a battle, and yet a war had begun. The United States was born in an act of violence lasting but fifteen or twenty minutes.

For that matter, the war could just as easily have commenced five miles farther down the road at Concord. Long before word of the shooting at Lexington had arrived, Concord militiamen were tumbling out of their beds in response to the frantic ringing of the alarm bell.

Characteristic of the diffusion of military responsibility in colonial society is the fact that the Reverend William Emerson, gun in hand, was
the first man to reach Wright's Tavern, the assembling point. But the
two Concord minute companies were hardly able to contest the advance of Pitcairn and Smith. They retired across the Concord River to
watch as Smith's column entered the village, about eight o'clock in the
morning. Since news of a British march had leaked out, the Americans
had carted away or concealed much of their military equipment. Moreover, Smith's searchers were none too thorough in destroying what they
found. Several barrels of flour thrown into the mill pond were later
salvaged, as were most of the five hundred pounds of musket balls also
deposited in the water.

All the while, the Concord units beyond the North Bridge were reinforced by several companies and some unattached volunteers from
nearby villages. Colonel James Barrett, exercising temporary command, ordered the militia toward the bridge. Three British light infantry companies standing guard there withdrew across the span and
delivered a volley that killed two of the approaching Americans. The
militiamen were better shots than that: a blast of rebel musketry killed
one redcoat, mortally wounded two, and hit four officers and five enlisted men. The light infantry now fell back into the town, followed
by the Americans at a cautious distance. Then occurred the war's first
atrocity, lending impetus to the myth of the American barbarian;
and not unlike similar happenings, it grew with the telling. A country
youth, possibly on his way to join the provincials, crossed the North
Bridge and saw two of the wounded regulars lying on the ground. Perhaps one of them called out or attempted to rise, whereupon the frightened boy drove an ax into the man's skull and left him dying. He was
still alive a few minutes later when a British party searching for patriot stores stumbled upon the poor man, his head and face covered
with blood. One need not doubt the report that the horrified regulars
offered their comrade no relief but "ran with great speed" to inform
Smith of the dreadful spectacle. The soldiers asserted that the victim
had been scalped and his ears cut off. As the story leaped through the
ranks the number scalped increased, and it was affirmed that the rebels
were gouging those who fell into their hands.[8]

At noon, the morning's work behind them, an apprehensive line of
redcoats wound its way back through the low hills outside Concord
toward Lexington and Boston. But their real day's work—escape from
annihilation—lay ahead. The remarkable battle that developed, as
Christopher Ward has written, would be fought on a field almost sixteen miles long and seldom more than a few hundred yards wide.[9] A
mile from Concord, near a fork called Meriam's Corner, the road nar-

rowed for a bridge spanning a meandering creek. The redcoats were bunched together; their flanking parties had come down from a ridge to get over the stream. The provincial militia—approximately 500, including those from Concord and a flood of later arrivals from other towns—opened a withering fire on the British flanks and rear. To the returning British, already tired and suffering from delusions of American barbarity, their assailants seemed to be everywhere, firing from behind trees, shrubs, and rocks. "There could not be less than 5,000" of them, claimed Ensign Henry de Berniere of the 10th Infantry. The redcoats, accustomed to fixed-position fighting and volley formations, faced a continuous rain of musket balls from unseen marksmen in shifting positions. Doubtless some of the older officers remembered this kind of warfare from their earlier American service. Not so the younger ones like Lieutenant William Sutherland of the 38th Regiment, who castigated the militiamen as "concealed villains" who made "cowardly disposition . . . to murder us all."[10] Colonel Smith was painfully wounded, and, in the confusion, Pitcairn's horse threw him and darted away. The British force, no longer a marching column, was now a disorganized throng rushing toward Lexington, its wounded strung out along the road.

Smith's desperate hope of support was realized at Lexington. Gage had dispatched a reinforcement of 900 to 1,200 men under thirty-three-year-old General Hugh, Earl Percy, and they arrived not a moment too soon. On the return journey Percy experienced the continuous, nerve-racking musketry all too familiar to Smith and Pitcairn. Americans posted in houses along this stretch of the road brought down more than a few of the invaders. Percy sent scores of men out in front and on the flanks to clear these buildings and set fire to them. Undoubtedly the bloodiest combat of the day took place here. British soldiers, tormented by the constant sniping and enraged by the reputed scalping incident, displayed scant mercy toward their adversaries. These redcoats were masters of the bayonet, and they employed it with grim effectiveness against the Massachusetts farmers whose own weapons were not so equipped. Lieutenant Barker admitted that all who "were found in the houses were put to death." Atrocities, hand-to-hand fighting, burning houses, supposedly disciplined regulars carrying away armloads of loot—neither side was fighting by the standard rules of the eighteenth century![11]

The Americans kept on coming. Watertown sent 134 men; Roxbury, 140; Needham, 185; Danvers, 331, and so on. Had General Heath and Dr. Warren, both of whom appeared late in the afternoon, been able to coordinate the various militia contingents, Percy's column might well have been destroyed, a blow of crushing dimension to Gage; with half his entire army gone his position in Boston would have been wholly untenable. As it was, the wild, unorthodox battle continued until the British reached Charlestown, where dusk and the protecting guns of the royal navy concluded the mauling.

Even after the troops retired to Boston, the rebels remained and others joined them. To the excited spectators in Boston, it seemed as if the whole countryside was converging on the city, as though "men came down from the clouds." The *Newport Mercury* described the day's events as the beginning of "the American Civil War, which will hereafter fill an important page in History."[12]

The Americans—"intrepid, rural sons of freedom"—had fought with spirit and determination. Intellectually, they had been well prepared to give battle. For months and years, the New England clergy—Jonas Clarke of Lexington and William Emerson of Concord were typical— had preached the right and duty of resisting tyranny with helmet and shield if all other measures should fail.[13] (Half a dozen or more clergy- men participated in the fighting of April 19.) Moreover, veteran colo- nial militia officers, nourishing a rankling resentment of supercilious British officers at Louisbourg, Crown Point, and elsewhere in the last war, had instilled in their men the belief that redcoats and their officers were only human, that indeed they had only beaten the French with indispensable colonial aid. Earl Percy, who had previously spoken of the Americans as "cowards," conceded the day after the battle that "They have men amongst them who know very well what they are about, having been employed as rangers against the Indians and Cana- dians, and this country being much cov[ere]d w[ith] wood, and hilly, is very advantageous for their method of fighting." Lieutenant Barker also described the country around Lexington and Concord as "an amazingly strong one, full of Hills, Woods, stone Walls, &c." Though one does not normally think of the Eastern region of America as a frontier by the time of the Revolution, much of it was rugged terrain, covered with dense woods: British Captain James Murray, following the engagement at Brooklyn Heights in 1776, said the area was "cov- ered with woods and hedges, from which they [Washington's Conti- nentals] gave us several very heavy fires."[14] To be sure, most of the major battles of the War of Independence would not have the frontier flavor of Lexington and Concord; but the numerous hills, brambles, and thickets of the East, like the mountainous interior, would pose diffi- culties for British operations.

The militia were clearly at their best in fending off an assault upon their immediate liberty and property. Yet even in victory they revealed some traditional weaknesses. Displaying improvised tactics that boiled down to every man for himself, the militia scattered out, each man firing from cover, loading from a place of concealment, and then hurrying across the fields to intercept the British marchers at another vantage point. The Americans' lack of coordinated direction, plus the work of Percy's flanking parties in keeping many of the patriots at a respectful distance (their muskets were inaccurate beyond sixty yards), tells why the high British casualty figures did not reach even greater numbers than 73 killed, 174 wounded, and 26 missing. American losses in all categories totaled 93. The day of Lexington and Concord offered military lessons that both sides could ill afford to miss.

## Marking Time

While Gage, awaiting reinforcements from Britain, sat in Boston cooped up by an angry populace, Massachusetts' patriot leaders were having their own problems with those same citizen-soldiers. In an unending stream, militia companies from distant towns, fifty, seventy-five, one hundred miles away, poured into the Harvard Yard at Cambridge. By the evening of the 20th, there were, according to some estimates, over 20,000 militiamen in that vicinity, possibly the largest assembled military force in the history of the colonies. They had rushed from their fields and shops to repel an invader that had now retired to the safety of Boston. Most of them, having made no arrangements for their home responsibilities, could not be expected to stay. Besides, they lacked food and equipment for a military campaign. This situation confronted the Massachusetts Provincial Congress on April 22 as it met at Concord and then adjourned to Watertown to be near the patriot force at Cambridge.

In their preparations the Massachusetts leaders demonstrated their need for the direct support of the population. Unlike European wars, the bulk of the citizenry could not be indifferent to the struggle; the Provincial Congress, after all, was responsible to the people. To prove that the conflict was justified, whether it eventually terminated in independence or reconciliation, the Provincial Congress published broadsides and collected depositions from eye-witnesses stating that at both Lexington and Concord the British had begun the shooting. Neither law, custom, nor patriotism, however, could compel the militia to continue indefinitely outside Boston. So the Provincial Congress, adhering to the pattern of the colonial wars, enlisted a volunteer force from the milita, headed by forty-seven-year-old General Artemas Ward, strong in patriotism and military background in the French and Indian War but weak in energy and talent.[15]

Massachusetts, feeling itself aggrieved by British General Gage, accorded its own generals appreciably less authority over the newborn Massachusetts army than the Second Continental Congress would later bestow on George Washington. In fact, the Massachusetts committee of safety—an instrument of the Provincial Congress—sat continuously in Cambridge, where it could make the important military decisions and receive instructions from the legislators in nearby Watertown. Effective leadership of the patriot cause in those first weeks of the war rested in the sure hands of thirty-four-year-old Dr. Warren, president of the Provincial Congress as well as chairman of the committee of safety. With James Otis now mentally and physically incapacitated, and with Samuel Adams and John Hancock attending the Second Continental Congress in Philadelphia, Warren was more or less the chief executive of Massachusetts. Organizing regiments, settling disputes among cantankerous officers, securing supplies, caring for the wounded (British and American), negotiating with Gage for the free passage of patriots from Boston, and filtering spies into Boston itself to gather intelligence, Warren was a human dynamo, the kind no successful revolution can do without.[16]

Yet Warren and Ward exercised limited control over the other New England troops participating in the siege. From Rhode Island came a brigade of nearly 1,500 men headed by the youthful ex-Quaker Nathanael Greene, whose energy, intelligence, and familiarity with the military classics more than compensated for his lack of experience as a militia officer. Connecticut, promising 6,000 troops, selected steady Brigadier General Joseph Spencer to lead them, though he was somewhat overshadowed by the colony's veteran Indian fighter, colorful "Old Put," Brigadier General Israel Putnam. New Hampshire's force of 2,000 was commanded by a hard-headed farmer named John Stark, who knew his militiamen and who was himself as unpredictable as colonial militia so often were. Greene, Spencer, and Stark each directed a military establishment independent from the army created by the Massachusetts Provincial Congress. Thus each colony was responsible for enlisting its men, appointing its officers, procuring its provisions, and paying its troops. Though a fair measure of cooperation resulted among the New England military commanders, only the New Hampshire contingent had initial instructions to follow Ward's orders in conducting field operations.

The pressing requirement of a unified American military effort manifested itself in the squabble preceding the attack on Fort Ticonderoga, a once-mighty fortress at the juncture of Lake Champlain and Lake George. Built by the French in 1755, the crumbling and lightly garrisoned structure was a "gateway to the continent," from which a strong foe could press southward via the Hudson River all the way to New

York City, cutting the colonies in half. But that was a remote fear for the Americans in May, 1775; of more concern were the idle, rusting British artillery pieces there. Who first proposed the seizure of the guns and their transportation eastward to secure the rebel defenses ringing Boston is unknown. Connecticut leaders authorized Ethan Allen to assault the fort, about the time the Massachusetts Provincial Congress commissioned Colonel Benedict Arnold to do the same thing.

The short, stocky Arnold, a former apothecary and merchant from New Haven, Connecticut, and the tall, leather-lunged frontiersman Allen, leader of the vigilante Green Mountain Boys, would hardly have become boon companions under ordinary circumstances. Allen and his boys, after battling for five years against New York authority in the New Hampshire Grants (now Vermont), almost exploded when the aggressive Arnold appeared and coolly demanded that he take charge of the attack. Allen's men agreed to let Arnold join them, though there is some uncertainty as to whether they recognized Arnold as joint commander of the expedition, as he later claimed. The fracas over authority and the boat trip across the dark, squall-ruffled waters of Lake Champlain to the western shore were more troublesome to the Americans than the redcoat garrison at Ticonderoga: forty-five officers and men who were mostly sick, "old, wore out, and unserviceable." Just before daylight on May 9, Allen easily captured the sleepy garrison "in the name of the great Jehovah and the Continental Congress"—or so he wrote in after years. The rough, roistering Green Mountain Boys celebrated their victory by freely imbibing from the "flowing bowl." These untamed spirits, not unlike John Sevier's Watauga backwoodsmen or Thomas Sumter's South Carolina partisans, were scarcely cut out for being regular soldiers, whether American Continentals or British redcoats; but such groups had their moments of glory in the Revolution. In Allen's case, his capture of Ticonderoga's heavy artillery, sledged eastward the next winter, hastened the British departure from Boston.[17]

There were some smaller American victories that spring. Seth Warner, Allen's right-hand man, occupied the little British post at Crown Point, some miles northward; and Arnold, now with a band of his own followers, sailed in a captured sloop beyond Crown Point and took Fort St. John on the Sorel River before returning down the lake. Around Boston, too, there was renewed activity. The besieging force had swelled to perhaps 17,000 men, extended in a half circle around Boston from Dorchester to Charlestown. Some of these men landed on islands in the harbor to keep sheep, cattle, and hay from falling into Gage's hands. They were mainly successful, despite several sharp encounters with enemy raiding parties supported by royal navy vessels.[18] Even so, this was meager fare to the restless militiamen of the besieging forces. Camp routine was exceedingly boring; and as weeks passed with little action, their presence seemed to be of scant importance. No wonder, then, that Colonel William Prescott and Israel Putnam, concerned over the dissatisfaction in camp, were eager to channel the energies of their troops into an entrenching operation on one of the strategic hills on Charlestown Peninsula overlooking Boston, even if their enterprise should invite a British thrust.

## Bunker Hill

The almost total collapse of British authority in the thirteen colonies followed hard on the heels of Lexington and Concord. Virtually impotent before the explosion in Massachusetts, the royal governors, with few exceptions, now dashed for the protection of the nearest British man of war. Quickly the militias, under orders of provincial congresses, solidified the authority of patriot leaders. Gage had reluctantly turned a deaf ear to the cries of royal governors for military equipment and regular troops. The General himself was encountering enough trouble maintaining control in Boston, a city filled with hostile citizens and hemmed in by a rebel army. Far away in London the ministry, for no sound reason, attributed his problems more to a dearth of energy than to a lack of men. Instead of transporting the thousands of troops actually required to bolster Gage's position, the politicians felt he needed advisors to spur him to action.

Consequently, on May 26, 1775, the thirty-six-gun frigate *Cerberus* dropped anchor in Boston harbor to deposit a "precious cargo"—Major Generals William Howe, Henry Clinton, and John Burgoyne. They were, as Burgoyne expressed it, a "triumvirate of reputation." Howe, the senior officer by virtue of achieving his rank several months before Clinton and Burgoyne, had carved his record in America. Like his brother "Black Dick," the admiral, Howe was a dark-complexioned man who had participated in the capture of Louisbourg in 1758 and the next year had personally led Wolfe's advance guard up the hazardous trail to the Plains of Abraham and Quebec. Though softened by years of high living, the forty-six-year-old Howe was a brave and able combat officer. Lord George Germain entertained great hope for Howe, who understood the colonial method of fighting behind "trees, walls or hedges"; and more recently he had taught those tactics to light infantry in Britain. "Nobody understands that discipline so well as Howe," boasted Germain.[19]

Clinton, forty-five years old, had made his reputation largely on his service in Germany, 1760–1762. When his regiment arrived on the continent, he became a volunteer with the advance allied corps under Charles, Prince of Brunswick, who, respecting Clinton's talents, appointed the Englishman his aide-de-camp. Clinton saw heavy fighting on more than one occasion and displayed personal bravery in battle near Friedberg, where he received a painful wound. Of keen mind, he seems to have possessed real gifts as a strategist. Would they be vitiated by his very real defects as a human being? A sensitive, prickly man, he got along poorly with his fellow officers. "I am a shy bitch," he had written in conceding his reluctance to mix with Howe and Burgoyne aboard the *Cerberus*.[20] And whether he recognized it or not, Clinton was sometimes suspicious of himself, capable of being his own worst enemy.

The short, paunchy Clinton appeared colorless in the presence of theatrical John Burgoyne. Handsome, gay, and vivacious, "Gentleman Johnny" was master of the drawing room and, according to gossip, the boudoir. His fifty-three years had been anything but dull: he eloped with the daughter of a wealthy peer, wrote bombastic prose and poetry, delivered histrionic speeches in the House of Commons, and intrigued at court for influence and favors. Somehow, along with all this and a lusty taste for the gaming table, Burgoyne had found time for a military career. He was in some ways a soldier ahead of his period. In a treatise on the duties of an officer, he urged his fellows not to subject enlisted men to harsh and brutal treatment. Anticipating future developments in warfare springing from industrialism and technological advances, he recommended that officers study mathematics and familiarize themselves with changes in military equipment. Yet Burgoyne was no mere rulebook officer; he showed dash and vigor leading the 16th "Light Horse" in Portugal during the Seven Years' War.

These generals, destined to be directly responsible for Britain's military fortunes in America, had not witnessed combat for over a decade, nor had they ever commanded large forces in the field. Still, these were not insurmountable handicaps. Pitt had found a great soldier in a gangly, hollow-chested youth of only thirty: James Wolfe. And Washington would find near greatness, if not more, in two thirtyish men: Benedict Arnold and Nathanael Greene, who were among the most inexperienced of his officers initially.

There are no absolute standards for successful generalship; Marshall Saxe believed a general was born, not made. Perhaps the most vital quality in a general is something all the great commentators on war have called character. Character, in British generals during the Revolutionary War, called for, among other things, a burning desire to win, resolutely pursued with a combination of both imagination and prudence until the victory was secured. Would they respond to the challenge?

One thing was clear: they felt they could do better than the steady, methodical Gage, who, different from the triumvirate, had not distinguished himself in the Seven Years' War; nor, so far as the trio was concerned, had he acquitted himself well in Massachusetts. Carping and back-biting, endemic among British generals and admirals in the Revolution, began at Boston and, for some, would continue long after the war in their reminiscences—though apologies is a better word. Clinton soon concluded that Gage had erred in sending Smith's detachment to Concord; while Burgoyne embarked upon a campaign of subtle criticism of his superior in letters to London. The newcomers, apparently all bluster and advice, were of "a single sentiment upon the military conduct to be pursued," reported Burgoyne, who also declared that the besieged garrison needed "elbow room."[21] In short, the major generals demanded action, and they had the ministry on their side. First, however, Gage, under orders from London, issued a proclamation on June 12 imposing martial law and describing as traitors those in revolt against the King, but, simultaneously, promising pardon to all in arms except Samuel Adams and John Hancock. The overture, clothed in Burgoyne's pompous prose, aroused only anger and indignation among the Americans.

Finally Gage agreed to a limited offensive: to occupy the outlying heights of Dorchester and Charlestown which, if fortified by the rebels, could subject Boston to heavy bombardment. Once again the patriots got wind of the British scheme. The Massachusetts committee of safety proceeded to checkmate Gage, Howe, and company by instructing General Ward to entrench on Bunker Hill, highest of three principal elevations on the Charlestown Peninsula. Colonel William Prescott, who had only recently urged the building of works on the peninsula, now received the assignment and approximately 1,000 men, mostly from Massachusetts but including a small contingent of Connecticut troops and an artillery company boasting two fieldpieces. The men assembled on Cambridge Common in the late afternoon of June 16, equipped with packs, blankets, and twenty-four hours' rations. After hearing President Samuel Langdon of Harvard pray for divine blessing, the column waited for darkness and then marched silently across Charlestown Neck.

For reasons never made clear, possibly through a misunderstanding, the Americans passed over Bunker Hill and halted farther down the mile-long peninsula on Breed's Hill. On this steep, seventy-five foot eminence the patriots, though closer to Boston, were more exposed to British fire and farther from the safety of their own lines. Only a narrow isthmus joined the peninsula to the mainland. As the only means of retreat, this corridor could be raked by guns from British warships or sealed off by enemy landing parties.

In response to Prescott's crisp commands, detachments hustled to the wagons and distributed entrenching equipment. At the summit of the hill, the New Englanders dug furiously into the summer earth. These farmers, after years of clearing rocks and tree stumps from their own land, were experienced wielders of picks and shovels. Colonel Richard Gridley, a Louisbourg veteran and an excellent engineer, planned a redoubt approximately forty yards square. The militiamen, unsteady in formal, open combat, needed the maximum protection. "Americans were not afraid of their heads, though very much afraid of their legs; if you cover these, they will fight forever," boasted Israel Putnam.[22] So Gridley ordered the erection of a six-foot parapet containing firing platforms of earth and wood. Gridley and Prescott also supervised the construction of a breastwork running eastward from the redoubt down the hill and extending one hundred yards.

The word "sluggish" can well be applied to Gage's response to the bold American enterprise on the Charlestown Peninsula. That very night Clinton, making a reconnaissance, either saw or heard the Americans at work on Breed's Hill. His advice to Gage, an attack at daybreak, was rejected on the ground that the rebels were probably on a temporary foray. At four o'clock in the dim light of dawn, the watch aboard H. M. S. *Lively* saw the major undertaking that Clinton had suspected. The roar of the *Lively's* guns, followed by those of the entire fleet as it tested the provincial positions, awoke Boston to the emergency at hand.

Once again, in a hastily convened council of war, Clinton pressed for quick action: while Howe ferried a large force to the southern shore on the peninsula across from Boston, he himself would land 500 men on the western shore and hit the Americans from behind, sealing off their line of retreat. Moreover, as historians have frequently noted, the smaller vessels of the fleet and the floating batteries could have prevented American reinforcements from reaching Prescott by shelling Charlestown Neck. Why Gage rejected Clinton's idea is not evident, although one suggestion is that he may have been reluctant to interpose a portion of his command between two wings of the provincial army. Clinton suggested another reason as a partial explanation: he was a veteran of the German campaign; Gage, a veteran of American service. Like the friction that developed between Continental and militia officers in the course of the Revolution, British officers battle-tested on the European continent not infrequently were cliquish and openly disdainful of officers with a background in New World warfare, and the latter reciprocated in kind. Clinton wrote: "Mr. Gage thought himself so well informed that he would not take any opinion of others, particularly of a man bred up in the German school, which that of America affects to despise."[23] In any case, the council decided instead on a frontal approach to Prescott's entrenchments on Breed's Hill at high tide that afternoon. Commanded by General Howe, the expedition consisted of four regiments and an artillery company, with another regiment and a marine battalion held in reserve.

The British decision to postpone the attack for a number of hours gave Prescott's men precious time to continue their spade work. The cannonading from the fleet, though inflicting little harm, frightened the raw American troops, producing some desertions. Finally, a soldier outside the redoubt was hit and killed. Prescott, a tough-minded officer of the last war and perhaps as near a professional in thinking and training as almost anyone in the provincial army (he had once rejected a British commission), was momentarily startled when his citizen-soldiers insisted on suspending their work to give the dead man a formal burial. But Prescott resignedly bared his bald head. What a strange sight for British officers to witness through their binoculars, with shells exploding around and a land attack imminent.

The tall, broad-shouldered Prescott, cool and steady throughout the day, seemed to be everywhere, offering the men encouragement and lending a hand with the actual labor. But as Massachusetts Private Peter Brown reported, "We began to be almost beat out, being tired by our labour and having no sleep the night before, but little victuals, [and] no drink but rum."[24] Despite orders to the contrary, Prescott discovered many men had brought no food. In the forenoon he issued a plea to General Ward for provisions and additional units. Ward, fearing an assault by Gage on his weakened lines, offered little further support until prodded by the committee of safety into sending out two New Hampshire regiments.

Howe, the expert on amphibious operations, the authority on light infantry, the student of American fighting methods, landed at Morton's Point about one o'clock and slowly began deploying his regulars for an advance on the American entrenchments. He undoubtedly intended for the redcoats to recover their now-tarnished reputation resulting from the Concord retreat. Little else explains his peculiar determination to send his legions in their traditional open-field formation into the face of the American muskets. Notwithstanding Clinton's subsequent sour observation that Howe and several other colleagues understood nothing "other than a direct at[tack],"[25] it is more probable that Howe hoped to overpower the Americans with sheer British might for psychological reasons, sound military theory being less important in this instance. Let the rebellious colonists experience a full-fledged attack to destroy any misconceptions about regulars under fire, and the ill-clad, poorly organized, inexperienced provincial army might simply unravel and disappear.

The patriots on Breed's Hill were about to face such a test. As the crimson ranks formed below him, Prescott completed his preparations assisted by Joseph Warren, who fought as a volunteer; Prescott also received aid from Putnam who bolstered the smaller American positions established on Bunker Hill. Since the enemy overlapped the shoreline on his left, Prescott became concerned about the gap between the far end of his breastwork and the edge of the peninsula, which might become an avenue for flanking his main entrenchments. He stationed his artillery company and his Connecticut troops behind a stone-and-rail fence to the rear of the redoubt and stretching toward the Mystic River. Some time before three o'clock they were reinforced from the mainland by a New Hampshire regiment under John Stark, who, noticing a strip of open beach, now extended the fence down to the water's edge.

This was the situation when, about three o'clock, Howe was finally ready to move, having taken two hours or more in the leisurely military manner of his day. The years had not diminished the personal courage of this man who had ripped off his coat and fought alongside 400 regulars in holding off a relieving force of 2,000 Frenchmen at Quebec in 1759. Generals still not uncommonly led their men in battle; and Howe, addressing the regulars below Breed's Hill, announced that he expected them to "behave like Englishmen" and that he would "go myself at your head." "English courage," wrote the Boston tory Peter Oliver with this battle in mind, meant "standing undaunted in open field to be shot at."[26] Assuredly the terrain afforded no protection as the crimson mass set forth—Howe leading the élite light infantry and grenadiers, plus the 5th and 52d regiments, against the rail fence in the hope of smashing through and then hitting the redoubt from the rear; Brigadier General Robert Pigot directing the British left composed of the 38th, 43d, and 47th regiments along with Major Pitcairn's marines against the breastwork and redoubt. The outcome that afternoon rested upon the performance of these regulars, for the artillery was ineffectual. Most of the guns of the fleet could not be elevated sufficiently to bear upon the summit, and the rest did minimal damage to the thick-walled redoubt. Howe's own six-pounders had been carelessly supplied with twelve-pound balls.

As people in Boston crowded the rooftops to watch the onslaught, Pigot's heavily-equipped redcoats, in three long lines, slowly pushed through thick grass and climbed over the many fences seemingly stretching endlessly before them. Ignoring James Wolfe's maxim "it is of little purpose to fire at men who are covered with an entrench-ment,"[27] the British at intervals unleashed volleys which only gener-ated billowing clouds of smoke and drew no reply from the defenders. Whether one or more American officers admonished their men not to fire on the British until they saw "the white's of their eyes" is unanswer-able, but the remark portrays the spirit of their intentions: effective combat with muskets could not even commence until the opposing forces were nearly face to face. At last, when Prescott shouted the order, the parapet seemed to ignite in one gigantic burst of flame that tore gaping holes in the British front ranks. Surging forward again, Pigot's wing staggered under a second blast, then hastily retired to the foot of the hill.

On the British right, Howe's own wing, minus the light infantry, had similar trouble with fences and heavy grass. He had sent those crack companies down the beach along the Mystic, only to discover their flanking effort thwarted by Stark's projection of the stone-and-rail fence. All along the lengthy front the Americans quietly awaited the invaders. Here the events varied little from those of Pigot's attack on the redoubt and breastworks. There was the same senseless firing from the scarlet lines and then, within fifty yards of the Americans, the same lethal fusillade from the patriots' muskets. The first line swayed and stumbled back into the ranks of the advancing second line, the entire wing falling away in confusion, pursued by a second decimating blast from the American fence.

Pigot's men tried the hill again, no longer seriously distracted by a party of snipers in nearby Charlestown, for shells from a battery com-manded by Burgoyne on Capp's Hill in Boston had destroyed the vil-lage and smoked most of the rebel marksmen out—the place being "one great blaze; the church steeples . . . great pyramids of fire," exulted the prose-minded General.[28] Pigot, however, fared no better than be-fore; a steady stream of musketry drove the attackers down the eminence. When Clinton arrived from Boston with a five-hundred-man reinforcement, he found Pigot's officers unable to control the fright-ened men. Never in his thirty years in the army had Clinton seen "so great a want of order."[29]

Clinton's remark could almost apply to Howe's second thrust against Stark and Putnam on the American left. Though the regulars bravely came on once more, stepping methodically over dead and wounded comrades, the American muskets erupted again and again and again. "Most of our Grenadiers and Light Infantry," declared one English-man, "lost three-fourths, and many nine-tenths, of their men. Some had only eight and nine men a company left, some only three, four and five." Francis, Lord Rawdon, a young man with a bright military future, wrote that "the oldest officers say thay never saw a sharper action."[30] The regulars were at a vast disadvantage. The Americans would not come out and exchange volleys with them in European fashion. And the heavy fire, the troublesome fences, and the tall grass now strewn with carnage prevented their getting close enough to use the bayonet, infighting at which they were unsurpassed. Howe, though failing to steady his thinning red lines, displayed his old bravery and received more luck than his personal staff, all of whom were shot down. For that matter, the losses among the entire body of officers was "most dreadful," Howe admitted.

As the forces of Howe and Pigot reformed on the beaches, Howe stubbornly determined to make a third assault. No longer was the prime objective to give the band on Breed's Hill—and indirectly the New England army, and indeed all America—a blow that would forever destroy their will to resist. The sole aim now was to avoid one of the most shattering defeats to British arms in a century of warfare in the New World. Burgoyne went so far as to aver "that, perhaps, a defeat was a final loss to the British Empire in America." Fortunately for Howe, he now had Clinton's reinforcement; and, ordering the men to drop their heavy packs, he threw both Pigot's wing and his own in a final, concentrated assault on the redoubt and breastwork.[31]

Inside the redoubt, Prescott desperately needed ammunition and fresh troops. In a magnificent display of courage, he commanded his troops at the redoubt and breastwork to stand firm: to hold their fire until the last possible moment to make the most of their meager quantity of balls and powder. Then, with the advancing red line a mere twenty yards away—so reported Prescott, though to Lord Rawdon it seemed no more than ten—the American muskets spoke again; but this volley was their last. Stepping over their fallen comrades in their front, Howe's legions swept over the parapet, their bayonets at long last brought into play. Only the smoke and dust in the redoubt prevented a wholesale massacre. Yet thirty Americans, swinging their muskets as clubs, were bayoneted to death; and Dr. Warren, "the greatest incendiary in all America," received a fatal ball in the head. In the confusion Prescott and many of his men escaped to nearby Bunker Hill, their flight covered in some measure by the Americans who momentarily remained at the rail fence.

From Bunker Hill the retreat continued. Clinton reported that American sharpshooters, posted in abandoned houses, made it hazardous for the British to pursue at close range. By this time, however, H. M. S. *Glasgow* and *Symmetry*, supported by floating batteries, were raking Charlestown Neck as the patriots withdrew. During this concluding part of the battle the Americans suffered their severest losses, which, all told, amounted to 100 killed, 271 wounded, and 30 taken prisoner.

For Howe the misnamed Battle of Bunker Hill was a Pyrrhic victory, resulting in the heaviest British losses of the war: 228 dead and 826 wounded, or 42 per cent of the 2,500 troops engaged that afternoon. The ghastly appearance of many of the wounded vividly brought home to the British generals the grim price of their achievement. The smooth bore musket, deficient though it was, packed a frightful blow at close range, capable of ripping open great quantities of human flesh. In addition to this form of mutilation, some Americans were responsible for mangling still others by cramming their muskets with rusty nails and pieces of glass. In Boston, Peter Oliver, encountering "Carts loaded with those unfortunate Men," described them as "truly a Shocking Sight," to say nothing of "the piercing Groans of the dying." Howe, who looked "with horror" upon his many casualties, freely conceded the "success was too dearly bought."[32]

What more can be said of Howe's generalship on this occasion? He failed to employ the new light infantry tactics of which he was supposedly an authority. Whereas Wolfe had recommended that troops should attack an entrenchment "not in a line, but in small firing columns of three or four platoons in depth, with small parties between each column . . . to fire at the top of the parapet,"[33] Howe used instead the traditional extended front of two and three lines in depth, with platoons firing volleys in sequence. In the last analysis, however, the unusual thing about the contest was not that Howe's tactics were conventional; Wolfe, after all, was a genius. The unusual thing—given the rugged American positions and Howe's inability to roll up the American flank near the Mystic—was that the British General had continued the head-on assault. In the eighteenth century, open field battles, and especially attacks upon fortified positions, produced a casualty rate sometimes reaching 50 per cent. Military men may not all have agreed with Marshall Saxe's claim that the best commander was one who achieved his ends by maneuver rather than by engagement, nor would all accept the dictum that battle was "the remedy of the desperate." Nevertheless, a good general usually fought only if forced to or if the odds were heavily on his side. Victory would be hollow indeed if a commander sacrificed the cream of his small, highly trained professional army, the creation of years of work, with every man part of a tactical machine designed to function smoothly in the field.

Christopher Ward, an excellent military historian, contended that American writers have exaggerated the influence of this battle on Howe's subsequent conduct: little if any evidence exists that Howe's flanking operations against Washington's army in 1776 and 1777 stemmed from a caution born of his enormous losses at Bunker Hill. In any case, the feint, the parry, and the flanking movement were more in keeping with the military theory of the day than the smashing assault, and one finds it hard to believe that Bunker Hill did not strengthen Howe's fidelity to the European art of war. Howe's own remarks, made several years later, seem to cast light on the matter: "my opinion has always been, that the defeat of the rebel regular army is the surest road to peace. I invariably pursued the most probable means of forcing its commander to action," *but* "under circumstances the least hazardous to the royal army; for even a victory, attended by a heavy loss of men on our part, would have given a fatal check to the progress of the war, and might have proved irreparable." Had it always been his opinion? Or was it more likely a consequence of Bunker Hill?[34]

British blunders, which include Gage's failure to occupy the Charlestown Peninsula ahead of the rebels, were no more numerous than those of the Americans, who in taking post there had risked the grave chance of being nipped off at Charlestown Neck, as Clinton had proposed. In the battle itself, the striking American weakness was behind the lines, where Ward's staff demonstrated a wholesale lack of energy and initiative in forwarding men, supplies, and ammunition.[35] All things considered, Prescott's force on Breed's Hill and at the rail fence had performed as well as irregulars possibly could. Gage, presently called home and replaced by Howe, wrote that the Americans had demonstrated "a spirit and conduct against us they never shewed against the French." But if the war continued, would spirit, courage, and marksmanship suffice? Soon, whether the Americans desired it or not, some battles would inevitably be fought in the open. Americans might require well trained regulars in greater numbers than New England could always supply. Even before the engagement of June 17, 1775, the Massachusetts Provincial Congress and the Second Continental Congress had turned their attention to these problems.

## NOTES

1. Carter, ed., *Gage Correspondence*, II, 181. Until recent years historians had assumed that Gage had acted on his own in sending the troops to Concord. The matter was clarified by John R. Alden, "Why the March to Concord?" *American Historical Review*, XLIX (1944), 446–454. B. D. Bargar, *Lord Dartmouth and the American Revolution* (Charleston, S.C., 1965), 164–166, suggests that Alden may have exaggerated the meaning of this dispatch since Gage was also told that his actions should be governed by the situation at the time in Massachusetts. However, the real desires of the ministry leave no room for doubt. For support of

Alden's view, see Shy, "Thomas Gage: Weak Link of Empire," in *George Washington's Opponents*, ed. Billias, 27–28; and Gruber, "Illusions of Mastery," chap. iii, which also stresses the government's intention for a showdown.

2. Allen French, *General Gage's Informers* (Ann Arbor, 1932), 10–14, 29–33.

3. *Journals of Each Provincial Congress*, 12. It is true that Gage sent neither baggage nor artillery with Smith's column. Was he therefore hoping to lessen the likelihood of meeting armed resistance? In any case, Dr. Warren chose to ignore the letter of the Provincial Congress' resolve. The size of Smith's contingent and its aim of confiscating the Concord stores gave sufficient reason to arouse the countryside. John Cary, *Joseph Warren: Physician, Politician, Patriot* (Urbana, 1961), 179–180.

4. Arthur B. Tourtellot, *William Diamond's Drum: The Beginning of the War of the American Revolution* (New York, 1959), 44–46.

5. Harold Murdock, who swept away a good deal of myth and misinformation about the events at Lexington and Concord, was himself on hazardous ground in suggesting that Samuel Adams, "the great agitator," had instructed Captain Parker to take post on Lexington Common, in the hope of provoking hostilities that would lead to revolution and independence. Murdock, *The Nineteenth of April, 1775* (Boston, 1923), 23–25. The same interpretation of Parker's conduct is advanced in Tourtellot, *William Diamond's Drum*, 124–125. Certainly Adams and Hancock had spent several days in Lexington, and they remained there some time after receiving Revere's midnight message. Adams, who had no authority over the militia officer, could only have recommended that he act. In view of the mountain of contemporary literature on the subject, it is likely that any role of Adams would have come to light. General William Heath, commenting on the militia's presence on Lexington green, felt that they had been "too much braving of danger; for they were sure to meet with insult, or injury, which they could not repel. Bravery, when called to action, should always take the strong ground on the basis of reason." Heath, *Memoirs*, 12. Allen French, *The Day of Concord and Lexington* (Boston, 1925), 97, agreed with Heath and stated that the Lexington men, civilians rather than soldiers, failed to understand that their presence in arms would, so far as Pitcairn's regulars were concerned, be like waving a red flag in front of a bull. Since militia units had turned out in the two previous British marches to secure rebel stores and on both occasions Gage's officers had avoided any moves against the irregulars, French's position is open to question.

6. G. R. Barnes and J. H. Owens, eds., *The Private Papers of John, Earl of Sandwich, First Lord of the Admiralty, 1771–1782* (Naval Records Society, Publications, vols. 69, 71, 75, 78 [1932–1938]), I, 61.

7. "Diary of a British Officer," *Atlantic Monthly*, XXXIX (1877), 398–399. It seems safe to say that the question of which side fired the first shot will never be settled. The most thorough studies of this and related matters are from the pen of Allen French, himself a Concord resident and New England's most distinguished student of the military side of the Revolution. Many American testimonials, taken at the direction of the Massachusetts Provincial Congress, were published in Force, ed., *American Archives*, 4th ser., II, 487–550. Seven accounts of Lexington, three British and four American, are conveniently found in Henry S. Commager and Richard B. Morris, eds., *The Spirit of 'Seventy-Six: The Story of the American Revolution as Told by Participants* (Indianapolis and New York, 1958), I, 70–83. Additional reports are in Clark, ed., *Naval Documents of the American Revolution*, I, 195–201, 203, 218–221.

8. C. K. Bolton, ed., *Letters of Hugh, Earl Percy from Boston and New York, 1774–1777* (Boston, 1902), 51. Gage later found that only one British soldier was involved, although he too accepted the scalping part of the story—"his head much mangled, and his ears cut off, tho' not quite dead—a sight which struck the Soldiers with Horror." The Reverend William Gordon, future historian of the Revolution, learned from William Emerson that a youthful patriot had "very

barbarously broke" a soldier's skull, and "let out his brains with a small axe (apprehend of the tomahawk kind), but as to his being scalped and having his ears cut off, there was nothing in it." Force, ed., *American Archives*, 4th ser., II, 434–436.

9. Christopher Ward, *The War of the Revolution*, ed. John R. Alden (New York, 1952), I, 44.

10. Henry de Berniere, "General Gage's Instructions . . . with a Curious Narrative of Occurrences," Massachusetts Historical Society, *Collections*, 2nd. ser., IV (1816), 217; Tourtellot *William Diamond's Drum*, 178.

11. "Diary of a British Officer," 400; *Diary of Frederick Mackenzie* (Cambridge, Mass., 1930), I, 22.

12. *Newport Mercury*, April 24, 1775.

13. *Newport Mercury*, May 8, 1775; Alice M. Baldwin, *The New England Clergy and the American Revolution* (Durham, 1928), 125–126.

14. Bolton, ed., *Letters of Percy*, 31, 53; "Diary of a British Officer," 400; Eric Robson, ed., *Letters from America, 1773–1780* (Manchester, Eng., 1951), 33. See also Gage to Lord North, June 12, 1775, Fortescue, ed., *Correspondence of George Third*, III, no. 1663.

15. The committee of safety, in enlisting the army on the spot, rejected the older but slower method of assigning quotas to all the townships in the province. Charles Martyn, *The Life of Artemas Ward* (New York, 1921), 93–94. Problems of collecting and publishing depositions are the subject of Timothy Pickering to the Provincial Congress, April 25, 1775, Artemas Ward Papers, Massachusetts Historical Society.

16. Warren's activities are well described in Cary, *Warren*, 190–217.

17. Allen French, *The Taking of Ticonderoga in 1775: The British Story* (Cambridge, Mass., 1928), 43; *The Narrative of Colonel Ethan Allen*, introd. Brooke Hindle (New York, 1961), 5–10; John Pell, *Ethan Allen* (Boston and New York, 1929), 75–86; Stuart H. Holbrook, *Ethan Allen* (New York, 1940), 82–88.

18. Ward, *War of the Revolution*, I, 51–58; Richard Frothingham, *History of the Siege of Boston . . .* (Boston, 1851), 105–110; *Boston Gazette*, Sept. 25, 1775. A garbled version of one of these minor contests is probably the basis of a "rumor," passed on by young James Madison, "that the provincials have stormed Boston and with the Loss of 7,000 have cutt off or taken Gage and all his men. It is but little credited. Indeed the fact is extremely improbable: but the times are so remarkable for strange events; that improbability is almost become an argument for their truth." Madison to William Bradford, June 19, 1775, William T. Hutchinson and William M. E. Rachal, eds., *The Papers of James Madison* (Chicago, 1962—), I, 152. The war literature is replete with stories of battles that were never fought and inflated reports of those that did take place.

19. French, *First Year of the American Revolution*, 94; *Virginia Gazette* (Dixon and Hunter), Oct. 14, 1775; Germain to Lord Suffolk, June 16 or 17, 1775, Historical Manuscripts Commission, *Stopford-Sackville MSS*, II, 2.

20. Sir Henry Clinton, *The American Rebellion . . .*, ed. William B. Willcox (New Haven, 1954), xvii. Most histories give Clinton's age at thirty-seven in 1775. However, in 1958 the Clements Library acquired a Clinton notebook that proves 1730 to have been the year of his birth. William B. Willcox, *Portrait of a General: Sir Henry Clinton in the War of Independence* (New York, 1964), 5 n3.

21. Frothingham, *Siege of Boston*, 114 n1; Willcox, *Portrait of a General*, 46.

22. Frothingham, *Siege of Boston*, 116. With the possible exception of Lexington and Concord, Bunker Hill is the most written about battle of the Revolutionary War. (See the staggering quantity of literature on the subject in Justin Winsor, *Reader's Handbook of the American Revolution* [Boston, 1880]). New England historians once engaged in acrimonious disputes over the respective contributions of the different participating units and over the respective achievements of Warren, Putnam, and Prescott. Though the heat of regional partisanship has evaporated, a number of questions have not been completely resolved. Bernard

Knollenberg, "Bunker Hill Reviewed: A Study in the Conflict of Historical Evidence," Massachusetts Historical Society, *Proceedings*, LXXII (1957–1960), 84–100.

23. Clinton, *American Rebellion*, 19; Willcox, *Portrait of a General*, 46, 48. There was apparently some support among the field grade officers for Clinton's plan to hit the American rear, and after the battle there was considerable criticism of Howe and Gage. Willard Wallace, *Appeal to Arms* (New York, 1951), 36; Peter Oliver, *Origin and Progress of the American Rebellion*, eds. Douglass Adair and John A. Schutz (San Marino, Calif., 1961), 125; Harold Murdock, *Bunker Hill: Notes and Queries on a Famous Battle* (Boston, 1927), 10 n; Mrs. E. Stuart Wortley, *A Prime Minister and His Son* . . . (London, 1925), 69.

24. Commager and Morris, eds., *Spirit of 'Seventy-Six*, I, 123; George F. Scheer and Hugh F. Rankin, *Rebels and Redcoats* (Cleveland, 1957), 56.

25. Willcox, *Portrait of a General*, 48.

26. Frothingham, *Siege of Boston*, 137; Oliver, *Origin and Progress*, 132.

27. James Wolfe, *Instructions to Young Officers*, 2d edn. (Edinburgh, 1780), quoted in French, *First Year of the American Revolution*, 235.

28. The battle reports of Burgoyne, Howe, and Gage are in Commager and Morris, eds., *Spirit of 'Seventy-Six*, I, 131–135. Shipboard accounts of the day's events are in Clark, ed., *Naval Records of the American Revolution*, I, 700–704.

29. Wallace, *Appeal to Arms*, 42.

30. "A British Officer to A Friend in England," Massachusetts Historical Society, *Proceedings*, XLIV (1910–1911), 101–102; Historical Manuscripts Commission, *Hastings MSS* (London, 1930–1947), III, 154–155.

31. Authorities disagree as to whether both Pigot and Howe launched two or three separate attacks upon the American positions. This disagreement points up the fact that attempts to describe battlefield activities are not infrequently fraught with difficulties. Events may occur rapidly, making it nearly impossible to state precisely where and when certain happenings transpired. Battlefield participants, flushed with excitement, may not subsequently recall accurately the developments that took place around them.

32. Oliver, *Origin and Progress*, 127.

33. Wolfe, *Instructions to Young Officers*, quoted in French, *First Year of the American Revolution*, 235.

34. Ward, *War of the Revolution*, I, 97; William Howe, *Narrative in a Committee of the House of Commons* (London, 1780), 19.

35. Ward's brief, prosaic appeal for additional stores after the battle is indicative of his uninspiring nature: "Gentlemen, I am in immediate want of large Ordinance, a Quantity of Powder, and small Musket Balls. I am Gentlemen, Your Humble Servant [,] Artemas Ward." Ward Papers, Massachusetts Historical Society.

# 4. Congress Takes the Helm

U NDER THE CONSTITUTION, the President and Congress share military responsibility. Though the Congress may declare war, raise and support armies and navies, and perform other related activities, the President is "Commander in Chief of the Army and Navy of the United States." During the American Revolution there was no distinct executive branch of government to divide authority with the Continental Congress, which convened again soon after Lexington and Concord. In fact, until the ratification of the Articles of Confederation in 1781, the Continental Congress was an extralegal body, exercising only what powers the colony-states permitted. For this reason many Congressional military decisions reflected the whims and interests of the states. Sectionalism and states' rights—in large measure an extension of colonial localism and provincialism—played no small part in Congress' conduct of the war effort, along with a scrupulous adherence to republican principles. Washington spoke his uncertainty of whether "ours was *one* Army, or *thirteen*," or "a compound of *both*."[1]

Yet if we note at the outset Congress' inherent weaknesses in terms of legal jurisdiction and pressures from the states, to say nothing of its lack of key material resources for waging the conflict, then the salient point about the Continental Congress may well be that it accomplished as much as it did. And out of a bond forged by a common threat from the mother country, a bond not infrequently frustrated by politicians at the state level whose preoccupation revolved around state sovereignty instead of wartime efficiency, there emerged a group of *American* political leaders, genuine nationalists who echoed the plea of New York Congressman John Jay that the "Union depends much upon breaking down provincial Conventions."[2] Let us now see how Congress acquired an army, appointed a commanding general, and prepared for war.

### Adopting an Army

An extraordinary task confronted the delegates who, on May 10, 1775, gathered in the white-paneled council chamber of the State House in Philadelphia for the Second Continental Congress. The earlier inter-colonial meeting had devoted itself to hammering out agreements on constitutional positions. Now that they were committed to common principles and now that fighting had erupted in Massachusetts, the overriding question at Philadelphia was whether these colonial states-men could unite on a course of military action. If the Congress involved itself in the confrontation between New England and Gage's forces in Boston, the chances of securing an amicable reconciliation might suffer. Whatever hesitation may have existed for this reason evaporated when Congress took up its first business: a report showing that Crown and Parliament had rejected its appeals for a redress of grievances. The second item on the agenda likewise influenced the delegates: a long list of depositions submitted by Joseph Warren and the Massachusetts Provincial Congress demonstrating—in Massachusetts' view—that the regulars had begun the shooting at Lexington and had performed many barbarous acts during the long day of fighting.

Even so, obstacles to effective Congressional action clouded the hori-zon. No military genius stood among the delegates—no Hannibal, Turenne, Saxe, Wolfe—not even a Braddock or a Loudoun. Further-more, the delegates were singularly deficient as civilian planners and administrators. In their respective provincial assemblies, they had exercised, for all practical purposes, control over their militias. But appropriating monies for a few hundred men, overseeing construction of a handful of frontier forts, using their influence in the choosing of ranking militia officers hardly qualified them to raise and provide for an army of thousands of men to fight a war of continental dimensions against the mightiest nation on earth.

Franklin was less an amateur than most of the delegates. Arriving on May 5 from London, where he had long resided as a colonial agent for various colonies, he had the wisdom of seven active decades behind him. British-America's most famous citizen had earlier struggled against Quaker pacifism in his own Pennsylvania. For a time he almost alone managed the colony's military preparations during King George's War, and he had taken the lead in the French and Indian War in preparing his province for hostilities. In Philadelphia he played a leading role in the proceedings, finding that "my time was never more fully em-ployed." Franklin's background for military affairs can be contrasted with that of Thomas Jefferson and John Adams, two members of Con-gress destined to attain patriotic immortality. Neither the Virginian nor his fellow congressman from Massachusetts had ever seen militia duty, and neither was old enough for legislative service in the last French war. They were, in these respects, far more typical of Congress as a whole than the venerable Franklin.[3] Yet from Philadelphia Adams wrote his wife Abigail of his yearning to comprehend more about the art of warfare and of his reading on that subject; while New York delegate James Duane deplored his own deficiencies in military matters.

Despite Congress' inexperience, the colonies looked to this extralegal body for advice and direction, and the martial ardor of Philadelphia must have inspired the assembled delegates to take a forceful stand. "This City turns out 2000 Men every day," affirmed John Adams, who also observed that even a company of Quakers were among the men under arms.[4] Connecticut asked what should be done with the munitions captured at Crown Point and Ticonderoga. New York inquired whether it should resist a landing by British troops. Massachusetts sought sanction for establishing a civil government in the Bay colony, and urged the Continental Congress to assume responsibility for the New England forces outside Boston.

In Massachusetts, a full month and more before Bunker Hill, a crisis was brewing. The citizen-soldiers collected around Cambridge, trained in disputation by their town meetings, not disciplined in the heavy-handed fashion of Prussian regulars, fell to questioning the decisions —and at times the authority—of the provincial Congress and the committee of safety. Traditionally fearful of a powerful military establishment that might overshadow the civil authority, reluctant to carry the burden of America without the succor of the middle and Southern colonies, and acknowledging the necessity for a more energetic direction of war preparation, the Provincial Congress had become sufficiently concerned to make its appeal to the Continental Congress in a petition dated May 16 and carried in person by Dr. Benjamin Church. In the key portion of its missive, the Provincial Congress asserted that

the sword should, in all free States, be subservient to the civil powers . . . we tremble at having an Army (although consisting of our own countrymen) established here, without a civil power to provide for and control them. . . . We would beg leave to suggest to your consideration the propriety of your taking the regulation and general direction of it, that the operations of it may more effectually answer the purpose designed.[5]

Examined in one light, Massachusetts, beset with problems, acted from selfish considerations. Yet seen in another respect, the colony was taking a bold and unprecedented step toward greater American unity by placing its armed forces under the control of the Continental Congress.

Too much has been said of Congressional inaction and inconsistency in the spring of 1775. If Congress delayed in replying to Massachusetts, if its answers to queries from the colonies were in some instances vague or seemingly contradictory, that body was defended by no less than John Adams, who personally favored the strongest measures and who earnestly labored to make the cause of Massachusetts and New England the cause of all America. "Such a vast Multitude of Objects, civil, political, commercial and military, press and crowd upon us so fast, that We know not what to do first," he confided to his friend James Warren. "Our unwieldy Body moves very slow. We shall do something in Time, but must have our own Way."[6] And in that manner the Congress moved, resolutely albeit gradually, to put the colonies in a posture of defense—calling upon Connecticut to garrison the captured posts on Lake Champlain, advising New York to erect batteries on the Hudson River, requesting New England to furnish Ward's troops outside Boston "with as much powder . . . and other publick stocks as they can possibly spare," and recommending to Americans below the Hudson the collection of lead and saltpetre.[7]

The prickliest thorn for the delegates at Philadelphia was the armed body of New Englanders confronting General Gage. From an early date in their proceedings, a majority undoubtedly favored assuming responsibility for the troops in and around Cambridge. Action to that end had been delayed to gain the approval of all the delegates. Unanimity on such a momentous step was vital, not only to build a solid wall of American resistance but also to convince Englishmen and any likely foreign friends of the colonists' determination to stand firm until the great issues were resolved in their favor. (Congress, the following year, delayed its declaration of independence for the same reason: to secure unanimity.)

On June 5, delegate Joseph Hewes of North Carolina described the forces in Massachusetts as the "*American Army*," and he expressed a willingness for Congress to move its meeting place so "that we might be near the seat of Action." He noted, however, that "some of the Southern Gentlemen have not yet given their consent, nor do I think they ever will." Perhaps most of the congressmen never seriously contemplated an adjournment "to Hartford or New-haven in Connecticut." Yet Hewes' remarks indicate that among some Southerners there existed a degree of uneasiness if not suspicion. We know little about this, for the delegates pledged not to divulge their debates on the floor of Congress, and except for an occasional comment made "under the Rose," as John Adams phrased it, precious little information pierced the seven-foot walls surrounding the State House. In his autobiography, Adams asserted the presence in Congress of "a Southern Party against a Northern and a Jealousy against a New England Army under the Command of a New England General." It was "absolutely Necessary in point of prudence," wrote Eliphalet Dyer of Connecticut, to pick a non-New Englander to head the Continental army: "it removes all jealousies, more firmly Cements the Southern to the Northern, and takes away the fear of the former lest an Enterprising eastern New England Genll. proving Successful, might with his Victorious Army give law to the Southern or Western Gentry."[8]

That any significant cluster of Southerners really feared their brethren to the northward seems highly doubtful. But the matter of choosing a ranking general had become wholly intertwined with the subject of adopting the army; indeed, the latter had apparently become contingent upon a solution to the former. One way the New Englanders could demonstrate that the war was being waged for more than their own immediate ends would be to appoint a commander in chief from one of the distant colonies, a step that would also arouse additional support for the military effort in the middle and Southern parts of America. It was John Adams who set about to swing the Yankee congressmen away from their favorite, Massachusetts' Artemas Ward, and in line behind Colonel Washington of Virginia. The subsequent unanimous selection of Washington on June 15 "to command all the continental forces" was largely due to the wisdom and political sagacity of the Massachusetts' legislator. Too often portrayed as rigid and unbending, the short, rotund Adams actually helped engineer one of the first sectional compromises in American history.[9] Washington, bearing the proper regional credentials, also hailed from the "right" colony, prosperous and populous Virginia. It was a Virginian who served as first president of the Continental Congress, a Virginian who commanded the American army, a Virginian who introduced the Congressional resolution for independence, and a Virginian who wrote the Declaration of Independence. Still, Adams' solution to the problem of command would scarcely have been accepted had Washington lacked requisite credentials as a man, a patriot, and a soldier.

## The Soldier-Statesman

Washington does not seem by the lights of the twentieth century to be a typical leader of a revolution. The fiery-eyed, shirt-sleeved orator heaping contumely upon the present and mystically proclaiming the bright tomorrow finds no parallel in George Washington. Washington's colleagues accurately took the measure of the man: "discreet and Virtuous, no harum Starum ranting Swearing fellow but Sober, steady, and Calm"; "no pretensions to eloquence . . . a man of . . . solid judgment and information." Possessed of a large fortune and aristocratic lineage, Washington gave the Revolution the respectability it needed, a decidedly conservative flavor far removed from "Boston radicalism." Yet Boston could approve the selection: his commitment to American rights and liberties was unimpeachable. He had earlier stated his "full intention to devote my Life and Fortune in the cause we are engaged in, if need be."[10] An apocryphal story making the rounds of Congress had it that "on hearing of the Boston Port Bill, he offered to raise an army and lead one thousand men himself at his own expense."[11] Even at this early date legend was forming around him.

Washington more than looked the part of his new role. Height, proportions, bearing, and composure suggested the commander, a man who created trust and confidence by calmness and dignity. Equal to Washington's strength of mind and purpose was his physical stamina. Throughout eight and a half grueling years of war he never once took a leave from his troops except for ten days at Mount Vernon on the march to and from Yorktown in 1781; nor did he incur serious illness. Contemporaries were as struck by his horsemanship, "fine figure," and "soldier like Air" as by his sobriety and prudence. His wearing of his militia uniform at the sessions of Congress is no proof he was angling for the supreme command, though it indicates his willingness to serve in some military capacity.[12]

Distrustful of militarists and desirous to keeping the Continental army under its own control, Congress had dipped into its own membership to find a commander in chief. During the sessions at Philadelphia, Washington had chaired committees to plan the defense of New York, to consider problems of securing military stores, and to provide regulations for the army. On first glance his soldierly credentials seem meager. A forty-three-year-old colonel of Virginia militia, his military service had been chiefly confined to the Virginia frontier, where he had last seen active duty in 1758. Almost without exception revolutionary or civil wars give birth to generals who have had little or no opportunity for large commands.[13] At forty-three Cromwell was still a country squire. Napoleon's dictum that every man carries a marshal's baton in his knapsack was almost literally true in the case of Jourdan and Soult.

One can too easily exaggerate Washington's limitations as a soldier in 1775. Granted his lack of training in directing massive formations and in formulating strategy. Granted his inexperience with artillery, cavalry, and engineers. Yet in comparison with the British generals he opposed, his military background was not so deficient as it might appear. British officers in the eighteenth century were not specialists in the modern sense. Intensive training and discipline simply did not exist in any European army. Britain had no Sandhurst or West Point; France, no St. Cyr. Even quasi-specialists like engineers and artillerymen once beyond junior rank usually found their talents employed as administrators or field commanders. Lacking a common body of strategic doctrine, officers could scarcely analyze a problem in systematic fashion.[14] In fact, much military theory was romantic and antiprofessional. Guibert praised the "born general." Lloyd declared that while the mechanical part of war might be taught by rule or precept, the higher portion could only be mastered through natural, intuitive knowledge. Not until the great military reforms of Scharnhorst and Gneisenau in Prussia after 1808 can one mark the true beginning of military professionalism in Western society; Clausewitz, another Prussian, authored the intellectual rationale for the new profession.

Washington therefore lived in an age when exacting training was a less compelling requirement for command than later. Fortunately for him, armies in 1775 still fought and maneuvered as they had when he shed his Virginia uniform in 1758. If Douglas Freeman is correct, Washington read few if any military treatises during the following sixteen and a half years at Mount Vernon. But prior to then he had perused the important ones in English, and he was at least fairly familiar with their contents in 1775.[15] As commander in chief he constantly pleaded for a "respectable army" competent for every emergency—properly organized, officered (whenever possible) by gentlemen, and decently armed and accoutred. Though his own firsthand experience had mostly been with woodland warfare, he strove for a disciplined army, as trained and tried in line fire as the best European ranks to be hurled against it.

We have seen in an earlier chapter that Washington's Virginia background was of immense value to him in the Revolution. There were still other similarities between the frontier colonel and the commander in chief of an army endeavoring to defend a continent. While in charge of Virginia's western defenses from 1755 to 1758, Washington suffered from shortages of powder and food and inadequate numbers of troops with whom he was to guard a 350-mile line. He saw in bold relief the strengths and weaknesses of Americans as fighters, the militia's fickleness, the deep-rooted colonial provincialism illustrated by one county's balking at aiding another county. He also felt, not always justly, the sting of public criticism. There was scarcely a problem that plagued the youthful Colonel that did not trouble the mature General in the War of Independence. During the Revolution he complained—too often according to some historians—of his heartaches and disappointments, as he had done two decades before in the service of Virginia. But he was no longer the raw, strident young officer who had been overweeningly conscious of his own rectitude. Always proud and sensitive, he nonetheless became master of himself to such a degree that his biographers, from Mason Weems onward, have foolishly ascribed to him anything but lifelike qualities. Confronting greater adversities between 1775 and 1783, he never threatened resignation. (The Virginia Colonel had twice resigned from pique, and threatened to do so at other moments.) Cool and steady, Washington recognized the harsh realities of waging an *American* war—including the limited resources of the country and its inadequate organization for a major conflict—far more clearly than any other ranking general. As an ex-assemblyman and congressman, Washington understood the legislative mind, an essential attribute for one who had to plead and improvise to keep an army in the field at all; his wartime correspondence fills thousands of pages in his *Writings*, much of it with Congress and the states. (It is generally forgotten that Washington was a penman of merit who wrote with force and vividness.) Unflinchingly deferential to the civil authority, he was a rare combination of soldier and statesman.

If Washington the statesman excelled Washington the soldier, if he erred seriously in the actions of 1776 and 1777, he showed the capacity to learn from his mistakes; as campaign followed campaign, they became fewer and fewer. It is surprising that older histories depict him as a Fabius, a commander who preferred to retire instead of fight. This is the same General who sent Arnold to take Quebec, who desired to attack Gage in Boston, who sought battle at Long Island, Trenton, Princeton, Brandywine, Germantown, and Monmouth, and who raced southward to the Virginia peninsula in 1781 to snare Cornwallis. Marcus Cunliffe, in his brief but perceptive biography, remarks that while Washington has been criticized for excessive caution, he was actually too impetuous.[16]

Whatever his virtues and limitations, Washington became the first meaningful symbol of national unity. He acknowledged that his very appointment sprang partly from "a political nature": that of unifying a North and South that had no national flag or national anthem. Recognizing that the initial step for promoting American solidarity was to accord Washington a general welcome in their region, the New England congressmen wrote to their families and constituents praising the Virginian. Even so, no commander could have attained such prestige without the courage, perseverance, dignity, and loyalty he gave to the patriot cause. Despite an early aversion against New England troops (whom by 1777 he called the best in the army), Washington could honestly declare in December, 1776: "I have laboured ever since I have been in the Service to discourage all kinds of local attachments, and distinctions of Country, denominating the whole by the greater name of American."[17]

## Preparing for War

Politics and geographic considerations cropped up again in the choosing of Washington's lieutenants. Massachusetts, having bowed to Virginia, now demanded its plum; hence the naming of Artemas Ward, still commanding the troops around Boston, as "first major general." The steady if uninspiring Ward, characterized by Charles Lee as "a fat old gentleman" better qualified as a *"church-warden,"*[18] continued in the service until the British evacuated Boston.

Lee, who had impressed Congress the previous year by his expertise in military affairs, stood in the fore as an obvious candidate for high office in the Continental army. Virginia and Massachusetts delegates, with their colonies' initial aims achieved, pushed Lee as "second major-general"; and when Congress hesitated, Washington settled the issue by requesting Lee's appointment. As men knew Lee better, they saw another facet to this genuinely talented soldier, one that revealed a sharp tongue, a mercurial disposition, and slovenly personal habits. In time bitter controversy swirled around Charles Lee, aptly christened "Boiling Water" by Sir William Johnson's Mohawks during the French and Indian War. Faults he had, this tall, thin, ugly man, but his contributions in the first year of the war—when, in the opinion of some, his star shown brighter than Washington's—were of the first order. He was, commented Dr. Benjamin Rush, particularly "useful in . . . inspiring our citizens with military ideas and lessening in our soldiers their superstitious fears of the valor and discipline of the British army."[19] Congress picked as adjutant general Horatio Gates, whose life and fortunes closely paralleled those of his friend Charles Lee. Ex-British officers, veterans of the French and Indian War, imbued with republican principles, both returned to America and purchased estates in Berkeley County, Virginia, on the eve of conflict; both were to have their moments of glory in the Revolution, only to descend from the heights as suddenly as they had risen. Gates, short, ruddy-faced, and bespectacled, with thin graying hair, scarcely bore a martial appearance; Burgoyne allegedly spoke of him as an "old midwife." Despite shortcomings seen later in the war, Gates had real talent as an administrator. And in the dawning days of the struggle, Gates, like Lee, gave the new American army badly needed professional experience.[20]

In addition, Congress elected five brigadier generals, only to discover that it had not fulfilled political demands even though military requirements were momentarily satisfied. "The states insist, with great justice and sound policy, on having a share of the general officers in some proportion to the quotas of troops they are to raise," explained one congressman. Therefore Congress raised the number of major generals to four and the number of brigadiers to eight. The third major general, Philip Schuyler, came from the strategic colony of New York, likely to become a critical theater of military operations. Though Schuyler could boast of campaigning under Sir William Johnson, Bradstreet, and Abercromby in the 1750's, he had even more forceful credentials. As a Schuyler in New York, he ranked at the apex of the provincial aristocracy, not to mention his equally influential family ties with the Van Cortlandts and Van Rensselaers. All this was explicitly pointed out by the New York patriot leadership, which stated that Schuyler, because of "his property, his kindred and connections," would add "lustre" to the service. Thus when New York recommended Schuyler, Congress responded "to Sweeten and to keep up the spirit in that Province." While Schuyler attained a major generalcy, another New Yorker with less social and political standing, the exceptionally able Richard Montgomery, an ex-British officer, contented himself with a brigadier's commission. After a forthright explanation from New York Congressman James Duane as to why he ranked below Schuyler, Montgomery agreed to "submit with great cheerfulness to any regulation they [Congress] in their prudence shall judge expedient."[21]

Connecticut, requested to provide a substantial contingent of men in defense of the continent, was thus in an advantageous position to nominate the fourth major general; he was Israel Putnam, the only officer of that rank for whom Congress voted unanimously. Marriage to a prominent woman of some estate had not erased the marks of the farmer and tavern keeper from this energetic, warmhearted man. If "Old Put's" lack of social graces normally deemed requisite for a general officer was apparent from the outset, only time would reveal that the rough-hewn frontier fighter was out of his element commanding large bodies of troops. But Putnam was not to be the only American commander who failed to understand grand strategy or the administration of sizeable divisions.

Of the eight brigadier generals, New England gained seven, since most of the troops then in the field were from that region: Seth Pomeroy, William Heath, and John Thomas from Massachusetts; David Wooster and Joseph Spencer from Connecticut; John Sullivan from New Hampshire; and Nathanael Greene from Rhode Island. Only Richard Montgomery, the New Yorker, hailed from outside New England. This sectional imbalance of general officers continued throughout the war, but became less pronounced after the principal military operations shifted to the South in 1779 and 1780. Congress formally enunciated its position on promotions in the so-called "Baltimore resolution." It provided that "in voting for general officers, a due regard shall be had to the line of succession, the merit of the persons proposed, and the quota of troops raised, and to be raised, by each state." Even so, few officers appear to have been elevated solely on the basis of merit.[22] Below the rank of general officer Washington himself could make brevet appointments, although responsibility for permanent promotions among field and junior grade officers rested with the colony-state legislatures according to their own rules and practices.[23]

That June of 1775 Congress had chosen fourteen generals. Only Lee, Gates, and Montgomery could accurately be called veteran soldiers. Valuable as they were among their more inexperienced colleagues, none had climbed above the rank of lieutenant colonel. Eventually the army would benefit from the services of some European professionals and soldiers of fortune, particularly von Steuben, de Kalb, du Portail, Lafayette, Pulaski, and Kosciuszko (and it would encounter serious trouble in one way or another from a good many more). Of course the great majority of Continental generals were American amateurs, men with militia backgrounds, all the original appointees except Sullivan, Heath, and Greene having at least limited battle training before the beginning of hostilities in 1775. Two of the most promising selections, Thomas and Montgomery, might have achieved illustrious careers had not death cut short their lives in the Canadian campaign, soon to unfold. The real "sleeper" of the fourteen was the thirty-three-year-old Greene, with only a year's militia service behind him. The last of the generals to be named in 1775, he was so obscure to the delegates that Connecticut's Roger Sherman wrote of him as "one Green of Rhode Island."[24] Of all those selected, except for Washington, Greene would become the most distinguished. The entire fourteen emerged from the middle or upper classes, for the Revolution neither at the onset nor at the end produced a wholesale leveling of American society.

Congress, though according considerable latitude to Washington since "all particulars cannot be foreseen," reserved for itself ultimate control over the Continental army in keeping with its whig traditions. Washington was to "observe and follow" any and all orders from the lawmakers. As the civil government, Congress determined *policy*: it decided the objectives of the war, the number of troops, and the quantity of material for the Continental forces; in addition, it conducted foreign relations and financed military expenses. One eternal question of modern history has been where do governments of free men draw the line between the civil and military branches in formulating *strategy*, which involves the planning and executing of operations consistent with the purposes of the war. In authoritarian governments, whatever their form, the problem has scarcely existed. Before the American Revolution, England being the most striking exception, both the civil and military divisions of government were usually in the hands of one man: an Alexander, a Julius Caesar, a Gustavus Adolphus, or a Frederick the Great. At first Congress occasionally exercised the strategic function, most noticeably in ordering an invasion of Canada in 1775 and in calling upon Washington to defend New York City the following year; but later it intervened less in the formulation of stragegy.

A well-structured command system never emerged during the Revolution. Part of the difficulty sprang from Washington's being unable to oversee the strategic operations of all American armies, as Congress had originally intended. The commander in chief always headed a field army, a post large enough to consume almost all his energies. From 1776 to 1781 that army occupied at various times all or parts of New York, New Jersey, and Pennsylvania. This area (save upper New York), along with Maryland and Delaware, became the Middle Department. The two other main departments, the Southern and Northern, had their own immediate commanders, and though subject to Washington's instructions, they were usually beyond his effective jurisdiction. The result was that Congress intervened more in the North and the South than it did in Washington's own Middle Department. Yet on the whole controversy between the generals and politicians over strategy was not pronounced, partly because Americans were on the defensive most of the time: their actions mainly determined by the nature of British offensive strategy.

The colonial dignitaries at Philadelphia were not unmindful of the irony in their labors. After inveighing against British regulars and taxes for their upkeep, they now had their own military establishment for which monies must be provided. In Philadelphia "Caractacus," an essayist "On Standing Armies," prophesied virtuous American yeomen and artisans, associating "together in barracks or camps," would lose the "gentleness and sobriety of citizens." Congress believed nothing of the sort would happen if the troops' spiritual needs were guaranteed. For the regulation of the "grand army of America" the delegates approved sixty-nine articles of war, highly moralistic in tone. It was "earnestly recommended to all officers and soldiers, diligently to attend Divine Service." Penalties fell upon those who "behaved indecently or irreverently at any place of Divine Worship," as well as men who uttered "any profane oath or execrations." Congress prescribed moderate punishments for these and most other offenses. Except for a few major crimes expressly bringing the death sentence, a court-martial could not order a whipping to exceed thirty-nine lashes, nor a fine to include more than two months pay, nor imprisonment to extend beyond one month. Fines collected were to be "applied to the relief of . . . sick, wounded, or necessitous soldiers." A regimental commander had authority to pardon a soldier sentenced by court-martial or to lighten his punishment. An

enlisted man or junior officer, believing he had received unfair treatment from a superior, could appeal to his regimental commander or to
a general officer.[25]

This restrained military code reflected a citizen army, composed
chiefly of yeomen and artisans, the core of American society, rather
than a conglomeration of flotsam and jetsam thrown up by economic
tides. Congress deigned not to subvert the integrity and resilience of
the citizen while in arms. To do otherwise might produce easy-prey
robots for would-be Caesars. In fact, the congressmen made so many
concessions to the popular aversion against militarism they soon found
it imperative to put more teeth in the articles of war. Even so, John
Adams assured his constituents there existed no "design to new model
your Army,"[26] a reference to Oliver Cromwell's famous New Model
army, which subjected England to martial control after its victory over
Charles I. So long as American soldiers were little more than a reflection of American society, the Continental army posed no threat to free
institutions.

Besides caring for the mental and spiritual welfare of the new army,
Congress looked to its material requirements. Temporarily abandoning
a scheme to borrow on its own credit, the lawmakers turned to the
printing press, emitting two—and later three—million "Spanish milled
dollars . . . in bills of credit, for the defence of America."[27] Congress
might tread boldly at times but not with regard to taxation, a subject
that had stirred the continent in the previous decade. Having broken
the grip of one Parliament, the colonies were not about to put themselves in the grasp of another. But if funds were in sight, for the time at
least, Congress still lacked gunpowder. Since the emergency might not
wait for the development of local manufactures, the men at Philadelphia altered the Continental Association to permit American vessels to
export produce in trade for gunpowder, saltpetre, sulphur, and other
military stocks.

In all these endeavors Congress acted to sustain an American Continental army characterized by its clear-cut civilian control and humanitarian military code. Not surprisingly, the British imprint would loom
large on the new army. Its battalion and divisional organization imi-
tated the British system; so did the American artillery, whose commander, Colonel Henry Knox, recommended an academy to instruct
officers in gunnery modeled after the Woolwich school in England. In
fact, Congress entrusted principal responsibility for repelling the invader to an army that would fight much in the fashion of European conflicts. As Walter Millis observes, Congress, though aware of the need
for widespread citizens' support of the cause, never contemplated
"immolating men, women and children alike upon the altars of patriotism." Another scholar, John Shy, notes the conservative character of the

Revolution in both its political and military aspects. Besides a substantial degree of continuity in leadership and stability of institutions, the Revolution was "militarily conservative": Congress never contemplated a full scale guerrilla war likely resulting in the razing of towns and cities, the pillaging of fields and farms—all this spawning a genuine civil war replete with mass brutality, executions, and reprisals. Such a conflict would have destroyed the fabric of American life, so deranging the economy and the political process that victory in war under these circumstances would have been hollow indeed, if not ultimately fatal to the growth of American democracy.[28]

If Congress' scheme of fighting stressed the employment of field armies prepared to engage like forces of the Crown, the lawmakers also saw the necessity of activity at the grass-roots level. The militia, with all its limitations, had been an invaluable institution in the colonial era, and Congress displayed no thought of shucking it in 1775. The militia afforded a vast reservoir of manpower for the Continental army, and, it was hoped, the irregulars would at times assemble and serve alongside the Continentals. Moreover, the regular army could not be everywhere; the militia, operating on the local scene or behind the lines, simply had to handle problems of law and order, disaffection, and war weariness.

Experience suggested to Congress that the mere existence of the militia was not sufficient. It required organization, training, and leadership. Consequently, the Revolutionary statesmen recommended to the colonies a general plan for strengthening the militia, specifying the composition of a company, the combination of companies into regiments, and the requisite officers for them. One proposal called for one-fourth of the militiamen in each colony to be selected as minutemen. Congress likewise embraced this opportunity to urge each colony to appoint a committee of safety to superintend measures of security and defense during the recess of their assemblies or conventions.[29]

In this chapter we have, save for an occasional commentary covering a broader span, examined most of the noteworthy military activities in the opening session of the Second Continental Congress. That session came to an end on August 2, with the legislators agreeing to reconvene six weeks later. During their nearly three months in Philadelphia, their deliberations (if one included committee meetings) frequently lasted from early morning until midnight, and small wonder in light of their multiple undertakings. Occasional hesitancy or indecision pales against the sum total of their accomplishments in twelve short weeks—calling the colonies to defensive preparations, adopting an army, appointing its generals, providing for its regulations, printing paper money, authorizing limited foreign trade, and, among other things, bolstering the militia. No longer a temporary council of American leaders sitting to discuss theories and draw up petitions, Congress was actually the central government of a people at war and a revolutionary body in the fullest meaning of the term.

# NOTES

1. Fitzpatrick, ed., *Writings of Washington*, XX, 488.
2. Butterfield, ed., *Adams Diary and Autobiography*, II, 204.
3. Smyth, ed., *Writings of Franklin*, VI, 409. John Adams thus described Franklin's attitude in the Second Continental Congress: "He does not hesitate at our boldest Measures, but rather seems to think us, too irresolute, and backward. He thinks us at present in an odd State, neither in Peace nor War. neither dependent nor independent. But he thinks that We shall soon assume a Character more decisive." Lyman H. Butterfield,, ed., *The Adams Papers: Adams Family Correspondence* (Cambridge, Mass., 1963), I, 252–253.
4. *Ibid.*, 207, 312. In July, 1775, an essay on *Prussian Evolutions* was published in the Quaker City, containing information about formations, fortifications, and other aspects of the military art. Here as well as elsewhere Americans eagerly sought military literature, proposed the establishment of military schools, and advocated public exhibitions of model forts and redoubts. See especially *Pennsylvania Evening Post*, Aug. 3, 1775; *New England Chronicle*, May 9, 1776.
5. Force, ed., *American Archives*, 4th ser., II, 620–621. On May 26, 1775, Warren wrote to Samuel Adams: "The continent must strengthen and support with all its weight the civil authority here; otherwise our soldiery will lose the ideas of right and wrong, and will plunder, instead of protecting the inhabitants. . . . You may possibly think I am a little angry with my countrymen, or have not so good an opinion of them as I formerly had; but that is not the case. I love—*admire* them. The errors they have fallen into are natural and easily accounted for . . . it is not easy for men, especially when interest and the gratification of appetite are considered, to know how far they may continue to tread in the path where there are no landmarks to direct them. I hope care will be taken by the Continental Congress to apply an immediate remedy." Richard Frothingham, *Life and Times of Joseph Warren* (Boston, 1865), 495–496.

It has been argued that Warren exaggerated the rebellious spirit of the Massachusetts troops in order to exert pressure upon the Continental Congress to swing behind New England. Warren's fears, however, were not without some foundation. On May 18, 1775, efforts were undertaken to see that no further army officers be permitted to serve in the Provincial Congress; this was to restrain the power and influence of the military. Cary, *Warren*, 196, 199–200. For an extended discussion of relations between Massachusetts and the Continental Congress at this time, see French, *First Year of the American Revolution*, 129–142.
6. Burnett, ed., *Letters of Congress*, I, 95.
7. Ford, ed., *Journals of Congress*, II, 56–86.
8. Burnett, ed., *Letters of Congress*, I, 112–113, 127–128; Butterfield, ed., *Adams Diary and Autobiography*, III, 321. General Nathanael Greene, upon hearing of alleged Southern fears, wrote Congressman Samuel Ward on October 16, 1775: "I can assure the gentlemen to the southward, that there could not be anything more abhorrent to N. E. troops than an union of these Colonies for the purpose of conquering those of the South." Force, ed., *American Archives*, 4th ser., III, 1077. For similar expressions, see Alden, *The First South*, 25 n5.

The term "Southern" was not always restricted to the region below Pennsylvania. Some of the resentment against New England in 1775 may have come from the middle colonies. Though the word "Southern" began taking on a more restrictive meaning during the war, a quarrel involving troops from the Delaware

Valley and from New England was described as between Southerners and Easterners. Washington's own immediate command in the middle states was called "the southern army." *Boston Gazette*, Feb. 10, 1777. As late as 1786 Washington on occasion spoke of Virginia as one of the "middle states."

9. Ford, ed., *Journals of Congress*, II, 91. Adams' account is in his autobiography written years later, but there is no serious reason to doubt it. His correspondence during the period in question shows his high opinion of Washington, as well as the existence of some sectional tension. It seems likely that Adams received strong New England support from Elbridge Gerry and Samuel Adams. One of the last to accept the idea of Washington's appointment was his friend and fellow Virginian Edmund Pendleton. Butterfield, ed., *Adams Diary and Autobiography*, III, 322–323; Austin, *Gerry*, I, 79; Mays, *Pendleton*, II, 24–25. For a somewhat different interpretation, see Bernard Knollenberg, *George Washington: The Virginia Period, 1732–1775* (Durham, N.C., 1964), 114–115.

10. Burnett, ed., *Letters of Congress*, I, 128; Esmond Wright, *Washington and the American Revolution* (New York, 1962), 65; Fitzpatrick, ed., *Writings of Washington*, III, 277.

11. Burnett, ed., *Letters of Congress*, I, 28; Butterfield, ed., *Adams Diary and Autobiography*, II, 117. The tale seems to have originated with Congressman Thomas Lynch of South Carolina. Freeman, *Washington*, III, 377 n27, discusses the improbability of Lynch's account.

12. Virginians had earlier displayed some propensity for the use of military titles and dress. One traveler referred to the Old Dominion as a "retreat for heroes." Washington wore his colonel's uniform when Charles Wilson Peale painted his portrait in 1772. Washington in 1759 unsuccessfully ordered from London busts of military heroes: Alexander the Great, Julius Caesar, Charles XII of Sweden, Frederick II of Prussia, and the Duke of Marlborough. All the above raises a legitimate question as to whether Washington's military ambitions, so evident in the Seven Years' War, had wholly disappeared in the period that followed. Washington was "remarkably robust and athletic," wrote Edmund Randolph. *Virginia Magazine of History and Biography*, XLIII (1935), 127–131.

13. Katherine Chorley, *Armies and the Art of Revolution* (London, 1943), 186–187, develops the point.

14. For a view of the army as a "very amateurish service," see Namier and Brooke, *House of Commons*, I, 138–143. On receiving a commission, a man remained permanently in the army until he resigned or was dismissed for misconduct. Many were officers only in name, having little or no actual duty. In a day when staff organization was insignificant, there were generals without assignments. The extreme example of this system was that of Charles Moore, 6th Earl of Drogheda, who at the age of ninety-one became a field marshal—seventy years in the army and "no active service."

15. Freeman, *Washington*, I, xv; Oliver L. Spaulding, Jr., "The Military Studies of George Washington," *American Historical Review*, XXIX (1924), 675–680.

16. Marcus Cunliffe, *George Washington: Man and Monument* (Mentor edn., New York, 1960), 75, 109.

17. Fitzpatrick, ed., *Writings of Washington*, III, 299, VI, 405.

18. *Lee Papers*, IV, 177–178.

19. George W. Corner, ed., *Autobiography of Benjamin Rush* (Princeton, 1948), 155–156.

20. See Gates' clear, crisp, businesslike letters as adjutant general in the Artemas Ward Papers, Massachusetts Historical Society.

21. George Washington Greene, *Life of Nathanael Greene* (New York, 1867), I, 263–264; Edmund C. Burnett, *The Continental Congress* (New York, 1941), 78; *Journals of the Provincial Congress . . . of New York* (Albany, 1842), I, 33; Don R. Gerlach, *Philip Schuyler and the American Revolution in New York, 1733–1777* (Lincoln, Nebraska, 1964), 281–282; Burnett, ed., *Letters of Congress*, I, 137; C. Edwards Lester, *Our First Hundred Years* (New York, 1875), 260.

John Adams declared that "Nothing has given me more Torment than the Scuffle We have had in appointing the General officers." Burnett, ed., *Letters of Congress*, I, 137.

22. Washington explicitly made that point in July, 1780 with reference to brigadiers and state quotas: "Custom (for I do not recollect any Resolve of Congress authorizing it) has established a kind of right to the promotion of Brigadiers in State lines (where there are Regiments enough to require a Brigr. to command[)]." Fitzpatrick, ed., *Writings of Washington*, XIX, 225. The "Baltimore resolution" is in Ford, ed., *Journals of Congress*, VII, 132, 133.

23. Troops of a state in Continental service were referred to as the line of that state —the Pennsylvania Line, for instance. Thus, officers below general grade received promotions within their own state lines and seldom commanded men from other states.

24. Burnett, ed., *Letters of Congress*, II, 144. See also John Hancock to Artemas Ward, June 22, 1775, Ward Papers, Massachusetts Historical Society.

25. *Pennsylvania Packet*, August 21, 1775; Ford, ed., *Journals of Congress*, II, 111–122; *Rules and Articles for the Better Government of the Troops Raised . . .* (Philadelphia, 1775).

26. Quoted in Lynn Montross, *Reluctant Rebels: The Story of the Continental Congress* (New York, 1950), 77.

27. Ford, ed., *Journals of Congress*, II, 103.

28. Millis, *Arms and Men*, 26; John Shy, "Charles Lee: The Soldier as Radical," in *George Washington's Generals*, ed. George A. Billias (New York, 1964), 47.

29. It is not clear how many colonies complied fully with the Congressional proposals; but most of them established minute companies. French, *First Year of the American Revolution*, 54, n54.

# 5. Boston Gained, Canada Lost, Independence Proclaimed

I N THE YEAR after Bunker Hill (a battle which virtually coincided with Washington's appointment to head the Continental Army), the British were slow to mount an offensive. Instead, the patriots were the aggressors. Outside Boston, Washington's forces confined the redcoats to the city's perimeter. Meanwhile, the Continental Congress boldly expanded the war. To protect the Northern frontiers and to arouse added support for the patriot cause, two American expeditions were dispatched to "liberate" Canada. Success for the rebels before Boston was overshadowed by their failure to make Canada "the fourteenth colony." Notwithstanding the uncertain outcome of the struggle against the mightiest empire in the world, the Americans—already suffering from "a long train of abuses," as Jefferson phrased it—had little to lose by taking the ultimate step of all revolutionists: independence. If they were denied the rights of Englishmen, as they surely were, then there seemed to be no reason to remain Englishmen.

### Boston

Leaving Philadelphia on June 23, Washington arrived in Cambridge, Massachusetts, nine days later and took command of the Continental army. The American besiegers under Artemas Ward had thrown up a wide arc of fortification from the Mystic River on the north to Dorchester on the south. Washington resolved to erect additional batteries on advantageous ground in order to keep the British bottled up while he trained and provided for his army. He hoped that this feat and the conquest of Canada would bring the ministry to terms before the year ended;

American rights would be acknowledged and a violent separation of the empire avoided.

In Philadelphia, Washington had noted the difficulties of building an army on short notice. In Cambridge, he found the task even more formidable than he had imagined. General Charles Lee, who accompanied Washington from the Quaker City, complained of finding everything exactly the reverse of what had been represented. Cannon, supposedly numerous, were few. The army, supposedly "stocked with engineers," possessed "not one." How many rank and file were present and fit for duty? At first informed of 20,000 men ready for combat, Washington subsequently discovered the actual figure barely exceeded 14,000. How much powder was at hand? The store of powder, reported as 308 barrels, was a mere 90! There were shortages of muskets, tents, and clothing. Washington, familiar with the long, loose-fitting hunting shirt worn on the Virginia and Pennsylvania frontier, recommended it to Congress as a partial uniform. The lawmakers, however, decided to acquire brown cloth uniforms with individual regimental facings. Eventually eleven of the states selected dark blue as the most suitable color for military attire. Such plans in no wise met the immediate needs of the troops, who sometimes wore the king's scarlet coats obtained from captured British supply vessels.

In September, Washington proposed to his senior officers an attack upon Boston. Fearing that his shortages would increase and that his army might wither away from expiring enlistments, the commander in chief saw an advantage in assaulting Gage before the latter, strengthened by reinforcements, could overrun the American lines. Washington was to be criticized for undue dependence on his generals, who did not always accord him sound advice. But in this instance, with such confusion in the army, he may have been wise in bowing to their negative counsel. Washington, however, acted on his own in arming eight or more coastal vessels manned by New Englanders bred to the sea, including mariners from Colonel John Glover's Essex County, Massachusetts, regiment. That fall these vessels took twenty-three prizes of incalculable benefit to the hard-pressed patriots; one, the royal ordnance brig *Nancy*, contained 2,000 muskets, 100,000 flints, huge quantities of musketshot and roundshot, in addition to 11 mortar beds and a brass mortar. All told, the pesky Yankee privateers seized fifty-five enemy ships before Congress absorbed them into Continental service in 1777.[1]

The activities of American privateers, along with bad weather that delayed the passage of supply ships from Ireland and England, resulted in a critical food problem for the British in Boston. After hunger and scurvy came smallpox, a disease so widespread that redcoat officers felt it alone might deter Washington from a blow against the city. Howe, replacing the discredited Gage who sailed for England on October 10, contemplated no major foray against the rebel entrenchments. He had only 6,000 effectives, while wounds and sickness hospitalized another 1,400.

Thanks to Dr. Benjamin Church, the first important American traitor, the British knew they had small reason to fear their opponents that summer and fall of 1775. The forty-one-year-old Church had studied medicine in London, married an English woman, and returned to Boston, where, as an active whig, he delivered the Massacre Day oration in 1773. Member of the Provincial Congress and committee of safety, he became director general of hospitals for Washington's besieging forces. As early as May, 1775, if not earlier, Church had acted as General Gage's informer. In September, the director general wrote a letter in cipher to his brother-in-law, John Fleming, in Boston. The missive, which fell into Washington's hands, was carried by the doctor's mistress, who identified the author as Church. When patriot authorities decoded the letter containing somewhat exaggerated information as to the strength of the American troops, Church explained that his purpose was to deceive the British—to forestall an assault on the Continental positions. Yet in closing he wrote: "Make use of every precaution, or I perish."[2]

Perhaps because the ultimate purpose of the war was still unclear, Congress had never squarely faced the problem of disloyalty. All that existed for Washington were the articles of war drafted for the Continental army. In response to a query from the commander in chief, a council of war unanimously declared that Church had carried on a criminal correspondence with the enemy; and that the approved sentences of cashiering, whipping, fines, and brief imprisonment were deficient in view of "the Enormity of the Crime." While Washington notified Congress of Church's perfidy and suggested a stiff amendment to the articles of war, the Massachusetts House of Representatives took up the case. The law of treason in colonial Massachusetts, as in England, consisted of betraying allegiance owed the king. Could the Massachusetts patriots punish a man for an act in behalf of George III? (In his cryptic message Church spoke of his "warm affection to my King.") To do so would be the act of an independent state.

Massachusetts threw the hot potato back to the Continental Congress, which subsequently stiffened the articles of war to make death the maximum penalty for mutiny, sedition, or correspondence with the enemy. The regulation was not *ex post facto* so far as Church was concerned. In 1777 he received permission to leave the country on a ship that was eventually lost at sea. But by allowing the death penalty for soldiers who aided George III, Congress, prodded by the army, took a giant stride in the direction of independence.[3]

A more perplexing problem involved the treatment of loyal patriots in the Continental army. Americans, for all their knowledge of firearms, were at the outset ill-suited for regular soldiers. "To attempt to introduce discipline and subordination into a new army," observed Washington's secretary Joseph Reed, "must always be a work of great difficulty, but where the principles of democracy so universally prevail, where so great an equality and so thorough a leveling spirit predominates, either no discipline can be established, or he who attempts it must become odious and detestable, a position which no one will choose."[4]

Washington claimed this leveling spirit generated the ill discipline rampant throughout the New England regiments. "The private who marched in his company to reenforce the army about Boston," declared C. K. Bolton, "felt somewhat as a voter did at a . . . town meeting. The company to which he belonged was his, and the officers owed their authority in part to his favoring vote."[5] The strongest bar to discipline, in Washington's mind, was the most common type of officer, whose position appeared to rest on popularity rather than military ability. To keep their elected positions, some officers pooled their pay, placing it in a common stock along with enlisted men, from which all shared equally.

Both Washington and Lee believed that by dint of ceaseless labor the New Englanders, "very healthy" fellows, could become good soldiers, but only by reforming the officer corps.[6] It is no surprise to find Washington, a Virginia planter, insisting that only "gentlemen" were fit to lead enlisted men. By his very nature, courtly and retiring, he abhorred familiarity between men of high and low position. (A captain, perhaps an ex-barber, was discovered shaving one of his own men, perhaps a former customer!) Within six weeks of his arrival at Cambridge, the commander in chief could write that he had made "a pretty good slam" among the more mediocre officers. Two colonels, one major, four captains, and four subalterns had either been dressed out of camp for misconduct or were under arrest awaiting trial. As a result, the attitude of the officers improved, as did the conduct of the rank and file.[7] Aside from punishment, including the maximum thirty-nine lashes, the enforcing and wearing of ensignia—a light blue ribbon over the chest of the commander in chief down to a green strip on the left shoulder of a corporal—nurtured order and respect.

Though Washington might improve the appearance and conduct of the army (Reverend William Emerson thought the Virginian had wrought a near miracle in a few short weeks), he could not recruit a full complement of gentlemen officers. The army might attract better officers with adequate pay and other compensation, but to obtain sufficient leaders, from the regimental down to the company levels, from an aristocracy of planters, merchants, and lawyers was an impossibility. Unlike Europe, officers in America would simply be too few if drawn from upper elements alone. To have done so would have deprived the Revolutionary cause of a host of splendid junior grade officers, and, among others, Daniel Morgan, the muscular Virginia frontiersman-farmer who, with the possible exception of Benedict Arnold, became the outstanding combat officer in the Continental army.

Colonial jealousies, no less than misbehavior, confronted the commander in chief. But both problems were present in the case of the ten companies of frontier riflemen from Pennsylvania, Maryland, and Virginia. Raised by order of Congress, they were the first units outside New England to join the army and give it a more "Continental" appearance. The riflemen, like a March wind, blew into Washington's camp, all blusterous and eager to prove their prowess. Stories of their exploits along the way had preceded them. Captain Daniel Morgan's Virginia company, raised near Winchester, dashed to Cambridge, 600 miles, in only three weeks, winning by a few days a race with Captain Hugh Stephenson's company from neighboring Shepherdstown. The Maryland company of Michael Cresap, member of a famous family of Indian fighters, entertained curious throngs on their march with exhibitions of their backwoods skills. One onlooker described their performance at Lancaster, Pennsylvania:

Captain Cresap's company . . . have been in the late expedition against the Indians . . . and show scars and wounds which would do honor to Homer's Iliad. . . . Two brothers in the company took a piece of board five inches broad and seven inches long, with a bit of white paper, about the size of a dollar, nailed in the centre, and while one of them supported this board perpendicularly between his knees, the other, at the distance of upwards of sixty yards . . . shot eight bullets through it successively. . . . The spectators appearing to be amazed at these feats, were told that there were upwards of fifty in the company who could do the same thing. . . . At night a great fire was kindled around a pole planted in the Court House Square, where the company . . . all naked to the waist, and painted like savages . . . indulged a vast concourse of people with a perfect exhibit of a war-dance, and all the manoeuvres of Indians, holding council, going to war, circumventing their enemies by defiles, ambuscades, attacking, scalping, &c.[8]

The riflemen had ample reason to be proud of their marksmanship. With their long range weapons, deadly accurate at well beyond 100 yards, they initially took a heavy toll of British sentries who previously had stood up behind their lines and even walked along the parapets with little to fear. William Carter, a British participant, called the riflemens' sniping "an unfair method of carrying on a war"; while another redcoat described the frontiersmen as "the most fatal widow-and-orphan makers in the world."[9] At the Boston siege Gage and company saw, as they had at Lexington and Concord, that the Americans would not always play by the rules.

Unfortunately, these rough-hewn spirits were also reluctant to uphold Washington's own camp rules. They fired their weapons needlessly, fought among themselves, and quarreled endlessly with the Yankee farmers and fishermen who formed the bulk of the army. The "shirtmen," so dubbed by the New Englanders because of their hunting garb, were less obnoxious after thirty-three of the Pennsylvanians were fined for disobedient and mutinous conduct.[10]

In this unusual kind of coalition war, rivalries also manifested themselves between men of the various Yankee colonies. Washington complained that Connecticut wanted no Massachusetts men in its regiments; Massachusetts in turn grumbled about mixing Rhode Islanders with its own troops. Among the general officers, too, there was dissension over the order of seniority prescribed by Congress. Seth Pomeroy left the army out of disappointment, and Joseph Spencer expressed dissatisfaction because Israel Putnam outranked him. The able John Thomas, a lieutenant general in the Massachusetts establishment, was now junior in seniority to Pomeroy and William Heath, both of whom he had outranked in the Massachusetts service. "In the usual contests of Empire and Ambition," wrote Washington soothingly to the unhappy Thomas,

the conscience of a soldier has so little share that he may very properly insist upon his claims of Rank, and extend his pretensions even to Punctilio; but in such a cause as this, where the Object is neither Glory nor extent of territory, but a defense of all that is dear and valuable in Life, surely every post ought to be deemed honorable in which a Man can serve his Country.[11]

Washington's remarks foretold a new day in the history of warfare. Conflicts between nations, beginning with the American Revolution, were ceasing to be waged by a ruling prince to extend his dominions, or settle a dynastic squabble, or secure a commercial advantage. War was no longer merely the preserve of the warriors, long-service mercenaries who were divorced from the productive element in society. The American Revolution did more than prove the validity of Enlightenment ideals; it ushered in yet another revolution—in the aims and nature of warfare.

But if the state was asking more of its citizens, the citizens, in turn, were in the position to demand more of government. Faced with the task of recruiting a new army, since virtually all enlistments save the riflemen's expired by the end of 1775, Washington informed the President of Congress that the men would not re-enlist until they knew "their Colonel, Lt. Colonel, Major, Captain, &ca, so that it was necessary to fix the Officers the first thing. . . ."[12] Another difficulty was intense opposition among the troops to signing for more than an additional year; and on this point Congress, sensitive to political pressures back home, sided with the prevailing mood. It was argued that a long-term policy would result in filling the army with the scourings of society instead of the freeholders who constituted the hope of the country.

Furthermore, there was grumbling among the New England troops who were accustomed to receiving bounties upon enlistment in their respective colonial establishments. It was lamentable indeed, cried James Winthrop to Mercy Warren, "That in a cause which had (or ought to have) public virtue for its basis, men must be hired. . . . I wish it was possible to get an army of volunteers who would fight without pay."[13] Though patriotism was a more compelling force in America than across the Atlantic, it was usually not an adequate inducement to prolonged enlistment. The property-owning farmers and artisans, so eagerly desired for military duty, had much to lose by an extended separation from their livelihood. The very fact that they were not the sweepings of the poor-houses and gin mills put their services at a premium. Thus pay (and eventually bounties) was relied upon by recruiting officers in America as in Europe.

The sheer quantity of human resources, far greater than Britain could ever hope to transport to American shores, actually compounded the task of recruitment. A Congressional committee visiting Washington in October, 1775, estimated that 20,370 rank and file would suffice for the coming year, and that most of them could be obtained by re-enlisting the soldiers already on the lines. But, as Washington and Congress learned, many of these men felt they should not be asked to serve. Why should they re-enlist while their farms deteriorated and their families suffered when there were other men—thousands of them in New England, besides countless thousands to the southward—who had spared themselves a long and unpleasant period in the Cambridge entrenchments? Their argument, in spite of Washington's anger, was essentially valid, especially since there appeared to be no imminent danger of the American positions being overrun by the British.

It was the much berated militia that pulled Washington through the year-end crisis, when one army melted away and another slowly emerged. Called upon to supply irregulars to fill the gap, Massachusetts and New Hampshire responded admirably. Even the commander in chief, scarcely fond of such troops, could write on December 11:

"The Militia are coming fast, I am much pleased with the Alacrity which the good People of this province, as well as those of New Hampshire, have shewn upon this occasion."[14] Still other colonial units came forth to man the lines, so that by early March when Washington began his operation designed to bring the campaign to a head, 5,000 of his 14,000 troops available were militia.

The issue at Boston was resolved by artillery, a military arm then employed mainly in siege operations or in defense of fixed positions. Heading the American artillery was a portly, twenty-five-year-old Boston bookseller, Henry Knox, whom Washington sent after the heavy ordnance taken at Fort Ticonderoga. The huge guns were dismantled by hand, floated in boats over Lake George, and then sledded across snow and ice the nearly 300 miles to Cambridge. It was a feat that made men marvel. But it was matched by Washington's ingenuity in placing these cannon along with supporting entrenchments atop high and previously unmanned Dorchester Heights, where the heavy weapons could fire down upon the city of Boston and the enemy fleet in the harbor. The operation occurred on the night of March 4 when an exchange of artillery fire between patriot ordnance at Roxbury and Howe's batteries in Boston muffled the noise of American working parties.

Washington, doggedly persisting in the notion of bringing "on a rumpus between us and the enemy,"[15] hoped that Howe would strike at the heights, in which case Israel Putnam with 4,000 men would launch an amphibious attack against the town. Three times previously his council of war had opposed a sortie; this time the generals went along with his idea. But the destruction of an American city by an American army might generate political repercussions as well as military results. Consequently, Washington had earlier secured secret Congressional approval to storm Boston if he thought it desirable, "not withstanding the town and the property in it may thereby be destroyed."[16]

The new situation now bore some resemblance to the original setting at Bunker Hill. And Howe, despite his previous blood bath on the Charlestown Peninsula, was sorely tempted to hurl his redcoats up the steep Heights—to the point of ordering a detachment to prepare for action; but when a hurricane delayed the operation, he reconsidered. Howe, who had received Lord Dartmouth's permission to evacuate, actually felt that New York, the strategic center of the colonies, was a more likely spot from which to begin the job of subduing the rebellion. For the time being, though, he resolved to withdraw to Halifax in Nova Scotia to prepare for the coming campaign. Since Howe tacitly promised not to burn the city, Washington made no move to molest his adversary. On March 17, Howe's fleet lifted anchor and sailed away, carrying with it 1,000 loyalists.

The struggle was far from over. Washington discarded his theory of a short-lived war as he wrote Charles Lee, then in New York City, that Howe's next stroke would probably be in that direction. At the moment, however, there was room for genuine rejoicing. The first lengthy campaign of the war had ended happily for the patriots. Boston rested in American hands, and the retiring enemy had left behind valuable stocks of cannon, powder, tools, wheat, and oats. As for Washington, he remained untested in actual battle, but this much seemed clear: he would undoubtedly be a fighting commander. Already the General revealed qualities of determination and tenacity in carrying out his assignment; it was no mean achievement to build an army, see it disband before his eyes, and then build another, all the while watching an opponent whose well-trained regulars might sally forth without warning. That he had acquired the respect and support of the influential political leaders in the various New England colonies was crucial in a coalition war in which the states would frequently be appealed to directly owing to the inability of Congress to sustain many of the military's needs. His cordial relations with the Yankee politicians demonstrate that the tall Virginia planter was losing some of his provincialism, further evidenced by his growing respect for the Northern soldiers (if not always their officers). In November, 1775, James Warren averred that the commander in chief was "certainly the best man for the place he is in . . . that ever lived."[17] He was now, the ensuing March, more than that. Portraits, mezzotints, and verse appeared to honor him; Harvard presented him with a doctorate of laws; and Congress commissioned a gold medal for him in distant Paris. The "best man" had become the indispensable man.

## Canada

All dynamic revolutions are exported at the first opportunity, and the American upheaval ran true to form. Yet the exportation was confined by physical limitations. The thinly settled Floridas, only acquired by Britain in 1763, were too distant to send delegates to the Continental Congress, and they were dominated by British garrisons and the royal navy. Nor did Bermuda, Jamaica, Barbados, or the other British sugar islands send representatives to Philadelphia. The American Revolutionaries paid scant attention to these far flung outposts, although twice in the war New Providence in the Bahamas fell into rebel hands; and once a patriot landing party captured the governor of Prince Edward Island. Remote from the thirteen mainland colonies in revolt and dependent for sustenance and protection upon the mother country,

Britain's West Indian subjects appear to have overwhelmingly retained their loyalties to the Crown.[18]

Quebec was different. Through the military exploits of Wolfe, Amherst, and others that region fell into British hands by 1760; and the peace settlement of 1763 formally ceded the province to Great Britain. English newcomers, "old subjects," amounted to only a few hundred in 1775, compared to a French speaking population, "new subjects," of approximately 80,000. Yet Carleton, the able career soldier who became governor in 1768, shrewdly observed that a British colony composed of Frenchmen was less likely to support an American insurrection in the name of British liberties than a province made up of Englishmen. Canada, in fact, might prove to be the principal anchor of royal power in America.[19]

To the members of the First Continental Congress, meeting in 1774, political motives alone seemed to dictate an alliance with the French Canadians: let British North America stand as a solid phalanx against the encroachments of Parliament. Let these "Unhappy people, . . . not only injured but insulted" by the Quebec Act's denial of self government for Canada, dispatch delegates to the Second Continental Congress.[20] The appeal awakened little response, if for no other reason than that Carleton suppressed Congress' petition. By the following year, the empire was literally aflame, and military considerations prompted a second appeal, as well as an armed invasion.

Wars sometimes hatch strange bedfellows, and the rebellious colonists hoped the maxim would apply to the Quebecers and themselves. The revolutionists could have looked far and wide for more unlikely comrades than the Canadians—both French and Roman Catholic! To be sure, early America was a congeries of sects and sectarians, a fact that had made religious toleration a social and economic necessity before 1775. Despite the presence of anti-papist statutes in every colony, Catholics, fairly numerous only in Maryland and Pennsylvania, received at least nominal acceptance. In theory, though, Catholicism for most provincials remained inherently inimical. Ministers like Jonathan Mayhew and politicians like Samuel Adams belabored the Mass, indulgences, and purgatory. Clinton Rossiter states that Catholicism fostered fears and suspicions in colonial America somewhat comparable to those aroused by Communism today.[21] The four imperial wars between England and France intensified these traditional attitudes, as did passage of the Quebec Act, which guaranteed the Catholic church's favorable position in the former French area. Soon after taking command of the army, Washington, a respecter of all faiths, issued orders against the "ridiculous and childish custom of burning the effigy of the pope."[22]

In 1774, Congress itself, while urging French Canadians to protest their denial of political rights in the Quebec Act, turned in almost the next breath to informing "the People of Great Britain" of the statute's dastardly religious provisions. Their inconsistencies notwithstanding, Congress considered French Canadian aid highly desirable, as was the assistance of Catholics in Maryland and Pennsylvania; and, should the conflict wear on, so might the help of Catholic France be imperative. Catholic agitation must cease! And to a remarkable extent it did.[23] It is almost a universal that war breeds intolerance; but in the case of Catholicism, the American Revolution broke the rule. It seems unlikely that had Americans written a national constitution in the mid-1770's, it would have stated so categorically that "no religious test shall ever be required as a qualification to any office or public trust under the United States," as did the Federal Constitution of 1787.

The French Canadians, regardless of American entreaties, were not to be won over, even by a Congressional mission including Catholics Charles Carroll and John Carroll, the latter a priest. The Catholic hierarchy and the *noblesse*, their privileges restored by Britain, stood behind George III, their new master. For the most part, the more numerous peasants, the *habitants*, viewed the Anglo-American conflict with indifference or neutrality.[24]

But Congress persisted for military reasons: "The importance of Canada," John Adams told James Warren, was that in "the Hands of our Enemies it would enable them to inflame all the Indians upon the Continent . . . as well as to pour down Regulars, Canadians, and Indians upon the borders of the Northern [provinces]." A secondary motive, often overlooked, was that possession of Montreal and Quebec, the major Canadian towns, would effectually put the squeeze on Britain's posts in the North American interior. Largely cut off from supplies and reinforcements, they would likely be evacuated or else fall prey to patriot raiding parties.[25] Already expansion, if not Manifest Destiny, was in the air.

Prospects for an invasion seemed bright. Only 700 regulars garrisoned all of Canada, so widely dispersed that no more than a single regiment could be assembled at any one spot. Carleton could expect no help from Howe's forces cooped up like "a parcel of Chickens" in Boston. Moreover, once the campaign was underway, winter storms and the ice-clogged St. Lawrence would permit no reinforcements from Britain before the spring of 1776. On the other hand, there was reason to wonder whether the patriots had the military and economic resources to hold a large portion of Canada, much less all of it. Would they have done better by augmenting their posts at Ticonderoga and thereabouts as a means of guarding the vital Hudson?

The Canadian campaign demonstrates the hazards of a people inexperienced in organized warfare engaging in elaborate offensive strat-

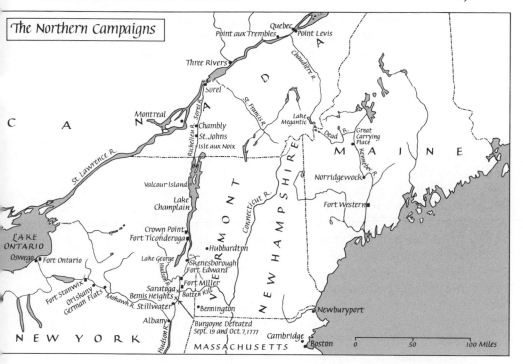

The Northern Campaigns

egy. At the end of June, 1775, after delaying for a month any decision on an invasion, Congress instructed General Philip Schuyler, commander of the Northern Department, to move northward from Ticonderoga to take Forts St. Johns and Chambly on the Sorel (or Richelieu) River, and then seize Montreal, along with other parts of Quebec. Congress' slowness in calling for an invasion was more than matched by Schuyler's dilatory tactics. Though a political general, Schuyler was not without ability, which he admirably demonstrated by his tenacious defensive operations in his own New York woodlands against Burgoyne in 1777. But Schuyler was vastly deficient in assembling and training an offensive army, even though one may sympathize with the disagreeable realities confronting this thoroughly loyal and devoted patriot. Far inland, away from centers of trade and commerce, he encountered innumerable hardships in acquiring supplies, munitions, and equipment. Good fortune in this venture depended much upon speed, for the enlistments of most of the New York and Connecticut irregulars, who constituted the core of the army, would expire on or before the year's end; and Schuyler, plagued by ill health, lacked both energy and decisiveness in his preparations. Only when Brigadier General Richard Montgomery, without orders from Schuyler, pushed the American van up Lake Champlain did the expedition get under way. As it was al-

ready September, with days exhilaratingly cool and the leaves displaying occasional splashes of red and yellow, Montgomery rightly foresaw
a "winter Campaign in Canada! Posterity won't believe it!"[26]

There was no planning or coordination between the Schuyler-
Montgomery forces and a second American invading column dispatched from Washington's camp. Most historians, through charity or
error, have ascribed American strategy as a systematic two-pronged
attack—a pincer's movement—against Carleton. But Washington ordered the expedition from Cambridge, under Benedict Arnold, without
authorization from Congress, though the lawmakers were presumably
superintending the invasion since they had ordered Schuyler's command into Canada.[27] Arnold was to advance northward up the Kennebec River in Maine, then over a "carrying place" leading to the Dead
River, westward on that stream, thence over the "Height of Land, and
finally northward down the Chaudière to the St. Lawrence, almost
directly opposite the city of Quebec. It was an exceedingly rugged
trail, doubly so due to the lateness of the season, and over it Arnold's
party of 1,050—ten companies of New England musketmen and three
companies of frontier riflemen—could count on no reinforcements, even
though most of Arnold's troops, like Montgomery's, would complete
their service in that year. Arnold's march, a distance of over 350 miles
from the Maine coast, has been celebrated in historical narrative and
fiction, and not without cause. The short, swarthy Colonel from Connecticut encountered more difficulties than either he or Washington
had anticipated. The six-week ordeal (originally estimated as three)
saw the men stumble along formidable portages, struggle against
swollen streams, wade snow-covered swamps, and, when provisions
gave out, eat their dogs and make gruel from shaving soap. That the
hearty band, gaunt and worn, eventually reached the St. Lawrence
on November 8 was a credit to Arnold's magnificent leadership, along
with that of Captain Daniel Morgan, the leader of the riflemen.

Meanwhile, Carleton had worked furiously to hamper the American
invasion. Failing to raise substantial numbers of French Canadians, he
assumed direction of the redcoats gathered at Montreal and hastened
preparations to shore up the defenses at St. Johns and Chambly.
Montgomery's force, proceeding down the Sorel in gondolas and
bateaux, appeared at the outskirts of St. Johns on September 5.
Schuyler, who had hurriedly overtaken Montgomery, was once again
in charge, and once again revealed his limitations. That night "a gentleman," possibly an "old subject" friendly to the patriots, convinced the
hesitant New Yorker that the St. Johns fort was "complete and strong,"
that a sixteen-gun vessel supported the garrison, that American senti-

ment was lacking in Canada, and that—instead of attacking St. Johns
—Schuyler should retreat to Ile aux Noix, a naturally imposing defensive position in the Sorel River. For Schuyler the withdrawal was an
incredible performance, even if allowance is made for his fear that
Carleton's vessel would demolish his small bateaux and gondolas. Soon,
however, the Americans regained their courage and returned to
besiege St. Johns. The retreat had gained them nothing. The effect
upon the morale of the green troops must have been shattering, as well
as the impact upon Canadians who might otherwise have been
tempted to join the American invaders. In fact, one tale spread through
that part of Quebec that a small party of Indians had decisively defeated Schuyler and sent his remnants scurrying for safety; the "victory"
was celebrated in Montreal by "a grand mass with a Te Deum."[28]
Schuyler, suffering from a bilious fever, returned to Fort Ticonderoga,
permanently relinquishing the army's direction to Montgomery. At
forty, Montgomery was only two years Schuyler's junior, but the Irish-
born Montgomery seemed youthful compared to the sluggish Schuyler.
One of Amherst's captains in the French and Indian War, Montgomery subsequently resigned from the British army and in 1772 migrated
to New York. A splendid officer, energetic and resourceful, it is tempting to speculate that had Montgomery been given the command in
the beginning, the outcome of the Canadian compaign might have been
different—if not completely victorious for the patriots, certainly not the
total disaster that eventually ensued.

The siege of St. Johns illustrates the point. The tardiness of the Northern army to move out from Ticonderoga, in addition to the later temporary withdrawal to Ile aux Noix, had enabled Carleton to bolster the
post at St. Johns. Throughout October the siege continued as the
weather turned cold and rainy, while the defenders, secure behind
newly built, heavy log walls, did not sally from the fort. The physical
discomfort ("like half-drowned rats crawling through a swamp") and
the sharp reduction of pork rations added to the dissatisfaction among
the Americans. Montgomery, like Washington at Cambridge, saw a
"leveling spirit" in his New England units. "The privates are all generals"; they "carry the spirit of freedom into the field, and think for
themselves."[29] Back at Ticonderoga, Schuyler, who had bestirred himself once divested of field authority, sent Montgomery reinforcements
along with powder and cannon to breech St. Johns' walls. Finally, the
fort's commander, Major Charles Preston, with only three days' food
left and sensing the imminent destruction of his works, ordered his
regulars to stack their arms in surrender. But for fifty-five crucial days
he had delayed the Americans.

Weak and disorganized though Montgomery undoubtedly was,

Carleton's condition was even worse. Fort Chambly had already capitulated to an American advance party, and only a bit of luck prevented
the British General from falling into Montgomery's hands. When
Montgomery's force crossed the St. Lawrence on November 12, Carleton's detachment fled eastward from Montreal toward Quebec, but not
in time to escape the patriot net. Carleton himself, dressed as a farmer,
slipped away in a rowboat. While the Governor made his way to Quebec, Montgomery halted at Montreal, refitting and reorganizing. In
fact, Montgomery originally had no intention of pressing down upon
Quebec just then, but planned to spend the winter at Montreal. The
very day he entered Montreal he learned for the first time that Arnold's
column had actually made its way through the forests of Maine. Two
weeks later, leaving a garrison behind, he floated down the St. Lawrence to unite with Arnold.

In the Canadian campaign, as in perhaps no other American operation of the Revolution, time was of the essence. Had Arnold's expedition been able to get over the St. Lawrence immediately upon emerging from the Maine wilderness the previous month, the Kennebec
column alone might have stormed the fortress city, sitting high on a
rocky promontory. Hector Cramahé, lieutenant governor of the province, was near despair, having but a handful of redcoats and royal
marines to man the city's walls. For several days Arnold delayed on the
south bank of the river, searching for boats and then waiting for rains
and wind-whipped waters to subside. Those were precious moments,
for Colonel Allen Maclean, a crusty Highlander with a small body of
regulars and British loyalists, arrived to reinforce the shaky Quebecers
after an unsuccessful effort to relieve St. Johns.

Maclean later boasted that he rather than Carleton had saved Quebec for the Crown; in any case, he contributed manfully to that end.
Taking charge within the city, he found he could scarcely build his
defense around troops of the line. With the exception of several detachments isolated in western stations, practically all British regulars had
been taken prisoner at St. Johns, Chambly, and on the St. Lawrence.
Besides about 100 redcoats and a few marines, plus seamen from war
and merchant vessels in the harbor, Maclean rounded up 200 of his
own loyalist followers, some English citizens in the town, and a contingent of French Canadian militia—all together, approximately 1,300
men. Restoring order and discipline in the city, Maclean cleared the
area around the walls by burning down outlying houses and buildings.
His cannon fire twice drove off a messenger from Arnold, who, having
eventually traversed the St. Lawrence on November 14, hoped to obtain Maclean's surrender without a struggle. After parading his men
below the parapets—to the jeers and taunts of spectators lining the

walls—Arnold also discovered that he could not persuade the British to come out and fight as Wolfe had done with Montcalm sixteen years before. Consequently, he retired to Pointe aux Trembles, twenty miles above Quebec, where Montgomery joined him on December 2. Because of expiring enlistments. the American General was able to bring only 300 men to add to Arnold's force.

Though the combined army of 975 troops returned to the Plains of Abraham before Quebec and immediately began siege operations, Montgomery had no illusions about their chances. The winter was bitterly cold, with snowdrifts reaching the second story of many houses; and digging entrenchments in the frozen earth was so difficult that the Americans built them instead from snow and ice. Under the circumstances a siege would have to be a drawn-out affair. American ammunition, food, and other supplies would not last until Montgomery could starve into submission the well-supplied defenders, whose spirits were now aroused by the appearance of the much respected Carleton. And, more important than anything else, most of Arnold's New Englanders would soon leave for home, their term of service ending on December 31.

The Americans were left with no choice but to assault the city—or else give up the ghost. The Montgomery-Arnold battle plan, to be carried out on the first stormy night, called for the two commanders to lead in person their inexperienced troops in striking from opposite directions against the Lower Town, a narrow strip along the river that lay outside the protecting walls. As the days passed, it seemed as though Carleton had gained an indomitable ally in General Time. But on December 30, with many of Arnold's New Englanders preparing to go home, the weather changed abruptly: snow, falling lightly in the late afternoon, whirled down in blinding intensity after nightfall. To prevail the outnumbered invaders needed both luck and the element of surprise. Unfortunately, they had neither. A deserter had betrayed to Carleton the scheme to hit the city on the first "wild night." The American columns, picking their way around ice cakes and stumbling through snowdrifts, reached the Lower Town, where Carleton's defenders, though forewarned, were frightened and badly disorganized. Here the American luck went from bad to worse. Montgomery, charging with his vanguard against a blockhouse obstructing their path, was shot down, at which point his timorous subordinate, Lieutenant Colonel Donald Campbell, beat a hasty retreat back to camp.

Arnold's fate was little better. Sighting a barrier at the end of a dark street, he cried for a frontal assault, since his only cannon had been abandoned in the deep snow. But a whirring musket ball tore into his leg, and while the vigorous Arnold reluctantly allowed himself to be

carried to the rear, Daniel Morgan took the lead. Morgan's performance in the next exciting minutes constitutes one of the great personal
performances of the war. Dashing forward ahead of the hesitant New
Englanders, Morgan, followed by his steady riflemen, hurdled the
barrier notwithstanding a bruised knee and powder burns, drove the
enemy back, and almost singlehandedly captured a house filled with
redcoats and French Canadian militia. Though Morgan wanted to
press on through an undefended second barrier, the other officers overruled him, arguing that they should halt until making contact with
Montgomery's column. Had the Americans followed the intrepid Morgan, the Lower Town might well have fallen to them; for in the midst
of the darkness, swirling snow, and blood-curdling yells of the riflemen,
confusion reigned supreme among the British defenders there. The
steady Carleton, however, quickly gained the upper hand as the Americans sacrificed vital minutes waiting for a supporting column that
never came. He dispatched troops to the previously unmanned barrier,
while at the same time he sent a Captain Laws out the Palace Gate
with instructions to hit Arnold's command from the rear.

At last, Morgan convinced his fellow officers to advance, but the
opportunity was no more. From behind the wall musket flashes lit up
the cold, gray dawn. In vain Morgan led scaling parties to the barrier;
bullets and bayonets drove them back. The tall ex-teamster was "brave
to temerity," declared an admiring rifleman. By this time, the outcome
was evident to all but Morgan, who, instead of surrendering with the
others, angrily dared the amazed redcoats to come and take his sword
from him. Finally, when they threatened to shoot him, he handed the
sword to a startled priest, proclaiming angrily that "not a scoundrel
of these cowards shall take it out of my hand."[30]

It has been a great temptation among students of the Revolutionary
War to dwell upon the "if's" of the Canadian campaign, particularly the
ill-fated Quebec assault: if Arnold had reached the city ahead of
Maclean, if Montgomery and Arnold had not been struck down, if Morgan had convinced Arnold's column to push on, and so forth. In spite of
valiant American efforts—in which the patriots lost 100 killed and
wounded and approximately 400 prisoners as opposed to 20 British
losses in all categories—the battle did not hold the ultimate fate of
Canada. The British vessels that eventually bucked through the icy St.
Lawrence in the late spring carried men and cannon more than adequate to rout the Americans, had they been fortunate enough to seize
Quebec.

Following the engagement Arnold, assuming full command from his
hospital bed, insisted on continuing the siege, though by this time his
remnant of the attacking force was but a fourth of Carleton's command.

His action was at once heroic and futile. Nor was it substantially aided by the Continental Congress' sending several thousand additional men to join the invasion. In May, upon the arrival of royal troops from Britain, the Quebec besiegers streamed westward in panic-stricken flight. A succession of American field commanders, David Wooster, John Thomas, and John Sullivan, failed to reverse the new tide. The last commander, Sullivan, a forty-five-year-old lawyer turned soldier, foolishly declared that his army would hold on in Canada or perish in the effort. Though Sullivan could "think only of a glorious Death or victory obtained against Superiour numbers,"[31] he at length fell back from Montreal and St. Johns southward along the Sorel and then to Fort Ticonderoga, the starting point of the invasion.

As Benedict Arnold soberly noted, "the junction of the Canadians with the Colonies" was "now at an End." It was time to "quit them and Secure our own Country before it is too late."[32] Congress could not have been given better advice. The cost of the Canadian campaign had been most high. All told, losses from battle, disease, and desertion came to 5,000 men. In addition, huge sums of money and vast amounts of supplies and equipment had been sucked down the Canadian rat hole. In the long run, the Americans may have experienced a blessing in disguise in being propelled out of Canada altogether. They were obviously incapable of withstanding such a continuing drain on their human and material resources, and they had dangerously overextended themselves. At best, the campaign had perhaps postponed a British thrust down the rivers and lakes stretching from the St. Lawrence toward the Hudson and New York City. Neither Congress nor Washington, however, relinquished the dream of making Canada "the fourteenth colony." In 1778 the lawmakers proposed an elaborate plan, originating with Lafayette, for conquering Quebec the next year. Washington, who did much to scotch the proposal as too complicated, himself suggested a Northern venture in both 1780 and 1781; but America's ally France, whose support was deemed essential, showed no enthusiasm for the scheme. And so ended—until the War of 1812— strenuous efforts to attach Canada to the new American union.

## Independence

Within the opening two paragraphs of the Declaration of Independence are the immortal phrases: "that all men are created equal," endowed with certain unalienable rights including "life, liberty, and the pursuit of happiness." The mere assertion of these rights was ample justification for Americans to assume "a separate and equal station" among the nations of the earth. But the timing of independence was the result of practical military considerations. The King and Parliament, continuing to scorn Congress' appeals for redress of grievances, were stepping up the war tempo. The burning of Falmouth (now Portland) in Maine by a British fleet in the fall of 1775 and the ravaging of the Virginia coast by the colony's Governor Dunmore at the year's end forecasted Britain's determination to resolve the imperial dispute by still harsher actions rather than by reconciliation. Moreover, Dunmore tried to enlist Negro slaves in the King's service and to bring Ohio Valley Indians down upon the frontiers of the Old Dominion. Almost simultaneously Governor Josiah Martin of North Carolina was raising the loyalists of that colony to serve in conjunction with a British fleet soon to arrive from Ireland for the purpose of striking at the Southern colonies. The Americans were also aware that London officials were negotiating for the hiring of thousands of foreign mercenaries to be used against the colonists.

In America opinion in favor of independence slowly crystallized in the first half of 1776. The incongruity of Washington's officers drinking toasts to George III at the same time they were giving battle to his scarlet legions did not escape the commander in chief or members of Congress. In January, 1776, the inconsistency was resoundingly pointed out in Thomas Paine's brilliantly devastating *Common Sense*, which berated monarchy in general and the House of Hanover in particular. In concluding his essay, suffused with emotion as well as reason, the youthful devotee of liberty expressed "strong and striking reasons" why a proclamation of independence would help bring about foreign support:

It is unreasonable to suppose, that France or Spain will give us any kind of assistance, if we mean only to make use of that assistance for the purpose of repairing the breach, and strengthening the connection between Britain and America; because, those powers would be sufferers by the consequences. . . . Under our present denominations of British subjects, we can neither be received nor heard abroad: the custom of all courts is against us, and will be so, until by an independence we take rank with other nations.[33]

In the army and in Congress men declared foreign aid to be imperative. General Nathanael Greene sought to embrace Frenchmen and Spaniards as brothers: "Their military stores we want amazingly."[34] In addition, Washington, Charles Lee, and Gates did not hide their pessimism concerning reconciliation and indicated their desire to seek money and weapons in Europe. Congress, from February 18 to April 6, took one decisive step after another—authorizing privateers, placing an embargo on exports to Britain and the West Indies, voting to disarm all loyalists, and opening American ports to the commerce of all nations except Britain. In March the lawmakers hastened Silas Deane, a Connecticut merchant, to Paris to buy war materials on credit and to determine the French attitude toward the American conflict.

These developments reflected changing sentiments in the colonies. One by one what might be termed state governments made their appearance and authorized their Congressional delegations to vote for American independence. New England and the South, already feeling or anticipating the war's direct effects, were out in front. But when Congressman Richard Henry Lee of Virginia introduced on June 7, 1776, a resolution calling for independence, an American confederation, and "measures for forming foreign Alliances,"[35] the delegates from the middle colonies generally held back, leading to an agreement to postpone action for at least three weeks. "It was argued," explained Jefferson, "That the people of the middle colonies . . . were not yet ripe for bidding adieu to [the] British connection but that they were fast ripening."

Jefferson's notes on the great debate, observes Julian Boyd, offer perhaps the best account of the final step to separation. According to the thirty-three-year-old Virginian, much of the discussion revolved around strategy: whether it was essential to demonstrate to prospective European allies that the states stood united in their determination for independence. Since attitudes between the Hudson and the Potomac "were fast advancing" toward a complete break, "it was thought most prudent to wait a while for them." The momentous conclusion to the drama came on July 2 when, with the divided New York delegation helpfully abstaining, Congress spoke with one voice for independence.[36]

During those hectic June days, Jefferson and a committee of four others including John Adams and Franklin had prepared an elaborate statement—the Declaration of Independence—to serve as an explanation and justification for the final severing of the imperial connection, a document Congress officially approved and adopted on July 4. In a study of the military side of the Revolution, the natural rights sections of the Declaration—the enduring portions as inspirational now as then —are not our principal interest. Of more immediate concern are a number of the specific charges made against the King.

He has kept among us, in Times of Peace, Standing Armies, without the consent of our Legislatures.

He has affected to render the Military independent of and superior to the Civil Power.

He has combined with others to subject us to a Jurisdiction foreign to our Constitution, and unacknowledged by our Laws; giving his Assent to their Acts of pretended Legislation:

For quartering large Bodies of Armed Troops among us:

For protecting them, by a mock Trial, from Punishment for any Murders which they should commit on the Inhabitants of these States:

He has abdicated Government here, by declaring us out of his Protection and waging War against us.

He has plundered our Seas, ravaged our Coasts, burnt our Towns, and destroyed the Lives of our People.

He is, at this Time, transporting large Armies of foreign Mercenaries to compleat the Works of Death, Desolation, and Tyranny, already begun with circumstances of Cruelty and Perfidy, scarcely paralleled in the most barbarous Ages, and totally unworthy the Head of a civilized Nation.

He has constrained our fellow Citizens taken Captive on the high Seas to bear Arms against their Country, to become the Executioners of their Friends and Brethren, or to fall themselves by their Hands.

He has excited domestic Insurrections amongst us, and has endeavoured to bring on the Inhabitants of our Frontiers, the merciless Indian Savages, whose known Rule of Warfare, is an undistinguished Destruction, of all Ages, Sexes and Conditions.

All told, approximately one-third of the grievances against George III deal with militarism, for they were undoubtedly freshest in the American mind in 1776. Jefferson, in singling out the King and largely ignoring the role of Parliament in imperial developments, was, of course, continuing the assault of Paine. Since Americans as early as 1774 had reached the point of denying any Parliamentary control over them, Jefferson sought to break the last remaining tie—with the monarch himself. At the bar of history, the charges have usually been termed severe if not false. It is true that the patriots had previously, before the appearance of *Common Sense*, leveled their attack upon Parliament while appealing to the King to intercede in behalf of his loyal American subjects. It is also a fact that in Britain, at least, George was no tyrant: he upheld rather than usurped the supremacy of Parliament.

Granting all this, Jefferson quite probably stood on sounder ground than has sometimes been recognized. The studies of Sir Lewis Namier and his followers reveal that the King necessarily played an active and crucial role in Parliamentary affairs in the absence of a party system; he was a cohesive and stabilizing force in a day when members of Parliament grouped themselves in factions revolving around families, personalities, and patronage. The ministers who fashioned the controversial laws and policies from 1763 to 1776 were really *his* ministers. The King favored, even urged, the use of force against his American subjects after 1773. Once the shooting began, George treated with contempt the Continental Congress' Olive Branch Petition, still another effort in which the colonists begged George III to protect their rights against Parliament. Two days after receiving it in August, 1775, he issued a proclamation declaring the thirteen provinces in rebellion. In December he approved an act of Parliament prohibiting all intercourse with them and ordering the seizure of their ships and crews on the high seas.

It is easy enough to understand the King's role in the war itself. Besides occupying an essential niche in the political spectrum, he had yet a further claim to ultimate responsibility for the conflict. In eighteenth-century Europe war was generally the peculiar preoccupation of the monarchy. Seldom did the aims and objectives of the struggle arouse broad popular interest or support. Indeed, to put arms in the hands of the population was to court serious danger. Here was a partial explanation for hiring foreign mercenaries. The so-called people's war in Europe lay in the future, in the era of the French Revolution. Thus George III's position in political and military affairs was rooted in tradition and precedent. But if the British scene called for such a monarch, then Americans had good reason to conclude that the Hanoverian was not the king for them.

After July 4, 1776, the air in America seemed to clear. As Joseph Barton of Delaware wrote on July 9, "I could hardly own the King and fight against him at the same time, but now these matters are cleared up. Heart and hand shall move together." The Declaration was first proclaimed before a large crowd in the State House yard in Philadelphia on July 8. The next day Washington had the Declaration read before his assembled troops, who responded with three cheers. No longer would they look to the King or the friends of America in England such as Pitt for any surcease. Washington reminded "every officer and soldier . . . that now the peace and safety of his Country depends (under God) solely on the success of our arms: And that he is now in the service of a State, possessed of sufficient power to reward his merit, and advance him to the highest Honors of a free Country."[37]

## NOTES

1. William Bell Clark, *George Washington's Navy* (Baton Rouge, 1960), 222.
2. French, *General Gage's Informers*, 155–157; copy of Church to Edward Kean in Ward Papers, Massachusetts Historical Society; Force, ed., *American Archives*, 4th ser., III, 1483.
3. Bradly Chapin, *The American Law of Treason: Revolutionary Origins* (Seattle, 1964), 29–33.
4. William B. Reed, *The Life and Correspondence of Joseph Reed* (Philadelphia, 1847), I, 243.
5. Charles K. Bolton, *The Private Soldier under Washington* (New York, 1902), 25.
6. Lee wrote: "As to the materials (I mean the private men) they are admirable—young, stout, healthy, zealous, and good humor'd and sober." Nathanael Greene echoed the same comments: "We want nothing but good officers to constitute as good an army as ever marched into the field. Our men are much better than the officers." *Ibid.*, 131–134.
7. Freeman, *Washington*, III, 520. On November 10, 1775, Washington gave Colonel William Woodford of Virginia his opinions on the subject of an officer's duty toward his men: "Be strict in your discipline; that is, to require nothing unreasonable of your officers and men, but see that whatever is required be punctually complied with. Reward and punish every man according to his merit, without partiality or prejudice; hear his complaints; if well founded, redress them; if otherwise, discourage them in order to prevent frivolous ones. Dis-

courage vice in every shape, and impress upon the mind of every man, from the first to the lowest, the importance of the cause, and what it is they are contending for." Fitzpatrick, ed., *Writings of Washington*, IV, 80.

8.  Frank Moore, ed., *Diary of the American Revolution* (New York, 1863), I, 121–123. See also *Newport Mercury*, Sept. 25, 1775; *Boston Gazette*, July 7, 1777; *Pennsylvania Packet*, Aug. 7, 1775.

9.  William Carter, *A Genuine Detail . . . in Letters to a Friend*, quoted in Freeman, *Washington*, III, 505; Willard M. Wallace, *Traitorous Hero: The Life and Fortunes of Benedict Arnold* (New York, 1954), 60; Thomas Mifflin to Artemas Ward, July 30, 1775, Ward Papers, Massachusetts Historical Society.

   As John Hancock remarked, Southern congressmen had already acquainted New Englanders with the virtues of the rifle: skilled marksmen "do execution with their rifle guns at an amazing distance." *Warren-Adams Letters* (Massachusetts Historical Society, *Collections*, vols. 72–73 [Boston, 1917–1925]), I, 58. But at what distance? On November 3, 1775, the *Virginia Gazette* (Purdie) reported that "a rifle-man killed a man at the distance of 400 yards." Likewise, Major George Hanger, a British officer, averred that the American sharpshooters were capable of hitting their mark at a "full 400 yards." *Colonel George Hanger to all Sportsmen* (London, 1814), 122–124, 144. Richard Henry Lee of Virginia asserted: "There is not one of these men who wish a distance less than 200 yards or a larger object than an orange—Every shot is fatal." Ballagh, ed., *Letters of Richard Henry Lee*, I, 130–131. James Madison, seldom thought of as a military type, claimed to be able to shoot accurately at 100 yards, and boasted that many could hit a man's face at 250 yards. Hutchinson and Rachal, eds., *Papers of Madison*, I, 153. In light of the fact that the accuracy of a musket seldom exceeded sixty-five yards, the above quotations seem, to say the least, open to question. It may be significant that General Charles Lee, a careful military observer who had witnessed the riflemen in Cambridge, issued the following orders concerning rifle fire while commanding at Charleston, South Carolina, in 1776: no man should fire his weapon at a distance greater than 150 yards. "In short, they must never fire without almost a moral certainty of hitting their object." Force, ed., *American Archives . . . ,* 5th ser. (Washington, 1848–1853), I, 99. See generally on the subject of Revolutionary firearms Warren Moore, *Weapons of the American Revolution* (New York, 1967); George C. Neuman, *The History of Weapons of the American Revolution* (New York, 1967); Harold L. Peterson, *The Book of the Continental Soldier . . .* (Harrisburg, Pa., 1968).

10. Disciplinary problems seem to have been limited to the Pennsylvania riflemen. Six of the ten companies, called for by Congress, were to come from Pennsylvania. Subsequently two additional companies were authorized for that colony; and as a result of some misunderstanding, Lancaster County, Pennsylvania, raised two companies instead of one.

11. Fitzpatrick, ed., *Writings of Washington*, III, 359.

12. *Ibid.*, IV, 83.

13. Freeman, *Washington*, III, 578.

14. Fitzpatrick, ed., *Writings of Washington*, IV, 156.

15. *Ibid.*, 359.

16. Ford, ed., *Journals of Congress*, III, 445. James T. Flexner makes the valid point that the fortifying of Dorchester Heights was distinctly secondary in Washington's thinking to an assault on the city. An amphibious blow by untrained troops would have been extremely hazardous; but Washington was determined to carry it out if Howe divided his own force and attacked the heights. "Had he at this early stage of the contest," writes Flexner, "well before the Declaration of Independence when so many Americans were still undecided, lost half of his army and with it his own prestige, the cause could either have collapsed or shriveled away." Flexner, *George Washington in the American Revolution* (Boston, 1968), 76–78.

17. *Warren-Adams Letters*, I, 186.

18. There were, however, statements from the Crown's West Indian subjects in favor of reconciliation between the Continental colonies and the mother country. See the memorial of the Jamaican Assembly in Force, ed., *American Archives,* 4th ser., I, 1072–1074. In Bermuda there was undoubtedly considerable sympathy for the patriots, but it fell far short of open rebellion. W. B. Kerr, *Bermuda and the American Revolution* (Princeton, 1936). See also David H. Makinson, *Barbados: A Study of North American-West Indian Relations, 1739–1789* (The Hague, 1964).

19. George M. Wrong, *Canada and the American Revolution* (New York, 1935), 237–238. At this time the words Canada and Quebec were often used interchangeably. In fact, the province of Quebec was organized in 1763 and covered much the same area as present-day Quebec. A. L. Burt, *The Old Province of Quebec* (Minneapolis, 1933), 74–78. By the terms of the Quebec Act of 1774, the boundaries of the province were extended south to the Ohio and west to the Mississippi. Nova Scotia and Newfoundland had separate governments.

20. Ford, ed., *Journals of Congress,* I, 105–113.

21. Clinton Rossiter, *The First American Revolution* (New York, 1956), 89.

22. Fitzpatrick, ed., *Writings of Washington,* IV, 65. Washington is best characterized as a deist. His genuine support of religious freedom—not merely gentlemanly indifference—is admirably set forth in Paul F. Boller, Jr., *George Washington and Religion* (Dallas, 1963). A Connecticut soldier of 1775 later recalled that the Quebec Act produced a "real fear of Popery" in New England; it stimulated many timorous people "to send their sons to join the military ranks. . . ." Daniel Barber *History of My Own Times* (Washington, 1823), 17.

23. Charles H. Metzger, *Catholics and the American Revolution* (Chicago, 1962), 48–70, 274–275. Metzger believes the laity developed an attitude of toleration more rapidly than the clergy, especially in New England. Consult also Sister Mary Augustina (Ray), *American Opinion of Roman Catholicism in the Eighteenth Century* (New York, 1936), chap. viii.

24. Though Nova Scotia contained many transplanted New Englanders, they, too, showed small interest in the struggle. John B. Brebner, *The Neutral Yankees of Nova Scotia* (New York, 1937). For Canadian attitudes, see the documents in G. A. Rawlyk, *Revolution Rejected, 1775–1776* (Scarborough, Ontario, 1968).

25. Burnett, ed., *Letters of Congress,* I, 355; see Force, ed., *American Archives,* 4th ser., III, 717.

26. Ford, ed., *Journals of Congress,* II, 74–75, 109–110; Burnett, ed., *Letters of Congress,* I, 146, 147; John C. Miller, *Triumph of Freedom* (Boston, 1948), 91.

27. Fitzpatrick, ed., *Writings of Washington,* III, 437–438. Freeman, *Washington,* IV, 66, says that Washington's most serious mistake during the siege of Boston "was the dispatch of Arnold's small, ill-equipped and poorly provisioned force" to Canada.

28. Ward, *War of the Revolution,* I, 152; *Boston Gazette,* Oct. 2, 16, 1775.

29. Justin H. Smith, *Our Struggle for the Fourteenth Colony* (New York, 1907), I, 418; Force, ed., *American Archives,* 4th ser., III, 1097–1098.

30. Journal of Joseph Henry, in Kenneth Roberts, *March to Quebec* (New York, 1938), 378. A fresh contemporary account of Morgan's part is in the *Maryland Gazette,* Oct. 24, 1776. The final quotation is from James Graham, *Life of General Daniel Morgan* (New York, 1856), 102–103.

31. Otis G. Hammond, ed., *The Letters and Papers of Major-General John Sullivan* (Concord, N.H., 1930–1939), I, 234.

32. *Ibid.,* 237.

33. Philip S. Foner, ed., *The Complete Writings of Thomas Paine* (New York, 1945), I, 39.

34. Force, ed., *American Archives,* 4th ser., IV, 572.

35. Ford, ed., *Journals of Congress,* V, 425.

36. Boyd, ed., *Jefferson Papers,* I, 299, 309–314.

37. John B. Hazelton, *The Declaration of Independence: Its History* (New York, 1906), 221; Fitzpatrick, ed., *Writings of Washington,* V, 245.

# 6. Britain at War

T HE BRITISH PHASES of the War of Independence long suffered from
scholarly neglect. Nineteenth-century American historians under
the influence of romantic nationalism lavished their full attention
upon the sufferings and triumphs of Washington and his heroic band of
Continentals. Historians in England usually steered clear of the American Revolution, the outcome of which reflected no credit upon the
parent country. Englishmen who did approach the subject generally
espoused the so-called whig interpretation of Anglo-American history:
they, too, found heroes on the American side and among the opponents
of the North ministry—Pitt, Burke, Rockingham, Fox, and the rest.
These whiggish writers did not ignore the military efforts of the King
and his cabinet. The Trevelyans and the Leckys wrote of corrupt and
incompetent ministers who sadly mismanaged a proven army and a
great navy and who failed to mobilize the wealth and credit of the
country.

Among the present generation of British historians there has been a
revival of interest in the American rebellion. These scholars have
drawn upon more reliable sources than the *Parliamentary History* and
the *Annual Register*, which are filled with the harsh criticisms of the
opposition. They have examined Britain's military effort within the context of eighteenth-century warfare. Moreover, they have doubtless
been influenced by the difficulties of recent imperial powers in undertaking military action in remote areas of the world where regular
military activities are handicapped by geography and by the unorthodox procedures of the local inhabitants. Indeed, as Piers Mackesy has
pointed out, Britain's task of putting down the American Revolution
was "never paralleled in the past, and in relative terms never

attempted again by any power until the twentieth century." Later it was compounded by the entrance of France and Spain into the war. Then "for the first time England faced what she had always dreaded and averted: a coalition of maritime enemies undistracted by war in Europe."[1]

## The Army

Britain appeared to have a formidable advantage in manpower. Her population came to roughly eleven million compared to fewer than three million colonials, of whom about a sixth were Negro slaves. Whereas America had no standing army in April, 1775, Britain's land forces in that year numbered on paper over 48,000 men—39,294 infantry: 6,869 cavalry; and 2,484 artillery.[2] Perhaps too much has been made of the background of the typical redcoat in the ranks. If he were an ignorant country boy beguiled by gin or other wiles of a recruiting officer into volunteering, if he were a criminal offered the choice of prison or the army (in 1776 ex-convicts filled three regiments), if he were an unruly Scottish Highlander, in time his regiment became his life. A professional fighting man, sturdy and courageous, he was proud of his unit's traditions that might rest upon the fighting fields of Blenheim and Fontenoy. Regiments such as the 20th, the 21st, and the 44th equaled the best of Frederick the Great's legions. In spite of early setbacks at Concord and Bunker Hill, the redcoat in America usually fought well when he could display his skill in the evolutions of European warfare.

Britain's problem in the Revolutionary War was not in the caliber of her soldiers but rather in her lack of troops in sufficient numbers. Ordinarily service was for life, a fact strongly militating against enlistment among the more productive elements in society, and the lot of the common soldier was far from easy. His superiors generally paid little attention to his physical and spiritual welfare; a notable exception to the indifference of the clergy—including chaplains—toward the army was John Wesley, who sought out soldiers in their barracks and elsewhere to win many souls. A popular saying, from a slightly later period, went this way: "A messmate before a shipmate, a shipmate before a stranger, a stranger before a dog, and a dog before a soldier."[3] Small wonder that authorities found it impossible to complete the increases voted by Parliament. On December 16, 1775, the *London Gazette* announced the subsequent limiting of enlistments to three years or the duration of the rebellion, "at the option of His Majesty." The government stepped up the practice of pardoning criminals in return for their entering the army and even forgave military deserters provided they re-enter the ranks. But as the war continued new measures came forth, such as extending the age range of eligibility to include men from sixteen to fifty. Parliamentary press acts of 1778 and 1779 stipulated that all able-bodied persons guilty of disorderly conduct who did not follow lawful trade or employment were to be inducted into the King's service. Significantly, the government excluded all voters. To do otherwise might mean—as it meant in America—that the electorate would demand a voice in public affairs in return for their service, a price the ruling classes of the eighteenth century refused to pay.

At the opposite end of the social scale from the common soldier was the officer class, the preserve of the aristocracy and the gentry. A military career open to talent alone, without regard for social origin, would have been unthinkable in a century when loyalty to the king was a necessary prerequisite for military command. George Grenville vowed that the King could never "trust his army in the hands of those that are against his measures." The army was a force on which the social order might depend, especially in the absence of a national police system.[4]

Notwithstanding a lack of formal training, Britain's regimental officers were generally competent and often superior in abilities. Francis, Lord Rawdon, Charles Stuart, and many others performed splendidly in the Revolutionary War. But they advanced through the officer ranks as much if not more as a result of wealth and station rather than because of their skill in handling regulars. Commissions were bought and sold through the rank of colonel. On October 8, 1775, Stuart, the son of Lord Bute, wrote his father that, surprisingly, he had purchased a majority in the 43d Regiment "without making use of your name, or being obliged to Lord Barrington," the secretary at war. After paying £2,600 to secure his advancement, Stuart told his father a year or so later that he was about to buy a lieutenant colonelcy for upwards of £5,000.[5]

General officers usually sprang from the aristocracy. Gage, Howe, Burgoyne, Cornwallis, and Clinton are examples, and the last four were politicians as well as generals, all holding seats in the House of Commons during their American service. (In 1780 there were twenty-three generals in that body.)[6] Lacking the discipline and sense of professionalism characteristic of a future period of warfare, Britain's general officers—and often field grade officers as well—behaved in ways that today would be considered grossly unpatriotic and insubordinate. Because of their influential positions at court or in the House of Commons they frequently managed to get away with it, for to censure a powerful military man with Parliamentary connections would likely drive him and his friends into the opposition, and there were moments in the American war, such as after Saratoga, when the ministry's majority was precarious indeed.

In the winter of 1775–1776, Burgoyne returned to England to attend the House of Commons. Cornwallis, preparing to depart on the same errand, cancelled his plans on hearing of the Hessians' mishap at Trenton. Early in 1777, Clinton, angry with Admiral Peter Parker and Sir William Howe, returned to England. He had previously written, "If I cannot serve with them I like, I had rather not serve at all"; but he resumed his American duties later in the year. Still other generals refused to go to America. This was true of Jeffery Amherst, the army's leading general, and of Lord Cavendish, who had fought ably in the last war. William Howe himself hesitated before agreeing to a New World assignment. The youthful Earl of Effingham regretfully tendered his resignation from the army: "I cannot, without reproach from my conscience, consent to bear arms against my fellow subjects in America in what, to my weak discernment, is not a clear cause."[7] Equally reluctant to take arms was General Henry Conway, who publicly criticized the war at every opportunity.

Independent of mind and spirit, Britain's generals divided on issues of court and factional politics, divided on the war itself. In America, their conflicts, principally over seniority and overlapping command, drove Colonel Stuart to comment acidly that they were "a pack of the most ordinary men . . . who give themselves trouble about the merest trifles whilst things of consequence go unregarded." Stuart found that by October, 1778, almost every general officer desired to return home and that this disenchantment had spread to many of the field officers. There was little glory attached to putting down a colonial rebellion, but the opportunities for disaster were great, particularly since London opinion took a dim view of American fighting talents. "This is an unpopular war," noted Colonel Frederick Mackenzie, "and men of ability do not chuse to risk their reputation by taking an active part in it." Given the attitudes of their superiors, the surprising thing about the British army in America may well be that the redcoat in the ranks performed as well as he did.[8]

## The Navy

While there has been little historical controversy over the state of the army at the opening of the Revolution, the same cannot be said of the navy. The Parliamentary opposition maintained that the fleet that won the Seven Years' War had wasted away while Lord Sandwich of the Admiralty spent his time fishing and cavorting with "Ladies of Pleasure." The public man's private life became grist for the partisan mill of politics; but Sandwich's moral transgressions—most notably embellishing his house with actress Martha Ray and her bastards—were hardly relevant to an evaluation of his Admiralty tenure. Though the navy in 1763 was the largest in English history, many of the newer vessels, hastily added during the final Anglo-French confrontation and constructed of green timbers, became unseaworthy some years before the American uprising. If Sandwich had allegedly inherited 139 ships-of-the-line (above fifty guns) on assuming his post as First Lord of the Admiralty in 1771, they were in "a most deplorable state" in 1775.[9]

Some blame for the navy's condition in 1775 should probably go to Lord North, who informed Sandwich in September, 1772, that the ministry would pursue a "judicious economy" in naval affairs.[10] Yet North's idea was a familiar one: all navies of the period deteriorated in time of peace. Parliament normally reduced the navy to the fewest ships and men compatible with its police activities. Men grew rusty for want of practical experience, and systematic peacetime training in naval strategy was uncommon. Virtually every war of the century began with the navies some distance removed from reaching their stride.

Recent scholarship indicates that Sandwich was industrious and dedicated. From the first, he foresaw a subsequent war against France and Spain in which, unlike previous contests, Britain might miss the opportunity to defeat them separately. His efforts to build up the naval establishment accomplished nothing spectacular, partly due to North's cutbacks (which Sandwich opposed), partly due also to a shortage of timber and skilled labor for shipbuilding. According to Sandwich, however, the timber problem was somewhat the result of lumber merchants artificially creating scarcity to keep prices high. Whatever the reason for the absence of seasoned British oak, so sturdy and durable that the *Royal William* saw active duty from 1719 to 1785, Sandwich turned to Germany for Stettin oak, obtained by floating logs down the Oder to the city of that name. But Sandwich soon discovered, at the beginning of the American war, that it was only about one-fourth as durable as British oak. Stettin oak, writes Michael Lewis, "was not . . . the only cause that brought us [Britain] to the verge of disaster and lost us our first empire, but it was certainly one cause, and a major one." Between 1775 and 1778 accidents resulting from inadequate fittings and mediocre material led to the loss of sixty-six ships.[11]

For the host of necessary repairs, as well as for the construction of new vessels, the navy had its own shipyards, though in the Seven Years' War the royal dockyards proved inadequate for the task of maintaining a growing fleet. A plan adopted by Sandwich for enlarging the naval yards had foundered for lack of funds, so that in the Revolutionary War

more than half of all shipbuilding occurred in private yards. Both
before and during the American Revolution, highly skilled shipwrights
were in great demand and were usually better paid in the merchant
yards. The persistent conflict of commercial interests with naval strategy was common in a century when England's wealth and power
rested on external trade and commerce. The government never
reached the point of seizing private shipyards or freezing shipwrights
in government service. "There is a line," declared Sandwich, "beyond
which the exertions of every country cannot go."[12] That line must
seem to have been drawn very short indeed. For the navy, as for the
army, limited rather than total mobilization characterized the years
between 1775 and 1783.

For the mother country's absence of an all-out homefront effort in
the earlier French wars there had been compensation in the colonies'
contributions, which by 1775 accounted for one-third of the total tonnage of British register. "It is from the American colonies," boasted an
Englishman during the Seven Years' War, that "our Royal Navy is supplied in a great measure with masts of all sizes and our naval stores, as
well as our ships[;] it is from them we have our vast fleets of merchant
ships, and consequently an increase of sea men; it is from them our men
of war in the American world are on any occasion man'd."[13] Though
the above was generally true in wartime when sea supremacy was
vital to victory, the royal navy under normal conditions favored tapping the superior pitch and tar of northern Europe.

But throughout the period, navy men acclaimed the stands of tall
New England *Pinus strobus*, or white pine, the most valuable sources
of all-important lower masts of ships-of-the-line. The royal navy sought
only the huge trees, usually twenty-five to thirty inches in diameter.
Authorities attributed the extraordinary resilience of pine masts to
their long-time retention of "the juices." Supposedly between 1694 and
1775 about 4,500 of these "great masts" were shipped to England for
the navy's use. Parliamentary acts in the 1720's forbade the colonists
from cutting *any* white pine, regardless of size or quality, regardless of
privately owned land, except for those trees lying within the bounds of
a township. Admiralty officials, however, secured almost all other (and
smaller) masts from the Baltic, with the result that only a tiny fraction
of 1 per cent of New England's white pines were actually earmarked
for the navy yards in Britain. In a real sense, an enormous "broad
arrow," the symbol of Admiralty attachment made with three blows
from a marking hatchet, lay over hundreds of thousands of trees. It was
a needless, selfish policy, which worked to the detriment of colonial
landowners, woodsmen, and millmen. Beyond doubt the Crown could
have met its needs without resorting to extreme restrictions upon its

American subjects. One historian asserts that Whitehall's harsh forest policy generated such feelings of anger and resentment in parts of New England that it was a factor in bringing the Yankee colonists to the "brink of rebellion" on the eve of the Stamp Act crisis.[14]

Though Britain possessed in home waters a reservoir of great masts at the beginning of the Revolution (the supply lasted until 1780),[15] she experienced trouble obtaining pine sticks and other naval stores for her vessels operating along the American coast. Of more significance, however, was the loss of American seamen who traditionally had swelled the navy and merchant marine in time of crisis. The *Annual Register* speculated that the break with the colonies robbed the mother country of at least 18,000 seamen, to say nothing of a sizeable portion of her merchant marine.[16] At the ourbreak of hostilities the navy's total strength stood at just that figure: 18,000, compared to 60,000 near the end of the Seven Years' War. Lacking an effective, organized system of recruitment, the Admiralty continued to pursue the age-old procedures of bounties and impressments. Bounties, though, never provided more than a fraction of the requisite manpower, for harsh discipline and high mortality were features of navy life known to all. "A man who went to sea for pleasure," proclaimed a contemporary doggerel, "would likely go to hell for a pastime."[17] Consequently, press gangs swept the streets of dockyard cities and boarded homeward-bound vessels in the channel and North Sea. But there were limits to impressing merchant seamen, and not because of the system's severity: the huge transport service, eventually supplying troops around the world, could not be wholly stripped of able seamen who could hand, steer, set up and repair rigging. Hence, there followed the conscription of landsmen who generally averaged from a quarter to almost half of every ship's complement.

Ships manned with inadequate crews frequently traced a poor performance to green, inexperienced hands. Probably these landed conscripts were the principal ones to suffer sickness and death at sea. Though only 1,243 seamen died in battle between 1776 and 1780, 18,541 died of disease (and 42,069 deserted).[18] Typhus and typhoid (yellow jack) were dread ailments, although scurvy continued to be the bane of the navy, the most malignant of all sea diseases in the eighteenth century. Admirals such as Lord Hawke and Lord Keppel maintained that a large fleet did well to stay at sea for six consecutive weeks without real suffering. This fact, along with the difficulty of securing adequate repairs in the New World, casts light on some of the naval peculiarities of the War of Independence: the disengagement of fleets in the midst of indecisive battles, the movement of squadrons back and forth between Europe and the West Indies, and the reluctance of commanders to undertake lengthy blockades. On the other hand, Captain James Cook in 1775 completed his second circumnavigation of the globe without the death of a single man from scurvy; careful victualing, including sauerkraut, was the explanation. But lemon juice was only slowly recognized as the best antiscorbutic. Unfortunately, the Admiralty left the problem to each captain, and in spite of the urging of Admiral George Rodney's physician, Sir George Blane, the Admiralty made no effort to issue seamen a regular supply of lemons until 1799.[19]

If the navy in 1775 was far below the desired two-power standard designed to keep it the numerical equal of the combined fleets of the Bourbon powers, and if the quality of its vessels was generally inferior to that of its arch enemies, then wherein lay the excellence of Britain's navy? Its performance depended upon its officers rather than its material. The mid-eighteenth-century navy boasted of a procession of splendid commanders in Vernon, Anson, Hawke, Boscawen, Saunders, and Stevens. Nor was it bereft of reputable figures during the American Revolution. Howe, Rodney, Hood, Peter Parker, Jervis, and Kempenfelt were in their prime. The navy was a more professional service than the army. While army officers acquired commissions without formal training, the potential navy officers first underwent instruction in seamanship and navigation. Starting their careers as cadets at the Royal Navy Academy (opened in 1732) or, more commonly, as captains' servants, their promotions depended upon the master of each vessel. Sharp competition among these young men led to hard work, a sense of responsibility, and the acquisition of a genuine knowledge of the sea. Family and influence, always important, were never quite what they were in the army; but to become a flag officer or admiral one resorted to the time-honored means of attaining preferment in the Hanoverian age.

The navy, like the army, manifested the internecine strife that marked the period. The captains and admirals too sat in Parliament, took part in factional battles, and reflected their politics in their relations with other naval men. Many officers felt that Lord Sandwich gave more weight to how a captain or admiral voted in the Commons than to his credentials for command.[20] When Admiral Keppel was court-martialed following the indecisive sea battle off Ushant in 1779, there were charges that Sandwich was motivated by Keppel's failure to back the ministry in Parliament. His friends interpreted his subsequent acquittal as a victory for the opposition.

Given the spirit and censorious nature of its military and naval commanders, the North ministry might have wondered who were its principal opponents—the American colonists or its own generals and admirals.[21]

## The German Allies

The Crown, refusing to call upon the productive elements in society, resorted to the familiar practice of hiring soldiers from the continent. Since troops seldom enlisted for reasons of patriotism, one might as well ask them to fight for a foreign sovereign as to bear arms for their own monarch. As early as October, 1774, General Gage had recommended that "foreign troops must be hired" in the event of open rebellion.[22] But with armed insurrection a reality the following year, the London government failed in its initial quests for mercenaries. Royal officials approached Catherine the Great of Russia, whose veterans, home from a victorious war against Turkey, might bolster British forces in the New World. The Empress demurred, impishly informing George III that she was doing him a favor, that to do otherwise would admit the King was too weak to put down his rebellious American subjects without outside aid. Nor did the ministry succeed in purchasing a Scottish brigade in the Dutch service.

Britain elicited a more favorable response from the German states. Hanover, whose elector was George III, lent the English monarch five battalions to garrison Gibraltar and Minorca, thereby releasing an equivalent body of redcoats for American duty. For years Germany had been an unfailing reservoir for European monarchs with ready cash. Germany, being a conglomeration of principalities whose rulers were anxious to emulate in their own courts the brilliance of Versailles, considered their soldiers one of the most remunerative commodities for export.

Hesse-Cassel could be counted on. Five times in the previous hundred years the landgrave had entered into a treaty for the single purpose of hiring out his troops, and England had been his best customer. Hessians shouldered arms on the continent for the British monarch in 1739, 1740, and 1742; and, in Britain itself, they participated in the Battle of Culloden against the Stuart Pretender in 1746. The current landgrave, with reputedly 100 children to succor, agreed in the winter of 1775–1776 to provide 12,000 mercenaries, and later an additional 5,000—out of a population of approximately 300,000. Though Hesse-Cassel sent the largest contingent of Germans to America (which accounts for the name *Hessian* to describe all foreigners in the King's pay), five other southern and western German principalities supplied, all told, another 12,800: Brunswick, 6,000; Hesse-Hanau and Anspach-Bayreuth each 2,400; Waldeck and Anhalt-Zerbst each slightly over 1,000. Of these six petty despots who profited from the labors of their soldiers across the seas, only Duke William of Hesse-Hanau and his

father Frederick II of Hesse-Cassel reduced taxes on their subjects who
had a father, son, or husband in British service.

Hesse-Cassel received the most favorable treaty from Britain; the
landgrave, a skillful barterer, acquired a subsidy per soldier roughly
twice that given the Duke of Brunswick.[23] And the subsidy was to
continue until one year after the regiments returned to Hesse-Cassel.
Yet the agreement with Brunswick contained a profitable, if infamous,
"blood-money" clause: the ruler won a lump sum for each man killed,
captured, or every three wounded. Less persuasive at the bargaining
table, but nonetheless determined to get any British sterling available,
was Prince Frederick August of Anhalt-Zerbst, a brother of Catherine
the Great, who ruled a domain of scarcely 20,000 inhabitants. The
Prince's subjects had lately suffered from famine and war and from an
economy devoted merely to agriculture. So doubtful was the North
ministry of Frederick August's ability to supply a body of recruits that
the treaty with Anhalt-Zerbst, unlike the others, specified that no funds
be handed over until the troops were actually mustered into British
service. Imagine the hardships imposed upon these simple farming
people to gratify their sovereign's lust.

Traffic in human flesh conflicted resoundingly with Enlightenment
ideals. To certain German intellectuals the American Revolution transferred the philosophical issues of the age from the salon to the battlefield. Goethe, Schiller, and Christian Schubart were among those who
criticized the ruling princes for sending Germans to fight and die in a
far-away contest of no concern to them, especially one waged for human freedom. A typical outburst of indignation came from the youthful Schiller:

> Look to the heavens, tyrant, where you sowed destruction,
> There from fields of blood
> Comes the stench of death.
> In a thousand storms,
> It beats about your head.
>
> Shudder, murd'rers, quake at every fleck of dust
> Which whirls into the sky.
> It is the dust of your own kin
> Which calls revenge upon your head.[24]

As Elisha P. Douglass writes, "The soldier traffic, therefore, served the
purpose of introducing romantic poets to the ideas of the American
Revolution, ideas they could manipulate to express their protest against
the many anachronisms in Germany which conflicted with the new

doctrines of the Enlightenment." Even in Germany, burdened with elements of feudalism and dominated by militarism, the ideal of war designed for freedom and fought by the citizens of the state was making its impact, albeit only among a fairly small group of intellectuals.[25]

In England, opponents of the ministry argued bitterly against the German treaties. Burke, denouncing Britain's buying of Germans to ravage her own subjects, asked how a war spawning such hatred in America could end in any gain for Britain. Further arguments stressing the cost of the foreign hirelings, the likelihood of desertion in America where there were large settlements of Germans, and the possibility of the alliances embroiling England in continental squabbles all fell on deaf ears. In the Commons the treaties carried by a vote of 242 to 88, and in the Lords by 100 to 32.

The caliber of Britain's mercenaries was, perhaps not surprisingly, of uneven quality. Some regiments compared favorably with the best in the British army, especially the Duke of Hesse-Cassel's Bodyguards. So did the *jägers*, particularly the corps organized in 1777 under Colonel Ludwig Johann Adolph von Wurmb composed mainly of men from Hesse-Cassel. Mostly recruited from huntsmen and gameskeepers, they were equipped with rifles and performed as light troops. This corps, as well as smaller *jäger* units, engaged in scouting and patrolling duties. Operating on the flanks of troops advancing in columns, they were effective in beating back American harassing parties and held their own in combat against Daniel Morgan's famous rifle corps, essentially their counterpart in the Continental army.[26]

In contrast, Colonel William Faucitt, sent to Germany as minister plenipotentiary in charge of recruiting, found that in one regiment destined for America the front and rear contained sound men, but that the center consisted of the very old and the very young.

To meet their quotas for George III, some of the princes almost literally rounded up every stranger in sight. Youthful Johann Gottfried Seume, a student from Leipzig, was kidnapped while passing through the domain of the landgrave of Hesse-Cassel, "this seller of human souls." His captors destroyed his "academic papers (proof that I had been a student), my only means of identification." Placed in a Hessian regiment, he found a student from Jena, a bankrupt merchant from Vienna, a lace maker from Hanover, a monk from Würzburg, and a magistrate from Meninger. A plot to escape involving a number of Seume's friends was discovered, and two were hanged; "the rest . . . were sentenced to run the gauntlet from twelve to thirty-six times. It was simple butchery." Once aboard British transports, Seume reported, they were "packed like sardines." Since sometimes as many as six men slept in a single bunk, the occupants all lay in the same position. "And when we thus had sweated and roasted enough on one side, the man on the right end called out, 'Everybody turn!' and so, everybody turned over."[27]

Seume's narrative and that of Hessian Major Baurmeister suggest that most of the German troops in the Revolutionary War were not the ogres portrayed in American school textbooks. General Wilhelm von Knyphausen sternly warned his men against plundering. Baurmeister stated that, while British General Clinton's troops looted their way across New Jersey in 1778, "there was no pillaging and plundering on the part of the Hessians, but it is my duty to report . . . that we had many deserters."[28] For the German officers, desertion was indeed a serious matter. Washington, Jefferson, and Franklin among other American leaders saw the mercenaries as a weak link in Britain's armor. Throughout the war the German troops received an incessant barrage of temptations. Congress and the states promised land, oxen, pigs, and cows, together with religious freedom and political liberty, if they would desert and make homes in America, where, they were told, thousands of their fellow countrymen were already living in security and contentment. Many responded, most notably during the march through New Jersey in 1778, during the confinement of Burgoyne's army after its capture at Saratoga, and prior to the British evacuation of New York in 1783. Only 17,313—about 58 per cent—of the 30,000 German troops returned to their native land, leaving 12,000 to be accounted for. Only a relative few of these died in combat, whereas a larger number succumbed to illness and disease. Additional thousands remained in America, in the words of the Pennsylvania Council of Safety, to "unite with ourselves in improving the fertile forests of America, extending its manufactures and commerce, and maintaining its Liberty and independency."[29] Thus the War of Independence added ore to the great American melting pot and provided an early instance of the use of psychological warfare to win converts among the enemy.

## The Loyalists

The British army and navy and the German mercenaries were all to be used in cracking the American rebellion, and so were the American loyalists, who affected British military policy to a much greater extent than usually realized. Their presence fashioned the expedition to the Southern colonies in 1776, influenced to a lesser degree the Northern campaigns of 1776 and 1777, and largely governed the final three years of genuine warfare.[30]

We shall probably never know precisely the size of the loyalist faction. The problem of giving figures and percentages for the Crown's followers is compounded by the so-called neutralists or passive colonists who lacked deep convictions, though perhaps hoping for the triumph of one side, but not to the extent of becoming vocal or taking to arms. Some historians, however, may have exaggerated the degree of apathy and indifference; by the standards of the time, the American was a remarkably sensitive political animal. There is hardly a parallel in the Revolutionary War to what happened during Napoleon's occupation of Prussia in 1806, as described by Gordon Craig:

> In 1806 all of the basic weaknesses of the absolutist system became manifest. When the victorious armies of Bonaparte entered Berlin after the battles of Jena and Auerstadt, they were greeted at the Brandenburger Tor by representatives of the Berlin magistracy and the local merchants; city officials voluntarily agreed to continue their services for the conqueror; and the burghers of Berlin served without demur in the national guard organized by the French. A similar reception was accorded the French in other Prussian towns; there were few signs of even passive resistance to the foreigner; and the Prussian press treated the shattering events of the recent campaign as indifferently as if they were writing of a war between the Shah of Persia and the Emir of Kasbul.[31]

Except for the Quakers and recent arrivals to the colonies, especially some of the German groups it is improbable that many Americans viewed the War of Independence with the indifference so prevalent in Prussia. Certainly the old symmetrical notion that a third of all Americans were revolutionists, a third tories, and a third neutralists[32] is too simple, and too high for the King's adherents as well as for the neutralists. The proportion of loyalists seems to have been highest among the cultural and religious minorities (including the Anglicans outside the South but generally excluding the whig-oriented Catholics and Jews). The rebels were an overwhelming majority in the colonies of purest English stock. Only in the heterogeneous middle colonies did the ranks of the loyalists come to possibly half the population; but in the South they amounted to scarcely a third or fourth of the total, and in New England no more than a tenth. One of the most intelligent estimates to date is that the tories were a third and the patriots two-thirds of the "politically active" American population.[33]

However, during the tumultuous years since the Stamp Act, the King, North, and their cohorts had never swerved from the opinion that the agitation in the colonies was a reflection of but a small minority spurred on by the ignoble ambition and avarice of a few demagogues. Indeed, William Howe in 1775 mirrored what would be the opinion of most London officials throughout the war when he assured a Mr. Kirk in England, "I may safely assert that the insurgents are very few, in

comparison with the whole of the people."[34] The loyalists themselves
added to the myth: Joseph Galloway of Pennsylvania claimed that the
faithful consisted of four-fifths of all the colonists. Equally guilty of disseminating false information were royal governors like Dunmore of
Virginia, Josiah Martin of North Carolina, and William Campbell of
South Carolina, who led Britain to underrate her task in bringing the
rebels to heel. Time and again commanders in the field, asking for reinforcements, received instructions to make greater use of the tories. This
illusion of loyalist support dictated more than a handful of military
decisions to the very end of the war.

At the onset of hostilities there was no dearth of local efforts to arouse
the King's friends. Colonel Allen Maclean, organizing a corps of "His
Majesty's Loyal North American subjects" in Quebec and Nova Scotia,
also hastened recruiting officers to New York and North Carolina.
Equally active was Governor Dunmore who, incredibly, declared that
the insurrection had such faint appeal in Virginia that, with two or
three hundred troops, plus the loyalists, he could hold his province for
the Crown. Dunmore even sent John Connally, his agent at Pittsburgh,
to see Gage at Boston with a proposal for raising a frontier army to
harry the western portions of Virginia, Maryland, Pennsylvania, and
New York. Connally never got the opportunity—sanctioned by Gage
—to implement his ambitious plan; captured on returning to the Old
Dominion, he remained in prison until any possibility of carrying out
his proposal had evaporated.

But the idea of a vast royal following in the Southland persisted and
remained to be tested. Acknowledging that the British army in New
England was as yet insufficient to throttle the rebellion there, Londoners felt an operation of modest dimensions below the Chesapeake
would attract support from thousands of loyalists in the back-country
districts and from the Scottish Highlanders who had lately settled in
North Carolina. Accordingly, in the summer and fall of 1775 a plan
evolved for tapping this reputed source of fidelity. A fleet under Sir
Peter Parker carrying five regiments and 10,000 stand of small arms for
the tories was to cross the Atlantic bound for Cape Fear, North Carolina, there to rendezvous with a smaller force under Sir Henry Clinton
arriving from Boston.

From the beginning, trouble beset the expedition. Contrary winds
and winter storms delayed Parker's leaving home waters for weeks.
Clinton, meanwhile, arrived off Cape Fear, where he found that a bar
at the mouth of the river of that name blocked the entrance of large
vessels. He also learned that two weeks earlier, on February 27, 1776,
the North Carolina militia had defeated a body of Highland loyalists at
Moore's Creek Bridge, seventeen miles from Wilmington. Governor
Martin, whose reports had built a roseate image of sentiments in his

colony, admitted that the whigs were in control all along the coast and
as far as 100 miles inland. Small wonder that Clinton developed
"gloomy forebodings of . . . success."[35]

When Parker finally united with Clinton in May, the General received his long-delayed instructions: "to re-establish order in four provinces" in time to rejoin Howe in the summer for an invasion of New
York! The two commanders decided to attack Sullivan's Island, protecting the harbor of Charleston, South Carolina. Charleston, on the
coast of the fiercely whiggish low country, had little bearing on the
purpose of the expedition, which was, in Clinton's own words, to assemble and arm *"the well affected inhabitants in such numbers as shall be
sufficient to restore and maintain order and good Government after the
King's Troops shall be withdrawn."*

This thriving commercial community at the juncture of the Ashley
and Cooper rivers had never been the object of the Southern expedition. Apparently a last-minute resolution on the part of Parker and
Clinton, the maneuver "would have produced no permanent advantage
even if entirely successful." Clinton lacked the manpower to hold the
city, and the loyalists were too remote to be of assistance. There is
good reason to believe that Clinton himself never thought of doing so,
that at most he contemplated occupying Sullivan's Island to salvage
something from a disappointing campaign before returning to New
York.[36]

The ensuing affair in Charleston harbor only gave Clinton and company another reversal. Luck immediately went against them. Though
the British warships and transports hove into view of the city as early
as June 1, 1776, stiff winds prevented them from entering the harbor
for over three weeks. During the wait Clinton debarked his troops on
Long Island, just outside the harbor, where they were to cross a ford
allegedly eighteen inches deep to smash the rebel defenses on Sullivan's
Island; to Clinton's "unspeakable mortification" the water measured
seven feet deep! American riflemen and field pieces moved into position to oppose Clinton should he collect boats and ferry his men
across. Charles Lee, speeded south by Congress, arrived with Continentals from Virginia and North Carolina to bolster the strength as well
as the spirit of the defenders. Disagreeing over strategy, as British
generals and admirals were apt to do, Parker and Clinton let valuable
days slip by. Finally, under more favorable winds on June 28, Parker,
largely ignoring Clinton, began a bombardment of a partially completed fort on Sullivan's Island. While three vessels sent to hammer the
unfinished western side of the fort all ran aground, the bulk of the fleet
hit at it from the south. For the most part the British balls were merely
absorbed in the spongy palmetto wood. Simultaneously, the American

guns were inflicting heavy damage to Parker's ships. With nightfall the
duel ended, and since further activities were out of the question, Clinton's troops re-embarked and the battered fleet limped away to the
north. Ill fortune, along with the breakdown in cooperation between
the services, which should have included improvisation to surmount
unforeseen difficulties, explains the outcome, plus, of course, the efforts
of Lee and the Carolinians.[37]

The termination of the first Southern campaign in no way dampened
Britain's optimistic view of the temper of the region. A campaign
founded on certain doubtful assumptions did not destroy those assumptions: namely, that loyalists would be able to rise on a schedule to
coincide with the landing of regulars and that they would be numerous
enough to create a viable regime. After all, the ministry could argue
that the attack on Charleston had never been the goal of the expedition. The futile rising of the loyalists at Moore's Creek Bridge only
served to convince London officialdom that had redcoats been present
the affair would have been significantly different. This vision of the
South, never abandoned, dominated British planning from 1778 to the
end of hostilities.

But what of other areas that early in the war came under British
control? What of endeavors there to utilize "the friends of government"? Colonial manpower had contributed to the empire's victory
over France in North America, but colonials often performed poorly
in conjunction with regulars and friction had resulted. British officers
looked upon the colonials as inefficient, ill-disciplined, and ignorant of
army life, while Americans deemed their British "protectors" imperious
and unschooled in wilderness warfare. A solution to the problem of
Anglo-American cooperation never came in the colonial era; and the
old antagonisms reappeared in the Revolutionary War, for neither loyalists nor redcoats were able to overcome their own heritage. Britons
too frequently revealed to the tories the professionals' aversion for
citizen-soldiers, in addition to a general contempt for Americans. On
the other hand, Edward Winslow, muster master-general of the loyalist
forces, acknowledged the reluctance of many provincials to fight outside their own colony (shades of the Seven Years' War!) and to enlist
for more than a short, fixed period. Massachusetts-born Winslow took a
kind of sadistic pride in Burgoyne's defeat by American farmers,
whom the British General had always scorned.[38] Many a loyalist, like
many a patriot, was a sensitive man; he, too, had rights and liberties,
and though loyal to the empire, he demanded recognition of them. In
Britain's newly established provincial service he often found them
wanting.

The British recalled from past experience the problems of American militia serving alongside redcoats, also the unlikelihood of colonists being smoothly integrated into regular units. Hence, the emphasis from 1775 onward was on raising provincial regiments "for rank," a system calling for a prominent loyalist to recruit his own corps. British officers predictably registered objections. Regular officers had their vested interests; few plums were more enticing than the colonelcy of a new regiment. A privileged group in a society of privilege, the army officers preferred incorporating tories into their regular forces instead of raising new corps, with their accompanying complement of American officers. In America, therefore, as in England, the British ruling classes looked askance upon offering partnership to outsiders as part of the price of total war. And though the idea of provincial units prevailed, the government, anticipating a quick end to the war, displayed an initial reluctance to make wholesale efforts to put regiments "for rank" into service—regiments which, wrote George III, would compete with established units for manpower and "annihilate all chance of compleating the regular forces which alone in time of need can be depended upon."[39]

Englishmen in authority naïvely assumed that the tories' enthusiasm for the cause was itself sufficient motive to entice loyal colonials to the standard, regardless of whether they received reasonable inducements. Provincial officers afford the best case in point. Denied hospital and nursing assistance as well as a gratuity allowance, all of which accrued to wounded British officers, the commissioned loyalists also received neither permanent rank nor half pay for life on the reduction of their regiments. In the absence of explicit regulations for the provincial service, some Americans were victimized by dishonest individuals such as Allen Maclean, who promised his officers permanent rank in the regular establishment and half pay. Consequently, many loyalists came *and went*, though their names might continue on the regimental rolls and give an inflated picture of the provincial line. Another loyalist complaint was that the British assigned them menial tasks and routine drudgery. Perhaps there was more truth than fiction in the patriot doggerel:

> Come, gentlemen Tories, firm, loyal and true
> Here are axes and shovels and something to do!
> For the sake of our king,
> Come labor and sing.[40]

Until 1778 Britain displayed an ambivalent attitude toward the loyalists characterized by a faith in their numbers and by a reluctance to gain their full participation. Reforms were slow in the provincial service chiefly because in the early years of the war British policy makers tended to minimize the need for loyalists in the field. But it would be inaccurate to assume they had insignificant impact on British policy in this period: military campaigns were usually formulated for areas where the regular army would bear the brunt of the fighting, but where it anticipated limited opposition because of the population's supposed fidelity to the Crown. When the war turned a more ominous color with the entrance of France, Britain became more dependent on the loyalists and brought about needed reforms in the provincial service, but not before irreparable damage had occurred. Loyalists' morale and faith in just treatment from the mother country had been permanently dimmed by their second-rate military status.

## The Machinery for War

The direction of the American war, like the ones with France, emanated from London, and the administrative machinery was the same that had served the mother country with varying degrees of efficiency throughout the century. Technically, as we have seen, war was the business of the monarch; and George III, though not a soldier as his grandfather had been, took his military obligations seriously. Proud of the army (and his title of captain general), he was genuinely interested in its efficiency and activities. A more aggressive monarch than his predecessor, George III, moreover, assumed the throne at a time when the Crown's patronage was on the increase because of the numerous wars of the century: wars which created a need for more ships and more regiments, more dockyards and more supplies, and more taxes (and tax collectors). All this fell in the sphere of military administration, and here the Hanoverian made his presence felt, either directly or through his ministers. If he did not actually choose military commanders, he demanded that they be acceptable to him. [41] The British nation was not yet ready to accept Charles James Fox's principle that kings should reign but not govern.

This does not mean that George himself planned campaigns and directed the movements of troops and ships. After insisting on the suppression of the rebellion, he left to his ministers the over-all strategy and the day-to-day decisions. His role was to encourage resoluteness in his officials, to give them energy for their tasks, to silence the fainthearted, and to ridicule the opposition. Most of all, the King needed to buoy up Lord North, first lord of the treasury and head of the cabinet, sometimes known as the prime minister, though in the eighteenth century the various ministers were primarily responsible to the King rather than to a cabinet leader. Outwardly dull and methodical, North was not one to infuse his colleagues with vitality or to manage the war effort. He confessed that "Upon military matters I speak ignorantly, and therefore without effect." Of his cabinet colleagues, he wrote, "I have never interfered in any of their departments. I have never clash'd with their views." Given to moods of depression and melancholia, North often talked of retiring, and after 1778, if not before, he doubted seriously the wisdom of continuing the fight against the American colonists. Yet through thick and thin the King, distrustful of politicians, kept North in office; it was easier to retain a man he could work with than to risk another. And North, a sound financier, was not without political skill. A veteran of the House of Commons, he knew that body inside and out; conscious of its procedures and traditions, he did not try to browbeat its members, but operated through patronage and debate to maintain majorities for the government.[42]

Whatever his weaknesses, North was a realist about the requirements for wartime leadership. As he informed the King, "in critical times, it is necessary that there should be one directing Minister, who should plan the whole of the operations of government, and controul all the other departments of administration so far as to make them cooperate zealously and actively with his designs even tho' contrary to their own."[43] Neither Secretary at War Lord Barrington nor his successor, Charles Jenkinson, had the competence or the authority to assume that role. Constitutionally, his position lacked definition, but he was subordinate to the office of commander in chief, a vacant post from 1770 until occupied by Amherst in 1778. The secretary at war seems to have been principally concerned with such technical aspects of military organization as preparing army estimates for the House of Commons and gathering stores and equipment for the troops. Without cabinet status, he had no part in planning broad strategy and individual operations. The best testimony of his impotence comes from Barrington himself, who stated as late as March, 1776, his unawareness of the destination and mission of the Clinton-Parker expedition to the Southern colonies. Possessed of much more authority was the first lord of the admiralty, Sandwich, who held a cabinet seat. But here, too, neither the officer nor the man was fitted to be a supreme director.

North's solution to handling the war amounted to installing another Pitt at the helm, a leader whose brilliant audacity, furious effectiveness, and inspirational qualities would once again galvanize the creaky and overlapping agencies of government to the high level of achievement of the late 1750's. In the palms of a lesser figure (though possibly capable enough) who lacked a popular mandate the machinery would likely revert to its older, cumbersome modes.

Supply and transportation disclose some of the system's infirmities. The navy's own victualling board acquired provisions for the fleet; the treasury performed this service for the army. The board of ordnance provided other stores and equipment for the navy and the army.

Though the victualling board secured the navy's victualling ships throughout the war, the navy board, subordinate to the Admiralty, hired victuallers for the army after the treasury gave up the job in 1779. The ordnance board saw to transporting engineers, artillery, and ordnance to America, but the navy board found passage for the infantry and cavalry, along with clothing, hospital supplies, tents, and camp equipage. When this division of authority was not maintained, a treasury transport might carry soldiers, a navy transport artillery, and an ordnance transport clothing. Competition between various boards and agencies for ships, food, and other supplies made serious delays and shortages. A careful student of British army organization finds it "sometimes remarkable that the troops received any food and clothing at all."[44] Unfortunately, food suppliers in England got slight relief from America: its sparsely settled areas, its hostile inhabitants, its poor roads and bridges all combined to make the theaters of rebellion generally undependable for provisions. Thus most food came directly from Britain, and it frequently arrived in sorry condition owing to sailing delays, poor quality to begin with, or careless stowage. To commissary officers in America, cargoes of mouldy bread, sour flour, rancid butter, and maggoty beef were the rule rather than the exception.

One would err to think that the government's only failures to function as a single coordinated instrument occurred in wartime; in other periods as well this was a government of loose organization, of departments, boards, and offices sharing jurisdiction in matters of importance and rivaling one another. Recall the management of colonial affairs in the decades prior to the American Revolution, when divided authority and overlapping responsibility had been characteristic of British control. War, therefore, was but a different manifestation of the inadequacies of government in the eighteenth century, attributable in some considerable degree to a process at work since 1689 if not before: the gradual transition from a highly personalized medieval monarchy to a more complex government in which functions and powers were widely distributed among offices and institutions whose areas of authority still lacked precise definition.[45]

In 1781, the younger Pitt, exasperated by military failures, asked how "the engine of government might be relieved from that load of machinery which rendered its movements so slow, so intricate, and so confused."[46] It may be difficult to explain why concerted endeavors were not undertaken to centralize and systematize, but this much is clear: government appears to have existed not to legislate—to create or innovate—but to maintain order, wage war, and conduct foreign policy with the materials at hand.

Military preparations became a collective enterprise of the cabinet.

During the War of Independence the eight or nine principal ministers met weekly for dinner after which business was attended to. When necessary there were special meetings to discuss developments requiring immediate solutions. The North cabinet was not the later cabinet of Gladstone or Disraeli; ministers were not immediately responsible to North, were not bound to place their problems before it. But, especially in time of war or other crisis, a department head protected himself by allowing crucial decisions to come from the cabinet as a whole. Lord Sandwich assured the House of Lords that every naval expedition "in regard to its destination, object, force and number of ships, is planned by the Cabinet, and is the result of the collective wisdom of all his Majesty's confidential measures." Sandwich himself was "only the executive servant of these measures."[47]

After the cabinet planned, it was the job of the secretaries of state to implement by issuing, as one official explained, "timely orders, to the Treasury, Admiralty, Ordnance and Commander-in-Chief of the Army on these heads, so that every necessary preparation can be made, and no delay nor disappointment happen when the services take place." One secretary presided over the Northern Department, another over the Southern Department. Between them they divided the execution of foreign policy and military affairs for Northern and Southern Europe respectively. The Southern secretary's jurisdiction had extended to North America and the West Indies until 1768, when a colonial secretary was appointed to head an American Department. Among the secretaries, as elsewhere in government, rivalries existed; from 1768 to 1775 the Southern secretary had unsuccessfully contested the colonial secretary's right to send orders to military commanders in the New World. Having withstood the "jarrings" and jealousies of the other secretaries, the American secretary became a kind of pivot on which the government's efforts to stamp out the American rebellion turned. Through his hands passed cabinet directives, and it was his responsibility to make the follow up—to push and pull to see that the wheels revolved and the machine moved. Any unity or coordination came about only through his labors. A well-provisioned force assembled on schedule with transports and naval support in readiness reflected the energizing influence of the American secretary. But though American affairs might be his province, the older secretaries could and did make their influence felt. Specific orders for embarkation of troops in Ireland were issued by the Southern secretary to the lord lieutenant of Ireland, though their destination was America. The Northern secretary superintended the negotiations for the German mercenaries and even saw to their arrival in England.[48]

The colonial secretary came closer than any other official to being the director of the American war. So it is easy to understand why the King was eager to fill the post with a minister favoring the sternest measures for the rebellious colonies. And in 1775 the head of the American Department, Lord Dartmouth, was not such a man. Indecisive and ineffectual, plagued with doubts about the government's American program, Dartmouth bowed out of office in November, 1775, accepting as compensation a less demanding assignment as lord privy seal. His successor, sixty-year-old Lord George Germain, a member of the House of Commons, had been a consistent advocate of force from long before the outbreak of hostilities. An energetic man with a military background and competent as an administrator, Germain was scarcely guilty of the manifold defects of character and sins of commission so frequently laid at his feet. But the very fact that gossip abounded regarding the American secretary lessened his effectiveness. Most damaging was his alleged conduct in the Seven Years' War, before which he had compiled a spotless military record. Serving in Germany under Frederick of Brunswick, he was accused of disobedience to orders in the Battle of Minden; returning to England, he demanded—foolishly as it turned out—a court-martial to clear his name. Service trials invariably generated political fireworks, or were from inception based on political behavior as much or more than military misconduct. Germain was an intimate of the Prince of Wales (later George III) and shared that young man's anti-Prussian views, all to the displeasure of German-born George II who was committed strongly to supporting Prussia and her allies against France. The officers composing the court-martial knew on which side their bread was buttered, and there is ample reason to accept the younger George's opinion that Germain's hearers were "both judge and party." The court found him guilty and declared him "unfit to serve His Majesty in any military capacity whatever." The King added insult to injury by forbidding him the royal court and directing the sentence to be read before all the regiments, with the added statement that it was "worse than death." The judgment was harsh if not totally without foundation, and during his six-year tenure as American secretary it haunted Germain.[49]

For a war leader he was dangerously vulnerable. "The Ghost of Minden" was ever trundled out by the opposition. Perhaps all of this contributed to his other limitations, a sharp and hasty temper and a measure of arrogance. Here then was an able man, often unjustly maligned, but one lacking wide prestige or the temperament to work smoothly with fellow ministers, a man whose tactless criticism of the navy led to a strained relationship with Sandwich and the Admiralty; and finally, a man whose incredible optimism about the war in America never seemed to flag, though in time the military men on the scene reported back to him the magnitude of their task.

## NOTES

1. Piers Mackesy, *The War for America, 1775–1783* (Cambridge, Mass., 1964), xiv.
2. Edward E. Curtis, *The Organization of the British Army in the American Revolution* (New Haven, 1926), 1.
3. Henry Belcher, *The First American Civil War* (London, 1911), I, 258. This work, though deficient in a number of ways, contains a wealth of useful information on "The Social and Military Conditions" of the army and navy between 1760 and 1800. See Vol. I, 242–350.
4. Richard Pares, *King George III and the Politicians* (Oxford, Eng., 1953 [1954]), 18–19. In fact, however, the army was used sparingly to quell local disturbances, because of public sensitivity on the issue. To call out the troops without the approval of local magistrates would evoke widespread criticism. For examples of the use of regulars, see D. B. Horn and Mary Ransone, eds., *English Historical Documents, 1714–1783* (London, 1957), 622–628. Namier and Brooke, *House of Commons*, I, 142, report that of the 208 army officers who sat in the Commons between 1754 and 1790, only one was a "self-made man": Major General William Phillips, born of humble parents, achieved a distinguished career in the royal artillery before dying in America in 1781.
5. Stuart Wortley, *A Prime Minister and His Son*, 71, 109.
6. Ian Christie, *The End of North's Ministry, 1780–1782* (London, 1958), 178–179.
7. Clinton, *American Rebellion*, xxiv; Commager and Morris, eds., *Spirit of 'Seventy-Six*, I, 240.
8. Stuart Wortley, *A Prime Minister and His Son*, 139; *Diary of MacKenzie*, I, 285. Lord Howe's secretary also noted an air of pessimism in 1777 and 1778 among officers in high places. Edward H. Tatum, Jr., *The American Journal of Ambrose Serle, 1776–1778* (San Marino, Calif., 1940), xxiv; Generals Charles O'Hara and Alexander Leslie also had deep misgivings about winning the war. George C. Rogers, Jr., "Letters of Charles O'Hara to the Duke of Grafton," *South Carolina Historical Magazine*, LXV (1964), 158–180.
9. M. J. Williams, "The Naval Administration of the Fourth Earl of Sandwich, 1771–1782" (unpubl. doctoral diss., Oxford University, 1962), 12–14, 42; Greig, ed., *Letters of Hume*, II, 318–319; *Newport Mercury*, Sept 7, 1772.
10. Barnes and Owen, eds., *Papers of Sandwich*, I, 19–23. Williams, "Naval Administration," has made effective use of this work in his sympathetic study of Sandwich. Williams' conclusions are reflected in Mackesy, *War for America*, *passim*. For other favorable estimates of Sandwich, see Esmond Wright, *Fabric of Freedom* (New York, 1961), 106, 118–121; Gerald S. Graham, *Empire of the North Atlantic: The Maritime Struggle for North America* (Toronto, 1950), 198–200. The only modern biography is George Martelli, *Jemmy Twitcher: A Life of the Fourth Earl of Sandwich* (London, 1962).
11. Michael Lewis, *The Navy of Britain* (London, 1948), 107; Gerald S. Graham, "Considerations on the War of American Independence," *Bulletin of the Institute of Historical Research*, XXII (1949), 28.
12. Barnes and Owens, eds., *Papers of Sandwich*, IV, 308. Commercial interests also interfered with army recruitment. North informed the King that the East India Company's campaign to secure men for overseas hampered the government's plans to find military manpower. Fortescue, ed., *Correspondence of George the Third*, III, nos. 1708, 1715.
13. *The Present State of North America* (1755), quoted in G. J. Marcus, *A Naval History of England: The Formative Years* (Boston and Toronto, 1961), 416.
14. Joseph J. Malone, *Pine Trees and Politics: The Naval Stores and Forest Policy in Colonial New England* (Seattle, 1964), *passim*, but especially 47–56, 141–143. Knollenberg, *Origin of the Revolution*, 127–137, discusses colonial resentment. There were widespread violations of the forest laws. Hundreds of thousands of

board feet of white pine emanated from New Hampshire and Massachusetts (including Maine) sawmills. In the 1760's John Wentworth, governor of New Hampshire and surveyor general of the woods, attempted to combat what he termed "backwoods anarchy" by inserting a degree of flexibility in British policy. Recognizing Parliament's statutes as "penal" in nature, he urged woodsmen and mill men to avoid trees literally marked with the "broad arrow" along with other stands of pine mapped as reservations; in return he agreed to close his eyes to other pine cutting. His solution appears to have met with considerable success until he and other Crown appointees were overwhelmed by events of the American Revolution. Malone, *Pine Trees and Politics*, 133–141.

15. Williams, "Naval Administration," 315–321, dispels the older view of R. G. Albion, *Forests and Sea Power* (Cambridge, Mass., 1926), 280–290, that the fleet's supply of white pines was exhausted by 1778, producing crippling effects on the navy's operations against the French in that year. Mackesy, *War for America*, 169, contains a more lengthy summary of Williams' conclusions on the matter.

16. *The Annual Register . . .* (London, 1778), 201. John Luttrell informed his Parliamentary colleagues that America before 1775 had been "a great nursery, where seamen . . . [were] raised, trained, and maintained in times of peace to serve this country in times of war. . . ." Clark, ed., *Naval Documents of the American Revolution*, I, 444–445.

17. Wright, *Fabric of Freedom*, 109. Pay on merchant vessels, always higher than in the navy, is said to have doubled in the first year of the war. Dora Mae Clark, *British Opinion and the American Revolution* (New Haven, 1930), 110.

18. The desertion figures are for the entire war. Full statistics on the other categories are apparently unavailable. Christopher Lloyd and Jack L. S. Coulter, *Medicine in the Navy, 1714–1815* (Edinburgh and London, 1961), 137.

19. Not 1795, the frequently cited date. *Ibid.*, 325–326. Lloyd and Coulter believe that "from a medical point of view," the British errors were as numerous and significant as those in tactics and strategy. *Ibid.*, 122. Admiral Kempenfelt declared that if a fleet could briefly put into port once every three or four weeks, it might otherwise remain operational for an entire year; "for, except for the scurvy, the men keep freer from diseases at sea than in port, as they have neither women or spirits, the chief causes of their diseases." J. K. Laughton, ed., *Letters and Papers of Charles, Lord Barham* (London, 1907–1911), I, 328, 331. See also Alan Villiers, *James Cook* (New York, 1968).

20. Namier and Brooke, *House of Commons*, I, 144, imply that Sandwich's critics were substantially correct. For a lengthy discussion of "Patronage and Promotion" presenting a more favorable view of Sandwich, see Williams, "Naval Administration," chap. iii. It might be appropriate to note here that, despite the talent and experience of certain key naval figures of the Revolutionary War, they were, by and large, rusty in 1775. In peacetime, naval squadrons—calling for admirals or flag officers to command—seldom engaged in operations; instead single ships commanded by officers of lower rank performed almost all the navy's work. Consequently, Rear Admiral Lord Howe, appointed commander in chief in American waters in 1775, had not been to sea since the Seven Years' War. Vice Admiral Keppel, given the channel fleet in 1778 and with it the task of thwarting a Franco-Spanish invasion, had not been to sea in fifteen years. It was asserted in the House of Lords that Sir Charles Hardy, Keppel's successor in 1779, had not been on ship in nearly twenty years.

21. On the death of Pitt, Captain Jervis wrote to his sister in 1778: "What will become of us now Lord Chatham is gone? The very name of Pitt kept the House of Bourbon in awe. This wretched, pitiful scoundrel, North, will act his underpart to our destruction." Marcus, *Naval History of England*, 414.

22. Carter, ed., *Gage Correspondence*, I, 380.

23 For the treaty with Hesse-Cassel and other illustrative documents on the use of German troops, see Morris and Commager, eds., *Spirit of 'Seventy-Six*, I, 264–270. The two standard accounts of German participation are now quite dated:

Max von Eelking, *Die Deutschen Hülfstruppen im nordamerikanischen Befrei-ungskrieg, 1775-1783*, 2 vols. (Hanover, 1863), translated by J. G. Rosengarten as *German Allied Troops in the North American War of Independence, 1775-1783* (Albany, 1893); Edward J. Lowell, *The Hessians and the Other German Auxiliaries of Great Britain in the Revolutionary War* (New York, 1884). Of more limited use is J. G. Rosengarten, *American History from German Archives* (Lancaster, Pa., 1904). Two recent works are worthy of note: Ernst Kipping, *Die Truppen von Hessen-Kassel im Amerikanischen . . . 1776-1783* (Darmstadt, 1965); Alfred Kröger, *Geburt der USA: German Newspaper Accounts of the American Revolution* (Madison, Wis., 1962).

24. James T. Hatfield and Elfrieda Hochbaum, "The Influence of the American Revolution upon German Literature," *America Germanica*, III (1900), 362.

25. Elisha P. Douglass, "German Intellectuals and the American Revolution," *William and Mary Quarterly*, 3d ser., XVII (1960), 204. Douglass provides a useful corrective to Lowell, *Hessians in the Revolutionary War*, 21-22, who underestimates the interest of the German intelligentsia in the American Revolution. Though Frederick the Great expressed concern to Voltaire over the fate of the "poor Hessians" hastened to America, his opposition to supplying Britain with manpower seems to have sprung from less lofty reasons than those expressed by the poets and other literary figures. Recruiting men for the New World battlefields interfered with Frederick's own recruiting program in Germany. He also harbored a grudge against England for her supposed ill treatment of Prussia near the end of the Seven Years' War. P. L. Haworth, "Frederick the Great and the American Revolution," *American Historical Review*, IX (1904), 460-478.

26. The best discussion of the *jägers* in English is J. F. C. Fuller, *British Light Infantry in the Eighteenth Century* (London, 1925), 134-151.

27. Margarete Woelfel, trans., "Memoirs of a Hessian Conscript: J. G. Seume's Reluctant Voyage to America," *William and Mary Quarterly*, 3d ser., V (1949), 553-570. The unpopularity of military service is strikingly revealed in instructions to Hessian officers prescribing extreme precautionary measures lest conscripts attempt to escape on the way to garrison camp. The instructions are paraphrased in Lowell, *Hessians in the Revolutionary War*, 42-43. Seume was not the only Hessian to call the Landgrave a "Soul-Seller." *Boston Gazette*, July 7, 1777.

28. Bernhard A. Uhlendorf, trans. and ed., *Revolution in America: Confidential Letters and Journals 1776-1784 of Adjutant General Major Baurmeister of the Hessian Forces* (New Brunswick, N.J., 1957), 22. For other comments on desertion see *ibid.*, 59, 167, 185, 202, 227, 248, 296, 502, 553, 557-558, 561, 564, 586.

29. Lyman H. Butterfield, "Psychological Warfare in 1776: The Jefferson-Franklin Plan to Cause Hessian Desertions," American Philosophical Society, *Proceedings*, CXCIV (1950); Carl Berger, *Broadsides and Bayonets: The Propaganda War of the American Revolution* (Philadelphia, 1961), 102-124; Miller, *Triumph of Freedom*, 15.

30. Paul H. Smith, *Loyalists and Redcoats: A Study in British Revolutionary Policy* (Chapel Hill, 1964), is excellent.

31. Craig, *Politics of the Prussian Army*, 21.

32. In 1954 John R. Alden noted that while this estimate has been attributed to John Adams, the New Englander was in fact discussing American divisions with reference to the French Revolution. On another occasion, however, Adams did remark that a third of Americans after 1776 were Tories, though he failed to follow this figure with estimates of patriots and neutralists. C. F. Adams, ed., *Works of J. Adams*, X, 87, 110-111.

33. William H. Nelson, *The American Tory* (Oxford, Eng., 1961), 92. For another highly suggestive analysis that puts the percentage of loyalists slightly lower (19.8% of white Americans), see Paul H. Smith, "The American Loyalists: Notes on Their Organization and Numerical Strength," *William and Mary Quarterly*,

3d ser., XXV (1968), 259–277. A recent study indicates the loyalists were a decided minority in New York. Bernard Mason, *The Road to Independence* (Lexington, Ky., 1966), chap. iii.

34. Troyer S. Anderson, *The Command of the Howe Brothers during the American Revolution* (New York and London, 1936), 49.

35. Clinton, *American Rebellion*, 26.

36. Willcox, *Portrait of a General*, 84; Smith, *Loyalists and Redcoats*, 26–28.

37. An article sharply critical of British planning of the Southern expedition and of the tactics at Charleston is Eric Robson, "The Expedition to the Southern Colonies, 1775–1776," *English Historical Review*, LXVI (1951), 535–560. A good account of the American side of the battle stressing the somewhat neglected role of Charles Lee is Alden, *Lee*, 119–135. Colonel Moultrie admitted that Lee's "coming . . . was equal to a reinforcement of 1000 men . . . he taught us to think lightly of the enemy, and gave a spur to all our actions." William Moultrie, *Memoirs of the American Revolution* (New York, 1802), I, 141; *South Carolina and American General Advertiser*, Aug. 2, 1776.

38. William O. Raymond, ed., *Winslow Papers* (St. John, New Brunswick, 1901), 40–44, 67–70.

39. Fortescue, ed., *Correspondence of George III*, IV, no. 2164.

40. Claude H. Van Tyne, *The Loyalists in the American Revolution* (New York, 1902), 147. Judge Thomas Jones, a New York loyalist, entitled a chapter of his book the "Illogical and Cruel Treatment of Loyalists by the British Military during the War." Jones, *History of New York during the Revolutionary War* (New York, 1879), II, chap v.

41. Fortescue, ed., *Correspondence of George III*, IV, nos. 2320, 2330, 2572, for examples. Requests for special assignments or leaves of absence often came directly to the King. See *ibid.*, no. 2599, for the Duke of Ancaster's request to go to America as Sir Henry Clinton's aide-de-camp. Pares, *George III and the Politicians*, 17–18, writes that the King "made the efficiency and contentment of the army, as an organized profession, his own concern—so much so, that his personal interferences, and resistances to interference, in military patronage were much more resolute than in civil."

42. Ritcheson, *British Politics and the American Revolution*, 198; Fortescue, ed., *Correspondence of George III*, IV, no. 2845.

43. *Ibid.*, no. 2446. For a statement by North almost identical to the above, see *ibid.*, no. 2327.

44. Curtis, *Organization of the British Army*, 149. See also David Syrett, "Lord George Germain and the Navy Board in Conflict: The *Adamant* and the *Arwin Galley* Dispute, 1777," *Bulletin of the Institute of Historical Research*, XXXVIII (1965), 163–171; Bernard Pool, *Navy Board Contracts, 1660–1832* (Hamden, Conn., 1966).

45. There is an admirable discussion of these changes in government in Charles M. Andrews, *The Colonial Background of the American Revolution* (New Haven, 1961), 75–79.

46. Donald G. Barnes, *George III and William Pitt* (London, 1939), 48.

47. Mackesy, *War for America*, 13.

48. *Ibid.*, 12; Margaret M. Spector, *The American Department of the British Government, 1768–1782* (New York, 1940), 67–73.

49. Gerald S. Brown, *The American Secretary: The Colonial Policy of Lord George Germain, 1775–1778* (Ann Arbor, 1964), 1–30; see also Brown, "The Court-martial of Lord George Sackville [Germain], Whipping Boy of the Revolutionary War," *William and Mary Quarterly*, 3d ser., XIII (1956), 3–25. The only full biography of Germain is Allen Valentine, *Lord George Germain* (London, 1962), useful and informative, but too critical of Germain at Minden and reluctant to acknowledge Germain's accomplishments as an administrator.

# 7. Campaign of 1776

I N THE DECADE before Lexington and Concord, the British government had viewed the American rebellion chiefly as a political problem. But in the year 1776 Whitehall saw the colonies as a military problem. Only the sword would bring the hard core of revolutionists to their knees. The appointment of Germain, an enthusiastic advocate of force, was thus in keeping with the martial spirit in London. Within the ministry there were exceptions. Prudent and practical Lord North favored another try at a political solution. To avert an expensive military undertaking, North would offer the colonists limited concessions, not on constitutional issues, but, most notably, the suspension of Parliamentary taxation if the American assemblies promised to ante up sums for imperial defense. It was mainly North, usually nonassertive, who won the consent of the King and Parliament for a peace commission to accompany a mighty expedition sailing to America to launch the campaign of 1776. But if George III approved, albeit skeptically, he felt it should not interfere with military operations; negotiations were only "to be attempted . . . whilst every act of vigor is unremittingly carried on."[1] North appointed as principal commissioner Admiral Richard, Lord Howe, free fom the taint of Whitehall's American policies. Howe, who had unsuccessfully tendered his good offices for the same purpose in 1774, had a genuine affection for New England, whose citizens had erected a monument in Westminster Abbey in memory of his older brother, George Augustus, slain at Ticonderoga in 1758.

A short time later the death of a senior admiral prompted Lord Howe to seek and obtain the naval command in America. The Admiral was now going to America in a double capacity, and he unquestionably found the role of the dove rather than the lion more appealing.

Germain distrusted the Admiral who insisted on being the sole commissioner, whereas the Colonial Secretary favored adding William Eden and William Knox, whose attitudes on the American question were not dissimilar to his own.[2] A compromise solution placed General William Howe on the commission with the Admiral, who agreed to accept and obey the exact terms of his negotiating powers. As the campaign opened, it took on both a coercive and a conciliatory character. This was never the intention of the King, Germain, and British officialdom in general, for to them the commission was a sop to North and Lord Howe or simply a vehicle for accepting American surrender.

The Admiral, to the contrary, emphasized moderation, resorting to muscle only in measured doses, a view he may well have in some degree impressed upon his brother. For, notwithstanding several military victories, the British General missed chances to strike what might have been fatal blows at Washington's army. Caution, lethargy, incompetence, and treason have all been advanced by way of explanation. The first two may partially explain the General's behavior, but none is wholly satisfactory. The desire to seek a political solution, with no more force than necessary, is yet another posible interpretation of the General's performance. In any case, the commission's search for peace had the effect of retarding the endeavors of Germain and the majority at Whitehall to achieve a military victory.[3] And Germain and company made their greatest effort in 1776: raising and sending to America the most imposing military expedition in English history, a feat never again equaled in the war.

## The Plan of Operation

In 1775 the British government had not formulated a strategy for conducting an American war: Clinton's Southern foray had only been a curtain raiser for 1776. Although Whitehall never systematically examined the various alternatives for a military decision over the rebels, there was no lack of discussion among Englishmen as to how to proceed. Declared Adjutant General Harvey in June, 1775: "it is impossible to conquer . . . [America] with our British army. . . . as wild an idea as ever controverted common sense." Harvey saw what escaped most of his countrymen. Invading a vast, sprawling domain like America was comparable to driving a hammer into a bin of corn; some kernels are damaged, but the hammer if not removed quickly runs the risk of getting lost.[4] Others contended, then and later, that a naval blockade would beat the Americans by strangling their commerce, while a minimum number of troops captured and garrisoned supporting naval bases along the Atlantic coast. This was a dubious assumption which few if any knowledgeable military and naval men swallowed. The possession of coastal, urban centers was not decisive. British armies occupied Boston in 1775, New York in 1776, Newport in 1776, Philadelphia in 1777, Savannah in 1779, and Charleston in 1780. Myriad coves, inlets, and streams from Georgia to Maine made the prospect of a rigorous blockade difficult at best. The military and political center of America was nonexistent, or everywhere and nowhere.

Yet geography did suggest New York City as a base from which British forces could fan out by land or sea. A decisive thrust up the Hudson might separate New England from the middle colonies. Furthermore, the city had a fine harbor; and there was undeniable sentiment for the Crown in the surrounding area. So many responsible Englishmen recognized these facts—Dartmouth, Germain, Gage, Burgoyne, and the Howes—that is impossible to ascribe the genesis of this, the plan for 1776, to any single individual. But an interchange of letters between General William Howe and Colonial Secretary Germain formalized the scheme. As early as June, 1775, while Gage's second in command, the General etched his thinking on the coming year: a landing at New York City and the seizing of the Hudson valley at the same time that a fleet blockaded all ports from New England to Nova Scotia. In October, Howe broadened his plan by advocating the advance southward from Canada of a second British army to meet his own force somewhere on the Hudson, from which point the two should spread out and overrun New England.

The idea of a British invasion from Canada also had deep roots. Talk of retaking Crown Point and Ticonderoga was prevalent in the summer of 1775; Guy Carleton had requested 10,000 to 12,000 redcoats for a southward penetration. Germain approved of Howe's two-pronged offensive, but he had doubts about the Canadian aspect until the patriot army under Arnold and Montgomery could be dealt with, and to accomplish that aim he dispatched reinforcements to Carleton. Then, on hearing in February, 1776, of Montgomery's defeat at Quebec, the Colonial Secretary ordered Carleton to pass beyond the lakes of upper New York and "contribute to the success of the army under General Howe."[5]

Supposedly General Howe in America displayed bountiful zeal in occupying land, preferring to outmaneuver Washington rather than to bring him to a decisive contest. Yet in the months before the onset of hostilities at New York, there was more to his scheme than splitting off New England and piecemeal recovery of territory. He repeatedly informed Germain that only an overwhelming military defeat would convince the Americans of the futility of their rebellion; "nothing is more to be desired or sought for by us, as the most effectual means to terminate this expensive war." A heavy reinforcement and an early beginning to the campaign were imperatives to that end. For the Americans, "knowing their advantages in having the whole country . . . at their disposal, . . . will not be readily brought into a situation where the King's troops can meet them upon equal terms."[6]

Germain, too, believed in the necessity of a climactic battle, and he put his shoulder to the task before him. Coordination was essential since forces had to be assembled from distances thousands of miles apart. And Carleton required additional support for his prong of the offensive. Howe, the other prong, was sailing from Halifax to New York, but he could not take the city until Clinton returned from Charleston and until the military and naval expedition arrived from Europe. From Germain's department flowed information and requests to the war office, ordnance board, treasury, admiralty, and navy board concerning recruits, tents, artillery, horses, wagons, landing craft, food, and other details of war administration. The most demanding chore was the Admiralty's search for transports, up and down the coasts of Britain, Holland, and Germany. By July 5, 1776, when the last contingent had embarked for America, there were 370 transports of 127,249 tons engaged, a figure never matched at the peak of the Seven Years' War.[7] Gradually the great concentration appeared off New York. General Howe's 10,000 troops from Halifax were spotted off Sandy Hook on June 29. Admiral Howe arrived ten days later with 150 transports convoyed by a naval squadron, followed on August 12 by the bulk of the European reinforcements, mostly Hessians who were thoroughly nauseated from the long sea voyage, wormy biscuits, maggoty peas, and corrosive, smelly pork. All the while vessels from the abortive Parker-Clinton Southern expedition dribbled in, the last ships looming on the horizon on August 15.

William Howe had sought 20,000 men to add to his Halifax detachment, and he now had more than that—32,000 troops, and mountains of supplies and equipment. Admiral Howe, simultaneously, could engage 73 warships manned by 13,000 seamen, "nearly 45 percent of all the ships and men on active service in the world's most powerful navy."[8] With the assistance of his brother, the General, Admiral Howe was to assault coastal towns, shelter loyalists, dismantle American merchantmen, destroy armed vessels, impress rebel seamen, and commandeer necessary stores—in sum, to carry a most vigorous war to the Americans. Meanwhile, approximately 10,000 men had been detached for Carleton's use in Canada. These, plus a body of foreign troops who arrived later in the year, brought the Canadian army to nearly 13,500 men.

It was a formidable assemblage that Britain had dispatched to New World shores, her finest effort up to that time, and one that would not be repeated in this war or paralleled in many wars to come. The ponderous, ungainly organism that was the British government had been galvanized for action, and most of the credit belonged to Germain and the Admiralty. Whether it might repeat the effort in a drawn-out struggle was another question. But Germain and the cabinet were bending every muscle to crush the revolt in a single campaign. They had acted literally in keeping with the words of Lord Rawdon when he remarked that the Americans could not last beyond 1776 "if you give us the necessary means of carrying on the war with vigour."[9]

## Disaster on Long Island

Howe's concern that Washington might retire inland without committing his army to a full-scale encounter turned out to be lliusory. Washington himself was eager to defend New York, as was the Continental Congress, which felt intense pressure on the matter from the New York Provincial Congress. Political considerations alone dictated a major show of force on Manhattan and its environs. In the spring of 1776 New York was a trimmer colony. Even the Provincial Congress exchanged communications with royal governor Tryon, who lingered on shipboard off Sandy Hook. Out-and-out tories were everywhere and by no means frightened into complete silence. Other New Yorkers, anticipating a British landing, were on the fence waiting to see the way the wind blew.

The patriots were as aware as their adversaries of the strategic possibilities of the area. The city itself posed serious problems for its defenders, surrounded as it was by various bodies of water which would allow the British not only to dominate its approaches, but also to envelop the exposed American flanks by amphibious assault. When Washington sent Charles Lee to shore up New York's defenses, the latter estimated that while New York could not be held in a sustained campaign against overwhelming British military and naval power, it could be so fortified that the enemy would be severely bled in the process of taking it. A series of forts and the fortification of specific rugged locations were called for by Lee, whose works were far from completion when Congress ordered him south to save Charleston, leaving Washington's army, which had come down from Boston, to finish the job. Washington initiated additional projects such as the building of Forts Washington and Lee to guard the Hudson, the barricading of key streets, and the forging of a huge chain to be extended across the Hudson near West Point. To make any kind of an effective fight for the city itself meant a dangerous division of the American army. Large contingents of men and a quantity of artillery had to be ferried across the East River to Long Island, where the heights of Brooklyn commanded lower Manhattan, just as Dorchester Heights overlooked Boston. Nothing could keep the British from making a landing on the big, sprawling island. And with a superior enemy land force in their front and the likelihood of a British fleet in their rear in the East River, the Brooklyn regiments were in danger of catastrophe.

Possibly his *éclat* at Boston created overconfidence in Washington and led him to believe that once again—under less favorable circumstances—he could match or surpass William Howe.[10] He had repeatedly spoiled for a bout with the British General without getting the opportunity. The American commander in chief could in some ways legitimately feel self-satisfaction. A year at the head of the army had taught him much, but at New York Washington would face his first battlefield command against an imposing military array.

Congress resolved to meet the present emergency in familiar, time-honored fashion by calling out the militia. As July turned to August, the irregulars filtered in, a regiment or two at a time. Some states, not unexpectedly, balked, particularly Maryland, which announced its militia was being held for duty at home. In the face of the swelling cloud of enemy sail in the harbor, Washington repeatedly urged that militia units be sent out with all haste. "Since the settlement of these Colonies," he wrote to a Connecticut colonel, "There has never been such just occasion of alarm or such an appearance of an enemy, both by sea and land." It took every bit of Washington's diplomacy and tact to persuade the states to provide him with 10,000 militia to serve as regular soldiers until the end of 1776, in addition to supplying him with about 7,000 short-term militiamen.[11]

The Howe brothers, meanwhile, showed no great speed in beginning the game. One can find excuses aplenty for their delay: the need to await the last arrivals, the admonition from Germain to attack Washington only at full strength, the unwillingness to risk an abortive strike that might dampen British prospects and bolster whig morale. All this, however, would scarcely have precluded a series of lightning raids up and down the coast by ships of Lord Howe's fleet, possibly in conjunction with units from the army. There was not even a serious effort in the month and a half after Lord Howe's arrival on July 12 to soften the American positions by naval bombardment.

During these weeks the Admiral was obsessed with other things; he preferred to temporize if at all possible. Neither Congress' decision for independence nor his restricted authority as a negotiator dimmed his determination. The significance of his commission seems to have escaped the Admiral, blinded by his zeal for reconciliation and by his opinion of his own persuasiveness. With pitifully little to offer, he could only grant pardons to those who renounced the rebellion; he could not end hostilities before the Americans disbanded their revolutionary assemblies, restored royal administration, and dissolved their armed forces. Only *then* could he mention what might be done: the inauguration of a system of American contributions for imperial defense in place of Parliamentary taxation for that purpose. Germain, ever skeptical about a negotiated peace, had effectually blocked the Admiral from whatever remote chance that may have existed. Undeterred, Howe issued a proclamation promising pardons and a secession of hostilities with the restoration of royal governments. Two emissaries from Lord Howe found Washington unwilling to treat, for as the Virginian put it, "those who had committed no fault wanted no pardon." In his enthusiasm to convince Congress of his good intentions, Howe violated a portion of his commission by divulging through an aide his desire to discuss a plan for substituting fixed colonial contributions for British taxation, a suggestion that fell on deaf ears.[12]

The Admiral's peace plans having so far misfired, it remained to be seen whether a mailed fist would bring the insurgents to their senses. One can only speculate as to the influence of Richard Howe upon William Howe, though before the arrival of the Admiral, the General had been eager for a decisive encounter with Washington's army; thereafter the General seemed preoccupied with the possession of territory. Witness his strategy for gaining New York City: a move from Staten Island—where British troops had landed unopposed as early as July 2 —to Long Island and an advance to a point on the East River northeast of New York City, from which the redcoats were to traverse the river to Manhattan.[13] Though this type of envelopment, not unlike "island hopping" in World War II, would surely make New York along with Brooklyn Heights untenable for Washington, it left plenty of time for the American army to flee northward. Any operation seriously designed to bring Washington to Armageddon on Manhattan had to seal off his only escape route; that meant the possession of the northern end of the island or the mainland around Kingsbridge in the Bronx. Rejecting Clinton's offer to lead an expedition up the Hudson to Spuyten Duyvil to block Washington's crossing the Harlem River to the Bronx, Howe now revised his own plan in order to devote exclusive attention to Long Island, where between the 22nd and 25th of August he put ashore an army more than twice the size of his opponent's in and around the Brooklyn entrenchments.

At this time Washington took one of his biggest gambles of the war. With his inexperienced, militia-dominated army already dangerously divided between Manhattan and Brooklyn, he ferried ten additional regiments to Long Island. In over-all command was the old Indian fighter Israel Putnam, the ranking major general then available, valiant as any man but incompetent for the assignment. Previously Nathanael Greene, who had risen from obscurity in only a year to become Washington's most trusted subordinate, had held the crucial post, only to relinquish it when a raging fever sent him to bed. While Greene was familiar with the ground, the troops, and their dispositions, Putnam was not. Moreover, Washington and his staff erred in their calculations, first in believing that Howe would not throw his full weight against Long Island, and second in expecting to slaughter the British before their strong defenses as at Bunker Hill. The Brooklyn redoubts and entrenchments, as Howe later admitted, were well constructed. But Putnam weakened his positions by sending forward about 4,000 men, divided between John Sullivan on the left and Lord Stirling (William Alexander of New Jersey) on the right, to guard the roads and passes leading toward Brooklyn. Then the Americans drew up a line along the Heights of Guana, a densely wooded ridge three or four miles long. Aside from the decision to defend Long Island, this advance proved to be the Americans' downfall. For the line was too thinly held, the distance too extensive, the terrain so rugged that units could hardly communicate with one another, and the American commanders—especially Sullivan and Putnam—were apparently uncertain of their precise responsibilities. When Washington inspected the forward positions on the evening of August 26, he found no fault with the arrangements or the command system, as indeed he should have. One result of all this was that the Jamaica Road on Sullivan's far left was held by only five men, a fact that caught General Henry Clinton's careful eye.

Though Howe is usually credited with originating the masterly tactics for the so-called Battle of Long Island, the plan was Clinton's.[14] It called for an advance against the American right by General James Grant's redcoats, a push at the center by General von Heister's Germans, and, while Stirling and Sullivan were accordingly engaged, a sweep by Clinton and Howe via the Jamaica Road into Sullivan's rear. In spite of their inexperience, the Americans were not so much outfought as they were outgeneraled. As the contest opened on the mornnig of the 27th, Stirling, a hard-drinking officer who claimed a lapsed Scottish earldom, battled heroically and, though greatly outnumbered, hurled back part of the enemy under Grant, who, as Stirling reminded his men, had boasted before Parliament that he could march from one end of America to the other with only 5,000 troops. In the center the Americans were resisting fiercely but beginning to give way when suddenly the British right, after a night-long march over the Jamaica Road, crashed down upon Sullivan's rear. For the Americans surprise soon turned to panic. All the while Stirling's Delaware and Marylander regulars fought tenaciously, even after being surrounded on three sides.

New York City, New Jersey,
Pennsylvania Operations

PENNSYLVANIA

Hudson R.

Morristown

Basking
Ridge

New York

Lo
Isla

Raritan R.

Delaware R.

New Brunswick

San
Ho

Princeton

Trenton

Monmouth
Courthouse

Assanpink Creek

Schuylkill R.

Whitemarsh

Bordentown

Valley Forge

Germantown

Burlington

Paoli

Brandywine Creek

Philadelphia

NEW JERSEY

Delaware R.

Chad's Ford

Wilmington

Chesapeake
Bay

ATLANTIC
OCEAN

DELAWARE

MARYLAND

DELAWARE
BAY

N

Miles

0    10    20    30

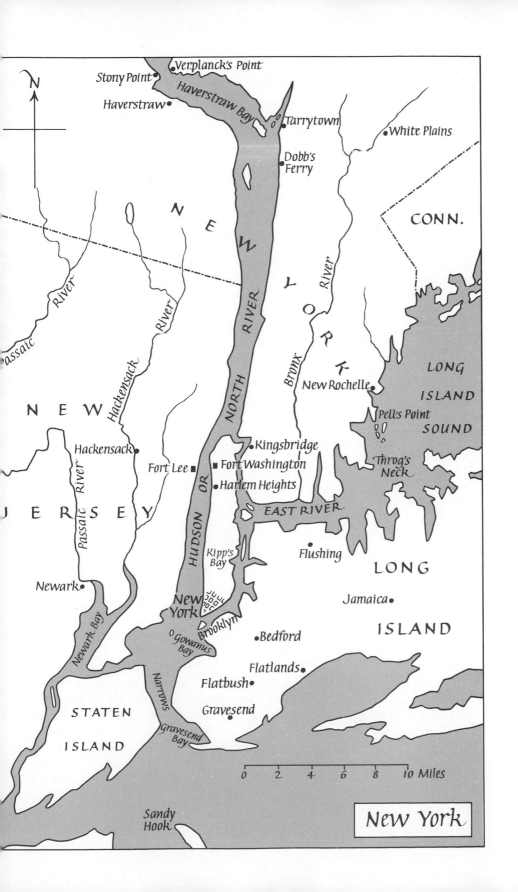

New York

Washington, seeing their predicament from a distance, is said to have exclaimed, "Good God, what brave fellows I must this day lose!" All told, American losses in various categories (including the capture of Sullivan and Stirling) amounted to roughly 1,500 as against Howe's fewer than 400.[15]

As survivors streamed back into the Brooklyn entrenchments, Washington shared in rallying the men. "Remember what you are contending for," he cried; but neither he nor the other officers could easily halt the mass confusion. Had Howe pressed his advantage, his chances of overrunning the Brooklyn defenders would have been excellent given their disorganized state. Howe said that had he given his regulars the go-ahead, they could have carried the day, but since "it was apparent the lines must have been ours at a very cheap rate by regular approaches, I would not risk the loss that might have been sustained in the assault." Was Howe thinking of the carnage at Bunker Hill? Was he mindful that regulars were too highly trained to sacrifice in any battle save the final one? Did he believe, as his subordinate Charles Stedman thought, that the patriots' bitter medicine on the Heights of Guana would sufficiently induce them to listen to sweet reasonableness? Or that a slaughter at Brooklyn itself would only deepen patriot resentment?[16]

Though Howe held Washington in the palm of his hand, two days later the Virginian slipped from his grasp. The British fleet, which could move freely in the East River, had not, in conjunction with the attack of August 27, sailed in behind Washington. Afterward it was too late. A nor'easter prevented the men-of-war from using the river.[17] To the amazement of historians ever since, Washington, instead of commencing a gradual evacuation while his sea lanes remained free, poured more troops from the mainland into the impending trap. But though the smell of gunpowder lingered in his nostrils, he and his council of war decided to avail themselves of the elements. On the night of the 29th they escaped, with the further assistance of an "American" fog. Washington, risking capture, supervised the silent loading of the boats as they plied back and forth across the bay. As Lieutenant Benjamin Talmadge boarded the last craft, he saw a tall, shadowy figure silhouetted against the ferry stairs; he thought it was General Washington.[18]

The rapid collecting of flat-bottomed boats and the subsequent ferrying of 9,000 men to Manhattan in less than nine hours was a remarkable feat.[19] Though in this operation Washington revealed his skill in small-scale amphibious activities (to be repeated at Trenton), there was little else to take pride in. In violation of a cardinal rule of warfare, he had divided his small army in the face of a superior foe. Greene, of course, would do the same thing in the South in 1780, but there was a crucial difference: Greene had room to maneuver, and Washington did not, exposing himself to the threat of having each wing of his army destroyed in detail. As for the Howe brothers, it is sufficient to say that, whatever the reasons, they did not exploit their victory.

## The Loss of New York

Washington could not have gleaned many insights from his near disaster on Long Island. He failed to recognize—or acknowledge—that potentially the same situation could be repeated on Manhattan, a bottle-shaped island with the Harlem River as its neck. British sea power, if properly applied, could cork the bottle. The Howes were equally obtuse, or else they thought the recent taste of British steel might have chastened their adversaries. Admiral Howe, instead of glancing at Kingsbridge and the Harlem, had his eyes on New York City with its docking facilities to refit his frigates and ships of the line. At first he tried to obtain it without a fight, offering this time to talk face to face with members of Congress. In conference on Staten Island, Benjamin Franklin, John Adams, and youthful Edward Rutledge, speaking for the patriots, demanded recognition of independence as a prior condition to negotiation, but the Admiral had to admit his inability to deal officially with the Congress, and the conference quickly terminated.

The abortive peace efforts gave a two-week respite to Washington's army, which was being riddled like a sieve by militia units decamping for home. Within a week after the Battle of Long Island, the 8,000 Connecticut irregulars had dwindled to 2,000. Nor could they be easily replaced as August and September were months when men were needed on the farms, a prime factor in the departure of the militia, along with the demoralizing defeat. The strengths of American society were not always wartime assets, especially the ease of finding gainful employment and the availability of land with its ceaseless demands on America's husbandmen.[20]

As Washington and his generals deliberated the question of whether to hold New York City, politics became intermingled with military considerations. If the Americans abandoned the city, wrote Washington to Congress, should they destroy it rather than leave the enemy a base and the loyalists a refuge? Congress, out of deference to the New York politicians, voted no. There was another factor: to put lower Manhattan to the torch, as advocated by Greene, Joseph Reed, and John Jay, would be, regardless of the tactical merits, in violation of the conservative character of the Revolution.[21] This was a war to preserve not only ideas and institutions but also society itself. There could be no return to Locke's wild state of nature. Thus there is a fundamental difference between the American Revolution and some of the recent Asian and African revolutions. Here was an insurgent movement by a people who were "have's" rather than "have not's." And in such a revolution "the have's" must always guard against losing much as well as endeavoring to gain much. Indeed, the opinion of many pessimistic colonists that the fabric of American life would be ripped apart explains their espousal of loyalism.[22] Congress was determined this should not happen, and Washington shared its resolution.

But if the commander in chief and the lawmakers rejected Greene's advice on demolishing the city, they would have done well to heed the Rhode Islander's warning that they get off Manhattan Island altogether. For Howe began a series of stabs designed to shut off the Americans' escape. After some hesitation Washington began withdrawing northward, albeit slowly, when Howe on September 15 landed a force at Kips Bay midway between New York City and the Harlem River. The Connecticut militia manning the coastal fortifications fled in terror; and two Continental brigades called out in support were soon smitten by the panic. Washington, spurring to the scene, exposed himself to enemy bullets and came close to being captured in an effort to hearten the men. But his cries of "Take the walls!" "Take the cornfield!" as he tried to form a defensive line, were of little avail before John Glover's Marblehead regiment appeared on the scene and checked the British forward troops. Even so, had Howe pressed continuously with his full force, he would have cut the island in two and probably isolated portions of Washington's retreating army that were still below that line, including Henry Knox's valuable corps of Continental artillery.[23]

The British had now driven the Americans into the wooded country of northern Manhattan. To dislodge them by direct assault would be costly at best, as a probing party of Hessians and redcoats discovered in the so-called Battle of Harlem Heights. The concentration of American troops around Kingsbridge indicated that the patriots were no longer susceptible to a direct flanking movement. A more feasible method of pushing them off Manhattan at this point would involve cutting their mainland communications by a landing farther north in the Bronx or Westchester. But for a month the Howes dawdled, content to enjoy the sweets of New York City. Throngs of loyalists turned out cheering their liberators, who marched through the streets to the tune of fife and drum. Finally, on October 12, William Howe commenced his move by threading through the treacherous waters of Hell's Gate and up into Long Island Sound, disembarking his troops at Throg's

Neck, virtually an island anchored to the mainland by a bridge. Since rebel forces promptly demolished the span, Howe re-embarked his regulars and landed them three miles northward at Pell's Point, a peninsula on Pelham Bay. Meanwhile, Washington saw the danger of his position and on the 18th his army started to retire beyond Kings-bridge to higher ground around White Plains, New York, though on Manhattan he left behind over 2,000 men at Fort Washington on the Hudson—a craggy, supposedly impregnable fortress—to tie down a large contingent of the enemy.

As Washington headed for White Plains, the only object across Howe's path was Glover's unit of Marblehead fishermen. The subsequent Battle of Pelham Bay, according to George A. Billias, was among the more crucial contests of the Revolutionary War. With his 750 Yankees squatting behind a series of stone fences, Glover held off the approximately 4,000-man British and German striking force for a full day. British battle casualties are uncertain, but deserters placed the number between 800 and 1,000. Had the British crossed the Bronx River on the evening of the 18th, they would have been directly in front of Washington's retreating Continentals, whose march was slowed by an absence of sufficient horses and wagons. Howe now took a circuitous route to White Plains, arriving five days after Washington. With Lord Howe's fleet sailing up the Hudson, and with regulars under Earl Percy in motion from Manhattan, William Howe missed a splendid opportunity to press Washington against the Hudson and crush him in a pincers movement.[24] As it was, Howe found the Americans strongly posted, and though he drew up a plan of battle, he seemed content to seize a hill on the American right.

While Howe dallied, Washington in the darkness of November 1 fell back to another imposing defensive position. Later before the House of Commons, Cornwallis claimed that "political reasons" explained the failure to follow through on the battle plan at White Plains. Was Howe once again mindful of conciliating the rebels and bringing them to terms? Was he merely acting like a typical general of his day, reluctant to seek a victory at more than the minimal price in casualties? It may be that his conduct at White Plains and his half-hearted attempts to envelop the rebels in the past month and a half were indicative of something else: the younger Howe and his brother the Admiral had given up hope of winning the war in 1776. A manifestation of this attitude was the Howe's decision to disperse their forces by seizing Newport, Rhode Island (accomplished by Clinton in December), a good winter naval station for part of Lord Howe's fleet, but unlikely to have a profound effect on the outcome of the rebellion. Possibly the Howes were looking ahead to the coming year and to a different kind of war. If annihilating the American army would be difficult and overrunning the continent even more so, then it is more than conceivable that the Howes were thinking of a naval war in which the fleet strangled American commerce and the army captured port towns for use as naval bases.

Whatever their thinking, the Howes, had they chosen to, could have pointed to the unrewarding land campaign of Carleton's Canadian-based army. Carleton, assisted by Burgoyne, pushed southward in the summer and fall, but lost valuable time as he constructed a fleet for service on Lake Champlain. Benedict Arnold, recovered from his Quebec wound and indomitable as ever, simultaneously built an American squadron. Fighting skillfully against great odds, Arnold suffered defeats in mid-October. More importantly, he delayed Carleton, a cautious officer, who on November 4 turned about and returned to St. Johns and Montreal for the winter.

Arnold's stopping Carleton and the Howes' pessimism, however, did not mean that Washington and his army were by any means out of the woods. William Howe, with winter in the air, saw his chance to wind up the campaign of 1776 on a bright note. Turning his back on the Virginian, Howe laid siege to Fort Washington, and with his command of the lower Hudson, he also menaced Fort Lee on the Jersey shore. Uncertain of Howe's exact plans, and possibly suspicious of a reverse move by the enemy, the commander in chief once again divided his forces. Leaving his New Yorkers and New Englanders—5,000 under Lee at Northcastle and 3,000 under Heath at Peekskill—Washington crossed the Hudson with 2,000 men from the region below that river. Though Washington favored evacuating Fort Washington, he deferred to Nathanael Greene, who believed the post could be held. The two American generals traversed the Hudson for a first-hand inspection on November 16, just as Howe began his assault. Before their own eyes they saw the defenses crumble, and they escaped to New Jersey only minutes before Colonel Robert Magaw surrendered his garrison of 2,900, a staggering loss, not to be equaled or surpassed before Clinton's taking of Charleston in 1780.[25] Howe had demonstrated that he would fight when the odds were in his favor, and now he dispatched Cornwallis over the Hudson to seize nearby Fort Lee, which Nathanael Greene consequently left in great haste.

## The Occupation of New Jersey

Now began Washington's famous retreat through New Jersey to the Delaware River, with Cornwallis and Howe in his rear. Contrary to popular notion, it was anything but a race. Cold, wet weather, muddy roads, and a shortage of wagons hampered both armies. Washington, searching for supplies and militiamen along the way, stopped for several days each at Camden, New Brunswick, and Trenton. Under the mistaken impression that Howe was headed for Philadelphia, Washington considered offering battle at various points, but owing to the condition of his army, raveling at the edges through desertions and expiring enlistments, he gave up the idea. With Cornwallis already following after Washington, Howe set out from Amboy on November 29, eventually overtaking his subordinate at New Brunswick. For Howe the pursuit represented no basic change in the campaign: the war was not to be won in 1776, nor in all likelihood was Washington to be destroyed; but East Jersey must be cleared of rebels so that part of his command could be cantoned there for the winter.[26] These are the salient facts about Howe's New Jersey operation, more important in explaining Washington's escape than the physical impediments along the route which Cornwallis later exaggerated, more important than Cornwallis' reluctance to punish his men with a hard-pressed march in violation of the slow, leisurely European manner of moving. Besides, there was to be another attempt at persuasion: the Howe brothers had announced a pardon to any and all who would take an oath of loyalty within sixty days of November 30.

Clinton, before sailing for Rhode Island, took vigorous exception to Howe's strategy. Ever keeping his sights trained on Washington, Clinton advocated a relentless chase, notwithstanding efforts at conciliation, the lateness of the season, or anything else that might damage the chance to crush the retreating Americans. Howe, on the other hand, was more intent upon removing Washington than defeating him. As has been suggested, the British General was uncertain that a land war would quell the rebellion. He seems to have found the vastness of the continent depressing. Such a war involved long marches, extended communications, scant use of his brother's fleet, and the risk of ambuscade by harrying parties. His redcoats were expensive commodities, not to be wasted in indecisive battles or frittered away in piddling skirmishes. But on uniting with Cornwallis on December 6, Howe heard that Washington, who had reached Trenton on December 3, was still on the Jersey side, again contemplating a stand and employing "Pioneers" to fell trees and place other obstructions in the British path. Momentarily Howe cast aside his idea of a mere clearing action in New Jersey. The old vision of destroying Washington's army reappeared and, if successful, the prospect of crossing the Delaware and effecting an easy occupation of Philadelphia. Unfortunately for Howe, Washington, getting wind of the Briton's now-rapid advance, rushed back to Trenton, where he ferried his troops over to Pennsylvania.

Howe, now Sir William, was not particularly disturbed that his quarry had flown. After all, he had fulfilled his original intention of shoving his adversary out of New Jersey. In defense against later critics, Howe said that Washington swept the river clear of boats, though a more zealous general probably could have constructed enough rafts from the lumber supplies at Trenton to propel his army into Pennsylvania. In any case, it was winter, unseasonable for campaigning; and Howe had a taste for snug quarters in hospitable New York, and reportedly a lust for blonde, blue-eyed Betsy Loring. Her husband Joshua seemingly did not mind; at least he did not forsake his profitable position as British commissary of prisoners, which frequently kept him away from his wife and the General.[27]

For the first time a British army had swept an entire American state. New Jersey, as American General Alexander McDougall reported, was "totally deranged": its government fled, and swarms of citizens availed themselves of Howe's offer of pardons. Among the defectors was such a distinguished personage as Samuel Tucker of Trenton, former president of the Provincial Congress. Repeated calls to the militia in the counties along Howe's line of advance had met with dismal failure. Washington complained that "the well affected, instead of flying to Arms to defend themselves, are busily employed in removing their Family's [*sic*] and Effects." Here was Howe's chance to prove by example his generous feelings toward the Crown's wayward subjects and to demonstrate "the difference between his majesty's government, and that to which they were subjected by the rebel leaders." For this reason Howe, after Washington's flight into Pennsylvania, departed from his earlier intention of stationing no garrisons farther west than New Brunswick, leaving—as he returned to New York—troops at Princeton, Pennington, and along the Delaware at Trenton, Bordentown, and Burlington.[28]

Lord Howe's secretary, Ambrose Serle, boasted that "the Heart of the Rebellion is now really broken." Its "dying Groans" were audible to all. Events soon demonstrated that Serle's opinion exceeded reality, even in New Jersey. In spite of Howe's repeated injunctions, perhaps the worst British pillaging of the war occurred during the eighty-to-ninety mile swath across the state. Although depositions later collected by the Continental Congress to validate such charges might be discounted to some extent as patriot coloration, responsible British authorities did not deny what Deputy Adjutant General Stephen Kimble described as "every species of Rapine and plunder" committed by Hessians and redcoats alike. Though tories joined in the fun of ravaging their whig neighbors, the loyalists themselves often fared badly, especially at the hands of Hessians who could not read a written pardon. In New Jersey, as along the road from Lexington and Concord, the conflict revealed a grim totality uncharacteristic of the Age of Limited Warfare. The practice in Europe was "very different," admitted British General James Grant, "even in an enemy's country." Grant placed blame for the depredations upon some of the officers who closed their eyes to the marauding of their men. Yet it was almost impossible to spare the civilian population when an army mainly cut itself off from outside supplies by plunging into the interior. Living off the countryside became virtually imperative. Taking a farmer's grain and horses, often without promise of payment, was more than sufficient to arouse his indignation and anger. Beyond all this, there was sheer wanton devastation: churches looted, homes burned, and women molested. John Hunt, speaker of the assembly, discovered his home desecrated, his wife murdered, and his children in hiding.[29]

As Grant conceded to the House of Commons, these events tended to "lose you friends and gain you enemies." A cowed and dispirited populace began to stir. "It is now very hard to travel in Jersey," complained a German officer in mid-December. "The peasant *canaille*" lay hidden in ditches, waiting to ambush soldiers journeying alone or in small groups. If chased, the rebels threw down their muskets and acted "as if they knew nothing about it."[30] The most ominous storm warnings emanated from the northern part of the state, where, in the mountainous vicinity of Morristown, Charles Lee's Continentals had moved, following a course roughly parallel to Washington's line of retreat. Though Lee had disobeyed Washington's repeated pleas to join his main army, his presence in upper New Jersey did much to revitalize the militia and silence the tories. Lee himself, unwisely staying at a tavern some distance from his camp, was taken prisoner on December 13; and his troops shortly after united with Washington. But other militia and Continental units from New York moved in to keep the flames alive. From the north militiamen swooped down on British parties who traveled the lonely roads between the long chain of posts stretching over the state. A British officer estimated on December 11 that the commissariat had lost to roving patriot patrols over seven hundred oxen and several thousand sheep and hogs. To overrun a province was one thing; to hold it securely was another matter.

### Trenton and Princeton

It is traditional to portray Washington's army in early December huddled on the Pennsylvania side of the Delaware in a state of near collapse, with the entire Revolution hanging on a thread. The picture was admittedly dark, a time to try men's souls, said Thomas Paine; but hardly as bleak as Washington limned it in that oft-quoted letter of December 18 to his brother John Augustine Washington. If the army were not enlarged, he warned, "I think the game will be pretty well up."[31] Washington, with his manifold burdens and his desire for long-service regulars, was understandably afflicted with outbursts of frustration and pessimism. Actually, the Virginian was spoiling for another fight, and four days before writing to his brother he was considering a lightning raid into New Jersey. Nathanael Greene, though conceding the critical state of affairs, was "far from thinking the American cause desparate."[32] Washington's numbers were now increasing. Sullivan arrived with Lee's overdue force the same day that Gates came from the Northern Department with 600 Continentals. Approximately 2,000 Pennsylvania militia were with the Commander in Chief, as were 1,000 Philadelphia short-term volunteers, the "Associators," and within co-operating distance on the opposite shore were bodies of New Jersey irregulars. One advantage of the American scene, as Washington found repeatedly, was that an army of sorts could be assembled and concentrated with considerable speed; and while it might not be kept together for a protracted campaign, it could be used effectively before it melted away. Since the enlistments of all but 1,400 of the Continentals expired with the year's end, Washington wasted no time in planning his only really brilliant stroke of the war.

After dismal reversals in New York the cause needed a psychological boost. Congress itself was in a slough of despondency as the legislators, fearing the loss of Philadelphia, adjourned to Baltimore. A solid blow against Howe's posts in New Jersey would keep alive the spirit of revolt in that state. Doubtless many Americans, postponing a decision on Howe's offer of pardon, would accept by the expiration of the sixty-day limit after November 30 unless the American army did something to revive its prestige.

At a council of war Washington outlined his plan for a descent upon West Jersey—to begin on Christmas night.[33] The focal point was Trenton, occupied by 1,400 Hessians under Colonel Johann Gottlieb Rall. While Washington himself would take 2,400 Continentals over the Delaware and swoop down on Trenton from the north, General James Ewing with several hundred Pennsylvania militia would pass over the river below the town and sever the road to Bordentown, a possible enemy escape route. A third body led by Colonel John Cadwalader would cross farther downstream to divert the Bordentown garrison. Flexibility characterized the whole operation, for if Trenton and Bordentown, isolated cantonments, fell to him, Washington was also prepared to drive against the British garrisons at Princeton and New Brunswick. The job of ferrying Washington's Continentals went to Colonel Glover's Marblehead men, who, besides their heroic stand at Pelham Bay, had evacuated the army from Brooklyn to Long Island; many of them, in the absence of uniform military dress, continued to wear their blue jackets, white caps, and tarred trousers, the typical fishermen's garb.

Few episodes are so familiar to Americans as Washington's crossing the Delaware, partly owing to the nineteenth-century painting by Emmanuel Leutze, a canvas filled with inaccuracies. The long boats of Leutze were not found on the Delaware. Twelve men crowded into such a small craft would surely have capsized it, especially had Washington been foolish enough to stand with one foot on the gunwale in the dark, ice-filled stream. Instead, Glover's mariners manned forty-to-sixty-foot flat-bottomed Durham boats, normally used on the river to haul grain and iron ore, each capable of transporting an entire company of men.[34]

The night was almost a replica of that stormy evening, nearly a year earlier, when Montgomery and Arnold had thrown their troops at Quebec. Here, too, the first phase of the contest was against the elements rather than the enemy. A fierce wind churned the waters of the Delaware. Chunks of ice swirled around the boats, whose crewmen pushed them away with oars and poles, an incredibly difficult labor, reported Colonel Henry Knox. At eleven o'clock snow set in, turning to sleet and wetting the priming of many flintlocks. Anticipating that very thing, Washington and Knox had brought along eighteen pieces of field artillery, which could be used in rain or snow if protected. (Usually no more than three cannon were employed with every 1,000 foot soldiers in the eighteenth century.) But the decision to rely on artillery also indicated the high quality of that military arm as developed by the able Knox. The former Boston bookseller, convinced by his trek from Ticonderoga that artillery could keep pace with marching men, had built new and improved gun carriages that resulted in greater mobility for the cannon with Washington's army.[35]

At three o'clock in the morning the last of Knox's guns had been landed, and then began the nine-mile trek through wind and sleet. "For God's sake, keep by your officers," shouted Washington above the whir of the storm.[36] Half-way to Trenton the army divided, Sullivan with one wing continuing on the road by the river, Greene with the other swinging to the left on another path, the two routes converging on different ends of King and Queen streets, Trenton's principal thoroughfares. Overrunning the unsuspecting Hessian outposts about eight o'clock, the two columns raced toward the center of town. Sleepy Germans, slow in rousing after a festive Christmas, stumbled out of their quarters just as Knox's artillery began raking King and Queen streets. The roaring wind, booming cannon, and wild confusion among the Hessians combined to give Henry Knox a vivid image of the trumpet's sounding on the Day of Judgment. Colonel Rall, drinking heavily until after midnight, was only awakened with difficulty. Then dressing in haste, he tried to form part of his men, many of them half-clad, in an open field, and ordered his band to strike up a martial tune! Washington, however, had no intention of sparring with his adversary in a game of drill field evolutions. Knox's guns bombarded the hapless enemy, while American riflemen, ensconced in upper windows of houses, hit them with a deadly fire. Attempting to fall back to an orchard, Rall fell from his horse mortally wounded. At the other end of the village, Sullivan was also making maximum use of artillery by placing his heavy weapons in position to command Assunpink Bridge, the only remaining avenue of retreat, but only after 400 Germans had escaped toward Bordentown.

An hour and a half after making contact with Rall's pickets, the battle was over, a signal victory for the Americans. Hessian losses came to 30 killed and approximately 918 taken prisoner, as compared to not a single American death in action and only three wounded—two of them officers, Captain William Washington and Lieutenant James Monroe. A difficult battle plan calling for simultaneous assaults from different directions under the worst of conditions had been executed to perfection. Obviously helpful was the Americans' knowledge of the town. And thanks to John Honeyman, a spy who posed as a loyalist butcher and cattle dealer, they were aware of Rall's dispositions as well as his low opinion of American fighting men.[37] The elements, the cool leadership of Washington and his lieutenants, the artillery's performance, and Rall's carelessness in guarding his post all contributed to the outcome.

At the moment Washington had no chance to savor his triumph. Neither Ewing nor Cadwalader had been able to traverse the ice-filled river. Consequently remnants of Rall's command reached Bordentown and alerted Hessian Colonel von Donop, who retired to Princeton. Burdened with captives, Washington and his weary troops fell back into Pennsylvania. But only briefly. He was still on the warpath, still eager, he informed Cadwalader, to "beat up the rest of their Quarters" in West Jersey.[38] Now he learned that Cadwalader had eventually gotten over the Delaware, that other irregulars under Generals Mifflin and Heath were assembling in lower New Jersey, and that "panic" had seemingly overtaken the enemy who had also abandoned Burlington, Black Horse, and Mount Holly. For all Washington's gloomy forebodings (and more than one historian has called him a chronic complainer), his pessimism seldom clouded his vision when an opportunity opened. The British appeared to be reeling, and the militia needed support. The expiring enlistments of most Continentals did not deter him. If he failed to convince a portion of his force to stay on temporarily, he resolved to unite his skeleton army with the state units and harry the enemy as best he could. Perhaps for the only time during the war the commander in chief contemplated becoming a guerrilla, if only until a new army might be raised and put in the field.

That course became unnecessary. On December 30, Washington once again crossed the Delaware and halted at Trenton, where he addressed each regiment, urging his veterans to remain for another six weeks in return for a bounty of ten dollars. Few episodes in the Revolution were more heart-warming than this, for half or more of the men agreed to stay, and Washington gratefully acknowledged that ten dollars was meager compensation for their sacrifice. The army, however, could no longer be an instrument for biting off further links in Howe's chain of posts. The British reaction to the fall of the Trenton garrison was more swift and decisive than Washington had imagined. Cornwallis, ordered back to New Jersey from New York, was hurrying to the scene with a column of 6,000 troops. To withdraw once more over the Delaware or to give battle at Trenton seemed Washington's only alternatives. But as he noted several days later, "to remove immediately was again destroying every dawn of hope" for the people of New Jersey.[39]

His determination to stay came perilously close to costing him his whole army. When Cornwallis' van pushed into Trenton at dusk on January 2, the Americans found their backs to the Delaware. Washington's numbers had swollen by militia arrivals; his ground—on the east side of Assunpink Creek—was strong; and he had brought along thirty to forty pieces of artillery. That evening it was his artillery fire that had discouraged Cornwallis from storming across the creek in the darkness.[40] Even so, the morrow might well bring destruction at the hands of Cornwallis' superior force, and the tall, portly Cornwallis reputedly boasted of bagging "the fox" next morning. At a council of war the American generals resolved not to give him the chance, but instead to hazard a maneuver as daring as the evacuation of Brooklyn or the Christmas raid on Trenton. While a special detail kept the fires burning brightly and clanged away with entrenching tools to produce the illusion of an army settling into position, Washington and his men, muffling the artillery wheels in heavy cloth, stole silently to the south and east by a side road, swinging completely behind Cornwallis. Ahead lay Princeton, and if successful there, Washington contemplated a raid on New Brunswick, where a £70,000 British pay chest beckoned.

At sunrise the British 17th and 55th regiments just outside Princeton on their way to reinforce Cornwallis were startled to see an American army rapidly approaching. With 350 Virginians, General Hugh Mercer, an ex-apothecary, took post in an orchard. Quickly ordering up the 40th, the guard regiment in the village, British Colonel Charles Mawhood opened up with his cannon and sent the 17th forward with the bayonet. The violent charge hurled the Americans back in disorder, leaving Mercer mortally wounded. Washington, fearing a rout, rode up and personally re-formed the Virginians. Calling up veteran Continentals, he led them in an extended line to within thirty yards of Mawhood's redcoats. Fire, he shouted. An American volley! A British volley! Smoke enveloped both forces. But the Americans had the better of it, and as the red line broke and scattered, Washington waved his men on, exclaiming "It's a fine fox chase, my boys!"[41] Roughly 200 of the enemy sought refuge in Princeton's Nassau Hall, home of the College of New Jersey. But Captain Alexander Hamilton's artillerymen drove them out, one cannon shot decapitating the portrait of George II hanging within. Most of Mawhood's regulars wasted little time in fleeing from the scene. Total British losses in the forty-five-minute encounter numbered at least 273 and possibly as many as 400, while American casualties amounted to 40 killed and 100 wounded.[42]

Compelling as was the lure of New Brunswick, Washington declined the temptation. His men were exhausted, and Cornwallis, enraged by his adversary's deception, was storming toward Princeton. Washington withdrew northward into the hilly, forested country about Morristown. With his recent victories having encouraged a heavy turnout of New Jersey and Pennsylvania militia, Washington was not interested in the European custom of suspending hostilities for the winter. Once Cornwallis retired eastward, the Virginian wished to continue his pressure on Howe's garrisons until the enemy abandoned New Jersey altogether; but the expiration of the six-week enlistments and the departure of the Pennsylvania irregulars canceled his hopes. As it was, the Americans had prompted the jittery Howe to relinquish all his gains in New Jersey except for a shallow bridgehead at New Brunswick and Amboy.

For Washington, the campaign of 1776 was over, a bit late by the calendar, but it ended on a note of optimism. The army had fought well, and, with new recruits, it would do so again. British Lieutenant Colonel William Harcourt conceded that the Americans could no longer be taken lightly as soldiers:

though they seem to be ignorant of the precision, order, and even of the principles, by which large bodies are moved, yet they possess some of the requisites for making good troops, such as extreme cunning, great industry in moving ground and felling of wood, activity and a spirit of enterprise upon any advantage. Having said thus much, I have no occasion to add that, though it was once the fashion of this army to treat them in the most contemptible light, they are now become a formidable enemy.[43]

It is doubtful that the fate of the Revolution prior to Trenton and Princeton was hanging as precariously as some have contended. For America was a huge, sprawling country, lacking a vital center yet possessing the capacity to raise new armies in the numerous areas outside British control. Undeniably, however, the sparkling victories over Rall and Mawhood pumped new life into Americans dispirited over the loss of Canada, Rhode Island, New York, and New Jersey. Critics of Washington were temporarily silenced, and the most ambitious carper, Charles Lee, was no longer a potential rival by virtue of his capture. Washington had committed errors in the campaign, some of them serious. But there was something inspiring about the man that went far beyond his stately presence. Brave often to the point of recklessness on the battlefield, he was a fighter, and when down, he bounced back. His opponents repeatedly underestimated him, as his stealthy nocturnal movements at Brooklyn, White Plains, and twice at Trenton so well illustrate.

An evaluation of Sir William Howe is more difficult, for though he clearly failed to reveal persistence and audacity in his quest of Washington, the explanation for his conduct will probably never be known. Howe's only really decisive attack was at Fort Washington, where the American garrison refused to escape or intially to surrender. If we are unable to gauge accurately the impact of his brother's conciliatory mood upon Sir William, we do know how that mood affected the Admiral's naval operations. The navy had begun the war in a state of ill-preparedness, and Howe's vessels were engaged in supporting the army in 1776. There was nevertheless valid criticism that at least some additional ships could have been employed in blockading the principal American harbors; certainly cargoes of munitions and other stores were passing almost at will between the West Indies and colonial ports. With the land campaign supposedly closing for the year, the Admiral, taking the initiative in December, sent Commodore William Hotham to blockade the Southern colonies. Howe's instructions seriously violated the spirit of his own orders from Germain. First, the Admiral desired his captains to be lenient—to "encourage and cultivate all amicable correspondence . . . to gain [the Americans'] good Will and Confidence . . . to grant them every other Indulgence which the limitations upon their Trade . . . will consistently admit" in order to "detach them from the Prejudices they have imbibed." Moreover, he forbade his officers to raid along the coasts.[44] But continued efforts at conciliation were to prove no more fruitful than in the past. To win, Britain would, as Germain maintained, have to rely on muscle alone. Could Germain and Whitehall repeat their impressive performance of the past year? And were the generals and admirals in America equal to the task of victory?

## NOTES

1. W. Bodham Donne, ed., *Correspondence of George III with Lord North, 1768–1783* (London, 1867), I, 293; Ritcheson, *British Politics*, 200–210.
2. Brown, *American Secretary*, 64.
3. Such is the conclusion of Ira D. Gruber, "Lord Howe and Lord George Germain: British Politics and the Winning of American Independence," *William and Mary Quarterly*, 3d ser., XXII (1965), 225–243; Gruber, "Richard Lord Howe: Admiral as Peacemaker," in *George Washington's Opponents*, ed. Billias, 233–242.
4. Sir John Fortescue, *A History of the British Army* (London, 1899–1930), III, 169; Eric Robson, *The American Revolution in its Political and Military Aspects* (London, 1955), 96, 96 n2.
5. Macksey, *War for America*, 60.
6. Gruber, "Lord Howe and Lord George Germain," 232 n27; Historical Manuscripts Commission, *Stopford-Sackville MSS*, II, 30; Anderson, *Command of the Howe Brothers*, 118–121.
7. Williams, "Naval Administration," 68.
8. Gruber, "Lord Howe and Lord George Germain," 232, 232 n25, citing abstract of monthly disposition, July 1, 1776, Admiralty Papers, Class 8, Vol. 101, British Public Record Office.
9. Williams, "Naval Administration," 55, 69; Macksey, *War for America*, 70; Historical Manuscripts Commission, *Hastings MSS*, III, 167. Horace Walpole, no friend of the ministry, could still give Germain due credit: "The year began with mighty preparations for carrying on the war in American with vigour. Lord George Sackville Germain, who had been brought into power for that end, was indefatigable in laying plans for raising and hiring troops, in sending supplies and recruits, and more naval force." Francis Stewart, ed., *The Last Journals of Horace Walpole . . . 1771–1783* (London, 1910), I, 510.
10. Douglas Freeman thus characterizes Washington on the eve of assuming command at New York: "a prouder man by far, and more self confident, than when he had arrived, nine months previously, to undertake his first campaign. He had won; he believed he could do it again." Freeman, *Washington*, IV, 76.
11. Burnett, ed., *Letters of Congress*, I, 485, 492, 526; Fitzpatrick, ed., *Writings of Washington*, V, 384.
12. *Ibid.*, 273–274, 321 n–323 n; Joseph Hewes to Samuel Johnston, July 24, 1776, Dreer Collection, Historical Society of Pennsylvania.
13. Clinton, *American Rebellion*, 40; Willcox, *Portrait of a General*, 104.
14. Clinton, *American Rebellion*, 41–43; Willcox, *Portrait of a General*, 105–106.
15. Freeman, *Washington*, IV, 166. The Americans' failure to employ mounted troops for scouting and reconnaissance is discussed in Charles Francis Adams, *Studies Military and Diplomatic, 1775–1865* (New York, 1911). Freeman, *Washington*, IV, 368–370, argues that Sullivan was chiefly responsible for the successful British flanking movement. But Ward, *War of the Revolution*, I, 227–230, is more critical of Washington. A brief, judicious analysis placing blame on both Sullivan and Washington is that of Charles P. Whittemore, *A General of the Revolution: John Sullivan of New Hampshire* (New York and London, 1961), 39–40.
16. Freeman, *Washington*, IV, 166; Anderson, *Command of the Howe Brothers*, 134; Charles Stedman, *History of the Origin, Progress, and Termination of the American War* (London, 1794), I, 198–199.
17. Why Lord Howe did not order his ships into supporting position earlier remains a mystery, as it was to one British naval officer, Sir George Collier, who had escorted von Heister's Germans across the Atlantic, and declared that he had been in "constant expectation" of being ordered to join the attack. Louis L. Tucker, ed., " 'To My Inexpressible Astonishment': Sir George Collier's Obser-

vations on the Battle of Long Island," *New York Historical Society Quarterly*, XLVIII (1964), 304.
18. *Memoir of Col. Benj. Talmadge* (New York, 1858), 11–14; Commager and Morris, eds., *Spirit of 'Seventy-Six*, I, 445–446.
19. A splendid account of the evacuation is George A. Billias, *General John Glover and His Marblehead Mariners* (New York, 1960), 100–104.
20. Washington was bolstered temporarily by militia from Massachusetts, with the result that some communities were perilously short of harvest hands. Butterfield, ed., *Adams Family Correspondence*, II, 135. On September 6, 1776, the *Virginia Gazette* (Purdie) reported that in some parts of Pennsylvania where the men were away in the army their women were taking to the fields.
21. Ford, ed., *Journals of Congress*, V, 733, VI, 866; Frank Monahan, *John Jay* (New York and Indianapolis, 1935), 90.
22. The point is made in Leonard W. Labaree, "Nature of American Loyalism," American Antiquarian Society, *Proceedings* LIV (1944), 15–58.
23. Greene's well-reasoned letter is in Force, ed., *American Archives*, 5th ser., II, 182–183; Victor Paltsits, "The Jeopardy of Washington," *New-York Historical Society Quarterly*, XXXII (1948), 267–268.
24. Billias, *Glover*, 110–123; Clinton, *American Rebellion*, 50. The Americans lost approximately six killed and thirteen wounded at Pelham Bay.
25. For a detailed analysis of the Washington-Greene correspondence concerning Fort Washington, see Bernhard Knollenberg, *Washington and the Revolution* (New York, 1940), 129–139. Though Knollenberg with some good reason accuses Washington of attempting after the war to shift the responsibility for the loss to Congress and Greene, the commander in chief was candid enough in a letter of August 22, 1779. He confessed to his own "hesitation which ended in the loss of the Garrison." Fitzpatrick, ed., *Writings of Washington*, XVI, 152.
26. Howe conveyed his intention to Germain, November 30, 1776, on the road toward New Brunswick. Historical Manuscripts Commission, *Stopford-Sackville MSS*, II, 49–50.
27. Leonard Lundin, *Cockpit of the Revolution: The War for Independence in New Jersey* (Princeton, 1940), 148–149, discusses the lumber situation. John R. Alden, *A History of the American Revolution* (New York, 1969), 503–505, believes the evidence concerning Howe's actual relationship with Mrs. Loring is inconclusive.
28. Force, ed., *American Archives*, 5th ser., III, 1364–1365; Fitzpatrick, ed., *Writings of Washington*, VI, 331–333; Howe, *Narrative . . . in a Committee of the House of Commons*, 9; Howe to Germain, December 20, 1776, Whitehead and others, eds., *Archives of New Jersey*, 2d ser., I, 368; Smith, *Loyalists and Redcoats*, 43, 43 n30. Curtis, *Organization of the British Army*, 102, errs in implying that the shortage of provisions elsewhere was the principal reason for establishing cantonments beyond New Brunswick.
29. Benjamin Franklin Stevens, ed., *Facsimiles of Manuscripts in European Archives Relating to America, 1773—1783* (London, 1889–1895), XXIV, no. 2046; Tatum, ed., *American Journal of Ambrose Serle*, 62; *The Stephen Kemble Papers* (New-York Historical Society, *Collections*, vols. 16–17 [1883–1884]), I, 96, 97–98, 99, 102; Commager and Morris, eds., *Spirit of 'Seventy-Six*, I, 528.
30. *Ibid.*, 527; Lundin, *Cockpit of the Revolution*, 178.
31. Fitzpatrick, ed., *Writings of Washington*, VI, 398. But, further in the same missive, he added: "under a full persuasion of the justice of our cause, I cannot entertain an idea that it will finally sink, though it may remain for some time under a cloud." In another letter of the same date to the Massachusetts legislature the commander in chief was much less doleful. Though "the whole of our affairs are in a much less promising condition than could be wished; yet I trust, under the smiles of Providence and by our own exertions, we shall be happy." *Ibid.*, 396.
32. *Ibid.*, 366; George Washington Greene, *The Life of Major General Nathanael*

*Greene* (New York, 1867), I, 280–289; Theodore Thayer, *Nathanael Greene: Strategist of the American Revolution* (New York, 1960), 136.

33. The idea of hitting Howe's isolated garrisons—in Washington's mind as early as December 14—was so obvious that it cannot be said that it originated with any one individual. Many Americans, in and out of the army, saw the virtue of such a thrust. Freeman, *Washington*, IV, 306 n15.

34. Marion V. Brewington, "Washington's Boats at the Delaware Crossing," *American Neptune*, II (1942), 167–170; Raymond L. Stehle, "Washington Crossing the Delaware," *Pennsylvania History*, XXXI (1964), 269–294.

35. Jac Weller, "Guns of Destiny: Field Artillery in the Trenton-Princeton Campaign," *Military Affairs*, XX (1956), 1–15, deals with American as well as British artillery.

36. Commager and Morris, eds., *Spirit of 'Seventy-Six*, I, 512.

37. John Bakeless, *Turncoats, Traitors and Heroes* (Philadelphia and New York, 1959), 166–170.

38. Fitzpatrick, ed., *Writings of Washington*, VI, 446.

39. Commager and Morris, eds., *Spirit of 'Seventy-Six*, I, 512, 519–520; Freeman, *Washington*, IV, 332–335; Alfred H. Bill, *The Campaign of Princeton, 1776–1777* (Princeton, 1948), 78–79; Jared C. Lobdell, ed., "The Revolutionary War Journal of Thomas McCarty," *New Jersey Historical Society, Proceedings*, LXXXII (1964), 29–46.

40. It is estimated that Knox's massed artillery fire was the heaviest displayed on the field of battle in America to that date. Weller, "Guns of Destiny," 2. For a description of the American positions, see Scheer and Rankin, *Rebels and Redcoats*, 217.

41. Freeman, *Washington*, IV, 353–354; Commager and Morris, eds., *Spirit of 'Seventy-Six*, I, 520; Scheer and Rankin, *Rebels and Redcoats*, 219.

42. Washington gave the higher British figure, Howe the lower. Bill, *Campaign of Princeton*, 113.

43. Edward W. Harcourt, ed., *The Harcourt Papers* (Oxford, Eng., 1880–1905), XI, 208. See also Gruber, "Lord Howe and Lord George Germain," 237 n45. The British recognized that Trenton provided patriot morale with a shot in the arm. Tatum, ed., *Journal of Ambrose Serle*, 163; Historical Manuscripts Commission, *Stopford-Sackville MSS*, II, 53; "Bamford's Diary," *Maryland Historical Magazine*, XXVIII (1933), 23–24; *Kemble Papers*, I, 107; A. M. W. Stirling, *Annals of Yorkshire House . . .* (London, 1911), II, 21.

44. Anderson, *Command of the Howe Brothers*, 233–235; Mackesy, *War for America*, 98–102; Gruber, "Lord Howe and Lord George Germain," 239. The tory historian Thomas Jones scornfully remarked that supposedly "Proclamations were to end an inveterate rebellion." Jones, *History of New York during the Revolutionary War*, I, 121. For other loyalists' criticism of the Howes, see "The Letters of Jonathan Boucher," *Maryland Historical Magazine*, IX (1914), 236, 335; P. O. Hutchinson, ed., *The Diary and Letters of His Excellency, Thomas Hutchinson* (Boston, 1884–1886), II, 247; Nelson, *American Tory*, 134–136.

# 8. Campaign of 1777

THE DRAMA OF the 1777 campaign was acted out on a broad stage with many scenes occurring simultaneously. See the theatrical, vainglorious "Gentleman Johnny" Burgoyne plunging southward through the tangled forests along the Lake Champlain-Hudson trough; the solemn, taciturn "Billy" Howe, his troops, sweltering in the summer heat, packed tightly into naval transports headed for Philadelphia; the fussy, quarrelsome Clinton sitting idly in New York; the haughty, supercilious colonial secretary, Lord George Germain, waiting confidently in London for word of his commanders' victories that would surely crack the rebellion. When the last curtain rang down, however, the finale had been far different from what Germain had contemplated. Burgoyne had lost an army, and while Howe had managed to keep his, he had accomplished little more than the occupation of Philadelphia, of no great strategic value to either side. Washington's Continentals, bruised but nonetheless a fighting machine, remained in the field. The Revolution waxed as strongly as ever; and France, encouraged by the patriots' performance, was preparing to enter the fray. In England opponents of the war became more vocal; and bitter controversy erupted over the question of responsibility for the ill fortune of the campaign. Burgoyne and Howe had been the principal planners as well as the principal actors, but Germain had failed to impose a measure of co-operation and co-ordination upon their endeavors. He had sanctioned a campaign without a unifying concept, one that rested upon the assumption that three widely scattered British forces—under Howe, Clinton, and Burgoyne—could operate successfully and without fear that the Americans could concentrate in force against one of the King's armies. The result, prophesied by Clinton and Charles Stuart, was disaster at Saratoga.

## "*Too Many Cooks*"

While from New York Howe was bombarding Germain with several different plans during the winter of 1776–1777, Burgoyne was in London on leave, presenting his single scheme for the coming year in person. Burgoyne rightly assumed, as did his superior Carleton back in Canada, that the ministry desired another invasion from the north in 1777. Discovering Carleton out of favor, partly owing to his setback with Benedict Arnold, Burgoyne wasted no time in criticizing his former chief. (He had also verbally knifed Gage in 1775.) Potentially a more serious rival to head the Canadian-based army was Clinton, Burgoyne's senior, who likewise was striving to butter his own bread during a visit to England. Clinton, protégé of the second Duke of Newcastle, could not be taken lightly by the ministry. Bold as a subordinate, Clinton had found Howe lethargic and had harassed Sir William with proposals for more aggressive endeavors. Though secretly coveting the post, Clinton did not push his claim. The actual possession of authority seemed to intimidate the man. Manufacturing excuses to keep from pressing for the Canadian plum, he accepted as recompense the red ribbon of the Order of the Bath and returned to New York as Howe's second in command.

Burgoyne in one respect might have seemed an ideal choice to accomplish what Carleton had been unable to do.[1] Having served for six months in Canada as Carleton's subordinate, Burgoyne should have understood the obstacles involved in a wilderness invasion. He was brave, energetic, and supremely sure of himself. But perhaps a more plodding, methodical soldier would have been a more likely selection than the gay, dashing former leader of light dragoons in the Seven Years' War. For Burgoyne in mind and body was always a cavalryman; and the exhausting grind of lakes and forests from the Richelieu to the Hudson was no place for a cavalryman. If Bunker Hill had imbued Gage and Howe with a grudging respect for American soldiers (at least for their marksmanship when in protected positions), Burgoyne, who had witnessed the battle from a Boston roof top, saw nothing admirable about their conduct on that occasion: history to him demonstrated that "mountainers and borderers have in almost all countries . . . done much more hardy things than defend one of the strongest posts that nature and art combined could make, and then run away."[2]

Burgoyne's "Thoughts for Conducting the War on the Side of Canada," a paper dated February 28, 1777, and submitted to Germain, illustrated the General's confidence: a main army of approximately 8,000 regulars was to plunge southward from Canada down Lake

Champlain, at the same time that a secondary force advanced by way of Oswego and the Mohawk River, the two to unite on the Hudson, presumably above Albany, the city that was his immediate objective. Upon accomplishing that, Burgoyne was uncertain as to his course of action, except that he was eventually, as everyone in London expected, to cooperate with Howe's army. Recent scholarship has demolished the notion that Howe was supposed to have marched up the Hudson for a juncture with Burgoyne. In fact, Burgoyne recognized that working with Sir William might take various forms. The most crucial sentence in Burgoyne's "Thoughts" states his purpose as "to effect a junction with General Howe or, after co-operating so far as to get possession of Albany and open the communication to New York, to remain upon Hudson's River and thereby enable that General to act with his whole force to the southward."[3] Did this imply that the very least expected of Howe was that he should clear the lower Hudson before driving on Philadelphia? Perhaps it did, but Germain, as we will see, did not so instruct Howe. Moreover, in London and later on the march, Burgoyne acted certain of being able to conduct his own movements without Howe's support.

How Burgoyne's army should operate on the Hudson while Howe took the Quaker City was not made clear, nor was the question of winter quarters given serious thought by either Burgoyne himself or by Germain, who easily persuaded the King and cabinet to accept the scheme. Germain likely hoped that at the year's end a British cordon would extend from Canada to New York, from the St. Lawrence to the Atlantic. However, this separation of New England from the rest of the colonies did not preclude Howe from making his initial offense elsewhere in 1777. No one in England in a position of authority appears to have given thought to the problems the Canadian army might encounter in the northern wilderness.

But assuming Burgoyne reached Albany unimpeded and assuming subsequently he, with or without the aid of Howe, extended control of the Lake Champlain-Hudson line to New York City, would the rebellion have folded? The isolation of New England, if followed by a massive land offensive and supported by a tight naval blockade, might have smothered resistance there, but only if the British were willing to leave thousands of redcoats to enforce royal rule. It is doubtful that the patriots to the south would have stood idly by while all this transpired. Clearly the mere possession of a string of posts along the Hudson would not necessarily have seriously endangered the American cause, for it would have been a most arduous, if not impossible, assignment to keep the patriots from re-establishing their communications.[4] Reflection after the fact, the preserve of historians rather than statesmen, points to the conclusion that the Canadian invasion was a dubious undertaking from its very inception, that at best it should only have been launched in conjunction with Howe's advancing from the south. In fact, a drive in force from New York City up the river toward Albany would have been a more realistic goal for a *single* British army than Burgoyne's expedition from Canada. For the principal rebel supply routes traversed the lower Hudson, and to protect them Washington might well have been drawn into a decisive encounter.

Sir William Howe, preparing his own campaign for 1777, expressed only fleeting interest in the Canadian invasion. Within a little more than four months—late November, 1776, to early April, 1777—Howe presented Germain four plans. First, he asked for 15,000 additional men. Stationing parts of his army to watch Washington in New Jersey and to guard his bases at New York City and Newport, he proposed to dispatch 10,000 troops up the Hudson to meet the force that he expected to penetrate from Canada. Even before Howe's first dispatch reached London, he outlined a radically different scheme: an overland advance on Philadelphia with the bulk of his army, leaving behind 4,000 to hold Manhattan and another 3,000 to garrison East Jersey and to "facilitate in some degree the approach of the army from Canada." How much help 3,000 could offer, Howe did not say, but he presumably believed the Canadian army would be largely capable of fending for itself. Besides, he felt that Burgoyne's expedition would need no assistance at all before mid-September, Howe's estimated time of Burgoyne's arrival at Albany.[5]

Howe, continuing to eye Philadelphia, kept shifting the details. He suggested in January, just after the British debacle at Trenton and Princeton, that while he headed on foot across New Jersey with the main army, a second contingent should approach the patriot capital by sea and the Delaware River. Now Howe upped his estimate of reinforcements to 20,000; however, if the ministry could not meet his quota, he would content himself with a single offensive across New Jersey. It has been contended that the General's proposals were prudent if unspectacular: moving a sizeable contingent by land, he could better maintain communications with Burgoyne and with his New York garrison; and should Burgoyne encounter unforeseen trouble, there was at least the possibility of sending him aid. It may be more significant, however, that this *third plan* contained no reference to cooperation with the northern army and that it reached England "long before Burgoyne left for Canada."[6] Burgoyne therefore could expect little succor without Germain's intervention in his behalf. If cooperation was necessary, and surely it was, then Germain needed to respond with all haste by impressing the point upon Howe before the British commander launched his campaign. We now are aware that between March 3 and April 19 none of Germain's eight or more missives to Howe referred to Burgoyne in any manner.[7] Germain had approved Howe's descent on Philadelphia via the Jersies; he considered it an easy task, one that would free Sir William to extend his posts to meet Burgoyne later in the season, but not that Howe need ever save Burgoyne from catastrophe. In light of the obviously foggy state of Howe's mind, flitting as it was from plan to plan, the Colonial Secretary had ample warning not to take Sir William for granted.

Not until May did Germain specifically raise with Howe the subject of coordinating the two armies, and only then in response to a *fourth plan* from the General; but by the time Germain's dispatch arrived in America it was too late.

Informed that substantial increases would not be forthcoming, Howe wrote in early April of his intention to lead in person 11,000 redcoats to Philadelphia, not through New Jersey but by sea in the vessels of his brother's fleet. He would leave 4,700 men at New York and another 2,400 at his Rhode Island base. And he would station 3,000 tories under Governor William Tryon in the vicinity of Manhattan to perform "upon the Hudson's River, or to enter Connecticut as circumstances may point out."[8]

Along with this letter to Germain, Howe enclosed a copy of a message to Carleton. Amazingly enough, Howe did not even mention to the Canadian official his recent decision to proceed to Philadelphia by sea instead of by land. Though Howe could not part with a detachment to advance up the Hudson for some months, he hoped that by the time the Canadian army neared Albany he could spare troops from New York to overrun the rebel forts in the New York Highlands to open communications for shipping.[9] Howe had guarded his language to Carleton, avoiding any hard and fast promise. Considering his defensive commitments in the New York City area, his low opinion of his provincial regiments, and his awareness of the American fortifications in the rugged highlands, he could scarcely have entertained a major push by Clinton, in command at New York. And in mid-July, in his first direct communication with Burgoyne, he said nothing of assistance from Clinton—only that on reaching Albany the Canadian army should govern itself according to "the movements of the enemy."[10]

Why had Howe decided to transport his entire expedition by sea, which would for some weeks isolate him from the outside world and permit Washington to maneuver between Burgoyne and himself, allowing the American to shift his units as the occasion demanded? Previously in contemplating a trek through New Jersey, Howe had counted on a heavy reinforcement with which to establish posts along his route to maintain his communications with New York. But the cabinet, after making great labors for the campaign of 1776, felt it impossible to repeat its performance each year.[11] Thus inadequate numerical strength may cast light on Howe's decision to abandon his cross-country jaunt.

In the dispatch containing his fourth and final plan, Howe conceded that the campaign would be late in starting because of the need to evacuate East Jersey. He also acknowledged that Philadelphia was not vital to the patriots; therefore Washington would quite probably avoid a decisive battle. As he put it, his hopes "of terminating the war this year are vanished." Why then did Howe persist in the idea of occupying Philadelphia, especially by sea? There are almost as many opinions as there have been analysts of the campaign.

There may well have been a lurking suspicion in Howe's mind that he was being neglected. After all, he was the British commander in chief in America and yet the campaign from Canada had been formulated without his advice; it was Burgoyne's whole show, and consequently he wanted little to do with it. With regard to Burgoyne's army, he would do only what was required of him (virtually nothing). Not to say that Howe would sit idly by while the Canadian army met disaster; but evidently it would not require his attention, for he still had heard nothing from Germain on the subject.[12] Moreover, to join in the Lake Champlain-Hudson operation in force would necessitate a movement deep into the interior. This strategy was foreign to the thinking of the General who the previous year had displayed not the smallest degree of interest in Carleton's invasion from Canada, the General who had mainly contented himself in 1776 with conquests along the coast at New York and Rhode Island. That the American continent, even the Atlantic fringe, imposed hazards to campaigning in Sir William's opinion can be seen from his later testimony before Parliament: "That part of America where I had been is the strongest country I was ever in; it is everywhere hilly and covered with wood and intersected by ravines, creeks, marshy grounds and in every quarter of a mile is a post fitted for ambuscades. Little or no knowledge could be obtained by reconnoitering."[13] More in line with Howe's thinking was the capture of Philadelphia, along with the curtailment of rebel shipping in the Delaware. These moves were analagous to his campaigning the year before and would result in extending the blockade down the coast; they must have found favor with his brother, if indeed the Admiral did not play a major role in their formulation.

In justifying his descent on Philadelphia, General Howe called attention to the reputed strength of loyalism in eastern Pennsylvania, an opinion shared by Germain. In substance, however, the two leaders visualized the tories' potential quite differently. Howe looked upon the loyalists as anything but a substitute for regular troops. They could provide a generally favorable atmosphere in which to conduct operations. Useful for obtaining provisions and intelligence, they could perform vital policing duties, and they could be enlisted in special units. Germain's opinion of provincials is well summarized in his reply to Howe's final plan of early April, though Germain's letter—which lingered three months in passage, perhaps because it was not mailed promptly—did not reach Howe until August 16, long after the General had embarked for Philadelphia. Germain consented to the invasion by sea (at that point he had no choice); but in this, his first direct reference to Burgoyne's campaign during his correspondence with Howe, he added the disturbing condition that the undertaking be completed in time to cooperate with Burgoyne. Howe had a more realistic opinion of patriot resistance than the Colonial Secretary, who spoke of the rebels' "weakened and depressed" state, of their inability to raise a sufficient force to oppose Howe. By stressing American weaknesses and the loyalists' numbers, Germain attempted to fend off criticism for not hastening additional regiments to the war fronts. He confidently asserted that so many loyalists would turn out in support of Howe that the regulars could go elsewhere. The chimera of loyalism continued to make Germain—3,000 miles away—starry-eyed to the point that he expressed confidence that the campaign would terminate the war.[14]

And now for the campaign itself. It began with Germain and Howe holding widely divergent views about reinforcements, provincial manpower, and prospects for victory in 1777. It began with Germain uncertain of Howe's whereabouts,[15] Howe unsure of Burgoyne's exact orders,[16] and Burgoyne unaware of Howe's precise intentions.[17] To pursue a war in a far-off part of the world was not simple. Problems of communication and coordination under any circumstances would not have been easy. But the architects of the 1777 campaign did little or nothing to overcome the inherent hardships. Vagueness characterized all the phases of planning, and words like "co-operation" and "conjunction" never received definition, thus allowing events to give clarity to the terms.

## Philadelphia

British leaders did not have a monopoly on optimism in 1777. The Continental Congress, heeding Washington's plea for long service regulars, authorized a vast army of 75,000 men. Recruiting for the Continental army, however, proceeded so slowly that Washington sent some of his best officers back to their own locales to spur enlistments. With warm spring weather the initial contingents of some 8,000 new Continentals trickled into Morristown to reinforce the core of regulars and New Jersey militiamen who had endured a winter of inadequate clothing and insufficient provisions.

To cope with the manifold burdens confronting him that winter, Washington had received from Congress virtually dictatorial power over military affairs for a period of six months beginning December 27, 1776. There was never, as Nathanael Greene told John Hancock, "a man that might be more safely trusted, nor a time when there was a louder call" for decisive measures to hold the tatterdemalion army together. Conscious of his unusual authority, Washington assured Congress that he would use his power temperately; but use it he did. He commandeered supplies when civilians balked at selling to the army for payment in depreciated paper securities; and he lodged sick and wounded soldiers in private homes around Morristown over the inhabitants' complaints. As much as Washington, the wealthy Virginia planter, may have favored a conventional war in order to spare American society and preserve whig ideals, as firmly as he believed the "sword" to be "the last resort for the preservation of our liberties," there were times when that sword must even be applied against his countrymen if their acts might cause the Revolution to falter. These included the well-affected along with the disaffected.[18]

Just as the balmy winds of April and May brought additions to the Continental ranks each year, so the commander in chief's letters took on an air of encouragement. Now in 1777, as the campaigning season approached, Washington's image of the militia, always somewhat fluctuating, likewise improved. The militia were turning out "in a very spirited manner," he assured Philip Schuyler, "and seemed determined, in conjunction with the Continental Troops, to harass and oppose the Enemy upon their march thro' the Country."[19] His optimism also increased as a result of important secret aid from France—thousands of muskets, tons of powder, and impressive quantities of clothing.

Where Howe would go remained a mystery to Washington, who bolstered his garrisons on the lower Hudson, and who, with most of his revived army, tramped south from Morristown to the heights of Middlebrook, where he could obstruct an enemy march toward the Delaware and Philadelphia. From Burgoyne's invasion alone, the commander in chief saw little to fear as he correctly predicted the physical obstacles to Burgoyne's making Albany. But several months expired before Howe's design became clear. Throughout June the British General, advancing in force to New Brunswick, played cat and mouse with Washington, who continually annoyed his foe with Morgan's riflemen, the militia, and regular units, just as he avoided three attempts by

Howe to lure him into an unfavorable position. To this day Howe's intentions remain clouded. Was he awaiting the readying of his transports, or seeking to secure his rear, or endeavoring to draw Washington into battle before departing by sea for the Quaker City? To the able Colonel Charles Stuart, his commander's meanderings were without rhyme or reason. But upon Howe's total evacuation of New Jersey and his boarding the men on vessels for Philadelphia, Stuart could only describe his commander's abandonment of Burgoyne as beyond comprehension; and he "tremble[d] for the consequences," as did Clinton, whose pleas to Howe to forsake the sea route were unavailing. Clinton, lately returned from London, knew, as Howe claimed he did not, that Whitehall intended this campaign to be decisive. And though Howe could argue that the ministry had approved his move on Philadelphia (but as yet not *by sea*), Clinton correctly maintained that the fall of the American capital would hardly be earth-shaking in its consequences. Their disagreement, enough to sever their already tattered relationship, reached its ultimate with Howe's decision to take an additional 2,000 men from the New York garrison (giving him a total of 13,000) and his subsequent call for five more battalions. At the same time, he granted Clinton permission to foray up the Hudson to clear the Highlands; but he did not so order it; and he had left his subordinate hardly more than enough troops to hold New York City, or—as Clinton phrased it—to conduct "a D . . . starved deffencive."[20]

Not until July 23, after keeping his troops sweltering aboard ship for two weeks, did the British armada of over 260 vessels clear New York Harbor. Reaching Delaware Bay on the 29th, the fleet entered the Delaware River as if to unload its 13,000 soldiers, but only to reverse its direction, return to sea, and, three weeks later, after sailing up Chesapeake Bay, land at Head of Elk on August 25. The Howes' behavior at sea, long a "perplexing feature" of the campaign,[21] has received a ray of light as a result of investigation of the papers of British Captain Andrew Snape Hamond, who commanded a small naval squadron off Delaware Bay at the time of the Howes' appearance there. Hamond was "mortified" to discover that Sir William was still in bed at ten o'clock on the morning of July 30 when he boarded the flagship *Eagle* to make an intelligence report. Hamond conceded that the Americans had erected defenses farther up the Delaware, the most prevalent interpretation of the Howes' decision to go further south.[22] *But* Hamond went on to assure the brothers that they could debark with ease on the lower river. A much more important influence on the General, according to Hamond, was the naval officer's report that Washington, marching southward, was already beyond the Delaware and nearing Wilmington, Delaware. (Washington, in fact, was a hundred miles or so away on the Jersey side of the Delaware at Coryell's Ferry seeking definite word of the Howes' whereabouts.) The General, apparently unwilling to fight except on his own terms, chose not to engage Washington immediately but to push on to the Chesapeake and advance more from the west of Washington, thus better enabling him to protect his left flank. Even had Hamond's information been correct, and it was not, Howe's decision is hard to justify. As Hamond averred, "the great length of time it would take to make such a detoure with so large a fleet, contrasted with the immediate opportunity of getting the whole army ashore in 24 hours." Hamond, amazed at Sir William's response, pled "to no purpose." The General "seemed resolved, and the Admiral would not oppose him; and to the astonishment of both Fleet and Army, the signal was made to turn away, and steer for the Capes of Virginia."[23]

From the Head of Elk, Howe, by the most circuitous route imaginable, was commencing his march on Philadelphia, fifty-seven miles away. He had lost more than a month at sea,[24] as well as June and July in New York. The campaigning season was advanced, and Washington's army remained to be dealt with. Perhaps time meant little to Howe, who only aspired to seize the patriot capital. It did, however, matter to Germain, whose letter of May 18—acknowledging Howe's resolution to move by sea—finally caught up with the General on August 15, between Delaware Bay and the Chesapeake, a letter that also urged Howe to return from Pennsylvania in time to cooperate on the Hudson. At last Howe had Germain's thinking first hand on the Burgoyne expedition, but by then, even had Howe desired to head northward (which he did not), it was too late.

Washington, meanwhile, was astonished at Howe's deserting Burgoyne, though the Virginian continued in the dark as to Howe's actual location. Nathanael Greene said the Americans were "compelled to wander about the country like the Arabs" in search of the British fleet and army.[25] After footsore days of marching and countermarching, Washington, learning of Howe's landing at the northernmost point in Chesapeake Bay, headed south to meet him. Sometimes criticized for not first joining with the patriot Northern army to smash Burgoyne and then returning with overwhelming reinforcements to oppose Howe, Washington, it will be recalled, was confident of Burgoyne's failure unless given additional support. Besides, for political reasons Washington could scarcely have turned his back on the American capital.

Howe, slowly making his way toward Philadelphia, felt anything but a liberator or conquering hero. The mirage of loyalism was coming home to roost. The people "excepting a few individuals are strongly against us," he complained to Germain. Word of British and Hessian pillaging in New Jersey the previous year prompted the local inhabitants to stream northward on foot and in wagons. Howe, short of food for his army and fodder for his horses after a debilitating voyage, saw clouds of smoke ahead of him as the retreating militiamen burned grain in the fields and in storage to keep it out of British hands. Howe's mood was further dampened by Germain's expectation that he actively assist Burgoyne. Almost simultaneously as Sir William wrote the Colonial Secretary of his inability to comply, the ever optimistic Lord George was penning a dispatch to the General informing him of "the fair prospect which you now have of an earlier junction [with Burgoyne] than you lately supposed likely to be effected."[26] There could be no better evidence of the earlier breakdown in communication between two men who came to misunderstand each other so completely.

As the Americans made repeated harassing strokes, Howe became fearful that the Virginian would retire toward the mountains to the west and dog his advance as he had done in New Jersey earlier that season. But Washington's countrymen expected him to interpose his army between Howe and the capital, and Washington himself showed not the slightest inclination to shy away. When Howe entered Kennett Square, Pennsylvania, he found Washington with 8,000 Continentals and 3,000 militia in position on the northern banks of Brandywine Creek. Washington anticipated a frontal assault across the stream, but he should have remembered Howe's flanking measure at Long Island. The American right wing under the ill-starred John Sullivan, victim of the earlier thrust in 1776, failed to reconnoiter or patrol adequately beyond its sector. While General Knyphausen with 5,000 men demonstrated before Chad's Ford on the main Philadelphia road, Cornwallis led the bulk westward, traversed the Brandywine at an unprotected ford above the American right, and crashed down upon Sullivan's flank and rear. As rumor of Howe's maneuver got to Washington before the assault itself, the American briefly considered a sudden plunge across Chad's Ford to destroy Knyphausen, and indeed he might have succeeded but at the risk of the total loss of Sullivan's force. Restraining his impulse, he hastened Nathanael Greene's division from his center to support the hard-pressed New Hampshire officer. Greene's men, some of them covering four miles in only forty-five minutes, fought splendidly as they held firm against repeated volleys and then bayonet charges, allowing Sullivan's disorganized regiments to escape. With darkness approaching, Greene retired in good order and joined Washington, who, denuded by Greene's departure from the center, had been thrown back by Knyphausen's Germans and redcoats.

At Brandywine as at Long Island, American intelligence proved defective, and for the second time Howe had outgeneraled Washington, but the Virginian had quickly recovered his presence at Brandywine by speeding Greene to the scene of potential disaster. Owing to fatigue among his own troops and the lateness of the hour, Howe did not pursue Washington, whose regiments finally were halted and reformed at Chester. Washington's casualties in all categories numbered about 1,000 men, Howe's approximately half that many.

The crucial point about the depletions on both sides was almost always this: though his losses were greater than Howe's, Washington could scrape up reinforcements, the Briton could not. And true to form, Washington in the next three weeks built his army up to better than its strength at Brandywine while Howe was occupying Philadelphia. General Alexander McDougall arrived from Peekskill with 900 Continentals, General William Smallwood appeared with 1,100 Maryland militia, and David Forman's 600 New Jersey irregulars were due momentarily.

For the first time in the war, Washington moved forward to attack the major part of a British army: 9,000 troops Howe had placed in quarters at Germantown, seven miles from Philadelphia. It was to be another of Washington's characteristic night movements. Since Howe had divided his army and had not required the Germantown contingent to erect defenses, the idea of an assault was militarily sound, but the plan may have been "too intricate for inexperienced officers and imperfectly disciplined troops."[27] Four columns—two of regulars, two of militia—started for Germantown on the evening of October 3 from their encampment near Skippack Creek, sixteen miles away. The two militia columns, moving on the outside, were to pass beyond the British front lines and assail the flanks and rear, while the Continental divisions under Sullivan and Greene were to hit the enemy's left and right fronts respectively. Although the militia, hardly trustworthy in such an operation, failed to execute their assignments, Sullivan's division at daybreak hurled the British advance parties back in wild confusion. Greene's division, having lost valuable time on the wrong road, finally arrived and drove all before it as far as the village market place. But the tide was already turning. Part of Sullivan's command had halted to flush several companies of the British 40th Regiment from the large stone house of Justice Benjamin Chew. Despite a heavy cannonading from Knox's artillery, the thick stone masonry served as an excellent fortress (though it took three carpenters all the next winter to restore the interior). Sullivan's delay and Greene's late appearance gave Cornwallis vital time to speed reinforcements from Philadelphia. Then, too, a heavy fog fell over the ravined, four-mile long battle front making it even more difficult for the American units to coordinate their actions. In the confusion General Adam Stephen, in disobedience to orders (he was drinking heavily), swung his Continentals out of line and, coming upon Anthony Wayne's rear, mistakenly opened fire upon fellow Americans.

Washington, who according to Sullivan exposed himself "to the hottest fire," turned to steady his officers and men, but the turmoil was too much for most of them. Panic overcame several of the American regiments, especially as ammunition in Sullivan's division began to run out. Since the Americans' luck was unbelievably wretched, Washington could take heart from the results, imperfect as they were. Actually defeated, for they had given up the field and suffered total losses of roughly 1,000 compared to Howe's 534 casualties in all categories, the patriots had nevertheless scared the daylights out of their opponents in several hours of vigorous action. It was a superior American army to the one that had fought the campaign of 1776. If the Continentals still had not worsted the enemy in formal combat, they made his victories highly expensive.[28]

Once more Washington's ranks expanded following defeat. From Gates' Northern army, triumphant over Burgoyne, came John Paterson's and John Glover's brigades and Morgan's invaluable riflemen; from elsewhere, came Varnum's Rhode Island brigade and militia units of various sorts and descriptions. Of course many of these, plus those from his own command, were ill-equipped and would soon leave. The reasons would vary—expirations of enlistments, illness, desertions, but go they would as they did each winter. But before that time, the commander in chief wanted another round with Howe. He had little to lose; Brandywine and Germantown indicated he was sufficiently resourceful to avert an utterly disastrous defeat. Howe, however, would not budge from his corner, having no inclination for another bloody, indecisive riposte. Yet Washington's continued presence in the Philadelphia area was embarrassing to Howe (who must have wished that the Virginian would quietly get lost for the winter).

For a month and a half Howe had good reason to let his adversary alone: he needed to clear the Delaware of rebel installations and open it as an avenue of supply from the sea. In the way were three forts and lines of *chevaux-de-frise*, iron-pointed timbers embedded in heavy cratelike structures anchored in the river and slanted upward so as to gash the bottom of an oncoming vessel. Howe found the task long and costly: on October 22, his casualties in attacking Fort Mercer were almost half his combined losses at Brandywine and Germantown, not to mention the destruction of one of Lord Howe's few ships-of-the-line. Not until the last of November, after batteries were brought to bear on the forts by land and water, was the Delaware cleared of the final rebel obstructions.

Washington tempted Howe to sally forth by remaining at Whitemarsh, a few miles from Germantown. Finally, with anything but enthusiasm, Sir William approached Washington's entrenchments on December 4. But after a lively skirmish, he drew away. Explaining his decision not to fight, Howe declared that he was unwilling to "expose the troops longer to the weather in this inclement season" and that the Continentals were strongly dug in. Howe was looking for an easy victory in a difficult war. Washington, somewhat amused by it all, explained the affair to Governor Livingston of New Jersey: "Gen. Howe after making great preparations, and threatening to drive us beyond the Mountains, came out with his whole force last Thursday Evening, and, after manoeuvering round us till the Monday following, decamped very hastily, and marched back to Philadelphia." The British army for the third consecutive winter settled down to city life, while Washington shifted to winter quarters among the desolate hills of Valley Forge, twenty-five miles away.[29]

## Saratoga

Burgoyne's campaign, meanwhile, had gotten underway earlier than Howe's, and it had ended before the finale in Pennsylvania. It began in mid-June, when the British General's army glided majestically down the blue waters of Lake Champlain, flanked on the west by the Adirondacks and on the east by the Green Mountains. First came 500 Indians decked out in paint and feathers paddling birch canoes; then the "advanced corps" of 650 Canadians and loyalists, followed by the British flotilla that had dueled Arnold the previous autumn, with the blue-coated German regiments toward the rear, and behind them the supernumeraries. Of the 6,000 regulars, 3,000 were foreign mercenaries, mostly Brunswickers, led by thirty-eight-year-old Major General Baron von Riedesel, an excellent soldier, who spoke fluent English.

Except for the multi-colored savages, this was a conventional army of its day that made meager allowance for the arduous physical tasks ahead. There was the cumbersome 138-piece artillery train, most of which might profitably have been left in Canada; the seemingly endless string of baggage vehicles, actually two-wheeled carts made of unseasoned wood, over thirty of them laden with Burgoyne's resplendent wardrobe and store of champagne; and the usual horde of women, children, dogs, and sutlers. Several officers brought along their wives —one, Christian Henrietta Acland ("Lady Harriet"), who was far along in pregnancy, a more cultivated person than her coarse, hard-drinking husband Major John Acland; another, the author of a delightful memoir of the campaign, Baroness Frederika Riedesel, petite, beautiful, and vivacious, who with children ages six, three, and one, braved the wilderness to be with her soldier-husband.[30]

The American Northern Department, whose job was to halt the invasion, could not have been more feeble or faction-ridden, partly due to Congressional shilly-shallying about the command. In 1776 the lawmakers had asked two temperamental generals, Schuyler and Gates, to serve together without spelling out their respective jurisdictions. Eventually Congress declared Gates subordinate to Schuyler, who, after a journey to Philadelphia to defend his position and his conduct, returned in June, 1777, to upper New York to prepare to meet Burgoyne's anticipated strike southward. Both Gates and Schuyler were politically oriented, and lobbied with Congress with as much enthusiasm as they ever devoted to stopping the enemy. It is improbable, however, that the two generals were more argumentative than their own later partisans in the historians' guild who still hotly debate their respective merits and ambitions. Too often forgotten is the fact that most Revolutionary generals were also solicitous of their own good standing with the politicians. Greene, Sullivan, Knox, Arnold, and Morgan are cases in point, as was Washington, who was anything but insensitive to potential rivals.

Schuyler, though a generous, selfless patriot, was pompous and overbearing; an aristocrat like Washington, he was not the Virginian's equal as a leader of plain people, and the Northern army consisted chiefly of New England farmers. Schuyler was disliked by congressmen from the New England states who felt, probably unfairly, that the previous year he had been ready to sacrifice New England had Carleton continued his offensive. There was a final bone to pick: Schuyler belonged to the class of New York landowners who had endeavored to gain jurisdiction over Vermont and had tried to have the Yankee settlers ejected. Schuyler was unmercifully vilified by his enemies, who even spread unfounded rumors that the proud Dutch patroon was disloyal.

Despondent and wanting to resign, Schuyler was a poor choice to rally the Northern states at this particular juncture. Fearful of further criticism, he resolved to hold Fort Ticonderoga, although its garrison of 3,000 poorly armed Continentals and militia had failed to secure Mount Defiance, a lofty and commanding eminence to the southwest. Schuyler's field commander at Ticonderoga was a competent ex-British officer, Brigadier General Arthur St. Clair, who hoped that Burgoyne would stage a foolish frontal assault in the manner of Howe at Bunker Hill. But when the British General planted heavy ordnance at the summit of Mount Defiance, the sandy-headed Scotsman wisely evacuated his works on the night of July 5, preserving his small force, which formed the bulk of the American Northern army.

Both sides exaggerated the magnitude of Burgoyne's wresting Ticonderoga from St. Clair, though the patriots sacrificed valuable munitions. George III is said to have rushed into the dressing room of Queen Charlotte, mother of his eleven children, but nonetheless an act shocking to the ladies-in-waiting, shouting, "I have beat them! I have beat the Americans." The Continental Congress voted to investigate the abandonment of Ticonderoga; and John Adams growled that the shooting of a cowardly general (St. Clair or Schuyler?) would serve as a warning to the others.[31] Washington, however, was far from despairing, and he agreed with Nathanael Greene that "General Burgoyne's triumphs and little advantages may serve to bait his vanity and lead him on to his final overthrow." Burgoyne appears to have concluded there was no great hurry to reach Albany, only seventy miles away. Consequently, after a sharp skirmish between St. Clair's rear guard and a body of Germans and redcoats at Hubbardtown, Burgoyne made a momentous error. At Skenesborough, where he destroyed a quantity of rebel supplies, Burgoyne resolved to continue south on an overland route in place of returning to Ticonderoga and advancing by way of Lake George, his original idea. The twenty-three miles from Skeneborough to Fort Edward on the Hudson lay through a dense wilderness of pine, spruce, and sycamore interlaced with streams and boggy marshland. Such a decision might have been justifiable had he sent a lightly equipped column ahead to seize Fort Edward, a move that would have increased the gloom in the dispirited Northern army. Instead, Burgoyne decided to keep his force *en masse*.[32]

While Burgoyne enjoyed the comforts of loyalist Philip Skene's stone mansion, the toil of his road-building crews became immeasurably heavier because of Philip Schuyler. The ring of American axes and the crash of giant trees felled across the enemy's path echoed through the wooded country. Schuyler's men also rolled rocks and boulders into Wood Creek, causing the overflowing waters to swirl across the wagon tracks that the British artificers were converting into a road. As a result of Schuyler's tactics, coupled with Burgoyne's lethargy, faulty planning, and superfluous paraphernalia, it took the Anglo-German army twenty-four days to travel the twenty-three miles to star-shaped Fort Edward, which the patriots had partly demolished. After a further delay, the British General plodded on another seven miles, down the east bank of the Hudson, halting at a blockhouse and abandoned trading post known as Fort Miller, where he remained until September 13, mainly for want of horses and supplies.

Philip Skene's assurances of assistance from the Hudson valley people proved to be fallacious. Men, women, and children—some undoubtedly tory by inclination—fled southward from solitary farms, driving, if time permitted, wagons bulging with household goods. Burgoyne's red-skinned allies, despite the General's admonitions about atrocities, were oblivious to the military subtleties that marked the Age of Limited Warfare in Europe. Friend and foe alike often fell before the tomahawk and scalping knife. Nine members of a family named Allen were surprised and massacred inside their house at dinner. A Barnes family was murdered in flight to Fort Edward. But it was the shooting and scalping of beautiful Jane McCrea, engaged to a loyalist officer with Burgoyne, that fanned the hatred for the advancing enemy more than any other incident of the campaign. Burgoyne, genuinely mortified by the act, made the affair all the more disastrous to the British by failing to execute the reputed murderer, appropriately named Wyandot Panther, for fear his Indians would desert.[33]

Burgoyne's troubles were mounting, but life for the General and the senior officers was outwardly pleasant enough. For the Riedesels these were "happy weeks" of "peace and quiet," broken only by the usual sounds of camp life, such as the tuba which daily awakened the Germans, and the fife and drum which aroused the British. There were picnics under the spreading trees, dinner parties for officers, and, at night as camp fires gleamed on hills overlooking the Hudson, card games. For the most part, the Riedesels remained outside the social circle of gay Gentleman Johnny, who developed a penchant for rattlesnake meat, and who scandalized the proper young Baroness by spending his nights in "singing and drinking and amusing himself in the company of the wife of a commisary, who was his mistress and, like him, loved champagne."[34]

Meanwhile, Burgoyne's supply and transport troubles kept him grounded. He was reluctant to cross the Hudson and push down the west bank to Albany before collecting enough provisions for thirty days. Of equal concern was his shortage of horses to bring up his artillery and small boats, which had taken the water route from Ticonderoga down Lake George. At this point, he should have left all but a few field pieces behind to provide greater mobility for his army that was already encountering almost insurmountable barriers in the rugged northland. But he elected to bring up a train of fifty-two cannon and to send out a large foraging expedition to round up food and horses. Still exuding optimism, he assured Germain that nothing had happened to change his prospects for an early termination of the immediate campaign, for reaching Albany before the end of August. Even the rebels' rear guard activities that included drawing off the cattle and population, burning the wheat fields, and leaving not a "morsel of grass" for the horses, as a German officer phrased it, did not dim the Briton's confidence. The Americans were merely revealing their "desperation and folly."[35]

Burgoyne could not have fallen into greater error. The civilian population gradually changed into a loosely arrayed body of irregulars of the sort unknown in the Old World. If Americans were reluctant to join the Continental army and serve in distant parts for as many as three years, Burgoyne soon learned they would protect their own areas of settlement. And it was the British General's ponderous pace that gave the inhabitants invaluable days to steel themselves and organize.

His truly novel experience of actually engaging the mass of the population was first brought home to Burgoyne soon after he detached Brunswicker Lieutenant Colonel Frederick Baum for a raid on Bennington, Vermont, to capture badly needed food and pack horses, which would eliminate using the fragile Canadian carts and allow the army to proceed more rapidly. Perhaps nothing illustrates Burgoyne's incompetence for a wilderness campaign more vividly than the composition of the force assigned to Baum, who himself spoke no English and thus was hardly a good candidate to march through a region of both friends and foes. Along with tories, Canadians, and Indians, plus a handful of grenadiers, light infantry, and *jägers*, Baum led Prinz Ludwig's horseless Dragoon Regiment, waddling along in their cumbersome twelve-pound thigh-high jackboots and entangling their tall sabers in the underbrush; and, to herald their arrival in Vermont, a German band.

To oppose Baum's 800 men, General John Stark gathered the militia from the surrounding Vermont and New Hampshire villages. Yankee improvisation was at its best, for dishes, plates, and spoons were melted into musket balls. Though Stark might thumb his nose at Schuyler, the hated Dutchman, who begged the temperamental Hampshirite to bring his following to the Continental camp, he would fight in command of his own kind, in defense of his own soil. On August 16, Stark's militia companies, like angry hornets, surrounded their prey. With the militia anything went, and on seeing an approaching column of men with the loyalist white paper badge on their hats, Baum assumed—until too late—they were friends. Suddenly assailed from all sides, Baum never had a chance, though his Germans fought bravely (after his Indians and loyalists scattered) until their ammunition was spent and their commander lay mortally wounded.

In the full flush of victory the militia once again became a motley throng as they broke ranks to loot and pillage. Stark, with the aid of fresh men under Seth Warner, barely managed to re-form them in time to ward off a blow from 600 Germans under Lieutenant Colonel Heinrich von Breyman, whom Burgoyne had sent out to assist Baum upon getting wind of possible trouble. Then the Yankee irregulars smashed Breymann too, though Breymann himself got away to give Burgoyne the bad tidings: 900 men lost, half of them regulars.

Burgoyne's setback at Bennington was all the more deeply felt since he failed to obtain men from Carleton to garrison Ticonderoga so as to permit his own troops at the post to bolster his ranks. Governor Carleton refused to let his bitterness toward Germain for removing him from the direction of the Canadian army stand in his way of assisting Burgoyne; but, as he pointed out, the Colonial Secretary had frozen all units then in Canada, an unsound act for a minister in London who could not possibly cope with unexpected developments on the scene. Furthermore, Continental Major General Benjamin Lincoln of Massachusetts, sent to New England by Washington and Congress, was aiding John Stark, rallying the militia, who subsequently severed Burgoyne's communications with Ticonderoga and Canada.[36] And there was further alarming news of the countryside in arms; this time from Lieutenant Colonel Barry St. Leger's diversionary expedition of 900 redcoats, tories, and Iroquois advancing via Lake Ontario and the Mohawk Valley toward a junction with Burgoyne at Albany. Along the Mohawk the Anglo-Dutch settlers, under picturesque leaders such as Colonel Peter Gansevoort and General Nicholas Herkimer, turned out to blunt the thrust. Though St. Leger beat back a body of New Yorkers near Oriskany, his siege of Fort Stanwix (only recently renamed Fort Schuyler) failed, largely because Schuyler hurried Benedict Arnold westward with reinforcements. In fact, when Arnold arrived the enemy had gone, for Britain's forest allies fell for an American story that Arnold's men were as numerous as the leaves on the trees. They decamped so suddenly that St. Leger had no alternative but to abandon the mission and return to Montreal.

While the campaign opened well for Burgoyne and ill for the patriots, the tables had turned. Nothing in irregular warfare beats success, and Burgoyne complained at this juncture that "Wherever the King's forces point, militia to the amount of three or four thousand assemble in twenty-four hours." There was indeed "a gathering storm" over the prose-minded Englishman who now, sensing the flight of Fortuna, began to grasp for an alibi. Complaining of the inflexibility of his orders, he asserted a willingness to halt his advance or retire northward if only "Had I latitude in my orders." No general worth his salt would blindly follow instructions in the face of absolute defeat, nor would Germain have demanded it. Burgoyne was not a great general, but a vain one. To give up short of victory would demolish his alter ego and would be equivalent to Carleton's turning back the year before, a step Burgoyne had roundly denounced. Arguing that Howe's success depended upon him,[37] a view sanctioned neither by his orders nor his knowledge of Howe's sailing for Philadelphia, Burgoyne on September 13 crossed the Hudson on a bridge of rafts. Gentleman Johnny, the gambler, was bidding for a slam with the lower cards in the deck.

The American Northern army, its morale perceptively better at the reversal of events, received fresh Continental regiments, including Colonel Daniel Morgan's frontier riflemen, who, as Washington declared, possessed the woodland skills to contain Burgoyne's free-wheeling savages. Washington was still unaware of the ruse worked upon St. Leger's redmen; but, an old frontier fighter himself, he recommended that news of the riflemen's coming should be circulated "with proper Embellishments . . . to the Enemy. It would not be amiss, among other Things, to magnify numbers." Schuyler, though his delaying tactics were bearing fruit, now gave way once more to Gates, whose appointment by Congress to direct the Northern Department was probably wise: Gates' popularity was unbounded in New England, and Schuyler's prestige had slipped in his own state of New York after being defeated in an election for governor.[38]

Gates accurately took the measure of Burgoyne whose snail-like progress gave the Americans opportunity to entrench on Bemis Heights, a densely wooded plateau north of Stillwater. With cool weather approaching, Gates resolved to let Burgoyne further deplete his supplies and thinning ranks with reckless assaults rather than chance an all-out battle suited to British military formations. And Burgoyne could not have responded more to Gates' liking. From this point onward, Burgoyne thrashed wildly about like a blind man as Morgan's forest-wise riflemen and bands of patriot militia drove in his scouts and so intimidated his Indians that "not a man of them was to be brought within the sound of a rifle shot." As Burgoyne's tribesmen departed in droves, Gates acquired his own aboriginal scouts, who delighted in swooping down upon British stragglers and—with Gates' sly indulgence—"hooting and hollowing" as they pretended to burn or bury their prisoners alive.[39]

With only the vaguest notion of Gates' whereabouts, Burgoyne groped forward for a showdown on the morning of September 19. Holding most of his force in position, Gates sent Morgan's corps—the "élite" of the army—northward into a wooded area to harass and delay the enemy, a stratagem that represented a compromise with Benedict Arnold who had favored a full-scale contest in the thickets and gullies toward which Morgan headed. While General Riedesel guarded the camp equipage on the river trail and a second column on the far right under Brigadier General Simon Fraser lost itself in the dense foliage, Burgoyne, in the middle, struggled across a deep ravine with 1,100 men toward the American center. Burgoyne had barely halted his column in a clearing at Freeman's Farm when the riflemen, now reinforced by Arnold's regiments from the American left wing, opened a withering fire from the trees and underbrush. That was as far as Burgoyne got. But each time the Americans rolled the enemy back, they themselves were pushed from the bloody clearing by vicious counterattacks with the bayonet. As the afternoon wore on, the riflemen in particular were taking a heavy toll of British officers and gunners and were equally "sedulous" in marking out the tories. "This misfortune," lamented redcoat Sergeant Roger Lamb, "accelerated their estrangement from our cause and army." It is not improbable that only last-minute relief from Riedesel's troops and gathering darkness saved Burgoyne from immediate disaster. The Americans, their job well done, prudently returned to their lines, leaving Burgoyne with approximately 600 casualties as against 320 of their own. As a Brunswicker observed, "In the open field the rebels do not count for much, but in the woods they are formidable."[40]

Two days later as Burgoyne contemplated a second probing of Gates' entrenchments, he got word from Sir Henry Clinton, who, hearing of Bennington, promised to dispatch a diversionary contingent up the Hudson against rebel fortifications in the highlands. But Clinton, left with what he deemed a deficient army for attempting both a defense of New York's sprawling environs and a sustained military operation, and under no positive orders to head north, had carefully qualified his proffered aid. And after his troops had seized American Forts Montgomery and Clinton by October 8, Sir Henry felt that was all he could do. Now to his astonishment came messages from the once confident Burgoyne that Gates had twice his number of men, that his supplies had dangerously diminished, and that he awaited Clinton's *orders*. With Clinton, as before with Germain, Burgoyne was seeking excuses for failing to accomplish his will-o'-the-wisp objectives. Sir Henry was unwilling to bear Burgoyne's cross. Not only lacking manpower, Clinton knew nothing of Washington's location or Howe's in Pennsylvania, for Sir William had not kept him informed. Even so, Clinton, too responsible to ignore Burgoyne's predicament, embarked Major General John Vaughan with 2,000 men for a push toward Burgoyne to help him in any way possible. As Vaughan felt his way upriver, he saw thousands of American militia observing him from the banks. His mission was hopeless. Besides, time had run out for Burgoyne. And Clinton, receiving a call from Howe for 4,000 men to compensate for casualties in Pennsylvania, recalled Vaughan, dismantled the highland forts, and withdrew to New York.[41]

For sixteen days Burgoyne dreamed of relief that never came as his men shivered in the autumn weather, ate reduced rations, and were bedeviled by American marksmen. Gates remained in his entrenchments, refusing to divide his army by sending a body of regulars back to assist in defending the highlands against Clinton. By now militia literally poured into Gates' camp. On October 5, Riedesel and Fraser to no avail urged their commander to retreat. Albany still beckoned

Burgoyne, who, two days later, set out with a reconnaisance in force to place cannon on an elevation overlooking the American left. As Burgoyne drew up his 1,500 men in a wheat field and searched in vain for the eminence (none existed!), Gates hurled Morgan's corps and Brigadier General Enoch Poor's brigade, both hidden in the woods, out upon the enemy's right and left flanks respectively.[42] Though his wings soon crumpled under the onslaught, Burgoyne's center occupied by Riedesel's Brunswickers held firm until General Fraser came forth with the light infantry and the British 24th Regiment to cover their retreat. Not content with a partial victory, the Americans drove against the British redoubts that had been constructed at Freeman's Farm after the first battle. By this time, if not earlier, Arnold, who had quarreled with Gates and lost his command, in disobedience to orders flung himself on a horse and raced into the melee. Arnold assumed direction of the battle that took on a different complexion from the limited action Gates had contemplated. But Gates did throw in additional units, although he could hardly see that had he committed his whole army Burgoyne would possibly have witnessed his denouement then and there. As it was, night once again terminated the battle, but not before Arnold had heroically led his troops in taking Burgoyne's far right redoubt; as a result Arnold, though himself wounded, had exposed Burgoyne's entire line of defense.

Gates had shrewdly calculated that the "old gamester," as he alluded to Burgoyne, would make another reckless stab at the works on Bemis Heights; and he had been ready for him, although credit for leadership on the battlefield belongs to Arnold and Morgan. Burgoyne, with Generals Phillips and Fraser, had scheduled a dinner engagement at the Riedesels that evening, but the only British general to arrive was Simon Fraser, mortally wounded, on a stretcher. While the Baroness shared her uneaten shoulder of pork with the wounded, Burgoyne began a withdrawal to the village of Saratoga. Gates, prudently declining his adversary's offer of another battle, hastened three columns forward to take post on the enemy's right and rear, at the same time that thousands of militia on the east bank prevented any British crossing of the Hudson. Discovering the futility of retreat, Burgoyne's only hope was a rescue by Clinton, and he knew that chance was slim.

The closing scenes of the campaign along the Hudson were horrifying to the British and their German allies, more in keeping with the fear and suffering of the destructive wars of a later period. Burgoyne's encircled army experienced ceaseless firing. Night and day musket shot and cannon ball rained down on them. Bodies of the dead, carcasses of horses, abandoned wagons, tents, ammunition, and baggage were strewed along the way. Wolves prowled among the corpses. The stench was indescribable. The soldiers—if they slept at all—lay on the ground, exposed to the cold night air and intermittent rain. Many of the expedition's women and children sought temporary shelter in a dark cellar. Upstairs the screams of the wounded on the amputating table rose above the sound of exploding shells. Baroness Riedesel reported that due to the confusion the wounded had almost nothing to eat and that the only water available came "from a very muddy spring." In desperation some "got water out of the holes the cattle made with their feet." She quenched her children's thirst with wine.[43]

As the Americans, said Sergeant Lamb, "Swarmed around the little adverse army like birds of prey,"[44] Burgoyne opened negotiations with Gates, whose forces were by this time roughly triple his own. After the commanders haggled for several days, Gates allowed generous conditions, partly because he had learned of Clinton's breaking through the highland defenses, partly too, perhaps, because his militia-dominated army might not remain through a protracted siege. Burgoyne, when hearing of Clinton's stroke, considered breaking the agreement, but, on the advice of a council of war, he signed the "convention" on October 17 at Saratoga, permitting his army to embark for England on condition it serve no more in North America. Congress with good reason feared that Burgoyne's troops might be used again or garrisoned in England so that equivalent regiments could be diverted to America. Therefore the "convention army" was kept in captivity until the war's end, many of its soldiers deserting to find a better life in America.[45] If Gates' terms of capitulation were unacceptable to Congress, he had nonetheless been a sound strategist, simply recognizing that, with fall in the air and the British on rough, unfamiliar ground, time and terrain were his all-important weapons, though, to be sure, they were implemented on the field by Benedict Arnold and Daniel Morgan.[46]

There were no laurels, only thorns, to bestow in England after the so-called Saratoga campaign. America had become a graveyard for British reputations. The cloud of disgrace had first enveloped Gage in 1775. Now it hovered over Burgoyne and the Howes. But there were always dangers for a weak ministry that attempted to censure admirals and generals graced with political influence. Burgoyne, who had left his army in captivity in America, could be obliquely condemned by offering him no new assignment across the Atlantic. The Howes posed a more ticklish problem. On October 22, 1777, Sir William, hearing rumors of Burgoyne's impending capitulation and realizing Germain considered him guilty of waging warfare too leniently, tendered his resignation, followed by that of his brother, the Admiral, a short time later. Friends of the Howes demanded the rejection of their resignations as a sign of confidence in the New World commanders. Lord Chancellor Bathurst, the Earl of Clarendon, the Howes' mother, and Lady Howe, the Admiral's wife, hurled verbal broadsides at the cabinet, particularly Germain, for failing to adequately sustain the brothers in quelling the revolt.

Germain, in fact, was harshly critical of the Howes, especially for their liberality in issuing pardons, their reluctance to batter the rebel coast with raids, and their willingness to permit American vessels in intercolonial trade to ply up and down the Atlantic more often than not without molestation. By 1777 the American Secretary saw clearly what he had failed to grasp the year before: namely, that the Howes, whatever their reasons, were not following the spirit of their instructions for cracking the American rebellion. Even so, North and Germain desired no formal investigation in Parliament that would fan the flames of the opposition and once again expose the vulnerable Germain to the "ghost of Minden." But the Howes, already subjected to pamphlet attacks and a verbal assault by Germain, obtained the Parliamentary inquiry they wanted as a means of clearing their record. A highly partisan review, marked by a great outpouring of invective and recrimination by both the friends of the Howes and the supporters of the government, the inquiry of May–June, 1779, terminated inconclusively, serving only to undermine a government increasingly weary of a war that now included France and Spain among England's foes.[47]

The Howes soon disappeared from the pages of the American Revolution. Hopeful of conciliation at the onset of their mission, they slowly despaired of achieving a peaceful rapprochement with the rebels, just as they grew steadily pessimistic of garnering a victory in arms. By some time in early 1777 the Howes became convinced that their assignment was hopeless, except perhaps by so vast an expenditure of manpower as to stagger the imagination of Whitehall. It is important to remember that the Howes were not removed from command as Gage had been; they resigned voluntarily. Perhaps they were lucky in that they did not lose whole armies to the patriots as did Burgoyne and Cornwallis. Yet the Howes, especially Sir William, contributed substantially to the British disaster in 1777.

## NOTES

1. Carleton has sometimes been acclaimed possibly the ablest of British commanders in America, a man frustrated and denied by his enemies at home. But A. L. Burt, "The Quarrel Between Germain and Carleton: An Inverted Story," *Canadian Historical Review*, XI (1930), pictures the Canadian governor as petty and ill tempered, and condemns him for failing to intercept the Americans retreating from Canada in the fall of 1776. That Carleton possessed serious defects of temperament is also the conclusion of Brown, *American Secretary*, 91–92; Paul H. Smith, "Sir Guy Carleton: Soldier-Statesman," in *George Washington's Opponents*, ed. Billias, 103–141. The circumstances surrounding Burgoyne's

appointment are analyzed in Jane Clark, "The Command of the Canadian Army for the Campaign of 1777," *Canadian Historical Review*, X (1929), 129–135. But Miss Clark's view that Clinton would have accepted the command if formally offered it is convincingly challenged in William B. Willcox, "Too Many Cooks: British Planning Before Saratoga," *Journal of British Studies*, II (1962–1963), 59, 59 n7; Willcox, *Portrait of a General*, 133 136.

2. Mackesy, *War for America*, 107–108; Claude H. Van Tyne, *The War of Independence: American Phase* (Boston and New York, 1929), 49.

3. Burgoyne's plan is printed in Hoffman Nickerson, *The Turning Point of the Revolution* (Boston and New York, 1928), 83–89, the only scholarly book-length study of the Burgoyne campaign, though more recent articles and biographies have significantly altered some of its interpretations. Harrison Bird's *March to Saratoga: General Burgoyne and the American Campaign* (New York, 1963) is highly entertaining but unreliable.

4. There is no more acute contemporary analysis of Britain's obstacles to holding the Lake Champlain-Hudson line than the one offered in April, 1777, by twenty-two-year-old Captain Alexander Hamilton, one of Washington's aides: "And as to the notion of forming a junction with the northern army, and cutting off the communication between the Northern and Southern States, I apprehend it will do better in speculation than in practice. Unless the Geography of the Country is far different from any thing I can conceive, to effect this would require a chain of posts and such a number of men at each as would never be practicable or maintainable but to an immense army. In their progress, by hanging upon their rear and seizing every opportunity of skirmishing, their Situation might be rendered insupportably uneasy." Harold C. Syrett, ed., *The Papers of Alexander Hamilton* (New York and London, 1961—), I, 220–221.

5. Howe to Germain, Nov. 30, Dec. 20, 1776, Historical Manuscripts Commission, *Stopford-Sackville MSS*, II, 49–50, 52–53; Anderson, *Command of the Howe Brothers*, 214–220.

6. Brown, *American Secretary*, 96.

7. Willcox, *Portrait of a General*, 145–146. The nearest thing to instructions that Howe received concerning the Canadian army was only a copy of a letter from Germain to Carleton of March 26, stating that Burgoyne was to make his way to Albany and there subject himself to Howe's authority. It was apparently sent with only a brief covering note by an undersecretary in the American Department. Willcox feels the information was not especially enlightening as to the purpose of the northern army. See also Brown, *American Secretary*, 111–113.

8. Historical Manuscripts Commission, *Stopford-Sackville MSS*, II, 63–65.

9. *Ibid.*, 65–66. Howe was somewhat disingenuous when he later assured Germain that in the above letter to Carleton he had "positively mentioned that no direct assistance could be given to the northern army." Anderson, *Command of the Howe Brothers*, 259.

10. *Ibid.*; John Burgoyne, *State of the Expedition from Canada as Laid before the House of Commons* (London, 1780), Appendix, xlix.

11. Howe received a 30 per cent reinforcement, or 6,000 men, compared to the 15,000 to 20,000 he desired. Not all of these were available in time for the Philadelphia offensive. The Canadian army received only 1,600 additional troops for the campaign. Mackesy, *War for America*, 117, 117 n, 118, shows that the figures commonly given for Howe's reinforcement—2,500—are in error.

12. The interpretation is in Anderson, *Command of the Howe Brothers*, 259–260; but Anderson and Willcox, *Portrait of a General*, 150, appear wrong in stating that the Canadian army acquired more reinforcements than Howe. See note 11.

13. Howe, *Narrative . . . in a Committee of the House of Commons*, 38. See also Willcox, *Portrait of a General*, 150.

14. Historical Manuscripts Commission, *Stopford-Sackville MSS*, II, 66–67; Smith, *Loyalists and Redcoats*, 45–47; Anderson, *Command of the Howe Brothers*, 227–229. Brown, *American Secretary*, 113–114 contends that had Howe not sprung the sea voyage to Philadelphia upon Germain and continued with the idea of a

land movement, then Howe might well have been able to cooperate in the fall with Burgoyne. Brown implies that from the moment Germain learned of Howe's proposed voyage he was greatly concerned. An apparent indication of this, according to Brown, is that Germain replied to Howe on the very same day (May 18) he received Howe's fourth plan, urging the General to complete his work in time to make contact with Burgoyne. Germain's apprehension may indeed have existed, but Mackesy, *War for America*, 122, 122 n3, points out that Howe's dispatch reached the colonial office on May 8, not the 18th, the date given in the Historical Manuscripts Commission, *Stopford-Sackville MSS*, II, 66. There is also the intriguing, if possibly unanswerable, question of why Germain's reply of May 18 required three months to reach Sir William at a critical juncture in the war.

15. Germain wrote William Knox, June 24, 1777: "I cannot guess by Sir Wm. Howe's letters when he will begin his operations or where he proposes carrying them out." Historical Manuscripts Commission, *Various Collections* (London, 1901–1914), VI, 131.

16. Clinton in conversation with his superior in New York discovered that Howe did not comprehend Germain's ardent desire that every effort be made to end the war in that year. Clinton also reported Howe uncertain of Burgoyne's objectives. Willcox, *Portrait of a General*, 155–156; Brown, *American Secretary*, 114.

17. On July 3, early in his campaign, Burgoyne was exceedingly optimistic about his chances of reaching Albany without great difficulty. Even so, he complained that "I have spared no pains to open a correspondence with Sir William Howe. . . . and I am in total ignorance of the situation or intentions of that general." Quoted in Fitzpatrick, ed., *Writings of Washington*, VIII, 499 n53.

18. Ford, ed., *Journals of Congress*, VI, 1045–1046; Thayer, *Greene*, 136; Fitzpatrick, *Writings of Washington*, VI, 464. "Happy it is for this country," wrote Hancock to Washington, "that the General of their forces can safely be entrusted with the most unlimited power." Burnett, ed., *Letters of Congress*, II, 198. A committee of Congress, with the approval of that body, dispatched a letter to the states explaining the necessity for the unusual grant of authority given Washington. Ford, ed., *Journals of Congress*, VI, 1047, 1053.

19. Fitzpatrick, ed., *Writings of Washington*, 263.

20. Gruber, "Illusions of Mastery," chap. viii; Stuart Wortley, *A Prime Minister and His Son*, 113; Jane Clark, "The Responsibility for the Failure of the Burgoyne Campaign," *American Historical Review*, XXXV (1930), 554; Brown, *American Secretary*, 125–126; Willcox, *Portrait of a General*, 153–168. Before sailing, Howe informed Germain that should Washington march northward against Burgoyne, he would have "no room to dread the event." However, he added vaguely that if the American General made Burgoyne his sole objective, "he may soon find himself exposed to an attack from this quarter"; but since Howe would be at sea, would he learn in time? Historical Manuscripts Commission, *Stopford-Sackville MSS*, II, 72–73.

21. Anderson, *Command of the Howe Brothers*, 277.

22. For examples, see Ward, *War of the Revolution*, I, 331–332; Fortescue, *History of the British Army*, III, 214, and to a lesser extent Wallace, *Appeal to Arms*, 136.

23. W. H. Moomaw, "The Denouement of General Howe's Campaign of 1777," *English Historical Review*, LXXIX (1964), 498–512. Moomaw shows that Hamond's testimony at the Parliamentary inquiry of 1779 into the campaign, in which he claimed the American defenses on the Delaware were too formidable for the fleet to breach in short order, was in flat contradiction to his opinions in 1777. Hamond, a protégé of the Admiral, was out to protect his chief. Even so, his answers were not always convincing, one contemporary calling them "artful misrepresentations to justify his Patron." *Ibid.*, 510. For a partial corroboration of Moomaw's account, see Tatum, ed., *American Journal of Ambrose Serle*, 241. Gruber, "Illusions of Mastery," chap. viii, stresses the "docile, passive role" of Lord Howe in the campaign. It is worth noting that William Howe had thought

of going by way of the Chesapeake before his conversation with Hamond, although his mind was apparently not made up prior to entering Delaware Bay. Clinton, *American Rebellion*, 65.

24. A little less than a year later Clinton moved overland from Philadelphia to Sandy Hook in twelve days.

25. G. W. Greene, *N. Greene*, I, 439. On July 30, Washington wrote Horatio Gates, "Genl Howe's in a manner abandoning Genl Burgoyne, is so unaccountable a matter, that till I am fully assured it is so, I cannot help casting my eyes continually behind me." Fitzpatrick, ed., *Writings of Washington*, VIII, 499.

26. John F. Reed, *Campaign to Valley Forge, July 1, 1777–December 19, 1777* (Philalephia, 1965), 71–72, 75, 85–86, 93; Uhlendorf, ed., *Revolution in America*, 97–99; Thayer, *Greene*, 190; Historical Manuscripts Commission, *Stopford-Sackville MSS*, II, 74–75; Brown, *American Secretary*, 126–127.

27. The opinion of Fortescue, *History of the British Army*, III, 221.

28. Whittemore, *General of the Revolution*, 74. If Howe was considering linking his own army with Clinton's by the end of the season, it is not unlikely that the contest at Germantown made him aware he would have his hands full in Pennsylvania for some time to come. On October 9, five days after the battle, he wrote Clinton: "As I shall probably be detained here this winter, I must beg of you not to think me unreasonable when I request you to continue in the command at New York." Anderson, *Command of the Howe Brothers*, 302.

29. *Ibid.*, 299; Fitzpatrick, ed., *Writings of Washington*, X, 149.

30. See Marvin L. Brown, Jr., ed., *Baroness von Riedesel and the American Revolution: Journal and Correspondence of a Tour of Duty, 1776–1783* (Chapel Hill, 1964). A lively biography containing a little new information is Louise Hall Tharp, *The Baroness and the General* (Boston and Toronto, 1962).

31. *The Proceedings of a General Court Martial . . . For the Trial of Major General St. Clair . . .* (Philadelphia, 1778); *Connecticut Courant*, Aug. 4, Sept. 1, 1777; Don R. Gerlach, "Philip Schuyler and 'the Road to Glory': A Question of Loyalty and Competence," *New-York Historical Society Quarterly*, XLIX (1965), 341–386.

32. *Correspondence of Mr. Ralph Izard of South Carolina . . .* (New York, 1844), 333; Brown, *American Secretary*, 123; G. W. Greene, *N. Greene*, I, 431.

33. For the McCrea episode, see W. W. Holl, *Old Fort Edward* (Fort Edward, N.Y., 1929), a careful local history; James A. Holden, "Influence of the Death of Jane McCrea on the Burgoyne Campaign," New York State Historical Association, *Proceedings*, XII (1913), 249–310; Commager and Morris, eds., *Spirit of 'Seventy-Six*, I, 558–561. According to a newly published British contemporary account by nineteen-year-old Lord Francis Napier, Jane McCrea's death occurred on July 26; but, as Napier's laconic entries show, Burgoyne's reprimanding the Indians "in very severe terms for their late behaviour" had minimal effect. On July 30, the redmen appeared in camp with five scalps, on August 3 with fifteen more. S. Sydney Bradford, ed., "Lord Francis Napier's Journal of the Burgoyne Campaign," *Maryland Historical Magazine*, LVII (1962), 306–308. Information from American Major Henry Dearborn suggests the patriots were beginning to reply in kind: on August 8 "an Indian Scalp was Brought in . . . By a Party of our men which is a Rareety with us." Lloyd A. Brown and Howard H. Peckham, eds., *Revolutionary War Journals of Henry Dearborn* (Chicago, 1939), 100. A most vivid description of the act of taking a scalp is set forth in Sydney Jackman, ed., *With Burgoyne from Quebec . . . Volume One of [Thomas Anburey's] Travels through the Interior Parts of North America* (Toronto, 1963), 168–169. This is to a considerable degree a paste-pot-and-scissors account, plagiarized from other contemporaries, so that, while interesting and valuable, it is questionable whether one should consider it a primary source. See Whitfield J. Bell, Jr., "Thomas Anburey's 'Travels Through America': A Note on Eighteenth-Century Plagiarism," Bibliographical Society of America, *Papers*, XXXVII (1943), 23–36.

34. Brown, ed., *Baroness von Riedesel*, 44–45, 55–56; Tharp, *Baroness and the General*,

176; Ray W. Pettengill, ed., *Letters from America, 1776–1779* (Boston and New York, 1924), 78–79. The Baroness, though unable to bring herself to sampling rattlesnake, ate bear meat for the first time and thought it delicious.

35. Mackesy, *War for America*, 133; Commager and Morris, eds., *Spirit of 'Seventy-Six*, I, 570.

36. Clifford K. Shipton, "Benjamin Lincoln: Old Reliable," in *George Washington's Generals*, ed. Billias, 195–196. Mackesy, *War for America*, 135, implies that Carleton used Germain's instructions as an excuse to drag his feet. However, Brown, *American Secretary*, 123, quotes Burgoyne's subsequent testimony that Carleton "could not have shown more indefatigable zeal than he did, to comply with and expedite my requisitions and desires." See also Smith, "Sir Guy Carleton: Soldier-Statesman," in *George Washington's Opponents*, ed. Billias, 127–128.

37. John Burgoyne, *State of the Expedition from Canada*, Appendix, xxv–xxvi; Mackesy, *War for America*, 136. Upon hearing of Burgoyne's difficulties in July and August, Germain confided to Undersecretary William Knox: "the best wish I can form is that he [Burgoyne] may have returned to Ticonderoga without much loss." Commager and Morris, eds., *Spirit of 'Seventy-Six*, I, 580.

38. Fitzpatrick, ed., *Writings of Washington*, IX, 71, 78. Soon American leaders were spreading the word that 1,000 riflemen were on the way. Horatio Gates to Benjamin Lincoln, Aug. 23, 1777, Gates Papers, New-York Historical Society. For Schuyler's mixing of politics and war, see Gerlach, *Schuyler*, 300–311; George Dangerfield, *Chancellor Robert R. Livingston of New York, 1746–1813* (New York, 1960), 95–96. Schuyler may have been as unattractive to the common people of New York as he was to the New Englanders in his army; for Gerlach, *Schuyler*, 309–311, states on the basis of partial election records that the soldiers' vote against Schuyler was likely a "decisive factor" in his defeat at the hands of George Clinton.

39. Burgoyne, *State of the Expedition*, 122; Brown and Peckham, eds., *Revolutionary War Journals of Henry Dearborn*, 105; James P. Baxter, *The British Invasion from the North with the Journal of Lieut. William Digby* (Albany, 1887), 269–270; "Journal of Oliver Boardman," Connecticut Historical Society, *Collections*, VII (1899), 224–227; Gates to Schuyler, Sept. 14, 1777, Gates Papers, New-York Historical Society. On September 18, Burgoyne, deploring the army's heavy attrition from the rebels' bushwacking activities, announced in general orders "That the first Soldier caught beyond the Advanced Centry . . . will be instantly Hanged," E. B. O'Callahan, ed., *John Burgoyne's Orderly Book* (Albany, 1860), 113.

40. R. Lamb, *Memoirs of His Own Life* (Dublin, 1809), 199; Pettengill, ed., *Letters from America*, 80–81. Burgoyne, *State of the Expedition*, 122, singled out the role of the American riflemen: "these . . . hovered upon the flanks in small detachments, and were very expert in securing themselves, and in shifting the ground . . . many placed themselves in high trees in the rear of their own line, and there was seldom a minute's interval in any part of our line without officers being taken off by single shot."

Gates' careful planning in the weeks before the battle, a reflection of his administrative talents, may be seen in his correspondence in the New-York Historical Society, especially beginning with his letter of Aug. 31, 1777, to Benjamin Lincoln. For a description of the battlefield, see C. W. Snell and F. F. Wilshin, *Saratoga National Historical Park* (National Park Service, *Historical Handbook* [Washington, 1959]).

41. Willcox, *Portrait of a General*, 174–196; Willcox, "Too Many Cooks," 78–90; Mackesy, *War for America*, 137–140.

42. In the House of Commons, Burgoyne subsequently called upon Earl Balcarres, a card-playing companion during the Saratoga campaign, to support his ill-conceived planning on October 7: "Q[uestion]. From the nature of the country, and the situation of the enemy's out-posts, was it possible to reconnoitre their

position? A[nswer]. From the nature of the country, the difficulties attending reconnoitering must have been very great. Q[uestion]. Were not the riflemen, and other irregulars, employed by the enemy at outposts and on scouts, an overmatch for the Indian or provincial troops that were with the army at that time? A[nswer]. They were." Burgoyne, *State of the Expedition*, 30. See also William L. Stone, ed., *Journal of Captain George Pausch* (Albany, 1886), 161–165. See also *Connecticut Courant*, Sept. 20, 29, Oct. 14, 1777.

43. Brown, ed., *Baroness von Riedesel and the American Revolution*, 50–63; Tharp, *Baroness and the General*, 204–225; Jackman, ed., *With Burgoyne from Quebec*, 190–194; Max von Eelking, *Memoirs and Letters and Journals of Major General Riedesel during his Residence in America*, trans. William L. Stone (Albany, 1868), I, 174; Burgoyne, *State of the Expedition*, 54.

A German described the nights as "bitterly cold and freezing." Pettengill, ed., *Letters from America*, 102. On the American side, Lieutenant Joseph Hodgkins complained that it was a "Cool Country & I should Be glad of a pr Mittens." H. T. Wade and R. A. Lively, *This Glorious Cause: The Adventures of Two Company Officers in Washington's Army* (Princeton, 1958), 115.

44. Lamb, *Memoirs of His Own Life*, 166.

45. William M. Dabney, *After Saratoga: the Story of the Convention Army* (Albuquerque, 1954); Jane Clark, "The Convention Troops and the Perfidy of Sir William Howe," *American Historical Review*, XXXVII (1932), 721–723; Knollenberg, *Washington and the Revolution*, 140–150.

46. For many years historians spilled much ink over which American leader deserves the greatest credit for Burgoyne's humiliation. Fortunately, many scholars can now examine the military performance of Gates and Arnold without looking ahead to Gates' alleged rivalry with Washington or to Arnold's treason. The Gates-Arnold animosity in the Saratoga campaign, probably born of ambition and temperament, as well as Arnold's friendship with Schuyler, is a sorry story, redounding to the advantage of neither man, and it will not be repeated here. At the same time, both have suffered unfairly at the hands of the most widely cited source for the campaign: James Wilkinson's *Memoirs of My Own Times*, 3 vols. (Philadelphia, 1816). Only twenty in 1777, Wilkinson was already displaying some of the defects of character that characterized his involvement with Aaron Burr. With regard to Gates and Arnold, Wilkinson, who denied them both the recognition they deserved in the victory over Burgoyne, might as well be laid to rest.

For the part of Morgan's riflemen, see Don Higginbotham, *Daniel Morgan: Revolutionary Rifleman* (Chapel Hill, 1961), 60–77. The latest and perhaps best summary of Gates' contribution is George A. Billias, "Horatio Gates: Professional Soldier," in *George Washington's Generals*, ed. Billias, 90–97.

47. An excellent account of the Parliamentary inquiry is Gruber, "Illusions of Mastery," chap. xi. See also Gerald S. Brown, ed., *Reflections on a Pamphlet Intitled "a Letter to the Right Honble. Lord Vict. H - E."* (Ann Arbor, 1959).

# 9. Civil-Military Tensions, 1777-1778

THE GREAT FRENCH LEADER Georges Clemenceau once declared that war was too important a matter to entrust to the military. Events of the last half century presumably indicate that the generals consider politics too vital a business for the politicians. No fewer than thirty-two of the fifty-one states that existed in 1917 have subsequently suffered military coups, while at least fifteen of the twenty-eight nations created between the Treaty of Versailles and 1955 have undergone the same experience. To determine the exact count of military revolutions more recently would not be easy, but that number, along with open or veiled rule by the sword, is undoubtedly large.

In the ancient world armies were generally less politically motivated than those in the modern era. Roman armies from the time of Marius and Sulla, lacking political and social programs, acted from individual self-interest—the desire to put their commanders in office and to gain rewards; they fought for a particular leader rather than for a definable object. With few exceptions, notably Cromwell's New Model army, it was only after 1789—and on a wider scale after 1917 or possibly 1945 —that the military has intervened in the name of the nation as a whole with a comprehensive program for change, variously including anti-corruption, anti-inflation, along with social and political reform for the people.

One can readily enough see why the experience of America—"the first new nation" in Seymour Lipset's phrase—was so counter to that of many of the twentieth century's emerging nations.[1] In lands of low political culture the cloth of legitimacy will seldom serve as a deterrent to the armed forces, for there is absent a tradition of civilian politics and self-government. The military, moreover, may provide a type of bureaucracy, men with professional training in organization and administration often wanting in societies not far above primitive status. America, to be sure, had its share of internal problems during and immediately following the War of Independence, some of them owing to an inadequate currency, a lack of sufficient industrialism, and the absence of adequate machinery and authority in the central government. But ethnically homogeneous, and without deep social or sectarian fissures, Americans were able to utilize their natural wealth and political experience to overcome the roadblocks inherent in the transition from colonialism to independence and to establish an administrative system more efficient than that of the mother country. We know additionally that no small fragment of the patriots' political philosophy condemned standing armies, quartering of troops on civilians, and uniting civil and military authority.

## The Army: A Threat or a Promise?

Hindsights, however, afforded no comfort for the living, for a John Adams, a James Lovell, or a Benjamin Rush. While sensitive Europeans feared standing armies in peacetime, wrote Washington, Americans were equally prejudiced against them in wartime. Such fears he deemed ridiculous: "they [the Continentals] are Citizens having all the ties, and interests of Citizens, and in most cases property totally unconnected with the Military Line. . . . We should all be considered Congress [,] Army, and as one people, embarked in one cause . . . and [with] the same End."[2] Congress agreed in theory, and similar statements emanated from that body on its adopting the New England regiments before Boston in 1775. But history showed, particularly with regard to soldiers and statesmen, that power often corroded even those who began with the most honorable intentions.

Jefferson, scarcely holding a Calvinist opinion of mankind, believed that "military habits" by their very nature inculcated monarchial attitudes. Benjamin Rush criticized the proposed constitution for Corsica drawn up by Mrs. Catherine Macaulay, the whig historian, because it permitted generals and admirals to vote in the legislature. "Men who have fought in the defense of their country," warned Rush, "claim superiority over the rest of their countrymen . . . and would render the transition from democracy to anarchy, and from anarchy to monarchy, very natural and easy."[3] Samuel Adams conveyed that same feeling to James Warren: "a standing army, however necessary it may be at sometimes, is always dangerous to the liberties of the people. Soldiers are apt to consider themselves as a body distinct from the rest of the citizens. They have their arms always in their hands. Their rules and their discipline is severe. They soon become attached to their officers and disposed to yield implicit obedience to their commands. Such a power should be watched with a jealous eye."[4]

Such predilections reverberated in all the state constitutions, which usually began with a declaration of rights enumerating, among other things, Americans' antipathy to peacetime forces, and calling for the control of civil authority over the military, the citizens' freedom from the quartering of troops in their homes, and the need to limit military appropriations to a given time. A typical provision, and indeed a model for subsequent documents in other states, was George Mason's statement in the Virginia Declaration of Rights "That a well-regulated militia, composed of the body of the people, trained to arms, is the proper, natural and safe defence of a free State; that standing armies in time of peace should be avoided as dangerous to liberty; and that in all cases the military should be under strict subordination to, and governed by, the civil power." The North Carolina constitution prohibited officers of the Continental army and navy, as well as those in the state forces, from occupying seats in the legislature. And the Continental Congress stirred uneasily because of a report that New York dared to elect Philip Schuyler a member of that assemblage without first demanding his resignation from the army.

The Articles of Confederation, the first constitution of the United States, also registered America's anti-militarist tradition. Though the document authorized Congress "to build and equip a navy," it spoke only vaguely of the army. The word *army* appears only once, where the articles proclaim that Congress may not "appoint a commander in chief of the army or navy, unless nine [of the thirteen] states assent to the same." There are several references to "the land forces of the United States," which were to be raised by the states and officered by the states below the rank of general. This first constitution forbade Congress from engaging "in a war . . . in time of peace," the meaning of which is scarcely clear. This much is certain: the right to maintain after the Revolution a permanent military establishment—a standing army—however small, though conceivably implied, was not expressly granted to Congress. In any event, Congress received proposals from Massachusetts, Pennsylvania, New Jersey, and Connecticut urging limitations on its military power, the last two states calling for an explicit amendment providing that the Confederation should sustain no armed body whatsoever in peacetime. Congress, however, eschewed all alterations that might delay presenting the articles to the states. But the subject of standing armies, including the original intention of the framers of the articles, appeared again in later years when the lawmakers turned their attention to postwar defense.[5]

During the war distrust of the military at times reached almost unbelievable lengths, as in the case of an appeal for clothing from Pennsylvania officers at Valley Forge to the civil authorities of their state. The politicians accused the officers of desiring to deck themselves out in beaver hats, gold lace, and other unbecoming finery, when in fact Washington's subordinates would have gladly settled for simple home-spun. When an officer in 1776 reputedly spoke abusively of Congress and its president, the lawmakers directed the man to make a public apology in their presence. Sam Adams dourly remarked that an officer who would drink a toast to the army before first downing a tumbler in honor of Congress exposed himself to suspicion of favoring a military dictatorship.

There were two periods in the war when Congressional apprehension of the military, and, conversely, the army's disapproval of Congressional doings, were most pronounced: first in the fall, winter, and spring of 1777-1778; second, in the final months of the war—a story relegated to a later chapter.

By 1777, Congress might readily consider the generals of the Continental army more than a little fractious. In that year alone friction cropped up between Sullivan and St. Clair, Greene and Mifflin, Gates and Schuyler, and Gates and Arnold. To John Adams, ever keeping "a watchful eye over the army," these service rivalries could well portend ambitious American generals leading their divisions against each other, as the Roman commanders Sulla and Fimbria had done. The American generals were not Romans; nor were they of a feudal nobility, the only class according to Frederick the Great truly worthy of officer status, men driven by a sense of honor and status to bear hardship, danger, and death without flinching or anticipation of reward. If Frederick's aristocrats evinced such stoicism in arms—certainly Britain's did not—they found no parallel in the American service. John Adams exclaimed that he was "wearied to Death with the Wrangles between military officers, high and low. They Quarrell like Cats and Dogs. They worry one another like Mastiffs Scrambling for Rank and Pay like Apes for Nuts."[6]

In a sense Congress in arrogating to itself full authority for naming generals was responsible for many of the military rivalries. Of necessity officers looked to the politicians for preferment rather than to Washington or the other senior generals. Some congressmen established a regular correspondence with certain officers and encouraged them to confide their innermost thoughts. Adams himself in the early years of the struggle exchanged frequent letters with Charles Lee, Horatio Gates, and Nathanael Greene.[7] In February, 1777, Congress debated the question of seeking advice on the appointment of several major generals from the general officers of the army. "If the motion is passed," declared Benjamin Rush sardonically, "I shall move immediately afterwards that all civil power of the continent may be transferred from our hands into the hands of the army, and that they may be proclaimed the highest power of the people." The motion failed, along with Washington's request that three lieutenant generals be selected from among the general officers. Congress did, however, choose five major generals —Lord Stirling, Thomas Mifflin, Arthur St. Clair, Adam Stephen, and Benjamin Lincoln—all of whom were inferior in rank and ability to the passed-over Benedict Arnold, whose state of Connecticut, to Congress' way of thinking, possessed sufficient officers of that grade for the regiments it had in service. When Congress belatedly, and at Washington's urging, advanced Arnold to equal rank with the others, it rejected the Connecticut ex-apothecary's plea for a restoration of his seniority. Henry Laurens, a member from South Carolina, thought Congress' "reasoning upon this occasion was disgusting." Arnold, he claimed, was turned down "not because he was deficient in merit or that his demand was not well founded but because he had asked for it and that granting at such an instance would be derogatory to the honour of Congress."[8]

For Washington this was a near-maddening time. General Andrew Lewis, his feathers ruffled at not receiving a major generalcy, resigned his commission, as did Colonel John Stark who resented the omission of his name from the list of officers raised to brigade command. The appointment of French and other foreign officers soon added fuel to the fire. Moreover, the lawmakers were after the scalps of several generals in late 1777, especially St. Clair, Schuyler, and Sullivan for alleged failures in the field. North Carolina's delegate Dr. Thomas Burke and Sullivan traded insulting epistles over the latter's conduct at Brandywine, prompting a feud that lasted until 1781.[9]

No civilian found more fault with the generals of the Continental army than the prominent Philadelphian physician Benjamin Rush, a sharp-tongued, highly opinionated man, who subsequently accepted a medical post in Washington's own Middle Department. To John Adams, a kindred spirit, he lambasted "the ignorance, the cowardice, and the drunkenness of our major generals." Congress, he proposed, should ration intoxicants to the American commanders, and any officer who consumed over a quart of whisky or got drunk more than once in twenty-four hours should be censured in front of his unit. Congress should also require the generals to sleep in their boots and order them to remain no more than 500 yards in the rear of their troops during battle. Few escaped Rush's vitriol: Sullivan—"weak, vain, without dignity, fond of scribling, in the field a mad man"; Stirling—"a proud, vain, lazy ignorant drunkard"; Edward Stevens—"a sordid, boasting cowardly sot." Rush concurred with John Adams' remedy: the annual election of all general officers, a step that would sweep away the deadwood, infuse the generals with "a Spirit of Enterprize," and keep the officers rooted to republican principles.[10]

## Washington: Caesar, Fabius, or Cincinnatus?

Quite predictably fears and criticism of the military in general in 1777 descended upon "one great man" in particular—the commander in chief. As Baron de Kalb said, Americans hailed "their General Washington . . . the first of all heroes ancient and modern; Alexander, Condé, Broglie, Ferdinand and the King of Prussia are not to be compared to him. . . . It is not only the lower classes;—clever people, or those passing for such, have the same opinion."[11] These were only normal sentiments among a people without a pantheon of heroes, a people groping for unity and national identity and lacking a president or other form of chief executive to symbolize the cause. It was equally understandable that particular congressmen, stout-hearted republicans and more than a trifle sensitive to slights toward their own body, would think that the veneration—"superstitious veneration," grumbled John Adams —was being carried too far. Already Americans were attributing heroic and inspirational qualities to the tall Virginian that would echo in the turgid prose of Parson Weems, who, it should be remembered, reflected the Washington image instead of creating it.[12]

Ironically, Washington's bitterest detractor, Dr. Rush, had his hand in the early near-deification of the commander in chief. In October, 1775, amidst his full flush of enthusiasm for the conflict, the Doctor boasted of Washington's "wonderful talents," "zeal," "disinterestedness," and "politeness," "one of those illustrious heroes whom providence raises up once in three or four hundred years to save a nation from ruin." There was "not a king in Europe that would not look like a valet de chambre by his side." That may have been the trouble; the tall, dignified Virginian did resemble a king. Repeatedly professing his belief in civil supremacy and deferring important military questions to Congress, he appeared too good to be true; so good that by 1777 Rush feared he would keep alive a respect for monarchy, and, urged on by myriad idolators, would assume an American throne as George I, successor to George III. John Adams thanked heaven that Gates, not Washington, had worsted Burgoyne; otherwise "Idolatry and Adulation" of Washington would have inundated the land. Adams himself conceded the commander in chief to be "wise, virtuous, and good, without thinking him a Deity or saviour."[13]

Rush was not so charitable. Weak, vacillating, dependent on advisors, Washington, thought the Doctor, was a likely tool or prop for designing men. And after Brandywine and Germantown, if not before, he concluded that the General was militarily incompetent to boot. It is doubtful whether more than a few shared Rush's fear of monarchy or dictatorship on Washington's part, but the sentiment that he had waged a disappointing campaign in Pennsylvania was more wide-spread. Even the most naïve armchair general—they were like leaves on the trees in the fall and winter of 1777–1778—could see that the Virginian's performance had fallen far short of Gates', whatever the explanation might be; Brandywine, Germantown, Philadelphia abandoned, and the Delaware River forts lost. It was claimed, curiously, that the Americans would not fight. James Lovell, former Massachusetts schoolteacher and a persistent critic, disparaged "our Fabius," and elsewhere in Congress there were at least occasional questions or complaints about the leadership of the army in the Philadelphia campaign.[14]

A crucial point, too often missed, is that the Washington fault-finders were mostly outside Congress rather than in its meeting halls. Those most deeply troubled by the posture of military affairs were the leaders of New Jersey and Pennsylvania, the two states that had borne the brunt of British depredations and occupation. And from them, along with Lovell, came the harshest strictures on Washington as a general. Jonathan Dickson Sergeant, attorney general of Pennsylvania and a former member of Congress, exploded to Lovell on November 20, 1777: "Thousands of Lives and millions of Property are yearly sacrificed to the insufficiency of our Commander-in-Chief. Two battles he has lost for us by two such Blunders as might have disgraced a Soldier of three months standing, and yet we are so attached to this Man that I fear we shall rather sink with him than throw him off our shoulders."[15]

Christopher Marshall, an affluent Philadelphia apothecary temporarily residing in Lancaster during the British stay in the Quaker City, learned from Rush and George Bryan, vice president of Pennsylvania, that throughout the state a general murmur arose against Washington's weak conduct. This was hardly startling news to the apothecary who had already confided to his diary this question: "O Washington, where is your courage?" In December, 1777, the Pennsylvania council and assembly protested to Congress against the army's encamping for the winter on the west side of the Schuylkill River, where the troops would feed off farms and towns already crowded with evacuees from Philadelphia, and where they would be in no position to defend eastern Pennsylvania and lower New Jersey from the ravages of the enemy.

There was also a movement in the state to circumvent Washington by calling out the militia and other citizens, a genuine "people's army," to wrest Philadelphia from its conquerors.[16] Dr. Rush who, with George Bryan, appears to have applauded the idea, had beforehand voiced his hope that militia rather than regulars would drive the enemy from American shores. "I should despair of our cause if our country contained 60,000 men abandoned enough to enlist for 3 years or more during the war."[17] Moreover, to civilians, uninformed of military affairs and nursing an aversion to standing armies, the exploits of John Stark and Gates' successful employment of militia tended to confirm their faith in irregulars as the country's first line of defense.

There were Continental officers who, while taking violent exception to relying heavily upon the militia, concurred with Lovell, Rush, and Sergeant that the army's performance had been disgraceful. A Pennsylvanian, Colonel Daniel Broadhead, joined Elias Boudinot of New Jersey, commissary general of prisoners, and Baron de Kalb in pointing an accusing finger squarely at Washington.[18] But for most critics, in Congress, in state government, and in the army, it is not always easy to determine where their chief complaints were directed. Were they aimed at Washington himself as an incompetent, at the officers surrounding him upon whom he relied for advice, or at the confusion and inefficiency that enveloped the army's administration, particularly its supply services? Only a bare handful of men are known to have attacked Washington directly. The most prevalent belief was that he suffered from bad advice in councils of war. The main culprits were "Beardless Youth," especially twenty-seven-year-old Henry Knox and thirty-five-year-old Nathanael Greene.

This criticism was not new, having already found expression in 1776 during operations around New York City. Charles Lee, no admirer of his superior, nevertheless believed Washington should exercise his own judgment and none other, the opinion also of Adjutant General Joseph Reed, Colonel Timothy Pickering, and Colonel John Haslet of Delaware.[19] The following year Anthony Wayne and several other Washington stalwarts voiced similar thinking: the reliance upon military councils, where divisions almost inevitably occurred, too often resulted in Washington's being unsure of himself—the Virginian would better trust to his own good judgment. Henry Laurens, elected president of Congress soon after joining that body, and an admirer of Washington, confided to his son John: "a good Heart may be too diffident, too apprehensive of doing right[,] righteous, proper Acts, lest such should be interpreted arbitrary." Since the charges came from friend and foe alike, it cannot be lightly dismissed. Until early 1777, when he obtained clarification from Congress, Washington mistakenly believed a majority vote in a council of war bound his behavior. By the time he learned otherwise, the habit of frequent councils was largely fixed. But here, as in the view of Washington the Fabian, the complaint of indecision rings somewhat hollow from our vantage point. The General who skillfully extricated his army from death traps at Brooklyn and Trenton, who repeatedly deigned not to let his sword grow rusty in its scabbard, who spent Christmas day, 1777, toying with the idea of essaying a repetition of the previous December's Yuletide blow ("Orders for a Move . . . Intended Against Philadelphia by Way of Surprise") appears to us anything but weak and timid.[20]

Washington indubitably relied greatly on Greene and Knox. If they dominated him, as was sometimes claimed, the proof still rests with their accusers. Except for Greene's error concerning the defense of Fort Washington, there is little evidence they gave him faulty opinions. Of the officers in Washington's immediate command, Greene and Knox were probably the ablest. Were the complainers, even those who were Washington's friends, jealous of these two New England men? The very complexity of the Washington criticism is well revealed in the displeasure of thirty-three-year-old Major General Thomas Mifflin, one-time member of Congress, aid to the commander in chief, and since August, 1775, first quartermaster general of the Continental army, a post he continued to hold—most reluctantly—until the fall of 1777. Plagued by ill health and frustrated by overwhelming supply difficulties, Mifflin retired to his home in Reading, Pennsylvania. Denied the field command he had long sought, Mifflin believed, rightly or wrongly, his influence with Washington declined with the ascendancy of Greene. The Pennsylvanian also saw (by this time through jaundiced eyes) the failure to defend Philadelphia to the last ditch the consequence of Greene's powerful hold on Washington. Mifflin, a loquacious type, continued to vent his spleen, and the Mifflin-Greene feud, soon common knowledge, broadened into the Mifflin-Washington "quarrel"; for an enemy of Greene could hardly be considered close to the commander in chief. But if Mifflin's word is to be taken, he opposed not Washington himself but Washington's favoritism.[21] As if to compound the task of historians in determining the issues, other Americans, in Congress and elsewhere, laid much blame for the army's misfortune at the doorstep of Quartermaster General Mifflin himself.

Confusing as the picture is, this much emerges. There was a plethora of complaining talk, not all of it informed, but most of it well meaning, by Americans in various walks of life who feared that the Revolution had reached a crisis. The sides were anything but neatly drawn; it was not simply hostility of civilians (i.e., congressmen and state politicians) toward some of the generals and the commander in chief. Yet Congress was clearly on edge. Its vanity was wounded by its less than graceful flight from Philadelphia. For months there had been no word from the American commissioners in France, for British war vessels had intercepted their dispatches. Moreover, since the army in the Middle Department had been far short of successful, it was only natural for the lawmakers to spend hours on end deliberating on the reasons for Howe's conquest of Philadelphia. Added to all this, an occasional military man had been quarrelsome and scarcely deferential to the representatives of the states, though on this point the civilians were undoubtedly hypersensitive.

## The Army Views Congress

The army, on the other hand, also had good reason to be touchy. Twice it felt the sting of defeat that fall. Given its mood, a question or rebuke by a single legislator was likely interpreted to mean condemnation of the military in general or a lack of confidence in Washington. The atmosphere at Valley Forge, marked by inaction, hunger, cold, and the absence of every necessity, was in itself sufficient to conjure up devils in the mind. It was said that officers as well as privates were "Covered with Rags and Crawling with vermin." A French officer learned that even some of the generals were reduced to wrapping blankets around themselves due to the absence of warm coats.[22] It became an easy matter for the distraught officers to place the chief blame for the army's failures upon a Congress that raised too few battalions and provided insufficient guns and ammunition.

More justly, the men huddled in tents and drafty huts beyond the Schuylkill found perplexing the legal niceties that could preoccupy the politicians in moments when the patriot cause seemed to hang precariously on a thread—when the strong nationalist James Wilson of Pennsylvania lost a heated debate with the arch-democrat Dr. Thomas Burke over the former's contention that Congress had the right to bypass state dignitaries by calling on constables and other local officials to apprehend suspected deserters; when Abraham Clark of New Jersey unsuccessfully proposed that Congress fault Washington for demanding of loyalists in his state "an oath of allegiance to the United States of America," which, to Clark, seems to have implied national citizenship as opposed to the only kind of citizenship then recognized: that of the separate states. "I have always been a Lover of Civil Law," vowed General John Glover, "and ever wish'd to see America govern'd by it —but I am fully of the Opinion that it would be the Salvation of the Country was Martial Law to take place, at least for 12 Months—and that Genl Washington was invested with power to call forth . . . all the male inhabitants (if wanted) at 24 hours notice; then . . . you would hear that they had compelled the enemy to quit this land, or had him cut to pieces."[23]

Congress was far from constituting an ideal government. Legislative bodies are scarcely characterized by their speed and efficiency, and rarely has one endeavored to direct a war so naked of formal authority as was the Continental Congress. But there were times, such as the winter of 1777–1778, when the dignitaries sitting at York could have demonstrated more understanding of the soldiers' thinking and of their needs. Congressional committees dispatched to Washington's head-quarters, seeing at firsthand conditions in the army, sometimes found the parent body unreceptive to recommended changes or else delayed in accepting them. And at the close of 1777 Congress still dallied over a much sought-after proposal of the officers for a grant of half pay for a period of years after the war and pensions for their widows as com-pensation for their manifold sufferings and hardships, not the least of which was the payment of their salaries in vastly depreciated Conti-nental money.

If the Congress did not always comprehend the army, the officers likewise were ignorant of insuperable handicaps that retarded prompt legislative action. Since the states sent men to Congress, they could and did recall their representatives at will, replacing them with others un-familiar with affairs before that body. Sometimes men chosen to serve declined or attended sporadically because of inadequate remuneration. Congress, in short, was a congeries of delegates, often coming, often going, few remaining the long periods necessary to keep abreast of the army's needs. Instead of the three or more representatives from each of the thirteen states deemed requisite to fill committees and handle general business, President Laurens at the onset of 1778 outlined the situation to the governor of Rhode Island. The "extra-ordinary and unreasonable" burdens of Congress, he complained, "Fall heavily upon a very few Members[.] from 17 to 21, who faithfully attend their duty at the expense of domestic happiness and the improvement of their private Estates." In fact, some sessions witnessed "barely 9 States on the floor represented by as many persons."[24]

The army, furthermore, scarcely realized that Congress faced thorny problems with the flood of soldiers of fortune—truly "citizens of the world" in the eighteenth century—who hammered at the doors of Con-gress in quest of high Continental commissions. The lawmakers ap-proved the employment of officers skilled in military areas where Americans lacked proficiency, particularly in the artillery and engi-neers. Unfortunately, however, Silas Deane, one of the American com-missioners in France, proved unable to withstand the deluge of appli-cants who descended upon him from all quarters. Deane, considering himself "well-nigh harassed to death," sent the unqualified and the scoundrels together with such admirable figures as de Kalb, von Steuben, Pulaski, and Duportail. When Congress instructed Deane to make no more of his ill-considered agreements, it still had to deal with the foreigners already on the scene. Most of them were Frenchmen, and the patriot leaders feared that mass rejections would impair relations with the government of Louis XVI. To accept them, on the other hand, meant prominent American officers stood to be outranked by some of the newcomers. Congress' *bête noire* turned out to be Colonel Philippe du Coudray, an adjutant general in the French army and an engineer highly acclaimed by Foreign Minister Vergennes. The thoughtless Deane signed the man to a contract stipulating him a major general, his commission pre-dated August 1, 1776, and making him head of the Continental artillery, all of which, if carried out, would have placed him above Greene and Sullivan in seniority and resulted in Knox's removal as artillery chief. The three American generals exploded in indignation, all writing Congress on the same day, promising or implying to resign if the promised favors were accorded the Frenchman. Congress, refusing to honor Deane's commitment, expressed equal indignation at the bargain but resolved to find the artilleryman another post; for du Coudray was supposed to be highly placed at court and in a position to acquire immense quantities of supplies for the army. Initially, however, Congress was more disturbed by Greene and company's alleged lack of respect for civil authority. John Adams, basically sympathetic toward the three New England officers, so upbraided Greene for his epistle that it terminated their correspondence for all time. Happily for all concerned, except du Coudray, that gentleman fell from a ferry and drowned in the Schuylkill.[25]

Along with the innumerable cases of embarrassment and irritation and the fewer cases of highmindedness and dedication, there was Lafayette, nineteen years old upon arrival, tall and thin, his reddish-brown hair pressed back from a distinctly receding brow. Years afterward Lafayette described his coming to America in terms of his love of freedom and human rights. The manner and deportment of the young man who joined Washington's army in 1777 would seemingly bear out his representation of half a century later. Awkward and ill at ease but eager to win friends and gain approval, he expressed a willingness to forego the promises of preferment from Silas Deane, offered to serve as a volunteer without reward. So apparently genuine were his professions of concern for the American cause that Congress straightway bestowed upon the reserve captain in the French army the rank of major general.

The Lafayette of reality, as he emerges from the exhaustive studies of Louis Gottschalk, was someone else. Reared in a rural setting and dominated by female members of his family, the young nobleman felt insecure in the world of Versailles and dreamed of military glories. Encouraged by his former commander, the Comte de Broglie (who hoped to supersede Washington), and filled with hatred of Britain, Lafayette departed for America. If at the time and even later he talked of fighting for freedom, he did little more than parrot a current phrase. It was during his stay in America, slowly and at times almost imperceptibly, that the young man learned to understand American ways and to comprehend the patriots' meaning of liberty. Eventually he was, perhaps, all that he had claimed to be in 1777, a man who returned to France to champion the abolition of Negro slavery, toleration of Protestants, a written constitution, and a bill of rights. But Gottschalk illuminates what was in truth an infinitely complex process.[26]

### The Conway Cabal

Considering the distraught mental state of Congress and the army, the Conway Cabal was not a surprising concomitant of developments in 1777. Contemporaries made so much of the handful of known facts that it was, until recent years, tempting for historians to conclude that the *whole* story was buried in the silence of the exposed conspirators. But what has been clear in legend remains cloudy in history. The legend is, basically, that there was a concerted effort to remove Washington as commander in chief in the fall and winter of 1777–1778. The list of participants included Mifflin and Rush; and in Congress, Richard Henry Lee, Francis Lightfoot Lee, John Adams, Samuel Adams, James Lovell, Elbridge Gerry, and William Duer. Their aim was the elevation of Gates; their method, the sowing of dissension and discord; their chief tool, General Thomas Conway, an Irish-born French officer, an alleged military expert, whose assignment was to expose Washington's grave defects as commander of the army.

Conway unfailingly nourished the qualifications for the role. Possessed of a sharp tongue, he evinced a willingness to use it against his new comrades in arms, such as his immediate superior, Lord Stirling, who was, as Conway apprised Congress, overly fond of liquor. If Conway, like most foreigners, boasted of his talents, his performance reinforced his pretensions. Appointed a brigadier in May, 1777, he demonstrated steadiness under fire and made his brigade one of the best drilled in the army. Jealousy may well have contributed to Conway's ultimate fall from grace. But given his imperious manner and biting sarcasm, coupled with a failing attempt to gain seniority over a number of equally deserving brigadiers, Conway became—with the death of du Coudray—the most unpopular officer, French or American, in the Continental service. One can almost conjecture that had Conway not played into the hands of the American officers at Valley Forge, they would have fabricated a cause célèbre with the Frenchman. As it was, what did happen may not have been far from that; at least few vouchsafed to give him the benefit of a doubt.

It was young James Wilkinson, Gates' aide, who touched off the explosion. Dispatched from Saratoga to bring the news of Burgoyne's capitulation to Congress in Philadelphia, Wilkinson told a Major McWilliams of Lord Stirling's staff of perusing a letter in Gates' papers from Conway casting aspersions on Washington's generalship. The Major passed the tidbit on to Stirling, who, angry, and doubtless glad of the opportunity to retaliate against Conway for his own injury, brought the matter to Washington's attention. In the weeks and months that followed, Washington acted far more human than his nineteenth-century biographers would admit. Normally poised and serene, the Virginian was a deeply sensitive man who never took lightly to criticism, not earlier as a militia commander on the frontier or later in the Presidency. Though more prickly than some, he was nonetheless on this point a child of his age—when the idea of a loyal, constructive opposition was little understood or appreciated. Yet in fairness to Washington, it can be said that not all of the criticism he encountered in many years of public service was of a healthy variety; certainly the cavilers in 1777–1778 were not always aware of the burdens and obstacles confronting him.

With regard to the already unpopular Conway, Washington refused to turn the other cheek. Without checking with Gates on the authenticity of Stirling's report, Washington dispatched a brief, stinging note to Conway on November 9: "Sir: A Letter which I receivd last Night, containd the following paragraph. In a letter from Genl. Conway to Genl. Gates he says: 'Heaven has been determined to save your Country; or a weak General and bad Councellors would have ruind it.' I am Sir Yr. Hble Servt."[27]

Conway promptly denied the reputed phrases, though he candidly acknowledged having made critical remarks on the general state of military affairs and of the officers on whom Washington relied for advice. Whatever Conway had expressed to Gates, he was free to state his opinions, as, of course, were Rush, Lovell, and other critics. And in a subsequent missive to Washington, Conway quite correctly observed that in European armies frank expressions concerning ranking officers were commonplace. "Must . . . an odious and tyrannical inquisition begin in this country? Must it be introduced by the Commander-in-chief of this army raised for the defence of liberty? It cannot be, and I am satisfied you never had such thoughts."[28]

Washington had responded perhaps intemperately, but he had no desire to expand and publicize the affair with Conway. Congress all unwittingly stoked the flames by raising Conway to major general to occupy the newly established office of inspector general, the date (November 6) virtually coinciding with Stirling's exposure of the Frenchman to Washington (November 8). Simultaneously Congress reorganized the Board of War, hitherto simply a standing committee of the lawmakers concerned with supply and administration, so that three nonmembers were added: Gates was selected president, the victor at Saratoga whose accomplishments that autumn were being contrasted to Washington's failures; Mifflin, former quartermaster general, the gossip who was hostile to Greene, if not to Washington himself; and (after Connecticut's Joseph Trumbull declined to serve) Timothy Pickering, whose earlier comments on the men around the commander in chief were apparently no secret.

With allowance for an occasional dissident, the officers of the Continental army were steadfastly loyal to Washington. Already somewhat disgruntled with some aspects of Congressional leadership, Generals Greene, Knox, Schuyler, Lafayette, Stirling, Cadwalader, Varnum, and Colonels Daniel Morgan, Henry Laurens, Alexander Hamilton, Tench Tilghman and others too quickly put two and two together and came up with a one-word conclusion: *conspiracy.* As to the purpose of the plotters the officers at first confessed they were in the dark; but at the very least the elevation of Conway amounted to a rebuke to the many brigadiers exceeding him in seniority and an effort to embarrass Washington, while the army's representation on the Board of War consisted of men who were suspect regarding their loyalty to the commander in chief. Congress, on the other hand, could point to the extensive administrative experience of the trio: Gates and Pickering were former adjutants general and Mifflin an ex-quartermaster general. As for Conway, his was a staff rather than a line appointment, which meant he would not actually command the brigadiers he now outranked.

If one can rightly feel compassion for Conway, who later apologized to Washington for any harm he might have caused him, the same is true for Gates. Yet the Northern commander's behavior on hearing of the rifling of his correspondence led Washington's supporters to implicate him in the cabal. Gates, of course, had only been the recipient of Conway's expressions—"a collection of just sentiments," declared Mifflin, who notified Gates of their disclosure to Washington. In a nervous letter to Washington, Gates acted as though there was plenty to hide. He begged Washington's aid in apprehending the "wretch" who "stealingly copied" from his letters; "but which of them, when, and by whom" was "as yet an unfathomable secret." There was no sympathy for Washington, no statement at all as to Conway's supposed aspersions, only the implication that Conway was Gates' regular correspondent. Gates had every right to be indignant, but not hysterical, and in closing he went from bad to worse, announcing his intention of informing Congress of the matter.[29]

There is no convincing evidence of Gates' participating in any scheme to turn out Washington. Why then the air of panic in his missive to Washington? Gates was highly susceptible to flattery, and following Saratoga he basked in a flood of congratulatory letters, many of which must have directly or indirectly pointed out how much more salutary were developments in the Northern Department than in Washington's Middle Department. Gates and Washington were not close, and Gates' estimation of the commander in chief by this time was evidently none too high.[30] Probably for these reasons, plus Gates' Northern victory, Rush, Lovell, and apparently Conway confided to him their blunt, unflattering opinions of Washington. Therefore any number of Gates' letters could well lead a suspicious mind to conclude that Gates fully shared the sentiments and ambitions of his correspondents. If Gates himself can be condemned, it is only because he failed to defend Washington against his detractors, which from the standpoint of unity and harmony (if not from his own personal conviction) was highly desirable.

Washington and Gates exchanged a series of letters dealing with Conway's epistle that would have been better left unwritten. Washington's redounded with sarcasm; Gates squirmed uncomfortably and protested his innocence, which was probably a fact, though his choice of language—"the spirit and import of your different Letters, and sometimes of the different parts of the same Letter with each other"—only increased Washington's antagonism. Rarely was Washington ever so ill-tempered, disposing of Conway as one "capable of all the malignity of detraction and all the meanesses of intrigue, to gratify the absurd resentment of disappointed vanity, or to answer the purpose of personal aggrandizement, and promote the interests of faction."[31]

It was anything but Washington's finest hour. By this time, however, he was convinced of the existence of a party that wanted not only to oust him from command, but that wished to humiliate and discredit him as well. The evidence, such as it was, amounted to guilt by association or by implication: the friends of Gates, the admirers of Conway, the enemies of Greene, the critics of anything that Washington had done—all stood convicted at the bar of justice. Perhaps the overriding reason Washington succumbed to this view of a plot was the fact that all those around him—his "military family"—thought one existed. From outside the army, too, Washington was bombarded with tales of conspiracy—by Joseph Jones, Patrick Henry, Dr. James Craik, the Reverend William Gordon. They seem to have taken literally the plea of Hamilton, as expressed to Governor George Clinton of New York, for "all the true and sensible friends of their country" to join the fight to expose the "monster" of party.[32]

The unveiling of the intriguers now took on the characteristics of a witch hunt, not too unlike episodes of hysteria and character assassination during periods of crisis in later American history. Tench Tilghman,

a Washington aide, denied to Gates any contribution to the victory
over Burgoyne, just as Colonel John Laurens stripped Conway of certain
soldierly qualities he had hitherto acknowledged. Brigadier General
James Varnum felt that a duel or two would set the conspirators back
on their heels, and, as if in response, General Cadwalader shot Conway through the mouth in an "affair of honor." Before that event, and
before the discredited foreigner returned to France, Lafayette refused
to lead an ill-conceived "iruption" into Canada early in 1778 because
Conway was to be his second in command. Congress, according to
Abraham Clark of New Jersey, who himself had questioned some of
Washington's decisions, recognized its tactical error in appointing
Conway inspector general, and for that reason decided to employ that
officer in Canada, far from the wrathful veterans at Valley Forge. But
Washington's admirers, now suspicious of anything and everything, saw
the matter as only another instance of Congress and the Board of War
engaging in unsavory machinations.

Small wonder that the members of the board were reluctant to visit
the army's encampment to talk over the military's needs, especially
after Colonel Daniel Morgan accosted its secretary, conscientious, hardworking Richard Peters, and informed him that camp talk indicated
his complicity in a plot against Washington. According to Peters, the
sinewy frontiersman shook with anger, their altercation ceasing just
short of violence. Peters had failed to regain his composure two days
later when he described the incident, referring to Morgan's assertion
as "the most villainous of all Falsehoods." Peters further declared (in
words that could as well have been uttered in the Joseph McCarthy
era) that if the charges and countercharges "continue to rage much
longer, I don't see how any Man of Feeling or Sentiment can continue
in a public Department where every measure is looked upon with a
jaundiced Eye and of course all Mistakes magnified into Sins political
and moral."[33]

Pleas for a return to sanity coupled with denials of conspiracy came
from many quarters. Peters observed that talk of a cabal was far more
prevalent at Valley Forge than at York, where Congress sat. Elbridge
Gerry of Massachusetts suggested that the generals' indignation concerning rank, seniority, and the appointment of foreign officers had
"some share in exciting this spirit." Pennsylvania's delegate Jonathan
Bayard Smith assured Joseph Reed that if and when Congress did not
always follow precisely Washington's wishes, the reasons were owing
to difficult circumstances and not "a design of injuring him." Eliphalet
Dyer of Connecticut, one of two men to remain continuously in Congress since Washington's election in June, 1775, declared there was
never "the most distant thought of removing Genll. Washington, nor
ever one expression in Congress looking that way."[34]

As early as 1837, in the first major edition of Washington's writings, the clergyman-educator-historian Jared Sparks, after steeping himself in documents bearing on the cabal, expressed doubt as to any "fixed design" or "concerted plan" to engineer a change in the leadership of the army.[35] But the conclusion of Sparks, really an able scholar who is usually castigated for adhering to the loose editorial standards of his age, was to fall mainly on deaf ears until well into the twentieth century. The verdict of recent research sustains Sparks, as well as the expressions of Smith, Dyer, and other contemporaries. In fact, only two Revolutionary leaders verging on the first rank, Lovell and Rush, are known to have positively stated the need to supersede Washington.[36] Why then were earlier investigators led so far astray? Because for the most part, as Bernhard Knollenberg says, historians tended to accept without question Washington's own statements and those of his partisans.

Furthermore, some students have stumbled because of their failure to understand the various meanings contemporaries accorded to certain key words in the eighteenth-century political lexicon. Colonial journalists had long found a popular topic in expounding on the evils of "faction," "cabal," and especially "party" ("party-heat," "party-malice," and "party-rage"). Though Samuel Johnson defined in one sense both cabal and party as "A body of men united in some design" (a cabal consisted of a few, a party of many), the words were as often used to describe any sort of obstructionism, wrangling, or dissension within a group such as a legislative body or an army.[37] Henry Laurens, who frequently spoke of "party" in describing the doings in Congress, is the most widely quoted source for the interpretation of an anti-Washington movement among the lawmakers. But to Laurens a "party-man" was evidently anyone who disagreed with him or wished to carry on prolonged and meaningless debate, or who displayed strong local or regional attachments. At least two months prior to the supposed Conway Cabal, prior to Brandywine and Germantotwn, Laurens maintained Congress was crippled by the activities of party. Laurens' most illuminating letter on this point is one dated January 12, 1778, and addressed to his son John's intimate friend, the youthful Lafayette, who had voiced alarm to the elder Laurens about a scheme against his chief. After devoting three paragraphs to the subject of "party in general" and in particular to differences between "the Eastern States" and New York, Laurens went on to deny categorically any opposition to Washington in the legislative halls. Laurens assured Lafayette of Washington's safety from his enemies, "if he has an Enemy, a fact of which I am in doubt of. . . . In a word Sir, be not alarmed."[38]

If Congress was riven by faction, if it was a wrangling, sometimes inept assemblage, "it had merely the faults of parliamentary bodies in time of crisis, and Washington did not suffer more from it than Lincoln did from its successors," observes Allan Nevins.[39] And as one Frenchman commented, "the members of Congress are like husband and wife, always quarreling, but always uniting when family interests are concerned." The arrival of spring, bringing balmy winds and green foliage to the gray, barren panorama that was Valley Forge, also worked its wonders on George Washington. Ever hostile to Conway, and doubtful of Mifflin and Gates, the commander in chief nonetheless could declare in May, 1778, that "no whisper" of his removal "was ever heard in Congress."[40] The army, too, developed a healthier frame of mind as new recruits marched into camp, as Baron von Steuben helped instill better order and discipline in the men, and as Congress showed signs of meeting the officers' demands for half pay after the war. Congress also emerged from the winter in healthier spirits owing to the arrival of many new members and owing to word of the formal alliance with France.

Barring the discovery of new information, we may assign the Conway Cabal to the realm of myth, though, to be sure, it was a troublesome thing while it supposedly lasted. From our twentieth-century vantage point, it reflects the kind of criticism, suspicion, and acrimony that are inevitably born in wartime, especially in free societies where men are accustomed to discussing the acts of their leaders.

## NOTES

1. Seymour Martin Lipset, *The First New Nation: The United States in Historical and Comparative Perspective* (New York, 1963). Perspective on the American experience is gained from S. E. Finer, *The Man on Horseback: The Role of the Military in Politics* (New York, 1962); Morris Janowitz, *The Military in the Political Development of New Nations* (Chicago, 1964); John J. Johnson, *The Military and Society in Latin America* (Stanford, 1964).
2. Fitzpatrick, ed., *Writings of Washington*, XI, 290–291.
3. Paul L. Ford, ed., *Writings of Thomas Jefferson* (New York, 1892–1899), I, 157; Lyman H. Butterfield, ed., *The Letters of Benjamin Rush* (Philadelphia, 1951), I, 70.
4. *Warren-Adams Letters*, I, 197–198. See also *Pennsylvania Journal*, Feb. 24, 1779; Arthur Lee to Richard Henry Lee, Oct. 4, 1777, Lee Family Papers, Alderman Library, University of Virginia.
5. Ford, ed., *Journals of Congress*, XI, 640, 649, 654.
6. Butterfield, ed., *Adams Family Correspondence*, II, 245. The state of North Carolina threatened to bar any officer who resigned his commission "at this critical period" from ever holding civil or military office within the state. *North Carolina Gazette*, Nov. 28, 1777.
7. Adams wrote Charles Lee on April 27, 1776: "Pray continue to write me, for a Letter from you Cures me of all anxiety and ill Humour . . . and besides that, leaves me better informed in many Things." Burnett, ed., *Letters of Congress*, I,

433. See Bernhard Knollenberg, "The Correspondence of John Adams and Horatio Gates," Massachusetts Historical Society, *Proceedings*, LXIV (1941–1944), 131–151.

Congressman Stephen Hopkins, disgusted with long, tedious letters from the officers explaining their conduct, reputedly exclaimed he "never knew a General Quillman good for any thing." Corner, ed., *Autobiography of Benjamin Rush*, 145.

8. Burnett, ed., *Letters of Congress*, II, 262–263, 448; Wallace, *Traitorous Hero*, 124–127, 133–136.

9. Whittemore, *Sullivan*, 76–77.

10. Butterfield, ed., *Letters of Rush*, I, 163–165; *Pennsylvania Magazine of History and Biography*, XVII (1903), 147; Burnett, ed., *Letters of Congress*, II, 300.

11. B. F. Stevens, *Facsimiles of Manuscripts in European Archives Relating to America, 1773–1783* (London, 1889–1895), XXIII, no. 1987.

12. For examples of Washington praise in this period and later in the war, see Massachusetts Historical Society, *Proceedings*, VII (1863–1864), 167; *Archives of New Jersey*, 2d ser., II, 135–137; *Belknap Papers* (Massachusetts Historical Society, *Collections*, Vols. 42–43 [1877]), II, 91, 300; *Lee Papers*, III, 322, 372, 400–401; Jack P. Greene, ed., *The Diary of Colonel Landon Carter* (Charlottesville, 1965), II, 1042–1043. See also Thomas Minns, "Some Sobriquets Applied to Washington," Colonial Society of Massachusetts, *Transactions*, VIII (1902–1904), 275–286. There is a good discussion of Washington as the chief symbol of American nationalism in Marcus Cunliffe's introduction to the John Harvard Library's edition of Weems' *Life of Washington* (Cambridge, Mass., 1962).

13. Butterfield, ed., *Letters of Rush*, I, 92; Butterfield, ed., *Adams Family Correspondence*, II, 361.

14. Knollenberg, *Washington and the Revolution*, 191–194; Burnett, ed., *Letters of Congress*, II, 570–571.

15. Knollenberg, *Washington and the Revolution*, 194.

16. William Duane, ed., *Extracts from the Diary of Christopher Marshall . . .* (Albany, 1877), 159, 153; *Pennsylvania Colonial Records* (Harrisburg, 1851–1853), XI, 386, 394, 464; *Pennsylvania Archives*, 1st ser. (Philadelphia, 1852–1856), VI, 104–105, 109, 111, 153–154; John J. Stoudt, *Ordeal of Valley Forge: A Day-by-Day Chronicle* (Philadelphia, 1963), 27; Fitzpatrick, ed., *Writings of Washington*, X, 195–196. There is evidence that some Pennsylvania and New Jersey officials were already sensitive toward Washington before his setbacks in the field. They claimed he had not been sufficiently deferential to their opinions and authority during operations in their theater. Kenneth R. Rossman, *Thomas Mifflin and the Politics of the American Revolution* (Chapel Hill, 1952), 87; Ford, ed., *Journals of Congress*, VII, 95; Burnett, ed., *Letters of Congress*, II, 292. One of the carpers was Jonathan Sergeant, at the time representing New Jersey in Congress.

17. Butterfield, ed., *Letters of Rush*, I, 157.

18. Knollenberg, *Washington and the Revolution*, 195; George A. Boyd, *Elias Boudinot: Patriot and Statesman, 1740–1821* (Princeton, 1952), 42–43; Henri Doniol, *Histoire de la participation de la France, à l'établissement des États-Unis d'Amérique* (Paris, 1884–1892), III, 226–227.

19. Haslet declared, "The Genl I revere, his Character for Disinterestedness[,] Patience & fortitude will be held in Everlasting Remembrances; but . . . Beardless Youth, & Inexperience . . . are too much around him." George A. Ryden, ed., *Letters to and from Caesar Rodney, 1756–1784* (Philadelphia, 1933), 112. See also *Archives of New Jersey*, 2d ser., I, 522–526.

20. Burnett, ed., *Letters of Congress*, II, 522; Fitzpatrick, ed., *Writings of Washington*, X, 202–205.

21. Rossman, *Mifflin*, 90–98.

22. Miller, *Triumph of Freedom*, 221.

23. Burnett, ed., *Letters of Congress*, II, 275–279, 243, 292; Ford, ed., *Journals of*

*Congress,* VII, 95, 165–166; Fitzpatrick, ed., *Writings of Washington,* VII, 62–63; Merrill Jensen, *The Articles of Confederation: An Interpretation of the Social-Constitutional History of the American Revolution, 1774–1781* (3d printing: Madison, 1959) 172–173, 174; Freeman, *Washington,* IV, 389–391; Billias, *Glover,* 133.

24. Burnett, ed., *Letters of Congress,* III, 11, 63; Cornelius Harnett to William Wilkinson, Nov. 20, 1777, Cornelius Harnett Papers, Southern Historical Collection, University of North Carolina Library.

25. Francis Wharton, ed., *Revolutionary Diplomatic Correspondence of the United States* (Washington, 1889), II, 198; *Rhode Island History,* II (1943), 80–81. John Adams, who had hailed du Coudray as "the most learned and promising officer in France," now breathed a sigh of relief. Butterfield, ed., *Adams Diary and Autobiography,* II, 263. Also see André Lasseray, *Les Français sous les Treize Étoiles* (Paris, 1935), I, 344–354.

26. Louis R. Gottschalk, *Lafayette Comes to America* (Chicago, 1935); *Lafayette Joins the American Army* (Chicago, 1937); *Lafayette and the Close of the American Revolution* (Chicago, 1942). It is not generally known that a Russian citizen fought in the Continental army. Gustav Rozenthal, who became John Rose, studied medicine in Baltimore before his military service at Valley Forge and in the Ohio country. See his "Journal of a Volunteer Expedition . . .," *Pennsylvania Magazine of History and Biography,* XVIII (1894), 129–157. My colleague David Griffiths has found considerable information on Rozenthal in the Estonian State Archives.

27. Fitzpatrick, ed., *Writings of Washington,* X, 29. It would seem that Conway's letter was common gossip before Stirling notified Washington, for on October 21 Rush discussed its contents, and Wilkinson himself implied as much. To John Adams, Rush confided: " 'A great and good God,' says General Conway in a letter to a friend, 'has decreed that America shall be free, or ——— and weak counselors would have ruined her long ago.' " Butterfield, ed., *Papers of Rush,* I, 161, 162 n4; Jared Sparks, ed., *Writings of George Washington . . .* (Boston, 1834–1837), V, 516. For much of the correspondence relating to the Conway Cabal, see Sparks' Appendix 6 in vol. V, 483–518.

28. *Ibid.,* V, 494.

29. *Ibid.,* 485, 487.

30. Freeman, *Washington,* IV, 545–546, sees an "abrupt change in attitude" on the part of Gates toward Washington, the result of Gates' recent praise and flattery: Gates corresponded more infrequently with Washington and did not inform him of the triumph over Burgoyne.

31. Washington to Gates, Feb. 9, 1778, Fitzpatrick, ed., *Writings of Washington,* X, 437–441. The letter contains approximately 3,600 words and is devoted solely to the Conway episode. For a different interpretation of this letter, see Freeman, *Washington,* IV, 600 n89, 600–602, who strongly defends Washington's conduct throughout the cabal episode.

32. Syrett, ed., *Papers of Hamilton,* I, 428.

33. Burnett, ed., *Letters of Congress,* III, 45 n6–46 n6. An aide to Gates "heard it . . . asserted that Col. Morgan has lately flabigastured [sic] Mr. R. Peters so unmercifully as to oblige to cry out 'Murder.' " Robert Troup to Gates, Apr. 18, 1778, Gates Papers, New-York Historical Society. That it was hazardous to say anything favorable to Conway is seen in a letter from John Jay to Gouverneur Morris. Jay expressed a complimentary remark concerning Conway's services at Albany early in 1778, but then added: "of this say nothing." Henry P. Johnston, ed., *The Correspondence and Public Papers of John Jay . . .* (New York, 1896), I, 180–181.

34. Knollenberg, *Washington and the Revolution,* 71; Rossman, *Mifflin,* 126–127, 130; Burnett, ed., *Letters of Congress,* III, 93–94, 122.

35. Sparks, ed., *Writings of Washington,* V, 517.

36. For examples, see Lovell to Gates, Nov. 27, 1777, Burnett, ed., *Letters of Con-*

*gress*, II, 570–571; Rush to Patrick Henry, Jan. 12, 1778, Butterfield, ed., *Letters of Rush*, I, 182–183, 184 n1–185 n1. Next to Conway's epistle to Gates, Rush's letter was probably the most talked-about piece written during the time of the cabal. Rush dispatched it unsigned, and he urged Henry not to reveal his identity if the Virginia Governor recognized the handwriting. But Henry promptly sent it to Washington, who easily made out Rush's penmanship. Lyman Butterfield calls the letter "the rashest act" of Rush's life. It had a profound effect on Rush's reputation and helps to explain the reluctance of his sons to have their father's papers published. Even so, Butterfield observes that the letter in some degree absolves Rush of being a part of an organized plot. Rush was not an intimate of Henry; the two had previously corresponded only once since August, 1775. "A plotter of treachery does not communicate his hopes and fear by mail to a mere acquaintance." For a full discussion of the Rush-Washington relationship, see *ibid.*, II, Appendix, I, 1197–1208; also note Louis Gottschalk and Josephine Fennell, "Duer and the Conway Cabal," *American Historical Review*, LII (1946–1947), 87–96.

37. Samuel Johnson, *A Dictionary of the English Language* (London, 1818), I, n. p.; James A. H. Murray, ed., *A New Dictionary on Historical Principles* (Oxford, Eng., 1888–1925), VII, 514–517.

38. Burnett, ed., *Letters of Congress*, III, 28–31. On Sept. 5, 1777, Laurens confided to John Lewis Gervais: "when I first arrived here I was told by way of caution that in Congress there were parties. I soon perceived there were. [I]n the short space of Seven Weeks I have discovered parties within parties, divisions and Subdivisions to as great a possible extent as the number 35 (for we have never more together) will admit of . . . it is wholly contrary to my genius and practice to hold with any of them *as party*." *Ibid.*, II, 477. On January 5, 1778, Laurens castigated with the term "party" those congressmen who prolonged the debate over a replacement for Joseph Trumbull as commissary general. *Ibid.*, III, 14, 20–25. See also Henry Laurens to William Livingston, April 19, 1779, Henry Laurens Papers, South Carolina Historical Society.

39. Allan Nevins, "Pater Patriae: the Washington Theme," *Saturday Review of Literature*, Feb. 24, 1940.

40. Fitzpatrick, ed., *Writings of Washington*, XI, 494.

# 10. The International Conflict

AMERICANS IN 1775 knew well of the European rivalries for domination of the New World and the control of its trade, developments and circumstances that had added new ingredients to the nexus of international affairs. American awareness came partly from direct experience: participation in the series of "world" wars between England and France. The product of mercantile and dynastic ambitions, these rivalries, as the Americans realized, were not extinguished by the peace of Paris in 1763. The colonists' information regarding international affairs came from such varied sources as travel in Britain, books or tracts published abroad, and conversations with English visitors or residents. None, though, was more useful than the American newspaper, which, it is claimed, devoted more attention to the international scene than at any time before the twentieth century.[1]

Americans and Europeans by 1750 agreed that the balance of power in the Old World depended on an equilibrium among the nations with imperial interests in the Western Hemisphere.[2] This was a century addicted to Newton, to ordered "systems," physical and philosophical, to not only balance of power in international affairs but "mixed government" in internal political affairs. It was, additionally, a mercantile age, when a maritime nation's strength and security supposedly rested upon having a colonial empire from which it derived the preponderance of its external commerce and trade. The expulsion of France from North America in 1763 seemingly tipped the scales in favor of Britain—only so long, however, as she held on to her colonial possessions. This was the thinking of Benjamin Franklin—American; of the Duc de Choiseul and the Comte de Vergennes—Frenchmen; of Charles III—Spaniard; and of George III and Lord George Germain—Englishmen. If this analysis of the international situation contributed to cementing France and America together in 1778, it also casts light on Britain's reluctance —until driven to the wall—to grant American independence.

## America Looks to France

The dozen-year controversy prior to Lexington between the colonists and the parent country over taxation and other policies had not occured in isolation. It transpired in a Western world where happenings in one country and its dominions could influence events in The Hague, Paris, Madrid, Lisbon, Berlin, Vienna, and St. Petersburg. Initially this truth offered no comfort to the colonists, who had hoped to keep their quarrel within the Anglo-Saxon family. That France and Spain, inveterate enemies of Englishmen everywhere, would rejoice in any weakening of Britain's position was all too obvious. Rumors were rife of Bourbon plots to seize several of Britain's American appendages while the King's house was divided against itself, something those two Catholic states had been unable to do when Britons on both shores of the Atlantic stood shoulder to shoulder. Franklin, a great British-American imperialist, felt that such storm warnings from the Old World might be the most compelling reasons for the colonists and the mother country to patch up their quarrel.[3]

From the beginnings of the Anglo-American discord, then, the colonists thought of Europe, but with the lengthening of the dispute American opinions of Europe generally shifted from fear to hope: hope that the continental nations would assist them in the event of war with England, a possibility colonial publicists repeatedly held up as a threat against Great Britain should she continue to trample upon American rights. That in itself was one of the "revolutionary" features of the American Revolution. Bred on a hatred of Catholicism and political absolutism associated with France, American writers for decades had shrilled for the permanent removal of the Gallic peril from North America not only to preserve British liberties, but also because the presence of the fleur-de-lis blocked their egress to the lusher parts of the North American interior. By a twist of circumstances, however, the removal of France from Canada meant that she was no longer the threat of old. France and her ally in the Family Compact, Spain, might be more tolerable from afar than in the day when the influence of Louis XV loomed at the back door of the English mainland colonies.

At first American opponents of Whitehall's new imperial program were content to issue a reminder to Britain of the importance of her New World possessions, and how those colonies had contributed to the *éclat* of 1763. Had Britain lost her provinces instead, declared Daniel Dulany, she "could not long subsist as an independent Kingdom." It was "at our Expence of Men and Money chiefly," asserted Franklin, "that the Balance of Europe has been kept." Here was the kernel of a point, historically dubious without severe qualification, that would soon appear as a major theme in patriot literature: America, far removed from the Old World and its interests, had fallen prey to European self-ishness; it would not again succumb to exploitation and save Britain's chestnuts from the fire. One of the first warnings came in the *Boston Gazette*, where a contributor wrote that in any future Anglo-Bourbon war, the colonists would not help Britannia until their rights were restored.[4]

But what if Whitehall remained impervious to American grievances, then could the colonists fail to take cognizance of other alternatives for relief? As "An American" warned, the patriots "well knew their weight and importance in the political scale"; an alliance with America and the privilege of its trade "will be courted by all the powers in Europe; and will turn the balance in favour of any nation that enjoyes it." Some writers, Franklin among them, displayed an ambivalence until 1774 or later about looking to traditional opponents for aid. Not so John Adams, who, after the ministry's investigation of the burning of the revenue cutter *Gaspee*, wished "the whole Bourbon Family was upon the Back of Great Britain." Implicitly the native American colonial agents, representatives of the various colonies in London, contributed to such thinking by sending reports back to the provincial capitals that little relief was to be obtained there: the colonies would have to look to their own resources and sustain themselves by other means. One agent was Arthur Lee of Virginia, a man of paranoiac disposition, though pos-sessed of considerable abilities, fluent in several foreign tongues, and knowledgeable about conditions abroad. From 1771 on, Lee kept a keen ear open for European reactions, which he described as decidedly sympathetic toward the colonies. Both Lee and his younger brother William, engaged in mercantile business in London, reported to their older brother Richard Henry as well as to other Americans their will-ingness to court foreign aid in case of a showdown. American opinion, in fact, had undergone an about-face regarding the Bourbons, especi-ally France, by the end of 1775. And the sentiments for outside support expressed in Paine's *Common Sense* at the beginning of 1776 were al-ready long under discussion in the colonial press and in letters from Americans abroad.[5]

Not all, of course, partook of the new sentiments, those whose stand after July, 1776, earned them the name "loyalist," along with those whigs who feared that if American trade were thrown up to the world, the nascent country would be fought over as were the Dutch in the previous century; or those who warned of an effective British blockade to keep out vessels from Europe, a point challenged by Alexander Hamilton, then an undergraduate at King's College, in *The Farmer Refuted* (1775).[6]

As we have indicated in an earlier chapter, the need for foreign assistance was a powerful catalyst for independence in 1776; and only a handful of patriots desired the new nation to go it alone. Arthur Lee, "the last of the colonial agents and the first national diplomat," became the confidential representative of the Continental Congress after that body established a committee of secret correspondence in November, 1775—to make contacts with "our friends in Great Britain, Ireland, and other parts of the world"; and the following March, with the incipiency of independence, it dispatched Silas Deane to Paris to purchase war stores and to explore the possibilities of a French alliance.[7]

The word "alliance" did not necessarily imply to Americans of 1776 the present meaning of close cooperation in a political or military sense. Patriot leaders at this time favored a limited relationship with France, characteristic of their distinctly ambivalent state of mind. If Europe's trade and military chest beckoned, and if an Anglo-French rupture was desirable, Europe also repelled: too intimate a connection meant becoming interlocked in the future strife of the Old World, whose peoples—often attractive as individuals—*en masse* mirrored a society and way of life that seemed incompatible with the free, republican institutions flourishing on the Atlantic's western shores. Regarding France, John Adams insisted on "No Political connections" ("Receive no Troops from her"). Paine put his finger on the foreign policy aspirations of a free America: "Our plan is commerce," the true interest of his countrymen being "to steer clear of European contentions." Thus by 1776 the American Revolution had added to its objectives a campaign for commercial freedom, and, with the simultaneous publication of Adam Smith's *Wealth of Nations*, it heralded the decline of mercantilism and the emancipation of trade. After analyzing Congress' suggested "Model Treaty" of 1776 with France—limited solely to commercial offers—which, in fact, the lawmakers were willing to extend to other nations as well—Felix Gilbert writes: "What is astounding is how little the Americans were willing to offer. Political and military cooperation with France was to be avoided even if France should enter the war against England." And surely Britain's rebels believed that a treaty of any sort would involve France in present hostilities.[8]

If it was hardly the accustomed practice of a state struggling for its very existence to propose such a one-sided arrangement with a mighty monarchy, one has to remember the immense value then attached to the trade of non-European parts of the globe. This was the theme emphasized by the three American commissioners to France, Franklin and Arthur Lee having been selected in September, 1776, to join Deane at the court of Louis XVI. Repeatedly the Congressional diplomats warned the dignitaries at Versailles that if Britain recovered her provinces, she would "become in a few years the most formidable power by sea and land that Europe has yet seen."[9] Compelling as was the argument of the intimate relationship between commerce and power, it alone was not to be decisive. France revealed no haste to acknowledge America's sovereign status, to conclude the treaty of amity and commerce, and to intervene in the war—all objectives sought by Franklin and his colleagues.

## *The Attitude of France*

To the French Foreign Ministry, the fruits of American commerce were not warranty enough for pursuing a bold foreign policy; after all, the new republic had no intention of confining its postwar intercourse to France. Yet to strip Britain of her colonial trade, on which so much of her advantage seemed to rest, was a matter of the highest importance. Such an enfeeblement of England would destroy the superior weight that kingdom exercised in the balance of power and would restore France to primacy in Europe. The diminution of British power had been France's ultimate goal since 1761, on the eve of overwhelming defeat. Not for a moment did the Foreign Minister, the Duc de Choiseul, favorite of Madame de Pompadour, intend to live by the promise contained in the treaty of 1763 for "a Christian, universal and perpetual peace." As a result of the terms therein, Choiseul paid a humiliating price for peace, but the Duc was bidding for time: to build up the Franco-Spanish alliance, the Family Compact; to strengthen the armed forces, especially the navy; and to plumb American discontent with Britain, which, after 1763, led him to send secret agents to the thirteen colonies to foment discord, just as he maintained an espionage service in London for that and additional reasons.[10]

The dominant figure in the French government, Choiseul was remarkably adroit in reviving his country's energies and prestige: by annexing Corsica, a bitter pill for British pride, and France's final extension in the *ancien régime*; by helping to scotch England's scheme for a "League of the North" to counter the Bourbons; and by assisting in warding off an Anglo-Spanish war over the Malouine Islands (Falklands), a resumption of hostilities that would have found the military rebuilding of the Bourbons still far from completion. In 1770, the Duc fell from office, not through failure or incompetence as was once alleged but because of palace intrigue.[11] His ambitions were carried forth by his apt pupil in diplomacy, the Comte de Vergennes, who assumed the portfolio for foreign affairs in 1774. In the American insurrection, Vergennes recognized two distinct possibilities: the re-establishment of French prestige and the likelihood of war with England. Cautious and prudent, a tough-minded career diplomat, no messenger of Enlightenment idealism, the head of the Foreign Office plotted for his sovereign, the young Louis XVI, a judicious course; for the Americans might suffer defeat, or compromise their quarrel by joining Britain in a blow against the French and Spanish islands. Still, Vergennes correctly saw an opportunity that could not be ignored. For the time being, though, until the picture cleared, only clandestine support for the Americans would be forthcoming.

Vergennes obtained from the Marquis de Grimaldi, Charles III of Spain's pro-French foreign minister, His Most Catholic Majesty's promise to afford the revolting colonists a small amount of surreptitious assistance. Grimaldi in 1776 was replaced by the proud, independently minded Conde de Floridablanca, who intended to see Spain pull her weight in the Family Compact, and who personally was contemptuous of the American rebels. Beyond her initial agreement Spain would not venture. She feared an independent American republic as a threat to Charles' dominions beyond the seas. Spanish thinking had no small influence upon Vergennes and his countrymen, who were further restrained from jumping over the traces by intelligence of American military reverses in 1776. Nevertheless, the year 1777 marked France's deepening commitment to the patriots. The increasing stream of supplies from France to America, the opening of French ports to American privateers and warships, the procession of Gallic officers bound for Washington's army, the unremitting pressures of Silas Deane and the more subtle blandishments of Benjamin Franklin all combined to move France toward the patriot orbit. To have turned back would have been hard and humiliating. Had France in truth traveled so far that, short of the patriots' suffering disaster, she was bound to enter the fray? Word of Saratoga reaching Paris December 4, 1777, made the question academic, as did the resultant reports of Britain's willingness now to accede to American grievances, ammunition which Franklin used to play on Vergennes' fear of a separate peace.[12]

The Franco-American alliance of February, 1778, however, illustrates that Congress had climbed down from its high pedestal in eschewing political and military ties with Europe. Congress, fearing disaster in the dark days of late 1776, had empowered the commissioners in Paris to hold up the British West Indies as bait for French entry

into the war. To accompany the Americans' eagerly desired Treaty of
Amity and Commerce, containing as it did most of the lawmakers'
proposals in the Model Treaty for distinct liberalization of trade along
principles foreign to mercantilism, Vergennes insisted on a "conditional
and defensive alliance." Perhaps the Continental Congress had contemplated this much in its about-face of 1776. Predicated on the belief
that France's recognition of American independence, contained in the
first treaty, would bring Britain and France to blows, the Treaty of
Alliance stipulated mutual guarantees: the United States assured
France her West Indian islands, France promised America's independence, and both stood by the other's territorial gains resulting from
the war with one exception—Louis XVI, His Most Christian Majesty,
renounced forever any pretensions to the Bermudas, Canada, and all
other parts of the North American continent east of the Mississippi.
Neither nation would lay down its arms before American independence
was assured, and neither was to make a separate peace. Notwithstanding their aversion to "foreign entanglements" and to the cynical rivalries
of the Old World, Americans, owing to the exigencies of the time, had
gone against the grain and concluded an alliance in the language of
old-fashioned diplomacy.[13]

The war that began between France and England in the summer of
1778 saw Spain on the sidelines. But the following year, when Vergennes induced the court at Madrid to take the plunge, the American
republic was swept even more fully into the vortex of European power
politics. For indirectly the nation's wagon became hitched to the star of
Spain. In return for his government's entry, astute Foreign Minister
Floridablanca wrung a high price from Vergennes: no peace until
Spain regained Gibralter, lost to Britain in 1713, plus efforts to wrest
Minorca, Mobile, and other plums from George III. No ally of America,
whose sovereignty she steadfastly refused to recognize, Spain had won
from France concessions to some degree incompatible with her commitments to America; America could not make peace without the consent of France, and that nation could not agree without meeting her
obligation to Spain.

## French Aid

To Americans of later generations the expression "foreign aid" connotes
their country's economic and military assistance to other nations, many
laboring for survival. How different from the first days of our national
history, when the United States stood on the receiving end.

Deane and Franklin, for all their accomplishments in forming a
Franco-American alliance, had no hand in France's earlier decision to

afford the rebellious colonists secret aid. Before a single patriot commissioner reached Paris, Louis XVI directed that one million livres be extended to Caron de Beaumarchais, playwright, poet, darling of the salons, sometime secret agent. Beaumarchais, working with Vergennes, played a part in influencing the King, even to proposing the form that clandestine support would take: creation of a fictitious mercantile firm, Roderique Hortalez and Company, actually Beaumarchais himself, who would spend the million livres to buy munitions for the Americans from French arsenals.[14] Spain promptly advanced a like sum, and the next year France repeated her initial contribution. To this day some of the circumstances surrounding Beaumarchais' doings are a mystery. Was the government's money that went for the war materials considered a loan or a gift to the revolutionists? Later Beaumarchais demanded substantial payments and seemingly for good reason. Regardless of the King's intention, Beaumarchais himself and French merchants had invested handsome sums in his ventures. (Eventually the United States in 1835 settled with his descendants for 800,000 francs.) His greatest effort came at the beginning of 1777 when mountains of goods were loaded on chartered vessels: 200 brass cannon, 300 fusils, 100 tons of powder, 3,000 tents, and heavy stores of bullets, mortars, and cannon balls, together with necessary articles of clothing for 30,000 men. Of this fleet of eight ships, all but one, captured off Martinique, safely reached their destination on the western side of the Atlantic.[15]

No way exists of measuring accurately the total value of the infinite forms of French assistance: of official funds extended to Beaumarchais, of Vergennes' permitting Deane and Franklin to contract independently with French merchants for American orders, just as French authorities prior to the alliance winked at the purchasing activities of American mercantile firms such as Willing and Morris and the agents of the various states seeking to fill orders for local needs, military and otherwise. Most American purchases were acquired on the credit of the United States. Congress hoped to meet much of its foreign indebtedness through the sale of agricultural commodities in France. These products, especially tobacco, were bulky and required fair-sized vessels to carry a paying cargo; but big ships, if available, proceeded at so ponderous a speed as to make them easy prey for British cruisers.

Increasingly therefore French subsidies and loans directly to the United States became important as a means of meeting obligations abroad to exporters and contractors supplying the patriots with the implements of warfare. If Silas Deane, a shrewd Connecticut merchant, was successful in dealing with French mercantile houses, where men spoke his language of trade, Franklin worked at obtaining cash from the court at Versailles. To the beginning of 1781, French loans and subsidies, counting 846,000 livres from the Farmers General and at least 4,555,000 in supplies from Hortalez and Company, amounted to 15,400,000 livres—or $2,852,000. The year 1781 heralded France's resolve to deepen its commitment. On the fighting fronts the commitment bore witness in the role of Rochambeau and de Grasse at Yorktown. At home it was manifested in grants and loans equaling almost $1,000,000 more than all previous allocations to that time. A loan of 4,000,000 livres was followed by a gift of 6,000,000. This gratuity, Franklin's achievement, came shortly before an equally spectacular development: persuading Louis XVI's government to guarantee repayment of a loan of 10,000,000 livres to be subscribed in Holland; and the French court agreed to advance immediately the full amount of the loan! All told, France had been generous indeed in what became the most crucial year of the war: 20,000,000 livres—or $3,700,000.[16]

Franklin's wariness about pressing France still harder, interpreted by John Adams as a sign of the venerable Philadelphian's subservience to France and willingness to compromise America's best interests, was sensible. Master of tact and finesse, qualities notably wanting in the flinty Adams, Franklin recognized that impertinence would likely redound to America's disadvantage, though in certain instances he applied the correct admixture of supplication and veiled coercion. And as a friend of the fiscal wizard Turgot, an opponent of French economic contributions to the patriots, Franklin must have known of the financial strains of France at the time, increased by the American War of Independence and ultimately contributing to the fall of the French monarchy.[17]

Americans were generally optimistic about securing advantages in other corners of Europe as well. Arthur Lee, who had hungrily devoured Adam Smith's recently published *Wealth of Nations*, thought the states of the Old World would fall over one another in their eager quest for the American raw materials that had made Britain wealthy and powerful. Patriot emissaries hastened to various European courts to spread their economic gospel of the liberalization of commerce. At Madrid, Berlin, St. Petersburg, and elsewhere the message was the same: Americans produced more raw materials than could be consumed at home; they needed foreign markets, just as they sought foreign imports since they turned out comparatively few manufactures. There was order and symmetry—"reason" in the rhetoric of the day— to this American way of thinking, a picture of nations trading among themselves with a harmony of interests, each turning out what nature allowed it to do best. American diplomats, certainly not all of them, were scarcely as naïve as to believe they could bring about a kind of commercial revolution all by themselves. But the fact is they genuinely believed in the new principles of economic intercourse they expounded; they would continue to pursue them after the war. More-over, trade was the most potent weapon in the American armory.[18]

Nations, however, do not conduct their external relations exclusively in terms of foreign trade, as Arthur Lee discovered in March, 1777, when he sought recognition and an alliance in Spain. At a border town Spanish officials turned back the eager diplomat, after politely listen-ing to the Virginian discuss the advantages of sharing in Britain's for-mer American monopoly, "this great . . . source of her commerce and wealth."[19] In fact, American commercial goals and general expansion-ist aspirations squarely conflicted with the attitudes of Madrid; even so, Charles III's ministers extended modest sums to the Americans, funneled partly through the Gardoqui brothers, members of a Bilbao firm en-gaged in trade with the revolutionists.

The geopolitical differences (today's terminology) between America and Spain proved insurmountable, even after Spain entered the war, and even though the Continental Congress modified its position. First, the patriot lawmakers not only publicly renounced their previously known desires for the Floridas, which Britain had seized from Spain in 1763, but the United States would also guarantee Spain's possession of her former colonies if she captured them. In September, 1779, just after Spain's taking up arms against Britain, Congress dispatched John Jay, former president of that body, to Madrid on a two-fold mission: sub-stantial financial support and an alliance from the Bourbon monarchy. Jay found that Spain's line had actually hardened since Lee's earlier effort at persuasion. Foreign Minister Floridablanca, exceedingly dis-trustful of America as a potential New World rival, extended only a pittance in additional monies; none at all during Jay's last eighteen months there, except for what had been already promised. Continuing to reject American recognition or any formal relationship, Spain looked upon her occasional handouts as a gift rather than a subvention. (It is estimated that the French government's total financial contribution to the United States amounted to $8,167,500, compared to $611,328 in Spanish contributions.)[20] In truth, though the Foreign Minister did not say so, an alliance was out of the question. However, Floridablanca, who secretly favored an ultimate dependency for America under Franco-Spanish auspices, now and then indicated that a change in Congress' attitude on the use of the Mississippi River might well lead to a fruitful accord. Before Jay's sailing for Europe, Congress had spelled out its ambitions regarding the Southwest: to terminate the war with nothing less than the Mississippi as its western boundary, includ-ing "the free navigation of the river Mississippi into and from the Sea"; and the line of north latitude 31° as the southern demarcation of American territory.[21]

British victories in Georgia and South Carolina in 1780, combined with severe American shortages of cash and equipment, appear to have been more important than pressure from the Bourbon powers in prompting Congress to make a *volte-face* on the Mississippi issue.[22] To remove every obstacle to an alignment, the lawmakers authorized Jay to drop their insistence on the right of American settlers in the West to have free navigation of the Father of Waters in order to exit their crops via New Orleans and the Gulf. Here, as in the case of the Franco-American military pact of 1778, wartime exigencies took precedence over the national interest.

Significantly, and brilliantly on his part, Jay advanced the relinquishment of the Mississippi as conditional upon Spain's agreeing to an alliance between the two nations. It can be argued that His Most Catholic Majesty, already engaged in the conflict, had nothing to lose and much to gain by a proposal that could very conceivably have retarded westward expansion and made Americans in the transmontane region dependent upon Spain for favors; but his servant Floridablanca refused to grasp the opportunity, and Jay precipitately withdrew Congress' bargain.[23] Thus Spain remained only the ally of France, for even Yorktown wrought no improvement in the political climate of Madrid toward the United States. Left behind was an issue disturbing to Hispano-American relations in the next two decades.

Embittered by his ill-starred mission to Spain, "one continued series of painful perplexities and embarrassments," Jay counselled his countrymen "to rest content with the treaty with France."[24] Franklin as early as the consummation of the French alliance adhered to the same view. Sending envoys scurrying hither and yon lacked dignity; better to get the sentiments in a particular capital before dispatching an envoy. For Arthur Lee in Prussia, William Lee in Austria, and Ralph Izard seeking to enter Tuscany found themselves unwelcome. Problems of the European continent such as the Bavarian succession and the fear of antagonizing the court of St. James bulked larger to the crowned heads than American tobacco and rice; but this would not be the last time that American diplomats would equate the interests of their country with those of the world.

Momentarily the prospect brightened in 1780. As American agents reported from their various listening posts, Europe hummed with rumors about Catherine the Great's newly formed League of Armed Neutrality. Since the beginning of the conflict, British officials had complained bitterly of Dutch merchants selling arms to the patriots, who more often than not received them at the tiny Dutch West Indian island of St. Eustatius. Russia, on the other hand, permitted no direct trade with the patriots, but with the spreading conflagration she found the Bourbon belligerents better customers than ever for her naval stores.

Having only a small merchant fleet, it was essential to the Russian Empress that foreign ships have access to her ports to load their cargoes. Created on paper in March, 1780, and subsequently joined by almost all the nonaligned maritime states of Europe, the League of Armed Neutrality called for free navigation along the coasts of warring nations and for a strict and limited definition of contraband goods that could be seized on neutral vessels. A *parvenu* power, Russia enjoyed her role, considered in many continental quarters to be that of holding the balance between the great powers, along with that of being a potential leader of the smaller states. Russia's action constituted a rude awakening for Britain, a nation that had been deceived by its wildly optimistic Ambassador James Harris in St. Petersburg into believing that Catherine was preparing to link herself with George III in the current struggle. For Britain the key country was Holland: Dutch trade with her enemies was voluminous compared to that of Russia or any other continental sovereignty. When the Dutch refused to accede to London's stipulations on contraband, Britain cast the die for war. But by clouding the issue, making the pretext for hostilities negotiations between Congress and the Magistracy of Amsterdam, England's Declaration of War gave the League of Armed Neutrality no excuse to intervene. The Anglo-Dutch conflict was hardly worth the name, and with the grinding down of the smaller state a valuable source of American trade was chiefly eliminated. As for the League, its founder never seriously contemplated drawing the sword in defense of trade, and the interests of its members were too diverse for a concerted military undertaking.

The Continental Congress as a staunch advocate of the liberalization of commerce applauded Catherine's stand in favor of freedom of the seas. America, offering to back the Empress' cause, commissioned Francis Dana to seek a treaty at St. Petersburg. Against Franklin's advice, Dana proceeded to the Russian court, where his reception was no less frigid than the Nordic winter. Catherine was no friend of revolution, and commercial freedom was not the only string to her bow. She now saw herself in the role of grand arbitrator between England and the Bourbons and her plan precluded recognition of the United States.

Still, the League indirectly benefited America. It enjoyed a greater impact upon European affairs than has usually been recognized, declares the most careful student of the subject.[25] It created a kind of third force in Europe, a system into which neutrals could fit. Embarrassing to Britain, it helped to frustrate her endeavors to obtain allies or even friends, not an easy task in any event. So far had Britain's prestige slipped that before the advent of peace even Portugal, long a satellite of Whitehall, joined Catherine's League.

## Britain in Isolation

Why did Britain, never wanting for allies in the four Anglo-French wars between 1689 and 1763, stand alone against America and the Bourbon powers? Pitt, though predominantly interested in advancing England's commercial and colonial aims in the last war, had not neglected the continent: he bolstered Britain's recently formed connection with Prussia, a rising state, which replaced Austria as England's ally against France. But on Pitt's resigning from the ministry in 1761 and Frederick the Great's desire to expand the conflict, George III terminated the expensive relationship with Prussia, leaving Frederick to claim subsequently, and somewhat unfairly, that he had been abandoned.[26] Israel Maudit's *Considerations on the Present German War* (1760) expressed sentiments of untold thinking Englishmen: Britain's interests and strength lay in her commerce and her colonies, not in weakening herself in needless continental entanglements. Maudit even maintained that by remaining aloof from the German states, including the King's own Hanover, England would cease to keep alive the anarchy there. The result would be the unification of Germany, a perfect counterweight against France. On the continent the balance of power, "the perennial panacea of British diplomacy," would come about without the loss of British sterling or blood.

Maudit's pamphlet ran through six editions. Horace Walpole, wit and inveterate gossip whose barbs escaped few men in public life, confessed it was almost "the only work . . . I ever knew that changed the opinions of many." What was involved has been interpreted as a controversy between "colonial" and "continental" schools of thought, the latter advocating British involvement to secure a "just equilibrium" by a system of "equipoises," the former—represented by Maudit—calling for a drastic curtailment of ties across the channel. The "colonial" idea, really a kind of isolationism, was not new, dating from William III's time. But such thinking was never more popular than in the 1760's; for a kingdom saddled with a burdensome public debt by the standards of the period, partly owing to subsidies granted European friends, it had a bread and butter appeal.[27]

The young monarch George III, no slave to Hanover, that "horrid electorate," was himself bitterly anti-Prussian. He had opposed the sending of an expeditionary force to assist Frederick in Germany, where, it will be recalled, his friend George Sackville—later Germain —had in the King's view fallen prey to "continental" politicians who sought to wound the then Prince of Wales by attacking his follower Sackville. In fact, comments Richard Pares, George III's "isolationism"

Washington at the Battle of Princeton, by C. W. Peale. *Courtesy of The Art Museum, Princeton University*

Battle of Lexington, engraving by C. Tiebout, after the drawing by E. Tisdale. *Courtesy of The New York Historical Society, New York City*

Yorktown in the Eighteenth Century, sketch by a British naval officer.
*Courtesy of The Mariners Museum, Newport News, Virginia*

Gathering of the [King's] Mountain Men at Sycamore Shoals, by Lloyd Branson. *Courtesy of the Tennessee State Museum*

Recruits for the British Army in America, engraving, 1780. *Courtesy of The New York Public Library*

Evacuation Day, lithograph by
E. P. and L. Restein. *Courtesy of
the Library of Congress*

George Washington, by James Peale. *Courtesy of the Independence National Historical Park Collection*

Nathanael Greene, by C. W. Peale. *Courtesy of the Independence National Historical Park Collection*

Daniel Morgan, by C. W. Peale. *Courtesy of the Independence National Historical Park Collection*

Anthony Wayne, after the portrait by Peter F. Rothermel, based on John Trumbull's study. *Courtesy of The Historical Society of Pennsylvania*

Horatio Gates, by C. W. Peale.
*Courtesy of the Independence National Historical Park Collection*

John Sullivan, by Richard M. Staiff.
*Courtesy of the Independence National Historical Park Collection*

Benjamin Lincoln, by C. W. Peale.
*Courtesy of the Independence National Historical Park Collection*

Philip Schuyler, by John Trumbull. *Courtesy of The New York Historical Society, New York City*

Charles Lee, anonymous caricature. *Courtesy of The New York Public Library*

Benedict Arnold, engraving by B. L. Prévost, after the drawing by Pierre Eugène du Simitier. *Courtesy of The New York Historical Society, New York City*

Steuben, by C. W. Peale. *Courtesy of the Independence National Historical Park Collection*

Lafayette, by C. W. Peale. *Courtesy of the Independence National Historical Park Collection*

Rochambeau, by C. W. Peale. *Courtesy of the Independence National Historical Park Collection*

John Adams, by C. W. Peale. *Courtesy of the Independence National Historical Park Collection*

Robert Morris, by C. W. Peale. *Courtesy of the Independence National Historical Park Collection*

Henry Laurens, by C. W. Peale. *Courtesy of the Independence National Historical Park Collection*

Lord North, by Rinke, after Dance. *Courtesy of Clements Library, University of Michigan*

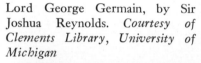

Lord George Germain, by Sir Joshua Reynolds. *Courtesy of Clements Library, University of Michigan*

The Earl of Sandwich, by Thomas Gainsborough. *Courtesy of the National Maritime Museum, Greenwich*

Admiralty Office, London, engraving by D. Cunego. *Courtesy of the National Maritime Museum, Greenwich*

Richard Howe, by J. Chapman.
*Courtesy of Clements Library,
University of Michigan*

William Howe, by J. Chapman.
*Courtesy of Clements Library,
University of Michigan*

John Burgoyne, engraving by A. H. Ritchie. *Courtesy of Clements Library, University of Michigan*

President's chair during the Constitutional Convention. *Courtesy of the Independence National Historical Park Collection*

Guy Carleton, engraving by A. H. Ritchie. *Courtesy of Clements Library, University of Michigan*

was also shared by "nearly all British statesmen after 1763."[28] It was easier, of course, to be an isolationist if, as was generally assumed by mid-century, the key to the balance between the maritime nations lay in America rather than in Europe.

All this does not mean that British leaders ignored the continent in the 1760's, nor does it indicate a revulsion against all involvements. The theory of treaties to maintain a continental equilibrium was so engrained that, notwithstanding past expenditures aimed at gluing a coterie of states to Britain, successive ministries in the 1760's and early 1770's occasionally went through the motions of seeking defensive alliances. The point is that Britain was unwilling to pay the price, involving as it invariably did subsidies to further the schemes of her allies. George Grenville's devotion to sound fiscal management and to the interests of the British taxpayer had consequences not only for the American colonies and for the royal navy but also for foreign policy in general.

Furthermore, the great issues after 1763 were in Eastern Europe, where Austria, Prussia, and Russia concerned themselves with Poland and Turkey, two once-prestigious powers that now faced the prospect of being melted down and fused with their powerful neighbors. In this region Britain had no vital interests other than trade, and she refused a tie-up that might ensnarl her in the escapades of the Eastern monarchs. Nor were these Eastern nations driven to Britain on Whitehall's terms by fears of French aggression. This familiar British cant now fell on deaf ears; European diplomats quite rightly believed the court at Versailles to be no longer enamored of European territorial expansion. Indeed, French foreign policy under Choiseul and Vergennes was no longer brusque or belligerent, but, generally speaking, soothing and conciliatory, well exemplified by Vergennes' rapprochement with Russia which had traditionally considered Poland and Turkey as the clients of France. And Vergennes went to lengths to point out to the crowned heads and their ministers that Britain had upset the European balance by her lopsided victory in the last war.

So Britain fought alone in the American War of Independence, partly because of an inept foreign policy but more because of changes in Europe mostly beyond her control. From 1775 onward the government received from a multitude of quarters reports of Dutch, French, and Spanish aid to the rebellious colonists. So widely known were the activities of patriot merchants and diplomats that much of the information obtained by the ministry's spies on the continent—the most celebrated were Paul Wentworth and Dr. Edward Livingston—was already public knowledge by the time it reached London. Englishmen knew as well of France's long-term program of *revanche*.[29] Why therefore did

Britain allow herself to be caught with her back to the wall in 1778 and after? First, there was her unbounded optimism that the American rebellion would be crushed no later than 1777. Partly for this reason the government had pretended to take little official notice of France's encouragement of the rebels. A smashing defeat would compel France and her other neighbors to draw away from the revolutionists.

There was an alternative—a negotiated settlement—if the British Goliath failed to slay the American David, as the King's ministers and most of the British press had so confidently predicted. But the alternative came too late, after Saratoga. Or rather it might be more accurate to say the alternative was not pushed to its logical conclusion: to make a peace with America that conceded independence, the only terms the patriots would have considered, buoyed up as they were by Saratoga and the increasing prospect of a French alliance. After Burgoyne's fall, a cessation of American hostilities was urgently needed to prepare for the pending confrontation with France that Chatham and others among the Parliamentary opposition were now predicting. In spite of the elder statesman's plea for urgency, Parliament recessed for six long weeks, until January 20, 1778; and it was nearly a month later, on February 17, that North admitted "it was possible, nay probable," that France had officially recognized the United States of America. That same day the King's first minister, conceding the dismal state of affairs, introduced in the House of Commons his proposals for a negotiated settlement with America.[30]

There is small value in repeating here the familiar story of the response: the mission of the so-called Carlisle commissioners who only reached America in June, 1778, several months after the signing of the Franco-American treaties.[31] Dispatched too late and offering too little, in the American view, their terms of revoking Parliamentary measures that had provoked the revolt and of renouncing the mother country's right to tax the colonists, fell upon deaf ears. While the King's friends had resolutely rejected granting independence, the opposition, divided mainly between the followers of Rockingham and Chatham, had itself reached no consensus on the question of sovereignty over America. The Chathamites, though feeling genuine sympathy for America, would not retreat beyond the practical relationship prior to 1763, essentially the overture of the Carlisle delegation. Rockingham in the course of the debate in 1778 came out for the independence of the thirteen colonies, the position of his ally Burke, the Duke of Richmond, Franklin's friend David Hartley, and such pro-Americans as Charles James Fox and Matthew Robinson-Morris.[32]

If a termination of the American war meant independence, was the price too high to pay? Could Britain, unable to subdue America in two and a half years, now take on the Bourbons as well and escape disaster? Even Germain, ever the advocate of a hard line toward America, conceded that if America had literally to be conquered, the subsequent cost of holding her would be ruinous to Britain. (Yet apparently without facing up to his inconsistency, he continued to consider a majority of provincials loyal to the King.) Simultaneously, the Colonial Secretary thought, as did most opponents of relinquishing America, that to give up the colonies would lead to commercial ruin, not only by losing the areas in question but also by leading to a further unraveling of her empire in the Western Hemisphere.[33]

It was a cruel choice: to fight a different kind of war, one vastly more arduous than the previous ones with the Bourbons; or to recognize the United States of America among the nations of the earth. The historian can sympathize with leaders circumscribed by the mental framework of their day. But there were men who transcended their day, who argued that Britain's commerce would not die, that America would continue to trade with Britain, that, in short, the balance of power would not be lost with the breaking of *political* bonds between England and the thirteen citadels of rebellion. Piers Mackesy has correctly reminded us that the opposition was often disposed to the low road, traducing the character of Germain, accusing the ministry of willfully subverting the constitution, and possessing a limited vision of the manifold problems encountered by the North administration. All the same, regardless of whether the antis were driven by ambition and the spoils of office, they hit a handful of nails squarely on the head. The war had not been well managed, and, as Rockingham quoted from a letter of Horatio Gates written in 1777, "The United States of America" were still "willing to be friends," though independent. "They are by consanguinity, by commerce, by language, and by the affection which naturally springs from these, more attach'd to England than to any country under the sun."[34]

The crucial task, as Englishmen of every political faction realized by March, 1778, was to prepare for the impending onslaught of "Perfidious Gaul," the "antient foe." Even with their disagreements over America, Britons might have presented a relatively solid front regarding war with her European rivals had North, Germain, and company enjoyed the full confidence of the country. Fox assailed the leaders of his government in time of war with a viciousness that to the modern ear sounds treasonous. So did part of the London press, the *Evening Post*, the *Packet*, the *Public Ledger*, all of which called for Germain's removal. North, sickened by "this dammed war," appears to have lost whatever faith he may have had in a complete victory. He spoke of stepping down and turning over the reins to Chatham, as Britain had done in her last hour of trial, to forestall further disasters and reconcile

America short of total independence. And beyond doubt the vision of Pitt again in command on Downing Street was as frightening to Vergennes as it was urgent to Englishmen who felt the Great Commoner could bind up the empire's wounds. Chatham, though, remained anathema to George III, and, in any case, his death occurred almost before his elevation could have been effected. George's concept of the proper relationship between the monarch and *his* public servants made a significant alteration in the cabinet impossible. It was the obligation of men of good will to accept a post at Whitehall before discussing policy. Since the opposition spokesmen demanded immediate changes in policy and personnel, they could hardly consider taking up the seals of office. North's very weaknesses, his lack of spine and need for pounds to shepherd his sizeable brood in court society, kept the unhappy minister at his desk. Germain also remained, not so much because of the King's confidence in him but more because of George's determination not to capitulate to the government's critics. Moreover, Germain had been associated with a vigorous prosecution of the war; and the civil war that had broadened into an internal conflict would demand more forceful measures than ever.[35]

## The Royal Navy in Global Strategy

The King and cabinet reconsidered the strategy of the war now that it would take place in a global context. Britain, as Pitt repeatedly exclaimed, was ill-prepared for the tasks before her. Available manpower fell short of necessary requirements. More important was naval power —or its lack; it determined the nature of the conflict in its second and final phase. To 1778, the navy's role was mainly that of transporting the men and supplies of the armies, blockading the rebel coasts, and conducting occasional raids on seaport towns. The blockade, owing something to Lord Howe's leniency but perhaps more to what may have been an insuperable assignment of patroling the extensive Atlantic coastline, had been less than effective. Whether, in fact, the job was beyond the realm of possibility can never be adequately answered. In the eighteenth century blockading vessels needed relatively easy access to fresh water and provisions; and no vigorous move to acquire sufficient bases was undertaken. Abandoning Boston before capturing New York, the British did not take Newport until 1776 and Philadelphia until the next year; and the halfhearted stab at Charleston in 1776 accomplished nothing. The navy was also fettered by the fact that British boarding parties, finding contraband aboard vessels bound for the West Indies (there to transfer their cargoes to smaller blockade runners), could not engage in confiscation if their captains were able to produce French papers. The London government might remonstrate against these and other unneutral acts before 1778, but it did not retaliate. It was chiefly the navy's inadequacy, its lack of tonnage equal to the combined Bourbon fleets, that prompted North and his colleagues to hope against hope that an expansion of the war could be avoided, to gamble on vacillation at Versailles. France's great problem of the Seven Years' War was Britain's two decades later: to defend with insufficient naval resources a vast and scattered colonial empire. To commit herself simultaneously in America, the West Indies, and perhaps elsewhere on the world scene would, as John Adams had warned in one of his famous *Novanglus* papers in 1775, invite a blow at the home island.[36]

Why then did Whitehall not resort to her customary strategy so salutary in the past: (1) to subsidize a European ally to hold France's attention on the continent; and (2) to choke off French activities overseas by a naval blockade in continental waters? Previously in this chapter we have seen the unlikelihood of buying a satellite in Europe. In 1780 Britain dangled before Catherine the Great a long-sought Mediterranean base, the island of Minorca, in a bid for Russian intervention against France and Spain. Catherine, preoccupied with Eastern questions and planning her League of Armed Neutrality, turned down the bait; nor could the ministry find ways of enticing Austria into its orbit.[37]

A meaningful explanation of the cabinet's failure to establish a continental blockade is not so clear-cut. Frederick called it an act of folly to engage in hostilities without containing the French fleet, "which was very possible in the beginning." Historian William Willcox analyzes the decision as "the most important and disastrous made in London during the war. . . ." To have sealed off the enemy fleet would have reduced the royal navy's commitment from the Indian Ocean to the Caribbean, while the squadron in American waters, though smaller because of the assignment in Europe, could have operated unchallenged on the American coast. In short, the French would pose no threat to Britain's three remaining American bases at Newport, New York, and Philadelphia in 1778; nor presumably would Cornwallis have met his downfall at Yorktown at the hands of Washington and de Grasse in 1781. According to this point of view, the British could still have won the war: "their prospects in the colonies would have been little impaired." Followed to some extent in the wars of the Spanish and Austrian Succession, this British blockading strategy attained its peak in Admiral Hawke's investment of Brest in the summer and autumn of 1759.[38]

British planning for 1778, as outlined in March to Sir Henry Clinton, the new commander in chief in North America, appears to have involved little thought of keeping French war vessels in Europe. Clinton was to make a wide dispersion of his forces by dispatching a contingent of 5,000 to capture the French West Indian island of St. Lucia and an additional 3,000 to St. Augustine and Pensacola for the purpose of either defending Jamaica or assaulting New Orleans. Weakened by this sacrifice to his army, Clinton, with his immediate command, was to abandon Philadelphia and return to New York; or, if it proved hazardous to hold the latter city, Sir Henry received the option of leaving his garrison at Newport and withdrawing the New York forces to Halifax.[39]

All of this meant that to the royal advisors on Downing Street the West Indies was to be the focus of subsequent warfare in the New World. Though a retreat in America would hearten the patriots and would destroy the faint ray of hope for the Carlisle commission, the West Indies, as in past colonial wars, took precedence. Considered more valuable than America, represented in London by powerful political and economic interests, the sugar islands had to come first.

Britain, accordingly, was to pay a substantial price for failing to try to hold the Bourbon men-of-war at bay: a wide dispersal of her forces in the New World; that in itself was an invitation to enemy squadrons to assail and capture her various American and West Indian bases in detail. Some historians, however, feel that Whitehall had no alternative. Not only was the size and condition of the fleet inadequate, the navy had always needed luck to make a French blockade work, including little or no sickness among the ships' crews and the absence of westerly gales. Rather than seeing the move against St. Lucia as a pointless diversion of already overextended forces, these authorities contend that the best defense in the Caribbean was the offensive—against French outposts that would offer succor to any future Bourbon naval squadron in those waters.[40]

A stationary blockade was, to be sure, hardly likely. The preponderance of French naval power resided at two extremely separated points: a squadron under Admiral d'Orvilliers at Brest on the western tip of Brittany, and a second commanded by Admiral d'Estaing at Toulon in the Mediterranean. By virtue of mighty labors on the part of Sandwich and the Admiralty, the British home fleet had received an increase in serviceable vessels by the early spring of 1778. It is not at all inconceivable that detachments from this fleet could have sallied forth to engage the respective parts of the enemy and drive them back to port. After making allowance for Britain's handicaps, the distinguished naval historian Alfred Mahan observed: "In truth . . . the surest way for the weaker party to neutralize the enemy's ships was to watch them in their harbors and fight them if they started." But Sandwich and Admiral Augustus Keppel, commander of the channel fleet, seem to have lived in dread of the spectre of a Bourbon invasion of the home island. Keppel's caution was somewhat born of political reasons. Having opposed the American war and declined to serve in the colonies, Keppel, a stouthearted man and admired by his seamen, refused to stick his neck out far enough to be chopped off by a ministry hostile to his personal opinions.[41]

Sandwich, however, had the dominant voice, and cold logic was on his side. The French navy was an improved fighting array over the last duel between the two powers. It had new, bigger ships, and the naval renaissance initiated by Choiseul had inspired learned essays in tactics like Moroque's *Tactique Naval* (1763) and Villehuet's *Les Manoeuvres* (1765), superior to similar British studies in the same period.[42] And though the British fleet in Europe was approximately comparable to the two French detachments at Brest and Toulon, it might be severely hard pressed if the Spanish squadron at Cadiz united with the French forces. Yet there is always a need now and then for a gamble or an attempt at derring-do in warfare on the part of the underdog if he is to walk off with the marbles. In 1778 the gamble may have been well worth the exertion. It was known in London that d'Estaing's ships at Toulon were about to put to sea. Was the Frenchman joining d'Orvilliers at Brest, the Spanish at Cadiz, or heading for America? By hastening a force to block his exit from the Straits of Gibraltar, the British could have prevented him from effecting any juncture at all.

The French Admiral was actually headed for America; and, at length, on getting word of d'Estaing's course, the cabinet, led by Germain, overruled Sandwich. Vice Admiral John Byron (the poet's uncle) was ordered to the New World to reinforce Lord Howe, who continued to hold his station while awaiting his replacement. Though rejecting the idea of a blockade, the government still had had to detach a squadron from the home defense, just as it would do so almost every time later in the war that it learned of a French squadron making sail for the colonies. But the initiative was usually with the enemy, who had the advantage of a head start and whose destination was not precisely known. The British detached squadrons, moreover, were seldom of sufficient strength to guarantee a favorable showing because of the obsession of Sandwich and Keppel for the safety of the British Isles.[43]

## The Campaign of 1778

In Philadelphia, Sir Henry Clinton busied himself with the government's objectives for the year, while his predecessor, Sir William Howe, sailed for England after his splendid farewell party, the extravagant Mischianza. Clinton and Admiral Howe knew of the potential threat from d'Estaing at Toulon, but they had no inkling that the government would fail to have him intercepted at sea. Consequently, with a powerful enemy fleet descending on him, Clinton prepared to embark his army on transports, some to head for Florida and the Caribbean, others to make for New York. Fortunately for him, so many loyalists flocked to the wharves to be carried to New York that the British General had scant room for the troops and equipment. Skirting the letter of his orders, he decided to march the army, impedimenta and all, overland across New Jersey instead, postponing the St. Lucia and Florida expeditions as well until he reached New York. A division of the already small naval complement in the face of the approaching d'Estaing could have been little short of disastrous. As it was, Lord Howe narrowly escaped from Philadelphia with his small fleet and bevy of tory-laden transports. The French Admiral, who anchored off the Delaware Capes on July 8, had missed confronting the elder Howe by approximately ten days.[44]

It is almost a universal fact of the War of Independence that the British fared poorly in their inland operations. Sir William Howe had displayed little enthusiasm for such endeavors. And now Sir Henry Clinton felt uneasy as he struck off through New Jersey with his 10,000 men, his long wagon train extending over twelve miles and therefore his flanks inviting attack from Washington's army and the New Jersey militia. Washington, previously in the dark as to Clinton's intentions, would not let the opportunity elude him. The Continental army, with the ordeal of Valley Forge behind it, with new recruits and new spirit engendered by the French alliance and the drill field labors of Friedrich Wilhelm von Steuben, overtook the slow-paced enemy at Monmouth Courthouse on June 28. Prior to making contact, Washington had held two councils of war that showed the commander in chief more disposed to fight than most of his generals, some of whom expressed reluctance to venture beyond the harassing tactics of the New Jersey irregulars and Daniel Morgan's riflemen, which, coupled with the extreme heat, were impeding the enemy's progress. On the 27th, Charles Lee, recently exchanged, moved out in response to orders to assail the British rear guard bivouacked at the courthouse. The indecision in the American command was mirrored the following morning as Lee, dubious from the beginning about the undertaking, went at the enemy, both Lee and Washington being unaware of the terrain or the enemy's strength—Lee's approaching van of 5,400 against 6,000 available to Clinton, who suspected a blow and prepared to meet it. Lee, having traversed three ravines in his line of march, was in danger of being pinned against any one of them before he could make his escape or before Washington, several miles away, could make his way over the route to rescue Lee's vanguard. Largely because of the terrain, hampering communications and making military formations difficult, Lee's troops, after initial probes, fell back. Under the circumstances

Lee did well enough—a good deal of confusion was inevitable. Managing to withdraw to the westernmost ravine, Lee during the last phase of the retrograde movement encountered Washington, who sharply criticized his subordinate.

Washington drew up a line of battle on a ridge just beyond the west ravine, and a general engagement ensued lasting the better part of the afternoon. Clinton made repeated stabs at the American left, right, and center. Americans were fighting a European army on European terms. The long Continental line stood fast, loosed volley after volley, and, here and there, counterattacked with the bayonet. It was now Clinton's turn to withdraw to higher ground, and some of the Americans pressed forward, only to halt as darkness enveloped the combat area. In the night Clinton decamped for Sandy Hook and New York, arriving several days later. The outcome of Monmouth was indecisive but heartening to American regulars who had stood face to face with Britain's best and given a good account of themselves.[45]

Had Baron von Steuben wrought a marvelous transformation in the Continental army? Washington, of course, had not been a bushwhacking general to begin with, and a healthy part of the army had fought before, sometimes quite well. Steuben had gained results at Valley Forge partly because he had experienced human material to work with. The chief contribution of the stout, balding baron, whose pretensions to being a lieutenant general and a twenty-two-year veteran in Prussian service were soon found out, was this: he imposed uniformity of evolutions, simultaneously simplifying them, where previously officers had often followed their own preference for the Prussian, British, or French system. Perspiring, cursing alternately in German, French, and eventually English, the baron personally saw to it that his system—the basis of his famous *Blue Book* of 1779—was drummed into the regiments at Valley Forge.[46]

If Monmouth bolstered the prestige of Steuben, the battle led to the downfall of the stormy Lee, who, after writing intemperate letters to Washington in defense of his honor, got the court-martial he demanded. Convicted of disobeying orders by not attacking, making an unnecessary retreat, and showing disrespect toward the commander in chief, Lee may well have fallen because he crossed swords with Washington. Interestingly and perhaps significantly, the youthful officers who so recklessly castigated Washington's critics, real and imagined, in the Cabal episode now blew the trumpets loudest for Lee's conviction, which resulted in a one-year suspension from the army, a humiliation Lee disdainfully rejected, prompting Congress to remove him from the service.[47]

Having derived the first benefits from France's coming openly to

America's side, Washington soon took his army over the Hudson and encamped at White Plains, New York. The situation, wrote Washington, was not a little surprising "that after two years Manoeuvring . . . both Armies are brought back to the very point they are set out from"; more lyrical was the London *Evening Post*'s description of British maneuvers in the colonies:

> Here we go up, up, up
> And here we go down, down, downy
> There we go *backwards* and *forwards*
> And here we go round, round, roundy.[48]

Washington confidently predicted even bigger and better things from the French alliance, especially since d'Estaing's fleet lay off Sandy Hook. But the French had not arrived in time to prevent Lord Howe from ferrying Clinton's column over to Manhattan, and since d'Estaing's largest ships drew too much water to cross the bar, he made no effort to force his way into New York harbor. The Admiral, though the essence of courtesy and lavish in his praise of Washington, the "Deliverer of America," pursued the interests of France and only within that framework the interests of America. This is understandable enough to a people accustomed to reading of *realpolitik* and national interest in the conduct of affairs. It was less so to certain exuberant patriots in 1778. Richard Henry Lee had boasted that the Admiral would "Act with and for us so long as the enemy by continuing here renders it necessary."[49]

When d'Estaing agreed to join the Americans in a *coup de main* against the British garrison in Rhode Island, General John Sullivan, commanding the Continental forces, proceeded to act as though d'Estaing were his subordinate. Then as Sullivan and d'Estaing (who had debarked 4,000 French troops) hit the island from land and sea, Lord Howe crowded sail from New York to relieve the Franco-American pressure on British General Robert Pigot and his defenders. Howe's squadron had been reinforced by stray war vessels, but it was not the equal of d'Estaing's. After d'Estaing put out of Narragansett Bay to engage Howe, and as the opposing admirals maneuvered for position, a fierce storm broke over them, damaging and scattering both fleets. The temperamental Sullivan exploded on learning from d'Estaing that the Admiral was not only going to Boston for his repairs, but he intended to take his French regulars with him. Sullivan, fearful of being stranded and then annihilated, managed to evacuate Rhode Island and American hopes of taking Newport collapsed. Before departing, though, Sullivan created his own fireworks by publicly condemning the French, and he expressed the hope "the event will prove America

able to procure with her own arms that which her Allies refuse to assist
in Obtaining."[50] Lafayette remonstrated at the abuse heaped upon his
native country, and d'Estaing, though one may cavil at his precipitous
withdrawal, had ample reason to deplore the public airing of the alliance's dirty linen. Washington's talents as a diplomat, often employed
to calm state jealousies, were now brought to bear. Conscious of the
differences in the French and American political systems, and fearful
his Gallic friends were not, Washington soothingly explained that "in a
free and republican government, you cannot restrain the voice of the
multitude"; here "every man will speak as he thinks," and the commander in chief stated that, if anything, Americans would have been even
more critical of their own forces had d'Estaing's fleet been an American
squadron.[51]

The military alliance was scarcely a spectacular success in this opening venture in joint operations. Nor were d'Estaing's soldiers and sailors
in Boston received with open arms. Rioting erupted in the Massachusetts capital between Americans and Frenchmen, and one of
d'Estaing's officers died of injuries. Massachusetts officials quickly acted
to placate French feelings. The officer was interred in a vault under
King's Chapel, and the legislature voted funds for a statue in his memory. No amount of good will would long detain d'Estaing once his refit-
ing was completed. On November 4, the charming visitor hoisted sail
with his entire fleet and passed over the horizon, leaving Washington
unsure of his objectives. Washington did not lose confidence in the
French, but the Rhode Island failure proved a sobering experience,
perhaps in the last analysis even a profitable one: France's entry was
not the millennium. In this spirit Washington persuaded Congress to
turn thumbs down on a proposal by Lafayette, temporarily sanctioned
by the lawmakers, to request French soldiers and ships for an allied
invasion of Canada. As Washington wisely pointed out, France, even
though an ally, was not to be trusted beyond her own interest, which
might well include regaining her former colony, the treaties of 1778
notwithstanding.

The French, for that matter, were not interested in Canada for themselves or for the Americans.[52] Versailles saw d'Estaing's foray as mo-
mentary relief, more psychological than anything else; and the Admiral's brief return to American waters in 1779 to participate in the
siege of Savannah was to be no more fruitful than the Rhode Island
operation. The preoccupation of France was with the West Indies, to
which d'Estaing repaired in November, 1778. Only in the hurricane
season could a French naval detachment be coaxed northward, then
to return to the Caribbean with the approach of winter.

The war in the Northern states was at a stalemate, and so it remained. The British retained only New York and Rhode Island (abandoning the latter in 1780). Nevertheless, Washington had fewer troops than Clinton, who, after saving Rhode Island in 1778, finally detached his expedition against St. Lucia. It was not easy for Washington to maintain a large army after three and a half years of fighting, especially when the British for the most part seemed to pose no immediate threat to New England and the middle states. Low pay and inadequate supplies and provisions continued to be deterrents to obtaining enlistments. Washington's qualities of patience and resolution were perhaps more called for in the "dull" period than ever before when apathy and war weariness were on the rise. Clinton, as we shall see, concentrated his attention on restoring royal control in the Southern states. Yet Washington and Clinton stayed alert; neither could read the other's mind. The Virginian could not prevent the enemy's occasional destructive coastal raids against New Bedford, New Haven, and elsewhere; but he could counter, as when Anthony Wayne stormed Clinton's advance post at Stony Point and when Henry (Light-Horse Harry) Lee raided Paulus Hook.

Let us end the chapter by returning momentarily to the campaign of 1778, to its final scene enacted in the West Indies. On November 3, the day before d'Estaing cleared Boston, Clinton's long-delayed expedition for St. Lucia sailed southward from New York, his transports accompanied by a small naval escort under Commodore William Hotham. Luckily for the Commodore, though he and d'Estaing traveled on a parallel course, the Frenchman with his superior squadron never got wind of the nearby enemy. Reaching Barbados early in December, Hotham's transports and war vessels united with the ships of Rear Admiral Samuel Barrington's West Indian command. Several days later they seized St. Lucia. Only after landing on the island did the British naval officers learn that d'Estaing too was in the Lesser Antilles and at the instant bearing down on them. A day earlier d'Estaing would have caught the smaller force in the open sea. Drawing his vessels close to shore, occupying a *cul-de-sac*, Barrington vitiated d'Estaing's superiority in numbers and his concentrated firepower repelled the enemy, just as afterward British troops on the island hurled back French regulars put ashore. D'Estaing withdrew, and soon afterward, on January 6, Admiral Byron's squadron with eight ships-of-the-line put in its appearance.

This was the same Byron, appropriately dubbed "Foul Weather Jack," who had been ordered six months previously to set out from England "without one moment's" loss in pursuit of the American-bound d'Estaing! While making for Halifax, hardly d'Estaing's objective, Byron's fleet was separated by severe storms, and Byron, after touching Halifax, finally reached New York in October. But the crisis in Rhode

Island was over; Clinton and Howe, with some aid from the elements, had held that beachhead. And when d'Estaing had slipped out of Boston in November, Byron once again had to give chase. Here the events bespoke an indictment of trusting in detachments to meet every French threat.

Superficially, it seemed that Britain had done well enough against her combined enemies in 1778—Philadelphia safely evacuated, New York secure, Rhode Island held, and, now, for the time being at any rate, naval superiority in the West Indies. Yet for Britain the ledger sheet for 1778 contained a warning: notwithstanding the accomplishments of Clinton, Lord Howe, and Barrington, lady luck had been her greatest warrior. The failure to contain the French fleet had time and again come close to resulting in disaster. In contrast, fortune never smiled on d'Estaing: he arrived off Philadelphia too late to trap Clinton's evacuating fleet; he failed to cross the bar into New York harbor; he saw a storm demolish his better than average chance of defeating Lord Howe off Narragansett Bay and pinning down Pigot's army on Rhode Island, its position analogous to Cornwallis' at Yorktown; and he missed nabbing the St. Lucia expedition while still at sea.[53] Given the continuation of the same naval policy in London, would Britain's luck continue to be so good? Would France's continue to be so bad?

## NOTES

1. Arthur M. Schlesinger, *Prelude to Independence: The Newspaper War on Britain, 1764-1776* (New York, 1958), 60.
2. Gerald Stourzh, *Benjamin Franklin and American Foreign Policy* (Chicago, 1954), 113; Max Savelle, "America and the Balance of Power, 1713-1778," in *The Era of the American Revolution*, ed. Richard B. Morris (New York, 1939), 158; Savelle, *The Colonial Origins of American Thought* (Princeton, 1964), 88-89. Professor Savelle, the leading authority on the subject, has written widely on early American foreign policy thinking. In addition to these studies, see his "Colonial Origins of American Diplomatic Principles," *Pacific Historical Review*, III (1934), 334-364; "The Appearance of an American Attitude Toward External Affairs, 1750-1775," *American Historical Review*, LII (1947), 655-666; *The Origins of American Diplomacy* . . . (New York, 1967).
3. Smyth, ed., *Writings of Franklin*, V, 254; on the subject generally, cf. Stourzh, *Franklin and Foreign Policy*, 114-116.
4. Dulany, *Considerations on Imposing Taxes*, in Bailyn, ed., *Pamphlets of the American Revolution*, I, 622; Crane, ed., *Franklin's Letters to the Press*, 185; *Boston Gazette*, Dec. 9, 1771. Franklin, urging the Stamp Act's repeal, told the House of Commons that the late Anglo-French conflict was of no vital interest to the colonists, that it "was really a British War." Smyth, ed., *Writings of Franklin*, IV, 439.
5. *Boston Gazette*, Jan. 1, 1772; *Newport Mercury*, July 13, 1772; *Virginia Gazette*, Jan. 5, 1776; Butterfield, ed., *Adams Diary and Autobiography*, II, 76; Michael G. Kammen, "The Colonial Agents, English Politics, and the American Revolution," *William and Mary Quarterly*, 3d ser., XXII (1965), 260-261. The concluding

sentences reflect the conclusion of Wonyung Hyun Oh, "Opinion of Continental American leaders on International Relations, 1763–1775" (unpubl. Ph.D. diss., University of Washington, 1963). This exceedingly valuable and important study successfully refutes certain assumptions of recent investigators, including Arthur M. Schlesinger, *Prelude to Independence*, and Felix Gilbert, *To the Farewell Address: Ideas of Early American Foreign Policy* (Princeton, 1961). Both Schlesinger and Gilbert believed, as Gilbert expressed it, that before Paine's piece almost no American had stated expressions in favor of independence (p. 40). In contrast, Mrs. Oh finds that the word independence "was not only voiced by the colonists but ideas similar to those of *Common Sense* were already advocated nearly five years before the publication of the pamphlet, and that all the arguments of the radicals in the second Continental Congress in the fall and winter of 1775 were included in *Common Sense*" (p. 170 n125). John Adams could only call Paine's work "a tollerable Summary of the Arguments which I had been repeating again and again in Congress for nine months." Butterfield, ed., *Adams Diary and Autobiography*, III, 333. The diminishing of Paine's originality, however, does not necessarily lessen the impact of his publication; his popularity may have been greater owing to the fact that the same notions were already under consideration. For an earlier statement anticipating some of Oh's investigations, see C. H. Van Tyne, "French Aid before the Alliance of 1778," *American Historical Review*, XXXI (1925), 33–34.

6. Syrett, ed., *Papers of Hamilton*, I, 154, 155.

7. Kammen, "Colonial Agents, English Politics, and the American Revolution," 261; Ford, ed., *Journals of Congress*, III, 392.

8. Butterfield, ed., *Adams Diary and Autobiography*, II, 236; Foner, ed., *Writings of Paine*, I, 20; Gilbert, *To the Farewell Address*, 53.

9. Franklin, Deane, and Lee to Vergennes, Feb. 1, 1777, Wharton, ed., *Revolutionary Diplomatic Correspondence*, II, 258, is typical of this idea.

10. On French agents, see Josephine F. Pachero, "French Secret Agents in America, 1763–1778" (unpubl. Ph.D. diss., University of Chicago, 1950). For a lengthy document in the French archives containing Choiseul's "Means for France to employ in order to reduce England . . . in the Balance of Europe," see Savelle, "The American Balance of Power and European Diplomacy, 1713–1778," 164–165.

11. John F. Ramsey, *Anglo-French Relations, 1763–1770: A Study of Choiseul's Foreign Policy* (Berkeley, 1939), chaps. vi–vii, x. Choiseul met with ill fortune in his aspirations to improve the colonies remaining in French hands in 1763: five trading posts in the dominion of the Great Mogul, Guiana, and a handful of islands scattered about the globe. This failure undoubtedly bolstered the government's willingness to eschew regaining its old New World territories during the American Revolutionary War. Carl L. Lokke, *France and the Colonial Question: A Study of Contemporary French Opinion, 1763–1801* (New York, 1932), 15–62. Lafayette later maintained that closer ties between the West Indian provinces and the new American republic would reinforce their economies. Louis R. Gottschalk, "Lafayette as a Commercial Expert," *American Historical Review*, XXXVI (1931), 561–570.

12. If American historians have usually overestimated Saratoga as almost the sole explanation for France's final plunge, Richard W. Van Alstyne, *Empire and Independence: The International History of the American Revolution* (New York, 1965), 133, may have proceeded too far in the opposite direction. He asserts that by September, 1777, the die was cast: that tension in the West Indies, where American commerce with the French was threatened by increased British power, "was the determining factor, not Saratoga." This valuable study, incorporating new information, is somewhat marred by its intemperate attacks on Samuel F. Bemis, *The Diplomacy of the American Revolution* (New York, 1935), still the best survey of the subject.

The motives for France's entry have been the subject of endless speculation. Five theories are enumerated and described in Arthur B. Darling, *Our Rising*

*Empire, 1763–1803* (New Haven, 1940), 22–26. A popular view, venerated by time and close Franco-American ties, has it that sentiments of liberal idealism motivated France's coming to the assistance of the rebellious colonials; its fullest expression is Bernard Fay, *The Revolutionary Spirit in France and America: A Study of Moral and Intellectual Relations between France and America at the End of the Eighteenth Century*, trans. Ramon Guthrie (New York, 1927). For a sharp and convincing dissent, elucidating the nature and complexity of French liberal thought in the 1770's, not all of which favored America, see Frances Acomb, *Anglophobia in France, 1763–1789: An Essay in the History of Constitutionalism and Nationalism* (Durham, N.C., 1950), 69–88. Miss Acomb further suggests that Fay and others have "apparently read back into the 1770's both that efferverscence of revolutionary sentiment that belongs rather to the 1780's and the utopian image of America" (p. 88).

That France was moved chiefly by a desire to regain her prestige in Europe, and at the expense of an old and bitter foe, with advantages in trade as a very secondary motive, is my own view. For perhaps the best statement of the prestige theme, see Edward S. Corwin, "The French Objectives in the American Revolution," *American Historical Review*, XXXI (1915), 33–61, and more generally the same author's *French Policy and the American Alliance of 1778* (Princeton, 1916).

13. The best edition of the full treaties is David Hunter Miller, ed., *Treaties and Other International Acts of the United States* (Washington, 1931–1948), II, 3–47. This supersedes Gilbert Chinard, ed., *The Treaties of 1778 and Allied Documents* (Baltimore, 1928).
14. John J. Meng, "A Foot-note to Secret Aid in the American Revolution," *American Historical Review*, XLIII (1938), 791–795; Elizabeth S. Kite, "French 'Secret Aid' Precursor to the French American Alliance, 1776–1777," *French American Review*, I (1948), 143–152.
15. The arrival of Beaumarchais' transports, sailing individually and in pairs, received wide publicity in the colonies: *Continental Journal*, April 24, Dec. 15, 1777; *Pennsylvania Packet*, April 1, 1777; *Boston Gazette*, April 28, 1777.
16. E. James Ferguson, *The Power of the Purse: A History of American Public Finance, 1776–1790* (Chapel Hill, 1961), 40–41, 126–127.
17. Stourzh, *Franklin and Foreign Policy*, 158–166, 299 n63. In Franklin's view, "these disputing, contradicting and confuting People are generally unfortunate in their Affairs. They get Victory sometimes, but they never get Good Will, which would be of more use to them." Leonard W. Labaree, ed., *The Autobiography of Benjamin Franklin* (New Haven, 1964), 213.
18. Wharton, ed., *Revolutionary Diplomatic Correspondence*, II, 508; *New-York Journal*, May 25, 1778; *Pennsylvania Journal*, May 21, 1777.
19. Wharton, ed., *Revolutionary Diplomatic Correspondence*, II, 282.
20. Samuel F. Bemis, *Pinckney's Treaty . . .*, 2d edn. (New Haven, 1960), 334, and 325–334 for a general account of the Spanish "debt," which Alexander Hamilton insisted on paying in the 1790's, though the court at Madrid never presented a claim against the United States. For a statistical breakdown of Spanish aid on a year-to-year basis, see J. F. Yela Utrilla, *España ante la independencia de los Estados Unidos* (Lérida, 1925), II, 375–378. The difficulties involved in unsnarling and evaluating the Revolutionary foreign debts, a problem for historians as it was for Hamilton's Treasury Department, are outlined in Ferguson, *Power of the Purse*, 193.
21. Johnston, ed., *Correspondence and Public Papers of Jay*, I, 249–250.
22. The conclusion of Richard B. Morris, *The Peacemakers: The Great Powers and American Independence* (New York, 1965), 239. The opinion seems valid, especially since the momentum for sacrificing the river traffic came from Southern congressmen, who, notwithstanding the value of the Mississippi to their agriculturally oriented section, initiated the "surrender" to Spain in the face of a British invasion of the lower South.

23. The most provocative treatment of the relationship between commerce and American foreign policy thinking in the early years of American independence is Paul A. Varg, *Foreign Policies of the Founding Fathers* (East Lansing, 1963), whose conclusions have influenced this study.

24. Quoted in Morris, *The Peacemakers*, 241, 237.

25. Isabel de Madariaga, *Britain, Russia, and the Armed Neutrality of 1780: Sir James Harris's Mission to St. Petersburg during the American Revolution* (New Haven, 1962), *passim*, especially chap. xviii. There is a good account of Catherine's rebuff to America in Varg, *Foreign Policies of the Founding Fathers*, 32–35. See also David M. Giffiths, "Nikita Panin, Russian Diplomacy, and the American Revolution," *Slavic Review*, XXVIII (1969), 1–23.

26. A revisionist view of the break with Frederick appears in Frank Spencer, "The Anglo-Prussian Breach of 1762: An Historical Revision," *History*, XLI (1956), 100–112. The author, who denies Frederick's charge of desertion, also asserts that British-Prussian difficulties did not lead European states to distrust and isolate George III's government. Prussia's reluctance to join Britain in a subsequent alliance rested more on a lack of common interests than on the breach in 1762. Echoing this outlook is J. Steven Watson, *The Reign of George III, 1760–1815* (Oxford, Eng., 1959), 73–78, 87. For a recent survey of British postwar foreign relations, emphasizing the 1760's, see the introduction to Frank Spencer, ed., *The Fourth Earl of Sandwich: Diplomatic Correspondence, 1763–1765* (Manchester, Eng., 1961), 3–66.

27. Mrs. Paget Toynbee, *The Letters of Horace Walpole* (London, 1903–1905), V. 7 n7; J. Richard Pares, "American versus Continental Warfare, 1739–1763," in Pares, *The Historian's Business and Other Essays*, eds. R. A. and Elisabeth Humphreys (Oxford, Eng., 1961), 130–172.

28. Pares, *George III and the Politicians*, 5.

29. That even the details of foreign aid to America were more or less public knowledge is the theme of Richard W. Van Alstyne, "Great Britain, the War of Independence, and the 'Gathering Storm' in Europe, 1775–1778," *Huntington Library Quarterly*, XXVII (1964), 311–346. Consequently, Van Alstyne attaches less significance to British intelligence efforts than does Samuel F. Bemis: "British Secret Service and the French-American Alliance," *American Historical Review*, XXIX (1924), 475–495; "Secret Intelligence, 1777: Two Documents," *Huntington Library Quarterly*, XXIV (1961), 233–249. See also F. P. Renaut, "Le secret service de l'amirauté britannique," *L'Espionage naval au XVIII siècle* (Paris, 1936). Certainly British naval officers felt there was great likelihood of a break with France a year or more before it came.

30. For Chatham's masterful analysis of the Bourbon danger and the reasons for accommodating the colonies, see William Cobbett, ed., *Parliamentary History of England* . . . (London, 1806–1820), XIX, 597–602, 741, 762–775.

31. On May 2, a month before the commission's arrival, the French treaties were delivered to Congress, which unanimously ratified them two days later. Washington's army celebrated the news on May 5.

32. George H. Guttridge, ed., *The Correspondence of Edmund Burke* (Chicago, 1961), III, 390. Editor Guttridge explains the "very few letters to or from Burke during the first three months of 1778" in terms of the feverish activity of Burke and his Rockingham faction in attacking the American war in Parliament (p. 418). See Carl B. Cone, *Burke and the Nature of Politics: The Age of the American Revolution* (Lexington, Ky., 1957), 299–303; Eliot R. Barkan, ed., *Edmund Burke on the American Revolution: Selected Speeches and Letters* (New York, 1966), xxiv; George H. Guttridge, *David Hartley, M.P., an Advocate of Conciliation, 1774–1783* (Berkeley, 1926), 287–288; George Thomas, Earl of Albemarle, *Memoirs of the Marquis of Rockingham and His Contemporaries* (London, 1852), II, 347–348.

33. Stuart, ed., *Journals of Walpole*, II, 80; Guttridge, ed., *Correspondence of Burke*, III, 409; Mackesy, *War for America*, 155, 220; Historical Manuscripts Commis-

sion, *Stopford-Sackville MSS*, II, 218. A West Indian wrote that those islands could not survive without maintaining the connection with the thirteen colonies. Samuel Estwick, *Letter to Tucker* (London, 1776), 55, cited in Dora Mae Clark, "British Opinion of Franco-American Relations, 1775–1795," *William and Mary Quarterly*, 3d ser., IV (1947) 306 n6.

34. Quoted in Van Alstyne, *Empire and Independence*, 141.

35. Lord John Russell, ed., *Memorials and Correspondence of Charles James Fox* (Philadelphia, 1853), I, 142–159, *passim*; Solomon Lutnick, "The American Victory at Saratoga: A View from the British Press," *New York History*, XLIV (1963), 111; Pares, *George III and the Politicians*, 119. In March, 1778, when Germain was piqued over the King's offering a sinecure to his arch-antagonist Carleton, George III referred to Germain's alleged forthcoming resignation as "a most favourable event." The Colonial Secretary would be "a heavy load whenever the failure of the expedition under Lt. G. Burgoyne came to be canvassed in Parliament, yet I never would have recommended his removal unless with his own good will[.] Now he will save us all trouble. . . ." Fortescue, ed., *Correspondence of George III*, IV, no. 2202.

36. Adams wrote: "Let her send all the ships she has round her island. What if her ill natur'd neighbours, France and Spain, should strike a blow in their absence?" *Boston Gazette*, Feb. 2, 1775.

37. Madariaga, *Britain, Russia, and the Armed Neutrality*, chaps. x–xii; Mackesy, *War for America*, 382–384.

38. Marvin L. Brown, Jr., trans. and ed., *American Independence through Prussian Eyes* (Duham, 1959), 17; William B. Willcox, "Why Did the British Lose the American Revolution?" *Michigan Alumnus Quarterly Review*, LXII (1956), 321. Willcox expresses the same sentiments, perhaps less emphatically, elsewhere: "British Strategy in America, 1778," *Journal of Modern History*, XIX (1947), 100–101; *Portrait of a General*, 211–215.

39. Some fairly recent secondary accounts confuse Clinton's instructions with an earlier order dated March 8. The King's final orders, along with a letter from Germain, both dated March 21, 1778, are in Stevens, ed., *Facsimiles from European Archives*, XI, nos. 1068–1069.

40. Williams, "Naval Administration," 87–90, 157–158; Mackesy, *War for America*, 186–187, 192–193.

41. A. T. Mahan, *The Influence of Sea Power upon History, 1660–1783*, 12th edn. (Boston, 1949), 527. If Keppel had a morbid fear of service trials, as is sometimes suggested, he had sufficient reason. Lord Albemarle, his oldest brother, had sat on Germain's court-martial, and Keppel himself had sat in judgment of Admiral John Byng, who was sentenced to death for the loss of Minorca in 1756, a most unjust verdict, one that Keppel and others tried unsuccessfully to get set aside. Dudley Pope, *At Twelve Mr. Byng Was Shot* (Philadelphia, 1962), chaps. xx–xxv.

42. Marcus, *Naval History of England*, 349; Graham, "Considerations on the War of American Independence," 29–30.

43. A harsh but warranted indictment of Sandwich on this matter is Gerald S. Brown, "The Anglo-French Naval Crisis, 1778: a Study of Conflict in the North Cabinet," *William and Mary Quarterly*, 3d ser., XIII (1956), 1–25; and in slightly more detail in Brown, *American Secretary*, 49–173, 221–232. Sandwich's chief antagonist was Germain, who asserted that "in all military operations of importance some risk must be run"; in this excellent document, dated April 29 and printed in *ibid.*, 163, Germain pointed out to the cabinet the dangers involved in failing to cope with French naval activity in the Western Hemisphere. Mackesy, though not unsympathetic to Sandwich and skeptical of the feasibility of a close blockade, admits that the First Lord of the Admiralty was constantly tempted "to forget the Channel fleet's role in global strategy: to over-insure in home waters and detach late and reluctantly." Mackesy, *War for America*, 194.

44. Willcox, *Portrait of a General*, 224, notes that any number of writers have erroneously stated that the decision to abandon Philadelphia was in anticipation

of d'Estaing's arrival. Clinton's orders went out from London before this threat was recognized.

45. Washington's casualties were at least 72 killed, 161 wounded, and 132 missing. Clinton reported his own losses as 294 dead and wounded—some of the former from the intense heat—and 64 missing. In addition to further casualties at the hands of American skirmishers before and after the battle, Clinton was minus 600 deserters, mainly Germans, during the trek across New Jersey. Freeman, *Washington*, V, 33, 43, and notes.

46. Alvin R. Sunseri, "Frederick Wilhelm von Steuben and the Re-Education of the American Army: A Lesson in Practicality," *Armor*, LXXIV (1965), 40–47. As to the baron's background, young John Laurens, really an enthusiastic admirer of the new drillmaster, confided to his father: "I must tell you tho', by the bye, that Congress has mistaken his rank in Prussia. . . . He had never any higher rank in the Prussian service, than that of colonel." William G. Simms, ed., *The Army Correspondence of Colonel John Laurens in the Year 1777–8* (New York, 1867), 137–138.

47. Alden's *Charles Lee*, chaps. xiii–xxvi, is sympathetic to Lee in this final phase of his patriot career. Clinton, never fond of Lee, gave his opinion that Lee's "whole corps would probably have fallen into the power of the King's army if he had . . . not retreated with the precipitancy he did." Clinton, *American Rebellion*, 96.

48. Fitzpatrick, ed., *Writings of Washington*, XII, 343; Lutnick, "American Victory at Saratoga," 126.

49. Lee to Jefferson, Aug. 10, 1778, Boyd, ed., *Jefferson Papers*, II, 208–209. *Pennsylvania Packet*, Aug. 4, 1778, predicted the "arrival of the French fleet . . . must soon terminate the American war, at least by land."

50. Hammond, ed., *Sullivan Papers*, II, 243–246, 264–265, and especially III, 645.

51. Fitzpatrick, ed., *Writings of Washington*, XII, 382. Alexander Hamilton believed "The stigmatizing an ally in public orders and one with whom we mean to continue in amity was certainly a piece of absurdity without parallel"—the "summit of folly." Syrett, ed., *Hamilton Papers*, I, 545–546. There are good accounts in Willcox, *Portrait of a General*, 234–249; Gottschalk, *Lafayette Joins the American Army*, 251–269; Thayer, *Greene*, 249–258; Whittemore, *General of the Revolution*, 83–111.

52. Although France under Article VI of the Treaty of Alliance renounced forever any aspirations for Canada, the United States, according to Article V, was permitted to keep Quebec and other British possessions to the north if they were taken in the course of the war. But from the beginning (and extending through the final treaty of peace) Vergennes opposed American expansion northward. Vergennes believed the money and manpower needed by Britain to hold Canada would diminish her strength in the European balance of power. At the same time, American fears of Britain on her northern border would keep the new nation in the arms of France. Doniol, *Histoire de la participation de la France*, III, 153–158; Georges Lacour-Gayet, *La marine militaire de la France sous le règne de Louis XVI* (Paris, 1905), 174–175.

53. One can but speculate as to what extent d'Estaing's cautiousness influenced the above-mentioned episodes. A soldier turned sailor in 1759, he quite possibly felt less confident than an admiral brought up in the navy. In any case, prudence was his chief characteristic. An unflattering, unidentified contemporary estimate —"Remarks and Comments on What Took Place During M le Comte d'Estaing's Campaign in America"—is in Freeman, *Washington*, V, appendix I, 503–505. Gerald S. Graham, "Considerations on the War of American Independence," 30, declares that even with the recent improvement in French naval science, "A century of . . . numerical inferiority had left an indelible mark on the French naval mind."

# 11. Loyalties and Liberties

I T CAN BE REASONED that the best gauge of a society's devotion to its expressed principles occurs in time of crisis—in war, for instance, when adhering to ideals comes at a price. Did the American patriots who so eloquently proclaimed the rights of mankind hold those very freedoms in contempt during the War of Independence? Through outpourings from the press, thunderings from the pulpit, and a welter of laws and edicts, they mounted a campaign to enforce substantial conformity on the home front. The Revolutionary regimes stifled free expression, ordered arrests, impressed goods, confiscated land, and exiled their opponents.

The role of the revolutionists in setting precedents is of the first moment for later Americans fearful of what they consider a growing atmosphere of conformity at the expense of basic civil liberties. Superficially, at least, the anti-communist affidavits of the Taft-Hartley and National Defense Education Acts seem analogous to the loyalty oaths enacted by most of the state legislatures in 1776 and 1777, just as present-day accusations about subversion are sometimes couched in language that might well have been used by those responsible for ferreting out loyalists and other obstructionists nearly two hundred years ago.

But there are fundamental differences between the atmosphere of 1776 and that of nearly two centuries later. Earlier Americans were endeavoring to create and sustain *revolutionary* governments. Until the war terminated in victory, they lived, in a very real sense, in Locke's wild, turbulent state of Nature. They faced a potentially overwhelming threat *at home*: from the loyalists and from British armies. The demands of self-preservation are indubitably greater in such an atmosphere— where a nation is struggling to be born—than in an old, established nation with vast means for protecting and sustaining its existence.

## The Press

With the passage of the Stamp and Townshend Acts, both directly hitting the American newspapers, the first imposing taxes on printed matter, the second levying duties on the commodity of paper, Britain offended a class of Americans—the pressmen—whose ability to influence colonial thinking was to be dramatically revealed. The printers did not engineer the protests against the mother country, but certainly they stimulated and articulated the resistance. Strongly sympathetic to the patriot cause, they filled their columns with pseudonymous tracts (as was the custom of the day) castigating the ministry and Parliament. Benjamin Edes' and John Gill's *Boston Gazette*, Isaiah Thomas' *Massachusetts Spy*, John Holt's *New-York Journal*, William Bradford's *Pennsylvania Journal*, and Peter Timothy's *South-Carolina Gazette* were unsurpassed in their whiggish proclivities. Their writers usually wielded abler pens than did the essayists for the smaller tory press, which was generally timorous unless assured of British protection.[1]

The spectacular growth of the newspaper is highly suggestive as to its influence in fostering anti-British thought and sustaining it during eight wearisome years of war. By 1764, the year of the Sugar Act, there were twenty-three newspapers in the colonies, a number that swelled to thirty-seven by early 1775. Though fifteen of them expired during the contest and eighteen new ones died in infancy during the same period, another fifteen hatched amidst the din of conflict survived. The country claimed thirty-five going journals when Cornwallis capitulated at Yorktown. And people did read the papers! In 1778 the *Connecticut Courant* boasted of an amazing 8,000 readers.[2] Letters to the printer from the back country attest to a wide circulation. Newspapers passed from hand to hand, reserved a prominent spot on tavern walls, and served as topics of endless conversation. Friend and foe alike agreed on the newspaper's part in fanning the flames of resistance. "It was by the means of Newspapers," wrote John Holt in January, 1776, "that we receiv'd and spread the Notice of the tyrannical Designs formed against America, and kindled a Spirit that has been sufficient to repel them." Likewise, Ambrose Serle, Lord Howe's secretary and temporarily editor of the tory *New-York Gazette and Mercury*, ascribed much of "the present Commotion" to "this popular Engine."[3]

The performance of the newspapers during the war itself is even more remarkable considering the vicissitudes of the struggle. The king's army at some time occupied almost every major American city, forcing the patriot printers to flee. In mid-April, 1775, the presses of the *Boston Gazette* and *Massachusetts Spy* were quietly moved at night—the *Gazette* to Watertown, seat of the Massachusetts Provincial Congress;

the *Spy* farther west to Worcester, which became its permanent home. When redcoats descended upon New York City the following year, John Holt transplanted his *Journal* upriver to Kingston, only to switch his establishment—this time to Poughkeepsie—when Howe's regulars burned the town.[4] Spiraling inflation, joined with acute shortages of paper in bulk, increased the cost of some newspapers and brought the death of others. The influential *Maryland Gazette* suspended publication for a year and a half owing to the scarcity of paper, and several journals reduced their size from a sheet to a half sheet. The printers of the *Massachusetts Spy* and the *Connecticut Courant* implored all fair daughters of liberty to save their cotton and linen rags; and Washington gave a publisher a supply of tent cloth in order that the soldiers might have an opportunity to read a newspaper. Military campaigns, physical destruction, and abominable colonial roads also frustrated American newspapermen, hampering the gathering of intelligence, just as they slowed the delivery of newspapers to distant subscribers. The Constitutional, or American, postal system, fathered by William Goddard of the *Maryland Journal* and subsequently taken over by the Continental Congress, worked as well as could be expected under precarious circumstances.

As the Revolutionary newspaper ventured full sail into the opinionmaking arena, the issue of freedom of the press predictably reared its head. Nine of the eleven states to frame constitutions during the war adopted statements resembling article XII of the Virginia Declaration of Rights: "That the freedom of the press is one of the great bulwarks of liberty, and can never be restrained but by despotic governments." It is not easy to say precisely what this "grand palladium of liberty," in the *Pennsylvania Journal*'s phrase, meant to Americans of the Revolutionary generation. Recently taking issue with most authorities past and present, Leonard Levy has denied that American leaders of the last quarter of the eighteenth century adhered to a broad concept of free expression. Neither the state constitutions nor the Bill of Rights expressly precluded the criminal law of seditious libel that had emerged in England—and had found application in the colonies—during the seventeenth and eighteenth centuries. According to Levy, an enlightened mind of the age would probably have understood freedom of expression to mean one's right to speak or print all that was accurate and well meaning, so long as that fell short of being considered seditious or libelous by the community and the courts.[5]

Quite predictably the rod descended upon the tories, who were regarded as enemies of the state. As Arthur M. Schlesinger so aptly said, "liberty of speech belonged solely to those who spoke the speech of liberty." Of course no government permits open succor to its opponents. Thus the relevant question concerning the press in the War of Inde-

pendence is to what extent was unfettered discussion permitted within
the patriot camp itself? It is well to keep in mind that the cardinal
tenet of the American Revolution was that government rests upon the
consent of the governed, a proposition that involved the right of selecting between opposing opinions and reviewing the conduct of public
officials. One cannot escape the feeling, after perusing the newspapers
of the war years, that many Americans had formulated libertarian theories of freedom of speech and press that went far in the direction of
free rein to criticize the government and its officials, despite the continued presence of the common-law theory of seditious libel. Indeed,
the willingness of people to risk prosecution for supposedly calumniat-
ing public men and uttering false statements implies a "popular" view
of free expression.[6] Some excellent statements in behalf of open, unin-
hibited discussion adorned the newspapers of the Revolutionary war:

> It is the birthright of Freemen to examine the conduct of public men,
> and to deliver their Sentiments on public measures. The present crisis of
> our affairs requires every friend to his country to Speak his mind freely,
> and with a jealous eye to watch the proceedings of those to whom he has
> committed the sacred trust of maintaining his liberties.
>
> I consider the freedom of the press as one of the greatest bulwarks of
> the liberties of a people; and, happily for this state, it is secured by an article
> in the declaration of rights. I must confess, this freedom is apt to degenerate
> into an extreme; the most respectable characters are sometimes traduced;
> the solemn deliberations of public bodies are exhibited in unfavourable lights,
> and the basest of motives imputed to the worthiest of men. These are incon-
> veniences, which every enlightened mind will easily submit to, when he
> reflects, what a powerful check this liberty exerts on the public and private
> conduct of every individual, who respects at all the opinions of liberty.
> I have had the honour to experience the little malice of writers; but am
> so far from willing to destroy, or abridge this invaluable right of free citizens,
> that I would as soon renounce the trial by jury.
>
> . . . thank God, my countrymen are not yet, and I trust they never will
> be, such flatterers of men in power as to hesitate a moment to point out
> any mistakes or faults either in the civil or military departments. Good
> magistrates, and good officers, will thank and esteem the man who has
> honesty enough to show them their errors. . . .[7]

There were instances when these professions were put to the test. On
February 25, 1777, William Goddard's *Maryland Journal* printed an
essay by Samuel Chase, a future justice of the United States Supreme
Court, who, signing himself "Tom Tell-Truth," satirically advised rec-
onciliation: "My soul overflows with gratitude to the patriotic virtuous
King, the august incorruptible Parliament, and wise disinterested Min-
istry of *Britain*." The humour of the piece escaped the Whig Club of
Baltimore, "a set of men not remarkable for their penetration and

sagacity." When Goddard, "with *mulish obstinancy*," refused to repudi-
ate the tract and reveal its author, the zealous Whig Club ordered him
out of town. Goddard appealed to the lower house of the Maryland
legislature, which upheld the redoubtable printer and cited in his defense the state Declaration of Rights. Two years later Goddard was
again in hot water after publishing an anonymous diatribe—by General
Charles Lee—against George Washington, and for a second time authorities backed him up. "It is surprising to what extent the Whig
printers asserted their independence of outside pressure," observes a
careful analyst. "Considerations of political expediency, it would seem,
should have barred many an item that was printed. Published criticisms
of public officials and policies were remarkably outspoken."[8] And while
armies maneuvered and fought, battles raged behind the lines on such
diverse subjects as the treatment of Quakers, the morality of slavery,
the relationship of religion to the state, the means of creating a stable
currency, and the provisions of the state constitutions and the Articles
of Confederation.

More importantly, it was the newspaper that brought home the war
and its implications to the American people. Printers crowded their
columns with detailed accounts of battles and campaigns, frequently
in the form of letters from eyewitnesses including official communiques
from Washington and other generals to the Continental Congress. They
publicized proclamations of Congress and acts of the legislatures,
printed appeals for recruits and provisions, and tacked on desertion
lists.[9] The depravity of the British, the perfidy of the loyalists, and the
dangers of war weariness were perpetual themes. Joining Thomas
Paine as literary propagandists of a high order were Philip Freneau,
Hugh Henry Brackenridge, David Humphreys, William Henry Drayton, James Iredell, and Francis Hopkinson, the last named probably the
most skillful war satirist on the American side.[10] But second only to
Paine in his proficiency to depict the ravages of the enemy was Governor William Livingston of New Jersey, who cried that the war had

opened the eyes of those who were made to believe, that their impious
merit in abetting our persecutors, would exempt them from being involved
in the common calamity. But as the rapacity of the enemy was boundless;
their rapine was indiscriminate, and their barbarity unparalleled. They have
plundered friends and foes. Effects capable of division, they have divided.
Such as were not, they have destroyed. They have warred upon decrepit
age; warred upon defenceless youth. They have committed hostilities against
the possessors of literature; and the ministers of religion. Against the public
records; and private monuments; and books of improvement. . . . They have
butchered the wounded, asking for quarter; mangled the dying, weltering in
their blood; refused to the dead the rights of sepulchers; suffered prisoners

to perish for want of sustenance; violated the chastity of women; disfigured private dwellings of taste and elegance; and in the rage of impiety and barbarism, profaned edifices dedicated to the Almighty God.[11]

In line with the canons of the century, the most frequent and probably the most inspirational literary form was the letter or the essay, ranking well above poetry and song. Myriad pieces appeared to stimulate morale, patriotic ardor, and national consciousness. The newspapers show, as is generally known, that the American Revolution introduced ideological conflict into warfare. "The Consequences of this Struggle," prophesied "Cato" in the *South-Carolina Gazette*, "will determine, whether Americans will be Freemen or Slaves"; whether there was "room upon the earth for honest men," declared Paine. The "nature of the American Revolution," assured William Henry Drayton, was such that it promised greater freedom than men had achieved in modern history. It was, wrote "a Soldier," a "most just and holy war, in defence of our country, our wives, children, parents, and sisters, and to secure to ourselves and our posterity the inestimable blessings of *Liberty*."[12]

Seldom if ever had a civilian population lavished such attention upon its military forces. The Continentals were *their* soldiers; they were citizens—"the boys from home." Their solicitude found expression in an assortment of communications to the press. People wrote to suggest drill procedures, sanitation methods, and dietary habits. An opponent of spirituous liquors vowed that a small quantity of vinegar mixed with water would have the same "stimulating" results (without the ill effects) as demon rum upon tired soldiers. A resident of the Old Dominion reminded the "Officers of the Virginia Army" that the parents throughout the state would hold the military leaders strictly accountable for the "moral conduct" of their sons, who should be protected from "gaming, profaneness, and debauchery."[13]

Nor were the daughters of liberty inattentive. "An American Woman" boasted that the fairer sex "manifested a firm resolution to contribute . . . to the deliverance of their country. . . . This sentiment is universal from the north to the south of the Thirteen United States." Anne Terrell of Bedford County, Virginia, reminded wives why they must temporarily sacrifice their husbands; they were "nobly supporting the glorious cause of liberty." Reportedly "the young Ladies of the best Families" in Mecklenburg County, North Carolina, formed a "voluntary Association" not to entertain the addresses of any young gentlemen unwilling to fight in defense of their country. In Philadelphia and Boston females, working in teams, canvassed the cities collecting goods and money for the benefit of Washington's army. "The shilling offered by the widow or the young girl, will be received as well as the most considerable sums. . . ." Women thoughout Maryland, Pennsylvania, and Massachusetts were urged to work to the same end, with a treasurer selected for every county—the proceeds to be forwarded to each governor's wife, who in turn would send them on to Mrs. Washington at camp. This undertaking bears a remote relationship to the U.S.O. and other philanthropic agencies of recent wars. For the purpose of these distaff patriots was not to contribute supplies and equipment that were the responsibility of Congress and the states: instead their aim was to make "conditions more pleasant" for the soldiery.[14]

In arousing Americans for the cause of freedom, the newspapers of the Revolutionary War were simultaneously spurring a spirit of American nationalism. Though colonial Americans spoke the same language, shared a common culture, and enjoyed the same historical traditions, their sense of oneness had not propelled them to independence. They had only undertaken that step in 1776 when Britain failed to meet their demands within the framework of the empire. Thus, whereas nationalism has been the potent instigator of revolutions in Europe, Africa, and Asia, it has pursued a different course in America by becoming the product—not the cause—of revolution. But though the war witnessed a conversion from a colonial to a national psychology, the change came slowly. Americans were not yet ready for the creation of "a well planned Continental Government," as Joseph Hawley of Massachusetts expressed it. In speaking of the proposed Articles of Confederation, Samuel Johnston of North Carolina, himself a nationalist, conceded that "the only object of importance at present is the Defence of the Country, [and] till that is effectually insured Leagues [,] Confederacies and Constitutions are premature except as temporary expedients." The kind of union envisaged by Hawley and Johnston would not come to pass until the writing and ratification of the Federal Constitution a decade or so later. But Americans were building the bricks and mortar of nationality out of their common beliefs and wartime experiences. The newspapers diffused this knowledge to Americans everywhere. Battle reports told of Virginians fighting at Quebec and Saratoga, of Delaware men holding the lines at New York City, of Massachusetts regiments performing at Brandywine and Germantown, and of Marylanders marching to assist South Carolina. There emerged a cluster of *American* heroes. A Bostonian proclaimed, after the Battle of Bennington, that "General Stark has immortalized his name. . . . Every man that fought there will be dear to his country." In distant New Bern, North Carolina, the tidings of Burgoyne's surrender at Saratoga met with "great Acclamation" as "the whole Town . . . waited on his Excellency the Governor at the Palace, where many patriotic toasts were drank, under a Display of the continental Flag, and the Evening concluded with a festive Joy that testified the Feelings of Americans. . . ."[15]

Nationalism, especially the budding variety, is deeply in need of tangible signs; and the press played a part in making Washington a symbol of American ideals and virtues. The journals enlightened the public about the man who commanded their armies, the general whose shoulders bore such burdensome responsibilities. An experienced officer, he had fought for America in the French and Indian War. Returning to "the delights of peace" and "the pleasures of domestic felicity," he had cultivated his acres before duty once more elevated him to the service of the people, this time with no personal compensation except the cost of his necessities. Washington loomed as no potential despot, but bore the marks of a "free and independent Citizen" whose natural inclination would ever be to sit under his own vine and fig tree. A great soldier beyond doubt, who combined "the coolness of a Fabius, the intrepedity of an Hannibal, and the indefatigable ardour and military skill of a Caesar," Washington ranked equally high as a statesman and shone "with unrivalled splendour in every department of life." "Brave without ostentation, magnificent without pomp, and accomplished without pride," he was "an honour to the human race, and the idol of America," truly "raised by Heaven to . . . guide the chariot of War."[16] Here indeed were the ingredients of legend intertwined with considerable truth.

The public response was predictable. As early as 1775 babies were christened after him; as early as 1779 his birthday was publicly celebrated, the same year of the first Washington biography. Prints of Washington paintings adorned American homes in Philadelphia and elsewhere. Toasts to the tall Virginian, wishing him health and success, were a part of every fourth of July observance.[17] The anniversary of independence itself helped to further fulfill the country's lack of national symbols; and the papers invariably gave space to the recurring festivities. The ringing of bells, the displaying of flags, the military review, the firing of cannon (thirteen or seventy-six), the toasts (usually thirteen) and speeches—all these constituted the form of celebrating "the fourth" well into the nineteenth century.[18]

## The Pulpit

When South Carolina's politician-physician-historian David Ramsay testified that the "press had a merit equal to that of the sword" in winning independence, he could have easily added that the pulpit could not have been far behind. The clergy from the birth of the colonies had commanded respect and influence; they had often guided their flocks in politics as well as religion; and they traditionally had exercised a role of unofficial leadership in time of crisis. Congregationalists, Presby-

terians, Baptists, and the other multiplying sectarians of Calvinist origin might still cross swords as in the past over fine points of doctrine
and worship, just as single denominations divided into "New Lights"
and "Old Lights" during the Great Awakening; but they could all agree
that both religious tyranny and political tyranny were blasphemous in
the sight of God. His American children saw in the 1760's and 1770's
threats not only from the British state but also from the Anglican
church, where certain zealots were striving to create a complete episcopal establishment in America. The colonists' spiritual mentors
thundered from their meetinghouses against both unlawful taxation
and bishops who might stifle religious diversity as in the days of
Charles I. The actual threat from the established church, somewhat
exaggerated by the colonists, was small compared to the danger from
the king's government that culminated in war.[19]

The chief contribution of the patriot clergy in steeling Americans
for the protracted military struggle was not in the arena of political
thought. Though many clergymen were familiar with theories of social
compact, natural rights, fundamental law, and the virtues of republican
government—and though they articulated these ideals to their congregations—they left the principal intellectual battle of political theories
and principles to the laity: to the holders of public office and the essayists for the press.[20] The American Revolution required religious
foundations to match the political underpinnings provided by Jefferson
and Paine. Americans needed to know God's attitude concerning war in
general and the current hostilities in particular. And to provide the
answers clerics turned for the most part from the recent past; they went
far beyond the seventeenth century of Locke and the commonwealthmen—so popular with the political intellectuals of the American Revolution—to Old Testament times.

The employment of the sword was a familiar part of man's behavior.
The Reverend Samuel Cook, delivering a Lexington anniversary oration in 1777, explained that "wars and fightings, destruction and bloodshed, from the beginning, have arisen, in all ages and countries. . . ."
Brutal and merciless, sparing neither age nor sex, human conflict as
seen in the tribulations of the Israelites bore no relationship to the
leisurely, even gentlemanly warfare characteristic of Europe in the
eighteenth century. Prey for the tyrants of Assyria, Persia, and Rome,
the Israelites, like the Americans—God's chosen people of a later day
—were abused and persecuted. In a 1777 thanksgiving sermon, Timothy
Dwight compared King Sennacherib's invasion of the Jewish homeland,
supposedly seven hundred and five years before the birth of Christ, to
George III's turning his legions upon the thirteen states. Wars stemmed
from the evil in mankind. Neither reason nor religion had ever restrained ambitious men from "invading the persons, liberties, and pos-

sessions of their neighbors. . . ." Both the looters of Israel and the redcoats desecrating America revealed an "insatiable lust of unrighteous
gain. . . ." Britain's moral decay had rent the empire asunder; her
"luxury, effeminancy, and irreligion" were manifestations of her fall.
Calvinist traditions continued to wax strong in America, whereas a
sense of man's depravity and the threat it held for government had
been sapped in England and Europe by the Enlightenment. Consequently, Americans recognized that depravity was a universal affliction,
not simply a British abomination. The imperfections of Americans,
though less glaring than those of Englishmen, nonetheless posed problems for a people hoping for the Lord's support. The fact was acknowledged in the middle states and in the South as well as in Puritan New
England; for most protestant denominations (even low-church Anglicans) believed that human hardships were in some measure divinely
inspired by man's imperfections, by failure to keep his covenant with
God[21]

American shortcomings helped to account for the present calamities.
The distressing situation would remain unchanged unless Americans,
singly and *en masse*, confessed their iniquities and engaged in acts of
repentance. A vast stream of clerical messages called for a spiritual
rejuvenation that was essential to arouse patriotic zeal and to insure the
blessing of Providence. In Massachusetts in 1775, Zabdiel Adams admonished his listeners that God had from time to time allowed the
ancient Jews to be conquered because they had practiced idolatry with
certain of their neighbors. The moral was obvious: "a people can have
no well grounded confidence of success in war, notwithstanding the
justice of their cause . . . unless their own character be righteous and
good. . . ." At Philadelphia in the same year clergyman David Jones also
warned his hearers of how, when evil set in among the Hebrews, they
lost their martial spirit and fell prey to the king of Babylon. Below the
Mason and Dixon line people also looked "to their Spiritual pastors with
great respect," stated Congressman Joseph Hewes of North Carolina;
"truths from their mouths come with redoubled influence upon their
minds." Hewes might also have noted that the message was in many
cases the gospel as unfolded by the Presbyterians of Philadelphia and
the Congregationalists of New England: one could not defeat British
depravity from abroad without first getting the upper hand over
wrongdoing at home.[22]

The civilian leaders of the Revolution and the whig clergy found a
common denominator in their conviction of human depravity. Morality
was as vital to the state as it was to the church, for neither institution
could flourish in the face of vice and corruption. The nonimportation
movements of the 1760's and 1770's had perhaps first illuminated the
puritanical strain that was a part of the American Revolution by calling

for a simpler and self-sufficient mode of life. Like numbers of civilian leaders, Washington was scarcely orthodox in religion, but he joined Congress in the belief that organized religion was essential to the morale and conduct of American fighting men. Congress annually in the course of the war set aside days for humiliation, fasting, and prayer, as the New England colonies had done for a century and a half. In 1780, five years after the first such proclamation, the lawmakers conceded, as they had in 1775, that Americans' manifold offenses had brought the ravages of the sword, that only by earning God's favor would victory crown the patriots' efforts.[23] It may be no exaggeration to state, as does Perry Miller, that "What carried the ranks of militia and citizens was the universal persuasion that they, by administering to themselves a spiritual purge, acquired the energies God had always, in the manner of the Old Testament, been ready to impart to His repentant children. Their first responsibility was not to shoot redcoats but to cleanse themselves; only thereafter to take aim."[24]

It was the Christian duty of Americans, once transfused with religious and moral spirit, to resist stoutly the immoral British onslaught, just as Moses, Joshua, and David had repelled God's foes in days of old. America need not quake because of her relative military weakness in comparison to her oppressors; God had regularly invigorated the just so that they could slay their powerful enemies. But woe unto those who would not fight in behalf of America's righteous cause. When the noble Barak had gone forth to battle against the hordes of Jabin, ruler of Canaan, the people of Meroz, "state or town in Israel," had denied Barak men and supplies. As a consequence an angel of the Lord afflicted them with a terrible curse. A multitude of patriot preachers drove home the point for the benefit of the apathetic and the neutralists that God scourged them not for aiding His enemies but for denying His friends.[25]

There were visible signs of God's concern for His American children. His hand was seen at Lexington and Concord, at Trenton and Princeton. The 28th of November, 1777, a day of "General and Solemn Thanksgiving" occasioned by Burgoyne's denouement at Saratoga, was to serve as a reminder that "the interposition of Divine Providence" rather than "our own Strength" had determined the glorious outcome. God revealed Himself just as naturally in adversity and defeat; only His influence had kept America on her feet.[26]

Members of the "black regiment"[27] frequently responded with deeds to match their words. Many served as chaplains in the Continental army, while others joined General Peter Henry Muhlenberg, a Lutheran, in taking directly to arms. In Virginia and possibly South Carolina, even the Anglican clergy overwhelmingly backed the Continental cause. At least five Virginia clerics exchanged the surplice for a military

uniform. In twenty counties of the Old Dominion, priests of the established church served as members of local committees of safety.[28]

It was only in a sense that the patriot preachers sold the War of
Independence to the American people. As was true of the politicians
who spoke of natural law and social compact, the Revolutionary ministers were expounding beliefs already widely held. But seldom has
the message been so stimulating to a people in need of wartime
resolution.

## *Laws and Machinery*

General Nathanael Greene hailed patriotism as "a glorious principle"
essential to a nation at war; but, he admonished, "never refuse her the
necessary aids." Greene, Paine, and other Revolutionary stalwarts
recognized that sonorous appeals to the glorious future of republican
America and to the words of the Scriptures were insufficient to draw all
Americans into the patriot orbit.[29] Some of their countrymen were
fence-sitters, and others openly refused to cut loose from their British
moorings. The outcome of the Revolution hinged on the Americans'
ability to succeed on the homefronts as well as on the battle fronts. If
the civilian authority crumbled, the collapse of Washington's army
would inevitably follow. Except for the occasional employment of Continental troops, the states led the assault against the enemy within, for
the Continental Congress lacked the requisite power and machinery
for action at the grass-roots level. The procedure varied from the pattern of future years when the national government assumed the brunt
of responsibility for coping with subversion.

Initially, however, Continental action served to spur the states into
the arena. The defection of Benjamin Church, the Congressional authorization of the death penalty for soldiers adhering to George III, the
revelation of a tory plot to assassinate Washington, these and other
episodes prompted Congress on June 24, 1776, to urge the states to de-
fine disloyalty and to enact measures to counteract it.[30] Most of the
states responded quickly, though the phraseology of their statutes
varied widely. If levying war against the state and adhering to its foes
generally constituted treason, what did the language mean specifically?
New Jersey, New York, and Delaware fell back on English common and
statutory law in enumerating treasonable activity. Pennsylvania, North
Carolina, Connecticut, and New Jersey went so far as to embrace almost all manner of cooperation with the enemy, including trade, within
their definition.

The states also defined crimes that amounted to less than treason. A
heavy hand descended upon those guilty of recognizing the sovereignty

of George III, encouraging persons to forsake American allegiance, discouraging enlistments in the patriot service, advising against resistance to armed invasion, expressing hostility to the state government, disseminating false information, and affording the enemy intelligence. For these offenses the statutes usually prescribed fines, detention, imprisonment, hard labor, and compulsory military service. The severity of this legislation sometimes bore a relationship to the course of the war. Thus Virginia in 1780, menaced from the outside, levied a maximum fine of one hundred thousand pounds' weight of tobacco and a five-year prison term upon anyone writing, printing, preaching, or saying that he was loyal to the King or that the King enjoyed any jurisdiction over America.[31]

The patriots, unwilling to wait for the royalists to expose themselves by hostile conduct, took steps to bring to public view those inimical to the Revolution. The *South-Carolina and American General Gazette*, speaking for state authority, commanded all nonresidents of Charleston as well as all from outside the state who had arrived in the city during the past month to register with the secretary of South Carolina, giving him adequate identification and making known their business. Subsequently, newcomers were to register in the prescribed manner within forty-eight hours of arrival. "Cato" in Maryland advised the states' whigs to keep a sharp eye on their suspicious neighbors to prevent them "from rendering you the very mischief they most assuredly would do you, were they at will." The printer of the *Connecticut Courant* believed it absolutely essential that "All Persons inimical to the country" be "hung up to view."[32]

Loyalty oaths have been a commonplace response when people are fearful of subversion, and the American Revolutionaries resorted to such tests to distinguish friend from foe. The first Revolutionary yardstick of fidelity was adherence to Congress' Continental Association, a uniform boycott regulation for all the colonies. Some Americans gladly signed the association, some subscribed out of duress, and still others did so in the hope of keeping the movement for American rights in moderate hands. The rapid pace of developments after Lexington and Concord generated new thought and action concerning loyalty procedures. Temporarily Washington entered the field of loyalty testing, twice sending expeditions to Long Island and once to Rhode Island and Connecticut. Continental officers worked with local patriots in rounding up the supposedly disaffected, compelling them to profess their allegiance or languish in jail. Approval by county committees of Washington's endeavors was not matched by state authorities, who informed the army that determining fealty was their business. Similarily a Washington-directed loyalty-testing campaign after Trenton and

Princeton prompted prerogative-conscious state politicians to lodge
such strong complaints that never again did the army or Congress impose tests upon civilians. Tests for the army were another matter, and
Congress, backed by the states, required in October, 1776, that every
soldier take an oath to uphold the United States and to obey Continental officers. In February, 1778, Congress drafted a stronger declaration that all Continental officials, civil and military, were obliged to
swear.

The states preempted for themselves the field of civilian loyalty testing, and by 1778 every one boasted enactments in this area. In Virginia
all free male inhabitants over the age of sixteen were to subscribe to
an oath renouncing loyalty to George III and his successors, agreeing
to do nothing harmful to the freedom and independence of America,
and promising to divulge all known treasons or traitorous conspiracies.
Nonjurors faced the loss of weapons and the franchise, sacrificing as
well all right to public office, jury duty, sue for debt, and purchase
property. Subsequently, they were compelled to pay double and eventually triple their regular taxes.[33] Throughout America those persisting
in abjuring state oaths, whatever their real motives, were often labeled
tories and faced the possibility of arrest, fines, and exile with the confiscation of their property—all this, not to mention the vengeance of
their whig neighbors. The contents of the oaths and the procedures for
taking the tests were publicized by newspapers and by an assortment
of local and state functionaries.[34]

Civil libertarians, with a glance to the present, have faulted the patriots for resorting to loyalty oaths; but the Revolutionary oaths, asking
for the renunciation of a prior allegiance to Britain and calling for adherence to a new state, have much in common with naturalization
oaths. It is worth recalling that the requirement was not confined to
suspected tories. John Adams considered such a declaration to be positive rather than negative in that it would inspire the friends of the
Revolution to live up to a sacred obligation to defend freedom.[35]
Moreover, the oaths were not without relevance to the social contract
doctrine embodied in the Declaration of Independence. It was essential
to know who would and who would not subscribe to the new contract.
Within the framework of Revolutionary thought, men could easily
enough justify loyalty oaths and other measures aimed at protecting
those who joined the contract from those who chose to remain outside.

A congeries of committees, commissions, courts, and officials provided the muscle to back legislature preachments. The pattern of Revolutionary justice directed at the enemy differed to some extent from
state to state, and it might change markedly within a single state. Only
when the legal records of the period are thoroughly analyzed—and
the process is still in the infantile stage for towns and counties—will

we have a comprehensive picture of how Americans prosecuted the Revolution. Though the pattern varied and the story is incomplete, there is sufficient evidence to show that in many areas enforcement was exceedingly effective; and the legal (and extralegal) aspects of the conflict have been underrated.

Amidst the turmoil between the Coercive Acts and the Declaration of Independence judicial processes were disrupted almost everywhere. Justice was predominantly in the hands of the local whig committees that were created to enforce the Continental Association and to bring about military preparedness. Loyalty enforcers, those extralegal bodies, publicized and enforced the edicts of provincial congresses, threatened trimmers, and meted out punishment to the disaffected. Some provincial congresses likewise established colony-wide committees of safety that functioned as the central government when the parent body was not in session.

The North Carolina committee, an itinerant group, traveled from county to county, issuing orders to the county committees and acting on charges—brought forth by the local committees—of corresponding with the enemy, inciting disorders, speaking favorably of Britain, rejecting Revolutionary currency, and engaging in other hostile endeavors. A number of prescriptions hit the supposedly guilty. The North Carolina committee allowed many to escape with promises of good behavior; those of dubious veracity posted bond to insure their future conduct. Some were jailed; others were paroled under the supervision of local committees in distant locales (usually westerners to the east, and easterners to the west). So it was with James Child of Anson County, a "New Light Baptist" preacher, who had threatened excommunication to all in his congregation that took arms against the King, and who was hastened eastward to Edenton. The state committee further recommended to local organizations that they inventory the farms and plantations of those suspected of less than fidelity. Few recipients missed the point: confiscation might quickly follow if they stepped far out of line.[36] The promulgation of a constitution and the re-establishment of regular courts, which had not existed since 1773, led to a greater reliance on traditional legal procedures in dealing with the loyalists in North Carolina. But elsewhere state committees functioned vigorously after 1776, sometimes working with the courts and sometimes exercising functions normally belonging to the courts, especially where the war made normal legal proceedings difficult if not impossible.

Perilous times, highlighted by British invasion and punctuated by open tory defiance, wrought drastic responses. With William Howe threatening New York City in September, 1776, a state public safety committee came into being. It set up a secret service to eye suspected civilians and coordinated the work of community committees. For several months the state body sat daily and in slightly over a year heard and decided as many as five hundred cases embracing a multitude of subjects. Its successor, established early in 1777, was a commission for detecting conspiracies, which in turn gave way to a larger, thirty-man commission, whose members in groups of three ranged over the state.[37] It was also the arrival of General Howe, this time at Philadelphia, that caused the supreme executive council of Pennsylvania to transform itself into a council of safety to act against the tories, who were emboldened by the British presence in the eastern part of the state. The revamped body retaliated against the disloyal and the suspicious in the fashion of its New York counterparts. In New Jersey, where the Revolution had genuine characteristics of a civil war, the thirteen county courts could scarcely function properly, even after Howe withdrew his forces following Washington's twin miracles at Trenton and Princeton. Early in 1777, New Jersey joined her sister states in adding a council of safety. The council bolstered and supplemented the county courts. Traveling about the state, the twelve-man body encouraged local personnel and clarified points of law and procedure for untrained justices. This council on its own heard a variety of cases concerning loyalism and subversion when the courts were derelict or unable to perform their assigned responsibilities.

Formal legal action for serious wartime crimes against the Revolutionary regimes usually fell to the attorneys general. Particularly in treason cases that official presented the state government's charge, usually before the highest tribunal (either known as the supreme court or superior court) but now and then before courts of oyer and terminer or other specially convened judicial organs. The importance of the highest court declined sharply in New Jersey during the war years; the bulk of security proceedings began at the county level and few appeals reached the top bench. In contast, North Carolina's highest tribunal led a busy existence, moving about the state holding sessions of superior court. Though their legal procedures differed, both in New Jersey and North Carolina the burden of significant prosecutions rested with the attorney general. During the years 1777–1779 Irish-born Attorney General William Paterson of New Jersey, a self-made man, brought close to 200 indictments in Hunterdon and Somerset counties alone (a minority of them for failing to report for military service). The courtroom tide, however, had turned in 1778, the year of the last weighty military engagement in the state. By 1780 loyalty cases dwindled to almost nothing in the two counties, a pattern that probably held true for the remaining counties; the battle against subversion was won.[38]

When the most strenuous part of William Paterson's work terminated, Attorney General James Iredell of North Carolina, a fine legal scholar and the state's best political essayist, found his duties of Revolutionary import becoming almost overwhelming. Between 1779 and 1781 North Carolinians lived under the shadow of enemy invasion. Tories who earlier had been silenced now became insolent and obstreperous. Spies for Generals Clinton and Cornwallis operated ahead of the British army, spreading rumors and calling on people to assist actively the King's troops. As the state's chief prosecutor and legal advisor, Iredell traveled in the company of superior court judges as they crisscrossed the state to handle cases in the various superior judicial districts. Through Iredell's efforts at Salisbury in the fall of 1779 "Upwards of eighty persons . . . were indicted for capital crimes among whom the greatest number was for high treason." Iredell acknowledged that the military crisis had spun a web of hysteria over the state. Many complaints and reports of wrongdoing, he suspected, were prompted more by old feuds and personal rivalries than by tangible evidence of disloyalty. William Paterson of New Jersey had complained of the physical dangers involved in his travels. Repeatedly Iredell made the same point. In the summer of 1781 he declared that a twenty-five-to-thirty-man escort would be needed to see him safely to Hillsborough for a superior court session. Luckily for Iredell, his good judgment warned him to forego an appearance altogether. Had Iredell continued he would undoubtedly have been captured in loyalist David Fanning's subsequent Hillsborough raid that bagged Governor Thomas Burke. A conscientious public servant in Iredell's position discovered that loyalists and redcoats were not the only enemies. Another was galloping inflation. Food, lodging, and other expenses during a week on the road in May, 1780, cost him $600 in North Carolina paper money.[39] In the campaign behind the lines, civilians like Iredell and Paterson made their sacrifices as did the fighting men of the Revolution.

The state militias were equally indispensable in the war against the Revolution's internal enemies. Governors, legislatures, and committees of safety resorted to the states' military establishment to maintain order, seize dangerous suspects, and battle disaffection in its various forms. Governors George Clinton of New York and John Rutledge of South Carolina agreed that suppressing loyalism was the most vital function the militia could perform. In this capacity, as on the field of conflict, the militia revealed itself as less than an efficient, smoothly operating military arm. Yet most of the undertakings were feasible for irregulars: they operated within the state, they served for short periods, and they not infrequently generated real enthusiasm for tory hunting; none is so dastardly in a civil war as the brother who chooses the other side.[40]

Western Connecticut was possibly the only part of New England where hostility to the Revolution reached the danger point. Several

New Haven and Fairfield County militia officers were stripped of authority for expressing opposition to taking up arms. The time for more vigorous action came when the bulk of a militia company in the town of Fairfield spoke defiantly of patriot authority. Wasting no time, the Connecticut assembly secretly organized a body of 200 whig militiamen who swooped down on the recalcitrant irregulars and others suspected of disloyalty at three o'clock in the morning. Taken by surprise, the dissidents offered no resistance, and outward opposition to rebel rule collapsed. On at least one instance Connecticut militia assisted the patriots of New York City by riding into town and destroying James Rivington's tory press.[41]

Despite the prevalence of loyalism in New York State and the threat from British regulars, the militia repeatedly took coercive action against the internal foe. In October, 1775, the New York Provincial Congress, informed of a pro-British conspiracy in the lower Hudson valley, summoned the militia, which took into custody a body of tories who were gathering arms around Peekskill. A short time later the menace of loyalism upstate in Tryon County drew General Philip Schuyler into the field. In January, 1776, Schuyler escorted several thousand militia on a march that caught the malcontents, mostly Highland Scots, unawares. Disarming the enemy, Schuyler returned with six hostages for the subsequent good conduct of Tryon County. That same month the state's revolutionists, aided by New Jersey forces, disarmed 600 loyalists on Long Island. Burgoyne's campaign in 1777 aroused the tories anew, but the local militia, posted at key roads and waterways, blocked scores of royalists from proceeding northward to join the British.[42]

Elsewhere in the middle states local military contingents were alert. Besides making life unpleasant for Howe's foraging parties, Pennsylvania irregulars harassed loyalist traders and profiteers attempting to do business in Philadelphia during the British occupation. At mobile checkpoints along roads leading to the Quaker metropolis, patriots in arms checked the credentials and possessions of passers-by. Maryland, though never occupied by redcoats, lay exposed to invasion from the sea. State troops, functioning smoothly with county committees of observation, watched the eastern shore, where dissidents endeavored to communicate with nearby British vessels. During Cornwallis' Southern campaign several Maryland loyalists went about enlisting men who were to rise on the approach of their British deliverers. Getting wind of these machinations, the state council sent out local units that arrested the leaders and terminated the threat.[43]

To the south the militia time and again proved to be the downfall of British sympathizers and other obstructionists. In the early phases of the war Virginia irregulars herded clusters of alleged enemies inland from the coastal frontier. In 1781 the militia on the western frontier quelled riots triggered by impressments and a recent draft law. War weariness, not disloyalty, figured as the basic cause of the disturbances.[44] Far more troublesome were the elements at odds with the Revolution in the Carolinas. In February, 1776, over 1,600 loyalists, predominantly Highland Scots, assembled at Cross Creek, North Carolina. Here was one of the most menacing tory uprisings of the war. More impressive, however, was the whig counterthrust. Not only did approximately an equal force of North Carolina militiamen rout the Scots; there were another 7,000 or more patriots under arms and still others were available.[45] Loyalism was also potent in the South Carolina back country, though in both states the amount of disaffection has been exaggerated.[46] In the absence of initial British support, some of the King's adherents bided their time by professing neutralism or outwardly displaying obedience to the local whig congress. Robert and Patrick Cunningham and Moses Kirkland preferred to hoist their true colors. They seized a back-country fort and stole a cache of arms bound for the Cherokee. Military retaliation administered by Colonel Richard Richardson and Major Andrew Williamson and combined with the artful persuasion of William Henry Dayton smothered the insurrection.[47] For the time being, at least, the tories posed no threat in the palmetto state.

The failure of loyalism as a bedrock of British military power rests upon several factors. But assuredly prompt whig civil and military action, especially in the opening phases of the conflict, rates a high priority. Threatened, disarmed, and defeated, the King's friends never recovered, except in certain areas overrun by royal armies; even then their resilience was often wanting—partly, of course, owing to shabby treatment from their rescuers; but the whigs had given many a taste of bitter medicine, and more than a few had no desire for a second and bigger dose.[48]

## To Try Men's Souls

When Thomas Paine visualized the war as a time to try men's souls, he had in mind patriot souls. For countless other Americans as well, the conflict brought hardships and sufferings. Even some who preferred a position on the sidelines had their bitter cup, finding truth in John Adams' aphorism that in politics the middle way is no way at all. The Quaker formula of obedience to authority placed over them by God smacked of unfettered loyalism in patriot eyes. So did the Friends' passive opposition to loyalty oaths, military service, and payment of substitutes—all on grounds of conscience. Despite laws subjecting Quakers to arrest, double taxation, and other punishments, they usually experienced harsh public criticism rather than actual persecution before Howe's invasion of Pennsylvania. Then in September, 1777, with Sir William's menacing shadow over Philadelphia, violence against the Friends increased; and Pennsylvania authorities exiled to western Virginia twenty-one Quaker leaders accused of engaging in communications prejudical to the American cause.[49]

Though there were exceptions, including pro-British James Pemberton, one of the exiles to the Old Dominion, most Quakers seem to have strived for genuine neutrality. Lending weight to this view is the general absence of serious charges against the Quakers of collaboration with the enemy during the British occupation of Philadelphia. In time Quakers took a more practical position regarding the new order: after all, Americans constituted the government *in power*, and Quakers themselves were Americans. In 1780 the Philadelphia Yearly Meeting boasted to its London counterpart that America was a separate nation, more virtuous than Britain. The Quakers' task was how to determine their own role in the society of the fledgling republic. If most Friends stood fast on the matter of nonviolence and other issues of principle, they nonetheless resolved to give service to the community by amplifying their doctrine of charity, previously limited to the intercourse of Quakers. During the Revolutionary War they extended relief in the form of money, clothing, and provisions to thousands of suffering noncombatants. Peace in 1783 did not witness the disbanding of this holy army, which increasingly fought for the Indian, the Negro, and, generally, the humanitarian reforms inspired by the Revolution. The Revolution, notwithstanding the torment it gave the sect, prompted the Friends to find means of conveying the values of their religion to outsiders and sustaining the importance of their church in American life.[50]

Of the smaller religious bodies, some of the German pietist sects preferred not to involve themselves with either warring camp. In Pennsylvania, according to Ambrose Serle, the Germans who were "disposed to be quiet" received a hard time at the hands of whig committees. Francis Asbury, the leading American Methodist, counselled his coreligionists to toe the neutral line. The pacifism of Asbury and certain other Methodist preachers, together with John Wesley's well-known hostility to the Revolution, placed Methodism under a pall of suspicion. Yet except for a very few instances, chiefly in Maryland, the remarkable itinerant Asbury traveled thousands of miles through the South and middle states without intimidation or violence. Methodists, with more aplomb than the Quakers, made the adjustment to the new order. Asbury himself took an oath of allegiance to the state of Delaware in 1780; while the Reverend Jesse Lee, a genuine pacifist, refused to bear arms but agreed to drive a wagon for the Continental army and wound up as an unofficial chaplain. After the war the Methodists, not hitherto a distinct denomination, organized the Methodist Episcopal Church, which, in the words of Asbury, now thanked George Washington for his leadership in "the glorious revolution."[51]

For the tories the story had no happy ending. The harshness of rebel treatment combined with their fealty to the British accounted for the exodus of more than 60,000 royalists to neighboring parts of the empire and to Britain itself.[52] Recent generations of Americans have found it easier than did their forefathers to look with tolerance, even sympathy, upon a troubled people whose sufferings often exceeded the misfortunes of Tom Paine's patriots. The revisionist approach gained impetus in 1902 from the first modern comprehensive study of loyalism by Claude H. Van Tyne, who, along with authors of several state studies, accused the revolutionists of shocking mistreatment of fellow Americans, themselves devoted to a cause. That threats, confiscations, mobbings, tarring and feathering, and loss of life befell the tories is a matter of indisputable record, as it is also true that now and then the whigs played fast and loose with the definition of patriotism. The Anne Arundel, Maryland, safety committee branded as an enemy anyone who, on application, refused to make a cash contribution for the purchase of arms. Cullen Pollok of Edenton, North Carolina, falsely accused of loyalism because of an innocuous remark, spent two days in jail before being released. Afterward a body of drunken militia, hearing Pollok was "an Enemy to America," split the door of the Pollok house with axes and dragged the scantily clad man from his bed and down the street "on the coldest night of the year," while his screaming wife ran barefooted for help.[53]

Some Americans penned eloquent pleas in behalf of conscience. "I do not assume any pretention to Controul the opinion of others," the disillusioned whig Daniel Dulany assured the Anne Arundel safety committee, "but I claim the right of judging freely, and of acting freely according to my Judgment." So did the respected New Yorker, Peter Van Schaack, an individualist torn by conflicting ties, but who found neither Revolutionary conformity nor absolute separation from the empire to his taste. He claimed for himself and all men the "right of private judgment," the "right to choose the State of which he will become a member." An interesting if unprovable suggestion is that more lenient treatment might have eventually swung over to the Revolutionary side Joseph Galloway of Pennsylvania and others of intellectual accomplishment who were embittered by public pressure. Certainly much has been written of the quality of many who left America, among them Benjamin Thompson, Count Rumford, later a distinguished scientist (though Thompson outwardly seemed a willing enough patriot before

Washington's army refused to honor his majority in the New Hampshire militia!).[54]

It is easy today for us to take an overview of the loyalist problem, to say the tories' numbers were inflated, their organization weak, their support from Britain inadequate. The men of '76 did not benefit from our perspective. A revolution is never a milk toast affair, and the patriots had no choice but to pull out all stops behind the lines. "Lenity is a most excellent virtue," conceded "Plain Truth," in the July 18, 1776, *Newport Mercury*; "but there are certain seasons when it may betray us . . . by encouraging the determined enemies of the country to cabal and prosecute . . . measures for the destruction of our liberties." Toryism would have been a far greater menace had the revolutionists responded less decisively. As it was, tories did aid and abet the British side by serving as spies and guides, spreading false rumors, providing food and supplies, and enlisting in the royal ranks; and from centers of royal control they poured forth a verbal onslaught comparably virulent to anything from the rebel presses. There also were serious defections, only a few but enough to excite extreme fears: especially Benjamin Church and later Benedict Arnold, who, prompted by a combination of avarice, vanity, legitimate if exaggerated grievances, and perhaps wifely influence, failed in his scheme to deliver West Point and its garrison into Sir Henry Clinton's hands in 1780.[55]

If one is mindful of the ravages normally associated with civil wars, of the savagery of so many revolutionary zealots in modern times, and of the fantasies brewed by near-hysterical American fears of domestic communists in recent decades (after generations of orderly government and democratic development!)—then the remarkable fact about the treatment of the loyalists was its relative mildness, not its severity. To be sure, there is in the papers of most of the great trustees of the Revolution the harshest of anti-tory language; but much of this, and it is invariably quoted, is limited to private correspondence. Congress early in the war set its face against violence and disorder by resolving that no one accused of loyalism should be punished except by Continental or state authority. Congress' action seems to have been chiefly aimed at private citizens, militias, and very probably town and county committees too. The committees, usually self-constituted, were not easy to control and many of the complaints of their witch hunting and disregard for justice were doubtless all too true. The Maryland council warned its town and county organizations that "extrajudicial and disorderly proceedings" tended "in their consequences to prejudice the common cause, and the destruction of order and regular government." But there is no reason for a sweeping indictment of the entire ground level structure. The Edenton, North Carolina, body publicly exonerated the unfortunate Cullen Pollok and responded against his persecutors. The Hanover, New Hampshire, committee, praising President Eleazer Wheelock of Dartmouth College, described accusations of disloyalty against the educator as "false, groundless, and malicious," and then proceeded to lecture the public on tolerance and the danger of wild accusations. Several essayists averred that "FURIOUS Whigs injure the cause of liberty as much by their violence as the timid Whigs do by their fears."[56]

By no means all known loyalists suffered severe chastisement. Goldsbrow Banyar lived quietly on his New York estate, Ralph Wormley remained at his plantation Rosegill in Virginia, and Peter Kemble, father-in-law of British General Gage, escaped molestation in New Jersey. Another prudent tory, though his sentiments were no secret, was Daniel Dulany; despite protests from the Baltimore Whig Club and the Anne Arundel safety committee, state leaders—the same officials who had sheltered William Goddard from the same zealous Whig Club—countermanded an order for Dulany's banishment, allowing one of Maryland's most distinguished sons to sit out the Revolution at his Hunting Ridge retreat.

Bradley Chapin has discovered that, except for some use of bills of attainder, the revolutionists in prosecuting treason cases were conscious of procedural rights to a degree that is seldom recognized. The great preponderance of cases were heard before supreme courts or at regular circuit, and the accused were in many instances defended by the finest legal minds in America. Commissions of oyer and terminer handled relatively few treason trials, and for a variety of reasons such specially constituted bodies were generally frowned upon. Military trials for civilians were also anything but popular. Though in 1777 New York, beset by large scale disaffection and enemy invasion, empowered the military to try alleged traitors, Chapin stresses that the state legislators scrutinized these courts-martial, reprimanded the officers on occasion, and exercised generously their pardoning power. Alexander Hamilton, a tory-despiser but no terrorist, regretted that the "unsettled state of government" in New York would not permit the use of civil authority in judicial matters with the "exactness which every friend of society must wish." In Pennsylvania, also afflicted with internal and external foes in 1777, the Continental army received authorization to bring civilians before military tribunals if they indulged in treasonable crimes. Washington, however, favored civil trials, and he delivered some of the most notorious offenders over to state leaders.[57]

Remarkable as it may seem, only a small fraction of those seized on suspicion of treason were ever indicted, only a sprinkling of those indicted were convicted, and only a few of those convicted were put to death—usually by hanging, none by the barbaric English legal prescription of drawing and quartering. In New England, a region that

escaped most of the alarms and excursions of war after 1776, the treason statutes were almost a dead letter; one Connecticut man so convicted is known to have been executed. Jefferson proudly wrote in his
*Notes on Virginia* that "not a single execution for treason" occurred in
the Old Dominion. Nor in war-ravaged New York and Pennsylvania
was there a hangman's harvest; the courts sent four men to the gallows
in the latter state, and perhaps no more than that in the former. Even
the loyalists' claims for compensation submitted to Britain after the
Revolution add up in their testimony to the conclusion that while the
King's friends encountered violence in an assortment of forms, there
was minimal bloodshed and few authenticated instances of loss of life.[58]

There is more room for criticism when one examines the circumstances of the revolutionists' confiscations of loyalist estates. The
Americans, it is true, were scarcely innovators in claiming that property
rights rested upon allegiance to the state. It was a Lockeian concept
that the desire to protect property drew men together in a social
contract and that a party who broke the contract lost the protection of
his property. And as a practical matter, sequestration was the only
manner of retaliation available against multitudes of tories who had
fled. But the Revolutionary government acted with a zeal that implies
some of those possessions caught the covetous eye of patriots hoping to
enrich themselves at the expense of their neighbors. If state treasuries
profited from the sale of confiscated farms and plantations, so did those
rebel purchasers who sometimes obtained choice holdings owing to
shady transactions. Not all the patriots approved of wholesale, indiscriminate seizures, some of which resulted in the punishment of innocent persons out of the country when the storm broke. They saw in
these practices as did the *Maryland Gazette's* "Plebian" an inconsistency between whig theory and practice.[59]

Yet when allowances are made for human frailties—for the cynicism
and materialism inherently engendered by war, and for the fears and
hatreds normally spawned by protracted conflicts where the stakes are
high—it is still possible to assert that Americans generally fought the
Revolution, as they had earlier stood up to Britain in the decade before Lexington, within the framework of their expressed principles.

## NOTES

1. The most famous tory printer was James Rivington, who fled from New York in
1775, only to return during the British occupation when he established his
*Royal Gazette* and resumed his lampooning of the patriots. For reasons now
beyond our comprehension, Rivington eventually became an American spy as
he continued to publish under the royal banner. Catherine S. Crary, "The Tory

and the Spy: The Double Life of James Rivington," *William and Mary Quarterly*, 3d ser., XVI (1959), 61–72.

2. Isaiah Thomas, *The History of Printing in America . . .*, 2d edn. (Albany, N.Y., 1874), II, 8–9, 90; Philip Davidson, *Propaganda and the American Revolution* (Chapel Hill, 1941), 395–400; J. H. Trumbull, *Memorial History of Hartford County, Connecticut* (Hartford, 1886), II, 450.

3. Victor H. Paltsits, "John Holt—Printer and Postmaster: Some Facts and Documents Relating to His Career," New York Public Library, *Bulletin*, XXIV (1920), 494.

4. *Massachusetts Spy*, Nov. 26, 1778; *Boston Gazette*, April 28, 1777; *Connecticut Courant*, Sept. 22, 1777, June 16, 1778. By January, 1778, the cost of a year's subscription to the *Courant* had risen from seven to eighteen shillings. In Williamsburg, printer Alexander Purdie informed his readers that "Paper is lately risen to more than triple its former value, and now can hardly be procured at any price. . . ." *Virginia Gazette*, Dec. 6, 1776.

5. *Pennsylvania Journal*, Feb. 17, 1779; Leonard W. Levy, *Legacy of Suppression: Freedom of Speech and Press in Early American History* (Cambridge, Mass., 1960), 186.

6. Arthur M. Schlesinger, *Prelude to Independence: The Newspaper War on Britain, 1764–1776* (New York, 1958), 189. I am indebted for this last sentence to James Morton Smith's review of Levy's *Legacy of Suppression. William and Mary Quarterly*, 3d ser., XX (1963), 158–159.

7. *Pennsylvania Packet*, July 29, 1777; *Maryland Gazette*, June 16, 1780; *Virginia Gazette* (Dixon and Hunter), Sept. 21, 1776. Further representations are in the *Pennsylvania Packet*, Sept. 26, 1777; *New-York Journal*, Sept. 14, 1778; *New-Jersey Gazette*, Oct. 7, 1778; *Maryland Gazette*, Sept. 19, 1776, Nov. 24, 1780, Dec. 1, 1780; *Connecticut Courant*, March 19, 1780; *Pennsylvania Journal*, May 1, 1776, Feb. 17, 1779, Aug. 25, 1782.

8. Sidney I. Pomerantz, "The Patriot Newspaper and the American Revolution," in *The Era of the American Revolution*, ed. Richard B. Morris (New York, 1939), 330. Pomerantz's study is of "the patriot newspaper in the New York-New Jersey area during the actual period of hostilities." For Goddard, see W. Bird Terwilliger, "William Goddard's Victory for the Freedom of the Press," *Maryland Historical Magazine*, XXXVI (1941), 139–149; Lawrence C. Wroth, *A History of Printing in Colonial Maryland* (Baltimore, 1922), 135–140. Writing in the *Continental Journal*, Dec. 3, 1778, "Vigilantus" pled for "decency" in expressing differing opinions, lest the arguments weaken the patriots and hearten the tories.

9. A close examination of John Holt's *New-York Journal* shows what was roughly true of most newspapers. Of the *Journal*'s contents, 40 per cent was devoted to advertisements, 20 per cent to official war news, 35 per cent to unofficial war news, and 5 per cent to articles unrelated to the conflict. E. M. Thomas, "The Publication of Newspapers during the American Revolution," *Journalism Quarterly*, IX (1932), 363–364. See also R. A. Brown, "New Hampshire Editors Win the War," *New England Quarterly*, XII (1939), 35–51. On November 11, 1775, "A Constant Reader" criticized the *Virginia Gazette* (Dixon and Hunter) for emphasizing trivia at the expense of military intelligence.

Pamphlets, so influential in the earlier verbal encounter with Britain, steadily declined in quality and quantity after Lexington and Concord. Broadsides too fell off in popularity, but they occasionally ground from the presses when military news arrived too late for inclusion in the local gazettes, and when public officials desired a proclamation to receive wide circulation. From Philadelphia, on February 10, 1776, a North Carolina congressman informed an unnamed correspondent: "We have searched almost every Booksellers Shop in this City for pamphlets but have made a poor Collection; few are Written, none read, since the Appeal to Arms." Hayes Papers, Southern Historical Collection, University of North Carolina Library. Good accounts of the pamphlet as a means of expression are in Homer L. Calkin, "Pamphlets and Public Opinion during the American Revolution," *Pennsylvania Magazine of History and Biography*, LXIV (1940), 22–42; Bailyn, ed., *Pamphlets of the Revolution*, chaps. i–ii.

10. Bruce I. Granger, *Political Satire in the American Revolution, 1763–1783* (Ithaca, 1960), 23.

11. *Pennsylvania Packet*, March 4, 1777; Moses C. Tyler, *The Literary History of the American Revolution, 1763–1783*, 2 vols. in 1 (New York, 1905), II, 17–20.

12. *South-Carolina Gazette*, July 25, 1775; Foner, ed., *Writings of Paine*, I, 105; *South-Carolina and American General Gazette*, Nov. 21, 1776; *Maryland Gazette*, Aug. 4, 1780; *Virginia Gazette* (Dixon and Hunter), Feb. 7, 1777; *Continental Journal*, July 25, 1777; *Boston Gazette*, March 25, 1776, Jan. 6, 1777, April 20, 1778, May 29, 1780.

13. *Continental Journal*, May 15, 1777; *Pennsylvania Packet*, April 22, 1777; *Boston Gazette*, Jan. 19, 1778; *Virginia Gazette* (Dixon and Hunter), Aug. 30, 1776. See also *Newport Mercury*, Dec. 18, 1775, March 18, 1776. Ezra Sampson, *A Sermon Preached at Roxbury-Camp* (Watertown, 1775), 22–24.

14. *Continental Journal*, July 13, 1780; *Connecticut Courant*, Feb. 19, 1776; *Virginia Gazette* (Dixon and Hunter), Sept. 21, 1776; *South-Carolina and American General Gazette*, Feb. 9, 1776; *Pennsylvania Gazette*, June 12, 1780; *Maryland Gazette*, June 23, 1780, July 14, 21, 28, 1780, Jan. 5, 1781; *The Sentiments of an American Woman* (Philadelphia, 1780); Mason L. Weems, *The Life of Washington*, ed. Marcus Cunliffe (Cambridge, Mass., 1962), xliv. Ezra Stiles reported that women everywhere were making cartridges and bidding their loved ones "to behave like men and not like cowards. . . ." Dexter, ed., *Literary Diary*, I, 476–485.

15. Force, ed., *American Archives*, 4th ser., V, 1169; Samuel Johnston to Thomas Burke, April 14, 1777, Thomas Burke Papers, Southern Historical Collection, University of North Carolina Library; *Continental Journal*, Aug. 28; *Boston Gazette*, Oct. 27, No. 10, 1777, June 19, 1780; *North-Carolina Gazette*, Nov. 7, 1777. A Connecticut soldier publicly informed the people of his state of the kindness and patriotism he encountered in New Jersey. *Connecticut Courant*, Aug. 4, 1778.

16. *Pennsylvania Packet*, Oct. 16, 1775, Oct. 9, Dec. 31, 1777, March 4, Dec. 24, 1778; *Connecticut Courant*, Jan. 13, 1777; *Newport Mercury*, Jan. 20, 1781; *Pennsylvania Gazette*, July 25, 1781; *Virginia Gazette* (Dixon and Hunter), Jan. 24, 1777; *Continental Journal*, Jan. 30, 1777, March 12, 1778; *Boston Gazette*, Aug. 14, 1775, April 15, 1776, Sept. 1, 1777, June 8, 1778, June 12, 1780; *Maryland Gazette*, Nov. 29, 1781; *New-Jersey Gazette*, April 2, 1778, Aug. 18, 1779; John J. Stoudt, "The German Press in Pennsylvania and the American Revolution," *Pennsylvania Magazine of History and Biography*, LIX (1935), 85; Davidson, *Propaganda and the American Revolution*, 362.

17. *Virginia Gazette* (Dixon and Nicholson), Feb. 26, 1779; *Newport Mercury*, July 7, 1781; Charles Henry Wharton, *A Political Epistle To His Excellency George Washington, Esq. . . . To Which is Annexed, A Short Sketch of General Washington's Life and Character* [by John Bell] (Annapolis, 1779); *A Primer Adorned with a Beautiful Head of General Washington . . .* (Philadelphia, 1779); *Pennsylvania Gazette*, June 20, 1781; *Boston Gazette*, Feb. 18, 1782. "We have the satisfaction . . . to acquaint the publick, that his Excellency general Washington continues to enjoy an uninterrupted share of health and vigour. . . ." *Virginia Gazette* (Purdie), Jan. 10, 1777. Washington, already holding an honorary doctorate from Harvard, added another one from Yale. *Connecticut Courant*, May 8, 1781.

18. Compare the celebration in Charleston, South Carolina, in 1777 with the one in the same city in 1843. *South-Carolina and American General Gazette*. July 10, 1777; Ralph H. Gabriel, *The Course of American Democratic Thought*, 2d edn. (New York, 1956), 99–100. On the night of July 4, 1781, a French fleet treated celebrating Rhode Islanders to a display of rocketry. *Newport Mercury*, July 7, 1781. See also *Boston Gazette*, July 28, 1777, July 27, 1778, July 10, 1780, July 9, 1781.

19. David Ramsay, *The History of the American Revolution* (Philadelphia, 1789), II, 319. The Anglican issue was first explored in depth in Arthur L. Cross, *The Anglican Episcopate and the American Colonies* (New York, 1902), a work now supplemented by Carl Bridenbaugh, *Mitre and Sceptre: Transatlantic Faiths, Ideas, Personalities, and Politics, 1689–1775* (New York, 1962). Bridenbaugh sees religious questions as a fundamental cause of the Revolution and a potent ingredient in the growth of American nationalism. Another recent treatment of the episcopate controversy is Knollenberg, *Origin of the American Revolution*, 75–86, 311–316. Upon the elevation of Thomas Secker, an earnest proponent of an Anglican establishment for America, the Reverend Ezra Stiles of Newport, Rhode Island, in 1760 advanced a proposal for a union of the New England Congregational churches and a loose association of dissenters throughout America and Britain to combat the Anglican menace. Morgan, *Gentle Puritan*, chap. xvi.

20. Edmund S. Morgan, "The American Revolution Considered as an Intellectual Movement," *Paths of American Thought*, eds., Arthur M. Schlesinger, Jr., and Morton White (Boston, 1963), 22–24.

21. Samuel Cooke, *The Violent Destroyed: and Oppressed Delivered* . . . (Boston, 1777), 8–9; Zabdiel Adams, *The Grounds of Confidence and Success in War, represented* (Boston, 1775), 4, 5; Timothy Dwight, *A Sermon Preached at Stamford in Connecticut upon the General Thanksgiving* (Hartford, 1778), 4, 13–14; Samuel Cooper, *A Sermon Preached* . . . (Boston, 1780), 2, 8; *Connecticut Courant*, Dec. 16, 1776; Samuel Langdon, *Government Corrupted by Vice* . . ., in Frank Moore, *The Patriot Preachers of the American Revolution* (New York, 1862), 56–60; Nathan Strong, *The Agency and Providence of God Acknowledged in the Preservation of the American States* . . . (Hartford, 1780), 12; *Boston Gazette*, Jan. 20, Oct. 20, 27, Nov. 3, 1777. "The Biblical conception of a people standing in direct daily relation to God, upon convenanted terms and therefore responsible for their moral conduct, was a common possession of the Protestant peoples." Perry Miller, "From the Covenant to the Revival," *Religion in American Life*, eds., James W. Smith and A. Leland Jamison (Princeton, 1961), I, 325.

22. Adams, *Grounds of Confidence*, 18; David Jones, *Defensive War in a just cause Sinless* (Philadelphia, 1775), 12; Joseph Hewes to Elihu Spencer and Alexander McWhorter, Dec. 8, 1775, Samuel Johnston Papers, North Carolina Department of Archives and History. There are voluminous references to the need for moral rejuvenation. For other instances, see John J. Zubly, *The Law of Liberty*, in Moore, *Preachers*, 14; Dexter, ed., *Literary Diary*, I, 103, 158; Ezra Sampson, *A Sermon Preached at Roxbury-Camp* . . . (Watertown, 1775), 5; Thomas Coombe, *A Sermon* . . . (Philadelphia, 1775), 11–12; Elam Potter, *A Second Warning to America* . . . (Hartford, 1777), 5; Dwight, *A Sermon Preached at Stamford*, 15; Jacob Duché, *The American Vine* . . . (Philadelphia, 1775), 24–26; Samuel Langdon, John Hurt, and Nathaniel Whitaker, in Moore, *Patriot Preachers*, 55–56, 157, 191; Eliphalet Wright, *A People Ripe for An Harvest* (Norwich, 1776), 16. See also *Pennsylvania Packet*, June 10, 1776; *Continental Journal*, Oct. 31, 1776; *Connecticut Courant*, June 16, Oct. 9, 1775, Sept. 16, Nov. 18, 1776, Jan. 13, Sept. 5, 1777, June 19, 1779; *South-Carolina and American General Gazette*, June 30, 1775; *Virginia Gazette* (Dixon and Hunter), July 20, Aug. 24, 1776. Some Americans believed that the practice of slavery was a sin that called for eradication before the Lord would smile on patriot fortunes. George H. Moore, *Notes on the History of Slavery in Massachusetts* (New York, 1866), 147; *Connecticut Courant*, May 19, 1777; David Avery, *The Lord is to be praised for the Triumph of his Power* (Norwich, 1778), 12; Samuel Stillman, *A Sermon* . . . (Boston, 1779), 34–35; David Ramsay, *History of the Independent* . . . *Church in Charleston* (Philadelphia, 1814), *passim*; David Austin, ed., *The American Preacher* (Elizabethtown, N.J., 1791–1793), II, 331; Jacob Green, *A Sermon* . . . (Chatham, 1779), 17–18.

23. Paul F. Boller, Jr., *George Washington and Religion* (Dallas, 1963), 49–59. Congress proclaimed: "It having pleased the righteous Governor of the World,

for the punishment of our manifold offences, to permit the Sword of War still to harass our Country, it becomes us to endeavour, by humbling ourselves before Him, and turning from every evil way, to avert His anger and obtain His favour and blessing." *Pennsylvania Journal*, March 15, 1780. References to fast days are in Ford, ed., *Journals of Congress*, XIII, 343, XIV, 252, XV, 1191, XVIII, 950, XIX, 284, XXI, 1074.

William Livingston believed the idea of a fast day was exceedingly valuable to the cause: "I cannot but think that such a measure is our indispensable Duty, & I dare affirm that it would be very agreeable to all pious people, who are all friends to America; for I never met with a religious Tory in my life." Quoted in Davidson, *Propaganda and the American Revolution*, 355.

24. Miller, "From the Covenant to the Revival," 333. Interestingly enough, some of the soldiers' songs have a distinct moral quality to them; but, as two historians observe, many of the British lyrical contributions were drinking songs and scarcely any were religious. Commager and Morris, eds., *Spirit of 'Seventy-Six*, II, 907.

25. The passage is from Judges 5:23. The reference is in many of the pamphlets cited in note 6; and in William Stearns, *A View of the Controversy . . .* (Watertown, 1775), 31; John Carmichael, *A Self-Defensive War Lawful* (Lancaster, 1775), 11–12; sermon of Samuel West, in John W. Thornton, *The Pulpit of the American Revolution*, 2d edn. (Boston, 1876), 309; *New-Jersey Gazette*, June 2, 1779; *Boston Gazette*, Nov. 3, 1777.

26. *North-Carolina Gazette*, Nov. 14, 1777. The Reverend William Gordon, reflecting on two years of war, called it unbelievable that "instead of being galled to the bone with the yoke of slavery, we are keeping the anniversary of our independency." Moore, *Patriot Preachers*, 176. So did a contributor to the *Continental Journal*, March 12, 1778.

27. This name for the Revolutionary clergy, especially the New England dissenters, was coined in the prewar friction with the mother country by James Otis; at least that was the opinion of Peter Oliver, who, along with other tories, made considerable application of it. Oliver, *Origin and Progress of the American Rebellion*, 29, 41–45, 53, 63, 106, 163; also *Connecticut Courant*, Dec. 14, 1772. Oliver readily acknowledged the influence of the patriot clergy upon the American people, as did Ambrose Serle. Tatum, ed., *American Journal of Ambrose Serle*, 115–116, 135.

28. George M. Brydon, *Virginia's Mother Church . . .* (Philadelphia, 1952), II, 422. At least 70 of the 122 known Anglican clergymen in Virginia supported the Revolution. Of the remaining number, most of whom cannot be classified for want of information, 17 were loyalists; but only 6 actively disloyal. Sylvia R. Frey, "Loyalist Anglican Clergy of Virginia in the American Revolution," (unpubl. M.A. thesis, Louisiana State University, 1965). Notwithstanding recent tensions between Baptists and Anglicans in Virginia, both Jefferson and Governor Patrick Henry praised these dissenters for their martial spirit. Boyd, ed., *Jefferson Papers*, I, 662; *Virginia Gazette* (Dixon and Hunter), Aug. 24, 1776. It is claimed that only five of twenty-three Anglican priests in South Carolina were loyalists. Raymond W. Albright, *A History of the Protestant Episcopal Church* (New York, 1964), 113–114. Sketches of many clergymen mentioned in this section are in J. T. Headley, *The Chaplains and Clergy of the Revolution* (Springfield, Mass., 1861).

29. Bernhard Knollenberg, ed., "The Revolutionary Correspondence of Nathanael Greene and John Adams," *Rhode Island History*, I (1942), 50; Foner, ed., *Writings of Paine*, I, 97.

30. Ford, ed., *Journals of Congress*, V, 475–476. The background of the resolution is examined in Curtis P. Nettels, "A Link in the Chain of Events Leading to American Independence," *William and Mary Quarterly*, 3d ser., III (1946), 36–47.

31. W. W. Hening, ed., *The Statutes at Large: Being a Collection of All the Laws of Virginia, 1619–1792* (Richmond, 1809–1823), X, 268–270; Boyd, ed., *Jefferson Papers*, III, 493, V, 593; William Thompson, "Anti-Loyalist Legislation during

the American Revolution," *Illinois Law Review*, III (1908), 81–90, 147–171; Van Tyne, *Loyalists in the Revolution*, 318–341.

32. *South-Carolina and American General Gazette*, July 10, 1777. In December, 1779, the same paper warned its readers of the state's treason law: any person who "withdraws . . . from the defence of this State [then under invasion] & go— or attempt to go—over to the enemy, shall        suffer death as traitors . . ." See also *Maryland Historical Magazine*, LIX (1964), 348; *Connecticut Courant*, April 8, 1776; *Newport Mercury*, April 3, 1776.

33. Hening, ed., *Statutes of Virginia*, IX, 351, 549; Boyd, ed., *Jefferson Papers*, II, 219.

34. For instances, see *Virginia Gazette* (Dixon and Hunter), Sept. 19, 1777; *South-Carolina and American General Gazette*, April 2, 1778; *Connecticut Courant*, Nov. 18, 1776; Boyd, ed., *Jefferson Papers*, II, 130. In November, 1777, the North Carolina assembly announced that all persons who failed to voice the prescribed oath within sixty days must leave the state. Nonviolent tories were allowed to sell their property, or face confiscation, before departing. By that time the most prominent loyalists had already left, sailing from New Bern. *North-Carolina Gazette*, July 25, 1777.

35. John Adams to Nathanael Greene, June 2, 1777, *Rhode Island History*, I (1942), 74. This is not to say that the terminology of every oath was above reproach. The Pennsylvania statement contained provisions that many ardent whigs quite rightly found objectionable.

36. William L. Saunders, ed., *The Colonial Records of North Carolina* (Raleigh, 1886–1890), X, 618–619, 627–628, 631, 666, 699–700, 826–830, 833; Adelaide L. Fries, ed., *Records of the Moravians in North Carolina* (Raleigh, 1922–1947), III, 1032.

37. Dorothy C. Barck, ed., *Minutes of the Committee and of the First Commission for Detecting and Defeating Conspiracies in the State of New York . . . to Which Is Added Minutes of the Council of Appointment . . .* (New York Historical Society, *Collections* [New York, 1924]), I, *passim*.

38. Chapin, *American Law of Treason*, 48–50, 63; Paterson's public service is admirably treated in Richard C. Haskett, "Prosecuting the Revolution," *American Historical Review*, LIX (1954), 578–587. See also "Loyalism in Bergen County, New Jersey," *William and Mary Quarterly*, 3d ser., XVIII (1961), 558–571.

39. James Iredell to Hannah Iredell, Sept. 20, Dec. 8, 1779, May 18, 1780, Sept. 3, 1781, Charles E. Johnson Papers, North Carolina Department of Archives and History.

40. Hugh Hasting, ed., *Public Papers of George Clinton* (Albany, 1899–1914), II, 251; *South Carolina Historical and Genealogical Magazine*, XVII, 131–133. According to Governor Jefferson, "Militia do well for hasty Enterprises, but cannot be relied on for lengthy Service and out of their own Country." Boyd, ed., *Jefferson Papers*, V, 54. Local units were also put to work repairing roads and constructing fortifications. *Connecticut Courant*, Sept. 28, 1779; Richard Upton, *Revolutionary New Hampshire* (Hanover, 1936), 89, 101–102.

41. C. J. Hoadley, ed., *Public Records of the Colony of Connecticut* (Hartford, 1850–1890), XIV, 391–393, XV, 51–52; Force, ed., *American Archives*, 4th ser., I, 1202, 1216, 1236–1239, 1270, II, 575, III, 852; Moore, ed., *Diary of the Revolution*, 173–175; *Connecticut Courant*, July 3, 1775.

42. Force, ed., *American Archives*, 4th ser., II, 661–662, 1669, III, 1305, 1763, IV, 660–661, 667–668, 818–819, 828, 829; E. B. O'Callahan, ed., *Documents Relative to the Colonial History of the State of New York* (Albany, 1853–1887), VIII, 663; Alexander C. Flick, *Loyalism in New York during the American Revolution* (New York, 1901), 63, 68, 87–88, 119; Barck, ed., *Minutes . . . for Detecting and Defeating Conspiracies, passim*.

43. Browne and others, eds., *Archives of Maryland*, XLV, 467, 469, 482, 492, XLVII, 328–330, 382, 425–426, 568; Dorothy M. Quynn, "The Loyalist Plot in Frederick," *Maryland Historical Magazine*, XL(1945), 201–210; Force, ed., *American Archives*, 4th ser., III, 1571–1585, IV, 716–717, 719, 733–734, V, 1515, VI, 833.

44. Isaac S. Harrell, *Loyalism in Virginia* (Durham, N.C., 1926), 47–48, 52, 60;

Higginbotham, *Morgan*, 160–61. "No frontier area of Colonial America surpassed the Valley [of Virginia] in its zeal for the Revolutionary movement," concludes Freeman Hart, *The Valley of Virginia in the American Revolution, 1763–1789* (Chapel Hill, 1942), 83.

45. *Boston Gazette*, April 15, 1776; Samuel Johnston to Joseph Hewes, March 10, 1776, Hayes Transcripts, North Carolina Department of Archives and History; Force, ed., *American Archives*, 4th ser., V, 60; Walter Clark, ed., *The State Records of North Carolina* (Winston and Goldsboro, 1895–1907), XI, 286–287. The best accounts of the battle are Robert O. Demond, *The Loyalists in North Carolina during the Revolution* (Durham, N.C., 1940), 88–97; Hugh F. Rankin, "The Moore's Creek Bridge Campaign, 1776." *North Carolina Historical Review*, XXX (1953), 30–56. The loyalism of the Highlanders is no longer explained simply by their prior oaths of allegiance to the House of Hanover following the Jacobite rebellions of 1715 and 1745. For many the course of action in 1776 was arrived at slowly and painfully, and was based on a variety of factors. Duane Meyer, *The Highland Scots of North Carolina, 1732–1776* (Chapel Hill, 1961), *passim*.

46. A case in point is the former Regulators. Both Carolinas had experienced unrest and violence in the back country in the decade before independence owing to insufficient or inadequate governmental institutions. Recent research has pretty well destroyed the once-popular notion that a majority of the frontier Regulators, still supposedly resentful of Eastern domination, cast their lot with Britain. Elmer D. Johnson, "The War of the Regulation: Its Place in History" (unpubl. M.A. thesis, University of North Carolina, 1942), 115, appendix iii; Brown, *South Carolina Regulators*, 123–126, 213 n35; Wallace Brown, *The King's Friends: The Composition and Motives of the American Loyalist Claimants* (Providence, R.I., 1965), 196, 202–204, 217–218, 225–226. See also Robert W. Barnwell, Jr., "Loyalism in South Carolina," (unpubl. Ph.D. diss., Duke University, 1941).

47. Force, ed., *American Archives*, 4th ser., II, 1715–1716, III, 180–182, 214–218, 1606, IV, 215–260, 316, 950; Edward McCrady, *The History of South Carolina in the Revolution, 1775–1780* (New York, 1902), 33–98. James H. O'Donnell, "A Loyalist View of the Drayton-Tennant-Hart Mission to the Upcountry," *South Carolina Historical Magazine*, LXVII (1966), 15–28. Henry Clinton, sizing up the situation in early 1776, complained that the King's friends "had been . . . precipitate in showing themselves [and] consequently [had been] overpowered, disarmed, and many imprisoned." Clinton, *American Rebellion*, 26.

48. For example, Cornwallis expressed disappointment to find that the Highlanders in North Carolina were unwilling to join his standard in 1781. Meyer, *Highland Scots*, 161; Clinton, *American Rebellion*, 268–269, 509.

49. Foner, ed., *Writings of Paine*, I, 83, 91–95, 97; *To the Inhabitants of Pennsylvania* (Philadelphia, 1777); *Pennsylvania Packet*, Nov. 13, 1775, Sept. 9, 1777; Thomas Gilpin, *Exiles in Virginia* (Philadelphia, 1848).

50. Sydney V. James, *A People Among Peoples* (Cambridge, Mass., 1963); James, "The Impact of the American Revolution on Quaker Ideas about Their Sect," *William and Mary Quarterly*, 3d ser., XIX (1962), 360–382; Mack Thompson, *Moses Brown: Reluctant Reformer* (Chapel Hill, 1962), 107–145. A fairly recent investigator believes that most of the Friends were actually neutral. Arthur J. Mekeel, "The Society of Friends (Quakers) and the American Revolution" (unpubl. Ph.D. diss., Harvard University, 1940), 380, cited in Brown, *The King's Friends*, 268. Yet the "example of the neutral" was "not only dangerous, but infectious," warned "RATIONAUS." *North-Carolina Gazette*, Aug. 22, 1777.

51. Tatum, ed., *Journal of Serle*, 109; William W. Sweet, *Methodism in American History* (New York and Nashville, Tenn., 1953), 78–99; Elmer T. Clark and others, eds., *The Journal and Letters of Francis Asbury* (London and Nashville, Tenn., 1958), I, *passim*. During the war itself, Asbury seemed totally uninterested in the outcome. *Ibid.*, 198–199, 204, 227–228, 249, 277, 307. For Asbury and Washington, see Paul F. Boller, Jr., "George Washington and the Methodists,"

*Historical Magazine of the Protestant Episcopal Church*, XXVIII (1959), 165–186. See also Jesse Lee, *A Short History of American Methodism* (Baltimore, 1810), 60.

52. Robert R. Palmer reminds us that percentage-wise the rate of exodus was five times that of the emigrés of the French Revolution. *Age of Democratic Revolution*, I, 188–190. The point is well made, however, that these comparative figures must be used cautiously in drawing generalizations. For the British government frequently assisted the departing loyalists, who found close by a number of His Majesty's dominions in which to settle. These factors were absent from the French experience. William H. Nelson, "The Revolutionary Character of the American Revolution," *American Historical Review*, LXX (1965), 1007 n32.

53. Force, ed., *American Archives*, 4th ser., I, 1141–1142; Mrs. Cullen Pollok to Joseph Hewes, Hayes Papers, Southern Historical Collection, University of North Carolina Library; *North-Carolina Gazette*, Dec. 22, 1775.

54. Aubrey C. Land, *The Dulanys of Maryland* (Baltimore, 1955), 315; Commager and Morris, eds., *Spirit of 'Seventy-Six*, I, 343–345; Henry J. Young, "Treason and Its Punishment in Revolutionary Pennsylvania," *Pennsylvania Magazine of History and Biography*, XC (1966), 292–293; Moses C. Tyler, "The Party of the Loyalists in the American Revolution," *American Historical Review*, I (1895), 31. Dulany and Van Schaack are treated sympathetically, along with other moderate tories, in William A. Benton, *Whig-Loyalism: An Aspect of Political Ideology in the American Revolutionary Era* (Rutherford, N.J., 1969).

55. Washington, after expressing his "mortification" over Arnold's treachery, added philosophically: "traitors are the growth of every country, and in a revolution of the present nature it is more to be wondered at that the catalogue is so small. . . ." Washington to Rochambeau, Sept. 27, 1780, Fitzpatrick, ed., *Writings of Washington*, XX, 97; *Newport Mercury*, Nov. 23, 1780.

56. *Virginia Gazette* (Dixon and Hunter), July 6, 1776; *Newport Mercury*, July 1, 1776; *North-Carolina Gazette*, Dec. 22, 1775; *Maryland Gazette*, Dec. 19, 1776, March 29, 1781; *Pennsylvania Packet*, March 18, 1777; *Connecticut Courant*, March 25, 1776, Dec. 15, 1778; *Continental Journal*, April 10, 1777. One town committee chairman wrote of his members, "I want them to Act in such a manner as may be Justifiable in the eyes of the whole world. . . ." Robert Smith to [Samuel Johnston?], May 29, 1775, Hayes Papers, Southern Historical Collection, University of North Carolina Library. The Maryland Council warned printers "to be cautious how they suffer in their papers against any person without good and sufficient grounds. . . ." *Pennsylvania Journal*, Nov. 29, 1775. See also Eleazer Wheelock, *Liberty of Conscience . . .* (Hartford [1776]).

57. Chapin, *American Law of Treason*, chaps. iv–v; Syrett, ed., *Papers of Hamilton*, I, 233, 236, 243. Alexander Flick, critical of the Americans' handling of tories, nonetheless admits that the patriots almost invariably placed a mantle of legality over their treatment of the Crown's allies. *Loyalism in New York*, 91. Governor George Clinton of New York refused a request to allow the state militia to punish tories for violations of New York law.

58. Thomas Jefferson, *Notes on the State of Virginia*, ed. William Peden (Chapel Hill, 1955), 155; Harrell, *Loyalism in Virginia*, 59; Young, "Treason and Its Punishment in Revolutionary Pennsylvania," 312–313; Brown, *The King's Friends*, 7, 34–35, 47–48, 64–66, 78–79, 87, 115–117, 134–135, 158, 168–169, 183, 197, 214–215; Brooke Hindle, *David Rittenhouse* (Princeton, 1964), 148–149; Chapin, *American Law of Treason*, 50–59, 64–69, 77; E. Wilder Spaulding, *His Excellency George Clinton* (New York, 1938), iii; Land, *Dulanys of Maryland*, 325.

59. *Maryland Gazette*, March 10, 30, 1780.

# 12. The Economic Front

A FAMILIAR THEME OF nineteenth-century historians was the American Revolutionaries' gross mismanagement of economic affairs. Engaged in a battle for sound dollars against silverites and other inflationists, contemporaries of the Gilded Age depicted the fiscal policies of the patriots as disastrous, leading to general disorder on the home front and to the near destruction of the Continental army. Assuredly Congress and the states emitted millions of dollars from the printing presses. One can easily agree with Curtis Nettels' remark that paper issues "exerted a more pervasive influence on the economic life of the states than any other factor of the Revolutionary War."[1]

Earlier writers found it incomprehensible that the revolutionists should resort to the same fund-raising method that had supposedly been invariably inflationary and unsound in the colonial period. Perhaps the presence of fiat money and managed economies in recent times has made it easier for a revised assessment of colonial and Revolutionary finance to emerge. We now are aware that paper money had usually been a sound and successful method of obtaining a medium of exchange for provincial governments without resources and a stable system of public finance. In the colonial wars many merchants and creditors as well as debtors (not infrequently substantial property owners themselves) approved the use of commercial paper. Hence, the Continental Congress resorted to an old and generally satisfactory mode of acquiring revenue.[2]

This is not to say that American merchants, planters, and other investors who sat in Congress saw commercial paper as a panacea. They were under no illusions as to the possible pitfalls involved. But whatever the results, Congress had no other choice lacking as it did the power to tax and to compel contributions from the states. The army had to be paid and supplied. If the American pattern was familiar, following the response to the imperial conflicts since 1689, it was nonetheless a revolutionary expedient without parallel for a "national" government. Cast aside were the theories of the mercantile era which called for disturbing the domestic sector as little as possible and which had customarily seen a monarch suspend military operations when his war chest ran dry or his opportunities to borrow had become exhausted.

## Paying for the War

From the moment the Second Continental Congress assumed the direction of the war it wallowed in a sea of financial distress. The total quantity of coin in circulation in 1775 was inadequate to meet the army's upkeep for a single year. Most of America's wealth was tied up in lands and commodities. Banks and business corporations were not existent.[3] In 1775, and throughout the war, the colony-states jealously guarded their right to tax, which they refused to share with Congress under the Articles of Confederation. Naturally enough, Congress turned to printing bills of credit—the total reaching $191,552,380 by 1779. Redemption was acknowledged as a serious problem, and the lawmakers did what was possible given the circumstances of an agricultural economy and their absence of power. Pledging the faith of America to redemption, Congress asked each colony-state to assume responsibility for withdrawing a quota of the total emissions, principally by accepting Continental bills in payment of taxes.

During the first year and a half Continental paper held its value reasonably well, probably because cash payments replaced the credit transactions characteristic of the colonial period, and because the growing wartime economy created a need for an expansion of circulating medium. Unfortunately, the continuation of the conflict and increased military demands made any kind of balance between emissions and withdrawals an impossibility. But the states might well have alleviated the problem by early launching a program of taxation that would have withdrawn Continental currency and thus have preserved in some measure the amount left in circulation. John Adams urged his beloved Abigail to "pay every tax that is brought, if you sell my books or clothes or oxen, or your cows to pay it." It was a "sacred Truth, that it is . . . [our] Interest to pay high taxes!" "The man who paid his taxes," declared Thomas Paine, "does more for his country's good than the loudest talker in America."[4] It is not surprising that Americans shrank from this form of finance. They carried unpleasant memories of British taxation, and their pockets had only been lightly tapped by their colonial governments. Not until 1780 did the states collect an appreciable amount of taxes, long after they too had gone the paper money route; the emissions of all the states exceeded $200,000,000, even surpassing Congress in that respect.

The mounting cost of military operations and the delinquency of the states in rendering meaningful assistance led to additional Congressional issues, eventually every month, then every fortnight. As emission followed emission, accompanied by the rising tide of state paper and an undeterminable quantity of counterfeit money, the purchasing power of Continental bills declined. Contempt for Congressional money gave rise to the first national slogan—"not worth a Continental." The revolutionists were determined men: if stuffing the country to the gills with paper money—debilitating as that might be—was the only course short of capitulating to Britain, then they would continue to stuff. "Is there any principle of religion or morality which forbade a weak and infant nation, driven into war for the avoidance of slavery, to arm itself by the best means in its power?" asked Edmund Randolph of Virginia, who went on to admit that depreciation was hardly unforeseen. "Yet to stop would have been political suicide." And as Franklin said in further justification, the depreciating currency served as a tax upon those persons in whose possession the money dwindled in value. It was for many a fair tax, Franklin thought, because the richest people had the most money passing through their hands. Add to these the commentary of an astute economic historian, Ralph V. Harlow, that modern warfare has demonstrated the inability of various governments to persist in a struggle without confiscation in some form: "the least painful method of achieving this result is the issue of paper money and repudiation. It was here that the leaders of the American Revolution made an involuntary contribution to the history of public finance."[5]

Congress also authorized other methods of securing revenue and supplies. One was domestic borrowing, so-called loan-office certificates that have been called the government bonds of the Revolution. Purchased almost wholly by wealthy citizens, since none was to be issued for less than $300, the recipients received a bond calling for interest at 4 per cent and later at 6 per cent. Though these bonds attracted some buyers, especially after Congress voted to apply funds acquired from France in payment of the interest, the enterprise fell far short of expectations. For the certificates could be purchased with depreciated Continental paper, which the lawmakers proceeded to pay out again. Furthermore, the bonds served as a form of money, adding to the total paper currency in circulation. Still other interest bearing certificates were issued by army purchasing agents in exchange for goods supplied the Continental forces. These too passed from hand to hand and served in many cases as a kind of currency.

If soaring prices were chiefly due to cheap money, the scarcity of goods and profiteering also played some part in accounting for the inflationary spiral. The rate of depreciation is not easy to establish for any given moment or place; but there was a relationship between the value of Continental currency and the demand for commodities and services; and the worth of Continental emissions was usually less in Pennsylvania and the middle states, where much of the war was fought and where the central government conducted most of its various operations. In 1779, Pennsylvania prices of beef, flour, wheat, corn, and pork skyrocketed. Between January and August of the same year advertisements in the *Pennsylvania Journal* show that rewards for runaway slaves jumped from $100 to $300. Congress quite possibly would have taken up quarters elsewhere to escape the worst of the inflation except that such a departure would have unnerved American morale.[6] High prices, exclaimed "A Continentalist," are "an offense against the laws of reason and morality." Governor Patrick Henry condemned those who went about offering high prices for commodities in order to inflate the dollar. Endless writers for the press warned that only if farmers and merchants kept prices down could Continental emissions be slowed or discontinued. "A Financier" begged people in the name of patriotism to accept paper dollars at their face value. "The Continental money is to be considered as a debt on the person and estate of every member of the United States, a debt of great honour and justice, not barely empty honour. . . ."[7]

Mutual recriminations burst forth as agriculturists and mercantilists accused each other of profiteering. "A Carolina Planter" complained that it was six of one and a half dozen of the other as to whether the tories or the merchants exercised the more pernicious effect upon the patriot cause. "A Merchant" replied, not without some justification, that "those who bring provisions to market, fix the price, and the merchants in common with others are forced to submit to it." Inflation, in fact, may have rejoiced the heart of many a farmer whose obligations—predominantly taxes and debts—did not increase at the rate of his produce; he might often sell only a part of his crop to meet obligations, then hold back the remainder in anticipation of still higher prices later. In contrast, the merchant profited from the volume of his business, which necessitated a constant turnover in goods and a constant turnover of ever depreciating currency before it became valueless.[8]

Nonetheless, some merchants grew rich from the contest. Those who engaged in privateering and importing military stores often performed a public service in the course of making a private gain. Merchants who marketed the privateers' cargoes made lucrative profits, especially when they had luxuries and other scarce domestic items to dangle before the public. The continuing requirements of the army for food, clothing, and other items offered the trader opportunities to exploit the service to his own advantage by cornering urgently needed items. So it was in 1778 with Samuel Chase, member of Congress from Maryland, who, acting on privileged intelligence, formed a secret combination with several friends to corner Philadelphia flour, a commodity that an approaching French fleet was known to need. Youthful Alexander Hamilton, a despiser of money grubbing and avarice, castigated Chase in three "Publius" essays printed in John Holt's *New-York Journal*. Hamilton felt confident that Chase had "acquired an indisputed title to be immortalised in infamy," but he ruefully conceded that the Marylander would be in the company of no mere handful of his fellow countrymen: "notwithstanding our youth and inexperience as a nation, we begin to emulate the most veteran and accomplished states in the arts of corruption."[9]

In all probability the government's insolvency worked only relatively minor hardships on most of the citizenry. Where suffering did occur, people usually had the means of persevering and making the best of the situation. It is important to remember that the social and economic health of the eighteenth-century colonies had been remarkably good. No yawning chasms, only shaded gradations, separated the various classes of free, white Americans. "It is clear," says Jackson T. Main, "that revolutionary America produced enough wealth to save even its poor from suffering, to permit the great majority to live adequately, even in comfort. . . ." Therefore, "economic abundance together with high mobility" united to minimize or eliminate the severe tensions and dire want that might have been spawned during the war by a rigid class structure and a lopsided concentration of wealth. Though clerks, craftsmen, shopkeepers, clergy, and teachers living on fixed wages were perhaps the civilians hardest hit, they fortunately constituted a small fraction of the population. For some of these wages did increase sharply, and there were strikes for better pay in New York, Pennsylvania, and North Carolina.[10]

## Turning to the States

Congress was not so innocent of economics as to imagine that something other than paper money was at the root of runaway inflation. Every effort to cope with that evil seemed to speed its progress. State price-fixing laws that made it illegal to reject fiat currency, to discriminate in preference for coin, or to charge in excess of stipulated legal prices had failed dismally.[11] The dislocation of agriculture and commerce, the shortage of manufactured goods, and the disruption of manpower owing to military requirements had all served to deepen the inflation. A final conclusion from all the evidence was that people had lost faith in their money, even though many sustained it as best they could. It was necessary, cried the Reverend Charles Chauncy in giving title to a Thursday lecture in Boston, that *The Accursed Thing* [paper issues] *be taken away from a People if they would reasonably hope to stand before their Enemies* (1778).[12]

Congress refused to be stampeded into a precipitate course. It was patently clear that no pay-as-you-go scheme was possible when Congress had no accumulated wealth to draw upon. On the other hand, with confidence in governmental credit at the vanishing point, could the paper money procedures of approximately four years' standing be continued?

Finally, on September 3, 1779, Congress resolved to stop printing when its total emissions reached $200,000,000, which would occur within a few weeks. Then, on March 18, 1780, Congress drastically revalued the Continental debt, declaring forty paper dollars equal to one specie dollar. A flourish of the pen had reduced the domestic obligation from almost $200,000,000 to $5,000,000. From outward appearances this seems a drastic act by the Revolutionary government. It is possible, though, to view the debt reduction quite differently: "The losses involved in this repudiation would have been staggering," admits Ralph V. Harlow, "had they been inflicted suddenly, but that was not the case. As the money passed from hand to hand the ordinary individual suffered little. The merchant, and even the laborer, could charge enough to protect himself. . . . For those who could pass the bills of credit on to another victim without delay the paper structure was perhaps distinctly advantageous. As long as the output of bills and notes continued, there was no burden of taxation. The governments were drawing their resources from depreciation, rather than income."[13] Even most of those who were finally saddled with large quantities of Continental paper when it reached the point of worthlessness had conceivably realized a modest to healthy return on their overall paper transactions. And its contribution to the cause of freedom was not ignored: "Common consent has consigned it to rest with that kind of regard, which the long service of inanimate things insensibly obtains from mankind," said Thomas Paine. "Every stone in the bridge, that has carried us over, seems to have a claim on our esteem, but this was a corner-stone and its usefulness cannot be forgotten."[14]

The financial measures of 1780 signaled the intention of a debilitated and dispirited Congress to rely more heavily upon the states, which now were asked to tax the old Continental currency out of existence at the forty to one ratio within a period of thirteen months. The states were empowered to issue one new dollar for every twenty they returned: the fresh bills not to exceed $10,000,000, which hopefully would remain fairly steady in worth since the quantity of the emission would be in line with the needs of the economy. With its currency at rock bottom, Congress turned to the states in two other ways: for commodity requisitions, a system where each state was expected to raise and deliver a greatly increased part of the sinews of war—chiefly food and clothing—to Continental agents and officers who would assign and transport them to the army; and for paying their own troops on the Continental establishment.[15]

In relinquishing its prior functions to its constituents, was Congress now wasting away? Was nationalism declining instead of growing, taking a back seat to localism and states' rights? Washington saw "one head gradually changing into thirteen." Twenty-nine-year-old James Madison of Virginia, a newcomer to Congress in the spring of 1780, observed that "the situation of Congress has undergone a total change from what it originally was. . . . Since the resolution passed for shutting the press, this power has been entirely give up, and they are now as depending on the States as the King of England is on the parliament." To many the Revolution by 1780 had descended to its nadir. The winter of 1779–1780 for the army was more fearful than the one of hunger, cold, and sickness at Valley Forge. The Continental line seemed to lack everything—pay, provisions, clothing, medicines, weapons, and transportation. To compound the gloom, British regulars overwhelmed the lower South.[16]

Some Americans cherished the hope that the states might rise nobly to the occasion. A Massachusetts essayist implored the states to "Fill up your battalions—be prepared in every part to repell the incursions of your enemies—place your several quotas in the Continental treasury —lend money for public uses—sink the emissions of your respective states—provide effectually for expediting the conveyance of supplies for your armies and fleets, and for your allies—prevent the produce of the country from being monopolized. . . ." A Marylander beseeched the states to "esteem a requisition of congress as binding and obligatory on all the states in the union. Congress is, and ought to be the judge of the number of men, & the sums of money, necessary to carry on the war. If one state may refuse or delay to raise its proportion of the supplies required, another may do the same, and by such conduct endanger the safety of the whole."[17]

Washington was not optimistic. On May 31, 1780, he wrote: "One State will comply with a requisition of Congress, another neglects to do it[,] a third executes it by halves. . . ." For the disarray in the economic and manpower sectors there are multiple and complex reasons. Congress' inability to tax, regulate commerce, deal directly with the citizens, and compel the states to adhere to its requisitions and other demands is fundamental. Nor would the eventual ratification of the Articles of Confederation in 1781 extend Congressional power into these areas. The Articles may well have been a healthy step toward a permanent form of American government; but only a first step, as David Ramsay pointed out in his *History of the American Revolution*: "No coercive power was given the general government, nor was it invested with any legislative power over individuals. . . ."[18]

Troubled though Congress was, one should avoid the extreme position taken by C. H. Van Tyne that the assemblage at Philadelphia amounted to nothing more than a council of ambassadors from the thirteen states, "merely the central office of a continental political signal system."[19] Congress' achievements have also been minimized by advocates of states' rights and Washington's admirers who have tended to place at the doorstep of the lawmakers all the great man's woes from 1775 to 1783. No better proof can be found for Congress' need to exercise paramount leadership, to reassert itself in 1780–1781, than in the states' failure to shoulder the heavy burdens that had devolved upon them.

In her careful study of the Revolutionary war governors, Margaret B. Macmillan finds that with the advent of spring in 1780 a new note was trumpeted in Continental-state relations. "More governors objected more often to the state quotas of money and supplies. They also complained that the special problems of their section of the country were either ignored or not understood. It became increasingly difficult for Congress to obtain any response from some of the executives." Certain chief executives waited months at a time to inform Congress whether anything at all had been done to meet requests from Philadelphia. Congress' plan for the states to replace its old bills of credit fell far short of the mark; only $4,468,625 in new bills were emitted under the scheme of 1780. State money continued to circulate which, along with Continental certificates for goods and stores, tended to draw down the new money, as did the continued presence of much of the original Continental paper that had never been exchanged. (By 1783, however, all the states had withdrawn their own paper from circulation, mainly through tax payments, and had repealed their legal tender acts.) Simultaneously the soldiers voiced their complaints concerning state pay, usually in the form of military certificates which fluctuated in value as did other types of paper instruments. These certificates in most cases constituted the largest form of state indebtedness after the war.[20]

The record of the states in responding to the new system of supply requisitions was, perhaps predictably, uneven. The administrative machinery of the states was cumbersome or altogether inadequate. Compelled not infrequently to confiscate in the absence of cash to pay for goods, local authorities often drew in their reins when their operations provoked a storm of protest from their own citizens. Meat, flour, and forage, if collected, usually reached the army off schedule, and those that arrived were generally deficient in quantity and quality. Alexander Hamilton complained that the "mode of supplying the army—by state purchases—is not one of the least considerable defects of our system."[21]

A backward glance enables us to see that if Congressional authority was weak, the same was true of state authority. Factors of geography and transportation hampered local officials, and so did the nature of state governments. One of the gravest weaknesses in the early state constitutions was the rigid limitation imposed upon the governors. Continental requests were normally sent to the state executives, who were invariably hamstrung by councils of state which had to approve any significant step undertaken by a governor. James Madison, who had served on Virginia's eight-man council before entering Congress, felt that this body reduced the governor to little more than a cipher and paralyzed executive action. "A modern parallel," says Irving Brant, "would be for the President of the United States to conduct a war with every step requiring the advance approval of a cabinet chosen for him by Congress and with that cabinet able to act without him whenever he left the capital city." At one juncture the North Carolina legislature placed all war measures in the hands of a board of war that was not obliged to consult with the governor at all. A remark of Governor Benjamin Harrison of Virginia applies to almost all the original state constitutions: "the Constitution . . . may do in Peace but is by no means adapted to war."[22]

Though governors of ability and experience such as George Clinton of New York and William Livingston of New Jersey might see a respectful legislature expand the boundaries of their jurisdiction, wartime conditions, especially by 1780, were liable to constrict their endeavors in behalf of the Continental Congress. George Clinton, on July 8, 1780, replied to a Congressional request:

> From the acts of the Legislature for raising monies, it will apear they . . . intended to have complied with the Requisitions of Congress and punctually to have paid the sums required . . . we were obliged by subsequent appropriations to apply the monies to different purposes. Hence I suppose our arrears are considerable. How far we are to be considered as defaulters, we submit to the justice and generosity of Congress. The enemy in the entire possession of our capital and four counties; our Southern, Western, and Northern frontiers exposed and ravaged; the staple of the country restricted from exportation and limited in price, for near three years past, solely with a view to retain it for the army. All purchases and impresses for the Continent . . . for many months past upon credit and still unpaid. . . . . In short if our peculiar situation, difficulties . . . former exertions and present efforts . . . are considered, I trust we shall stand acquitted and that none of the public embarrassments will be imputed to us.[23]

## The Nationalists' Ascendancy

The final years of the Revolutionary War witnessed a revival of energy on the part of Congress. The decline in public affairs brought to the fore in the council chambers of the republic men who were ardent nationalists. James Duane, Robert R. Livingston, ex-General John Sullivan, James Varnum, Joseph Jones, James Madison, Alexander Hamilton, Samuel Johnston, and John Mathews were convinced that Congress must once again become the main theater of action where the war would be won or lost. The motives behind their avowed nationalism have provoked endless scholarly debate. Some of these men, along with their allies in and out of Congress, have been charged with political and economic opportunism. Supposedly deeply conservative and therefore hostile to the democratic features of the Revolution, they have been accused not only of attempting a grab for personal power, but also of seeking to consummate a marriage between government and wealthy interests who had amassed quantities of unredeemed land office notes and other Continental securities, and who in some instances were speculators in Western lands.[24] Undoubtedly, a wedge of Revolutionary leaders saw gains for themselves and for others should Congress acquire the power to tax and collect revenues. Assuredly there were nationalists who saw the influence and prestige of this creditor group as a dynamic force to employ in behalf of a stronger union. As Alexander Hamilton said in his oft-quoted analysis in 1781, "A national debt if it is not excessive will be to us a national blessing; it will be a powerful cement of our union."[25]

Whatever else motivated the personnel at the helm, they faced the task of trying to win a war, not an easy assignment at any time against a formidable foe, and doubly arduous when both the states and Congress seemed more inefficient and impotent than ever. The pressure of adversity combined with a vision that America's future rested upon more effective governmental machinery and greater national solidarity were formative elements in fostering nationalist thinking in the early 1780's. There is small room for doubt that the nationalism of Madison and Hamilton was born of their immediate wartime experiences. As a state office-holder, first in the assembly and then on the governor's council, the shy, retiring Madison—he habitually dressed in black—had chafed at the tardiness of the Old Dominion in providing its share of supplies and equipment for the army. Of slight physical physique like Madison, but of erect military bearing, Hamilton (who did not reach Congress until 1782) had his experience at Valley Forge and elsewhere to convince him of the evils of state peculiarities and Congressional diffidence. But what is intensely interesting, and seldom mentioned, is that the agonies of prolonged conflict could convert a man who is normally depicted as a doctrinaire, states' rights democrat into an apostle of more centralized authority. That man was Dr. Thomas Burke, delegate from North Carolina. It was he who had authored the second clause of the Articles of Confederation, that "Each state retains its sovereignty, freedom and independence, and every power, jurisdiction and right, which is not by this confederation expressly delegated to the United States, in Congress assembled." While Madison's nationalism antedated the British invasion of the South, it was the threat to Burke's own region and state that apparently led the Carolinian who had earlier derided the idea of a permanent union as a "Chimerical project" to speak in terms of national power: to urge in 1781 that the states award Congress the authority to levy a 5 per cent import duty.[26]

Congress never traveled the long road that both Hamilton and Madison desired. (Hamilton called for "complete sovereignty in all that relates to war" by either the doctrine of implied powers or by a special convention assembled for that purpose; Madison also pushed for "arming Congress with coercive powers.")[27] But its members bestirred themselves by agreeing to a reorganization of the army that met some (but not all) recommendations by Washington, and they exhorted the states to make greater efforts to enlist men for three years or the duration of the war. If they shunned the motion of South Carolina delegate John Mathews that they bestow upon Washington near dictatorial powers from the fall of 1780 to the conclusion of 1781, the lawmakers joined Mathews and Madison in voting for a strongly worded impressment act, thereby formally returning to a practice they had earlier turned over to the states (actually, throughout the war the army had always relied to some degree on this method). Congress also beefed up the old embargo against trade with Britain by striking out all previously allowed exceptions, chiefly the King's West Indian colonies, just as it provided tough penalties for crimes on the high seas, forbade unchartered privateering, and stipulated the distribution of prize monies.[28]

The executive departments that superseded the Congressional committee system in 1781 represented another positive step, a modest triumph for the nationalist group in Congress over those who had an instinctive dread of centralized power. Congress, in its administrative evolution, had passed from special committees initially to a standing committee system. But this arrangement had its serious limitations, for a delegate might serve on several major committees at the same time that he sat on a number of *ad hoc* committees, in addition to his regular Congressional duties. Gradually boards composed of both congressmen and outsiders appeared to replace the older set-up. But combining executive and legislative business was not always easy, and the ever changing make-up of Congress meant that inexperienced men were entrusted with affairs beyond their competence.

When a legislative body is also an executive one, confusion is inevitable. So to bring better efficiency and management, Congress in January, 1781, created the department of foreign affairs and in February, departments of war and finance, each to be headed by one man who would be responsible to the lawmakers and hold office during their pleasure. The first secretary of foreign affairs was Robert R. Livingston, a wealthy New York landed aristocrat. Able and energetic, he got on well with the astute French minister, the Chevalier de la Luzerne, though the Gallican found that the New Yorker refused to serve as a mouthpiece for French interests. Livingston had, in fact, little real authority; he was in some ways scarcely more than a Congressional clerk or errand boy. (Once he was to arrange with a tavern keeper a dinner—his own name had been omitted from the list of guests!—in honor of the French minister.)[29]

General Benjamin Lincoln of Massachusetts, appointed secretary at (not *of*) war, was to keep precise returns of troops, supplies, and stores, to make estimates of the army's manifold needs, and to transmit the instructions and resolutions of Congress to the military forces in the various war theaters.[30] Lincoln did not take office until after the Battle of Yorktown. His duties, like those of Livingston, were predominantly clerical in character. Even so, the mild reformation in administration enabled the Confederation government to function more smoothly and efficiently. The heads of the departments of war, finance, and foreign affairs, joined by the secretary of Congress and occasionally Washington, met periodically to confer on public business; in this procedure they resembled a semi-official cabinet.[31]

The dominant voice in these sessions belonged to Robert Morris, superintendent of finance, a man of highly sanguine temperament, who wielded more power than any other civilian leader during the Revolution. The reason for Morris' influence was that financial considerations held the center of the American stage in 1781, dwarfing all other aspects of the war. There was a sensible explanation for Congress' turning to Morris rather than another to overhaul the financial affairs of the Confederation. The richest and most prominent merchant in America, he had earlier been a leading figure in Congress, serving as chairman of the secret committee of commerce, the chief agency in the acquisition of foreign war goods, along with holding key assignments on other preeminent committees. If some contemporaries questioned the Philadelphia merchant's business ethics and believed him to have an exorbitant appetite for authority, they doubted not his boundless energy, zeal for detail, and influential connections in the realm of business. John Adams, never one to mince words, believed Morris to have "a masterly Understanding, an open Temper and an honest Heart. . . . He has vast designs in the mercantile way. And no doubt pursues mercantile ends, which are always gain; but he is an excellent Member of our body."[32]

"Bob Morris," unanimously chosen by Congress, set "a high price upon his services," complained Colonel John Armstrong. Reluctant to accept the proffered honor, one that he felt would expose him "to the Calumny & Detraction of the Envious and Malicious," Morris insisted on the right to appoint all officers in his department and to oversee and dismiss anyone involved in spending money; his demands included control over the monetary transactions of the quartermaster, commissary, and medical departments of the army. Morris stipulated a final condition that is strongly unfamiliar to us today: permission to retain his personal mercantile connections. A present-day secretary of defense or occupant of another cabinet chair is expected to sever all his business ties, salaries as well as investments, on entering the government. That was not a hard and fast rule of conduct two hundred years ago, when a merchant might accept official duty while continuing to involve himself in his personal counting house ventures. Merchants, given their administrative background and given the lack of a trained professional bureaucracy, were much sought after men who also had the wide-ranging connections necessary to transact the government's commercial business.[33]

These facts are important in understanding why Congress permitted men like Morris to exact such demands in return for their services. But there is additionally something to be said for the merchants' thinking. Their network of correspondents and associates, the product of years of effort, would be hard to rebuild if allowed to unravel. Then, too, what would the entrepreneur do with his capital if he "retired" from business when banks and other liquid means of investment of our time were generally non-existent? This is not to say, however, that the practice of multiple representation was flawless. Morris and merchants like him in working for Congress had mingled their Congressional and personal transactions, even using the same vessels for private and public affairs. The result was that their accounts became almost hopelessly ensnarled, especially when inadequate bills of lading accompanied the cargoes, placing a heavy strain on eighteenth-century bookkeeping. One of the best known cases is that of Silas Deane, the Connecticut merchant and American commissioner in France, who not only did business for himself but acted as agent for the firm of Willing and Morris, besides engaging in his primary assignment of procuring military paraphernalia for the Continental army. It is undeniable that many such men, including the merchants who staffed the quartermaster and commissary departments, took advantage of their positions. They were known to buy

*V. L. Mitchell*
*1975*

government goods from themselves and their partners; even the most scrupulous ones often favored their friends, if not themselves.[34] Yet there was another side of the coin. Merchants generally worked for Congress on a commission basis that might be dramatically affected by scarcities, prices, and British seizures. They might incur debts in the course of their operations for which they were personally responsible, and they occasionally were compelled to advance their cash or credit for public purposes.

Merchants such as Morris therefore were not always unreasonable in extracting their pound of flesh from Congress. The lawmakers, in fact, may well have eventually plied Morris with more responsibilities than he had bargained for, though he undoubtedly relished the whirlwind of activity that engulfed him. Besides a vast array of accounts to consider, including an adjustment of loan office certificates, he corresponded with American diplomats in Paris and elsewhere; he disposed of monies obtained in Europe in accordance with Congress' directions; he provided supplies for the army and arranged for their transportation. As time wore on, his official burdens increased as he dispatched circulars to the states on innumerable financial and military topics, sent necessities to Nathanael Greene's Southern army, prepared six-month statements on funds borrowed and bills emitted, drafted a plan for protecting commerce, and assumed the direction of naval administration. Once the financier pledged his personal credit for a quantity of badly needed flour. So trivial a matter as compensating a farmer for the loss of a horse and oxen used by the army came to his attention. As Morris confided to his diary, people were "constantly applying even down to the common express riders and give me infinite interruption so that it is hardly possible to attend to business of more consequence."[35]

Against the ominous background of military and financial reverses in 1781, Morris postponed long-range economic reform in order to stave off immediate calamity. Though Morris had not anticipated putting his hand directly to supplying the troops, he now devoted his energies predominantly to that task. In the emergency he did what almost any department head of mercantile background would have done: he turned to his friends and associates connected with commerce and trade, to those individuals he could trust and rely upon. If this amounted to particular favors for a sector of private enterprise, the overall results could be measured in tangible benefits to the public: the army was adequately provisioned for the Yorktown campaign. Cash had not come from the states, except Pennsylvania, at this critical juncture; it was French livres and credit that enabled Morris to meet the army's needs in the summer and fall of 1781.

The last year and a half of the war witnessed only inconsequential raids and skirmishes on the American mainland, a time in which Morris turned to permanent remedies. After Congress abolished the unsuccessful method of states' supplying their own troops, the financier instituted a system of purchasing army goods through contractors in place of governmental commissary agents. Instead of allocating general contracts, individual agreements were made with one dealer for obtaining rum, with another for salt, and yet another for flour. By distributing business, Morris kept prices down and, by avoiding exorbitant debts to a few, could postpone his payments. On the whole, the scheme worked reasonably well.[36]

The restoration of the government's credit was the real mission of Robert Morris. The essentials of his program were later known as Hamiltonianism. Had he succeeded, the course of American development in the 1780's would likely have been quite different, and Hamilton, at least as a fiscal wizard, might well have remained in the shadowy wings of American history. As Morris saw it, the country's two primary needs were to acquire a sound paper currency redeemable in specie and to pay in coin the interest on most of the Continental debt. These measures would meet with the enthusiastic approval of the wealthy class, which, once confident of the government's financial stability and integrity, would sustain the Confederation with loans in times of trial. Accordingly, Congress approved Morris' proposal for creating the Bank of North America, a quasi-public institution. The government, using foreign loans, provided the bulk of the capital and enjoyed the right of supervision, but management was in the hands of private stockholders. The bank issued notes redeemable in specie, over $1,272,842 of which went to the Confederation government in loans by 1784. To supplement the bank notes that performed as a kind of paper currency, the Superintendent of Finance issued so-called Morris Notes and Morris Warrants, orders bearing the Superintendent's signature and directing the Treasurer of the United States to pay specific sums: the Notes to the bearer on demand, the Warrants to a designated individual at a certain time. These circulating media held up reasonably well for the duration of the conflict—supported as they were by the presence of foreign loans—and were a pump to draw supplies for the army out of the hands of farmers and merchants.[37]

With foreign aid but a stop-gap measure, since loans from abroad were likely to dry up with the conclusion of hostilities, Morris urged that Congress impose taxes directly upon the people to pay the interest on the union's indebtedness. By 1782 it consisted principally of sums due France, Spain, and Holland, together with loan office obligations and a bewildering variety of certificates given the citizens when agents bought or impressed goods in behalf of the army. Morris also suggested assuming part of the war debts of those states making financial contributions in excess of their sisters. Morris' plea for poll taxes, land taxes, a liquor excise, and tariff duties upon imports was indeed a bold proposal; shocking would be a more accurate description of contemporary reaction. Yet when Congress had requested $8,000,000 from the states to meet the Confederation's obligations for 1782, Continental receivers were able to collect only $400,000. Congress had already agreed to a recommendation of a tax on imports—the so-called impost —that would allow the government to levy a 5 per cent duty upon outside commodities imported into the United States. Requiring the unanimous approval of the states as stipulated in the Articles of Confederation, the impost failed of ratification when, with twelve approvals, Rhode Island remained intractable: "the most precious jewel of sovereignty [is] that no State be called upon to open its purse but by the authority of the State and by her own officers."[38]

In the absence of foreign loans and the failure to secure direct Congressional taxation, Morris' program broke down. The financier had made a notable contribution toward winning the war, but the country, seeing the prospect of victory, was not yet ready to execute the methods and objectives of Robert Morris in building the peace.

## Domestic Production

We have observed that foreign goods were invaluable in underpinning the Revolution. Some cargoes came directly from Europe to America, but the vast preponderance arrived in the West Indies, at Cape François, Port au Prince, Martinique, St. Eustatius, Havana, and St. Croix: from which they were transshipped on small, fast-sailing schooners and brigs owned by American mercantile firms or private traders. The great emporium for this traffic was St. Eustatius, a tiny Dutch island lying near the northeastern corner of the West Indian chain, its roadstead perpetually filled with vessels of almost every nation, its warehouses crammed with European-manufactured munitions and American tobacco, indigo, flour, and naval stores.[39] All the same, there were limits to foreign trade imposed by such factors as the country's inelastic credit resources, the hazards of blockade running, the course of the war on land, and the eventual British sacking of St. Eustatius. American initiative in the area of domestic production was essential in order to feed, clothe, and equip the Continental army. "Let those who stay at home, unite and exert themselves, to furnish every comfort and assistance to their brethren in the field," exhorted a Connecticut patriot.[40]

Food in particular had to be grown locally. New Englanders did well by the patriot forces surrounding Boston in the dawning months of warfare, and the troops continued to operate on full stomachs until the evacuation of Manhattan in the fall of 1776. Generally throughout that time pork, beef, bread, rice, corn meal, and various kinds of farm and garden produce were in plentiful supply. Later, while the quantity of meat and flour fluctuated between good and bad, there were few vegetables. Congress adopted a resolution on June 10, 1777, calling on the Continental military commanders to encourage the troops to raise "Quantities of potatoes[,] Turnips and other Vegetables,"[41] a scheme that evidently bore few positive results. Perishable food, of course, could not be carried during a campaign as easily as beef. The severest shortages of meat—and virtually all other provisions as well—took place during the winters of 1777–1778 (Valley Forge) and 1779–1780. In February, 1778, the soldiers stretched their meager ration of three ounces of meat and three pounds of bread over an entire week. Once or twice in the latter winter the men went two days without either mainstay.

It is a familiar saying, not without some foundation, that the Continental army endured hunger and near starvation in the midst of plenty. An overwhelmingly agricultural society, America collectively could produce the foodstuffs to nourish its fighting men.[42] New Englanders raised cattle, hogs, and sheep; they grew an array of fruits and vegetables, besides corn, a staple everywhere; and they made an abundance of cider. The middle states are appropriately labeled the grainery of eighteenth-century America. Along with their livestock, they had exported their flour and wheat in sizeable quantities before the Revolution. In the South, however, small farmers engaged in diversified agriculture and had only meager surpluses for sale, though cattle from that region proved a valuable asset to the Revolutionary forces. There are elements accounting for this apparent paradox that go beyond the reluctance of some farmers and merchants to sell their produce for depreciated paper currency and the sluggishness of the states in responding to Continental requisitions. None exceeded the formidable obstacles of the transportation services in obtaining adequate procurement and distribution. Washington calculated that in a single year 15,000 soldiers required 100,000 barrels of flour and 20,000,000 pounds of meat. Rivers were seldom helpful, more often harmful, for military movements and supply shipments normally crossed rather than followed the principal waterways. Thus horses, oxen, and wagons took precedence over boats in the Continental transportation pattern. It befell the quartermaster general and his staff to obtain, commonly by hiring, teams for the hauling services, an arduous assignment that was doubly imposing at harvest time when country people were reluctant to part with them. Farmers were not necessarily unpatriotic when they raised doubts as to whether they would ever see their animals again. One winter, with forage almost unattainable, 1,500 horses starved to death. The travail at Valley Forge was partly due to a shortage of wagons and teams to fetch pork from New Jersey and flour from wharves along the Susquehanna. Even with available transport, progress was hampered by roads that were primitive enough under satisfactory conditions but well-nigh impassable quagmires after snows or heavy rains.

Since it was patently beyond the realm of possibility to assemble the army's entire campaign needs at a single point, supply depots or magazines dotted the areas surrounding the main camp and lined the route of the army's proposed advance or retreat. (When Washington moved precipitately, as in his unplanned exit through New Jersey in December, 1776, then acute shortages and hunger afflicted his command.) Without salt, however, there was no point in storing meat behind the lines. Mostly imported from the Cape Verde Islands and the British West Indies prior to 1775, Americans relied on salt to maintain the New England fisheries, sustain cattle, and preserve meat. Even with the states' endeavors to regulate prices, combat hoarders, and establish saltworks, the valuable commodity remained distressingly scarce. If housewives and rural folk were pinched, and sometimes mobbed monopolizers, it was the army that was most intensely pained by the absence of salt. In some instances cattle were herded all the way to the camps to be slaughtered. Occasionally farmers living near army posts were asked to take care of recently arrived cattle—invariably thin if driven far—by fattening them on hay and corn until commissary officials were ready for the slaughter.[43]

The creation of saltworks was one of the many forms of manufacturing urgently requested by the Continental Congress in a key resolution introduced by John Adams in March, 1776. There was no shift of emphasis or sentiment at that time; since the Stamp Act and the nonimportation agreements, patriot leaders had pled for self-sufficiency and home manufactures. Ambitions for internal improvements in agriculture and industry were also Enlightenment themes, long mirrored in the writings of Franklin and the activities of the American Philosophical Society. In fact, Congress' above-mentioned resolution proposed the formation of societies for the promotion of manufactures in all the colonies.[44]

Aside from armaments, the most persistent cry was for multiplying the output of linens and woolens. Though the art of making cloth and clothing was widely known, and though the emphasis was upon heightened self-sufficiency in the pre-independence decade, English woolens had continued to enjoy a thriving American market. From a value of £645,900 in woolens shipped to the colonies (excluding New York) in 1774, British exports of this product to America fell to approximately £2,540 in 1776. Congressional and state leaders encouraged farmers to fatten rather than slaughter their sheep and to breed them as well. In spite of a profusion of patriot schemes, "The United Company for Promoting Manufactures" in Philadelphia, employing as many as 700 at a time, appears to have been the only large, organized cloth-making undertaking of the time; but by 1779 it was no longer in existence. Most workers labored in their own homes or in the homes of someone else. A Maryland contractor announced that he was ready to operate a new clothing business consisting of sixteen looms in a single house. In all, domestic production jumped sufficiently, coupled with imports from continental Europe, to take care of civilian necessities. The South, previously lagging behind, increased its activity. Jefferson wrote that many people manufactured their necessary articles of clothing throughout the war.[45]

Household industries faced a more imposing assignment in outfitting the Continental army. In June, 1776, Congress petitioned the states to furnish two pairs of clothing for each of its soldiers in service; state agents were to turn over their collections to the Continental clothier general with headquarters at Lancaster, Pennsylvania. No state consistently met its obligations, but Connecticut drew praise from Washington, who assured Governor Jonathan Trumbull that none of the men too poorly clad for duty at Valley Forge hailed from his state. Connecticut had instructed the towns to attire every man sent to the army with one suit. Massachusetts asked of each town a specified quantity of blankets, coats, shirts, and so on. After a period of experimentation, New Hampshire permitted its citizens to pay their taxes in clothing appropriate for the troops. Some prospective suppliers, who were to employ local weavers, received government contracts and secured loans in order to set up operations. There is no way of determining the amount of army clothing that came from domestic looms as compared to that imported from abroad. In any event, local textile production never reached the heights that Congress seemingly anticipated when, on October 8, 1776, it promised each long-term enlistee four shirts, two pairs of overalls, one pair of breeches, one leather or woolen coat, and a hat or leather cap. Yet carelessness, inefficiency, and confusion all contributed to the gap between needs and accomplishments, as when a local manufacturer turned out 300 hats too small to wear, when another producer delivered a consignment of supposedly two-man blankets, each of which would not satisfactorily cover a single soldier; as when imported clothing sufficient to fill 100 wagons languished for months in New Hampshire awaiting teams, when—according to Washington—10,000 uniforms lay in French warehouses because of a bureaucratic mix-up between Congressional diplomats and representatives of American mercantile firms. If the army was almost invariably ill-clad, genuine hardships were, except for shoes, minimal in summers, although the ragged appearance of the Continentals never ceased to be an object of embarrassment and resentment to Washington and to many of the men themselves. In winter, the average Continental would have been happy enough to settle for one warm suit of clothing.[46]

Improvisation and self-help also characterized the patriots' quest for powder and guns. The scramble for powder in 1774–1775 underlined the scarcity of this essential item at the outset of hostilities and explained Benjamin Franklin's recommendation of bows and arrows, the venerable Pennsylvanian reminding Congress that a bowman could launch four arrows in the time a musketman could load and fire a single projectile; going a step further, Franklin's friends Thomas Paine and scientist David Rittenhouse experimented with arrows dipped with fire vial and shot from steel crossbows. The most critical ingredient in gunpowder was saltpetre (potassium nitrate), which the colonies had not previously produced. Patriot appeals backed by substantial rewards were made everywhere for this valuable resource. David Ramsay, John Winthrop, Benjamin Rush, and David Rittenhouse were among those who conducted experiments, disseminated information, and superintended state-directed enterprises.[47] In Virginia, Charles Carter of Stafford rode from plantation to plantation instructing his countrymen in the process of extracting saltpetre from the "Sweepings of their Tobacco-Houses," which, along with stable deposits and other nitrate-bearing materials, were "exceedingly useful" in making the valuable commodity. Soon recognizing there were limits to what one man and one horse could do, Carter published a list of others who could teach the same process. Though the overwhelming preponderance of gunpowder between Lexington and Saratoga came from foreign markets, American exertions yielded 115,000 pounds of gunpowder by late 1777, compared to a stockpile of only 80,000 pounds in the spring of 1775.[48]

A distinguished economic historian believes that the "Revolution could have succeeded if the states had not possessed a vigorous iron industry," accounting in 1775 for a seventh of the world's output. Not a moment was wasted in some parts of America in converting this industry—concentrated in Pennsylvania and New Jersey but present everywhere save Georgia—to a martial footing. Nicholas Brown of Providence, Rhode Island, implied that cannon were cast in Maryland, New Jersey, and Pennsylvania as early as November, 1775. Nicholas and his brother John, two of colonial America's most versatile entrepreneurs, witnessing the wartime dislocation of their lucrative spermaceti candle business, allowed their Hope Furnace (established a decade earlier) to come into its own as a producer of cannon. Selling chiefly to owners of privateers and to a lesser extent to the Continental navy and to the states, John Brown claimed, with what may have been a slight but pardonable exaggeration, that the Hope works

had cast "about 3000 . . . of the best Cannon ever made in the Nation."
The war also drew into the iron business venturesome beginners who
geared their talents and capital to the making of armaments. Two Virginians, John Ballendine and John Reveley, erected Westham Foundry
on the James River, which funished shells, grape, cannister shot, and
some cannon to Virginia's military forces. Most of the states made serious, if sometimes failing, exertions in trying to fashion new works or to
lease or confiscate going concerns. The Connecticut council of safety
took over loyalist-owned Lakeville Furnace, which soon contributed
guns for the New York forts and supplied batteries for Continental
warships. It was at the state foundry at Stirling, New York, twenty-five
miles above West Point, that iron workers forged in six weeks the 180-
ton chain that was stretched across the Hudson to prevent enemy vessels from ascending the river. Continental or state inducements in one
form or another provided the stimulus for foundries that went up at
Springfield, East Bridgewater, and Easton in Massachusetts, at Lancaster in Pennsylvania, at Trenton in New Jersey, and at Principio in
Maryland.[49]

British captures of large Continental detachments, as at Fort Washington in 1776 and Charleston in 1780, added to the strain on scattered
American resources. At Fort Washington and nearby Fort Lee, which
had been evacuated, William Howe took 146 pieces of artillery, over
12,000 cannon shot, 2,800 small arms, and 400,000 musket cartridges.
One incentive that prompted Washington to make winter camps in
New Jersey was to protect the invaluable cluster of forges and furnaces
in the northwestern part of the state just above Morristown. Information is spotty relative to the quality of American cannon in relation to
those coming from France. In 1777, Alexander Hamilton described to
New York revolutionists a new three-pounder cast and bored in Philadelphia. As a test, it had "fired twenty times as fast as possible"; Washington deemed it "a great acquisition." Though American-made artillery pieces were not infrequently defective, European guns also
brought death to their crews because of muzzle explosions, defective
caps, and unexpected backfiring. (Any number of American gunners
became fatalities for these reasons, and a similar explosion had deprived artillery chief Henry Knox of two fingers.)[50]

Small arms factories and individual gunsmiths did their bit to keep
America in the fight, experiencing ups and downs akin to those of the
cannon-casting establishments. North Carolina's overly ambitious
scheme to set up six small arms undertakings apparently brought neg-
ligible results, but Virginia's armament plant at Fredericksburg enjoyed
a reputation for considerable accomplishment. Local shops or state-
encouraged factories turned out muskets at Providence, Rhode Island,
Sutton and Springfield, Massachusetts, Waterbury, Connecticut, and

elsewhere. Their volume, combined with the arrival in 1777 of 23,000 French "Charleville" muskets, were of no mean consequence to state and Continental forces, which, despite the fact of a "population in arms" in 1775, found hand weapons invariably in short supply. For flintlocks wore out, needed new parts, and the bores of older guns varied so profusely that each man often needed a separate mold to shape bullets for his own weapon. Some soldiers left their muskets at home for the benefit of their families. Indeed, a man who contributed his own firearm made a notable sacrifice if it were damaged or destroyed; its worth was most likely equal to two weeks' pay for a laborer. Local Revolutionary committees scoured the countryside bargaining for every available musket, 800 of which were deposited with the Fredericksburg factory for repair in 1781.[51]

American war industries required skilled artisans and laborers, and, in keeping with the practice of colonial times, the states exempted workers in vital occupations from military service. These were not blanket deferments, instead being parceled out according to necessity. New York's procedure was typical, exempting one miller to each gristmill, five iron workers per furnace, three powder makers in each powder mill, three journeymen in each printing office, and a ferryman for every public ferry. Additional deferments resulted from appeals of entrepreneurs who claimed that labor shortages would result in damage to the cause. Boatbuilders, shoemakers, blacksmiths, nailmakers, linen workers, and flax seed mill employees now and then fell into this category. The army, however, often contributed to the labor scarcity by hiring carpenters, blacksmiths, and other artificers. Not surprisingly, advertisements for artisans and laborers and mechanics were commonplace. Various expedients were sought. The New York Provincial Congress paid the passage from Britain of a number of gunsmiths and locksmiths. Virginia, desiring to do the same thing for munitions makers in France, found that Louis XVI's government refused to allow their departure. At Fredericksburg and Westham scores of slaves were put to making arms. At times Continental officials allowed regular troops to lend a hand in such essential war industries as shoes and salt, just as they permitted manufacturers of shoes and nails to borrow German prisoners. Withal, complaints of inadequate human resources to man the homefront never ceased.[52]

## Science and Technology

American accomplishments in the economic sector—even after due allowance for waste, mismanagement, and inefficiency—are not to be ignored, especially in view of the material and technological restraints imposed upon American efforts. Financing a war without a stable currency and without a centralized administrative system, and depending upon small units of production scattered about a huge wilderness of a country, Americans revealed a bent for improvisation that united with foreign assistance to see the contest to its victorious conclusion. The absence of governmental centralization, large-scale production, and adequate transportation made it out of the question to harness simultaneously a really imposing part of the population, either as soldiers or civilian workers. There were many times when Washington cried for additional men; but more often he appealed simply for clothing and equipment to maintain the troops at hand.

At this juncture one can observe both a comparison and a contrast between the military features of the American Revolution and the French Revolution. Frenchmen of the 1790's discarded the notion of restricted manpower, adopted the Americans' concept of the citizen in arms, providing in theory and in fact for a vast reservoir of fighting men. But, as John U. Nef has shown, in France, unlike America, the brakes upon mobilization were, by the standards of the day, becoming weaker or were missing altogether. Technological limitations clearly impeded American efforts, nowhere more glaringly than in the tiny corps of engineers. Always distressingly deficient in trained officers, it was commanded by a Frenchman, Brigadier General Louis Duportail, whose staff included Pierre Charles L'Enfant, future designer of the federal capital. (In 1782 only one of fourteen officers in the corps was an American.) Duportail encountered failure in his plan to establish a military academy for the education of engineers and artillerists, its curriculum to call for a heavy concentration of mathematics and chemistry. In France, however, Nef tells us that the general mobilization of manpower and the accentuated industrial output "combined with a growing desire to put the work of scientists and engineers to the most practical use." One of the most rewarding fruits of that union brought improvements in the accuracy and frequency of gunfire and the mobility of artillery, traceable directly to Gaspard Monge, Lazare Carnot, and other mathematical experts. Acting under the revolutionary committee of safety in 1793 and 1794, Monge drew up a scheme for a national war effort that included producing guns, metal, and saltpetre in quantities sufficient to beat back the anti-French coalition. His *Description de l'art de fabriquer les canons* explained how to convert village churches into cannon factories.[53]

For the most part this sort of wartime interaction between government and scholar came much later in America. Yet Americans had done demonstrably more than send their men of intellectual attainments to Congress or to Europe on diplomatic assignments. The best scientific minds had experimented with the making of saltpetre and munitions. David Rittenhouse had also helped locate fortifications, surveyed portions of the Delaware River, investigated ways of grooving cannon, and experimented with telescopic sights and built-in ammunition compartments for rifles. But Rittenhouse, Benjamin Rush, and men like them found that they were equally in demand for holding office, and thus faced a lack of leisure time as well as financial backing for conducting experiments in the public interest. However frustrating these circumstances might be, Franklin, whose own scientific reputation was a monumental asset in France, had earlier expressed an opinion with which most devotees of science probably concurred. "Had Newton been Pilot but of a single common Ship," averred Franklin, "the finest of his Discoveries would scarce have excus'd, or atton'd for his abandoning the Helm one Hour in Time of Danger; how much less if she carried the Fate of the Commonwealth."[54]

If the American Revolution antedated the period of profound technological change in the United States, it nonetheless suggested some of the trends of the future. The increased production of shot, muskets, cannons, cannon balls, iron chains, *chevaux-de-frise*, nails, camp kettles, and pots and pans pointed the way to the phenomenal interaction between war and industry that marked the next two centuries. It was the stimulating pressure of critical times that fostered the mechanical creativity of fourteen-year-old Eli Whitney, who converted his father's tool shed into a two-man nail factory at Westborough, Massachusetts, the same Whitney who subsequently made the first large-scale attempt at mass production in America by manufacturing muskets in unheard-of quantities.[55]

Another New England youth with a bent for mechanics was Yale student David Bushnell, inventor of a submarine. Built in 1775 to "pulverize" the British navy, Bushnell's "American Turtle" was an oaken cask, caulked and coated with tar and bound with iron bands. Protruding from its top were two ventilating tubes and a glass-covered "head," or conning tower. The craft was submerged by pulling a hand spring that admitted water to a compartment at the bottom, while a foot pump pushed the water out enabling it to surface. Other gadgets operated by hand and foot propelled the submarine forward and backward or to either side. Approaching a British vessel underwater, it was to attach to the enemy's hull, by means of a long screw, an egg-shaped bomb (containing 130 pounds of gunpowder) set to explode after the submarine had withdrawn a safe distance. Though the submarine worked and actually made contact with a British warship in New York harbor in August, 1776, the operator, an army sergeant, was unable to screw the bomb to the hull, probably for lack of adequate pressure.

Subsequent experiments were similarly unproductive; but the principle of submarine navigation had taken a forward step in the Revolution.[56]

More positive were certain advances that flowed from the medical demands of the struggle. While modest in scope, usually reflecting knowledge already held in European circles, the achievements were all the same beneficial to the republic. The mixing of American physicians on a previously unapproached scale was in itself helpful in the dissemination of medical information; and it contributed to the eventual organization of the medical profession and the setting of professional standards. A spate of handbooks made their appearance on gunshot wounds, fractures, dysentery, small pox, and an array of other subjects. Benjamin Rush's *Directions for Preserving the Health of Soldiers* (1778), containing sensible directions on dress, diet, cleanliness, and exercise, was reprinted as late as the American Civil War. Rush's later medical investigations concerning such ailments as tetanus were traceable to his wartime experiments. American medical men also profited from their exposure to outside influences. Dr. James Thatcher admired the techniques of British surgeons in operating on their own wounded following Saratoga. Jean-François Coste, chief physician with Rochambeau's French army, not only gave freely of his time and knowledge to American practitioners, but also encouraged his hosts to put American medicine on a respected and independent footing, commensurate with the political goals of the new nation.[57]

There is, however, a danger of overstating the case. Medicine was still predominantly in a primitive state, with no understanding of infection and anesthetics unknown. Purging, bleeding, emetics, and blisters were standard treatments. Smallpox, dysentery, jaundice, cholera, and typhoid headed the grim list of diseases that exacted a higher death toll than British bullets. The wounded not infrequently suffered cruelly from a lack of medicines, surgical instruments, bandages, and adequate hospital facilities. Disturbing, to say the least, was the internecine strife over the post of director general of the medical services. The successor to the first appointee, the traitor Benjamin Church, was Dr. John Morgan, Edinburgh educated and a founder of the Philadelphia College of Medicine. Victimized by professional rivals and intolerable conditions, he was summarily dismissed in favor of Dr. William Shippen, also trained at Edinburgh and affiliated with the fledgling medical school at Philadelphia. Though Shippen outlasted Morgan, he too succumbed to the hazards of a thankless task and the machinations of a third Philadelphian, the versatile Benjamin Rush. Shippen's replacement, instead of Rush, was Dr. John Cochran of New Jersey, who served out the remainder of the war. The gains in medical know-how obviously do not redound to the credit of the disorganized and distraught medical department; they rest on the accomplishments of individuals, though some of them were involved in the bickering and emerged with tarnished honor.[58]

In other ways the American War of Independence had wrought changes—some far-reaching—on the economic front. The metallurgical and clothing industries obviously spurted sharply, although we do not know if the immediate gains were always permanent; for there is a dearth of sound monographic literature on manufacturing in the Revolutionary era. The administrative, financial, and commercial burdens of the struggle encouraged reform in the central government with the creation of executive departments responsible to Congress. Nationalists such as Alexander Hamilton and Robert Morris had opened a discussion—to be continued in the years ahead—on the need for even more governmental power in order to invigorate the economic sector. The Revolution heralded the emergence of banking and the growth of incorporation. (While a half-dozen business charters were issued in the colonial period, fifteen were granted between 1781 and 1785.) The tempo of economic life was quickened or altered by foreign investments in the United States, loans from abroad, the search for fresh market outlets, and the quest for new trade routes. The discontinuance of archaic land laws and the confiscation and distribution of tory estates were other concomitants of independence. Wars invariably create problems in the course of solving others. The organization and sale of the public domain in the West, the interest and principal of the war debt, and the desirability of a hard-money supply were among the issues that awaited resolution in the years following the peace settlement.[59]

## NOTES

1. Nettels, *Emergence of a National Economy*, 23.
2. E. James Ferguson, "Currency Finance: An Interpretation of Colonial Monetary Practices," *William and Mary Quarterly*, 3d ser., X (1953), 153–180; Theodore Thayer, "The Land Bank System in the American Colonies," *Journal of Economic History*, XIII (1953), 145–159; *Continental Journal*, June 17, 1779.
3. "To expect loans within the United States," cautioned Robert Morris, "presupposes an Ability to lend, which does not exist in any considerable number of the inhabitants. The personal property, not immediately engaged in commerce or the improvement of lands, was never very considerable." Wharton, ed., *Revolutionary Diplomatic Correspondence*, IV, 532–533.
4. Miller, *Triumph of Freedom*, 457; *Pennsylvania Evening Post*, Oct. 5, 1776; *Boston Gazette*, Oct. 28, 1776.
5. "Edmund Randolph's Essay on the Revolutionary History of Virginia, 1774–1782," *Virginia Magazine of History and Biography*, XLIV (1936), 36; Smyth, ed., *Works of Franklin*, VII, 292–294, VIII, 151–152, IX, 231–236; Ralph V. Harlow, "Aspects of Revolutionary Finance, 1775–1783," *American Historical Review*, XXXV (1929), 46. When British authorities forged American money, declares

Kenneth Scott, it was the first time in history that "counterfeiting was resorted to by a government to undermine confidence in the currency, and thereby the credit, of the enemy." Scott, *Counterfeiting in Colonial America* (New York, 1957), 253; *Boston Gazette* (supplement), Oct. 20, 1778.

Congress and several states made small sums of money from the use of lotteries. John S. Ezell, *Fortune's Merry Wheel: The Lottery in America* (Cambridge, Mass., 1960), 59–68; *Boston Gazette*, Feb. 2, July 13, Oct. 20, Nov. 2, 1778, Feb. 14, Aug. 28, 1780. The final Massachusetts lottery was "For the sole Purpose of Cloathing the Army." *Ibid.*, July 2, 1781.

6. The only in-depth study of depreciation in a single state is Ann Bezanson, *Prices and Inflation during the American Revolution: Pennsylvania, 1770–1790* (Philadelphia, 1951). A chart on p. 322 shows the percentage changes in prices of fifteen commodities from year to year. Congressman James Madison spent $21,373 a third for room and board in Philadelphia between March and September, 1780, plus $605 for two cords of wood, $1,776 for washing, and $6,611 for the care of his horses. Hutchinson and Rachal, eds., *Papers of Madison*, II, 97. On the other hand, David Ramsay reported that in 1775–1776 paper issues were "of real advantage to the state of South-Carolina; for the whole money then in circulation was inadequate to the purposes of . . . trade." Ramsay, *History of the Revolution in South Carolina* (Trenton, N.J., 1785), II, 77–81.

7. *Pennsylvania Packet*, Dec. 24, 1777; *Virginia Gazette* (Purdie), July 18, 1777; *Maryland Gazette*, Oct. 24, 1776.

8. *North Carolina Gazette*, Dec. 12, 26, 1777, Jan. 30, 1778; *Newport Mercury*, March 25, 1776; *Boston Gazette*, Feb. 2, 1778. Ralph V. Harlow, "Economic Conditions in Massachusetts during the American Revolution," Colonial Society of Massachusetts, *Publications*, XX (1917–1919), 163–190, stresses the prosperity of farmers in a state little touched by military operations after early 1776.

9. Ramsay, *Revolution in South Carolina*, II, 75–77; Syrett, ed., *Papers of Hamilton*, I, 562–563, 567–570, 580–582. Michael Hillegas, treasurer of the United States, emphasized as a factor in inflation "a Scarcity of foreign Articles (and which scarcity was by the Traders made somewhat Artificial by secreting the Goods we really had). This the retailers as well as the Importers availed themselves of, and Continued to raise their prices (till lately) higher & higher." Hillegas to Franklin, March 17, 1778; *Pennsylvania Magazine of History and Biography*, XXIX (1905), 233–234. Abigail Adams testified that approximately one hundred women assaulted a merchant who monopolized coffee. Butterfield, ed., *Adams Family Correspondence*, II, 295. Certain flour merchants in the middle states were reportedly "Speculators . . . as thick and as industrious as Bees, and as Active and wicked as the Devil himself [.]" George H. Ryder, ed., *Letters to and from Caesar Rodney, 1756–1785* (Philadelphia, 1933), 324.

10. Jackson T. Main, *The Social Structure of Revolutionary America* (Princeton, 1965), 163. Hamilton, in proposing schemes for obtaining revenue in 1781, commented on "the much greater equality of Fortunes" in America than in Europe. Syrett, ed., *Papers of Hamilton*, II, 610. See also Marquis de Chastellux, *Travels in North America in the Years 1780, 1781 and 1782*, ed. Howard C. Rice, Jr. (Chapel Hill, 1963), I, 130. "A Mechanic" charged that apprentices as well as merchants and farmers had sped the course of inflation by demanding additional goods and cash in exchange for being taught a trade. *Connecticut Courant*, June 8, 1779.

11. Robert A. East, *Business Enterprise in the Revolutionary Era* (New York, 1938), 203–206; Richard B. Morris, *Government and Labor in Early America* (New York, 1946), 29–125; Oscar and Mary F. Handlin, "Revolutionary Economic Policy in Massachusetts," *William and Mary Quarterly*, 3d ser., IV (1947), 3–27. Price-fixing and the feasibility of enforcement by local committees provoked considerable disagreement among the patriots. Some felt such endeavors drove scarce items into underground markets; others argued that local committees had grown too powerful. Local authorities usually put little heart into enforcing price

conformity. *Maryland Gazette*, May 23, 1776; *Pennsylvania Journal*, July 7, 1779; *Connecticut Courant*, Aug. 3, 30, 1779; *Continental Journal*, June 17, 24, Sept. 25, 1779; *Virginia Gazette*, (Dixon and Nicholson), July 17, 24, 1779; Commager and Morris, eds., *Spirit of 'Seventy-Six*, II, 779–787.

12. For a typical debate over paper issues, a recurring theme in the American press, see *Virginia Gazette* (Dixon and Nicholson), Nov. 6, 13, Dec. 11, 1779, Feb. 5, 1780. Harsh observations by Gouverneur Morris are in the *Pennsylvania Packet*, Feb. 17, 24, 29, March 4, 11, 23, 1780.

13. Harlow, "Aspects of Revolutionary Finance," 63.

14. Foner, ed., *Writings of Paine*, II, 228.

15. Ford, ed., *Journals of Congress*, XV, 1044–1045, XVI, 196–201.

16. Fitzpatrick, ed., *Writings of Washington*, XVIII, 453; Hutchinson and Rachal, eds., *Papers of Madison*, II, 20.

17. *Continental Journal*, June 17, 1779; *Maryland Gazette*, March 3, 1780; see also *Connecticut Courant*, Nov. 14, 20, 28, Dec. 5, 12, 20, 1778.

18. Fitzpatrick, ed., *Writings of Washington*, XVIII, 453; Ramsay, *History of the American Revolution*, II, 342–343; Chastellux, *Travels in North America*, I, 74.

19. Claude H. Van Tyne, *The American Revolution, 1775–1783* (New York, 1905), 188; Van Tyne, "Sovereignty in the American Revolution," *American Historical Review*, XII (1907), 529–545.

20. Margaret B. Macmillan, *The War Governors in the American Revolution* (New York, 1943), 114; Ferguson, *Revolutionary Public Finance*, 65–66; Ferguson, "State Assumption of the Federal Debt During the Confederation," *Mississippi Valley Historical Review*, XXXVII (1951), 408–409.

21. Syrett, ed., *Papers of Hamilton*, II, 406.

22. Irving Brant, *James Madison* (Indianapolis, 1941–1961), I, 316–317; Macmillan, *War Governors*, 61.

23. Hastings, ed., *Papers of Clinton*, V, 938–943.

24. Several studies contain this somewhat critical interpretation of the nationalists: Merrill Jensen, "The Idea of a National Government During the American Revolution," *Political Science Quarterly*, LIII (1943), 356–379; Jensen, *The New Nation: A History of the United States During the Confederation, 1781–1789* (New York, 1950), 3–84, *passim*; Ferguson, *Power of the Purse*, 109–178, *passim*; East, *Business Enterprise*, 207–208. For a decidedly more favorable vignette of the nationalists, see Brant, *Madison*, I, 370–400, 442, appendix entitled "American Nationhood During the Revolution," 453–458, II, 11–33, 104–133.

25. Hamilton to Robert Morris, April 30, 1781, Syrett, ed., *Papers of Hamilton*, II, 635. The best statement of Hamilton's nationalism at this time, united with a trenchant critique of the Confederation's ills, is *ibid.*, 400–418.

26. Elisha P. Douglass, "Thomas Burke, Disillusioned Democrat," *North Carolina Historical Review*, XXVI (1949), 172–173, 183–185. "Every Member of Congress seems to wish for a Confederacy except my good friend Burke," complained Cornelius Harnett to Richard Caswell. March 20, 1778, Preston Davie Papers, Southern Historical Collection, University of North Carolina Library. Even Samuel Adams, the personification of Revolutionary radicalism, acquiesced to stepped up Continental demands upon the states and to a long-term army. Burnett, ed., *Letters of Congress*, V, 440. "We must cast off our prejudices, rise above our circumstances and divest ourselves of a pitiful regard to our interests whether pecuniary or political." This was "Hard talk indeed!" admitted the author, Gouverneur Morris, writing as "An American" in the *Pennsylvania Packet*, Feb. 17, 1780.

27. Syrett, ed., *Papers of Hamilton*, II, 408; Hutchinson and Rachal, eds., *Papers of Madison*, III, 310.

28. Ford, ed., *Journals of Congress*, XX, 516, XIX, 270–272, 313–316, 354–356, 374–375, XXI, 861–873, 961–968, 1151–1158, XXII, 377–380.

29. Dangerfield, *Livingston*, 144.

30. Harry M. Ward, *The Department of War, 1781–1795* (Pittsburgh, 1962), chap. iii.

31. Jennings B. Sanders, *Evolution of the Executive Departments of the Continental Congress, 1774–1789* (Chapel Hill, 1935), 142; Fitzpatrick, *Writings of Washington*, XXIV, 71.

32. Burnett, ed., *Letters of Congress*, I, 433. Clarence Ver Steeg, *Robert Morris: Revolutionary Financier* (Philadelphia, 1954), a first-rate study of Morris' tenure as superintendent of finance, is distinctly sympathetic to the controversial Philadelphian. Ferguson, *Power of the Press*, is less favorable to Morris. Two older works are still worthy of attention: William Graham Sumner, *The Financier and the Finances of the American Revolution* (New York, 1891); Ellis P. Oberholtzer, *Robert Morris: Patriot and Financier* (New York, 1903).

33. Sanders, *Evolution of the Executive Departments*, 128; Joseph S. Davis, *Essays in the Earlier History of American Corporations* (Cambridge, Mass., 1917), 111–123.

34. E. James Ferguson, "Business, Government, and Congressional Investigation in the Revolution," *William and Mary Quarterly*, 3d ser., XVI (1959), 293–318; Ferguson, *Power of the Press*, 70–105; East, *Business Enterprise, passim*, especially chap. iv.

35. Sanders, *Evolution of the Executive Departments*, 134–136; Ver Steeg, *Morris*, 69–76.

36. East, *Business Enterprise*, 211–212; Ver Steeg, *Morris*, 141, 152, 184; Hatch, *Administration of the American Revolutionary Army*, 113–117.

37. Lawrence Lewis, Jr., *A History of the Bank of North America* (Philadelphia, 1882), chaps. ii–iii; Bray Hammond, *Banks and Politics in America from the Revolution to the Civil War* (Princeton, 1957), 46–53; Nettels, *Emergence of a National Economy*, 32–33. In a thoughtful essay that remained unpublished for many years James Madison accurately denied that the amount of paper issues necessarily determined the worth of them. "If the circulating medium be . . . paper currency, still its value does not depend upon its quantity. It depends on the credit of the state issuing it, and on the time of its redemption. . . ." Hutchinson and Rachal, eds., *Papers of Madison*, I, 304. "An American" rendered the same vedict in the *Pennsylvania Packet*, Feb. 17, 1780.

38. Ver Steeg, *Morris*, 130–131, 136.

39. R. G. Albion, *Sea Lanes in War Time* (New York, 1942), 51–54; Eileen Arnot Robertson, *The Spanish Town Papers* (New York, 1959), *passim*; David Hannay, ed., *Letters Written by Sir Samuel Hood* (London, 1895), 21–23; John Franklin Jameson, "St. Eustatius in the American Revolution," *American Historical Review*, VIII (1903), 683–708. British Admiral George Rodney complained in 1780: "This rock of only six miles in length and three miles in breadth, has done England more harm than all the arms of her most potent enemies, and alone supported the infamous American rebellion." Quoted in G. B. Mundy, *Life and Correspondence of Lord Rodney* (London, 1830), II, 97. One vessel reportedly made the voyage from St. Eustatius to a Massachusetts port in seventeen days. *Continental Journal*, Oct. 31, 1776. Almost all the gunpowder imported to America in the first two and a half years of the war came from the West Indies. Orlando W. Stephenson, "The Supply of Gunpowder in 1776," *American Historical Review*, XXX (1925), 279.

40. *Connecticut Courant*, June 20, 1780.

41. Ford, ed., *Journals of Congress*, VIII, 439.

42. "With respect to Food," complained Washington in 1777, "considering we are in such an extensive and abundant Country, No Army was ever worse supplied than ours. . . ." Fitzpatrick, ed., *Writings of Washington*, VIII, 441.

43. Methods of salt-making were much publicized: *Virginia Gazette* (Dixon and Hunter), Dec. 9, 1775, July 13, 1776, Nov. 21, 1777; *South-Carolina and American General Gazette*, May 20, 1777; *North-Carolina Gazette*, Sept. 22, 1777; *Maryland Gazette*, April 19, 1781; *The Art of Making Common Salt* (Philadelphia, 1776). Food and transportation for the Continental army are covered in Victor L. Johnson, *The Administration of the American Commissariat During the Revolu-*

*tionary War* (Philadelphia, 1941). Briefer treatment of these subjects is found in Macmillan, *War Governors*, 190–218; Hatch, *Administration of the American Revolutionary Army*, 88–92, 98, 104–105, 112; Nettels, *Emergence of a National Economy*, 34–40; Edmund C. Burnett, "The Continental Congress and Agricultural Supplies," *Agricultural History*, II, (1928), 111–128.

44. Ford, ed,. *Jourials of Congress*, IV, 224; Stuart Bruchey, *The Roots of American Economic Growth, 1607–1861* (New York, 1965), 106–107.

45. Joseph Hewes to Samuel Johnston, July 24, 1776, Dreer Collection, Historical Society of Pennsylvania; Diary of Josiah Smith, *passim*, Southern Historical Collection, University of North Carolina Library; *South-Carolina and American General Gazette*, Feb. 9, 1776; J. L. Bishop, *A History of American Manufactures* (Philadelphia, 1864), I, 390; Victor S. Clark, *History of Manufactures in the United States, 1607–1860* (Chicago, 1917), 56–59; Arthur H. Cole, *The American Wool Manufacture* (Cambridge, Mass., 1926), I, 63–64; Brooke Hindle, *The Pursuit of Science in Revolutionary America, 1735–1789* (Chapel Hill, 1956), 246; Browne and others, eds., *Archives of Maryland*, XII, 278; Jefferson, *Notes on Virginia*, 164–165.

A Scottish indentured servant, serving as a plantation school master in 1775, wrote that "before this year there has been little or no linen made in the Colony." Edward M. Riley, ed., *The Journal of John Harrower . . .* (Williamsburg, 1963), 121.

46. Ford, ed., *Journals of Congress*, V, 467, 885; Fitzpatrick, ed., *Writings of Washington*, XI, 182–183; William B. Weeden, *Economic and Social History of New England, 1620–1789* (Boston and New York, 1891), II, 790–791; Tryon, *Household Manufactures*, 115–117; Hatch, *Organization of the American Revolutionary Army*, 86–88, 93, 98–102, 116–117; Bolton, *Private Soldier*, 89–104; *Connecticut Courant*, Nov. 5, 1777; *Boston Gazette*, Sept. 30, 1776.

47. Ford, ed., *Journals of Congress*, II, 218–219, III, 296, 345–348, 511; Smyth, ed., *Writings of Franklin*, VI, 438–439; Timothy Dwight, *A Valedictory Address . . .* (New Haven, 1776), 8–9; Hindle, *Rittenhouse*, 188–189; Force, ed., *American Archives*, 4th ser., V, 593; *Winthrop Papers* (Massachusetts Historical Society, *Collections*, vol. 44 [1878]), 5th ser., IV, 306; Butterfield, ed., *Letters of Rush*, I, 92–94; Benjamin Rush, *Essays upon the Making of Salt-Petre and Gunpowder* (New York, 1776); *New-York Journal*, Aug. 24, 1775; *Massachusetts Spy*, Jan. 5, 1776; *Continental Journal*, Aug. 22, 1776; *Pennsylvania Packet*, July 24, 1775; *Pennsylvania Gazette*, Jan. 24, March 20, 1776; *Maryland Gazette*, Dec. 21, 28, 1775; *Connecticut Courant*, July 3, 8, 1776; *Boston Gazette*, Oct. 23, Dec. 4, 1775, Jan. 1, 22, 1776.

48. Mays, *Pendleton*, II, 45; Donald E. Reynolds, "Ammunition Supply in Revolutionary Virginia," *Virginia Magazine of History and Biography*, LXXIII (1965), 56–60; Stephenson, "Supply of Gunpowder in 1776," 277.

49. Nettels, *Emergence of a National Economy*, 42; James B. Hedges, *The Browns of Providence Plantations: Colonial Years* (Cambridge, Mass., 1952), 269, 276, chap. xii, *passim*; Clark, *History of Manufactures*, 220; Morris, *Government and Labor*, 300–302; Kathleen Bruce, *Virginia Iron Manufacture in the Slave Era* (New York and London, 1930), 42–50, 52–54; Charles S. Boyer, *Early Forges and Furnaces in New Jersey* (Philadelphia, 1931), 29–30, 94–97, 120, 137, 161, 181–184; Albert H. Heusser, *George Washington's Map Maker: A Biography of Robert Erskine* (New Brunswick, N.J., 1966), 175–182; *Boston Gazette*, Jan. 7, 1782; *New-Jersey Gazette*, March 4, 1778.

50. Syrett, ed., *Papers of Hamilton*, I, 240; North Callahan, *Henry Knox . . .* (New York, 1958), 162; Jac Weller, "The Artillery of the American Revolution," *Military Collector and Historian*, VIII (1956), 61–65, 97–101; M. V. Brewington, "American Naval Guns, 1775–1785," *American Neptune*, III (1943), 11–19, 148–158; John Muller, *A Treatise of Artillery* (Philadelphia, 1779).

51. East, *Business Enterprise*, 73; Weeden, *Economic and Social History of New England*, II, 792–793, 795; Bruce, *Virginia Iron Manufacture*, 28–42; Boyd, ed.,

*Papers of Jefferson*, V, 515–516, Bolton, *Private Soldier*, 106–107, 113–115; Mays, *Pendleton*, II, 49. Washington reported that 2,000 men were without firearms on June 13, 1776. Fitzpatrick, ed., *Writings of Washington*, IV, 235.

52. Morris, *Government and Labor*, chap. vi; *Pennsylvania Gazette*, Feb. 2, 1780; Bruce, *Virginia Iron Manufacture*, 36, 50–52; Weeden, *Economic and Social History of New England*, II, 795; Hedges, *Browns of Providence Plantations*, 269; Hindle, *Rittenhouse*, 162; *Virginia Gazette* (Purdie), May 16, 1777.

53. Hindle, *Pursuit of Science in Revolutionary America*, 241–243; Elizabeth S. Kite, *Brigadier-General Louis Lebeque Duportail* (Philadelphia, 1933), 266–270; Nef, *War and Human Progress*, 318–326. See also Harold T. Parker, "French Administrators and French Scientists during the Old Regime and the Early Years of the Revolution, in *Ideas in History* . . . , ed. Harold T. Parker, Chicago, 1965), 85–109. The first country to do anything seriously in an institutional sense for the training of engineering and artillery officers was Great Britain. In 1741 the Royal Military Academy at Woolwich was established. The curriculum stressed algebra, geometry, fortifications, mining, gunnery, and bridge building. Sir John Smyth, *Sandhurst* (London, 1961), 5–34.

54. Hindle, *Rittenhouse*, 128; Hindle, *Pursuit of Science in Revolutionary America*, 228–230; Labaree, ed., *Papers of Franklin*, IV, 68.

55. Two excellent biographies of Whitney assess the extent of American technological development in the last quarter of the eighteenth century: Jeannette Mirsky and Allan Nevins, *The World of Eli Whitney* (New York, 1952); Constance McL. Green, *Eli Whitney and the Birth of American Technology* (Boston, 1956). Whitney's idea was seemingly original with him, but several Europeans had been laboring after the same objective in the manufacture of arms. While minister to France in the 1780's Jefferson reported the presence of such activity. Boyd, ed., *Papers of Jefferson*, VIII, 455.

56. *American Journal of Science and Arts*, II (1820), 94–101; American Philosophical Society, *Transactions*, IV (1799), 303–312.

57. Hindle, *Pursuit of Science in Revolutionary America*, 234, 236–240, and notes for the most important published pamphlets; Commager and Morris, eds., *Spirit of 'Seventy-Six*, II, 835–843.

58. The friction plaguing the medical service is judiciously chronicled in Whitfield J. Bell, Jr., "The Court-Martial of Dr. William Shippen, Jr., 1780," *Journal of the History of Medicine and Allied Sciences*, XIX (1964), 218–238; and in the same author's *John Morgan:Continental Doctor* (Philadelphia, 1965). For a little-researched topic, see George B. Griffenhagen, *Drug Supplies in the American Revolution*, United States Natural Museum Bulletin no. 225 (Washington, D.C., 1961). Documents bearing on the above paragraphs are in Commager and Morris, eds., *Spirit of 'Seventy-Six*, II, 815–835. Medicine is analyzed in terms of its American setting in Richard H. Shryock, *Medicine and Society in America, 1660–1860* (New York, 1960).

59. A provocative essay demonstrating that some aspects of Revolutionary economic history have scarcely been scratched by scholarly research is Clarence L. Ver Steeg, "The American Revolution Considered as an Economic Movement," *Huntington Library Quarterly*, XX (1957), 361–372. J. Franklin Jameson, *The American Revolution Considered as a Social Movement* (Princeton, 1926), is a classic, but it has been demonstrated that Jameson exaggerated the degree of some social and economic changes, probably because he failed to recognize certain dynamic forces already at work in the late colonial era. See Frederick B. Tolles, "The American Revolution Considered as a Social Movement: A Re-Evaluation," *American Historical Review*, LX (1954), 1–12. Jameson's impact may be seen in Evarts B. Greene, *The Revolutionary Generation, 1763–1790* (New York, 1943), chap xi, entitled "The War's Economic Effects."

# 13. War on the Frontiers:
# The West and the High Seas

THE AMERICAN REVOLUTION gave birth to a minor war as we are inclined to think of wars in the twentieth century. And certainly it was small in terms of the sizes of the opposing armies and the populations of Great Britain and the thirteen states. Yet the conflict extended over a far-flung theater of operations. Even in 1779, with direct French and Spanish involvement scarcely felt by the struggling revolutionists, Hugh Henry Brackenridge, one of the prominent orators and penmen of the day, could exclaim that the war "has been fought from Canada to Georgia, and from Georgia to Canada; from the ocean to the mountain, and from the mountain to the ocean."[1] It is easy to lose perspective in describing American fighting on the fringes, easy to magnify the significance of the dramatic achievements of a few colorful personalities, of a George Rogers Clark on the Western frontier, of a John Paul Jones on the seaboard frontier. Still, their stories and those of "frontiersmen" like them deserve to be retold, and they are not without importance.

### The West

We saw in an opening chapter that events associated with the Western frontier had helped to produce the Revolution, but not to the extent that historians claimed a generation or more ago. Nor can it be demonstrated that the campaigns in the interior wrought momentous strategical benefits to either warring camp. In that vast arena we may term the Revolutionary West, white men, soldiers and civilians, were clustered mainly on the periphery. The British military retrenchment in the

West, beginning in 1768, left only a handful of garrisons girding a huge expanse in the name of George III when hostilities erupted. Redcoats retained Forts Niagara, Detroit, and Michilimackinac on the northern rim, Kaskaskia in the Illinois country, and Mobile and Pensacola in the lower Mississippi-Gulf region. Spain, owner of the sprawling Louisiana colony since 1763, also had posts on its side of the perimeter, stretching from New Orleans upriver to the distant St. Louis station.

From the Mississippi to the lofty barriers of the Appalachian Mountains, British-Americans were few and far between, except for traders and trappers and for such French-speaking enclaves as Kaskaskia and Cahokia on the middle Mississippi and Vincennes on the Wabash. But along the crest of the towering ranges, the situation was shifting even before the day of Lexington and Concord. The failure of British Western policy and the colonists' insatiable lust for land gave rise to settlements in Kentucky and on the Holston and Watauga rivers in Tennessee. Many a newcomer came via the Cumberland Gap, while to the north, Wheeling (West Virginia) and Pittsburgh overflowed with farmers and frontiersmen intent upon possessing lands beyond the Kanawha River. Generally, northwest of the Ohio the human tide advanced more slowly although estimates have it that the white inhabitants of western Pennsylvania (beyond McConnelsburg) multiplied threefold between 1760 and 1770, fivefold by 1780.[2]

The Indians, as in the colonial wars, were in a position to influence the balance of power in the hinterland. The Iroquois, or Six Nations (Mohawk, Oneida, Cayuga, Onondaga, Seneca, and Tuscarora), lived in central New York and northern Pennsylvania. About the Great Lakes lay the Wyandot, Ottawa, Miami, and Wabash tribes, all influenced by the British post at Detroit. Closer to Fort Pitt and the Ohio River were the Shawnee and the Delaware. Along the Southern frontier dwelled the Cherokee and the Creek Indians and, deeper in the interior, the Chickasaw and Choctaw. Though both sides eagerly solicited the Indians' good will, the advantage clearly rested with the British, who, besides having an Indian Department with officials well versed in the redmen's affairs, were better able to supply the tribes with favors and necessities; and they stood to profit from the Indians' ancient resentment of colonial encroachments, recently heightened by white expansion in the early 1770's. At the outset, however, most British and American leaders displayed scant enthusiasm for calling the Indians to take up the hatchet, each antagonist concentrating on gaining from the natives a sympathetic neutrality for its own side. Conscious of being at a decided disadvantage, the Continental Congress accorded a high priority to the problem by creating an Indian Department divided into three districts, with commissioners and agents of each district responsible to Congress' committee for Indian affairs. To Iroquois representatives, Congressional agents termed the war a "family quarrel between us and Old England," which prompted the sachem, Little Abraham, to express the mood of the assembled tribesmen: to "sit still and see you fight it out."[3]

The Indians, of course, did not "sit still," and historical opinion remains divided as to whether Britons or Americans must bear the onus for initially inciting the redmen. Some tribes were ready to ravage outlying American settlements, with or without British encouragement. Against the advice of British Southern Indian Superintendent John Stuart, the Cherokee struck along the frontiers of Virginia and the Carolinas. In a rare example of cooperation, the three states collected several thousand militia, launching a crushing, three-pronged retaliatory offensive that ended with the Cherokee signing treaties ceding large tracts of land to their adversaries.[4] Guy Carleton, governor of Canada, was reluctant to encourage Indian forays against the frontier villages, favoring instead occasional service from pro-British tribesmen as guides and scouts directed by royal officers. Lord Dartmouth and Governor Dunmore of Virginia advocated a no-holds-barred policy toward stirring up the redmen. Even before Lexington, however, Massachusetts took the first step by enlisting men from the Stockbridge tribe in the colony minute companies; they later took part in the seige of Boston. Both Montgomery and Arnold resorted to Indian guides and auxiliaries during the Canadian campaign. Had the patriots held the St. Lawrence line, the savages would most probably have been less receptive to British blandishments, dependent as they would likely have become on Americans for sustenance.

Fearing the possible loss of Canada, Gage urged Guy Carleton to amass every available savage to retake Ticonderoga, secure the surrounding river-and-lake country, and descend upon the New England frontier. The patriots' alliance with the Stockbridge Indians provided Gage with his justification for rallying the Iroquois to the northward, but even the General recognized that the semi-civilized Stockbridge enlisted in regular military units were hardly the equivalent of the warlike Iroquois. Soon afterward, in ordering John Stuart to galvanize Indian power in the Southern back country, Gage repeated his weak analogy to the whig-led Stockbridge. Even so, given the Indians' proximity to the hostilities, their grievances and their militant disposition, their involvement was perhaps inevitable, just as there was never serious doubt as to which of the contending parties would have the upper hand in soliciting the abrigines.[5]

Allowing for infrequent variations, the war in the West pursued a general pattern. With Washington's army invariably tied down in the

East, frontier defense fell to the states; but more often than not the settlers were actually responsible for their own protection. Their customary procedure was to erect stockades and maintain the defensive. Thus the Indians usually struck first, relying heavily upon surprise, their basic offensive stratagem, since they were seldom proficient in executing movements of a complicated nature, even when guided by white officers. Rarely did the Indians try to storm a fortification; they scored their greatest gains when the defenders foolishly came forth to attack or pursue the invaders and were pounced upon from ambush. In time many frontiersmen concluded that the best defense was a good offensive: destroying the Indians' villages and fields upon which their way of life depended, the one tactic most likely to compel the tribesmen to stand and fight in the white man's fashion. Neither the Indians nor the frontiersmen were much disposed to give quarter and little was expected. Despite the warnings, half hearted or genuine, of their leaders, both sides took the lives of noncombatants. No more grisly episode can be found than the massacre of ninety defenseless, Christianized Delawares at Gnadenhütten by Colonel David Williamson's Pennsylvania militia in March, 1782; herded into two cabins, the victims, mostly women and children, were systematically scalped and hacked to death. At Sandusky, the Delaware retaliated for Gnadenhütten— Colonel William Crawford, a frontier veteran and friend of Washington, was methodically roasted at the stake, the details too grotesque to bear repeating.[6]

By 1778–1779, all along the flaming frontier, moves were afoot to roll the Anglo-Indian tide back. While Kentucky pioneers huddled together at such stations as Harrodsburg and Boonesborough following the bloody year of the "Three 7's," a twenty-five-year-old surveyor, George Rogers Clark, obtained authorization from Kentucky's parent state of Virginia to raise a force to overwhelm the anchor points of British influence north of the Ohio. Clark perceived his immediate objectives to be the taking of Kaskaskia and Cahokia in the Illinois country and, to the east, Vincennes on the Wabash—all French communities whose inhabitants might be receptive to American entreaties. Eventually he hoped to seize Detroit, where British Lieutenant Governor Henry Hamilton had dispatched raiding parties of British-led warriers to destroy the American back settlements. Whether Hamilton specifically paid the savages for white scalps, or whether he merely rewarded his allies for fruitful missions has been a matter of historical controversy. If the Lieutenant Governor's claim of actually discouraging cruelties and warfare against women and children is accurate, as historian John D. Barnhart believes, the same scholar accuses the British administrator of a certain callousness to Indian warfare in his eagerness to please his royal master, of an awareness that "twice as many scalps as prisoners were being brought to Detroit."[7]

The sinewy Clark, a six-foot redhead and a dynamic leader with a flair for the dramatic, may not have achieved all that his overly enthusiastic admirers have claimed for him, but the genuine accomplishments of his small band were more than sufficient to catch the fancy of his countrymen. With approximately 175 men recruited in western Pennsylvania and the Kentucky and Tennessee settlements, Clark floated down the Ohio and, before its juncture with the Mississippi, set off across 120 miles of river-bottom forest land in southern Illinois. Early in July, 1778, the hamlets of Kaskaskia and Cahokia fell to Clark without bloodshed. The Kentuckian acted to win over the French and impress the Indians as well. Good treatment and word of the Franco-American alliance brought most of the villagers to an enthusiastic acceptance of "the —Bostonnais," their generic term for the American rebels. After sending an influential priest, Father Pierre Gibault, to persuade the residents of Vincennes to accept American jurisdiction, Clark detached a corporal's guard to garrison the fort there. Soon the entire region became known as the county of Illinois in the state of Virginia. As for the Indians, Clark performed no miracles, no permanent weaning of most of the tribes from British influence; but he won the respect of many and strengthened his own precarious position for the moment. Skilled in the high-flown, metaphorical vein of Indian oratory, Clark (Long Knife) gave assembled chiefs and other leaders (Brothers) assurances of American power, not neglecting to spin a highly original interpretation of George III (the British Great Father), who soon would tax all the Indians (Children), just as he had demanded unjust tributes from the colonists.

Clark's venture in diplomacy proved short-lived, for Lieutenant Governor Henry Hamilton, with a detachment of 130 French militia, 70 Indians, and 35 regulars, swept down from Detroit to restore royal authority throughout the Illinois country. The advantage did not belong to Clark, who had acquiesced to the demands of some of his frontiersmen to return to Kentucky; it belonged to Hamilton, who easily wrested Vincennes from Clark's detachment, and who persuaded the quixotic townspeople to renew their fidelity to the English king. The most significant feature of the Clark-Hamilton duel was the Briton's decision to postpone until spring his planned attack against George Rogers Clark at Kaskaskia. True enough, the flooded rivers across Illinois and the inadequacy of food stores made Hamilton's delay understandable, but only if he could rely on holding his mixed complement together during a raw winter far from their own villages and settlements. It should have come as no surprise to the Lieutenant Governor, after three years at Detroit, to find that most of his Indians and many of the French militiamen soon insisted on taking their leaves, and that he had no real alternative to bowing to their intentions. To make matters worse, Hamilton's haughty demeanor thoroughly antagonized the Vincennese, at the same time the Lieutenant Governor found himself unable to entice the tribesmen of the lower Wasbash to do his bidding.

Clark, in contrast, was not one to let adversity bar the door when spring might bring reinforcements for Hamilton. Believing, as he told Patrick Henry, that "Great things have been affected by a few Men well Conducted,"[8] he struck off in the first week of February on the 180-mile trek to Vincennes. His 172 men ("My Boys"), half of them French volunteers, sloshed through torrential rains, traversed four swollen rivers, camped without tents, and once went two days without food. Arriving at Vincennes on April 23, Clark warned the inhabitants to stay indoors; then under cover of darkness the Americans opened fire on the fort, dispersing themselves in such a manner as to exaggerate their true numbers. Though at first Hamilton refused to capitulate, his situation was ominous, doubly so after his remaining Frenchmen bluntly informed him of their unwillingness to fight alongside his thirty-odd redcoats. When Hamilton attempted to stall, Clark showed "The Famous Hair Buyer General" that he was of no mind to tarry: having captured a small party of British Indians with white scalps swinging from their belts, he ordered that four be tomahawked in sight of the garrison and their bodies thrown in the Wabash. Clark and his hearty frontiersmen might wreak vengeance on Hamilton's redskin followers, but not on the Lieutenant Governor himself, who pulled down his colors on February 5, 1779. Whatever the truth about the so-called "Hair Buyer," Hamilton was one of the most hated Britons in the War of Independence, a man that Virginia's normally humane Governor Thomas Jefferson permitted to languish in irons in a cold, damp cell for months in Williamsburg.[9]

Clark's conquest of the Illinois country stood as a dramatic feat accomplished under tremendous physical and material handicaps by a bold and resourceful leader. In a war where clear-cut American victories were scarce, the besting of Hamilton provided a boost to patriot morale. Technically, it had been a state project, organized and financed by Virginia, which considered Clark's recruits a part of the state militia. Clark owed almost as much to the merchant and patriot agent, Oliver Pollock, in New Orleans. Usually bereft of official funds, the merchant advanced his own credit and other resources; all told, Clark drew upon Pollock for $25,000 in cash and supplies, far more than he could squeeze from Virginia authorities, who, incidentally, were unconsciously slow in reimbursing the hard-pressed New Orleans merchant.[10]

If British power tottered in the far interior in 1779, it did not come tumbling down. For the Indians remained dependent on the white man, and Britain could do what the Continental Congress could not: recognize the tribal land claims and provide a relatively efficient trading system. Moreover, Clark failed to receive the reinforcements from Virginia that would have enabled him to pursue his ambitions against Detriot, although as late as 1781 he nursed plans for assaulting the enemy stronghold. Therefore, it seems dubious to accept the time-worn adage that Clark's exploits "won the Northwest," insuring that trans-Appalachia would be America's in the peace of 1783.[11] In fact, Clark was on the defensive along the Ohio during the last two years of the war as the Indians resumed their devastation of the frontier. In 1782 at Bryan's Station in Kentucky, dusky warriors and Detroit militia, unable to wear down the occupants of the local fort, slowly retired, followed in pell-mell fashion by Colonel John Todd's hastily assembled Kentucky volunteers. Daniel Boone's warning went unheeded as Todd stumbled into an ambush at the Blue Licks, losing seventy killed and seven captured.[12] Once again the frontiersmen turned to Clark, whose counter-offensive encouraged the marauding Shawnee to retire into central Ohio. Far to the west the hero of the Revolution and the very real savior of Kentucky was the flaming redhead, George Rogers Clark, who ultimately met a pathetic end in alcohol, indebtedness, and mental disintegration.

On the upper Ohio, as in Kentucky, Americans were hard pressed by 1778. Virginia's string of forts below Fort Pitt served as no real deterrent to Shawnee raiding parties. The situation was even worse along the Pennsylvania-New York frontier. As Kentucky suffered because of Detroit, so the Northern frontiersmen suffered because of Fort Niagara: from there Iroquois warriors led by Mohawk chieftain Joseph Brant and supplied by the Johnsons, John and Guy, son and nephew respectively of Indian Superintendent Sir William Johnson, wrought havoc and destruction. Their accomplices were loyalist rangers commanded by still another family team, Major John Butler and his son Captain Walter Butler, both of whom had joined the St. Leger expedition of 1777. Re-grouping and adding followers in the year after Burgoyne's debacle, John Butler advanced southward into the Wyoming valley of Pennsylvania, a fertile region left virtually without protection by the departure of men for duty in the Continental army. Many of the valley's inhabitants were crowded into a large palisade, Forty Fort, near present-day Wilkes-Barre, when Bulter's over 1,000 redskins and tories reached the vicinity late in June, 1778. Inside the works Colonel Zebulon Butler made a classic error of frontier warfare. Sallying out to meet the invaders, the American officer discovered himself enveloped by a

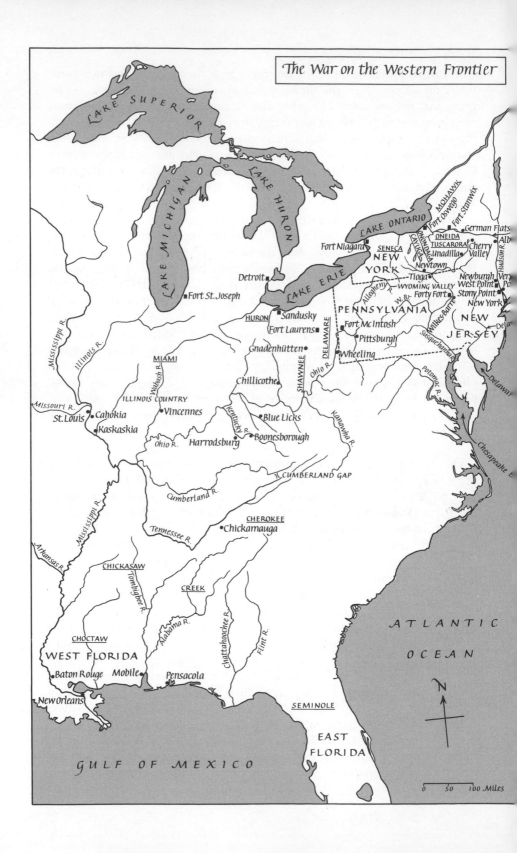

The War on the Western Frontier

LAKE SUPERIOR

LAKE MICHIGAN

LAKE HURON

LAKE ONTARIO

Fort Niagara

LAKE ERIE

Detroit

Fort St. Joseph

MOHAWK
Fort Oswego
Fort Stanwix
German Flats
ONEIDA
ONONDAGA
CAYUGA
SENECA
NEW
YORK
TUSCARORA
Unadilla
Cherry
Valley
Alb
Newtown
Tioga
Newburgh
WYOMING VALLEY
West Point
Forty Fort
Stony Point
Wilkes-Barre
New York
NEW
JERSEY

Allegheny R.
W. Br.
Susquehanna R.
Potomac R.
Delawar
Chesapeake B

HURON
Sandusky
Fort Laurens
DELAWARE
Fort McIntosh
Pittsburgh
Wheeling

Gnadenhütten

PENNSYLVANIA

MIAMI
Chillicothe
SHAWNEE
Ohio R.

Wabash R.

ILLINOIS COUNTRY
Vincennes
Kentucky R.
Blue Licks

Missouri R.
Cahokia
St. Louis
Kaskaskia

Ohio R.
Harrodsburg
Boonesborough
Kanawha R.

Mississippi R.
Illinois R.

CUMBERLAND GAP

Cumberland R.

Tennessee R.
CHEROKEE
Chickamauga

Arkansas R.

CHICKASAW
Tombigbee R.

CREEK

ATLANTIC
OCEAN

CHOCTAW
Alabama R.
Chattahoochee R.
Flint R.

WEST FLORIDA
Baton Rouge
Mobile
Pensacola

New Orleans

SEMINOLE

EAST
FLORIDA

GULF OF MEXICO

N

0    50    100 Miles

superior force. The result was the "Wyoming Massacre." The destruction of most of Zeb Butler's militia—no quarter was given—and the
subsequent burning and pillaging of hundreds of fields and farmhouses
turned the beautiful valley into a wasteland. That fall the tory-Indian
avalanche struck again at German Flats and Cherry Valley in New
York.

There is good evidence that the Butlers and Brant discouraged
butchery and the assaulting of women and children, and that they were
genuinely distressed by the behavior of their redskinned charges.
Brant, a remarkably well-educated Indian for his day (who had already taken a whirl in London society), was a devout Anglican and
had aided in translating the Bible into the Mohawk language. Noncombatants fared well, it seems, at Wyoming, and there were few
deaths of any kind at German Flats, where Brant had warned the
settlers ahead of time to evacuate their community. At Cherry Valley,
however, the savages got completely out of hand. Fearing for the safety
of the women and children who had thus far escaped being hacked to
death, John Butler escorted most of them into patriot hands. For all
the excesses directly or indirectly attributable to the Butlers and the
Mohawk chieftain, there is this to be said for them: they too were fighting for their homelands. Most of the loyalists and Iroquois were themselves from western New York; they had sometimes been dispossessed of
their property, and they had in still other ways felt the heavy hand of
the patriots.[13]

Even before war whoops resounded through the upper borderlands,
the Continental Congress slowly retreated from its notion of leaving the
defense of the fringes completely to the states. Aggressive warfare, not
the defensive, would drive back the enemy hordes. A first step was
Brigadier General Edward Hand's appointment to command the new
Western Department at Pittsburgh in 1777. Hand's militia were ill-
equipped and unmanageable, and the frontiersmen generally were so
hostile to all Indians that it was impossible to gain the cooperation of
normally friendly tribesmen. Hand's tenure at Pittsburgh was marred
by the infamous "squaw campaign." Designed to capture military stores
for British Indians deposited near the Cuyahoga River, it terminated
not in confiscating supplies or defeating warriors, only in the murder
of four Indian women and a boy by Hand's "brave[,] active lads."[14]

Hand's successor, General Lachlan McIntosh, could agree with
American Colonel John Campbell's observation that the "West[ern]
country is under a bad character for quarreling with the generals sent
to command them." Partly for that reason McIntosh attempted a different policy. Rather than relying upon a string of inadequate militia posts
along the Ohio, which were all too often attacked without adequate

warning, McIntosh believed that several forts erected in the Indian heartland, if adequately garrisoned and backed by Continental resources, might provide the most advantageous means of holding the tribesmen at bay. A series of forward stations would also serve as links in a chain stretching toward Detroit. American parties built Forts McIntosh and Laurens in the Ohio country in the fall of 1778, and two Continental regiments joined the Western Department. Yet McIntosh's grand scheme of additional forts and a blow at Detroit died abruptly. Indian depredations to the eastward at Wyoming, Cherry Valley, and other points required the diversion of Continental manpower and placed a restraint on Congressionally sponsored military operations in the Northwest.[15]

Washington, considering a push against Niagara beyond his thin resources, decided instead to detach an expedition under John Sullivan into the Iroquois region of western New York. The campaign that ensued, though unpretentious in its aims and accomplishments, was one of the best planned and best executed operations of the Revolution. The commander in chief collected maps and assembled intelligence on the terrain and the means of gathering and transporting Sullivan's necessities. Washington, an old Indian fighter, instructed Sullivan to conduct a scorched-earth campaign. Only by devastating the Indian villages and fields would the redmen's effectiveness be impaired; and only by such a threat to their livlihood would the Indians expose themselves to the prospect of defeat or annihilation. The Virginian who had witnessed Braddock's disaster nearly a quarter of a century before cautioned against close-rank formations, advised in favor of a "loose and dispersed" arrangement. Nothing, he added, would "disconcert and terrify" the savages more than "the warhoop and fixed bayonet."[16]

Setting out in May, 1779, Sullivan's three brigades of regulars, supported by light infantry and riflemen, cut a road northwestward from Eaton, Pennsylvania, to the Wyoming valley, proceeded thence to Tioga (Athens, Pennsylvania), where a smaller wing of the army under New York Brigadier General James Clinton united with the main body. Sullivan's army took all the requisite precautions for traversing enemy territory as his rifle companies and other light units ranged far and wide on all sides of the slow moving column. Before crossing the Susquehanna River, Sullivan directed his cannon to rake the edge of the forest on the far shore, then threw his light troops over the stream with orders to fan out and form a line to protect the brigades during their passage.

On August 27, at Newtown, the Butlers and Brant were overruled by Delaware and Seneca warriors who, tired of futile delaying measures, insisted on making a stand. Sullivan had 4,400 available men as against

600 to 800 tories and Indians. For the Butler-Brant forces the only hope was surprise, and even then it is hard to visualize more than a temporary American setback. But the enemy's preparation for an ambush—a camouflaged breastwork on rising ground near Sullivan's line of march —was detected by an American advance rifle corps. Sullivan, on the afternoon of August 30, opened the Battle of Newtown with an artillery barrage, followed by an advance of the infantry and light troops in the center, while Enoch Poor's brigade swung around to a flanking position on the right. The defenders broke and scattered after offering token resistance; casualties on each side were a bare handful. So ended the only real encounter of the campaign, with the Butlers and Brant falling back to Niagara as Sullivan's army devastated the beautiful and bountiful land of the Seneca, Cayuga, and Onondaga, leveling 40 villages, cutting down orchards, and burning or otherwise destroying the equivalent of 160,000 bushels of corn.[17]

Although Sullivan's expedition provided Americans with an example of how to conduct Indian warfare, it was no more decisive in its outcome than Clark's dazzling stroke along the Wabash. And once again flames lit up the New York-Pennsylvania frontier, as well as the Kentucky settlements. Repeatedly in 1780 the Iroquois tribes hit the Mohawk and Schoharie districts of New York; between February and September 59 war parties killed 142, captured 160 (including 81 women and children who were released), destroyed 4 forts and 157 houses, and captured 247 horses and 422 cattle.[18] Even after Yorktown in 1781, the frontier war swayed brutally back and forth, not only in New York where the militia under General Robert Van Rensselaer and Colonel Marinus Willett had their hands full repelling the dusky invaders, but also on the upper Ohio, where a succession of commanders—Daniel Brodhead and William Irvine followed Hand and McIntosh—were never able to bring the Wyandot, Shawnee, and Delaware tribes to heel.[19]

Neither Britain nor America gained outright ascendancy in the West. Both faced too many problems and burdens to seize the upper hand and maintain it. Congress, in undertaking to pacify or neutralize tribe after tribe, found itself frustrated by some of the factors that had hamstrung British Western policy in the 1760's. Congress received reports of settlers preempting Indian lands and mistreating the natives in trade. Continental agents could not even protect friendly and pro-American Indians from Americans! Senecas beckoned to Pittsburgh for a conference in 1775 had hardly arrived before several in their party were shot down by whites enraged by recent murders on the frontier. A procession of Delawares invited to treat with Congress in Philadelphia needed a heavy guard along the way, and even after their arrival, there were rumors of a plot to slay them in the City of Brotherly Love. Several Shawnee, including Chief Cornstalk who had striven to keep his tribe from succumbing to British favors, were seized as hostages during a visit to Fort Randolph (Point Pleasant, West Virginia) and subsequently killed by local militiamen. "From this event," predicted General Hand, "we have little reason to expect a reconciliation with the Shawanese . . . for if we had any friends among them, those unfortunate wretches were so."[20]

The Delaware had leaned strongly toward the Americans, and Congress made numerous gestures in their behalf. But the Delaware, like most of the red nations, desperately needed goods and supplies, and Congress was never able to provide them, though it had several times promised to make permanent trade arrangements. Former trader George Morgan, a genuine friend of the Indians and Congress' ablest wilderness diplomat, found that around Pittsburgh many whites actually welcomed and encouraged Indian warfare as a means of conquering choice lands. Mistreatment by frontiersmen and unkept promises by Congress combined to drive the Delaware into British arms in 1779, just as similar promises by George Rogers Clark about American trade could not be kept with the Illinois tribes. All things considered, it is not startling that the feats of Clark and Sullivan failed to bear lasting fruit.[21]

If virtually all the participating Indians fought on the British side, does that fact necessarily prove an overwhelming advantage for His Majesty in the West? Not at all, since Britain too did not realize its Western objectives. With only a sprinkling of redcoats available for forays from Detroit and Niagara, Britain depended on allies of questionable reliability: French inhabitants, small clusters of tories, and the Indians. Henry Hamilton's surrender at Vincennes exposed the wavering loyalties of the French and the fickleness of the tribesmen. When under capable leaders like the Butlers and Brant, the loyalists and Indians were a distinct military advantage to Britain, even though personal jealousies among these three leaders impaired their effectivness. But the Indians, for all the fear they spread through the borderlands, may have been in the long run a psychological disadvantage to Britain. Sometimes failing to make a subtle distinction between patriots and loyalists, the hatchet-men inflamed opinion, drawing many less than whiggish Americans into the patriot camp. In England, Burke and Pitt made the practices of Britain's redskinned allies a subject of embarrassment to the ministry. In France, Benjamin Franklin shocked the French court with one of his most famous hoaxes: a New England newspaper account of a captured British "document" describing "eight Packs of

Scalps, cured, dried, hooped, and painted," each packet neatly labeled with the quantity and nature of its contents—62 farmers "surprised in the Night"; 88 women, "hair long . . . to shew they were Mothers"; "29 little Infants' Scalps of Various Sizes," and on and on.[22]

Monetarily, too, Britain paid a steep price for Indian involvement. The winter of 1777–1778 at Niagara presaged the winters to follow. The 2,300 Indians gathered there for protection and sustenance consumed such staggering quantities of supplies that the post commander expressed the conviction that the Indians were a far greater burden than benefit. The situation paralleled that at Detroit, where the population, normally fewer than 2,500 people, had jumped to "about 5,000 Souls," complained Henry Hamilton in 1778.[23]

Important as was the West in the Revolution, developments there, comparatively speaking, constituted a side show, since neither opponent possessed the means to make it otherwise. Had Britain been able to unify and consolidate the warriors from Illinois to New York, they would undoubtedly have wiped out the frontier settlements and possibly placed Washington's army in a squeeze. On the other hand, had American armies based in the West overrun Niagara and Detroit, thus posing a serious threat to Canada, Howe, Clinton, and company might have retrenched their operations in the middle states and the Southern campaign of 1778–1781 might never have left the planning table. Only in story and legend did the West hold the center of the stage, as it has in other periods of our history.

## The High Seas

Most Revolutionary Americans deemed the seaboard frontier even more vital to their well-being and safety than the Western frontier. Relatively few people lived beyond the reach of the sea. Foreign commerce, intercolonial trade, whaling, and the fisheries depended upon the Atlantic and the rivers and harbors that it touched. War exposed these enterprises to disruption and destruction, as it did the principal cities, which were seaports. The very configuration of the seaboard posed a threat, for an enemy astride Chesapeake Bay, Delaware Bay, or the Hudson might choke off American north-south communication and transportation both by water and land. "In point of safety," inquired the author of *Common Sense*, "ought we to be without a fleet?" "No country on the globe is so happily situated, or so internally capable of raising a fleet as America," Paine boasted. "Tar, timber, iron, and cordage are her natural produce." Moreover, there would be no doctrinaire fear of standing navies; whig philosophers had habitually pictured sea forces as posing none of the threats to civil liberties that were inherent in permanent army establishments.[24]

But financial inadequacies and other limitations dictated a moderate Continental naval program that would be supplemented by state navies and by individual initiative in the form of privateering. The American navy was destined to be no instrument of national expansion as it became in the 1890's and later. No American entertained the notion of the patriot navy seriously coping with the mighty royal navy. American aspirations were to engage in coastal and harbor defense and to plunder the commerce of Britain.[25] Warring nations, of course, sought to protect their commerce from just the sort of strategy that America's fledgling naval leaders had in mind. Europeans believed that a fleet's most crucial function was not to seek out and destroy the men-of-war of the enemy but to defend the colonies and seaborne trade of one's state and to annoy or capture those of its adversary. Hence, the preoccupation of both British and French admirals with the West Indies (and the indecisive engagements there) during the War of Independence.

Advocates of John Paul Jones, Esek Hopkins, George Washington, and John Adams have debated endlessly the question of who was the father of the United States navy. The honor belongs to no single individual. The first initiative for naval warfare came at the colony level. A few days after Lexington and Concord, citizens of Martha's Vineyard, Massachusetts, recaptured two sloops taken earlier by H. M. S. *Falcon*. Shortly thereafter patriots at Falmouth, Maine, tried unsuccessfully to seize at anchor a British war vessel, which retaliated by burning the greater part of the town. On August 26, 1775, Rhode Island's revolutionary legislature resolved that the Continental Congress superintend the construction of an "American fleet." This step transpired even before Washington had chartered and armed several fishing schooners and small merchantmen to harass the enemy's supply line.[26]

Despite the apparent necessity for naval prowess to many in and out of Congress, there was, as John Adams phrased it, "very loud and vehement" opposition. To attempt to launch a fleet to oppose Britain's sea power was described as comparable to an infant taking a mad bull by the horns. Though no one seems to have feared a navy itself as a direct threat to the freedom of America, it was stressed that colonial sailors would become debauched by a lust for booty and plunder. Samuel Chase of Maryland thought the cost of a navy prohibitive; it would "mortgage the whole Continent." Materials on the debates are thin, but it appears that some delegates from the Southern and middle colonies visualized the outfitting of armed vessels as principally a scheme to protect the maritime interests of the Northeastern states. At

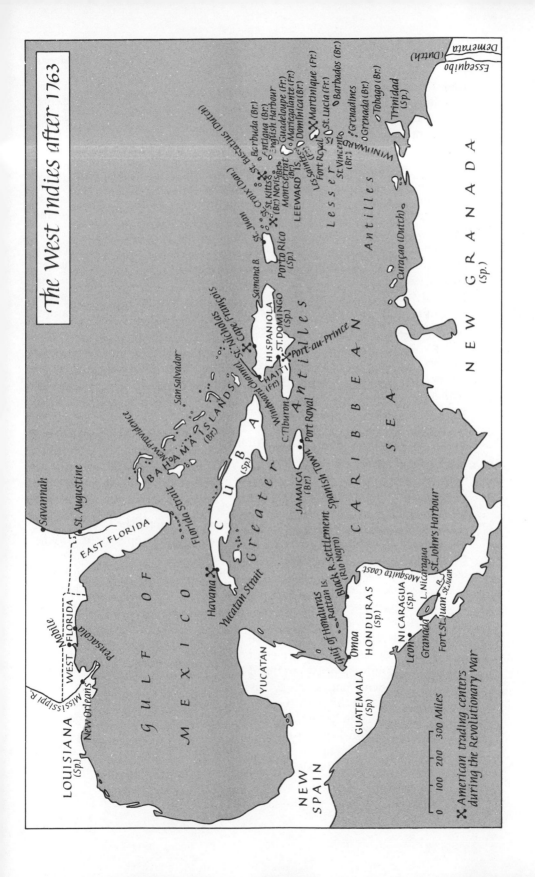

The West Indies after 1763

least a few Southerners were staunch navy men, notably Joseph Hewes, the North Carolina merchant, and Virginia's George Wythe, who, citing Roman history, expostulated that a nation with vast maritime interests could not afford to be without a naval arm.[27]

The modern American navy traces its official birth to Ocotober 30, 1775, when Congress appointed a seven-man navy committee and authorized the acquisition and maintenance of armed vessels "for the protection and defence of the United Colonies." During the next month Congress created the marine corps and drew up "Rules for the Regulation of the Navy," principally framed by John Adams.[28]

From January, 1776, to December, 1779, the marine committee, successor to the naval committee, managed maritime affairs. The marine committee, said Adams, had "the Care of every Thing relating to the Navy. . . ." Its orders and instructions convey something of the committee's spirit and outlook. American ships "should never be Idle," warned the members. "Expedition and vigilance are excellent qualities in a Sea Officer," they advised one captain. And no officer had the right to violate his instructions from the marine committee. We have seen in an earlier chapter how Congressional diplomats prefaced their endeavors with the thought that the New World trade was essential to Britain's survival in war or peace. That point of view found expression in the marine committee's preponderant concern for the capture and destruction of enemy commerce. Ambitious plans called for attacking sugar vessels in the West Indies, Newfoundland fishing craft, the Hudson Bay fleet of furs and peltries, the Guineamen and the East Indiamen, along with disrupting the Baltic trade and destroying the Atlantic whaling fleet.[29]

To assist the marine committee, Congress established two navy boards (one at Boston, the other at Philadelphia) composed of prominent local and regional leaders not serving in Congress. As a "board of assistants to the Marine Committee," each was to handle the business of the part of the Continental fleet "Built, bought, or fitted" within the area of its jurisdiction. Responsible for holding courts of inquiry and courts-martial, the navy boards also allocated sums of money for shipbuilding and repairs and salaries for officers and their crews. Since the boards were distant from most coastal towns and cities, a ship's captain in need of provisions or disposing of prize vessels sought out the Continental naval agent, one or more having been appointed for every state. Even with the help of naval boards and naval agents, the marine committee staggered under an excessive amount of work. Its members served on additional Congressional committees, and its composition was continually changing as states altered the make-up of their delegations at Philadelphia. The close of 1779 brought a new turn in naval administration: the lawmakers replaced the marine committee with the so-called Board of Admiralty, consisting of three commissioners not in Congress and two more who were members of that body. Until naval administration receives close scholarly scrutiny, any conclusive evaluation of its machinery is a hazardous undertaking. It seems, however, that complaints concerning the Commissary and Quartermaster Departments, as well as other areas of administration, were generally echoed concerning the navy. It was said, for instance, that Continental naval agents employed their offices for nonpublic ends. Moreover, the movement for single-headed executive departments extended to the navy; a Department of Marine, theoretically created in 1781, never really functioned, although Robert Morris, the financier, exercised the duties that would have fallen to a secretary of marine.[30]

Factors of geography and family influenced the selection and ranking of officers of the Continental navy, just as those considerations bore a relationship to the appointment of Washington and the generals of the army. Command of the infant fleet went to Esek Hopkins of Rhode Island, a veteran merchant captain and skipper of privateers in the last French war, and a brother of Stephen Hopkins, chairman of Congress' original naval committee; Esek's son John received the brig *Cabot*. *Alfred*, another vessel commissioned at the outset, did not go to her former master in commercial service, the able John Barry; instead it became the plum of prominent but incompetent Dudley Saltonstall of Connecticut, brother-in-law of naval committeeman Silas Deane. John Paul Jones early suffered at the hands of what S. E. Morison aptly terms *localitis*. According to Congress' seniority list of October 10, 1776, Jones was ranked below seventeen officers, most of whom were appointed to command new frigates under construction: and virtually every captain was a native of the city or state where his vessel was being built. It was not merely sectional or other prejudice on the part of the delegates that prompted Congress to exclude the recent Scottish immigrant John Paul Jones, concludes Morison. With seamen for each frigate to be recruited from the place it was fitted out, "men would enlist only under a master mariner or other local character whom they knew."[31] In that respect they differed little from the militia or even from some of the Continentals.

Information about common seamen in the Revolutionary era is scanty; or, in any event, historians over the years have told us little about them. The leading specialist on the maritime history of Massachusetts asserts that the Bay commonwealth never had a "native deep-sea proletariat": its merchant fleets were manned by adventuresome youths, chiefly farm lads, who made a few voyages to satisfy their wanderlust before returning to the soil. Possibly such a clear composite image is an oversimplification not only for Massachusetts but also for the other colonies. For there were, as best estimates have it, an average of 33,000 mariners employed annually in the colonies by the last quarter of the eighteenth century.[32] To have had such a manpower supply consistently available suggests, to say the least, that many made their livelihood more or less continuously from the sea.

In fact, a present-day historian has lately argued that the seamen were a rather distinct element or class, that there were fewer loyalists in the Revolution among the seafarers than among other laboring groups, and that it was the harsh British practice of impressment that gave colonial seamen a particular disdain for the mother country. The same scholar contends that impressment riots in the decades preceding the Revolution represented a kind of political reaction to indignities and injustices felt by the inarticulate mariners.[33] Even among British authorities there was confusion and uncertainty, stemming from different interpretations of a statute in Queen Anne's reign, as to the legality of impressing seamen in American waters. After 1765 the matter was usually left to the determination of squadron commanders and individual captains. But the practice did continue, although not always noticeably since seizures occurred off the coasts rather than in the combustible seaport cities, where riots were a predictable response to the appearance of an impressment gang.[34]

The most publicized episode of the next decade was the killing in 1769 of a British naval lieutenant allegedly in the act of impressing sailors off Marblehead. The defendants received a court verdict of justifiable homicide as defense lawyer John Adams attacked the constitutionality of such methods of obtaining crews. To Adams the case was more important than the Boston Massacre trials of the following year, and he always remembered the honesty and courage of the royal navy seamen who testified against their own officers. The issue flamed again in the opening months of 1775 as British boarding parties stepped up their odious activity, leading Massachusetts patriots to brand Vice Admiral Samuel Graves, commanding in American waters, a traitor and to demand his dismissal from the royal navy. Instead Parliament expressly repealed the confusing legislation of Queen Anne's time to clear the way for large scale efforts to man Grave's vessels, which were then intent upon stopping the smuggling of arms and munitions into the colonies. The tougher attitude further revealed itself in Graves' order for the inclusion of fishermen, who had traditionally been exempted from impressment owing to the dependence of New England coastal communities upon their livelihood.[35]

With such a reservoir of anti-British seamen at hand, one might be tempted to assume that the Continental navy failed to encounter the manpower shortages that perpetually bedeviled the Continental army.

Nothing could be farther from the truth. Seamen probably feared that life in the American navy would be as harsh and brutal as they knew it to be in the royal navy. Congress endeavored to counter this prejudice in its navy regulations, which were written in the moderate spirit of the army's articles of war. Whereas in the British service flogging was the standard form of correction, up to 1,000 lashes, though between 100 and 200 were more in the normal course of events, American regulations prescribed a maximum of 12 lashes; only a court-martial, convened with the consent of the "Commander in Chief of the navy," could exact a stiffer penalty. Moreover, "the sentence of a court martial for any capital offence shall not be put in execution until it be confirmed by the Commander in Chief of the fleet. . . ."[36]

Conditions in the American service were not ideal. A seaman's life was always hard and hazardous in the eighteenth century. Even with a fair-minded captain in command, sailors found bad food, unsanitary conditions, and overdue pay grounds for complaint. Like all navies of the time, the American service had its mutinies, prompted by a variety of complaints, although often the instigators were captured English and Irish sailors who had chosen to join the Continental standard in order to escape confinement. At other times, American Revolutionary principles served as a justification for insubordination and dissent. Many "Jovial Tars" considered John Paul Jones an unduly hard taskmaster. It was said that Jones' "mode of Government" was such that "no American of spirit can ever serve with cheerfulness under him," and that he had persecuted a Lieutenant Thomas Simpson (actually, a demagogue) for preaching to the crew that in a fight for American liberty the captain should heed the voice of the people. There can be small doubt that a part of the American seamen were politically sensitive, whatever the origins of Jones' discomfort. When in English prisons or prison ships they almost universally preferred their cells in favor of offers to exchange their status for duty on British men-of-war. One group of incarcerated rebels occupied themselves by drafting a constitution to govern their behavior in prison.[37]

A seasoned mariner risked making a handsome monetary sacrifice if he enlisted for a voyage on a Continental frigate instead of signing on a privateer—a privately owned armed vessel sailing under a license (letter of marque) issued by a state or by the Continental Congress. Besides higher pay on privateers, the total value of captured vessels ("prizes") went to the captors and their financial backers; while Continental officers and sailors received only one-half the proceeds when the prizes were enemy warships, one-third when they were merchantmen, transports, and storeships. To make the regular service more attractive, Congress increased the shares of naval personnel to the whole amount in the former category and to one-half the complete worth in the latter.

Even had the lawmakers put the navy on an absolute par with privateers, the "militia of the seas" would have retained their popularity over
the regular establishment. Seamen preferred to be free from military
discipline, and the prospects for profits were greater: engaged almost
exclusively in commerce raiding, privateers were more likely to take
numerous prizes over an extended period. It is small wonder that many
a Continental crew was literally scraped together, with landsmen of
various backgrounds and British prisoners forming a substantial part of
the aggregate. (John Paul Jones' crew of the *Bon Homme Richard*
contained men of eleven nationalities; of the 144 nonofficers, 41 are
listed as "Boys.")[38]

Although American naval warfare in the Revolution is primarily a
chronicle of single-ship actions, there were fairly important exceptions.
In the spring of 1776, Esek Hopkins with eight ships swooped down on
Nassau in the Bahamas. This was also the first taste of combat for the
new marine corps led by its senior officer, Samuel Nicholas, a Philadelphia tavern owner. Nicholas' 268 marines dominated the landing
party that occupied the town and two forts, then joined the sailors in
loading the loot—invaluable munitions—into Hopkins's vessels. Another exception, the most disastrous one, was a state rather than a Continental expedition. In 1779 the Massachusetts state navy escorted
transports carrying militia for an assault on the British-held Penobscot
Bay region of Maine. Commodore Saltonstall, heading the navy, failed
to support the landing parties, nor did he engage three nearby enemy
ships. A British squadron, arriving in mid-August, drove off the Massachusetts invasionary force, whose discreditable performance brought an
abrupt end to Saltonstall's service. For the most part, the state navies
(only New Hampshire did not commission ships) confined themselves
to their territorial waters, where their gunboats, row-galleys, and other
small craft guarded against plundering forays and prevented tories
from provisioning cruisers off shore.[39]

All told, Congress put together, though not simultaneously, a navy of
fifty to sixty ships. Besides converted merchantmen purchased at home
and several warships acquired in France, Congress pursued a modest
program of naval construction that showed small regard for the ship-
of-the-line (a unit in the line of battle), the equivalent of a twentieth-
century battleship. Approximately 170 feet long and mounting 60 to
120 guns, with a crew of 450 to 1,000 men, the ship-of-the-line seemed a
needless extravagance for a small commerce-raiding navy. William
Ellery summarized the sentiment of the marine committee on the subject: "These huge ships are too costly and unwieldy, and it will require
as many men to man one of them as to man three or four frigates. Besides, we cannot with all the naval force we can collect be able to cope

with the British navy. Our great aim should be to destroy the trade of Britain, for which purpose frigates are indefinitely better calculated than such large ships."[40] Predominantly for these very reasons, the American navy for years to come followed the "frigate tradition." Stressing speed under sail and maneuverability vital to single-ship engagements, frigates, similar to cruisers of today, were roughly 140 feet long, carried 200 to 300 men, and 24 to 50 guns. They stood mid-way between the heavy ships-of-the-line and the lighter sloops of war, 80 to 120 feet in length, with 150 men and 16 to 20 guns.

Congress resolved on December 13, 1775, that thirteen frigates be constructed at various shipyards from Portsmouth, New Hampshire, to Baltimore, and that they be ready to put to sea in slightly more than three months' time. Although in Europe naval construction had become a specialized field under governmental control, colonial shipyards had occasionally given birth to vessels for the royal navy, commencing with H.M.S. *Falkland* at Portsmouth, New Hampshire, in 1690. It is evident, says Howard Chapelle, that many a colonial shipwright had been trained in British dockyards or had been apprenticed to maritime craftsmen themselves trained in those facilities. In addition, local artisans reaped invaluable knowledge during the colonial wars by refitting and repairing men-of-war. From Boston, Captain Charles Knowles wrote in 1747: "There will be no repair wanting to any of the Stationed Ships but what may be done here and with as much Expedition as in any Yard in England and I think full as well."[41]

The informed reader may ask, granted all this, whether American-built frigates of the Revolution were not poor specimens of their class? This is a common assumption; but Chapelle, after gathering the master plans of the new vessels which have survived, concludes that they were excellently drawn and that some of the frigates were actually well constructed.[42] We should bear in mind that haste was called for, and probably as a consequence there was truth to the allegation that in several of the shipyards inadequately seasoned timbers were used. But most of the ill-fortune encountered by the cruisers was not caused by inherent defects. The British blockade and the loss of New York and Philadelphia combined with shortages of men and guns kept all but four of the thirteen frigates from rendering active service as late as 1777; and one, the *Hancock*, had been captured by the enemy. Two others had been destroyed on the stocks to avoid their falling into British hands, and two more soon met the same fate.

The frigates and smaller warships available to the United States navy had not dared to engage the fleet of Admiral Howe as it supported General Howe's land campaigns of 1776–1777. But Captains John Barry, Lambert Wickes, Nicholas Biddle, Seth Hardy, and John Young had demonstrated their competence as naval officers as they ranged the

Atlantic from Newfoundland to the West Indies, taking prizes, exchanging occasional blows with British men-of-war, convoying merchant vessels, and carrying supplies. We need to remember these relatively unheralded warriors[43] who far too long were almost completely obliterated in the heavy shadow of John Paul Jones, recipient of more than thirty biographies.

Like all legends, that of John Paul Jones has been grossly inflated by all save the tiniest fraction of his admirers. There is fascination and glory aplenty in the literal record of the Scottish-born John Paul, a seafarer since the age of twelve, who added the protective surname Jones and turned up in Virginia after killing a mutinous sailor in self-defense at Tobago in 1773. Early in the war Jones distinguished himself while operating from American ports. Capturing sixteen prizes, he later raided the coastal region of Nova Scotia, destroying the fisheries at Canso and Île Madame and taking nine more ships; on another cruise off Cape Breton he added new plunder, including the 350-ton transport *Mellish* with a cargo of winter uniforms for the British army in Canada. It was in the European theater, however, that Jones won his lasting acclaim. In May, 1777, the Continental commissioners in France recommended the sending of several cruisers across the Atlantic "to intercept and seize the great part of the Baltic and Northern trade," along with the returning Greenland whaling ships and the Hudson Bay merchantmen. A crowning blow, of the highest economic and psychological import, called for the "burning or plundering" of Liverpool or Glasgow.[44] These were "bold and extravagant" schemes, admitted the commissioners. Captains Wickes, Henry Johnson, Gustavus Conyngham, and James Nicholson who proceeded Jones to Europe had found times not yet propitious for anything so grandiose as their country's diplomats had in mind. Louis XVI still pursued a theoretical if precarious neutrality in 1777, and Vergennes' attitude toward allowing American warships the freedom of French ports for themselevs and their prizes fluctuated in response to the protests of Lord Stormont, George III's ambassador to Versailles, whose agents diligently collected intelligence of collusion between America and France.

Jones' arrival in France, commanding the sloop-of-war *Ranger*, virtually coincided with the signing of the two treaties between the Bourbon monarchy and the United States. If the thirty-year-old Captain met disappointment in his quest of a new frigate to be purchased or built by the Continental commissioners, he found himself welcomed in Paris, and he discovered the septuagenarian Franklin agreeable to his strategical objectives: hit-and-run attacks on "the enemies' defenceless places"—leaving most of the commerce-destroying to the Yankee privateers—in order to tie down British warships that otherwise would be engaged in blockading the American coast or in sustaining George III's army contesting Washington. A secondary aim, besides destroying shipping in his path, was the capture of a prominent person to compel the British government to exchange American sailors rotting in English jails. Though the master of a single small cruiser is scarcely in a position to bring the impact of the war home to the enemy's civilian population, Jones sailed boldly into the Irish Sea and in April, 1778, struck at the port of Whitehaven, Scotland. With a party of men, he rowed ashore under cover of darkness, spiked the guns at the harbor entrance, and set fire to several vessels along the dock. The inhabitants quickly extinguished the flames. The raid's tangible accomplishments were inconsequential, but to the British people, the event proved disconcerting, and to the royal navy the Whitehaven episode was positively embarrassing. Not since the Dutch attack at Sheerness in 1667 had an English seaport suffered such a humiliation. Jones performed two other indignities on the same cruise: one a somewhat farcical raid on St. Mary's Isle that failed to bag Lord Selkirk as a hostage, although several crew members did make off with Lady Selkirk's family silver; the other the conquest of twenty-gun H.M.S. *Drake*, a sloop-of-war.

For nearly a year after his sensational dash through the Irish Sea, Jones was grounded for lack of a ship. Polished and urbane, the handsome little Captain (almost five feet, five inches) scored a direct hit on the Parisian ladies; his conquests, platonic and otherwise, may well give him pre-eminence in a unique field of American Revolutionary leadership. Even so, fighting was uppermost in the mind of Jones, described by envoy John Adams as "the most ambitious and intriguing Officer in the American Navy." (It was apparently Captain Jones who advised the flinty New Englander, on the date he recorded the above impression, that the two best ways of learning the French language were to "take a Mistress" or "go to the Commedie.")[45] Jones sought a raiding squadron that would descend upon Liverpool with a landing force, then hastily depart for a cruise around Scotland and a stab at the great shipping port of Leith, before climaxing his venture by seizing the annual Baltic convoy carrying naval stores upon which British sea power depended.

As it was, Jones had to be satisfied with a good deal less than he had hoped for in men and ships from France. The Ministry of Marine gave Jones for his own use an old, clumsy East Indiaman, renamed *Bon Homme Richard* in compliment to Franklin, the "Poor Richard" of almanac fame; and three smaller French naval vessels that sailed as part of the American squadron, as did the Continental frigate *Alliance*, under vain, mercurial Pierre Landis, a former French officer now in American service. Owing to the small size and nature of his force, plus the unwillingness of Landis to obey orders, rebelliousness which soon infected the French navy captains, the voyage took on the prospect of abject failure. By the time the squadron had rounded Ireland and passed up and down the coasts of Scotland, Jones had only several small prizes to his credit, and his one effort to raid a port city—Leith—had been thwarted by his captains.

Then, off the chalk cliffs of Flamborough Head on September 23, 1779, Jones spotted forty-four sail atop the horizon to the northeast: the Baltic fleet escorted by H.M.S. *Serapis* (50 guns) and H.M.S. *Countess of Scarborough* (20 guns). The upshot was the most spectacular naval episode of the Revolution, a duel between aging, decrepit *Bon Homme Richard* and *Serapis* (under Captain Richard Pearson), a sturdy, new copper-bottomed frigate.[46] As the Baltic merchantmen scurried for safety, and as the French cruiser *Pallas* paired off with *Countess of Scarborough*, Jones and Pearson jockeyed for position. Since *Serapis* possessed greatly superior firepower, "it was as though a 14-inch-gunned battleship, with an additional advantage of speed, engaged an 8-inch-gunned heavy cruiser."[47] Each captain, in standard tactical fashion, attempted to maneuver his ship so that the full weight of either of his main batteries (located on the port and starboard sides) could be brought to bear without the opponent's being able to respond with a broadside. Each captain, in other words, sought to rake by getting his vessel across the enemy's bow or stern. To be able to steer for *Serapis*, without allowing *Serapis* to steer for her, *Richard* needed the advantage of the wind, which is called "the weather gauge" in sailors' lexicon. But *Serapis'* superior speed and maneuverability prevented Jones from gaining an advantageous position; and after exchanging two or three salvos, during which two of *Richard*'s heavy guns burst killing their crews (it was now too dangerous to risk firing the rest), Jones sought to board and grapple. His opportunity to clinch came when a sudden burst of wind caused both vessels to pivot crazily and then collide, bow to stern and stern to bow.

Although Jones himself grabbed a line to assist in lashing the ships together, shouting "we have got her now," the results of the embrace were anything but certain. On the *Serapis'* open deck her cannon were deserted owing to the rain of musket and grenade fire from Jones' sharpshooters; but her eighteen-pounders below deck roared on, turning *Richard*'s topsides into a mass of fragments and splinters. Jones, by this time, had only 3 nine-pounders on her quarterdeck still in operation. At this moment Captain Landis' *Alliance* loomed up through the smoke and flame—and "to my utter astonishment," exclaimed Jones, poured a broadside, later two more, into *Richard*, not only killing almost a score of men, but doing irreparable damage to her at the water

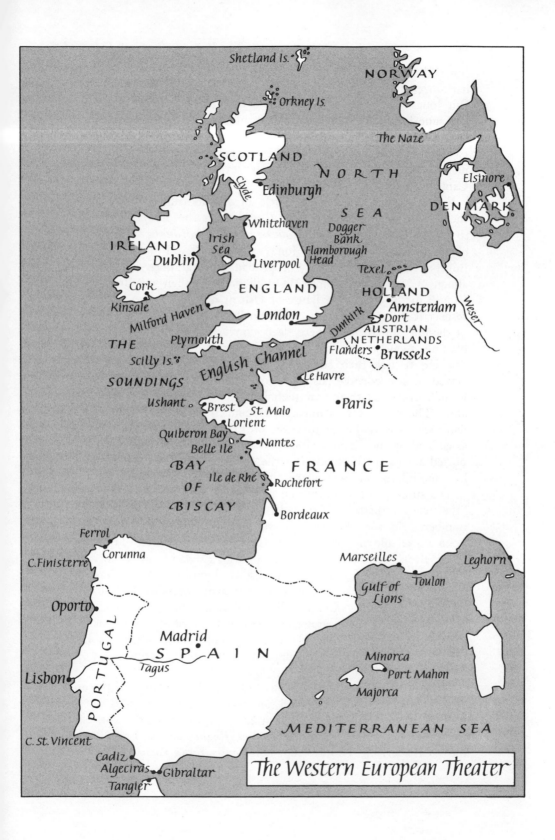

The Western European Theater

line and even lower. With water five feet deep in her hold and afire in a half dozen places, *Bon Homme Richard* seemed at the end of her tether. But Jones was a man of indomitable will. His marksmen were performing superbly, none better than seaman William Hamilton who, late in the battle, threw a grenade down *Serapis'* main hatch that killed twenty men. It was Pearson whose nerve finally gave way. When his main mast began to tremble after several indirect hits, the British Captain struck his colors.[48]

Following the three-hour Battle of Flamborough, Jones abandoned the sinking *Bon Homme Richard*, took over the *Serapis*, and sailed her to Holland, bringing along *Countess of Scarborough*, which had capitulated to *Pallas*. Word of Jones' victory gave France an uplift, for Bourbon naval fortunes in Europe had thus far been nothing to shout about. Admiral the Comte d'Orvilliers had taken on British Admiral Keppel in the indecisive Battle of Ushant on July 27, 1778. In only one respect it differed from the traditionally sterile clash of opposing ships-of-the-line squadrons, where fleets converged from opposite directions, blasting away as they passed each other in formation, and then withdrawing to lick their superficial wounds. Some of Keppel's vessels received unprecedented damage to their sails and rigging when the French practiced their new technique of concentrating much firepower aloft. The next year's campaign, as conceived by Vergennes and Floridablanca, was to be an invasion of England, for which 31,000 troops assembled at the French cities of Le Havre and St. Malo, to be transported across the channel after the combined fleets of France and Spain had annihilated or neutralized the smaller British home fleet.

The summer of 1779 seemed perilous to Englishmen as they awaited "the other armada." With both its regular sea and land forces outnumbered in the channel and the coastal fortresses, Britain fell back upon unreliable militia and home guard organizations. That the combined fleets returned to Brest, sparing England an enemy landing, owed something to the inadequate Franco-Spanish leadership: Admiral d'Orvilliers was sixty-nine, French army Marshal de Vaux seventy-four, and Spanish Admiral Cordova seventy-three. But the failure of the Bourbons is more understandable in light of the inherent obstacles to ambitious naval schemes in the age of sailing ships: shortages of stores, difficulties of revictualing, sickness among crews, and rivalries and suspicions among allies.[49]

If Jones' triumph contrasted sharply with d'Orvilliers' misfortunes, the American Captain's acclaim did not pave the way for fresh laurels. The years 1780–1783 in the American navy were distinctly anti-climactic. Scheduled to sail to America in the *Alliance*, since Franklin had removed the erratic Landis from command, Jones then saw the warship returned to Landis through the machinations of a personal enemy, Arthur Lee. Afterward in the United States, Jones faced more unhappiness. Awarded command of the *America*, the one ship-of-the-line built in this country during the Revolution, the Captain found that it would be transferred to France as a gesture of good will. Still another honor that seems to have barely eluded his grasp was promotion to rear admiral; but the jealous intervention of Captains James Nicholson and Thomas Read, who stood higher on the seniority list, caused Congress to back off rather than face an unpleasant scene. Not until 1861 was the navy to have its first rear admiral, David G. Farragut.

Jones' failure to bow out on a note of glory was substantially a reflection of the pathetic state of the United States navy in the waning period of the war. For the navy there was no *éclat* similar to that of Washington's army at Yorktown. Naval events to be sure were the vital ingredient in the decisive campaign on the Virginia peninsula, but it was the French fleet of the Comte de Grasse that combined with Washington to bring the downfall of Cornwallis. Congress dismissed its ranking naval officer Esek Hopkins from the service on grounds of incompetence, a fate he shared with several other captains. The frigate *Randolph* blew up, taking the life of capable Captain Biddle. Atlantic storms sent other fine captains to watery graves, Wickes in the *Reprisal* and Young in the *Saratoga*. In 1778 alone five new frigates had to be burned or scuttled to keep them from falling to the enemy. Four other Continental cruisers were captured when Charleston surrendered to Sir Henry Clinton in 1780. The next year witnessed, among others, the loss of the *Trumbull*, last of the thirteen frigates of 1776. By early 1782 frigates *Alliance* and *Deane* were the only ships of the United States navy in commission.

As the navy decreased in numbers and effectiveness, privateering, as late as 1781, expanded in scope and volume. All told, it is probable that 2,000 vessels of almost every conceivable description received commissions to prey upon British commerce; but the average raider, if one can generalize, probably carried about eight or nine guns and a crew of thirty-five men. They accounted in all for the loss of roughly 600 enemy prizes compared to slightly fewer than 200 credited to the Continental navy.[50]

It was a simple matter for historians of Alfred Mahan's generation a century or more later to read into the naval failures of the American Revolutionaries the necessity for a big navy. It was particularly easy because such a requirement seemed to be essential in their own time when America was increasing her colonial and commercial commitments within and without the Western Hemisphere. Even if one accepts the highly dubious assumption that a much larger fleet was not beyond the physical and financial resources of Revolutionary America, the American navy could have done no more than place a dent in British sea power. Whatever the faults or faults or virtues of future naval policy under the Federalists and the Jeffersonian Republicans, Americans fought the War of 1812 at sea as they had engaged the British in the Revolutionary War by employing frigates and privateers in commerce raiding.

## NOTES

1. Hugh Henry Brackenridge, *An Eulogium of the Brave Men Who Have Fallen in the Contest with Great-Britain* (Philadelphia, [1779]), 10.
2. Francis S. Philbrick, *The Rise of the West, 1754-1830* (New York, 1965), 81.
3. Ford, ed., *Journals of the Continental Congress*, II, 174-183; *Pennsylvania Packet*, Dec. 11, 1775; Force, ed., *American Archives*, 4th ser., III, 473-496. Two useful studies of British Indian agents are Consul W. Butterfield, *History of the Girtys* (Cincinnati, 1890); Reginald Horsman, *Matthew Elliott: British Indian Agent* (Detroit, 1964).
4. John R. Alden, *John Stuart and the Southern Colonial Frontier . . . 1754-1775* (Ann Arbor, 1944), 170-171, 171 n75; Philip M. Hamer, "John Stuart's Indian Policy during the Early Months of the American Revolution," *Mississippi Valley Historical Review*, XVII (1930), 351-366; Hamer, "The Wataugans and the Cherokee Indians in 1776," East Tennessee Historical Society, *Publications*, no. 3 (1931), 108-126. The best account of the Cherokee War is James H. O'Donnell, "The Southern Indians in the War of Independence, 1775-1783" (unpubl. Ph.D. diss., Duke University, 1963), chaps. i-ii. The war years form only a single chapter in Walter H. Mohr, *Federal-Indian Relations, 1774-1788* (Philadelphia, 1933).
5. French, *First Year of the Revolution*, 403-410, is a severe indictment of Gage, far more so than Alden, *Gage*, 257-259. A recent appraisal stresses the inevitability of Indian involvement, but is nonetheless mildly critical of the British General. Jack M. Sosin, "The Use of Indians in the War of the American Revolution: A Re-Assessment of Responsibility," *Canadian Historical Review*, XLVI (1965), 101-121. Still pertinent is Andrew McF. Davis, "The Employment of Indian Auxiliaries in the American War," *English Historical Review*, II (1887), 709-728. Dartmouth expressed his opinion in favor of arousing the tribes to Guy Johnson, Superintendent of the Northern Indian Department, July 24, 1775, O'Callaghan, ed., *Documents Relative to the Colonial History of New York*, VIII, 596: "lose no time in taking such steps as may induce them to take up the hatchet against His Majesty's rebellious subjects in America"; and to Gage, Aug. 2, 1775, Saunders, ed., *Colonial Records of North Carolina*, X, 138b.
6. For Williamson's massacre of the Delaware, see Elma E. and Leslie R. Gray, *Wilderness Christians: The Moravian Indian Mission to the Delaware Indians* (Ithaca, 1956), chap. vi; Paul A. W. Wallace, ed., *Thirty Thousand Miles with John Heckewelder* (Pittsburgh, 1958), chap. xxii. There are grim portrayals of Crawford's death in Consul W. Butterfield, *An Historical Account of the Expedition against Sandusky under Col. William Crawford in 1782* (Cincinnati, 1873), 379-384; [John Knight and John Slover], *Narratives of a Late Expedition against the Indians with an Account of the Barbarous Execution of Col. Crawford* (Philadelphia, 1773 [1783]), 9-13, 21-22.
7. John D. Barnhart, *Henry Hamilton and George Rogers Clark in the American Revolution with the unpublished Journal of Lieut. Gov. Henry Hamilton*

(Crawfordsville, Ind., 1951), 21–36, 93–95; Barnhart, "A New Evaluation of Henry Hamilton and George Rogers Clark," *Mississippi Valley Historical Review*, XXXVII (1951), 643–652. More detailed and slightly more cautious in offering the same revisionist interpretation on the "hair buyer" question is Orville J. Jaebker, "Henry Hamilton: British Soldier and Colonial Governor" (unpubl. Ph.D. diss., Indiana University, 1954), chap. iv. Though Lord George Germain gave the order for unleashing the Indians of the Northwest (Carleton had not complied with Gage's call), the Colonial Secretary declared that the idea had originated with Hamilton; if so, Hamilton's letter to Germain no longer seems to exist. However, as early as September, 1776, Hamilton appears to have been unopposed to such a step. It would be "a deplorable sort of war, but [one] which the arrogance, disloyalty, and imprudence of the Virginians has justly drawn down upon them." Michigan Pioneer and Historical Society, *Collections* (Lansing, 1887–1929), IX, 346–347, X, 268.

The colonists themselves had adopted the practice of paying for scalps in previous wars, and it was not completely discontinued in the Revolution. In May, 1777, the North Carolina assembly, responding to new Cherokee depredations, offered its militiamen £15. per prisoner, £10. per scalp. Clark, ed., *State Records of North Carolina*, XXIV, 15.

8. Clark to Henry, Feb. 3, 1779, James A. James, ed., *George Rogers Clark Papers, 1771–1784* (Illinois State Historical Library, *Collections*, vols. 8, 19 [1912, 1926]), VIII, 97–100, and 208–302 for Clark's memoir of his frontier services during 1773–1779.

9. Hamilton's accounts of the scalping are in Historical Manuscripts Commission, *Stopford-Sackville MSS*, II, 234; Barhart, ed., *Hamilton and Clark*, 203–205; Boyd, ed., *Papers of Jefferson*, II–IV, *passim*; *Virginia Gazette* (Dixon and Nicholson), June 19, 1779.

10. Macmillan, *War Governors in the American Revolution*, 186–189; James A. James, "Oliver Pollock, Financier of the Revolution in the West," *Mississippi Valley Historical Review*, XVI (1929), 67–80; James, *Oliver Pollock . . .* (New York, 1937), chaps. ix–xi.

11. Clark's admirers have generated much heat and little light in their claims that the Kentuckian's campaigns had a momentous impact on the peace commissioners who awarded the Northwest to the new republic. See especially James A. James' *George Rogers Clark* (Chicago, 1928) and the same author's several articles: "To What Extent was George Rogers Clark in Military Control of the Northwest at the Close of the American Revolution?" American Historical Association, *Annual Report for 1917* (Washington, 1920), 313–329; "An Appraisal of the Contributions of George Rogers Clark to the History of the West," *Mississippi Valley Historical Review*, XVII (1930), 98–115; "The Northwest: Gift or Conquest?" *Indiana Magazine of History*, XXX (1934), 1–15. A more recent Clark biographer writes: "It is probably true that he added three—perhaps five—states to the Union." And "It is arguable that his rear-guard operations in the 'back country' saved the American Revolution from collapse." John Bakeless, *Background to Glory . . .* (Philadelphia and New York, 1957), preface. A dissenting opinion is registered by Clarence Alvord, "Virginia and the West: An Interpretation," *Mississippi Valley Historical Review*, III (1916), 19–38, though his case is not well stated. According to one scholar (in 1934), only one document had turned up to show that any of the American peace commissioners had heard of Clark's exploits, a letter that actually disclosed very little. Lewis J. Carey, "Franklin is Informed of Clark's Activities in the Old Northwest," *Mississippi Valley Historical Review*, XXI (1934), 375–378. But two new studies indicate that there was some general awareness in Paris of happenings in the Illinois country. Yet, affirms Richard B. Morris, "For all the diplomats in Paris seemed to care, the Virginians who had waded the icy waters of the Wabash in their heroic march to Vincennes might just as well have remained by their own firesides." Morris, *The Peacemakers*, 320, 323, 524; also Van Alstyne, *Empire and Independence*, 217.

12. Two excellent articles are by Milo M. Quaife: "When Detroit Invaded Ken-

tucky," Burton Historical Collection, *Leaflet*, IV (1925), 17–32; "Detroit Battles: the Blue Licks," *ibid.*, VI (1927), 17–32.

13. A generally convincing defense of Brant's method of warfare is given in Marc Jack Smith, "Joseph Brant: Mohaw Statesmen" (unpubl. Ph.D. diss., University of Wisconsin, 1946), 30–33, 35, 43–44. A revisionist view of the Butlers, though less judicious than Smith's dissertation, is Howard Swiggett, *War Out of Niagara: Walter Butler and the Tory Rangers* (New York, 1933; reprint, 1963), chaps. vi–vii. Swiggett makes the valid observation that many of the worst atrocity tales make their appearance years later in county histories of New York, hardly the best of sources. Also relevant is Ernest A. Cruikshank, *The Story of Butler's Rangers and the Settlement of Niagara* (Welland, Ontario, 1893), 44–50.

14. Ford, ed., *Journals of Congress*, VII, 247; Mohr, *Federal-Indian Relations*, 50–51, 70–71; Reuben G. Thwaites and Louise P. Kellogg, eds., *Frontier Defense on the Upper Ohio, 1777–1778* (Madison, 1912), 193, 201–202, 215–222.

15. Mohr, *Federal-Indian Relations*, 71; Louise P. Kellogg, ed., *Frontier Advance on the Upper Ohio, 1778–1779* (Madison, 1916), 54–59, 87–88, 125–274, *passim*.

16. Fitzpatrick, ed., *Writings of Washington*, XV, 190–191. Sullivan's command received 1,000 frontier hunting shirts before departing. Board of War to Congress, Aug. 11, 1779, Papers of the Continental Congress, no. 147, III, 558.

17. Reports of the numbers engaged are in Whittemore, *General of the Revolution*, 138, 141; Jones, "Brant," 40. Scarcely a Revolutionary campaign was so well recorded on the American side as this one, chiefly through the eyes of many diarists. Particularly valuable are Alexander C. Flick, comp., *The Sullivan-Clinton Campaign in 1779* . . . (New York, 1929); Albert H. Wright, comp., *The Sullivan Expedition of 1779* . . . (Ithaca, 1943).

18. Jones, "Brant," 45. James Madison learned that "The inroads of the Enemy on the frontier of N. York have been most fatal to us in this respect. They have almost totally ruined that fine Wheat Country, which was able and from the energy of their Govt. most likely, to supply Magazines of flour both for the main Army & the NW posts. The settlemt. of Schoarie which alone was able to furnish . . . 80,000 bushels of grain for public use has been totally laid in ashes." Hutchinson and Rachal, eds., *Papers of Madison*, II, 173.

19. Randolph C. Downes, "Indian War on the Upper Ohio, 1779–1782," *Western Pennsylvania Historical Magazine*, XVII (1934), 93–115. "To speak of a 'conquest' of the Northwest from the Indians during the Revolution," warns Downes (p. 93), "is to speak idly. The Indians never considered any of this territory as conquered, annexed, or legally occupied until the Treaty of Greenville of 1795." See also Milo M. Quaife, "The Ohio Campaigns of 1782," *Mississippi Valley Historical Review*, XVII (1931), 515–529. American difficulties are documented in Louise P. Kellogg, ed., *Frontier Retreat on the Upper Ohio, 1779–1781* (Madison, 1917).

20. Thwaites and Kellogg, eds., *Frontier Defense*, 126, 149, 157–163, 176–177, 188–189.

21. Two excellent monographs find considerable fault with America's handling of the Indians: Max Savelle, *George Morgan: Colony Builder* (New York, 1932); Randolph C. Downes, *Council Fires of the Upper Ohio* (Pittsburgh, 1940).

22. Smyth, ed., *Writings of Franklin*, VIII, 437–439.

23. Michigan Pioneer and Historical Society, *Collections*, XI, 363, 634–646, IX, 400, 441, 469, X, 311–327; Jaebker, "Henry Hamilton," 80–81.

24. Foner, ed., *Writings of Paine*, I, 34, 33; Robbins, *Eighteenth-Century Commonwealth*, 104; Blackstone, *Commentaries on the Laws of England*, I, 417–418. A navy, Madison assured readers of Federalist no. 41, "can never be turned by a perfidious government against our liberties." Jacob E. Cooke, ed., *The Federalist* (Meridian edn., Cleveland, 1961), 275. Even Thomas Burke, suspicious of militarism and a devotee of states' rights until late in the war, spoke out for a strong, permanent navy. Burke to Elbridge Gerry, July [?], 1778, Preston Davie Papers, Southern Historical Collection, University of North Carolina Library.

25. "What Think you of an American Fleet?" wrote John Adams to James Warren on October 19, 1775. "I don't Mean 100 ships of the Line, by a Fleet, but I suppose this Term may be applied to any naval Force. . . ." Burnett, ed., *Letters of Congress*, I, 235. One of the earliest—if not the first—appeals for an American navy issued from Major Adam Stephen of the Virginia militia to Richard Henry Lee, Feb. 1, 1775: "What can we do, if united? We only want a Navy to give law to the world, and we have it in our power to get it." Clark, ed., *Naval Documents of the American Revolution*, I, 77. By August of that year Franklin and Silas Deane were anxious to have a naval establishment. *Ibid.*, 243–244.

26. John R. Bartlett, ed., *Records of the Colony of Rhode Island and Providence Plantations in New England* (Providence, 1856–1865), VII, 369; Clark, ed., *Naval Documents of the American Revolution*, I, 1236; Clark, *George Washington's Navy*.

27. Butterfield, ed., *Adams Diary and Autobiography*, II, 198, III, 342–343; Samuel E. Morison, *John Paul Jones: A Sailor's Biography* (Boston and Toronto, 1959), 35–36. A possibly revealing letter as to Southern thinking is from Robert Morris to John Paul Jones, dated February 1, 1777. Morris informed Jones, on returning home from a West Indian voyage, that "The southern Colonies wish to see part of their Navy . . . you might recruit and refit at Georgia, South or North Carolina, there make sale of such part of your prize goods, etc., as would be useful to them. . . ." Charles O. Paullin, ed., *Out-Letters of the Continental Marine Committee and Board of Admiralty August 1776–September 1780* (New York, 1914), I, 69–70.

28. Ford, ed., *Journals of Congress*, III, 311–312, 348, 364, 375–376, 378–387, 393, 513; *Rules for the Regulation of the Navy of the United Colonies of North-America . . .* (Philadelphia, 1775); Frederic H. Hayes, "John Adams and American Sea Power," *American Neptune*, XXV (1965), 35–45. Printed Congressional rules and edicts on naval affairs are listed in Evans and Shipton, comps., *American Bibliography*, nos. 14582, 14848, 15135–15143, 15154, 15637–15641, 15688. The origins of the naval committee are considerably more involved than it would appear from the above paragraph. See the heavily annotated notes in Burnett, ed., *Letters of Congress*, I, 216–217; Butterfield, ed., *Adams Diary and Autobiography*, II, 201–202.

29. Burnett, ed., *Letters of Congress*, II, 59; Paullin, ed., *Out-Letters of the Continental Marine Committee and Board of Admiralty*, I, 109–114, 123, 125–129, 138–139, and *passim* for commerce raiding.

30. Paullin, ed., *Out-Letters of the Continental Marine Committee and Board of Admiralty*, I, 148–149; Ford, ed., *Journals of Congress*, XIV, 708, XV, 1133, 1204, 1216–1218, XIX, 126, 127–128, 133, 203, XX, 724–726, 764–767, XXI, 943. Many Board of Admiralty letters are in Hutchinson and Rachal, eds., *Papers of Madison*, II.

31. Ford, ed., *Journals of Congress*, VI, 861; Morison, *Jones*, 87–92; *Memoirs of Andrew Sherburne: A Pensioner of the Navy of the Revolution* (Utica, 1828), 19. In obtaining a midshipman's berth for his son aboard the sloop-of-war *Saratoga*, Governor William Livingston declared that the public interest "requires our navy to be officered by the children of respectable families." But he reminded his son that officers should treat their men with respect and dignity. Theodore Sedgwick, Jr., *A Memoir of the Life of William Livingston* (New York, 1835), 345–347.

32. Samuel E. Morison, *The Maritime History of Massachusetts* (New York, 1941), 105–106. Estimates of the seagoing population are in Morris, *Government and Labor*, 225, 225 n1.

33. Lemisch, "Jack Tar in the Streets," 381–400.

34. Dora Mae Clark, "The Impressment of Seamen in the American Colonies," in *Essays in Colonial History Presented to Charles McLean Andrews*, 198–224; Neil R. Stout, "Manning the Royal Navy in North America, 1763–1775," *American Neptune*, XXIII (1963), 174–185.

35. Wroth and Zobel, eds., *Legal Papers of John Adams*, II, 276–335; Clark, ed.,

*Naval Documents of the American Revolution*, I, especially 82, 91, 93–94, 98, 492, 493–494, 704, 714, but see many more references to the subject in the index. During the Revolution only two states legalized the impressment of seamen, and then for only short periods. Congress received occasional complaints against Continental officers impressing sailors; but Captain Seth Harding was evidently the only serious offender. Elizabeth Cometti, "Impressment during the American Revolution," in *The Walter Clinton Jackson Essays in the Social Sciences*, ed. Vera Largent (Chapel Hill, 1942), 99–100; Ford, ed., *Journals of Congress*, XV, 1204; *Pennsylvania Archives*, 1st ser., V, 328; James L. Howard, *Seth Harding Mariner* (New Haven, 1930), 100–104, 133, 135–136, 258–259.

36. *Rules for the Regulation of the Navy of the United Colonies*, 3–4, 8; Gardner W. Allen, *A Naval History of the American Revolution* (Boston and New York, 1913), II, appendix ii, prints in full the American naval regulations.

37. Morison, *Jones*, 167–172; Lincoln Lorenz, *John Paul Jones: Fighter for Freedom and Glory* (Annapolis, Md., 1943), chaps. xxiii–xxiv; Allen, *Naval History of the American Revolution*, I, 198–199, 350–351, II, 527, 534; Hyman, *To Try Men's Souls*, 102. Fitzpatrick, ed., *Writings of Washington*, XXIII, 258; John K. Alexander, "Forton Prison during the American Revolution . . .," *Essex Institute Historical Collections*, CIII (1967), 365–389. Though Americans in British prisons might deem life in the royal navy harsh and forbidding, they had no chance of being exchanged for British seamen in American hands until late in the war. The London government permitted the exchange of army personnel, but treated Americans captured in privateers or warships as pirates or marauders without belligerent status. Finally, in 1779, after John Paul Jones had a parcel of navy prisoners in hand, the first exchange of seamen took place. See also Jesse Lemisch, "Listening to the Inarticulate: William Widger's Dream and the Loyalties of American Revolutionary Seamen in British Prisons," *Social History*, III (1969), 1–29.

38. Morison, *Jones*, 205. Captain James Nicholson of the frigate *Trumbull* complained in 1780 that most of his crew, exclusive of officers, "were green country lads, many of them not clear of their sea-sickness. . . ." Commager and Morris, eds., *Spirit of 'Seventy-Six*, II, 957.

39. A new account of Hopkins' raid is John F. McCusker, Jr., "The American Invasion of Nassau in the Bahamas," *American Neptune*, XXV (1965), 189–217. Marine Captain Nicholas' report of the marines' role is in a letter to an unidentified friend, dated April 10, 1776, in *The Remembrancer*, Part II (1776), 212–214. Interesting remarks about the Continental marines are in J. Fenimore Cooper, *The History of the Navy of the United States of America* (Paris, 1839), 164–167. There are few histories of state naval operations; a good one is Robert A. Stewart, *The History of Virginia's Navy in the Revolution* (Richmond, 1934). See also Louis F. Middlebrook, *Maritime Connecticut during the American Revolution* (Salem, Mass., 1925), I.

40. Commager and Morris, eds., *Spirit of 'Seventy-Six*, II, 922–923.

41. Quoted in Daniel A. Baugh, *British Naval Administration in the Age of Walpole* (Princeton, 1965), 342.

42. Howard I. Chapelle, *The History of the American Sailing Navy: The Ships and their Development* (New York, 1949), chaps. i–ii; M. V. Brewington, "The Design of our First Frigates," *American Neptune*, VIII (1948), 11–25. John J. McCusker, Jr., "The Tonnage of the Continental Ship *Alfred*," *Pennsylvania Magazine of History and Biography*, XC (1966), 227–235, contains thoughtful remarks on methodology of evaluating ship construction.

43. The task of restoring these captains to the public eye has been taken on almost singlehandedly by William Bell Clark, author of *Lambert Wickes: Sea Raider and Diplomat* (New Haven, 1932); *Gallant John Barry* (New York, 1938); *Captain Dauntless:The Story of Nicholas Biddle of the Continental Navy* (Baton Rouge, 1949); *The First Saratoga: Being the Saga of John Young and His Sloop-of-War* (Baton Rouge, 1953). These and Clark's other naval studies of the Revo-

lution are evaluated in the *William and Mary Quarterly*, 3d ser., XVIII (1961), 146–148.

44. Commager and Morris, eds., *Spirit of 'Seventy-Six*, II, 939–940; Wharton, ed., *Revolutionary Diplomatic Correspondence*, II, 325–326.

45. Butterfield, ed., *Adams Diary and Autobiography*, II, 370–371.

46. In the eighteenth century ships were periodically laid up for the time-consuming task of cleaning away the accumulation of marine growth that progressively slowed their movements. To avoid such delays, the Admiralty in 1778 began a large-scale program of nailing thin copper plates to the bottoms of its vessels. Maurer Maurer, "Coppered Bottoms for the Royal Navy: a Factor in the Maritime War of 1778–1783," *Military Affairs*, XIV (1950), 57–61.

47. Morison, *Jones*, 216.

48. American contemporary reports of the battle are in Commager and Morris, eds., *Spirit of 'Seventy-Six*, II, 946–953.

49. A. Temple Patterson, *The Other Armada* (Manchester, Eng., 1960); P. del Perugia, *Le tentative d'invasion d'Angleterre en 1779* (Paris, 1940).

50. See Edgar S. Maclay, *A History of American Privateers* (New York, 1899), chaps. iv–xvi; William B. Clark, *Ben Franklin's Privateers* (Baton Rouge, 1956); Clark, *George Washington's Navy*; Stanley G. Morse, "Yankee Privateersmen of 1776," *New England Quarterly*, XVII (1944), 71–86; Commager and Morris, *Spirit of 'Seventy-Six*, II, chap. xxiv; Charles W. Farnham, "Crew List of the Privateer *Independence*, 1776," *Rhode Island History*, XXVI (1967), 125–128.

# 14. Defeat and Victory in the South

**T**HERE IS A GLAMOROUS image to the war in the South in much of our literature, the theater to which the British shifted the brunt of their military activity after 1778. One sees it in the seven novels of the Southern campaigns written by William Gilmore Simms, the high priest of Charleston antebellum literary circles. There are fiery young aristocrats forming partisan bands, bitter blood feuds between virtuous whigs and decadent tories, courageous women of gentle birth sacrificing loved ones and plantations in liberty's cause, and dutiful slaves standing manfully on the side of their patriot masters. To be sure, there are flesh and blood heroes as well, fighting against the variegated backdrop of the Southern landscape of oak and hickory, pine and palmetto, swamps and rivers, sand barrens and red clay piedmont, overlooked by the towering Blue Ridge. There are the ubiquitous guerrillas of South Carolina, Francis Marion, Thomas Sumter, and Andrew Pickens; the dashing, plume-decked cavalrymen Henry Lee and William Washington; the hardy "over-mountain" men, John Sevier, William Cleveland, and Isaac Shelby; the redoubtable woodsman Daniel Morgan; and the nimble strategist Nathanael Greene. Even so, the war in the South before 1781 added up to an uninspiring catalogue of American reversals that included the loss of two Continental armies. Until that year Britain ostensibly had the upper hand. Yet the British too committed errors, even in their early victorious phases of the struggle. Certain false assumptions and miscalculations underlay the Southern campaign from the very beginning; scarcely evident for many months, they were to reap their harvest at Yorktown.

## A Chain of Defeats

For Britain the year 1778 clearly called for a strategic reappraisal. The impending threat from the Bourbon monarchies and the failure thus far to bring the rebels to heel prompted the London ministry to turn its attention to the American Southland. Since the abortive Clinton-Parker expedition to the Carolinas in 1776, and except for occasional raids against the Georgia frontier by Florida-based loyalists, the vast region below the Potomac had been spared the agonies of the upper states. If Washington could not be brought to a climactic battle, then why not give up the North, at least New England, for the time being if not forever? Armchair strategists in the mother country expressed these sentiments with a fair amount of logic. In the North, the Americans were thickly settled, reasonably well armed, and far less inclined toward reconciliation than once assumed. Charles Jenkinson, a Treasury subminister, went a step further by arguing that for commercial reasons New England could be sawed off from the empire with relatively small harm to Britain: the only American products crucial to the empire's well-being were those of the Southern provinces. Possession of the deep South would also bolster the British hold on the Floridas, currently menaced by the rebels to the north and by the Spanish to the south in the Caribbean.

Up to a point Washington and Lord George Germain were of one mind concerning the prospects for British mastery in the South. So long as New York City remained a center of British power, the American General would probably be unable to march his troops below the Susquehanna to aid the inhabitants against invasion. Even if manpower and supplies were available to send southward, South Carolina and Georgia in particular were virtually inaccessible by land routes from the North. Thus a region thinly populated (compared to the North), fearful of slave uprisings, and heavily dependent on the outside for goods and markets might be conquered more easily than New England. Germain and other policy-makers at Whitehall made two additional assumptions: namely, that the loyalists were exceedingly numerous in the South and that Britain could maintain superiority on the sea. Both assumptions are worthy of closer analysis. Optimism concerning the potency of loyalism rested on no more than the long-held opinions of deposed royal officials and prominent loyalists that had underlain the expedition of 1776 to the Carolinas. In still another way the tories figured in the ministry's enthusiasm for a Southern campaign. In response to mounting criticism from the Parliamentary opposition, whose ranks were augmented by the disaster at Saratoga and the growing burden of debt and taxation, North, Germain, and company concocted a persuasive reply. Not only would it be dishonorable to forsake the King's friends in the South, but the government could actually expand the war to that theater at a minimal expense and at a small increase in the army; for the loyalists themselves were a mighty reservoir of untapped military strength. Political considerations, chiefly the maintenance of a Parliamentary majority, came to weigh heavily upon military considerations affecting the Southern campaign.[1]

Naval supremacy was vital to Britain in a Southern campaign that would see her military resources dispersed between Manhattan and the Floridas. Such a scattering of her forces created the potential danger of their being beaten in detail if Americans gained the aid of an enemy fleet. Since supplies and reinforcements could come only by sea, royal army commanders could scarcely push inland to the point where they lost effective contact with His Majesty's Atlantic squadrons. Was it reasonable for British leaders to assume they could perpetually dominate the waters adjacent to the American states? Perhaps so in March, 1778, when Germain first proposed to Sir Henry Clinton a campaign to the southward. But by the conclusion of 1779, when only Georgia was securely occupied, there was good cause to fear that the policy of dispatching detachments from the home fleet or the West Indies offered inadequate protection from French naval threats.

Although Germain was eager to recapture Georgia and South Carolina, he informed Clinton in August, 1778, that Sir Henry was responsible for making the final decision to invade the South;[2] Germain, after the Burgoyne fiasco, refused to put himself in the position of once again becoming a scapegoat for the opposition. Clinton, too, was of a cautious mind, already preparing to detach a force to attack the French West Indian island of St. Lucia. Feeling safe enough to undertake a limited Southern offensive, Clinton in November, 1778, embarked 3,500 men under Lieutenant Colonel Archibald Campbell for the coast of Georgia; there they were to join General Augustine Prevost with 2,000 troops from Saint Augustine.

Georgia, youngest and weakest of the thirteen former colonies, loomed as an inviting target. Always aware of Georgia's vulnerability, Continental officials encouraged the state's authorities to recruit Georgia troops in Virginia and the Carolinas. The commander of the American Southern Department, Major General Robert Howe, had difficulties in dealing with sensitive South Carolinians and had fought a bloodless duel with fiery Christopher Gadsden, "the Sam Adams of South Carolina." In Georgia, both Governor John Houstoun and Colonel George Walton, head of the state militia, considered the regular officer as an intruder upon their prerogatives. "It is impossible for me to

give an account of the confused, perplexed way in which I found matters in this state," wrote Howe to South Carolina General William
Moultrie, "nor has it been in my power to get them . . . in a better
train."[3]

The reduction of Georgia began on December 23, when Campbell
landed near Savannah, then occupied by Howe with an inferior body
of Georgia and South Carolina Continentals and irregulars. Without
delaying for Prevost, Campbell easily took the Georgia capital. Soon
after the arrival of the redcoats from Florida, Augusta fell to the British in late January, 1779. In spite of Campbell's claim of taking the
"first stripe and star from the rebel flag of Congress,"[4] the British found
the back country not as easily controlled as the coast. Because of patriot militia raids in the interior, Campbell retired from Augusta, whose
loyalists were left to the mercy of their opponents. In the South, from
the outset, British commanders consistently made two mistakes: they
failed to digest their acquisitions before gulping down more territory,
and they neglected to give the tories adequate protection.

At the moment, however, Prevost measured the abandonment of
Augusta as a temporary loss, as indeed it was. Already he meditated an
invasion of South Carolina and an assault upon Charleston. When
portly Major General Benjamin Lincoln, Howe's successor, advanced
toward Augusta with a contingent of South Carolinians, Prevost coun-
tered by crossing the lower Savannah River and driving toward Charleston. Lincoln, steaming to the rescue, saved the city, and after fierce but
inconclusive fighting at Stono Ferry below the town, Prevost returned
to Savannah. Following a typically oppressive summer in the Carolina-
Georgia low country, it was Prevost who came perilously close to
destruction at the hands of the Comte d'Estaing. The French Admiral
hastened from the West Indies in response to appeals from Southern
patriots who pled that he alone could save Charleston. A naval blow in
September, 1779, the height of the hurricane season, was wholly unexpected by Prevost and the ministers in London, and Clinton had so far
been unable to detach reinforcements to the lower South. Once again
lady luck and poorly executed Franco-American operations combined
to bail the British out, although Prevost's stubborn defense itself was
meritorious. Shoring up their fortifications and slipping in units from
nearby posts, the outnumbered British held off their opponents. Disagreements between the allies, slow progress of siege operations, a
disastrous assault, and the threat of Atlantic storms prompted d'Estaing
to call off operations and set sail for France.[5]

Up to now the Georgia campaign was still a British sideshow, somewhat comparable to operations in Rhode Island. It might have been
worthwhile for Clinton and the ministry to contemplate keeping it that

way. In Prevost's narrow escape from destruction at Savannah, there was further evidence that British naval preponderance would be tenuous at best. Instead, Clinton, with the encouragement of Germain, prepared to disperse his army more widely than ever. Unable to lure Washington into decisive battle as he seized two American posts along the Hudson, Clinton personally turned his energies to the South—after evacuating Rhode Island, receiving modest reinforcements from Europe, and learning of d'Estaing's departure for France.[6] The first great British offensive since 1777 witnessed Sir Henry, with 8,500 troops, sailing southward in December, 1779, accompanied by a fleet under Vice Admiral Marriot Arbuthnot. Landing thirty miles below Charleston on February 11, 1780, the British General slowly pushed northward to besiege the city.

Lincoln, shoring up the capital's defenses, encountered Continental-state friction similar to that experienced by his predecessor Robert Howe. He discovered his forces, "to use General Howe's own words," utterly dependent "on the civil authority," which refused to equip North Carolina Continentals sent by Washington. Already Lincoln knew the South Carolina militia to be a doubtful commodity in orthodox campaigning. As South Carolina's historian David Ramsay conceded in portraying this period of the war, the militia "had not yet learned the implicit obedience necessary for military operations. Accustomed to activity on their farms, they could not bear the languors of an encampment. Having grown up in habits of freedom and independence on their freeholds, they reluctantly submitted to martial discipline. When ordered on command, they would some times enquire 'whither they were going?' and 'how long they must stay?' "[7]

As the shadow of Clinton's army fell across the beleaguered city, the state legislature invested Governor John Rutledge with extraordinary powers. Some historians of the Palmetto state have referred to Rutledge as "the Dictator." But the Dictator's proclamation that all available rural militia repair to the defense of Charleston fell almost wholly on unresponsive ears, some of the back-country irregulars averring that they feared the danger of smallpox if cooped up in an unhealthy city.[8] In truth, this agrarian distrust of urban life was shaped by another consideration: Charleston was doomed, whether reinforcements increased its garrison or not. By late March, Clinton was pounding on its gates with 10,000 troops. Notwithstanding obvious differences, the contest for Charleston bore a striking resemblance to the Manhattan campaign of 1776. Lincoln was under pressure to defend the Southern metropolis as Washington had been to hold New York. Situated at the end of a marshy peninsula between the Ashley and the Cooper rivers, the city was vulnerable to an enemy advance around the peninsula that would seal off all the possible American escape routes to the north. Lincoln faced a cruel dilemma: to evacuate and earn the ire of the hotheaded Carolinians who might consequently throw in the towel, or to remain and risk the loss of his 5,500 men, roughly half of them Continentals, the rest low-country militiamen. By mid-April the choice was no longer his. The ring about Charleston closed, and daily it grew tighter as the British inched forward by digging trenches (both zigzags and parallels) toward the American lines. When in early May Clinton smashed the outer defense works, the fickle civilian authorities now clamored for Lincoln to capitulate. On May 12, the unfortunate General surrendered his entire command, the most severe reversal suffered by an American army during the war.

"Afflicting as the loss of Charleston may be," Thomas Paine consoled his countrymen, "yet if it universally rouse us . . . and renew in us the spirit of former days, it will produce an advantage more important than its loss." But agonizing months were to pass before the patriots could express well-founded optimism over affairs in the South. As the flame of insurrection appeared to die out in South Carolina, British regiments overran the state, garrisoning a chain of posts dominating the interior from Augusta on the Savannah River and Ninety-Six on the Carolina frontier, northward to Rocky Mount and Camden, and eastward to Cheraw and Georgetown on the coast. At Cheraw, Baptist minister Evan Pugh, "much terrified about the English light horse coming," surrendered himself to the conquerors (June 11) and accepted parole (June 12). Plagued by guilt feelings, the former whig contemplated renouncing his parole (June 22), but resigned himself to taking a British oath of allegiance (June 29). Pugh's case was typical. Inhabitants by the hundreds came forth to announce their fealty to the crown, including militia General Andrew Williamson, who handed over Ninety-Six to the King's representatives. Clinton embodied the loyalists and repentant whigs into a royal militia organization under Major Patrick Ferguson, with some units to police the countryside and others to serve with the army[9]

More misfortune was in store for the revolutionists, this time at the hands of Lord Cornwallis, left in charge of the lower South when Clinton and Arbuthnot—concerned over reports of a French fleet headed for New York—departed in June for their Northern stronghold. Cornwallis' new opponent was Horatio Gates, appointed by Congress to replace the captured Lincoln. On July 25, 1780, on Deep River in North Carolina, Gates assumed direction of a small, newly formed Southern army: 1,400 veteran Maryland and Delaware Continentals under the self-styled "Baron" Johann de Kalb, and detachments of regular cavalry and artillery. For the very reason that the Southern army was so woe-

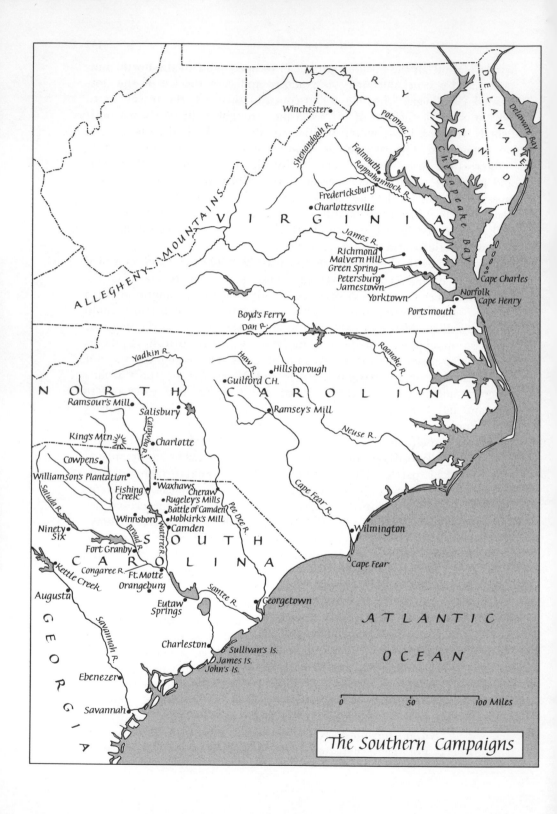

The Southern Campaigns

fully inadequate, faced as it was with the task of defending a region already drained of men and supplies during the American reversals in Georgia and South Carolina, the choice of Gates seemed an excellent one. A talented organizer and administrator, popular with enlisted men, Gates was a builder of armies. Hitherto prudent in the face of adversity, the diminutive Horatio had conserved his resources in the Saratoga campaign and played a waiting game, allowing Burgoyne to act rashly and then taking advantage of the Briton's mistakes. Washington, to no one's surprise, evinced skepticism at Gates' appointment in the South; after the Conway Cabal, the commander in chief was anything but objective about his supposed rival.[10]

Whatever the source of his opposition to Gates, subsequent events were to show that Washington was right, albeit for the wrong reasons. But only because Gates disregarded his customary caution and prudence, displaying such a reversal of military character as to make his conduct almost wholly inexplicable. It had been de Kalb's intention to advance his Continentals westward to pro-whig Mecklenberg and Rowan counties, where provisions were relatively plentiful. Then the German officer contemplated prudent harassing tactics against the enemy posts in upper South Carolina, with Camden—until "lately called Pine Tree Hill"—as his first target. To the amazement of his officers, Gates drastically altered the plan by beginning an immediate march for Camden through desolate, infertile loyalist country, which soon reduced his men to eating green apples, peaches, and half-ripened corn. Later, a member of the expeditionary force, writing in defense of Gates, claimed that the Southern commander was victimized by local leaders, who, frantic for a victory to boost morale, had insisted on a precipitate stroke and minimized every obstacle involved; that one such leader, if not the most insistent one, was General Richard Caswell of the North Carolina militia.[11]

Although up to this point one may possibly sympathize with Gates, whose ranks increased with the addition of Caswell's state units and General Edward Stevens' Virginia militia, his conduct seems indefensible after he stumbled upon a British column under Lord Cornwallis in the early morning of August 16, just north of Camden. It may have been no fault of Gates that he was unaware Cornwallis had wind of the threat to Camden, the main British supply depot in the interior and the point from which His Lordship intended to push into North Carolina; and that Cornwallis had hastened from Charleston with reinforcements for his outpost 150 miles away. But Gates' tactics as the two armies engaged in battle at dawn were absurd. Entrusting his untrained militia with the entire left side of the American line, with the bulk of de Kalb's Continentals on the right and the remainder of the regulars in the rear,

Gates put an incredible faith in irregulars to stand resolutely in open combat. The British right swept forward, yelling and flourishing their bayonets, driving the shaky militia before them. American officers reported it "out of the power of Man to rally them"; "they ran like a torrent and bore all before them." Colonel Otho H. Williams of Maryland recalled that "a great majority of the militia (at least two-thirds of the army) fled without firing a shot." The Continentals fought heroically, more than holding their own until the pressure created by the militia's panic-stricken flight became intolerable. In time they too broke and scattered, with British cavalry in pursuit.[12]

The death of de Kalb, the loss of still another Southern army (barely 700 regulars regrouped at Hillsborough), and the fall from grace of Gates were the results of Camden. Southern congressmen wasted no time before clamoring for the removal of Gates, who had seen his "Northern laurels turn to Southern willows." Upon the motion of South Carolina's John Mathews and North Carolina's Whitmill Hill, Congress voted to strip Gates of the Southern Department and to request Washington to name a successor.[13]

### The Front-behind-the-Front

Although one might visualize the expiration of the Revolution in the lower South from sheer exhaustion if nothing else, there were stirrings in the region both before and after Camden. The paralysis that afflicted South Carolinians following Charleston's fall was short-lived. For this development Clinton's pacification policy was partly responsible. Initially lenient in dealing with the Carolinians, Clinton, on June 3, 1780, abruptly took a hard line, forcing men who had accepted parole and withdrawn from participation in the conflict to swear an oath of allegiance and actively engage in upholding royal government. Compelled to choose between rebellion and collaboration, some shouldered arms for the patriots, others subscribed to the oath under duress and consequently felt no obligation to honor it.[14]

British dreams of a permanent atmosphere of good feelings were also dashed by mounting American resentment against the alleged brutalities of their enemies. Not infrequently loyalists embodied into detachments for policing the interior utilized their exalted status to settle old scores with whig neighbors and to confiscate valuables for their personal use in the King's name. Perhaps if the population of South Carolina had been overwhelmingly of a pro-British disposition, the misdeeds of the zealots would have generated no explosive repercussions; but in South Carolina, as everywhere, the conquerors grossly exag-

gerated the ranks of the well affected. Scholars, too, have inflated the
true strength of the Carolina loyalists, who probably constituted a
majority of the population only in the region between the Broad and
Saluda rivers.[15]

Enemy depredations, real and imagined, gave rise to the legendary
partisan movement in South Carolina and Georgia. It began in the lush
green Waxhaws country, slightly below the North Carolina line, where
British Lieutenant Colonel Banastre Tarleton's Tory Legion virtually
annihilated a column of retreating Virginia Continentals under Colonel
Abraham Buford. The details of the slaughter—at what point did
Buford offer a white flag, and did Tarleton try to restrain the Legion
from senseless killings—are hopelessly confused; but from that day forward "Bloody Tarleton" and "Tarleton's Quarter" were household
epithets in the South. Although the short, thickset, twenty-six-year-old
Tarleton may not have been a butcher, he nonetheless was ruthless by
the standards of warfare in his day, receiving condemnation from
some British officers like Charles Stedman as well as from his adversaries. He levelled houses and razed fields of suspected whigs. His
victims, according to Francis Marion, were often "Women & Children"
found "Sitting in the open Air round a fire without a blanket or any
Cloathing but what they had on. . . ." Sherman's march to the sea
nearly a century later had its counterpart in the raids of Banastre
Tarleton through the Carolinas.[16]

But Tarleton's harsh effectiveness came at a high price, spurring the
trimmers and the faint-hearted to join bolder patriots in the field.
William Hill, most influential citizen of the Waxhaws, unfurled the
standard of rebellion and, accompanied by a small troop of followers,
presented his services to another back-country grandee, Thomas Sumter. "The Gamecock" Sumter, an ex-Continental officer previously living quietly near Statesburgh, was "all sweat and fury" after Tarleton's
Legion burned his plantation house. For the remainder of the British
occupation Sumter held forth with his guerrillas in upper South Carolina, a proud, domineering man who fought on his own terms as though
he were a feudal lord, adhering casually to the instructions or advice
of Continental generals and Governor John Rutledge.[17]

While Sumter bedeviled the enemy to the west, another former regular, Francis Marion, gnawed at British posts and supply lines in the
vast swamps and tangled vegetation of the region between the Pee Dee
and Santee rivers. The forays of the elusive Marion, "the Swamp Fox,"
would later become a fascinating melange of fact and fiction in the
hands of his first biographer, Mason Locke Weems; his study of the
"celebrated partizan officer," written with the aid of Marion's subordinate Peter Horry, pictured Marion as the Robin Hood of the Revolu-

tion. Rounding out the trio of South Carolina's famous partisans was tall, lean Colonel Andrew Pickens of Long Cane Creek, near Ninety-Six. A veteran of colonial Indian wars, Pickens had routed a large contingent of tories at Kettle Creek in 1779; but after the collapse of Charleston and the surrender of Ninety-Six, he took a British loyalty oath, keeping his pledge until marauding tories plundered his plantation. A devout Presbyterian elder, he seldom spoke, and then only after he supposedly put his words "between his fingers and examined them." If Pickens' achievements were not as spectacular as those of Sumter and Marion, he was never a trial to Continental authorities, for he recognized the necessity of coordinating his own operations with the regular forces.

In 1780 and 1781 there were dozens, possibly hundreds, of skirmishes in the interior of the lower South. Probably no record exists of many of these encounters, especially those involving a handful of whigs and tories on each side. Many of our extant accounts are the highly colored reminiscences of patriot participants put to paper long afterward and collected by Lyman C. Draper of the Wisconsin Historical Society. It is safe to assume, in the absence of much sound source material, that the whigs committed their share of atrocities in the civil war of the back country. Colonel Isaac Hayne of South Carolina, striking at a convoy of sick and wounded redcoats bound for Charleston, performed "extraordinary acts of brutality," according to British soldier-historian Roderick MacKenzie. From the American side, an early historian of the Revolutionary period admitted that an irregular officer, Captain Patrick ("Paddy") Carr, never gave tories quarter "as prisoners, or as enemies in battle. . . . He hunted them down like wild beasts, and permitted no asylum to protect them."[18]

In the lower South, with the destruction of two Continental armies and the disappearance of state governments, the Revolution had taken a turn to the left, and guerrilla warfare had replaced orthodox fighting. Cornwallis discovered that the rear areas could no longer be treated in the traditional sense as zones of communication and supply; the front-behind-the-front became a theater of operations in its own right. These factors did not deter His Lordship from undertaking an invasion of back-country North Carolina in the fall of 1780. In fact, he contended that control of the Tar Heel state was essential to bringing about the termination of rebel resistance in South Carolina. Up to a point Cornwallis realistically assessed the war in the South. Gates' defeat and a recent setback to Sumter had scarcely dampened the partisan movement in South Carolina, and increasingly the loyalists were displaying reluctance to shoulder arms. East of the Santee, where disaffection was rampant, Marion roamed at will; and, as Cornwallis told Clinton, "the indefatigable Sumter is again in the Field . . . beating up for Recruits with the greatest Assiduity."[19] But even if the South Carolinians were receiving powerful support from the north, which certainly may have been a dubious assumption immediately after Gates' disastrous defeat, could Cornwallis, by spreading his thin, garrison-ridden army over still another state, meet with success in arousing the tories and subduing the North Carolinians?

Second guessing has its limits. The fact is that Cornwallis, restless and ambitious, had long wanted to invade North Carolina, had earlier believed that the only justification for a Southern campaign was to carry it all the way to Virginia and even to the middle colonies. When the British General had earlier expressed a desire to push northward, Sir Henry Clinton had voiced no objection, provided *"the safety of Charleston and the tranquility of South Carolina"* would not be endangered. More conservative than his subordinate, Sir Henry wished to pacify the region already theoretically under Crown control, then slowly and systematically enlarge the area in British possession. His approach was less dramatic than that of Cornwallis, who prepared to strike immediately into the remote piedmont country of North Carolina; but by solidifying control of captured territory, there was more reason to believe the loyalists would come forth and take an active hand, without having to fear that they soon might be left to fend for themselves. Moreover, Clinton favored a different route for an invasion of North Carolina: an advance to the east by the way of the Cape Fear River, so as to remain in contact with Charleston and to draw upon any available naval support.[20]

Although Gates' skeleton army at Hillsborough scarcely barred the door, Cornwallis still encountered more than he had bargained for. Delayed by malaria and yellow fever raging through his ranks, he then stumbled northward from Camden with his sickly army—finding, as Tarleton put it, that North Carolina's Mecklenburg and Rowan counties "were more hostile to England than any in America." The invaders were in the bailiwick of North Carolina's two most enterprising guerrilla fighters: William R. Davie, a dashing cavalryman, whose severity in dealing with roving loyalists had prompted his adversaries to speak of his horsemen as "the Bloody Corps"; and William Lee Davidson, once a Continental with Washington at Valley Forge, who now spurred his Scotch-Irish neighbors in the Catawba bottomlands to join with Davie in turning their region into a hornet's nest for the enemy. Gaining the village of Charlotte after a hot exchange in the streets with Davie's men, Cornwallis experienced constant harrassment as rebel snipers depleted his outposts and drove off his foraging parties. American irregulars employed in this manner were far more effective than when arrayed in close rank formation against redcoat veterans, as was the case at Camden.[21]

   Cornwallis' left wing, composed of Major Patrick Ferguson's loyalist troops and volunteers, advanced through equally hostile country to the westward along the foot of the Blue Ridge. Hunting down rebel raiders and punishing outspoken whigs, Ferguson aroused the wrath of the Watauga inhabitants in present-day east Tennessee. The "over-mountain men"—Ferguson called them "backwater-men"—swept through the mountain gaps and joined other settlers from North Carolina and Virginia. They were armed with hunting knives and rifles and led by Colonels Isaac Shelby, John Sevier, William Cleveland, and William Campbell. Displaying almost unprecedented cooperation for individualistic frontiersmen, the Americans caught up with their prey on October 7 at King's Mountain, thirty miles west of Charlotte and just inside the South Carolina border. For Ferguson, foolishly beyond effective contact with the British main army and seemingly unconcerned about the retaliatory ability of his enemies until almost the last minute, the end was swift and decisive. The British officer lost his life, over 300 of his men fell dead and wounded, and nearly 700 were captured; the Wataugans and their allies reported 90 casualties. Some of the American fighters were not content with this retribution. At Gilbert Town, North Carolina, a short time later, Colonel William Campbell had to forbid further "slaughtering and disturbing [of] the prisoners." A committee of colonels tried thirty-six of the loyalists on charges of breaking open houses, turning out women and children, and murdering fathers and husbands. All were convicted, nine of them executed. Grim and relentless, the strife in the back country falls outside all our generalizations about both camps in the Revolutionary struggle.[22]

## Greene Retaliates: North Carolina

   While developments at King's Mountain and at Charlotte convinced Cornwallis to withdraw from North Carolina and make winter quarters below Camden, Nathanael Greene took charge of the American Southern Department, its fourth commander in two years. At age thirty-eight, Greene was slightly older and infinitely wiser than the prickly young officer who had previously feuded with Congress over matters of seniority and his two-and-a-half-year performance as quartermaster general. When the lawmakers in 1780—seeking more supplies from the states—abolished the positions of two of his most valuable subordinates and made further reductions in the size of his staff and his funds, Greene indignantly resigned; but he remained in the army. Indeed, Greene in the South was a skillful diplomat in dealing with local politicians and partisan leaders. This was to be an overriding factor in the success of the Rhode Islander, who had never before set foot in the region below the Potomac. An ardent nationalist, he had in the opening shots of the conflict denounced the "prejudices" of those with strong "local attachments." "For my part," he announced, "I feel the cause and not the place. I would as soon go to Virginia as stay here" in New England.[23]

Greene endeavored to gather around him able subordinates with a "knowledge of the southern States and of the customs and manners" of the inhabitants. He had such an officer in Brigadier General Daniel Morgan, the muscular Virginia backwoodsman who had distinguished himself at Quebec and Saratoga, but who had not joined Gates until after the debacle at Camden because of illness. Popular with the frontier people who relished his style of fighting, Morgan, "the famous partisan," figured prominently in Greene's thinking, as did Sumter, Marion, and the other Carolina guerrillas. Greene was at pains to explain to these irregular chieftains that he did not intend to place Continental officers over them, although he did urge, as in the case of Sumter, that they synchronize their own undertakings with his: "You may strike a hundred strokes and reap little benefit from them, unless you have a good Army to take advantage of your success."[24]

Greene turned for advice to another Southerner, Washington, who, under authority granted by Congress, had chosen him to replace Gates. Since the time of his appointment, Greene had corresponded with the commander in chief on the subject of Southern topography. At Washington's recommendation, Greene sent details to inspect the Roanoke, Dan, Yadkin, and Catawba rivers as sources of transportation or a means of retreat. The same parties compiled information on the distances between towns and the condition of the roads in his theater. Greene's careful planning followed a decision he had made as early as November 2, 1780, a month to the day before he rode down the red clay streets of Charlotte to assume the reigns of the Southern army. As he explained to President Samuel Huntington of Congress, partisan-type operations would have to suffice until he could build a respectable force to oppose Cornwallis. His strategy would encourage "the militia," protect "the persons and property of the Inhabitants," and "check and restrain the depredations of the Enemy." Accordingly, Greene in mid-December divided his small command of approximately 1,600, most of them inadequately clothed and poorly equipped. With slightly over half his troops, Greene took post at Cheraw, South Carolina, on the Pee Dee River, there to raise, provision, and outfit an army, and from which point he could aid the guerrilla Marion and observe British movements from Charleston. The cream of his soldiers he entrusted to Daniel Morgan, who tramped southwestward into the South Carolina back country to sit on the enemy's left flank and rear. "It makes the most of my inferior force," said Greene of his decision, "for it compels my adversary to divide his, and holds him in doubt as to his own line of conduct."[25]

Greene had brilliantly hit the nail on the head. "Events alone can decide the future Steps,"[26] wrote Cornwallis to Clinton as the British General, like Greene, now divided his own army—detaching Tarleton's Legion across the Enoree and Tiger rivers to hammer at Morgan's corps, while "the Noble Earl" himself drove up the east bank of the Broad River to catch Morgan should he elude Tarleton. Although Greene's daring strategy had upset Cornwallis' timetable, the Briton was already preparing for a second excursion into North Carolina, not only to rally the loyalists but eventually to advance into Virginia and the Chesapeake area if all went well. Cornwallis' optimism sprang from the approach of reinforcements from Clinton: 2,500 men under Major General Alexander Leslie, who, after halting briefly at Portsmouth, Virginia, and Cape Fear, had proceeded to Charleston and were then marching to join Cornwallis in the interior.

Morgan, separated from Greene's division by 140 miles, hastily fell back toward the North Carolina line upon getting wind of Tarleton's movement. The "old wagoner" recognized that the guerrilla fighter normally avoids the challenge to positional combat. The value of his corps lay in harassment, and approximately half his force now consisted of militia unfamiliar with orthodox warfare. But with the enemy hard on his heels and darkness approaching on the afternoon of January 16, 1781, Morgan had no choice but to make a stand on the west side of the Broad River—at a place called the Cowpens, a popular grazing area of Carolina farmers. Morgan had long wanted a crack at Tarleton; and notwithstanding the disadvantages, he was confident of his ability to combine the particular talents of his militiamen and Continentals. Near the foot of a gently sloping ridge he stationed a body of frontier riflemen, and slightly to their rear he placed the bulk of his militia under Colonel Andrew Pickens, with his Continentals—under Colonel John E. Howard—behind his two advance lines at the crest of the elevation. Morgan's plan called for the riflemen, then the militia, to fire one or two well-aimed volleys and retire to the rear of Howard's troops, where they were to be re-formed as a reserve, along with Lieutenant Colonel William Washington's cavalry.

The battle that began at daylight the next morning revealed how splendidly Morgan had employed the sharpshooting abilities of the backwoods irregulars without compelling them to stand for long in regular combat. When Tarleton upon arrival foolishly ordered his legionnaires—exhausted by an all-night pursuit—to attack immediately, the American forward parties tore gaping holes in the British ranks before filing off as scheduled. Minutes later, after the green-jacketed Legion surged forward again and traded blasts with Howard's veterans, the Continentals slowly drew back, mistakenly believing the retrograde move had been ordered by Howard. To Tarleton's overly zealous troops, the prospect of another Camden loomed in sight, and they broke ranks and lunged pell mell after the foe. Morgan, sensing a climactic opportunity, ordered Howard's line to face about and deliver a sudden volley. Simultaneously, Morgan sent Washington's dragoons crashing down upon the unsuspecting British right, and he hurled Pickens' reorganized militia against the enemy left. The Legion was thrown into a "panic," admitted Tarleton, who fled with a handful of followers. As Morgan exclaimed to a friend, he had given Tarleton "a devil of a whipping, a more compleat victory never was obtained." Tarleton lost 110 killed and 702 captured as against Morgan's 12 killed and 60 wounded.[27]

From the moment they first learned of Cowpens, both Cornwallis and Greene played their strategy by ear. Cornwallis, having halted briefly at Turkey Creek (twenty-five miles from Cowpens) to allow Leslie to catch up, now set out after Morgan, who retreated as rapidly as possible into North Carolina. Cornwallis therefore had chosen not to stop and re-evaluate his North Carolina strategy as he had done earlier following King's Mountain and his difficulties at Charlotte. To be sure, he had the added muscle of Leslie's regiments; but he had lost, besides Ferguson's detachment, the most valuable unit of his army: Tarleton's Legion, fast and far-ranging, invaluable in scouting, guarding the flanks, and beating back the partisans, precisely the kind of force Britain was always lacking in sufficient numbers throughout the war, especially useful in the Southern terrain. The late Eric Robson, a perceptive English historian of the war, considered the destruction of the Legion "almost equivalent" to the loss of an entire army. Moreover, the insurrection in South Carolina had not diminished. Only a month before Cowpens, Cornwallis stated that, bad as the situation was on the remote frontier, home of the King's Mountain fighters, it appeared "much worse" beyond the Santee, an opinion echoed by Lord Rawdon. By this time, too, Cornwallis had come to doubt that his presence in North Carolina would necessarily bring a wholesale uprising of alleged loyalists. In short, he implicitly questioned the whole premise concerning Southern loyalism that had been behind the campaign, the view so optimistically expressed by Germain and others in London.[28]

There was, withal, a case for Cornwallis' return to North Carolina in pursuit of Morgan. His subordinate, General Charles O'Hara, stated it well: British prestige in the South, already severely diminished, would have evaporated had Cornwallis not followed up the Cowpens' debacle with some bold stroke, "however desperate."[29] And if he had overtaken and destroyed Morgan's corps and Greene's own division, which soon united with Morgan's, then the British General would have truly been hailed as "the Hannibal" of the South, a term already applied to him in derision.

Reaching Ramsour's Mill on January 25, and finding Morgan still beyond his reach, Cornwallis destroyed most of his heavy equipment and his food and baggage wagons, turning his entire army into a mobile striking force. It was a radically unorthodox decision to cast aside an army's supplies for a winter's campaign, as Sergeant Robert Lamb, Lieutenant Colonel Charles Stedman, and General O'Hara attested.[30] For European armies of the eighteenth century were prone to travel with formidable wagon trains designed to make them self-sufficient. Whatever his outward appearance—tall and handsome according to Gainsborough (who discreetly ignored the cast in one eye, the result of a youthful hockey game), or stout and ungainly with a dull countenance according to others—the forty-two-year-old Cornwallis was not hidebound by convention, and in that he differed from his fellow British generals, who seldom improvised although usually fettered by their cumbersome equipment and elaborate supply system. Having spared only his salt, ammunition, medical stores, and four ambulances, he pushed on after Morgan, his redcoats without tents to cover them and no more food than they could carry in their haversacks. Cornwallis, however, took too long at the task of shedding his impediments, so that the heavy rains he subsequently encountered made the North Carolina rivers in his path temporarily impassable. Morgan, already over the Catawba, put still another river, the Yadkin, behind him and on February 9 reached Guilford Courthouse, where he united with Greene's command.

Greene, having personally raced across country to join Morgan on the Catawba, had instructed General Isaac Huger to follow with his own wing of the Southern army at Cheraw. After combining his forces, Greene's principal concern was to save the small, ill-equipped Southern army from destruction. With Cornwallis nipping at his heels, Greene —thanks to his own foresight in having boats assembled on the Dan River for just such an eventuality—crossed over that turbulent stream and found relative safety in Virginia. So far, Cornwallis had nothing to show for his second invasion of North Carolina. Several hundred miles from his main base in South Carolina, he had lost 250 men by sickness and desertion, together with the invaluable stores and equipment voluntarily destroyed at Ramsour's Mill. He had no boats with which to get at Greene, whose army was still intact and preparing to return to North Carolina, if only the Rhode Islander could obtain additional manpower from the Southern states.

Ever short of Continentals, though his Delaware and Maryland regulars were among the best in the service, Greene, as he had done before in the South (and as he would do later), was compelled to rely heavily on militia. Greene, committed to a war of maneuver, has with some justification been called a guerrilla fighter in the Carolinas, but this did not mean he delighted in the employment of militia.[31] Ideally, Greene would have preferred 5,000 Continental infantry and 1,000 cavalry to drive the enemy from the Southland. Even for mobile operations such as reconnaissance and harassing the flanks, Greene favored, when they were sufficiently numerous, his own light infantry detachment formed under Colonel Otho H. Williams and his cavalry units under Colonels William Washington and Henry "Light Horse Harry" Lee. To Greene's way of thinking, the militia were wasteful; they consumed great quantities of supplies because they invariably appeared with inadequate clothing and equipment. Usually called out for short periods, sometimes only six weeks, they seemed to come and go with reckless abandon. He admitted to the exceptions: Pickens' South Carolinians had retired with the army into North Carolina and had performed invaluably as scouts and guerrilla fighters; militia Generals John Lawson and Edward Stevens were excellent officers; and he found much to admire in the small body of King's Mountain riflemen temporarily in his service. All the same, he believed that militia did not perform well with the regular army: they were at their best in small, detached bodies, for they "constantly lose their Comparative force as their numbers are Augmented."[32]

Still, it was necessary for a wholesale turnout of the militia if Greene was to challenge Cornwallis for supremacy in North Carolina, His Lordship having established himself at Hillsborough to refit and to assemble the Tar Heel loyalists. After dispatching harassing parties to the vicinity of the enemy, Greene led his army back into North Carolina, playing a game of cat and mouse with Cornwallis, attempting "by finesse"—as he told Jefferson—what "I dare not attempt by force."[33] Finally, appeals to state leaders brought results as the long-awaited militia arrived: over 1,600 Virginians and approximately 1,000 North Carolinians.

Greene, a highly flexible officer, discarded the role of guerrilla or partisan and took up positions at Guilford Courthouse, admirably suited for a formal eighteenth-century battle. Cornwallis, encamped only twelve miles away, accepted the challenge, assuming the superiority of his 2,000 veterans over Greene's combination of Continentals and militiamen, numbering 4,200. Greene's plan followed closely Morgan's formations at Cowpens: astride the Salisbury road that crested on an elevation near the courthouse were Greene's Continentals, who constituted the main line, with two lines of militia in their front. But Greene's forces were too widely separated—nearly 400 yards com-

pared to the 150-yard intervals between Morgan's men at Cowpens—to
allow the militia to fall back in orderly fashion when pressed. After the
North Carolinians in the most advanced position fired only one round
before fleeing from the field, the second line of Virginians thinned the
oncoming redcoats with a withering fire, then retired, hastily on the
American right but slowly and stubbornly on the left. Greene's regulars
under Huger and Williams took a heavy toll of the enemy, although a
newly recruited Maryland regiment collapsed, prompting the American center to turn somewhat to its left to cover the exposed flank, which
it did most effectively. Throughout the three-hour battle Greene declined to take risks, preferring to hold his ground rather than chance
counterassaults, and in his caution he may have passed up opportunities for a decisive stroke, as when he failed to call for a general advance after the 1st Maryland Regiment's bayonet charge had broken the
segment of the British line under Lieutenant Colonel James Webster.
As it was, when Greene halted the action and withdrew, he knew that
Cornwallis was severely battered by the affray. The Briton suffered the
loss of a fourth of his effective command: 93 killed, 413 wounded, and
26 missing as against Greene's 78 dead and 183 wounded.[34]

If ever a general won a Pyrrhic victory, it was Lord Cornwallis,
whose army virtually ceased to exist as a fighting force. Whatever his
alternatives, His Lordship's own decisions had shaped the results of
the duel with Greene's Southern army that had begun before Cowpens.
Abandoning his sustenance at Ramsour's Mill, subjecting his troops to a
chase of several hundred miles, and engaging in major combat without
the prospect of replacing his losses, all this he did in an unfamiliar
country in the midst of winter. Or to sharpen the point, he had put a
European military machine through stresses and strains collectively
too much for it to bear. The night following the battle of March 15 rain
fell on British regiments without tents, without surgical equipment,
and without food. Unable to remain in central North Carolina, Cornwallis limped eastward, hopeful of re-establishing contact with the sea
in order to acquire supplies and reinforcements. Halting temporarily at
Wilmington, the British General, as we will see in a later examination
of the Yorktown story, then set out to join General William Phillips'
diversionary force in Virginia and to enlarge the theater of operations
in the Chesapeake area. From Wilmington, General O'Hara penned a
fitting epilogue to the North Carolina campaign, which had not "produced one substantial benefit to Great Britain"; a campaign that had
"completely worn out" the King's soldiers, who in appalling numbers
were "barefoot" and "naked," sometimes either totally without provisions or at best reduced to eating uncooked carrion and "three or four
ounces of unground Indian Corn." In short, a campaign that had
"totally destroy'd this Army."[35]

Would a different British commander have achieved more? Perhaps so if he had attempted less than His Lordship did. A man on the order of the cautious, methodical Sir William Howe, no reckless gambler or exponent of derring-do, might have better carried out Clinton's strategy of solidifying existing gains and pacification before seeking new conquests. (And would the bold, aggressive Cornwallis have outdone Sir William in trying to hunt down and destroy Washington in the North?) Pacification failed in South Carolina where it was never thoroughly tested, and it was never even attempted in North Carolina owing to Cornwallis' very brief forays into that state in 1780 and 1781. But did all of this really matter so far as loyalism was concerned, given the apparently sound opinion of historians today that the nucleus of Crown support in the South was vastly overestimated from the beginning? It just conceivably could have counted had the genuine loyalists been sufficiently induced to make their presence felt, and had they sought to win over their fellow Americans with a spirit of forgiveness for past sins, rather than displaying a mood of vengeance against the whigs for earlier transgressions.[36] One thing is clear: naked force alone could not accomplish the job. The British army, an eighteenth-century fighting machine, was no more qualified for the role of meaningful pacification than this same army had been capable of policing the frontier in the 1760's. In this respect times have not necessarily changed. The mid-twentieth century has witnessed the repeated frustrations of foreign armies attempting to perform similar tasks in the so-called backward areas of the world, even though military forces of our day have lavished time and effort upon social and economic programs designed to win over the inhabitants of the countryside.

## Greene Retaliates: South Carolina

While confronting the British in North Carolina, Greene had kept in mind the possibility of returning to South Carolina, a step he took after trailing Cornwallis a short distance in the direction of Wilmington. His departure would "oblige the Enemy to follow us or give up their posts" in South Carolina, he confided to General Steuben.[37] At first glance Greene may have appeared overly optimistic: his Virginia and North Carolina militia had left him—they had returned home to kiss their wives and sweethearts, as he phrased it; and the rigors of the campaign had reduced his Continentals to a meager 1,500, as compared to the 8,000 British and loyalist troops under arms in the lower South. But the Crown's forces were thinly dispersed, holding important bases at Georgetown, Charleston, Camden, Ninety-Six, and Savannah; and occupying a string of lesser posts—Forts Watson, Motte, and Granby—on

the Santee and its tributaries, along with Orangeburg on a fork of the
Edisto and Augusta on the Savannah.

True to form, Greene was the careful planner who made the most of
his modest resources. During his absence from South Carolina he had
kept open his communications with the partisan leaders, whom he now
prepared to employ in a war of posts. He urged Sumter to isolate Camden from the west, Pickens to stab at Augusta, and Marion—with the
support of Henry Lee's Legion—to disrupt the enemy's communications
connecting Charleston with Camden and Ninety-Six.

At Camden there were 1,500 British troops, the only real striking
force at the disposal of Lord Rawdon, who had assumed command in
the Palmetto state upon Cornwallis' advance northward. To contain his
opponent while the partisans were striking elsewhere, Greene offered to
do battle with Rawdon, drawing up his Americans at Hobkirk's Hill,
two miles north of Camden. The numerical advantage was in Greene's
favor since Rawdon had detached 500 men to cope with Marion and
Lee. The youthful Rawdon, age twenty-six, was no novice, a veteran
of numerous engagements since Bunker Hill. Seizing the initiative on
April 25, he attacked the Americans; but Greene was ready, and as was
characteristic of most of his contests in the South, the Rhode Islander's
chances of winning seemed promising initially. After the American
artillery decimated the British forward units which were advancing
compactly on a narrow front, Greene sent Colonel John Gunby's Maryland Continentals and Colonel Samuel Hawes' Virginia regulars surging forward with fixed bayonets while other regiments flared out to the
left and right to close in on the enemy flanks. This time it was not the
militia but Gunby's Marylanders who denied Greene his triumph.
When three of his companies became disorganized, Gunby withdrew
his entire regiment to re-form, creating a gap in the line that led the
1st Virginia and the 2d Maryland to falter. The initiative now passed
to Rawdon, who drove his confused adversaries back. Greene, the daring strategist but cautious tactician, ordered a general retreat, which
was achieved in something less than good order.

Even so, persistence was Greene's middle name. "This repulse, if
repulse it may be called, will make no alteration in our general plan of
operations," he reassured Steuben. And to French minister La Luzerne,
he stoutly declared, "We fight, get beat, rise, and fight again. . . ."[38]
Having suffered approximately the same number of casualties as Rawdon, the American General saw no reason not to maintain the pressure.
Already his plans were reaping rewards. The combined corps of Lee
and Marion picked off Fort Watson, chiefly by erecting a forty-foot log
tower that enabled them to enfilade the stockaded work, thus making it
untenable to its occupants who laid down their arms. Greene next sent

Lee and Marion across the Santee to invest Fort Motte, a fortified brick-and-stone mansion, which capitulated when the besiegers set the shingled roof on fire with flaming arrows. With Camden virtually cut off and the interior of South Carolina in open revolt, Rawdon abandoned his advance base and fell back toward Charleston. Meanwhile, Sumter overran Orangeburg, and Andrew Pickens and Colonel Elijah Clarke of Georgia surrounded Augusta. As Greene himself headed for Ninety-Six, Marion scouted Rawdon's flanks to see that the Englishman did not turn upon Greene's rear, and afterward Marion led his swamp fighters in driving the enemy out of Georgetown. The aggressive Lee dashed thirty miles up the Congaree and captured Fort Granby; then, in response to Greene's order, he joined Pickens and Clarke before Augusta which capitulated to them on June 4.

Greene was not so fortunate as his subordinates. The star-shaped fort at Ninety-Six held out against the Americans, who resorted to such tactics as the wooden tower and the flaming arrows that had led to the downfall of British posts elsewhere. When Rawdon, after receiving reinforcements by sea, hurried to the rescue of his beleaguered garrison, Greene abandoned the siege. If his tactics again failed, his strategy once more succeeded; for Rawdon, unable to hold indefinitely such a remote base, soon withdrew his entire force to the low country.

In a whirlwind campaign, from April to July, Greene and his South Carolina allies had cleared the enemy from virtually all of the lower South except for a narrow belt between Charleston and Savannah. Captain Robert Kirkwood of Delaware calculated that the Southern army had marched 771 miles since Greene had parted company with Cornwallis and returned to South Carolina. The cliché to the contrary, this army had scarcely traveled on its stomach, being continually short of rations, which were predominantly rice and almost never meat, according to Henry Lee.[39] With his tattered legions bordering on exhaustion and suffering from malnutrition, Greene established a camp in the High Hills of the Santee, there to rest and reorganize. The next five weeks were put to good use training new recruits and searching for supplies, so that in late August he was again ready to draw his sword: against Lieutenant Colonel Alexander Stewart, Rawdon's successor, who had ventured out from Charleston to revive Britain's sagging prestige.

Eutaw Springs, where the armies met on September 8, was another of Greene's indecisive battles in which he left the field to his opponent after victory had barely eluded his grasp. With his militia composing the bulk of the front line and his regulars anchoring the rear, Greene hurled back the enemy; but a stone house similar to that at Germantown provided its British defenders a means of halting the Southern

commander while Stewart re-formed his battered regiments. Evidently
Greene believed this factor alone saved Stewart, although many of the
Americans took out time to loot the enemy camp and to gorge themselves on British rum. In any case, upon Stewart's return to action,
Greene called a halt to the four-hour encounter, which had nonetheless
been rewarding: he bagged 400 prisoners and inflicted upwards of
500 casualties upon Stewart, even if his own losses—nearly 500—were
not inconsiderable, as Philip Freneau lamented:

> At Eutaw Springs the valiant died;
> Their limbs with dirt are covered o'er—
> Weep on, ye springs, your tearful tide;
> How many heroes are no more!

Fighting on a large scale came to an end in the lower South after
Eutaw Springs, although Greene and his army stood guard until the
British evacuated Savannah and Charleston in 1782.

In his Southern campaign Greene showed signs of true greatness, and
not merely because he triumphed: a general may win a battle or a
campaign without being primarily responsible for its outcome.
Greene's laurels rest upon the "how's" and "why's" of his achievement.
The "how's" are easy to enumerate. He won with an army poorly provisioned, shabbily clad, and thin in numbers, reinforced by fiercely independent partisan bands and undisciplined militia. The "why's" are more
elusive. The most obvious ones—the failure of the loyalists to turn out
as expected and the errors of Cornwallis—were important determi-
nants, but it remained for Greene to capitalize on them with the means
at hand. His native intelligence, his selection of subordinates, and his
finesse in dealing with partisans and politicians were of a high order.
Tactically, he suffered from his own mistakes and bad luck, although
every battle that he lost hurt the enemy more than it did him. We have
noted that the essential quality of a great captain is what most perceptive students and practitioners of warfare have called "character." That
elusive quality, defying easy delineation, involves moral courage, plain
nerve, relentless determination, combined with (or producing?) the
ability to dominate any situation, to obtain a psychological initiative
over one's adversary. In varying degrees Greene revealed these com-
ponents when he divided his army at Charlotte and made Cornwallis
divided his own command; when he fell back into North Carolina and
drew the British General on a fruitless, debilitating chase; when he returned to South Carolina leaving His Lordship weak and dispirited
near Wilmington; when, one by one, he plucked Rawdon's bases in the
Palmetto state; and when he chose the time and place of every major
battle—Guilford Courthouse, Hobkirk's Hill, and Eutaw Springs—
which cut deeply into British manpower.

In short, Greene made up his own game and compelled Cornwallis and Rawdon to play it largely by his rules. It was predominantly a game of rapid movement highlighted by constant pressure applied to the enemy to keep him off balance. It involved an assortment of methods: hit-and-run raids, assaults on supply lines, sieges, and fixed battles. Greene was always bold but never rash, always flexible, always willing to give up the battlefield in order to return for a better day. "There are few generals," he remarked puckishly, who have "run oftener, or more lustily than I have done. But I have taken care not to run too far, and commonly have run as fast forward as backward, to convince our Enemy that we were like a Crab, that could run either way."[40] To the British, Greene and his partisan allies were a swarm of hornets. Drive them away and back they came, again and again, to sting in a new and often unexpected place. A single sting inflicted a minor wound to the British lion; but when the hornets were through the lion was all but dead.

There is another, lesser known, side of Greene's service in the South. He, with the possible exception of Washington, had a better opportunity than any other American general of the Revolution to make solid contributions in the area of civil government and domestic tranquility. For the lower South was ravaged by the war as no other section of the country. Its governmental processes had collapsed, and its society had disintegrated to the point that it approached John Locke's savage state of nature. Greene repeatedly expressed alarm over these developments, which he felt could do lasting harm to the future of the country and its republican institutions. He started the wheels rolling for the restoration of state government in South Carolina, gave sought-after advice, and helped prepare for the convening of the first assembly in many months. Though the record is lean, Greene on his own authority appears to have appointed an acting governor for the state of Georgia. Ordinarily his action would have been greeted as a dangerous infringement of the military in the civil sphere, but in Georgia whig political authority in every form had literally disappeared.[41] Greene recognized that the Revolution had been inspired partly by a concern for property rights, and he vigorously opposed pillaging and plundering of either friend or foe. For that matter, Greene did his best to stop mistreatment of the loyalists and believed that with encouragement many could be won over to an acceptance of patriot rule. The ex-Quaker from Rhode Island was a genuine humanitarian who hated all forms of human suffering, who on at least one occasion assigned the South Carolina partisans the task of collecting and distributing food to the destitute. All things considered, he could hardly have accomplished more. His principal regret was not to have been in on the capture of Cornwallis. He had earlier predicted that if he were free to head north, he could with the support of a French naval squadron seal off His Lordship on the Virginia peninsula. It was Washington, however, rather than Greene who united with French Admiral de Grasse to fulfill that prophecy.

### *Yorktown*

Cornwallis' decision to abandon the Carolinas, besides conflicting with Clinton's instructions to hold South Carolina at all cost, upended the strategy behind the Southern campaign: to rally and organize the loyalists as a means of holding areas overrun by the British army. In fact, for three months in 1781—from January to April—Clinton was largely in the dark as to the operations of Cornwallis, who finally wrote his superior from Wilmington, announcing his intention of marching to Virginia and urging Clinton to make that rebellious province the strategic focus, "the Seat of war"—even if necessary at the expense of abandoning New York.[42] It was true, of course, that there were already British forces in Virginia, but not for the reason that Cornwallis believed, or pretended to believe. It was never Clinton's purpose to make the Old Dominion a major center of offensive operations, at least not as long as the Carolinas remained outside firm British control. He had favored a base on the coast of Virginia for secondary reasons: to take some of the pressure off Cornwallis in the lower South and to provide a haven for loyalists in the area. To this end, Clinton sent a detachment under the turncoat Benedict Arnold to Virginia in December, 1780. Later, when a French naval squadron at Newport, Rhode Island, endeavored to sail southward and nip off Arnold on the Virginia peninsula, Clinton, after thwarting the French with British vessels from New York, reinforced his Virginia command and placed it under General William Phillips.

Clinton recognized that a force in the Chesapeake area was vulnerable to French naval power, as the attempt of the Bourbon squadron to capture Arnold had demonstrated. The region was fever-ridden as well, scarcely a fit location for summer campaigning. These considerations, if Cornwallis weighed them, brought no change in his determination to invade the Old Dominion, the possession of which—he maintained—was now crucial to subduing the Carolinas. By this time, writes William B. Willcox, Cornwallis was "a man driven beyond the limits of clear thinking."[43]

Clinton, all the same, was not blameless. He found it painful to communicate candidly with Cornwallis, to give him explicit orders and to elucidate his own intentions. The endemic friction in the British councils of war consumed these two generals as it had others. Willful and ambitious, Lord Charles had sought to advance his own cause over that of Clinton with the court and the politicians in London. Clinton knew this, just as he was aware that Germain, who continued to voice senseless optimism on prospects for victory in the South, had lost confidence in him. For any commander in chief, faced with such a lack of support in the ministry and in the army, the effect would have been disheartening to say the least. For the morbidly sensitive Clinton the result was lethal. He refused to deal forcefully with his principal subordinate, whose star seemed to be on the rise at Whitehall, and who might replace him at any moment. Germain, however, stopped short of calling for Clinton's removal before the supreme commander in America made an overt blunder. The ministry intended to avoid any controversial action that might shatter its delicate unanimity and its increasingly fragile majority in Parliament. Clinton, in turn, would do little or nothing that might play into Germain's hands, a resolution that came all the easier for a man who seemed to shun responsibility as commander in chief when the chips were down.[44] Consequently, Cornwallis went his own way, leaving Clinton to fuss and fume in New York. Clinton's relationship was as bad or worse with that aging incompetent, Vice Admiral Marriot Arbuthnot, who had commanded the naval contingent in American waters since 1779. At odds with his counterpart in the navy, overridden by his number two officer in the army, and denied the confidence of the chief war minister in London, Clinton was wholly ineffective, though he continued to hold the supreme command.

Meanwhile, Cornwallis arrived at Petersburg, Virginia, on May 20 and took command of the forces of Arnold and Phillips. Cornwallis' presence, with a combined army of 7,200 (including two newly arrived regiments by sea), terrified Virginia authorities, who had already witnessed the destruction of part of Richmond and the burning of invaluable military stores at the hands of the enemy. The rise of nationalist sentiment in Congress in 1781 had its equivalent in Virginia as that commonwealth lay under the threat of full-scale invasion. A group of citizens, in a petition to the general assembly, rejected the prevailing whig doctrine that the militia constituted "the cheapest and surest Defense, on whose protection we are ultimately to depend"; and proposed instead the division of the entire country into districts with specified military quotas for the Continental army. According to the editor of the *Papers of Thomas Jefferson*, "it is perhaps the earliest suggestion that, at least in respect to military organization, the government of the United States should operate directly on individuals rather than through the states." In the midst of the crisis, Richard Henry Lee, traditionally pictured as an opponent of centralized power at the expense of the states, urged James Lovell (of all people!) to favor Washington's returning to the Old Dominion to assume dictatorial authority.[45]

Much blame for the state's predicament was laid on the shoulders of

Governor Thomas Jefferson, whose ultimate humiliation came when a British raiding party routed the Virginia assembly from Charlottesville and almost captured the Governor himself, who—according to his later critics—fled with his "coattails flying in the wind." But the widely-held opinion that Jefferson's legalistic theories and philosophical temperament crippled his effectiveness is not supported by the evidence, which shows that the constitutional limitations upon executive action, the inadequate machinery of government, and the magnitude of the crisis all combined to hamper the state's response to the British challenge. A victim of circumstances, Jefferson actually interpreted his prerogative broadly on several occasions and contributed appreciably to collecting men and supplies for the American forces in the state commanded by Lafayette and Steuben. Moreover, contrary to the canons of whiggery, he later defended the legislature's choice of his successor, General Thomas Nelson of the militia, explaining that by combining the military and civil authority the executive could work with "more energy, promptitude and effect for the defence of the state. . . ."[46] Already, however, Jefferson's exertions were bearing fruit. Supplies and militiamen were arriving from western Virginia, where Daniel Morgan, who had temporarily retired because of ill health, had worked feverishly to bolster the troops under Lafayette. The Frenchman also received from the north a 1,000-man contingent of Pennsylvania Continentals under General Anthony Wayne. As Cornwallis fell back through Richmond and down the peninsula, he was closely followed by Lafayette. On July 6, at Green Spring near Jamestown, the Americans and British fought a fierce but indecisive skirmish, after which Cornwallis established a base at Yorktown and began erecting fortifications.[47]

While Cornwallis frittered away two months inconclusively campaigning in the Old Dominion, Clinton continued what was to be a long and laborious correspondence with His Lordship over the question of future operations—with particular reference to the troops under Cornwallis' command and to Clinton's desire to shift the focus from Virginia. There were fundamental differences between the two generals. Clinton still was hopeful of making considerable use of the loyalists. Favoring a scheme advanced by loyalist Colonel William Rankin of Pennsylvania, Clinton proposed an undertaking to arouse the King's friends in Maryland, Delaware, and southeastern Pennsylvania; but Cornwallis, embittered by his experiences with the tories in the Carolinas, would not buy it, and continued to press for a build-up in Virginia. This much at least may be said for Cornwallis: he had come to recognize, tardily to be sure, that an outpost on the Chesapeake "is for ever liable to become a prey to a foreign Enemy, with a temporary superiority at Sea." Consequently, he wished to abandon Virginia entirely if Clinton refused to make it the center of British military operations in America. Clinton had good reason not to adopt the Virginia strategy. He could scarcely stretch his thin resources effectively from New York to embrace Cornwallis' ambitions. On the other hand, he might have weighed more seriously the alternative of a complete abandonment of the Chesapeake; but the Rankin plan for calling out the loyalists remained in the back of his mind as a possibility for later in the year. It "was a fundamental reason why Cornwallis' entire army was not withdrawn from Virginia during the summer," declares Paul Smith. Throughout the summer, however, Clinton assaulted Cornwallis with requests that part of the Virginia command be transported to New York or employed in operations elsewhere. But since the matter was left to Cornwallis' discretion, and since he maintained he needed all his regiments to hold his defensive positions on the peninsula, his 7,200 men remained in and about Yorktown, idling away weeks and months, an inviting target for the Franco-American allies.[48]

If, before the Yorktown campaign, French aid had probably been vital to sustaining the patriots in the field, the military alliance with the Bourbon monarchy had produced no direct benefits, only a train of failures when Count d'Estaing operated in American waters in 1778 and 1779. The latter year was generally a bad one for France and *her* new ally, Spain, notably marred by the ill fortune of "the other armada" against England. The demise of the invasion, however, created an opportunity for French involvement elsewhere; and the Paris ministry, encouraged by Lafayette, dispatched its first land forces to America in the late spring of 1780: 5,500 troops commanded by the Comte de Rochambeau, under convoy of the Chevalier de Ternay's dozen naval vessels. Belatedly, as usual, a British naval reinforcement of six ships-of-the-line headed by Rear Admiral Thomas Graves set out in pursuit, hoping to unite with Vice Admiral Arbuthnot at New York in time to cope with de Ternay. Though the French Admiral arrived safely at Rhode Island, where Rochambeau made his permanent headquarters, the British still had a splendid opportunity to overwhelm the Bourbon forces. British naval preponderance was actually increased for a short time when crusty old Admiral Sir George Rodney put in at New York with part of his West Indian squadron. But the strife between Arbuthnot and Clinton led to a disagreement over planning a *coup de main*, and the matter was dropped, with Rodney subsequently returning to his Caribbean station.

Even so, de Ternay's fleet was bottled up in Newport for the remainder of 1780 and well into the following year; nor was Washington during the same period able to capitalize on the presence of Rochambeau's warriors, whom the King of France had put under his jurisdiction. For months Washington had contemplated an attack on New York City, a scheme Rochambeau had viewed with scant enthusiasm, although the two leaders agreed that any such endeavor should await French naval superiority.[49]

The realization of Washington's ambitions was soon to be in prospect as reports arrived in May, 1781, that Admiral François Joseph Paul, the Comte de Grasse, had sailed from Brest for the West Indies with twenty ships-of-the-line. In conference at Wethersfield, Connecticut, the Virginian was unable to determine from Rochambeau whether de Grasse would consent to joint operations with the Franco-American armies on the continent of North America. At the time plans were broadly outlined for Rochambeau's regiments to join Washington's army for a thrust at New York, which, if less than completely successful, might nonetheless compel Clinton to draw troops away from Cornwallis and consequently ease the pressure on Lafayette in Virginia. But Washington consented to terminate his efforts against New York when word arrived that de Grasse was sailing for the Chesapeake with 3,000 troops from the French garrison at Santo Domingo. On August 17, the American General and Rochambeau wrote the Admiral of their intention to march southward to join him in trapping Cornwallis.[50]

Timing and coordination were of the essence: orders went out to Lafayette to hold Cornwallis on the Virginia peninsula, supplies were assembled, a small force was left to hold the lines before New York, and the building of bake ovens and other measures were undertaken to keep Clinton and Cornwallis from determining the new plan of the allies. On August 21, Washington set in motion 7,000 men, over half of them French, overland toward Virginia, while almost simultaneously the Comte de Barras, now commanding the French Newport squadron, eluded the enemy and crowded sail for the Chesapeake, bringing along Rochambeau's heavy artillery. True to his word, de Grasse reached the Virginia capes on August 26, and after landing his French troops, he hastened up the bay transports which loaded the waiting regiments of Washington and Rochambeau and brought them to the James River on September 18.

The cooperation between Washington, Rochambeau, de Grasse, de Barras, Lafayette, and the Virginia authorities in a difficult and complex undertaking was virtually unparalleled in the history of eighteenth-century warfare. The allies' strategy was based upon certain calculated risks such as the ability of de Barras to escape from Newport, the unwillingness of Clinton to strike at the greatly reduced American forces outside New York, and the hazards of de Grasse's leaving the French West Indies unprotected. The British in contrast failed to pull together and refused to respond boldly to the threat. In London, Germain and the Admiralty had made no effort to prevent de Grasse's sailing from France in March, and not until June did they send out a feeble naval reinforcement of three vessels. Consequently, de Grasse had numerical superiority in the Caribbean over Rodney, whose responsibilities included protecting British North America from the very kind of danger that now was so imminent. Germain's complacency was matched initially even by Clinton, notwithstanding his long awareness of the significance of seapower in dispersing his army from South Carolina to New York, and also by Rear Admiral Thomas Graves, temporary successor to Arbuthnot at New York. Surprisingly, in view of his aggressive behavior throughout the Southern campaign, Cornwallis, too, reacted to the deepening crisis as if he were in something of a stupor, declining to attempt to drive his way past Lafayette and escape by land before the Franco-American regiments from the north were able to establish positions and begin siege operations.

As a result, Cornwallis' only chance of escape rested with the royal navy squadron of Sir George Rodney. The stouthearted veteran, a splendid officer and every inch a fighter, did not rise to the occasion. In ill health and preparing to return to England, he had wind of de Grasse's forthcoming departure for American waters but erroneously assumed that the French admiral would not take his entire fleet of twenty-eight vessels with him, and would instead leave behind a naval complement to protect the Bourbon West Indian possessions. Rodney himself had but twenty-three serviceable ships-of-the-line, of which he withheld nine—for convoy duty and other assignments—from Rear Admiral Sir Samuel Hood, whom he assigned fourteen vessels with orders to proceed northward.[51]

In the past lethargy, miscalculations, and interservice backbiting had snarled British operations, but now as much as anything the problem may have been in large part psychological: the inability in light of d'Estaing's failures in 1778 and 1779 to see the French naval menace as more than the yearly menace that invariably ended to Britain's advantage, that saw lady luck again and again bestow her smiles on Britannia. Disaster at the hands of the Bourbons was all but incomprehensible to the British mind of the eighteenth century. That state of mind was rudely shattered after Hood reached New York, gave his command over to Graves, and the two officers with a total of nineteen vessels hurried toward the Chesapeake in the hope of intercepting de Barras before he reinforced de Grasse. The British fleet was inferior in numbers to the French, and its ranking admiral was not the equal of the fiery-tempered de Grasse, who, according to his sailors, stood six feet two on ordinary days and six feet six on battle days. The Frenchman had the better of it in several days of skirmishing and maneuvering off the

Chesapeake, and on September 13, Graves headed back to New York. By then de Barras was on the scene, and with thirty-six ships-of-the-line at de Grasse's disposal, the fate of Cornwallis was sealed.

The allies' investment of Yorktown was performed by the book, by the maxims and rules that had remained standard since the days of Vauban, the eminent French military engineer of the seventeenth century. Present were all the ingredients to perform the art of siege-craft: water, food, easy soil, and superiority in artillery and manpower—roughly 5,700 Continentals, 3,200 militia, and 7,800 Frenchmen—excluding de Grasse's 15,000 seamen—as opposed to slightly more than 8,000 British, loyalists, and Germans. The wooded countryside furnished materials for fascines and gabions, which the soldiers made while waiting to begin formal operations. After Cornwallis abandoned his outer defenses and drew back to the immediate vicinity of Yorktown without contesting the ground, siege activities commenced. A parallel was constructed about six hundred yards from the enemy—"General Washington with his own hands first broke ground"—and cannon were pulled forward and emplaced. Five days later, on October 11, having run a zigzag (approach trench) forward, the second parallel was completed at approximately three hundred yards; the besiegers extended it almost to the York River after storming parties overran two British redoubts, Numbers 9 and 10. The engineers, sappers, and miners had done their part, and now the gun crews took over. The French were excellent artillerists, the best in Europe at the time, and for the siege they were well provided with a large assortment of field guns and heavier ordnance. This was not fortuitous. "The middle years of the eighteenth century saw a more rapid increase in the use of artillery, in proportion to other arms, than any other period from the sixteenth century to the twentieth," observes Robert R. Palmer. Yorktown also witnessed a fine performance by Henry Knox's corps of American artillery, which earned the praise of both friend and foe. All told, 100 allied siege guns fired an incessant rain of shot and shell into the enemy positions, pinpointing gun batteries, command posts, and ships in the harbor.[52]

As early as September 23, Clinton had received a warning from Cornwallis: "This place is in no State of defence. If you cannot relieve me very soon, you must be prepared to hear the Worst." The worst was not long in coming. In desperation Graves and Clinton set out with a fleet carrying 7,000 soldiers—scarcely equal to the task of rescuing Cornwallis—only to learn before reaching the Chesapeake that His Lordship had capitulated on October 19. The "irresistable wanderer," chuckled the *Maryland Gazette*, "hath at length periodicated his rambles, in the mode we could most have wished. . . ." And to the

Reverend Timothy Dwight the outcome had resulted from divine intervention. On the earthly side of the ledger, French naval power and skillfully executed operations had at last played a decisive role; but British errors in the field and certain faulty assumptions behind the Southern campaign had lent Washington and his comrades a helping hand.[53]

Technically, the War of Independence dragged on until 1783; but realistic Englishmen recognized that the former colonies were lost forever. Lord North, on hearing of the Yorktown disaster, reportedly exclaimed, "Oh God! It is all over!" On March 4, 1782, Parliament voted to "consider as enemies to his Majesty and the Country all those who should advise or by any means attempt to further prosecution of offensive war on the Continent of North America."

## NOTES

1. Smith, *Loyalists and Redcoats*, 94–99, contains the best account of the relationship between political and military factors in the origins of the Southern campaign.
2. The key pieces of correspondence behind the campaign are Germain to Clinton, March 8, 1778, Stevens, comp., *Facsimiles of Manuscripts in European Archives Relating to America*, IV, no. 396; Germain to Clinton, Aug. 5, 1778, Sir Henry Clinton Papers, William L. Clements Library, University of Michigan.
3. Richard Walsh, ed., *The Writings of Christopher Gadsden, 1746–1805* (Columbia, S.C., 1966), xxiv; *Historical Magazine*, IV (1860), 265–267; Kenneth Coleman, *The American Revolution in Georgia, 1763–1789* (Athens, Ga., 1958), 98–99, 105–106; Robert Howe to William Moultrie, Dec. 8, 1778, in Moultrie, *Memoirs of the American Revolution*, I, 247.
4. Coleman, *American Revolution in Georgia*, 122.
5. Alexander A. Lawrence, *Storm over Savannah: the Story of Count d'Estaing and the Siege of the Town in 1779* (Athens, Ga., 1951), is excellent.
6. Clinton, *American Rebellion*, 121–133, 139–140, 405–406, discusses his efforts to induce Washington to give battle.
7. Clifford K. Shipton, "Benjamin Lincoln: Old Reliable," in *George Washington's Generals*, ed. Billias, 198; Ramsay, *History of the Revolution in South Carolina*, II, 12; Brunhouse, ed., "David Ramsay, 1749–1815, Selections from His Writings," 58, 65. See also Moultrie, *Memoirs of the American Revolution*, I, 271–277. The British invasion came as no surprise to South Carolinians. *South-Carolina and American General Advertiser*, Nov. 6, 1777; *Charleston Gazette*, Jan. 26, 1779.
8. Ramsay, *History of the Revolution in South Carolina*, II, 48; Moultrie, *Memoirs of the American Revolution*, II, 47; R. W. Gibbes, ed., *Documentary History of the American Revolution* (New York, 1855–1857), II, 130–131; Joseph Kershaw to John Rutledge, April 25, 1780, in Thomas J. Kirkland and Robert M. Kennedy, *Historic Camden* (Columbia, S.C., 1905–1926), I, 127–128.
9. Foner, ed., *Writings of Paine*, I, 166–167; *The Narrative of Colonel David Fanning* (New York, 1865), 12; Evan Pugh diary extracts, in Alexander Gregg, *History of Old Cheraws* (New York, 1867), 302, 304; Clinton, *American Rebellion*, 175–176, 441.
10. The able Saratoga veteran, Colonel Daniel Morgan, a vigorous supporter of

Washington, praised the choice of Gates to lead the South. As Morgan wrote Gates, ". . . would to god youd a had it six months ago—our afairs, I am convinc'd, would have wore a more pleasing aspect at this day than they do. I wrote . . . last winter, that thay ought to send you to the southward, as I did not think Genl Lincoln capable of that command, he being a man of little experience . . . your character would stir up the people & put fresh life in them." Morgan to Gates, June 24, 1780, Gates Papers, New-York Historical Society.

11. "Extracts of a letter from Salisbury," dated Aug. 23, 1780, *Maryland Gazette*, Sept. 15, 1780; and reprinted in *Pennsylvania Journal*, Sept. 20, 1780; *Connecticut Courant*, Oct. 3, 1780; *Boston Gazette*, Oct. 23, 1780. Gates' proclamation to the people of South Carolina, announcing his taking the field, appears in *Virginia Gazette* (Dixon & Nicholson), Aug. 23, 1780; Moultrie, *Memoirs of the American Revolution*, II, 388–390.

12. Boyd, ed., *Papers of Jefferson*, III, 558, 595–597; Otho H. Williams, "A Narrative of the Campaign of 1780," in William Johnson, *Sketches of the Life and Correspondence of Nathanael Greene* (Charleston, S.C., 1822), I, appendix B, 494–498. British Lieutenant Colonel Banastre Tarleton, *A History of the Campaigns of 1780 and 1781, in the Southern Provinces of North America* (London, 1787), 109–110, criticized Gates' military formations and praised Cornwallis for capitalizing on his opponent's weakness.

13. Ford, ed., *Journals of Congress*, XVIII, 906. The quotation, if not apocryphal, supposedly came from Charles Lee, who warned Gates upon going to the South to "take care lest your Northern laurels turn to Southern willows."

14. Clinton, *American Rebellion*, 181–182; Stedman, *History . . . of the American War*, II, 198–199, Thomas Jones, the New York loyalist, considered the "proclamations of [British] Generals and Governors mere farces. The loyalists laughed at them, the rebels despised them, and by both they were held in contempt. They were great favourites with Governors, Generals, and Commissioners during the whole war. The American Rebellion was the first (I believe) in the universe attempted to be crushed, and reduced, by proclamation." Jones, *History of the American Revolution in New York*, I, 121.

15. Barnwell, "Loyalism in South Carolina," 130 and *passim*.

16. For the slaughter in the Waxhaws, compare Ramsay, *History of the Revolution in South Carolina*, II, 109–110, with Tarleton, *History of the Campaigns of 1780 and 1781*, 27–35. Stedman condemns Tarleton in his *History . . . of the American War*, II, 193. Marion's remarks are in a letter to Horatio Gates, Nov. 9, 1780, Jared Sparks Papers, Harvard University Library. John Rutledge echoed Marion on Tartleton's destructive raids. Joseph W. Barnwell, ed., "Letters of John Rutledge," *South Carolina Historical Magazine*, XVIII (1917), 44.

17. A. S. Salley, Jr., ed., *Colonel William Hill's Memoirs of the Revolution* (Columbia, S.C., 1921), 6–8. Andrew Pickens described his fellow guerrilla Sumter thusly: "He was self important and not communicative. I had little connection with him during the war." Andrew Pickens to Henry Lee, Nov. 25, 1811, Lyman C. Draper Papers, 1VV108, State Historical Society of Wisconsin.

18. Roderick Mackenzie, *Strictures on Lt. Col. Tarleton's History . . .* (London, 1787), 140; T. U. P. Charlton, *The Life of Major General James Jackson* (Augusta, Ga., 1809), 22. Later General Nathanael Greene complained, "There is not a day passes but there are more or less who fall a sacrifice to this savage disposition. The Whigs seem determined to extirpate the Tories, and the Tories the Whigs. . . . If a stop cannot be put to these massacres, the country will be depopulated . . . as neither Whig nor Tory can live." G. W. Greene, *Nathanael Greene*, III, 227n. For Greene's view, see also *Boston Gazette*, May 5, 1781. "The passions of both sides," admitted David Ramsay, "were kept in perpetual agitation, and wrought up to a degree of fury which rendered individuals regardless, not only of the laws of war but of the principles of humanity." Ramsay, *History of the Revolution in South Carolina*, II, 270.

19. Benjamin F. Stevens, ed., *The Campaign in Virginia, 1781: An Exact Reprint*

*of Six Rare Pamphlets on the Clinton-Cornwallis Controversy* . . . (London, 1888), I, 261–264. Recent scholarship has stressed the close link between the guerrilla bands of Sumter, Marion, and Pickens and the older militia structure in South Carolina. Cole, "South Carolina Militia," 89; Clye R. Ferguson, "General Andrew Pickens" (unpubl. Ph.D. diss., Duke University, 1960), *passim.*

20. Earlier expressions of Cornwallis' interest in the upper South appear in his letters to Clinton, June 30, Aug. 6, 1780, Stevens, ed., *Clinton-Cornwallis Controversy,* I, 225, 236–238. Clinton's concern for the security of South Carolina is seen in messages to Cornwallis, June 1, 1780 (two letters of that date), *ibid.,* 213–215; Clinton, *American Rebellion,* 186; Willcox, *Portrait of a General,* 348–353.

21. Tarleton, *History of the Campaigns of 1780 and 1781,* 162; Blackwell P. Robinson, *William R. Davie* (Chapel Hill, 1957), 49, 62–79; Chalmers G. Davidson, *Piedmont Partisan: The Life and Times of General William Lee Davidson* (Davidson, N.C., 1951), 78–83, 91.

22. Lyman C. Draper, *King's Mountain and Its Heroes* (Cincinnati, 1881); James G. de R. Hamilton, ed., "King's Mountain: Letters of Colonel Isaac Shelby," *Journal of Southern History,* IV (1938), 367–377; Sally, ed., *Colonel William Hill's Memoirs,* 19–24.

23. Force, ed., *American Archives,* 4th ser., III, 1077; G. W. Greene, *Nathaniel Greene,* I, 118–119.

24. Greene to Sumter, Jan. 8, 1781, Sumter Papers, Library of Congress; G. W. Greene, *Nathanael Greene,* III, 45. For Greene's initial effort to woo Marion, consult Dec. 4, 1780, Greene Letter Book, Oct.–Dec., 1780, Library of Congress. See the weight that Greene attached to diplomacy and personal leadership: "It has been my opinion for a long time that personal influence must supply the defects of civil constitution, but I have never been so fully convinced of it as on this journey. I believe the views and wishes of the great body of the people are entirely with us. But remove the personal influence of a few and they are a lifeless, inanimate mass, without direction or spirit to employ the means they possess for their own security."

25. Greene to Samuel Huntington, Nov. 2, 1780, Papers of the Continental Congress, no. 155, I, 459–460, National Archives; G. W. Greene, *Nathanael Greene,* III, 131. Possibly both William Davidson and Sumter recommended to Greene the sending of a detachment into South Carolina hinterland to rally the rural patriots, harass the tories, and threaten Cornwallis' post at Ninety-Six; both had advocated such a plan in November. Clark, ed., *State Records of N.C.,* XIV, 759; Davidson, *Piedmont Partisan,* 98–99; Anne K. Gregorie, *Thomas Sumter* (Columbia, S.C., 1931), 125, 127.

26. Cornwallis to Clinton, Jan. 6, 1781, Stevens, ed., *Clinton-Cornwallis Controversy,* I, 315–316.

27. Two letters, entirely neglected by scholars, are crucial to an understanding of Morgan's decision to fight at Cowpens: Morgan to Gates, Nov. 23, 1780, Jan. 26, 1781, Gates Papers, New-York Historical Society. See also Higginbotham, *Morgan,* chap. ix. Henry Lee erroneously asserted that Morgan's decision to engage Tarleton "grew out of irritation of temper, which appears to have overruled the suggestions of his sound and discriminating judgment. . . ." But Lee conceded that Morgan's "disposition for battle was masterly." Lee, *Memoirs of the War in the Southern Department . . .,* ed. Robert E. Lee (New York, 1869), 226–227.

28. Eric Robson, *The American Revolution in Its Political and Military Aspects, 1763–1783* (New York, 1955), 100. The British need for additional mobile units is treated in more detail in Robson, "British Light Infantry in the Mid-Eighteenth Century: the Effect of American Conditions," *Army Quarterly,* LXII (1950), 209–222. Cornwallis and Rawdon describe the disaffection: Cornwallis to Clinton, Dec. 3, 1780, Stevens, ed., *Clinton-Cornwallis Controversy,* I, 302–309; Rawdon to Alexander Leslie, Oct. 24, 1780, Clinton Papers, Clements Library. Cornwallis' thinking on the North Carolina loyalists is reported in letters of Rawdon,

temporarily in command during His Lordship's illness in the fall of 1780: ". . . we may have a powerful body of friends in North Carolina," commented Rawdon, "and indeed we have cause to be convinced, that many of the inhabitants wish well to his Majesty's arms; but they have not given evidence enough either of their number or their activity, *to justify the stake of this province, for the uncertain advantages that might attend immediate junction with them.*" Rawdon further reported that although "Earl Cornwallis forsees all the difficulties of a defensive war, . . . *his Lordship thinks they cannot be weighed against the dangers which must have attended an obstinate adherence to his former plan* [of conquering North Carolina]." Stevens, ed., *Clinton-Cornwallis Controversy,* I, 278–279; Rawdon to Leslie, Oct. 31, 1780, Clinton Papers, Clements Library.

29. Rogers, ed., "Letters of Charles O'Hara to the Duke of Grafton," 173–174.

30. Lamb, *Memoirs of His Own Life,* 346–347, 381; Stedman, *History . . . of the American War,* II, 326 n; Rogers, ed., "Letters of Charles O'Hara to the Duke of Grafton," 174; A. R. Newsome, ed., "A British Orderly Book, 1780–1781," *North Carolina Historical Review,* IX (1932), 284–296.

31. According to one writer, Cowpens proved the supremacy of "the armed yeomanry of America, for it is a fact established by reason and experience, that a respectable and well regulated militia is the safest palladium of the liberties of a state." Morgan's militia "had long been pupils in the school of adversity. Deprived of their property, banished from their domestic engagements, and fired with the remembrance of repeated injuries, aggravated by repeated insult, a noble spirit for revenge conspired with the love of country to impel them to the field." *Maryland Gazette,* Aug. 2, 1781.

32. Greene to Washington, Feb. 13, 1781, Greene Letter Book, Jan.–Feb., 1781, Library of Congress; Boyd, ed., *Jefferson Papers,* V, *passim,* especially 301, 360, 361 n–362 n, 570 n.

33. *Ibid.,* 111.

34. There are excellent accounts of the Battle of Guilford Courthouse in Ward, *War of the Revolution,* II, 784–794; Wallace, *Appeal to Arms,* 237–239; Thayer, *Greene,* 326–331. Readers are especially referred to M. F. Treacy's recent and provocative *Prelude to Yorktown: The Southern Campaign of Nathanael Greene, 1780–1781* (Chapel Hill, 1963). For Morgan's influence on Greene's tactics at Guilford Courthouse, see Higginbotham, *Morgan,* 156, 158–159. A sound and sprightly popular history is Burke Davis, *The Cowpens-Guilford Courthouse Campaign* (Philadelphia, 1962).

35. Rogers, ed., "Letters of Charles O'Hara to the Duke of Grafton," 177. Horace Walpole complained that "Lord Cornwallis has conquered his troops out of shoes and provisions, and himself out of troops." Mrs. Paget Toynbee, ed., *The Letters of Horace Walpole, Fourth Earl of Oxford* (Oxford, 1903–1905), XII, 13.

36. There are keen observations along this line in W. Stitt Robinson, ed., *Richard Oswald's Memorandum on the Folly of Invading Virginia . . .* (Charlottesville, Va., 1953), 8–9.

37. Greene to Steuben, April 2, 1781, Boyd, ed., *Papers of Jefferson,* V, 361 n–362 n.

38. G. W. Greene, *N. Greene,* III, 251–253; Thayer, *Greene,* 347–348.

39. *The Journal and Order Book of Capt. Robert Kirkwood* (Delaware Historical Society, *Papers,* LVI [Wilmington, 1910]), 16; Lee, *Memoirs of the War in the Southern Department,* 386. Throughout the campaign artillery was little used by Greene and his opponents. Jac Weller, "Revolutionary War Artillery in the South," *Georgia Historical Quarterly,* XLVI (1962), 250–273, 377–387.

40. Greene to Henry Knox, July 18, 1781, quoted in Thayer, *Greene,* 367. As one British officer exclaimed, "the more he is beaten, the faster he advances in the end. He has been indefatigable in collecting troops, and leading them to be defeated." *Diary of Frederick MacKenzie,* II, 273.

41. "From the end of May, 1780, until July, 1781, the whereabouts or existence of the Georgia state government is unknown." Coleman, *American Revolution in Georgia,* 161. See also Thayer, *Greene,* 358, 367; Greene to the Georgia dele-

gation in Congress, July 18, 25, 1781, Greene Papers, Duke University Library. During the British occupation royal government was re-established. New information on the subject is in Lilla M. Hawes, ed., "Somes Papers of the Governor and Council of Georgia, 1780–1781," *Georgia Historical Quarterly*, XLVI (1962), 280–296, 395–417.

42. Stevens, ed., *Clinton Cornwallis Controversy*, I, 318 321, 331, 395–399. Cornwallis argued that "Until Virginia is in a manner subdued, our hold of the Carolinas must be difficult, if not precarious. The Rivers of Virginia are advantageous to an invading Army, But North-Carolina is, of all the Provinces in America, the most difficult to attack, (unless material Assistance could be got from the Inhabitants, the contrary of which, I have sufficiently experienced) on account of its great extent, of the numberless Rivers and Creeks, & the total want of interior navigation." *Ibid.*, 399.

43. Willcox, *Portrait of a General*, 386. This section on Yorktown also draws heavily upon Willcox's "Rhode Island in British Strategy, 1780–1781," *Journal of Modern History*, XVII (1945), 304–331; and "The British Road to Yorktown: A Study in Divided Command," *American Historical Review*, LII (1946), 1–35. See also George W. Kyte, "Strategic Blunder: Lord Cornwallis Abandons the Carolinas, 1781." *The Historian*, XXII (1960), 129–144; Clinton, *American Rebellion*, chap. xxii.

44. Willcox, *Portrait of a General*, 510, believes that an inner conflict over the use of authority, going back to his childhood, provides the most plausible explanation for his ambivalent behavior as commander in chief. With the collaboration of psychiatrist Frederick Wyatt, Willcox had previously issued a report of their psychological findings. See their "Sir Henry Clinton: A Psychological Exploration in History," *William and Mary Quarterly*, 3d ser., XVI (1959), 3–26. Remarks of young Robert Biddulph, a British army contractor in New York, indicate that Cornwallis had his own following among the military men around Clinton: "We are upon no terms with the Clinton, but have every assistance from the C-s party. . . ." "Letters of Robert Biddulph, 1779–1783," *American Historical Review*, XXIX (1923), 100.

45. Robert Poage and others to the Virginia Assembly, [May, 1781], Boyd, ed., *Papers of Jefferson*, VI, 55–60. Lee to Lovell, June 12, 1781, Ballagh, ed., *Letters of Richard Henry Lee*, II, 537–538. Lee also wrote directly on this point to Washington, who declined to leave the New York area. As he noted, he was the only American general authorized to command the French land forces in America. *Ibid.*, 233–235; Fitzpatrick, ed., *Writings of Washington*, XXII, 178–179; Burnett, ed., *Letters of Congress*, VI, 105–106.

46. Paul L. Ford, ed., *The Writings of Thomas Jefferson* (New York, 1892–1899), I, 70. John Quincy Adams termed these sentiments "anti-republican." *Memoirs of John Quincy Adams, Comprising Portions of His Diary from 1795 to 1848* (Philadelphia, 1874–1877), VIII, 294–296. A convincing defense of Jefferson's conduct as governor, which also denies the near-collapse of Virginia's government, is found in Boyd's editorial notes to vols. V–VII of the *Papers of Jefferson*. The standard charges against Jefferson are in Paul A. W. Wallace, *The Muhlenbergs of Pennsylvania* (Philadelphia, 1950), 204, 205, 207, 208, 210, 220; Treacy, *Prelude to Yorktown*, 57, 131, 211 n17.

47. Emory G. Evans, "The Nelsons: A Biographical Study of a Virginia Family in the Eighteenth Century" (unpubl. Ph.D. diss., University of Virginia, 1957), chaps. vi–ix, illuminates the Revolutionary career of Jefferson's successor. Louis Gottschalk, *Lafayette and the Close of the American Revolution*, chaps. ix–xi, gives an in-depth treatment of the war in Virginia at this time.

48. George W. Kyte analyzes the Rankin plan in "A Proposed Attack on Philadelphia in 1781," *Pennsylvania Magazine of History and Biography*, LXXVI (1952), 379–393. Cornwallis' observation on the naval threat is in Stevens, ed., *Clinton-Cornwallis Controversy*, II, 57–58. The same source contains Clinton's numerous epistles to the Southern commander. *Ibid.*, 14–17, 18–23, 24–25, 26–28,

29-31, 41, 49-56, 61, 62-65, 73-78, 99, 100, 109-119, 123-124. Smith, *Loyalists and Redcoats*, 154-161, provides something of a revisionist assessment of Cornwallis. Clinton's later claim—that Germain ordered him to retain his Virginia base and not to draw away any of its garrison—was untrue. Willcox, *Portrait of a General*, 405 and notes.

49. As early as July 15, 1780, roughly a year before the Yorktown campaign, Washington had confided these sentiments to Rochambeau: "In any operation, and under all circumstances a decisive Naval superiority is to be considered as a fundamental principle, and the basis upon which every hope of success must ultimately depend." Fitzpatrick, ed., *Writings of Washington*, XIX, 174.

50. Many secondary accounts erroneously state that at the Wethersfield conference (May 22, 1781) Washington was told by the French that Admiral de Grasse was definitely coming north to cooperate with the allies. See Washington to La Luzerne, May 23, 1781, Fitzpatrick, ed., *Writings of Washington*, XX, 103-104. Though Rochambeau did have advance notice of de Grasse's plans, he felt obliged by his instructions not to disclose the information at that time. Freeman, *Washington*, V, 296 n87. Several very recent works, failing to consult Fitzpatrick or Freeman on this point, repeat the mistake.

51. Rodney assigned two other vessels to convoy duty at Jamaica. He also suggested to Sir Peter Parker, commanding the station, to put them in motion after Hood, along with four ships-of-the-line then at the island. Parker, lacking precise orders, failed to act until too late.

52. J. W. Wright, "Notes on the Siege of Yorktown in 1781 with Special Reference to the Conduct of a Siege in the Eighteenth Century," *William and Mary Quarterly*, 2d ser., XII (1932), 228-249. For pertinent information about the terrain, consult Charles E. Hatch, Jr., *Yorktown and the Siege of 1781* (National Park Service, *Historical Handbook* [Washington, D.C., 1957]). Martin, *Private Yankee Doodle*, 195, was the eyewitness to Washington's activity. Palmer's remark may be read in Earle, ed., *Makers of Modern Strategy*, 57. Numerous references to the splendid performance of the allied artillery are in Acomb, ed., *Revolutionary Journal of Baron Ludwig von Closen*; Chastellux, *Travels in North America*, ed. Rice.

53. Stevens, ed., *Clinton-Cornwallis Controversy*, II, 158; *Maryland Gazette*, Oct. 25, 1781; Timothy Dwight, *A Sermon Preached at Northampton* (Hartford, 1781).

# 15. The Continental Army

ALTHOUGH ONLY A small percentage of American manpower was under arms at any one time during the Revolutionary struggle, Secretary of War Henry Knox in 1790 estimated that the total enlistments in the Continental and state forces had come to 396,000 men. Most authorities consider Knox's figures to be highly inflated, failing—for example—to take into account the many individuals who enlisted on two or more occasions. We are additionally handicapped in analyzing the extent of military participation by the absence of reliable information about the American population at the time. Congress placed the number of inhabitants of the thirteen states at 3,000,000, whereas the British American Department made it under 2,500,000, of whom perhaps 600,000 were Negroes. Whichever numbers we accept, we must also subtract the loyalists, the neutralists, the seamen, the elderly, the women, and still others, an almost hopeless task so far as precision is concerned. In the late 1760's Franklin calculated that America had 250,000 men of prime fighting age. This is also the maximum estimate for the Revolutionary period made by Howard H. Peckham, a careful historian, who speculates that probably no more than 100,000 different men actually bore arms on the American side. Assuming for the sake of argument that Peckham's figure is correct, it might well be viewed as unflattering to the zeal of the revolutionists, even though it represents a far higher proportion of direct involvement than one would find in a European nation in the eighteenth century. It is worth recalling that some states—and some towns and counties—made greater contributions than others. Massachusetts put a larger percentage of her population in the field than any other state. Malden, Massachusetts, in 1776 gave 231 of her sons to the army out of an overall population of 1,030, while by the war's end New Ipswich, New Hampshire, had contributed 360 of its 1,033 citizens to the cause. For some states, especially in the South, the military records are less complete; undoubtedly many men performed occasional duty with the partisan bands under leaders such as Marion and Sumter without ever formally entering the service.[1]

### Filling the Ranks

Yet manpower was always in short supply, and Emory Upton and his followers have berated Congress for getting off on the wrong foot in not initially providing for an army on a long-term basis. But in the fall of 1775 when the lawmakers laid plans for the coming year, no one knew that the conflict would be a long one. There were real dangers to morale, with the Revolution still a tender reed, in suggesting to a people hoping for reconciliation that the struggle would be hard and protracted. Besides, would men have actually enlisted in impressive numbers for more than a year? John Adams said that in Massachusetts no more than a regiment "of the meanest, idlest, most intemperate and worthless" human beings would have joined for a longer time.[2] As it was, the army of 1776, based on a one-year term of service, fell far below the strength desired by Congress. Just as the lawmakers recognized the need for caution in creating anything resembling a professional army among citizens averse to old-fashioned militarism, so they also were mindful of the logistical hurdles to maintaining a large regular army; it was a sizable task merely to feed and clothe the few thousand stalwarts who remained with Washington each winter throughout the Revolution.

All the same, the continuation of the conflict necessitated bold new approaches and the modification of former attitudes. In the deepening crisis of 1776, marked by William Howe's army threatening New York City, Congress voted to raise eighty-eight battalions (equivalent to regiments) "to serve during the present war." It was no easy turn of mind, Robert Morris assured Washington, that led the legislators to surmount their prejudices against standing armies. But once the step was taken, they continued throughout the war to seek extended enlistments. Unfortunately for Washington and the other generals, the army never remotely approached its intended strength for 1777—about 75,000 men—or for any other year. Washington's own command in the Middle Department appears to have reached its maximum, with 18,472 reported "present and fit for duty" on October 1, 1778, more than twice the number of troops he had available around New York City just before the Yorktown campaign.[3]

A variety of expedients was tried to keep the army together. Con-

gress agreed to accept three-year Continental terms in place of enlistments for the war. This retreat was partly owing to competition from
the states, which were able to offer more tempting inducements for
brief periods in the local forces. As early as 1775, the New England
provinces had revived the colonial custom of awarding bounties for
military service. Congress, in planning for the army in 1777, had also
turned to bounties, promising every enlistee for the duration twenty
dollars and a hundred acres of land, or each three-year recruit ten
dollars.

That body and the states continued to bid against each other until
the central government in 1779 offered two hundred dollars for the
duration and a number of the states considerably higher sums. At
times, however, some of the states cooperated in recruiting. In 1777,
Harvard, Massachusetts, held out a bounty of thirty pounds to every
man who joined the Continental establishment for three years. Later
the same town changed its offer to eighteen calves for a similar period
in arms. State governments, too, were known to provide extra compensation for prospective Continentals. But these endeavors were at best
a mixed blessing, for as the states tried to exceed one another in their
inducements, the inflationary spiral soared higher and higher. More
lucrative rewards for new soldiers brought grumbling from Continentals
who had enrolled previously for smaller sums. Washington, convinced
of the justice of this complaint, persuaded Congress in 1779 to extend
an additional gratuity of one hundred dollars as a reward for the "services of those faithful and zealous soldiers who at an early period
engaged in the Armies of the States during the war."[4]

For a time Continental officers and enlisted men were detailed as
recruiters in their own states. Then in 1777 the assignment was turned
over to the states, which were divided into districts, with each local
official given a fee for every recruit secured. In their zeal to muster
men, recruiters frequently forgot or neglected their instructions that
every soldier must be healthy, able-bodied, at least sixteen years old,
and not under five feet two inches in height. At least two soldiers
serving with the Pennsylvania line in 1779 were little more than children. David Hamilton Morris of the 3d Regiment had been enlisted for
a year, but was still only twelve. Jeremiah Levering, fourteen or
fifteen, had already put in three years with the artillery. Occasionally
newspapers advertised for enlistees, stipulating where and when a man
could enter the service. Broadsides to the same effect were circulated,
such as one addressed "TO ALL BRAVE, HEALTHY, ABLE
BODIED, AND WELL DISPOSED YOUNG MEN, IN THIS NEIGH-
BORHOOD, WHO HAVE ANY INCLINATION TO JOIN THE
TROOPS, NOW RAISING UNDER GENERAL WASHINGTON,
FOR THE DEFENCE OF THE LIBERTIES AND INDEPEND-

ENCE OF THE UNITED STATES." Not unlike methods of later
periods, a young man was informed that the service offered him the
broadening opportunity for travel and seeing new regions "of this
beautiful continent, in the honourable and truly respectable character
of a soldier, after which, he may, if he pleases return home to his
friends, with his pockets full of money and his head covered with
laurels." A youthful farm boy, Joseph Plumb Martin of Milford, Connecticut, attested to the persuasiveness of several recruiters, who
"attacked me, front, rear and flank" with arguments for preserving
freedom. Although Martin had only recently completed a tour with
the Connecticut state troops, he enlisted in the regular establishment
in 1777 and served until the Continental army was disbanded six years
later. A skillful combination of political persuasion and rum were the
tools of the trade in recruiting. A martial speech before a crowd of men
and boys ouside a village tavern was followed by rounds of drinks,
and, hopefully for the recruiter, several signatures on his recruiting
roster. A Bernard Elliott, seeking to fill the ranks of the 2d South
Carolina Regiment of Continentals, besides treating potential soldiers
to wine and grog, served free barbecue at a "Virginia hop" to all the
country lads and their "Lasses."[5]

Voluntary enlistments, as Washington wrote in 1778, were the most
desirable way to maintain an army, but in practice he had found that
compulsion was essential if the Continental battalions were to be filled.
All of the "allurements of the most exorbitant bounties and every
other inducement that could be thought of, have been tried in vain,
and seem to have had little other effect than to increase the rapacity
and raise the demands of those to whom they were held out. We may
fairly infer, that the country has been already pretty well drained of
that class of Men whose tempers, attachments and circumstances disposed them to enter permanently, or for a length of time, into the
army. . . ."[6]

Drafts for the duration were patently impracticable, a policy that
would arouse the wrath of the property-owning farmers and artisans
constituting the largest productive elements of society. They and their
families would suffer from a prolonged absence from their livelihood.
Consequently, Washington advocated annual drafts for twelve months'
service from the militia—chiefly to complete Continental regiments—
and Congress consented after making several alterations in the commander in chief's proposal out of deference to the sensibilities of the
states. Massachusetts had already resorted to conscription in 1776, as
had New Hampshire in 1777, and most of the remaining states fell in
line in 1778 and afterward, but with scant enthusiasm. An officer
advised Governor Thomas Lee of Maryland that "Draughted men, who
are forced out will render very little assistance or rather do no good."[7]

Not uncommonly the draft followed a set procedure. After Congress called upon a governor or legislature to furnish a specified number of men for duty, the state would divide its quota among the militia regiments, whose colonels would in turn apportion men from the towns or counties in their commands. Sometimes local captains would draw names from a hat, which the statutes proclaimed should be held by a distinguished citizen who would regularly shake the hat to guarantee fairness. A typical Massachusetts draft notice was addressed to one John Sail:

To Dea. John Sail, SIR:
This is to inform you [that you] are this evening drafted as one of the Continental men to go to General Washington's headquarters, and you must go or find an able bodied man in your Room, or pay a fine of twenty pounds in law, money in twenty-four hours.

*Samuel Clark, Capt.*

To a degree, the drafting procedure involved two principles of later selective service in America: selection by lot and marriage exemption. Still, the system was never all-inclusive, as John Sail's orders show: men could avoid service by paying a fine or by furnishing a substitute. Affluent towns might spare all their citizens, as did Epping, New Hampshire, in 1777, by hiring soldiers from other communities to meet their quotas.[8]

The Continental army often accorded a unique position to skilled artisans, some of them formally in the army, others in a specified non-combatant status, their pay generally in either case exceeding that of ordinary soldiers. One company of artificers enlisted in 1776 consisted of a captain, a lieutenant, and twenty-five carpenters, boatbuilders, and wheelwrights. Responsible for acquiring their own tools, blankets, and clothing, they were "when occasion requires it . . . [to] act the part of Soldiers in either attack or defence as well as Artificers." Both Continental and state authorities favored the voluntary enlistment of artisans over the draft as a means of securing their services. Advertisements for forge men, nailers, carpenters, and wagoners were commonplace throughout the war. But owing to higher pay in the domestic industries and the overall scarcity of skilled workers, the army continually complained of a shortage of artisans.[9]

## "Rabble in Arms"

Try as they might, the patriots could not confine themselves to employing only their upstanding citizens in the fight for freedom. Manpower requirements coupled with the domestic responsibilities of the farmers and tradesmen inevitably led the Americans to scrape the bottom of the barrel of human resources. For the same reasons, the colonists had eventually taken such steps in the earlier intercolonial struggles, when, for instance, the Virginians during the Seven Years' War had resorted to the impressment of "idle, vagrant, or dissolute persons."[10] These measures may have been resorted to reluctantly by the revolutionists, whereas in Europe such procedures were a matter of course, but nonetheless they were taken.

British deserters and prisoners of war soon found their way into the ranks of the Continentals, even though recruiters were expressly enjoined to pass over such undesirable human flesh. In Massachusetts officials considered Burgoyne's captured army—the so-called "Convention troops"—fair game for filling depleted regiments, much to Washington's consternation. There was a grave danger, warned the commander in chief, in dredging up men "who are bound to us by no motives of attachment," whereas citizens had "ties of Country, kindred, and some times property . . . [as] securities for their fidelity."[11] By every standard, the former enemies made miserable soldiers. Understandably, they hung back in battle for fear of capture and vengeful retribution, or at other times they escaped to the enemy lines after hearing of a royal offer of pardon to defectors. But the practice continued, especially in the Pennsylvania line in 1778 and later in the Carolinas, where both sides drew upon the other's prisoners and deserters. In order to fleshen out skeleton regiments, Washington and Congress eventually moderated their opposition to using the enemy, the lawmakers in 1782 formally calling for the enlistment of Germans who in turn would be given citizenship upon taking the oath of allegiance.

Americans also turned to the recruiting of men in bondage, both white and black. At the outbreak of the Revolution, the number of white servants held by indenture to specified terms had reached an all-time high for the colonial period. The totals reflected the rising tide of immigration in the eighteenth century; thousands arrived as redemptioners bound to labor in return for their Atlantic passage. Such a human reservoir could not go untapped. Rhode Island, New Jersey, and Maryland permitted servants to enlist without their masters' consent, although the three nonetheless provided the masters monetary compensation. Other states, requiring the masters' approval, offered them no financial inducements. Not uncommonly, as in Maryland, vagrants were inducted into the army—in that state for a nine-month period; and so were convicted felons, who received pardons for satisfactory military duty.[12]

While bondage was a temporary status for whites, slavery constituted a permanent condition for the vast preponderance of Negroes in the Revolutionary era. The Americans made limited use of colored men in the opening phases of the war, displaying reluctance to deprive a master of his slave or to place arms in the hands of the black man. Slavery existed in all the thirteen states, although the institution was more firmly rooted in the South. It was a New Yorker, General Philip Schuyler, who asked whether it was "consistent with the Sons of Freedom to trust their all to be defended by slaves."[13] But opposition to Negro military participation was strongest in the lower South, and Congress refused to recommend the enlistment of colored men. On their own, most of the states gradually bowed to the pressure of man-power deficiencies. In 1777 Massachusetts included Negroes among those eligible for its draft. Rhode Island the following year voted to raise two battalions of blacks, and the rest of New England quickly fell in line. In the South, Maryland alone permitted the inclusion of slaves in her forces, but Virginia allowed free Negroes to join the standard. Many Negroes, both slaves and free men, served as substitutes for gun-shy whites.

Congress and Washington, all the while, accepted the states' recruit-ment of Negroes for Continental service with little comment. The British success in the lower South finally drove the lawmakers in 1779 to the unprecedented step of recommending to South Carolina and Georgia the taking of measures immediately for raising "three thousand able-bodied negroes." Congress dispatched a South Carolinian, Lieutenant Colonel John Laurens, back to his own state to arouse support for the new scheme. A devotee of human freedom partly owing to his educa-tional experiences at Geneva, young Laurens was also influenced by his father, the president of the Continental Congress, a planter and former slave trader, who had come to recognize the inconsistency between the thought of the Declaration of Independence and the condition of the bondsmen on his own estates. He was not "one of those who dare trust in Providence for defence and security of their own liberty while they enslave and wish to continue in slavery thousands who are as well entitled to freedom as themselves."[14]

Unfortunately, John and Henry Laurens were out of step with their fellow Carolina planter aristocrats, who, notwithstanding the per-suasiveness of the younger Laurens, turned a cold shoulder on the notion of thrusting muskets into the hands of their servile laborers. (An exception was Dr. David Ramsay, who deplored "White Pride and Avarice" as "great obstacles in the way of Black Liberty.")[15] The same was true of the Georgians, who also spurned Laurens' plea.

Outside the lower South colored men increasingly saw action under the newly unfurled stars and stripes. This was to be the pattern in most of America's wars, observes Benjamin Quarles; initially the Negro would be bypassed. Only when the conflicts grew arduous would authorities resort to the "one great remaining manpower pool, and the Negro would emerge from his status as a rejected inferior to become a comrade in arms." There are no reliable figures as to the number of Negroes who bore arms for the patriots. For the most part, the military records are silent as to racial identities, and colored combatants were interspersed with whites in military units. If Negroes were occasionally found in militia and other local units, they were more often seen in the Continental army, which was well sprinkled with blacks by 1778. A few Negroes fought in cavalry or artillery regiments, but most were in the infantry, and many of these received orderly duties or such semi-domestic assignments as waiters and cooks. Why did Negroes serve? Frequently slaves were drafted, usually as substitutes; some were promised manumission—"freedom with their swords," as Alexander Hamilton phrased it. A variety of motives influenced free Negroes—adventure, bounty money, a belief in the idealistic goals of the Revolution.[16]

Negroes also made contributions outside the army. In the South they were valuable spies, guides, and messengers. Even South Carolina went so far as to free a slave, "Antigua," and his family as a reward for his gathering valuable intelligence about enemy troop movements. As military laborers colored men were everywhere employed. Frequently procured by public levy, they were put to felling trees, destroying bridges, and erecting fortifications. In Virginia the state government purchased slaves for these and similar purposes, some to work at the Westham iron works, others to toil in the lead mines at Chiswell. South Carolina and Georgia authorities overrode local complaints and impressed bondsmen to labor at strengthening batteries and forts. Slaves confiscated from tory masters, considered public property, were put to the pick and shovel in the same fashion; but some Southerners whenever possible kept captured slaves as the plunder of war. James Madison reacted indignantly against a proposed scheme in Virginia to encourage enlistments in the army by offering recruits a bounty to be paid in slaves: "would it not be as well to liberate and make soldiers at once of the blacks themselves as to make them instruments for enlisting white Soldiers? It wd. certainly be more consonant to the principles of liberty which ought never to be lost sight of in a contest for liberty...."[17]

Indeed, the conscience of many patriots was stirred by the plight of the blacks, particularly those fighting in the army. Negroes themselves increasingly saw the need to apply Revolutionary theory to their own subordinate status. Individual slaves petitioned for manumission, and in groups they memorialized their legislatures to abolish human bondage. A Negro, "Vox Africanorum," summarized the sentiments of thoughtful, articulate members of his race: "Liberty is our claim. Reverence for our Great Creator, principles of humanity and the dictates of common sense, all convince us, that we have an indubitable right to liberty. . . . Though our bodies differ in colour from yours; yet our souls are similar in a desire for freedom. Disparity in colour, we conceive, can never constitute a disparity in rights."[18]

Above the Potomac, where slavery was less of an economic factor than in the South, sentiment against the "peculiar institution" resulted in positive action. During the war Pennsylvania and Massachusetts took steps to eradicate slavery, and within a year of the treaty of peace Connecticut and Rhode Island enacted gradual abolition measures. New York, one of the last Northern states to respond, finally adopted a gradual plan of manumission in 1799. Thus the ideals of the Revolution, combined with the service of blacks in the cause of freedom, brought a profound change in the legal status of Negroes above the Mason and Dixon line. Genuine equality in the North and freedom in the South for Negroes lay in the future, but the Revolution nevertheless began the painfully slow process of assimilating the Negro into the mainstream of American life.[19]

If the Revolution failed to produce any significant change in the status of women in America, females nonetheless played a role with the Continental army, not only in gathering clothing and other necessities but also by their presence in the camps. So-called camp followers were found among all the armies of the times. They included wives, sweethearts, homeless females, and ladies of easy virtue. In his general orders of August 4, 1777, Washington complained that "the multitude of women . . . especially those who are pregnant, or have children, are a clog upon every movement." A few days later, just before his army passed through Philadelphia, the commander in chief directed that the women be sent out around the city: "Not a woman belonging to the army is to be seen with the troops"—for fear of offending the sensibilities of the good Quaker residents. For a time American leaders attempted to limit rations to females on the basis of no more than one woman for every fifteen Continentals; but Washington generally followed a more flexible standard in his own command, chiefly because some soldiers had brought their families with them from British-occupied areas. "The Cries of these Women; the sufferings of their Children, and the complaints of the Husbands would admit of no alternative."[20]

Women were not without their considerable value to the army. They did washing, sewing, and cooking, adding a feminine touch to the life of men away from home. Without the distaff side, admitted Washington, some of the best soldiers in the service would have deserted. At Valley Forge women performed as nurses, and on occasion they manned the battlements everywhere. Of the two soldiers' wives who took part in Arnold's tortuous march to Quebec, one fell in combat before the walled city. Margaret Corbin, wounded at Fort Washington "whilst she heroically filled the post of her husband who was killed by her side serving a piece of artillery," received a pension from Congress. The most unusual performance was that of Deborah Sampson, who enlisted in a Massachusetts regiment as Robert Shurtleff and served from 1781 to 1783 by the "artful concealment" of her sex.[21]

## Restlessness in the Ranks

The suffering of the Continental army is a familiar story that hardly needs repeating in detail, and we have already examined the problems connected with administering the supply services. Even so, some of the soldiers' hardships should at least be mentioned prior to looking at the reaction of the men to their conditions. Officers and enlisted men alike were paid, habitually late, in paper money, which scourged them because of soaring prices and sinking currency. "What officer or soldier," asked one American, "will enter into the service in the future, if the common and immediate necessaries of life are denied because they have not in their power to lay down any other than Congress money?" Though the soldiers were supposedly supplied with wearing apparel, their garments were more likely to be their own. The shifting of clothing responsibilities back and forth between the states and Congress meant that at neither the state nor the Continental level was the problem dealt with effectively, even with allowances for shortages that could not be helped. Relatively few of the troops received the uniforms they were promised as a kind of bounty for enlisting. Americans even resorted to wearing captured British uniforms until Washington finally forbade the practice in 1781. For the most part it was an American army of scarecrows—of tattered hats, patched coats and breeches, and broken shoes. The sight of shoeless men in December prompted Lieutenant Colonel Ebenezer Huntington to exclaim, "Poor fellows, my heart bleeds for them, while I Damn my country as void of gratitude."[22]

Uniforms, of course, were occasionally to be seen; several states did reasonably well in outfitting their men. But it is a popular misconception that the first official uniform colors of the Continental army were blue and buff, for in the fall of 1775 Congress adopted brown as the color of American military attire. Blue coats, however, were very much in evidence after 1778 because of such shipments from France. The uniform question was explicitly settled with the adoption of blue as the basic color of army clothing in 1779, and so it remained until the beginning of the twentieth century. Yet it was not until the Yorktown campaign that a substantial portion of the American army was decently clothed in uniforms.[23]

The standard ration of food as established by Congress was generous for the time, and in essence it continued as the ration of the United States army for more than a century:

RESOLVED, That a ration consist of the following kind and quantity of provisions: 1 lb. beef, or ¾ lb. pork or 1 lb. salt fish per day; 1 lb. bread or flour, per day; 3 pints of peas or beans per week, or vegetables equivalent, at one dollar per bushel for peas or beans; 1 pint of milk per man per day, or at the rate of $\frac{1}{72}$ of a dollar; 1 half pint of Rice, or one pint of indian meal per man per week; 1 quart of spruce beer or cider per man per day, or nine gallons of Molasses per company of 100 men per week; 3 lb. candles to 100 Men per week for guards; 24 lb. soft or 8 lb. hard soap for 100 men per week.[24]

But after the first winter of the war, the cold months invariably found the army hungry. At Valley Forge, Washington feared that growling stomachs were likely to lead to mutiny. General James Varnum's division was without meat for two days and without bread for three days. During that winter of 1777–1778 the standard fare consisted of "fire cakes," made by baking a flour-and-water paste. "Nothing but Fire Cake & Water" for every meal, fumed Dr. Albigense Waldo. "The Lord send that our Commissary of Purchases may live on Fire Cake & Water, 'till their glutted Gutts are turned to Pasteboard." Two years later, during the winter encampment at Morristown, Baron de Kalb declared, "Those who have only been in Valley Forge or Middlebrook during the last two winters, but have not tasted the cruelties of this one, know not what it is to suffer." By New Year's day, 1780, Washington's army had been on a half ration of bread for six weeks, and one day some of the troops had no bread at all. Private Joseph Plumb Martin reported that a group of Continentals barbecued their shoes and attempted to eat them; several officers slew a pet dog and dined on him. One could scarcely disagree with Plumb's further observation that the Revolutionary War "not only tried men's souls, but their bodies too. . . ."[25]

By ones, tens, and even hundreds, Americans expressed their dissatisfaction with army life by the traditional means of desertion. Accurate statistics as to the number of desertions from the Continental army are almost completely absent. Washington, who repeatedly complained of the problem of unauthorized absences, never estimated the percentage of defections. He recognized that at times recruiting officers had padded their rosters with fictitious recruits and then had claimed that their nonexistent soldiers had deserted. The motives of the deserters are an equally difficult subject for careful analysis since men left the service without permission for a variety of reasons. Some joined the British, who offered pardons and promised land to any Americans in return for changing uniforms. The British diarist Frederick Mackenzie stated that on a single day nearly eighty Americans crossed the King's lines. In 1777, British General William Howe launched an intensive propaganda campaign to win Continentals over to the royal standard. In May of that year Washington admitted that these appeals had produced "an unhappy influence on too many of the soldiers; in a particular Manner on those who are not Natives."[26]

The vast preponderance of deserters, however, did not embrace the enemy. Many simply left their regiments and joined other American units in order to pick up additional bounty money. There were men who engaged in this practice time and again, making it "a kind of Business," complained Washington. They were willing, declared General Jedediah Huntington, "For the Sake of a Little ready Money" to "risque the Smart of a few Lashes (Shame they have none)." Countless others, troubled by inadequate pay and supplies, simply made their exodus when the opportunity availed itself. Although many of the absentees were guilty of irresponsibility and criminal conduct by any fair standard, there were numerous men who left the camps because of reasons that did not necessarily reflect upon their devotion to the cause. The need to take care of the spring planting and the fall harvesting drew soldiers away from their regiments, as did pathetic letters from home filled with accounts of the sufferings and deprivations of the families left behind. Shortly before Christmas of 1778 an officer declared that not a day passed but that some tearful-eyed soldier showed him a letter from his wife detailing his family's hardships and closing with "pray come home." There are even instances of men returning voluntarily to duty after having been absent without leave to deal with a pressing domestic matter. Troublesome as the problem was to American authorities, desertion was an infinitely greater difficulty to cope with in European armies of the age, when even in peace time the average annual loss sometimes ran in the thousands.[27]

It is doubtful that the majority of the officers of the Continental army fared appreciably better than the enlisted men. Officers were largely responsible for feeding and clothing themselves from their pay and private means. Their own resources were often scarcely equal to the task since so many men with commissions were from the middle orders of society. A French officer was amazed to find that "the several military grades . . . [are] granted here to every rank of people. There are shoemakers who are Colonels; and it often happens that the Americans ask the French officers what their trade is in France." Lieutenant Joseph Hodgkins, a cobbler from Ipswich, Massachusetts, depended on the needle of his wife for almost all his clothing. "I am afrade that I shall whare you out," he wrote, "By sending you so much work But I cannot git any thing Don hare so I must Bage your Patience. . . ." In the winter she sent him mittens, heavy shirts, boot soles, without which, he explained from Valley Forge, "I must go naked. . . ." Hodgkins later claimed that because of "his necessary expenditures in the army & to subsist his family," he "became empoverished & embarrassed by debts, as is well known to the people in his County."[28]

Officers of high rank also complained of financial hardships. "I despise my Countrymen," exclaimed Colonel Ebenezer Huntington, whose wages would "scarcely support" him a week. In the spring of 1781, General Daniel Morgan protested to Virginia authorities that his pay was months in arrears, which, combined with high taxes and army expenses, had reduced him to near poverty. He was so "bare of cloaths" as to be ashamed to appear in public. General John Glover complained of receiving no wages from 1780 to the day of his retirement from the army in 1782, his back pay then amounting to $2,343.[29]

There was no need for officers to desert the army to escape intolerable conditions; they were at liberty to resign their commissions at any time, and hundreds did just that. Other officers took leaves of absence and simply did not return, a practice so common that it provoked Alexander Hamilton to propose trial by court-martial for such offenders. Many officers advocated that they be given permission to sell their commissions—as was permitted in the British army—as a means of raising cash to allow them additional compensation for their services. When Congress refused, the officers demanded half pay for life upon retirement, pointing out that pensions of this kind were awarded to the military in Great Britain. At first both Washington and Congress expressed reluctance to go along with the proposal, viewing it, in the words of Congressman Elbridge Gerry of Massachusetts, as comparable to the creation of a distinct body of "placemen and pensioners," a system that had helped destroy independence and freedom in Great Britain, substituting in their stead corruption and the undermining of the constitution of the mother country.[30]

Washington, who was generally more flexible than is usually recognized, soon swung around to the officers' position, just as earlier he had dropped his opposition to bounties for enlisted men and had gone along with the recruitment of Negroes and prisoners of war. Washington informed Congress that the suffering and sacrifices of the officers more than entitled them to half pay. While such a measure might seem highly expensive, it would—by keeping officers in the service—heighten morale and efficiency and, consequently, would shorten the war. When the lawmakers procrastinated, Washington persisted. "I am ready to declare," he wrote, "that I do most religiously believe the salvation of the cause depends upon it. . . ."[31] The opponents of half pay did not

sway easily, President Laurens expressing only a willingness to compensate those officers whose needs and privations were demonstrable. For
the most part, vowed the South Carolinian, officers had eagerly sought
their commissions, knowing full well the stakes of the game and the
responsibilities and burdens of their stations. These deliberations
occurred in the early months of 1778, scarcely a time when the congressmen looked sympathetically upon the army that was wrought up
over the so-called Conway Cabal and the hiring of swarms of French
soldiers of fortune.[32] Even so, Congress rose above its prejudices against
standing armies, and notwithstanding fierce debate on the subject, all
but two of the delegates finally voted to grant the officers half pay for
seven years. The outcome was a compromise: less than the officers
wanted and more than Congress desired to give, although two years
later the lawmakers extended half pay for life.[33]

Although the hardships of the officers aroused serious discontent,
remarkably few of Washington's subordinates went over to the enemy.
Indeed, the only highly placed soldier to commit treason was Benedict
Arnold, the outstanding battlefield commander in the Continental
army. A proud, willful man, Arnold had repeatedly quarreled with
state and Congressional officials. In his eyes the Massachusetts legislature had failed to support his efforts to take Fort Ticonderoga in
1775, Congress had sacrificed him on the promotion lists and then had
only grudgingly made adequate compensation, and the Executive Council of Pennsylvania had interfered with his duties as military commander
of Philadelphia following the British evacuation of the city in 1778. If
Arnold had occasionally received shabby treatment from the politicians, he was also lacking the honesty to recognize his own faults of
ambition and temperament or the lack of patience to endure the unjust
criticisms that all men in public life must now and then accept.

But Arnold's motives in changing the colors of his coat were undoubtedly complex. To his way of thinking, the patriot leaders had discredited themselves by their treatment of him and by their inability to
prosecute the war with vigor; in short, he seems to have developed
serious doubts about the value of independence for a country that
seemed to be weak and poorly led by civilians in the states and in
Congress. It is possible that the French alliance further influenced
Arnold against his countrymen; he made such a claim after his defection, arguing that America had prostrated herself at the feet of a nation
inimical to the liberties of mankind and to the protestant faith. The
role of Arnold's beautiful young wife, Peggy Shippen of Philadelphia,
is at once illuminating and shadowy: illuminating in that she was from
the beginning privy to his negotiations with the British, shadowy in that

whether her complicity also included influencing Arnold to become a traitor remains in doubt. In any event, she had many British and loyalist friends, and she shared her husband's desire for the good life that came from ample finances and social prestige.

In the spring of 1779, Arnold, whose extravagance had put him heavily in debt, began his secret negotiations with Sir Henry Clinton that were to last for sixteen months. The result was that Arnold would join the enemy and also turn over the strategic fortress of West Point to the British for a commission in the royal army and the tidy sum of £6,000, well over $55,000 in current reckoning. Although Arnold himself escaped to obtain his compensation, the plot to deliver West Point was foiled. Major John André, sent by Clinton to make the final arrangements, was captured wearing civilian clothes and carrying incriminating documents, which gave Washington no choice according to military custom but to execute the charming young man as a spy. Arnold, who was infallible in his own eyes, appears to have suffered no remorse at breaking faith with his country. As a soldier he was superior to the other military leaders who were approached by the British: Israel Putnam, John Sullivan, Philip Schuyler, Ethan Allen, Daniel Morgan, and Samuel Holden Parsons of Connecticut; but the favorable comparison does not extend to character—all the rest were honorable men.[34]

### Mutiny in January

"It's with inexpressible pain that I now inform your Excellency of the general mutiny and defection which suddenly took place in the Pennsylvania Line, between the hours of nine and ten o'clock last evening." So wrote General Anthony Wayne to Washington, at half-past four on the moonless morning of January 2, 1781, from his winter cantonment at Morristown. Symptoms of wholesale discontent, of course, were scarcely new in the army. Washington repeatedly expressed amazement that the Continentals, unlike other armies, had stopped short of rebellion in the face of intolerable conditions and had instead endured their hardships with incomparable "patience and fidelity." Before 1781 there were no serious uprisings in the army, and only in the case of an unhappy New England brigade, in 1777, was there bloodshed. The Yankee troops, long unpaid, refused to march from the Hudson to join the main army in Pennsylvania. A captain killed one of the mutineers, and was himself then shot by one of the rebellious men before order was restored and the troops were paid. In 1780 two hungry Connecticut regiments quartered in New Jersey prepared to move out of their encampment and ravage the countryside, but they were checked by loyal troops and their leaders were arrested.[35]

The grievances of the Pennsylvania line were common to the earlier mutineers and to soldiers throughout the army—want of pay, provisions, and clothes—except for one additional complaint. These regulars claimed, contrary to the contention of state leaders, that they had enlisted for three years rather than for the duration of the war. The matter had not been settled by January 1, 1781, the month the men regarded as terminating their services. That day, which happened to be Wayne's thirty-sixth birthday, there arrived in camp Pennsylvania recruiting agents who paid twenty-five dollars apiece in hard money to six-months' troops who had agreed to enlist for the duration. The veterans were more eager than ever to be honorably discharged so that they might either return home or re-enlist for the new cash bounties being offered. In the evening, 1,000 troops marched out of camp, announcing their intention of placing their grievances before civilian authorities. Although two officers were wounded and one killed before Wayne and his subordinates gave up their attempt to halt them, the mass of the mutineers professed a desire to avoid violence if at all possible.

The revolt of the Pennsylvania line was a unique episode which could only have occurred in a country where many of the men were upstanding citizen-soldiers conscious of their rights and liberties. At Princeton, Wayne caught up with his disgruntled regiments, and there a board of sergeants, representing the rank and file, explained their position to the General. They had no desire to go over to the enemy, and they would hang any man who attempted it. They told of their great personal respect for Wayne, and they said they would drop everything and fight under him immediately if the British tried to capitalize on the controversy. But otherwise they would take no further orders from him or any officers until their wrongs were righted. Sir Henry Clinton, unaware that the Pennsylvanians' quarrel was strictly a family affair, sent spies to lure the men into the British ranks with promises of personal freedom and bounties for joining the King's army. The sergeants promptly turned the enemy emissaries over to state authorities for execution. As one American remarked, Clinton might "bribe such a mean toadeater as Arnold," but "it is not in his power to bribe an American soldier."[36]

The mutineers informed Joseph Reed, president of the Executive Council of Pennsylvania, that he would be treated with dignity if he met with them to discuss their grievances, that they would be gratified by a quick solution to this "unhappy affair." Indeed, the behavior of the troops on the march and at Princeton had elicited the sympathy and good wishes of the local residents. A British agent admitted that "the Pennsylvanians observe the greatest order, and if a man takes a fowl from an inhabitant he is severely punished."[37] Reed, who saw justice in many of the soldiers' grievances, made important concessions: acceptance of a Continental's oath concerning his enlistment if the original muster-rolls were lost or unclear, or, in the case of some, if they had been tricked by their officers into signing up for the duration; payment of back salaries as soon as possible; new issues of shoes, overalls, and shirts; and immunity for all the mutineers. At Trenton on January 9 these arrangements were carried out, with five-sixths of the men receiving their discharge from the army, many of whom were probably not entitled to it, although some who swore the required oath were honest in thinking so.

If the Pennsylvania line displayed self-restraint and patriotism, state and Continental authorities also came off well, employing wisdom and justice in dealing with the disgruntled soldiers. John Sullivan, former major general and now a member of Congress, declared, "Constitutionally, no concession has been granted them, that the critical state of our affairs did not warrant, and justice dictate." Washington, who had advocated conciliation, voiced his approval; he had judiciously remained aloof from the proceedings to enable the civilian leadership to bring about a peaceful settlement. The *Pennsylvania Packet* praised the loyalty of the soldiers and extolled their superiority over "mercenary troops, who bear arms for pay and subsistence only, uninspired by their country's rights, or the justice of the cause which they have engaged to support." Governor William Livingston of New Jersey thought that good had come out of evil: "Even this alarming mutiny has ended to our honor and the confusion of the enemy."[38]

The flare-up among the Pennsylvania troops had its sequel on January 20, when three New Jersey regiments at Pompton mutinied. This time Washington felt that a stern hand was imperative to keep the infection from spreading to other state lines. Major General Robert Howe, refusing to make concessions, promptly surrounded the New Jersey men with New England units and trained cannons on them. The revolt collapsed. Howe arrested the three most prominent ringleaders, formed a firing squad out of the twelve next most influential offenders, and compelled them to execute their comrades.

## Politics of Demobilization

Disbanding the army in 1783 posed problems concerning both the officers and the rank and file. There was an abundance of time for all to dwell on the hardships and injustices of their service, for the army continued to exist for roughly two years following the defeat of Cornwallis. With few exceptions there was little fighting anywhere in America. Washington's dwindling band of regulars along the Hudson chiefly confined itself to observing the enemy at New York and waiting for the diplomats in Europe to complete the arrangements for peace (a subject to be treated separately in the next chapter).

A pressing grievance of the officers dealt with the half pay promised by Congress in 1780. Two years later, with the war apparently won, nothing had been done to follow up Congress' decision. Some civilians, in and out of Congress, now argued that an agreement made under the duress of war was invalid and that, if such compensation were to be forthcoming, it should be undertaken instead by the states. Massachusetts officers resolved to appeal to their state legislature for compensation, but when a committee with a memorial went to Boston in September, 1782, it was turned down and informed that Congress should first consider the matter. Returning to Washington's camp at Newburgh, the Massachusetts men took the lead in drafting a list of grievances to lay before Congress. The smoldering discontent of the officers so alarmed Washington that he decided against returning to Mount Vernon to spend the winter. Their mood, Washington confided to Joseph Jones of Virginia, "has become more irritable than at any period since the commencement of the war. . . ."[39]

Yet the officers' demands—carried to Congress by General Alexander McDougall and Colonels John Brooks and Matthias Ogden—were not unreasonable, even though strongly worded. Besides enumerating their familiar complaints of inadequate food and clothing for the entire army, they urged that "as great a part as possible" of their back pay be provided before their discharge and that there be a general reckoning of all remaining accounts to prepare the way for later settlement. The officers at Newburgh, aware that the half-pay-for-life provision was unpopular with people who feared the creation of a distinct military caste, offered a conciliatory alternative, the commutation of their pensions into a cash sum. They did not stipulate whether they expected payment by Congress or by the states, but they requested that the representatives of the Confederation set the cash equivalent of their pensions and "point out a mode" of payment.[40]

By this time some of the nationalists—advocates of a stronger central government—saw the army as a valuable political instrument or pressure group. Let it join with the other principal public creditors, primarily the mercantile class which had acquired its certificates of indebtedness in the course of trade and supplying the army; together with the nationalists in Congress, they would be able to make that legislative body a power in the land. On the other hand, if the officers looked to the states rather than to the Confederation for justice, then the forces of localism would gain a significant victory and the cause of firm, effective national union might receive a fatal blow. Three civilian leaders especially sought to cement the army to the nationalists' cause: Robert Morris, Gouverneur Morris, and Alexander Hamilton. The advocates of additional federal control had recently failed in their effort to secure an amendment to the Articles of Confederation to allow Congress to levy a 5 per cent duty on foreign imports. The defeat of this "impost"—rejected only by Rhode Island—gave Superintendent of Finance Robert Morris an opening wedge in discussions with McDougall and the colonels. Congress, he said, favored paying the pensions instead of leaving the matter to the states; but little could be accomplished until the lawmakers received the power to tax.[41] In fact, Morris and his allies hoped that joining the weight of the army with that of the influential and increasingly restive civilian creditors might lead to the adoption of Morris' long-range financial program for funding all Continental debts and creating a permanent federal revenue. Hopefully, Congress would adopt several amendments to this effect and the states would ratify them. The states would likely be more difficult to persuade than Congress; but the Morris faction assumed that the recalcitrant Rhode Islanders and the state-centered politicians elsewhere would think twice before thumbing their noses at the arms-bearing Continentals as they had done in the face of Congress.

The Morrises may not necessarily have been opposed to a small measure of violence on the part of the army. Young Gouverneur Morris, a charming aristocrat, whose vigor was scarcely dampened by the recent loss of one leg, minced no words in expressing his feelings. Morris, assistant superintendent of finance but no kinsman of Robert Morris, was as skeptical of the wisdom of the mass of humanity as he was dedicated to a firm American union. "The army have swords in their hands," he bluntly notified John Jay. "You know enough of the history of mankind to know much more than I have said, and possibly much more than they themselves yet think of." Besides alerting Nathanael Greene to the impending crisis, Morris wrote Henry Knox that after the army brought the politicians into line, or "after you have carried the Post"—"if you will permit me a Metaphor from your own Profession"—then "the public Creditors will garrison it for you."[42]

Since not all of the nationalists were cut from the same cloth, there is no need to indict them *en masse* for willingness to risk the subversion of American liberties in order to obtain a government capable of coping with the country's financial needs. For instance, a very few at most would apparently have been willing to prolong the war as a means of goading the states into granting greater centralization of governmental authority. Once again the Morrises may be singled out. Two months after Yorktown, Gouverneur Morris informed Greene that "to reinforce the reasonings" behind more power for Congress, "to impress the arguments, and to sweeten the persuasions of the public servants, we have that great friend to sovereign authority, a foreign war." Robert Morris agreed; as a true patriot, he wished the conflict to last until the prestige and jurisdiction of Congress were elevated to higher levels. A nationalist himself, Washington was mindful of such sentiments, but could not fully share them since he desired an end to hostilities at the earliest possible date.[43]

Rumors flew thick and fast in the opening months of 1783. Hamilton and Madison reported that elements in the army were dissatisfied with Washington, who, it was said, failed to show sufficient sympathy for the welfare of the men in service. Madison believed the opinion "to be well founded, that the arms which have secured the liberties of this country will not be laid down until justice is secured. . . ." With each passing day "The discontents and designs of the army are . . . taking a more solemn form." Arthur Lee, back from Europe and now in Congress, complained to Samuel Adams that "Every Engine is at work here to obtain permanent taxes. . . . The terror of a mutinying Army is playd off with considerable efficacy."[44]

These reports are difficult to evaluate, partly because a faction of the nationalists was intent on spreading such stories, partly too because their opponents were fearful, perhaps unduly so. In any case, the disposition of the officers was scarcely improved by the return of General McDougall and Colonel Ogden with word that at the moment Congress felt it could do nothing in their behalf. Colonel Brooks, who remained in Philadelphia for another ten days allegedly for further indoctrination by the nationalists, then returned to Newburgh to prepare the junior officers for "manly, Vigorous Association with the other public Creditors." But Brooks, according to one of the chief malcontents, Major John Armstrong, Jr., was "a timid wretch" who failed to carry out his mission. Whatever their private views, several of the ranking officers were aware that the army's muscle was a potent weapon for good or ill. McDougall asked Knox about the feasibility of joining "the Army and the public Creditors to obtain permanent funds for the United States[,] which will promise most ultimate Security to the Army?" Knox, unlike McDougall, was no extremist. He predicted that the soldiers, if fairly compensated, would return to their homes "the lambs and bees of the community." Were they disbanded before a settlement, however, they would become "its tigers and wolves."[45]

Alexander Hamilton proposed to fish in these troubled waters: Washington would be his bait with which to land the army on the side of the nationalists and the public creditors. The use of violence, in Hamilton's mind, was absurd; force could not be kept within limits. It "might end in the ruin of the Country, and would certainly end in the ruin of the army." But with Washington's prestige unifying the army and joining it with the other advocates of a revitalized Confederation, the military could obtain its objectives "within the bounds of moderation." Hamilton made no bones about the role the commander in chief should play. "Your Excellency's influence," he instructed Washington, "should preserve the confidence of the army without losing that of the people." For the "great *desideratum* at present is the establishment of general funds, which alone can do justice to the Creditors of the United States (of whom the army forms the most meritorious class), restore public credit and supply the future wants of government. This is the object of all men of sense; in this the influence of the army, properly directed, may cooperate."[46]

Washington, refusing to be coached, was of a different mind. Though "No man in the United States" recognized more than he the need of "reform in our present Confederation," the commander in chief considered the army a "most dangerous instrument to play with," even for the laudable end of obtaining a general revenue. He believed that the quickest means of producing more discontent among the soldiers was to let them think they were being used as puppets to establish Continental funds. If Washington refused to manipulate the army to the advantage of certain politicians and public creditors, he nevertheless hoped that the military establishment would not be disbanded until the officers and men had their accounts ascertained and provided for by Congress.[47]

The next episode in the unfolding drama of demobilization was the Newburgh Addresses. The whole story will likely never be known, but the outline is clear enough. On March 10, 1783, two unsigned addresses were circulated among the officers at Newburgh. The first called a meeting of the officers to obtain a "redress of grievances," which the army's recent committee to Congress "seem[s] to have solicited in vain." Such a gathering was unauthorized and against regulations since the commander in chief had not been consulted. The second was a pamphlet, emotional and dramatic, probably written by Major Armstrong, an aide to General Gates, now the ranking general in the army next to Washington. Neglected in war, the army would soon be forgotten with the advent of peace, warned the author. "To be tame and unprovoked when injuries press hard upon you" would be fatal to the officers' cause. Events had demonstrated that theirs was "a country that tramples upon your rights, disdains your cries and insults your distresses." The anonymous counsellor advocated putting congressmen on notice that the officers' patience was at an end:

Tell them that, though you were the first, and would wish to be the last to encounter danger: though despair itself can never drive you into dishonor, it may drive you from the field: that the wound often irritated, may at length become incurable; and that the slightest mark of indignity from Congress now, must operate like the grave, and part you forever: that in any political event, the army has its alternative. If peace, that nothing shall separate them from your arms but death: if war, that courting the auspices, and inviting the direction of your illustrious leader, you will retire to some unsettled country, smile in your turn, and 'mock when their fear cometh on.'[48]

What sort of conspiracy, if any, lay behind the Newburgh Addresses? Two days earlier, on March 8, Superintendent of Finance Robert Morris had proposed an ultimatum to the states. On the basis of implied powers, he asserted that Congress had the authority to determine a plan for meeting the federal debt. Should the states fail to come up with their respective portions of the debt by a specified time, possibly a year, then the states would have to allow Congress to levy taxes and tariff duties necessary to discharge their quotas. Was pressure from "the financier" to be combined simultaneously with pressure from the army to secure a congressional revenue? Approximately the day of Morris' ultimatum to the states there arrived at Newburgh a Colonel Walter Stewart, who, according to Horatio Gates, was a "kind of agent from friends of the army in Congress." Washington himself believed that Stewart had taken an active part in arousing the officers, telling them that the public creditors looked to the officers for relief and would "even join them in the Field if necessary." Indeed, the commander in chief heard it said that "the Scheme" leading to the Newburgh Addresses "was not only planned, but also digested and matured in Philadelphia. . . ."[49]

It is no easy matter, however, to arrive at a neat, clear-cut explanation of the efforts to enroll the army in the drive for a more centralized political system. Although there were a substantial number of large security holders in the Philadelphia area, they were scarcely a monolithic group; some cordially detested others, and by no means all of them were close to Robert Morris.

Equally perplexing is the role of Horatio Gates in fomenting the discontent reflected in the Newburgh Addresses. There is a good deal of circumstantial evidence to implicate Gates as one of the chief troublemakers. Colonel Walter Stewart was Gates' former aide, and John Armstrong was currently serving Gates in that capacity. George Bancroft, the first historian to offer a detailed treatment of the events surrounding the Newburgh Addresses, placed the blame for the episode squarely upon "Gates and those around him." Bancroft presented no extensive documentation for his accusation, and most historians have shied away from such a forceful indictment of the victor at Saratoga. Yet Gates must surely have sympathized up to a point at least with the views of Armstrong in the Newburgh Addresses, for the latter wrote frankly to his immediate superior of his disgust with the politicians and officers, "fools and Rascals," who refused to stand resolutely behind the interests of the army. To Gates, he also lambasted Washington, "the Illustrissimo of the age"; and he vowed that, with "Mad Anthony [Wayne] at their Head," the soldiers would have resorted to every possible means to obtain their objectives.[50]

Even so, Gates was probably not closely allied with the Morrises and the nationalist faction in Congress. Previously, at least, the very reverse was true: hostile to Robert Morris and Hamilton, Gates, an ardent democrat, was a darling of the small government men and doctrinaire republicans such as Dr. Benjamin Rush.[51] If all this suggests anything, it is that no well-organized conspiracy existed, that the nationalists, the civilian creditors, and the army's dissidents were never of one mind as to means and ends.

The situation at Newburgh nevertheless was potentially dangerous. Many officers might follow the words of Armstrong and seek violent methods of resolving their grievances. Consequently, Washington's hand in calming the storm remains important. The commander in chief took quick and decisive action. He informed Congress of the Newburgh Addresses, he denounced these "disorderly proceedings" in his general orders, and he called a new meeting of the officers for March 15. Before the assembled group, he appealed to the officers to have faith in the good intention of Congress and not to undertake steps that would "lessen the dignity, and sully the glory you have hitherto maintained. . . ." He promised to support their just complaints "to the utmost" of his "abilities." If Washington did not win over all the malcontents, he definitely carried the majority with him. Some of his brothers in arms were visibly touched when, in reading his remarks, he faltered and reached for his eyeglasses, saying, "Gentlemen, you will permit me to put on my spectacles, for I have not only grown gray, but almost blind, in the service of my country."[52]

The denouement of the army crisis came about as a result of sensible actions on the part of both the officers and Congress. After Washington's speech, the men at Newburgh formed a committee, headed by Knox, that drafted resolutions affirming the officers' loyalty to Congress, their faith in an honorable settlement of their grievances, and their opposition to the ideas in the Newburgh Addresses. Congress, in turn, met the officers' proposal to commute the authorized bonus of half pay for life into a promise of full salaries for five years—in the form of federal securities at 6 per cent. The final two demands of the officers, full pay and the settlement of accounts, inevitably involved a delay, but neither officers nor enlisted men wanted to remain in the service longer than necessary. Congress decided that three months' pay would be an appropriate parting gesture in behalf of the army. But Washington, responding to a resolve from the lawmakers of May 26, had already furloughed part of the troops, their discharges to be automatic with the signing of the official treaty of peace. Some of the men marched away with only their muskets, which they were allowed to keep as a gratuity. A contingent of three-year enlistees remained with Washington until the British evacuated New York City.[53]

The complete settlement of the army's accounts was to be the work of many years. Because of the straitened financial condition of the Confederation government, military pay and bonus certificates—except for a fraction honored by the states—were not redeemed until the 1790's and were sometimes sold at a heavy discount by the original owners. The veterans of the Revolution were also frustrated in collecting their bounty lands voted by Congress. Even though the lawmakers displayed their good intentions toward the ex-soldiers eligible for land grants (enlistment for the duration of the war) in the Ordinance of 1785 and subsequent legislation, Congress could do little until money was at hand for the survey and administrative disbursement of the public domain. The country was at peace for a decade and a half before the first titles to bounty lands were conveyed, and by then most of the former Continentals' warrants were in the hands of speculators and other outsiders. Disabled veterans also had to wait until a later day for the cash allotments they were to receive, officers half pay for life, enlisted men five dollars a month. (In 1818 Congress pensioned all veterans in need, and ten years later all servicemen of the Revolution obtained pensions equal to their former military pay.)[54]

## A Republican Army

The Continental army, in the last analysis, was a republican army. Even with its tensions and flare-ups, it was remarkably loyal to the civil authority and to the goals of the Revolution. When officers and men complained of their ill fortune, they usually did so through constituted channels. If many soldiers became disenchanted with conditions and left the service, others continued to give their all for reasons of patriotism. The Continental was spending his blood in his own cause, for a country in which he had a share, a country where people had more rights and liberties than anywhere else in the world. To the English savant, Dr. Samuel Johnson, patriotism was the last refuge of a scoundrel; but to the youthful British officer Charles Stuart, who marvelled at the courage and determination of the American soldiers, a new day was emerging in the annals of warfare: when officers and their men must share common ideals, when to win they must be animated by something akin to "religious fervor."[55]

"I admire the American troops tremendously!" exclaimed Baron von Closen of the French army. "It is incredible that soldiers composed of men of every age, even of children of fifteen, of whites and blacks, almost naked, unpaid, and rather poorly fed, can march so well and withstand fire so steadfastly." American officers likewise praised the stamina and perseverance of their own lines. John Laurens, who was to give his own life in the final action of the war in the South ("a trifling skirmish," Washington noted sadly), "cherish[ed] those dear, ragged Continentals, whose patience will be the admiration of future ages, and [I] glory in bleeding with them." Laurens' dedication was matched by that of Lieutenant Joseph Hodgkins, who, though preferring the sweets of domestic life, recognized that he was engaged in a "glorious cause": he stood ready "to serve my Contery in the Best way & manner that I am Capable of. . . ." Lieutenant Colonel Lewis Morris of New York was another who had "embarked in this Cause from Principle." He sought "no other Reward but the approbation of having done my Duty."[56]

The commander in chief of an army, like the chief executive of a nation, may sometimes give a kind of tone and quality to the cause he leads. The Continentals were freedom-loving men to begin with, but the loyalty and patriotism of many of them must have been reinforced and heightened by Washington, whose own devotion to the Revolution was well known. No warm, outgoing person, he bound men to him by his own sense of justice and dedication. In fact, he has been criticized for expecting his troops to measure up to his own high standards of conduct—in particular, he is said to have been an excessively harsh disciplinarian. Undoubtedly, "Subordination and Discipline" were "the Life and Soul of an Army" in Washington's view. He not only heartily approved when Congress increased the authorized number of lashes from 39 to 100; he later tried unsuccessfully to have the maximum raised to 500. But as one historian reminds us, contemporaries did not fault him for resorting to such punishment; and it is well to remember that in the British army 1,000 lashes were not uncommon.[57]

At times Washington was surprisingly moderate as a disciplinarian—too lenient, according to Steuben, Henry Laurens, and Charles Carroll. Upon finding that a man convicted of sleeping at his post was normally a "well-behaved soldier" and was "probably unwell" at the time of his offense, the commander in chief reduced his sentence to twenty-five lashes. He was even more lenient in the case of two soldiers convicted of abandoning their stations; they received full pardons on the grounds they were young and did not comprehend their duties. On July 4, 1779, the Virginian pardoned all soldiers in the army under sentence of death, and four times he offered amnesty for all deserters who would rejoin their regiments by a certain date. Washington especially disliked the death penalty. Allen Bowman declares that, after taking a sample of 225 men given the ultimate sentence, only 40 can be said with certainty to have actually met their death as ordered.[58]

With rare exception, however, charity ended with men convicted of plundering, for which death was a common punishment. Washington knew that the army could scarcely have the confidence of the people if such predatory behavior were condoned to the slightest extent. The Revolution, after all, had begun partly in defense of property, and marauding Continentals had no more right to an American citizen's possessions than the British Parliament. It was imperative, he felt, to protect "the essential interests of any individual," even at the risk of sacrificing advantage; hence, his extreme reluctance to confiscate supplies for the army—an unpleasant task which, whenever necessary, should be undertaken by civilian authorities instead of by Continentals. His attitude was of the highest importance in a war that, to the civilian population, seemed endlessly long and fraught with severe hardships. Conscious of public opinion, he out-generaled his adversaries for the minds of his countrymen. His army displayed visible virtue: it was less destructive than that of the enemy.

Washington intended for his soldiers to know what the Revolution was all about, and in his general orders he acted as a teacher desirous of forming "enlightened opinions" among the troops. The struggle, he repeatedly reminded them, was for human freedom, not for the imperialistic and dynastic ambitions that customarily drove the European nations to arms. "The fate of unborn millions will now depend, under God, on the Courage and Conduct of this Army," he wrote on the day that Congress voted in favor of independence. Washington warned that if the American experiment in self-rule should fail owing to defeat on the battlefield or because of apathy behind the lines, then Americans would sacrifice not only their own country but all mankind as well, for the Revolution in its broad implications suggested that a better way of life was possible for men everywhere. Besides holding his army together and achieving victory with the aid of France, he had helped to pave the way for the transition to peace and domestic concerns: he and his countrymen had, in the words of New Englander Fisher Ames, "conducted a civil war with mildness and a revolution with order."[59]

# NOTES

1. *American State Papers. Military Affairs* (Washington, 1832), I, 14–19, Peckham, *War for Independence*, 200; Frederic Kidder and Augustus A. Gould, *The History of New Ipswich* (Boston, 1852), 102, 106. See also *Massachusetts Soldiers and Sailors of the Revolutionary War . . .* (Boston, 1896–1908), I, ix–xxxix.
2. Butterfield, ed., *Adams Diary and Autobiography*, II, 210.
3. Jared Sparks, ed., *Correspondence of the Revolution: Being Letters of Eminent Men to George Washington* (Boston, 1852), I, 348–349. Roger Sherman of Connecticut described "Long enlistment . . . [as] a state of slavery. there ought to be a rotation which is in favor of liberty." Burnett, ed., *Letters of Congress*, I, 360. However, Washington from the beginning of his efforts to secure a more permanent military establishment found considerable support in Congress. Knollenberg, *Washington and the Revolution*, 122–128.

   Congress realistically reduced the army from its authorized strength (which finally reached 104 battalions) to 80 in 1779, and the next year it further cut the number to 50 regiments of infantry, plus four each of artillery and cavalry, and one of artificers.

   See Revolutionary War Records, Record Group 93, microfilm rolls 137–138, National Archives, for returns of Washington's Middle Department.
4. Ford, ed., *Journals of Congress*, V, 483, 762–763, XIV, 758. John Hancock to Washington, June 26, 1776, Papers of the Continental Congress, No. 12A, I, 201–202; Washington to Jonathan Trumbull, Feb. 1, 1777, Washington to Patrick Henry, Nov. 13, 1777, Washington to John Jay, March 13, 1779, Fitzpatrick, ed., *Writings of Washington*, VII, 86, X, 54–55, XIV, 242. Unfortunately for Washington, the problem continued as late as 1782. "Those who desert are almost entirely of the old soldiers who are [enlisted] for the war," wrote General William Heath. *William Heath Papers* (Massachusetts Historical Society, *Collections*, vols. 64–65 [1904–1905]), 7th ser., V, 379–380.
5. Copy of broadside in possession of the author. Martin, *Private Yankee Doodle*, 66–67. Elliott's account is in *South Carolina Historical Magazine*, XVII (1916), 95, 96. Some of Washington's general officers seem to have condoned the enlisting of "Boys of Good Growth & firm Constitutions . . . altho' they shall not be of the age of Sixteen . . . ." Alexander McDougall to Washington, with enclosure, Feb. 24, 1779, Washington Papers, Library of Congress.
6. Fitzpatrick, ed., *Writings of Washington*, X, 366.
7. Ford, ed., *Journals of Congress*, X, 200; John D. Thompson to Governor Thomas Lee, Aug. 11, 1781, Browne and others, ed., *Archives of Maryland*, XLVII, 411.
8. Marvin A. Kriedberg and Merton G. Henry, *History of Mobilization in the United States Army, 1775–1945* (Washington, 1955), 15, compare conscription in the Revolution to selective service of more recent times. For Massachusetts, including John Sail's notice, consult Jonathan Smith, "How Massachusetts Raised Her Troops in the Revolution," Massachusetts Historical Society, *Proceedings*, LV (1921–1922), 351–356. Three useful articles are by Arthur J. Alexander: "Pennsylvania's Revolutionary Militia," *Pennsylvania Magazine of History and Biography*, LXIX (1945), 15–25; "How Maryland Tried to Raise Her Continental Quotas," *Maryland Historical Magazine*, XIII (1947), 184–196; "Service by Substitute in the Militia of Lancaster and Northampton Counties (Pennsylvania) During the War of the Revolution," *Military Affairs*, IX (1945), 278–282. See also Orville T. Murphy, "The American Revolutionary Army and the Concept of the Levee en Masse," *ibid.*, XXIII (1959), 13–20. Lynn W. Turner, *William Plumer of New Hampshire, 1759–1850* (Chapel Hill, 1962), 5, mentions Epping's conscription practices.

9. Morris, *Government and Labor in Early America*, 298; *Minutes of the Albany Committee of Correspondence, 1775–1778* (Albany, N.Y., 1923–1925), II, 1048–1050, 1056; "Journal of Joseph Joslin, Jr., . . . A Teamster in the Continental Service," Connecticut Historical Society, *Collections*, VII (1899), 299–369.

10. Hening, ed., *Statutes at Large*, VII, 70.

11. Fitzpatrick, ed., *Writings of Washington*, XI, 98–99.

12. Bernardo and Bacon, *American Military Policy*, 14. The county committee of Cumberland County, Pennsylvania, voiced opposition to the enlistment of servants without their masters' consent because "all Apprentices and servants are the Property of their masters and mistresses, and every mode of depriving such masters and mistresses of their Property is a Violation of the Rights of mankind, contrary to the . . . Continental Congress, and an offence against the Peace of the good People of this State." *Pennsylvania Archives*, 1st ser., V, 340.

13. Massachusetts Historical Society, *Collections*, 7th ser., IV, 135–136.

14. Ford, ed., *Journals of Congress*, XXIII, 387–388; Richard B. Morris, ed., *A Letter from Henry Laurens to His Son John Laurens, August 14, 1776* (New York, 1964). John Laurens' anti-slavery views are discussed in letters to his father, especially Jan. 14, Feb. 2, 1778, in Simms, ed., *Correspondence of John Laurens*, 108, 114–118. An unknown essayist declared, "The blacks are naturally brave as any people under heaven; their motives of fidelity, if liberated, stronger, if possible, than those which operate on the whites." *Connecticut Courant*, May 19, 1777. Similar sentiments appear in *Boston Gazette*, Oct. 13, 1777.

15. Ramsay to Benjamin Rush, March 21, 1780, Brunhouse, ed., "David Ramsay, 1749–1815; Selections from His Writings," 66.

16. Quarles, *Negro in the American Revolution*, vii; Richard B. Morris, ed., *Alexander Hamilton and the Founding of the Nation* (New York, 1957), 455. A French officer claimed that a fourth of Washington's army at White Plains, New York, in July, 1781, consisted of Negroes. He also noted, "Three-quarters of the Rhode Island regiment consists of negroes, and that regiment is the most neatly dressed, the best under arms, and the most precise in its maneuvers." Acomb, ed., *Journal of Baron Von Closen*, 89, 92.

17. Hutchinson and Rachal, eds., *Papers of Madison*, II, 209. See also *ibid.*, 182–183, 185 n6, 198, 219, 233.

18. *Maryland Gazette*, May 15, 1783.

19. Early American thought on the Negro is examined fully in Winthrop D. Jordan, *White Over Black: American Attitudes Toward the Negro, 1550–1812* (Chapel Hill, 1968). The process of manumission is detailed in Arthur Silversmit, *The First Emancipation: The Abolition of Slavery in the North* (Chicago, 1967).

20. Fitzpatrick, ed., *Writings of Washington*, IX, 17, 126, XXVI, 79.

21. See Walter H. Blumenthal, *Women Camp Followers of the American Revolution* (Philadelphia, 1952).

22. Rossman, *Mifflin*, 75; Worthington C. Ford, ed., *Correspondence and Journals of Samuel Blachley Webb* (New York, 1893), II, 231–232.

23. "The Continental Army Uniform," in John C. Fitzpatrick, *The Spirit of the Revolution* (Boston and New York, 1924), 117–138; Harold L. Peterson, *The Book of the Continental Soldier: Being a Compleat Account of the Uniforms, Weapons, and Equipment with Which He Lived and Fought* (Harrisburg, Pa., 1968). Other useful works on the subject include Charles M. Lefferts, *Uniforms of the American, British, French, and German Armies in the War of the American Revolution, 1775–1783* (New York, 1926); Frederick P. Todd, *Soldiers of the American Army, 1775–1954* (Chicago, 1954).

24. Ford, ed., *Journals of Congress*, III, 322. "Christopher Ludwig, Baker-General of the Army of the United States during the Revolutionary War," *Pennsylvania Magazine of History and Biography*, XVI (1892), 343–348, is pertinent.

25. "Valley Forge, 1777–78: The Diary of Surgeon Albigence Waldo of the Continental Line," *ibid.*, XXI (1897), 309–310. Baron de Kalb's remark is quoted in Erna Risch, *Quartermaster Support of the Army: A History of the Corps* (Washington, 1962), 56. See Martin's *Private Yankee Doodle*, 150, 149. The

army's second winter at Morristown is treated in S. Sydney Bradford, ed., "Hunger Menaces the Revolution, December 1779–January, 1780," *Maryland Historical Magazine*, LXI (1966), 1–23.

26. *Diary of Mackenzie*, I, 64; Fitzpatrick, ed., *Writings of Washington*, VIII, 8. Though one may seriously doubt Joseph Galloway's estimate that the winter of 1777–1778 witnessed the defection of 1,134 soldiers and 354 sailors to the British side, the Pennsylvania loyalist was perhaps correct in stating that the bulk of American defectors were foreign-born, "natives of Ireland, England, or Scotland." Stevens, ed., *Facsimiles of Manuscripts in European Archives Relating to America*, XXIV, 2094. Available records indicate that many deserters were from England, Scotland, Ireland, and Germany. See Roster of State and Continental Troops, Connecticut, Massachusetts, and South Carolina, Record Group 93, National Archives.

27. Rupert Hughes, *George Washington: The Savior of the States* (New York, 1930), 81, 86; "Letters of Ebenezer Huntington, 1774–1781," *American Historical Review*, V (1900), 721. Desertion and sickness together are said to have accounted for an average loss of 20,000 men (from a total of about 180,000) in the French army. Albert Duruy, *L'armée royale en 1789* (Paris, 1888), 34. Between 1713 and 1740, 30,216 men deserted from the Prussian army. A contemporary observer of mid-century Prussia wrote that the native half of the army was assigned the task of preventing the foreign half from deserting. Dorn, *Competition for Empire*, 98, 98 n24. Frequently American newspapers contained descriptions of runaways from the Continental Army. See the following references in *Boston Gazette* for examples: Aug. 16, 1776, Feb. 3, May 5, June 2, July 7, Oct. 13, Dec. 8, 1777, Jan. 18, 1779, May 7, 1781.

28. "Diary of a French Officer, 1781," *Magazine of American History*, IV (1880), 209; Wade and Lively, *This Glorious Cause*, 52–53.

29. "Letters of Ebenezer Huntington, 1774–1781," 721, 725; Daniel Morgan to Jefferson, March 23, 1781, Boyd, ed., *Papers of Jefferson*, V, 218–219; Billias, *Glover*, 190. Pertinent information on the social and economic background of Continental officers appears in Main, *Social Structure of Revolutionary America*, 213–215; Sidney Kaplan, "Rank and Status among Massachusetts Continental Officers," *American Historical Review*, LVI (1951), 318–326. Presumably, a substantial number of American officers were reasonably well educated for their day. A historian of higher education declared that out of 2,500 college graduates alive in 1775, about one-quarter entered military service. Charles F. Thwing, *A History of Higher Education in America* (New York, 1906), 165.

30. Syrett, ed., *Papers of Hamilton*, I, 415; Sparks, ed., *Correspondence of the Revolution*, II, 67–68.

31. Washington to the Committee of Congress, Jan. 28, 1778, and Washington to Henry Laurens, April 10, 1778, Fitzpatrick, ed., *Writings of Washington*, X, 363–365, XI, 237.

32. See chap. ix.

33. Ford, ed., *Journals of Congress*, X, 391–393, XI, 502, XVII, 771–773, XVIII, 958, 960.

34. The full story of Arnold's treason was first told by Carl Van Doren, *Secret History of the American Revolution* (New York, 1941), chaps. vi–xv, appendix. It was Van Doren who pointed out the involvement of Peggy Shippen Arnold, whereas contemporaries and previous historians had not known of her awareness of the conspiracy. A brilliant biography is Wallace, *Traitorous Hero*, who estimates the value of Arnold's monetary compensation in terms of modern currency as of 1954. Some new information on Arnold's treason is in James T. Flexner, *The Traitor and the Spy* (New York, 1953). The fidelity of Joseph Reed, Washington's aide and Pennsylvania political leader, was once seriously questioned. The matter seems to have been permanently resolved in favor of Reed's loyalty to the United States. John F. Roche, "Was Joseph Reed Disloyal?" *William and Mary Quarterly*, 3d ser., VIII (1951), 406–417.

35. Draft of Wayne's letter in C. J. Stillé, *Major General Anthony Wayne and the*

*Pennsylvania Line* (Philadelphia, 1893), 242–243. For the New Englanders' mutiny, see Hamilton to Washington, Nov. 10, 12, 1777, Syrett, ed., *Papers of Hamilton*, I, 357–362, *passim*.

36. *New-Jersey Gazette*, Jan. 17, 1781.

37. The British agent's observation is quoted in Carl Van Doren, *Mutiny in January* (New York, 1943), 56, the standard treatment of the Pennsylvania uprising.

38. Sullivan to Washington, Jan. 10, 1781, Sparks, ed., *Correspondence of the Revolution*, III, 198; *Pennsylvania Packet*, Jan. 28, 1781; *Pennsylvania Gazette*, Feb. 12, 1781; Sedgwick, *A Memoir of the Life of William Livingston*, 359.

39. William Health to Knox, June 24, 1782, Knox to John Hancock, Sept. 2, 1782, Knox Papers, Massachusetts Historical Society; Fitzpatrick, ed., *Writings of Washington*, XXV, 430.

40. The petition is in Ford, ed., *Journals of Congress*, XXIV, 291–293. See also Sidney Kaplan, "Pay, Pension, and Power: Economic Grievances of the Massachusetts Officers of the Revolution," *Boston Public Library Quarterly*, III, (1951), 129–134.

41. Alexander McDougall to Henry Knox, Jan. 9, 1783, McDougall and Matthias Ogden to Knox, Feb. 8, 1783, Burnett, ed., *Letters of Congress*, VII, 14 n2, 35–36 n3; Brutus [McDougall] to Knox, Feb. 27, 1783, Knox Papers, Massachusetts Historical Society; Ford, ed., *Journals of Congress*, XXIV, 43, XXV, 847–855.

42. Gouverneur Morris to John Jay, Jan. 1, 1783, Gouverneur Morris to Nathanael Greene, Feb. 15, 1783, Jared Sparks, *Life of Gouverneur Morris* (New York, 1832), I, 249, 250–251; Gouverneur Morris to Knox, Feb. 7, 1783, Burnett, ed., *Letters of Congress*, VII, 34–35 n3.

43. Gouverneur Morris to Greene, Dec. 24, 1781, Sparks, *Gouverneur Morris*, I, 238–241; Robert Morris to Matthew Ridley, Oct. 6, 1782, *The Confidential Correspondence of Robert Morris* (Stan V. Henkels, *Catalogue* no. 1183), 41; Washington to William Gordon, Oct. 23, 1782, Fitzpatrick, ed., *Writings of Washington*, XXV, 287–288.

44. Hamilton to Washington, Feb. 13, 1783, Syrett, ed., *Papers of Hamilton*, III, 254; Madison to Edmund Randolph, Feb. 13, 25, 1783, Arthur Lee to Samuel Adams, Jan. 29, 1783, Burnett, ed., Letters of Congress, VII, 44, 57–58, 27–28; Arthur Lee to James Warren, Feb. 19, 1783, *Warren-Adams Letters*, II, 190. See also Hutchinson and Rachal, eds., *Papers of Madison*, VI, 232–233, 285–287.

45. John Armstrong, Jr., to Horatio Gates, April 29, 1783, McDougall to Knox, Jan. 9, 1783, Burnett, ed., *Letters of Congress*, VII, 155 n3, 14 n2; Knox to Benjamin Lincoln, March 3, 1783, Francis S. Drake, *Life and Correspondence of Henry Knox* (Boston, 1873), 79–80. See also Knox to Lincoln, Dec. 20, 1782, Knox Papers, Massachusetts Historical Society.

46. Hamilton to Washington, March 17, 1783, Syrett, ed., *Papers of Hamilton*, III, 293, 253–255.

47. Washington to Hamilton, March 31, April 4, 1783, Fitzpatrick, ed., *Writings of Washington*, XXVI, 276–277, 291–293.

48. The Newburgh Addresses are in Ford, ed., *Journals of Congress*, XXIV, 294–297. Copies of the Addresses, along with the transactions of the meeting of March 15 and Washington's correspondence with Congress, are in Papers of the Continental Congress, No. 152, XI, 105–154.

49. Robert Morris to President of Congress, March 8, 1783, Wharton, ed., *Diplomatic Correspondence of the Revolution*, VI, 277–281; Gates to John Armstrong, Jr., June 22, 1783, quoted in George Bancroft, *History of the Formation of the Constitution* . . . (New York, 1883), I, 93; Washington to Joseph Jones, March 12, 1783, Fitzpatrick, ed., *Writings of Washington*, XXVI, 213–214.

50. Bancroft, *History of the Formation of the Constitution*, I, 84. Forrest McDonald, *The Formation of the American Republic, 1776–1790* (Boston, 1965), 27–28, repeats Bancroft's charge against Gates but offers no additional evidence. A contemporary effort to implicate Gates, based on hearsay evidence five years after the event, is in Charles R. King, *The Life and Correspondence of Rufus*

*King* (New York, 1894), I, 621–622. The closeness of the Armstrong-Gates relationship is revealed in Armstrong to Gates, May 30, June 26, 1783, Burnett, ed., *Letters of Congress*, VII, 175–176 n3, 199–200 n2. Since writing this section, a stimulating article has appeared on the subject by Richard H. Kohn, "The Inside History of the Newburgh Conspiracy: America and the Coup d'Etat," *William and Mary Quarterly*, 3d ser., XXVII (1970), 187 220. Kohn also implicates Gates, but he admits that his evidence is largely circumstantial.

51. See Rush to Gates, June 12, Sept. 5, 1781, Butterfield, ed., *Letters of Rush*, I, 263, 264–265.

52. Fitzpatrick, ed., *Writings of Washington*, XXVI, 208, 211–212, 222–227; Freeman, *Washington*, V, 435, 435 n39.

53. Ford, ed., *Journals of Congress*, XXIV, 206–210, 364, XXV, 926. For Knox's advocacy of moderation, see Knox to McDougall, March 12, 1783, Knox to Lincoln, March 12, 16, 1783, Knox Papers, Massachusetts Historical Society. Eighty enlisted men at Lancaster, Pennsylvania, refused to be put off by promises of a later settlement and set out for Philadelphia to demand an immediate adjustment of their accounts. Reinforced by troops already garrisoned in the capital, the mutineers barricaded Congress and the Executive Council of Pennsylvania in the State House. But the rebels failed to follow through on their threats of violence. Even before the arrival of reliable units under Robert Howe, the Pennsylvania soldiers bowed to pressure from the state's Executive Council and agreed to return to their quarters at Lancaster. Hatch, *Administration of the American Revolutionary Army*, 179–191.

54. Jean H. Vivian, "Military Land Bounties during the Revolutionary and Confederation Periods," *Maryland Historical Magazine*, LXI (1966), 231–256; Rudolf Freund, "Military Bounty Lands and the Origins of the Public Domain," in Vernon Carstensen, ed., *The Public Lands* (Madison, Wis., 1963), 15–34; William T. Hutchinson, "Military Bounty Lands of the American Revolution in Ohio" (unpubl. Ph.D. diss., University of Chicago, 1927); William H. Glasson, *Federal Military Pensions in the United States* (New York, 1918), chaps. i–iii. A recent publication contains considerable information on Revolutionary War pensions. Robert L. Meriwether and W. Edwin Hemphill, eds., *The Papers of John C. Calhoun* (Columbia, S.C., 1961—), II–III.

55. Stuart Wortley, *A Prime Minister and His Son*, 62.

56. Acomb, ed., *Journal of von Clossen*, 102; Fitzpatrick, ed., *Writings of Washington*, XXV, 271, 281; Simms, ed., *Correspondence of John Laurens*, 136; Wade and Lively, *This Glorious Cause*, 46, 47; New-York Historical Society, *Collections*, VIII (1875), 455. There are similar expressions in *Continental Journal*, July 13, 1780, Feb. 15, 1781; *Maryland Gazette*, May 17, 1781; *Connecticut Courant*, July 3, 1781; *Pennsylvania Gazette*, Aug. 1, 1781.

57. Knollenberg, *Washington and the Revolution*, 216–219, objects to Washington's employment of the lash. Congressional action is recorded in Ford, ed., *Journals of Congress*, II, 122, V, 806, XX, 658. A defense of Washington as a disciplinarian is in Stuart L. Bernath, "George Washington and the Genesis of American Military Discipline," *Mid-America*, XLIX (1967), 83–100. Equally pertinent to the subject is Maurer Maurer, "Military Justice under General Washington," *Military Affairs*, XXVIII (1964), 8–16.

58. Fitzpatrick, ed., *Writings of Washington*, IV, 108, VII, 364, 459, VIII, 214, 404, IX, 426, XIV, 429–430, XV, 364; Allen Bowman, *The Morale of the American Revolutionary Army* (Washington, 1943), 88–92.

59. Fitzpatrick, ed., *Writings of Washington*, V, 210, VI, 222.

# 16. The Revolutionary Impact: Europe

THE GUNS OF YORKTOWN were barely silent when Americans, sensing the termination of all hostilities, looked to the future and predicted great things for their aspiring country. At Brookfield, Massachusetts, the Reverend Nathan Fiske spoke for many when he foresaw America as "the late founded seat of peace and freedom. Here shall arts and sciences, the companions of tranquility, flourish. Here shall dwell uncorrupted faith, the pure worship of God in its primitive simplicity, unawed, unrestrained, uninterrupted. Here shall religion and liberty extend their benign influence of the American Revolution on the subsequent course of Europe."

Meanwhile, there was a more immediate concern regarding the Old World. Victory in the war was no guarantee that America would win the peace. Formal recognition of independence had yet to be gained from Britain, as did agreement on the vital question of the territorial boundaries of the United States. New Englanders sought a restoration of their fishing and curing privileges on the coasts of Newfoundland and Nova Scotia which they had enjoyed as British colonists. Americans could look forward to altruistic generosity from neither friend nor foe. France, leagued with Spain, hesitated to push American interests against the wishes of her Bourbon ally, which objected to any new rising empire in the Western Hemisphere. If England might prove somewhat conciliatory toward her wayward colonies, the motives of the mother country would be dictated by a desire to shatter the hydra of the Franco-American alliance. On the other hand, as events were to show, there were representatives of the belligerents who were not unwilling to work together surreptitiously to limit the territorial aspirations of the United States. Neophytes in the art of Old World diplomacy, and with their position undercut in the Continental Congress by French pressures, the American peace commissioners nevertheless won an impressive triumph at the conference table. They were the only diplomats with firm objectives from which they refused to budge, notwithstanding threats, cajolery, or the other machinations of eighteenth-century diplomacy. "Undisciplined as we were," recorded John Adams, "we were better tacticians than was imagined."[1]

## The Peace Settlement

In Britain, the last years of the war revealed mounting political unrest that was unparalleled since the Glorious Revolution. The influence of the American Revolution on these developments is not easy to measure, for the desire for change would have been "in the air" regardless of the upheaval across the Atlantic. But the proponents of reform found the North ministry especially vulnerable because of mounting taxes, failure in America, and danger from the Bourbons. Ireland, long smoldering in discontent, erupted with new protests against anti-Catholic laws, economic restrictions, and political corruption. In England, extra-Parliamentary opinion expressed itself in the Yorkshire Association, which, apart from its immediate attack on the North administration, represented the first presentation of the issue of Parliamentary reform on a national scale. Rotten boroughs, containing few or no voters, sent members to Parliament. Banbury's seventeen voters kept Lord North in the House of Commons, and Lord George Germain had a constituency of thirty electors. In the absence of changes in the electoral system, the cities were generally underrepresented, and manufacturing towns such as Manchester and Birmingham sent no members at all.

Opposition political leaders, however, were not really interested in making Parliament truly representative of the people but rather advocated steps to make that body independent of the King, whose influence—it was asserted—had been vastly increased through the use of jobbery in the enlarging of the army and the bestowing of military contracts. Edmund Burke's famous plan of "Economical Reform," which included clipping the civil list, purging Parliament of contractors, and reducing the King's household, was designed to leave the monarch with money and offices but not enough of either to practice the wholesale buying of votes and other forms of corruption. Rockingham and Shelburne, leaders of the opposition, temporarily closed ranks in an effort to topple the North ministry: with the aid of numerous defections from North's customary majorities, they rammed through the House of

Commons in April, 1780, a resolution of much-respected lawyer John Dunning "that the influence of the crown has increased, is increasing, and ought to be diminished." Herbert Butterfield, the historian of this internal crisis of 1779–1780, goes so far as to say there existed in Britain a "quasi-revolutionary" situation.[2]

If Lord North became unnerved and irresolute, George III took his customary hard line. Luck and good news from America sustained the King. In June, 1780, the Gordon Riots, anti-Catholic fanaticism prompted by concessions to the Irish, shocked Britons of various political persuasions into drawing rein on their reforming instincts and rallying behind the government. The capture of Charleston and the triumph at Camden added impetus to the conservative swing of opinion. So did the results of the general election of 1780, in which the Crown spent over £100,000 in paying expenses of government candidates and buying boroughs—collecting, in the process, a majority of over one hundred in the House of Commons.

Yet the recent mood of the country indicated that word of new reversals could again lower the clouds on the political horizon. Yorktown, combined with other ominous reports, revealed how fragile in fact was the ministry's edifice. St. Eustatius fell to the French, as did Minorca in the Mediterranean, while in the West Indies de Grasse captured Nevis and Montserrat and threatened Jamaica. Simultaneously, the British position in India was contested by the French, and West Florida was overrun by the Spanish. The administration's majorities steadily declined until, in February, 1782, a motion to renounce all attempts to regain America passed the House of Commons. Rather than face censure and a call for dismissal, North, Germain, and Sandwich resigned their posts.

When George III undertook to form a new government, he sought a ministry formed "on a wide basis" from the various political factions. Failing in his efforts to secure a "broad bottom," he considered abdicating the throne before finally agreeing to accept a cluster of ministers drawn mostly from the opposition forces of Rockingham and Shelburne. Rockingham, the first minister, favored recognizing American independence, but the King held out for holding whatever part of the former American empire that could be retained. Shelburne also bridled at a complete separation, hoping for a dependent America, still yoked to the mother country in some sort of federal and commercial union. Rockingham, without a real Parliamentary majority of his own, had to acquiesce.[3]

Moreover, there occurred a surprising upturn in Britain's military fortunes. The most spectacular event was Rodney's smashing victory over de Grasse in April, 1782—the Battle of the Saints—in the West

Indies. Rodney took five of the French vessels, made de Grasse himself a prisoner, and saved Jamaica, an action that pointed toward naval warfare of the future. "Eighteenth-century observers," writes M. S. Anderson, "often tended to believe that naval battles between opponents of more or less equal strength were almost certain to be indecisive, that naval warfare was by its nature unlikely to produce victories of the kind which might be expected on land. . . . Not until the Battle of the Saints in 1782 did a struggle between two fleets of approximately equal size produce a clear-cut victory for either of them."[4] Much to the embarrassment of Rockingham, he had, before learning of the battle, announced the removal of Rodney, a friend of Germain, for an admiral close to his own party. Likewise in India, Britain obtained the upper hand as a result of a series of fierce but indecisive naval engagements between Admiral Sir William Hughes and the Balli de Suffren, a splendid officer who lacked the ships and supporting troops to dislodge his opponents. There was also good news from Gibraltar, where General George Elliot's determined stand, combined with the assistance of Lord Howe's fleet, insured Britain's continued possession of the rocky fortress.

Britain, therefore, was down but far from out when, early in 1782, Lord Shelburne dispatched a retired merchant, Richard Oswald, to Paris to open peace negotiations with the Americans and to wean the revolutionists away from France. The British knew that all was not harmonious between America and the Bourbon powers. Spain, as we have found earlier, had no taste for another rival in the New World, especially a republican one; and, consequently, she sought to confine the troublesome interloper to the region east of the Appalachians. In fact, had Spanish Foreign Minister Floridablanca been given his way, he would have favored instead of independence for the United States a long-term truce, with both the Americans and the British holding the areas occupied by their respective forces. In 1780 the Spaniard had outlined such a scheme in secret conversations with Richard Cumberland, a British agent. Spain's disdainful attitude toward the United States was heightened by her military accomplishments on the North American continent. In September, 1779, Bernardo de Gálvez, the energetic, twenty-three-year-old captain-general of Louisiana, seized British posts at Manchac, Baton Rouge, and Natchez. Mobile fell to Gálvez the following March, and slightly more than two years later he took Pensacola after a two-month siege. In the meantime, Lieutenant Governor Francisco Cruzat at St. Louis detached Spanish militiamen who captured St. Joseph, a British station in present-day Michigan, which provided King Charles III with a claim—however tenuous—to the east bank of the Mississippi.[5]

French Foreign Minister Vergennes, though never personally hostile to his American allies, believed that the young republic's boundaries should be limited to reasonable proportions, so that America's strength and security should never be perfected to such an extent as to render the support of France dispensable.[6] For this reason as well as France's involvement with Spain, the Comte leaned toward the empire of Castile when the aspirations of his cobelligerents clashed. Twice in the year after making her alliance with the United States, France violated the spirit if not the letter of her American treaties: first, by promising to share the Newfoundland fisheries only with Spain;[7] and, secondly, by committing herself to fight until Spain obtained Gibraltar, which, in effect, constituted a unilateral change in the Franco-American military pact. In still another way Vergennes contemplated action at variance with the interests of America: when, in the winter of 1780–1781, he responded enthusiastically to the offer of Catharine the Great and Prince Kaunitz of Austria to mediate between the warring nations and to hold a peace conference at Vienna. But upon sounding out John Adams, commissioned by Congress to negotiate a peace settlement, Vergennes found that the New Englander refused to go to Vienna unless the participating nations would first agree to recognize American independence and unless Britain would withdraw all her troops from the thirteen states.

If New England's aspirations were threatened by the Bourbons' designs on the fisheries, those of the Southern states conflicted with Spanish objectives concerning the West and the Mississippi. Pressure from France at a time the South was reeling from Cornwallis' invasion drove Congress to pare down its territorial demands. When, in June, 1781, John Adams was replaced as the sole peace negotiator by a five-man commission (Franklin, Jay, Henry Laurens, Jefferson, and Adams himself), Congress instructed the commissioners to insist only upon American independence. Moreover, they were "to make the most candid and confidential communications, upon all subjects to the ministers" of France; "to undertake nothing . . . without their knowledge and concurrence; and ultimately to govern yourselves by their advice and opinion. . . ."[8]

Fortunately for America, her commissioners were tough-minded men who refused to sacrifice the country's best interests, even to the extent of ignoring at times Congress' words about notifying the French of all their doings. The point applies not only to Jay and Adams but also to Franklin, the lone negotiator in the initial peace talks, who has too often been described as subservient to Vergennes and willing to sacrifice his nation's ambitions to placate France. Franklin, it is worth stressing, was the first of the American commissioners to disregard his orders when they appeared to contradict America's vital concerns.

Although Franklin considered the French alliance a cornerstone of American foreign policy, an opinion he candidly advanced to Shelburne and Oswald, he nevertheless implied to the British that generosity on their part could bring about a restoration of Anglo-American good will, which he thought to be to the advantage of both nations. Franklin never revealed to Vergennes that in April, 1782, he confidentially suggested to Oswald the cession of Canada to the United States to salve the bitterness created by the war. Even more important, Franklin on July 12, 1782, gave Oswald his first concrete peace proposals (they were to form the basis of negotiation) without the knowledge of Vergennes. On the other hand, he insisted, in agreement with the Foreign Minister, that Anglo-American and Anglo-French discussions be carried forward simultaneously in the direction of a general peace settlement.[9]

For a time talks between American and British representatives stalled. The death of Rockingham on July 1 led to the elevation of Shelburne as head of the ministry. Though eager to bring about better relations between the English-speaking peoples, Shelburne, clinging to the hope of America's retaining some formal relationship with the empire, refused to acknowledge the independence of the United States before the signing of a peace treaty. Shelburne, to be sure, needed the support of George III and Parliament; and for bargaining purposes he and his cabinet would not concede American sovereignty in advance.

Meanwhile, John Jay, after lingering impatiently in Spain, joined Franklin in Paris, following a long encounter with "bad roads, fleas, and bugs." Negotiations were entirely in their hands. For John Adams, involved in securing a loan at The Hague, did not arrive until late October; Henry Laurens, captured at sea, was a prisoner in the Tower of London; and Jefferson, because of the fatal illness and death of his wife, declined to serve on the commission. As is well known, Jay took charge of the peace talks, but at a time when Franklin fell ill. Jay had learned in extensive conversations with the Spanish minister at Paris, the Conde de Aranda, that Spain's goals in the American West were wholly incompatible with those of his own country. Soon afterward Aranda and Vergennes' secretary, M. de Rayneval, presented to Jay a proposal that had the approval of the French Foreign Minister: Britain was to retain the Ohio-Great Lakes country while the area west of a line beginning at the Cumberland River and extending to the eastern boundary of West Florida was to be reserved for the Indians under Spanish protection. Consequently, the United States was to be excluded from almost all of the trans-Appalachian region.

Jay's distrust reached immense proportions when he discovered that Rayneval had departed for London after taking elaborate precautions to keep his destination a secret. When Jay conveyed his fears of a

French double-dealing to Franklin, and when the venerable Philadelphian failed to share his suspicions, Jay, unbeknownst to his colleague,
sent word to Shelburne that he was ready to open separate and confidential negotiations. Franklin, however, subsequently concurred in
Jay's move, and the two diplomats advanced proposals to Oswald and
Shelburne without informing Vergennes. The commissioners would
drop their demand for an explicit recognition of independence, provided the British made an implicit acknowledgment of the fact by
permitting her negotiators to treat with representatives of "the United
States of America." The Americans insisted on a share of the Newfoundland fisheries and the possession of the trans-Appalachian country to
the Mississippi River. In return Jay and Franklin assured their counterparts that America would not fight until Spain's lofty ambitions were
met, that British citizens would be given entry to the Mississippi trade,
and that—this was a hint—the United States might make a separate
peace if France did not accept such an Anglo-American settlement.

Shelburne, eager to pry the patriots apart from France, chose to favor
the Americans over the Bourbons. Thus he rejected Rayneval's suggestions that Britain retain the "Old Northwest" and that France would
not back American claims to the fisheries. After Oswald presented new
credentials acceptable to Jay and Franklin, the three men—on October
5—approved a draft treaty to take effect when Britain and France
reached terms. The patriots had abandoned their designs on Canada,
scarcely attainable under any circumstances, in return for satisfying
their desires in the West. Shelburne had insisted on certain changes.
Though personally favoring free trade between America and the
empire as provided in the draft treaty, he realized that a majority in
Parliament opposed his view. The American representatives agreed
instead to accept a simple statement that there would be no restriction
on navigation of the Mississippi. They also consented to validate American debts to British citizens, and they accepted a clause stipulating
Congress would recommend "earnestly" to the states that the loyalists
be compensated for the confiscation of their property. After ironing out
other points at issue, the parties gathered on November 30, 1782, in
Oswald's lodgings at the Grand Hotel Muscovite in Paris and signed
the preliminary treaty of peace.

Jay and his colleagues had avoided a literal compliance with the
French alliance, to say nothing of violating Congress' stipulation about
informing the French of all their proceedings. They did so with good
reason, for Vergennes had sought to discharge his obligations to Spain
at the expense of America and to keep the infant prodigy tied to the
lead strings of France. In the absence of modern instantaneous communications, the Americans had to act on the basis of sudden developments;
five or six months usually elapsed between the time a letter was sent

from Europe and a reply arrived from America. European diplomats, in contrast, could contact their own courts in a relatively short period of time. Therefore, as Franklin wrote in defense of the American delegation, they had to assume discretionary powers the European states were unaccustomed to granting their own plenipotentiaries. Jay put the matter bluntly to Secretary of Foreign Affairs Robert Livingston: "As we had reason to imagine that the articles respecting the boundaries, the refugees, and fisheries, did not correspond with the policy of this Court, we did not communicate the preliminaries to the Minister until after they were signed...."[10]

France, and indeed all Europe, was stunned by the liberal terms Britain had bestowed upon her former subjects. "Their concessions exceed all that I could have thought possible," exclaimed Vergennes.[11] The Comte was bitter that the commissioners had acted behind his back, partly because of a personal factor: his desire to preside over all the peace negotiations. A realist, he accepted the outcome—together with Franklin's deft apology—and sought to preserve the Franco-American axis, even advancing an additional 6,000,000 livres for the depleted American treasury. The Frenchman, besides, was no more eager than the Americans to fight indefinitely in behalf of Spain's "grandiose pretensions" to Gibraltar. Determined that peace should not founder on the rocky fortress, he persuaded the Conde de Aranda to disregard his own instructions from Madrid and settle for the Floridas instead. On January 20, 1783, the three principal European belligerents concluded preliminary treaties that were followed by a general armistice.

In England, Shelburne resigned from office, having suffered a vote of censure for conceding too much to his nation's enemies when, in fact, he had sheathed the sword on the best terms possible under the circumstances. Aided by British victories in 1782, he had held French gains to a minimum: the restoration of St. Pierre and Miquelon, the acquisition of Senegal and Tobago, and the right to dry fish on the coast of Newfoundland; and limited Spanish conquests to Minorca along with the Floridas. The new ministry led by former rivals, the stolid Lord North and the brilliant but erratic Charles James Fox, could not alter Shelburne's labors. The preliminary articles of peace that England had concluded with the United States, France, and Spain were all signed— with scarcely a change—as definitive treaties on September 3, 1783.

Although the American diplomats had benefited by the rivalries of the Old World in securing highly advantageous terms of peace, they had exploited their opportunities in the face of hostility and backstage dealings by both friend and foe. Without pre-war experience in the conduct of foreign affairs or previous systematic thought in the management of diplomacy, the "militia diplomats," as John Adams called them, had battled with skill and tenacity for every concession they received.

And they remained uncompromising on the vital objectives of independence, the fisheries, and the Western domain.

After word of the signings reached America, Sir Guy Carleton, now British commander in chief, evacuated New York City, finding shipping space for many of the loyalists who desired to leave the country. On November 25, Washington's remaining Continentals entered the city. Nine days later the tall Virginian bade farewell to his officers in a final gathering at Fraunces' Tavern. The emotional strain felt by all was in a sense repeated when, on December 23 at Annapolis, Washington likewise took his leave of the Continental Congress. In a three-minute address to the congressmen, he congratulated them on the "confirmation of our independence." Near the end his voice faltered; then regaining his composure, he concluded: "Having now finished the work assigned me, I retire from the great theater of action; and bidding an Affectionate farewell to this August body under whose orders I have so long acted, I here offer my commission, and take my leave of all the employments of public life." Departing, he spurred southward, reaching Mount Vernon on Christmas Eve. After eight and a half years of military service he was—he wrote Lafayette—"Free from the bustle of a camp and the busy scenes of public life. . . ." He was again "a private citizen on the banks of the Potomac, and under the shadow of my own vine and my own fig tree."[12]

## The Consequences of the War

What may we say of the long-range international significance of the War of Independence beyond the obvious facts that America emerged as one of the nations of the world, that Britain lost a large part of her empire, and that the Bourbons obtained revenge against an inveterate enemy?

American commercial and foreign policy aspirations were shaped by the war, but time was to show that the new nation fell short of attaining its goals. American diplomats, as we have seen, believed that, as an agricultural-commercial country, their interests lay in stimulating foreign trade and commerce. It was assumed that, with the termination of the war, states that had hesitated to deal with rebels would now be desirous to treat with a legitimate government whose policy called for a reign of free exchange and pacific intercourse. If America would profit by the new day in economic affairs, so would Europe. In their most optimistic moments, American diplomats went so far as to hope that the Revolutionary War was "a war to end all wars." For if mercantilism, that instigator of internal strife and imperial conflicts, could be replaced by free trade, nations would have far less to create tensions and rivalries between them, and peoples would find that their common interests exceeded their differences.

Americans wholly concurred with Lord Shelburne, who, in the bitterness of retirement, condemned war and irrational ambition: "I have long thought," he declared, "that people have but one cause throughout the world. It is sovereigns who have different interests. . . . If the people of different countries could once understand each other, and be brought to adopt half-a-dozen principles, their servants would not venture to play such tricks." No better example of an enlightened spirit with regard to a free exchange can be found than the passport Franklin issued during the war to the English explorer and navigator, Captain James Cook, once again off for the South Seas. Cook's undertaking would be of value to mankind, asserted Franklin, "as the Increase of Geographical Knowledge facilitates the Communication between distant Nations" and the "Exchange of useful Products and Manufactures." Accordingly, he encouraged the captains of all American vessels to offer Cook and his party "as common Friends to Mankind, all the Assistance in your Power, which they may happen to stand in need of."[13]

Unfortunately, from the point of view of the United States, Europe did not accept the commercial principles of the American Revolution. Trade continued to be burdened with monopolies and restrictions harmful to the peace and welfare of mankind. The failure of the American campaign began to dawn on the nation as early as July, 1783, when an order in council forbade United States shipping from the British West Indies. Combined with the restoration of old barriers in the French and Spanish colonies, the English restrictions sealed off the most lucrative part of America's foreign trade. Hard on the heels of these reversals came other setbacks as American diplomats sought trade treaties in the various courts of Europe and obtained nothing or, in a few instances, only the most minimal concessions. As Jefferson wrote later, "They seemed, in fact, to know little about us, but as rebels, who had been successful in throwing off the yoke of the mother country. They were ignorant of our commerce, which had always been monopolized by England, and of the exchange of articles it might offer advantageously to both parties."[14]

If Europe rejected the American foreign policy approach based on commercial rather than political relations, the United States in turn scorned political commitments abroad in the hope that it might avoid the blood-drenched rivalries of the Old World. Even before the signing of the definitive treaty of peace, Congress, in June, 1783, unanimously adopted a resolution that "the true interest of these states requires that they should be as little as possible entangled in the politics and controversies of European nations. . . ." Thus Congress warned its peace commissioners to avoid any agreements "which should oblige the contracting parties to support those stipulations by arms."[15] Congress was trumpeting a note of nationalism and political isolationism, attitudes which were reinforced by the country's failure to secure reciprocal trade agreements in the 1780's. Even in the case of France, America demonstrated in the separate negotiations of her peacemakers that she was a restless satellite, scarcely willing to remain unequivocally in the diplomatic orbit of Versailles. The French alliance, after all, had been a marriage of convenience, and following the war America's safety no longer rested on the French connection. In time the United States returned to a unilateral approach more in harmony with her world outlook.

In terms of basic interests, America still had much more in common with England than with France. Besides the obvious cultural and linguistic ties, America needed to sell Britain agricultural exports, just as Britain provided the new nation with large quantities of imports. Yet the permanent impact of the American Revolution upon England was predominantly negative. Americans lamented Britain's unwillingness to deviate from orthodox mercantilism and to accept the farsighted free-trade notions of the Earl of Shelburne. British rigidity also asserted itself in colonial affairs. The Canada Act of 1791, for example, supposedly extended the benefits of the British constitution to the émigré loyalists and other inhabitants, but it scarcely gave meaningful acknowledgment to the right of self-government, nor did it preclude attempts to impose imperial interests upon a colonial society. Britain, notwithstanding the loss of America, remained supreme in the colonial and maritime field. Thirty years before the peace of 1783 she had already begun to lay the basis for what Vincent T. Harlow has called "the Second British Empire," whose vital center was the great subcontinent of India, and which led to new fields of commerce in the Pacific and the South China Seas. "The Second Empire," as Harlow reminds us, "was predominantly a coloured Empire, ruled not through representative institutions, but by a strong benevolent bureaucracy directed from London."[16]

Lack of imperial reform matched the absence of political reform at home. In spite of the Yorkshire Association and the rise of other forms of extra-Parliamentary opinion, politics remained chiefly in a narrow framework, with the realities of influence and patronage continuing to take precedence over political theory, party loyalty, and public opinion. The Parliamentary opposition tended to reinforce the prevailing system; its purpose, aside from the rewards of office, was usually limited to preserving the country from maladministration and ill conceived public policies. Indeed, with few exceptions, the most avowed reformers were hardly radical but were concerned mainly with cleansing the *existing* constitutional system by such means as the abolition of placemen and sinecures. Even the followers of John Wilkes, whom George III considered a wild-eyed revolutionary, failed to advocate the extension of the Parliamentary franchise, although, to be sure, some of their methods and proposals—including oaths to bind representatives to the wishes of their constituents and petitions and remonstrances on a national scale—would be carried forward by campaigners for constitutional reforms in the next century. On the outer fringes of politics stood the commonwealthmen, the small knot of liberal thinkers who had inspired Americans in the pre-1776 controversies with Britain, and who, in turn, were almost alone among Englishmen in accepting the American view of an empire of equal parts and in calling for substantive changes in the British constitution.

Given the degree of complacency and unanimity at home on the fundamentals of politics and government, on traditional methods and established institutional forms, it is all the more understandable why the American colonists' arguments never received a fair hearing in the 1760's and 1770's; why new and imaginative leadership did not emerge in the course of the Revolutionary War; and why Britain fought with the same creaky, overlapping governmental machinery that had sustained the kingdom in the past. Simultaneously, it is easier to comprehend why the King and Germain—convinced of the worth of their own political system and its success in previous wars—were exceedingly optimistic about the prospects for obtaining victory in America, where, so they thought, only a small fraction of the population could find serious fault with the enlightened government of the mother country.[17]

Had there been no overconfidence and no divided counsels in London, no crippling limitations to the administrative apparatus, and no blunders of generals and admirals in the field, Britian would still have faced overwhelming, and perhaps insuperable, obstacles to regaining her thirteen colonies. Fighting a substantial war at 3,000 miles distance from home base against a people rather than a mere army, she experienced a greater problem of logistics and manpower than any European nation had ever faced—in a country thickly wooded and continental in scale. And after 1777 she fought on a world-wide theater against France, Spain, and eventually Holland, without the backing of her traditional European allies.

The role of France in relation to American independence calls for a further word. French assistance in terms of military stores and hard cash was undoubtedly of the highest importance to the patriots. But what of France's own participation in the war? Would Britain have overcome her other difficulties and put down the rebellion without direct Bourbon military intervention? The French threat led immediately in 1778 to a dispersal of British military and naval forces, thus lessening to some extent the pressure on America. It was, however, three and a half years after the signing of the Franco-American alliance before the French launched a successful land and naval offensive —the Yorktown campaign—in cooperation with the patriots. In fact, most recent authorities suggest that, regardless of formal French intervention, Britain had slight chance of permanently subduing America. Richard B. Morris goes so far as to speculate that the war might have ended favorably for America considerably before Yorktown if there had been no French alliance! He asserts that the French entrance into the fray saved the North ministry from collapse in the aftermath of Saratoga, undercut the "appeasers among the Whigs" and the Carlisle peace commission, and rallied Britons to prosecute the war with renewed vigor.[18]

But in weighing the historical imponderables, one can suggest other results less favorable to an America that fought alone. The struggle might have dragged on interminably, eventually ending with a British withdrawal because of war-weariness and bringing a kind of *de facto* recognition of American independence. In that case, the status of the West would certainly have remained up in the air, with the strong likelihood of Spain's seizing the lower Mississippi valley. Another result of a prolonged conflict might have been a stalemate in which the British attempted to hold the parts of America already occupied by their armies. In this situation Americans would probably have turned increasingly to guerrilla warfare, making British control of land areas in a meaningful sense impossible except for the coastal cities and their environs. Even in nearby Ireland, the British found after World War I that terrorist activities and partisan operations of the Sinn Fein made effective authority out of the question. Such an outcome in America, however, could quite conceivably have torn apart the fabric of society, have damaged irreparably the budding democratic social and political institutions of the new republic. Robert R. Palmer reminds us that "a country gaining independence in this way would not have been the country that emerged in 1783. The winners of the American war were not guerrilla chieftains. They were not obscure and hunted men out of contact with civilization. They not only made government impossible for the British: they made governments of their own. They did not represent the triumph of anarchy."[19]

All the same, we have seen that there were unique features to warfare in America, even though the patriots never turned to bush fighting as their principal means of resistance. What effect did the experiences of the American war have upon later European conflicts: specifically, those of the French Revolution and the Napoleonic era? In the

realm of military administration the Americans, without a truly centralized government, made no contribution. But the English, according to
Piers Mackesy, remembered the inadequacies of their own bureaucratic
system, as well as the follies of divided authority and insufficient cooperation between commands. The year 1793 brought a fundamental
overhauling of the war machine marked by the creation of the office of
Secretary of State for War to oversee army operations and to speak for
the military in the ministry and in Parliament. Administrative reforms
took place elsewhere, however, more in response to the remarkable military successes of the French, as in the case of Prussia, where, after
1807, Gerhard von Scharnhorst and his collaborators founded the ministry of war, the general staff, and the military academy.[20]

At the operational level of warfare in revolutionary Europe, certain
changes were scarcely a reflection of American observations, such as
the recasting of armies into relatively self-sufficient divisions and the
increasing of the mobility of artillery forces. But in regard to tactical
arrangements, many British and German officers returned from America convinced that somewhat open, flexible battlefield dispositions were
the new order of the day. Subsequently, the line, fire by volley, and
other close order methods were combined with skirmishing parties and
individual marksmanship—all a part of the same tactical command,
which now achieved greater coherence. (Earlier, specialized or detached units, where they existed, had performed the tasks of reconnaissance and flank protection.) These lessons were learned mostly from
small-unit engagements and woodland fighting, not from the major
battles of the Continental army, which fought the British largely in the
European fashion.

Assuredly one can exaggerate the consequences of the Revolutionary
War, even in the tactical area. Peter Paret has lately stressed that the
light infantry, the *chasseurs*, and the *jägers* provided a background for
the battlefield innovations at the turn of the century. Likewise, irregular or guerrilla fighters, though less common in Europe than in America, were not unknown. During the Seven Years' War Austrian partisans
slipped around the forces of Frederick the Great and temporarily occupied Berlin. There was, in short, an organic development to European warfare that extended back to the beginning of the eighteenth
century. Thus "colonial experiences . . . tended to reinforce existing
trends, not to initiate them," cautions Paret.[21]

But to judge from the diarists and journalists among the British and
German enlisted men and junior officers, they must have considered
these evolutionary developments to be painfully slow, if indeed they
were aware of all of them. They complained of the Americans' sniping, aiming at officers, night forays, hit-and-run raids, and winter cam-

paigning. They criticized British rigidity, especially their armies' slowness of movement and adherence to copybook tactics. It had been, in the European manner, a war of position, with the British seeking to secure fixed points, waterways, towns, even specific colonies; and it had brought few long-run advantages when, in America, the key to any real possibility of total victory lay in the destruction of the Continental army. Du Roi, a German officer, voiced widely held sentiments: "The rules of war should be changed by a general every time according to position and condition of the country in which the fighting is done."[22] The commanding officers and their ministerial superiors may not have fathomed the major lessons to be derived from the War of Independence; but the lessons were there, and they pointed the way toward warfare of the future.

So did the Americans' employment of productive citizens in defense of the nation. The patriots had rejected the notion of the soldier as distinct and divorced from his own countrymen, a creature without his stake in society. No longer was "the Life of the Soldier the Property of the King," as Burgoyne phrased it. And he fought for more meaningful things than monarchial abstractions. Daniel Morgan, the rugged backwoods veteran, implicitly denoted the difference in exhorting his throng of militiamen and Continentals on the eve of the Battle of Cowpens. They were fighting for their homes, their wives, and their sweethearts, he exclaimed; victory would send them back to their communities as heroes. In Europe, says Sir John Fortescue, the historian of the British army, there was no thought of turning the common soldier into a hero. When he had served his purpose, he was thrown aside and returned to his status of being the scum of society.[23]

To honor enlisted men, Washington created chevrons to be worn on the sleeves indicating length of service. He also established an award for outstanding merit: "not only instances of unusual gallantry but also of extra-ordinary fidelity and essential services in any way"—"the figure of a heart in purple cloth or silk" to be worn on the left breast. This "Badge of Military Merit" was the first such decoration in the history of the United States army.[24]

This was one example, the use of the citizen-soldier, that did influence the European imagination. If the pervasiveness of the wars between Valmy and Waterloo called for enrolling huge armies, if the technological advances by the 1790's made possible the equipping of additional thousands, the *levée en masse*, there was yet another advantage—seemingly confirmed by American experience—to harnessing hordes of citizens: they would be motivated by sentiments of patriotism in battling for national aims. Accordingly, they would fight with greater determination and dedication because they had a vital interest in the outcome. For an age dedicated to Enlightenment thought and devoted to the principles of nature, here was the natural way to wage war: here too was a political ideal—confidence in the individual as a trustworthy citizen—that would revolutionize not only warfare but other areas of human endeavor as well.

In fact, it was chiefly in the political arena rather than that of commerce, foreign policy, or military strategy and tactics—that the American Revolution influenced the French Revolution and related developments in Europe. Lafayette returned to his homeland a worshipper of Washington and an admirer of American institutions; so did General Chastellux, already an influential *philosophe*, who, like Rochambeau's chaplain, the Abbé Robin, wrote a book on his experiences highly flattering to the new nation. Jefferson, for five years American minister in Paris, informed the English liberal, Dr. Richard Price, of the relationship between the revolutions of America and France: "Though celebrated writers of this [France] and other countries had already sketched good principles on the subject of government, yet the American war seems first to have awakened the thinking part of this nation in general from the sleep of despotism in which they were sunk. The officers too who had been to America were mostly young men, less shackled by habit and prejudice, and more ready to assent to the dictates of common sense and common right. They came back with these."[25]

Jefferson was not far from the complete truth, at least about the officer corps. As Louis Gottschalk notes, such officers as Alexander de Lameth, Mathieu Dumas, the Comte de Segur, the Vicomte de Noailles, and the future socialist Saint-Simon all remembered later that their initial thinking on the subject of liberty came from their American contacts during the Revolutionary War.[26] In still another respect the American contribution was significant. Although the French upheaval was caused by many political, social, economic, and intellectual factors, some of long duration, French unrest did not surface dramatically until the national treasury verged on bankruptcy in 1789. That condition and the rising cost of living were brought on by governmental expenditures during the War of Independence, a conflict that cost France approximately 2,000,000,000 livres.

# NOTES

1. Nathan Fiske, *An Oration Delivered at Brookfield, November 14, 1781* (Boston, 1781), 7. For other examples, see Robert Smith, *The Obligation of the Confederate States of America to Praise God* (Philadelphia, 1782); Levi Frisbie, *An Oration Delivered at Ipswich* (Boston, 1783); David Tappan, *A Discourse Delivered at the Third Parish in Newbury* (Salem, 1783); Henry Cummings, *A

*Sermon Preached in Billerica* . . . (Boston, 1784); Israel Evans, *A Discourse Delivered in New-York* (New York, [1784]). John Adams' remark is in Adams to Elbridge Gerry, Dec. 14, 1782, quoted in Morris, *The Peacemakers*, 459.

2. Cobbett, ed., *Parliamentary History of England*, XXI, 347–348; Herbert Butterfield, *George III, Lord North and the People 1779–1780* (London, 1949), vi.

3. A detailed treatment of the activities of the opposition, including the formation of the Rockingham-Shelburne ministry, appears in Archibald S. Foord, *His Majesty's Opposition 1714–1830* (Oxford, Eng., 1964), chap. viii, especially 350–365. The basic study of the final years of Britain's wartime cabinet is Ian R. Christie, *The End of the North Ministry 1780–1782* (London, 1958), which finds that "the political extinction of [North's] . . . ministers was the due desert for the incompetence with which they had schemed and acted during the American war" (p. 371). The latest biography of the King's discredited first minister, Alan Valentine's *Lord North*, 2 vols. (Norman, Okla., 1967), presents disappointingly little that is new or incisive.

4. Anderson, *Europe in the Eighteenth Century*, 149.

5. Lawrence Kinnaird, ed., *Spain in the Mississippi Valley, 1765–1794*, American Historical Association, *Annual Report for 1945* (Washington, 1949), II, 418. The military operations from Spanish Louisiana are detailed in John W. Caughey, *Bernardo de Galvez in Louisiana, 1776–1783* (Berkeley, 1934), 85–242; N. Orwin Rush, *The Battle of Pensacola* (Tallahassee, Fla., 1966).

6. As early as 1778 Vergennes made his position clear: "We ask independence only for the thirteen states of America. . . . We do not desire that a new republic shall arise which shall become the exclusive mistress of this immense continent. . . . " Doniol, *Histoire de la participation de la France à l'établissement des États-Unis d'Amérique*, III, 561.

7. It is significant that although France agreed to renounce any territorial ambitions upon the continent of North America in the treaty of alliance with the United States, she did not mention the island of Newfoundland. Arthur Lee recorded that he, Franklin, and Deane had failed in their efforts to insert an additional clause whereby France would give up any designs on the northeastern island. Richard Henry Lee, *Life of Arthur Lee* (Boston, 1829), II, 378–379, 383. French ambitions were explicitly stated in Article V of the Franco-Spanish accord of 1779, the so-called Convention of Aranjuez. Article VI further stated that if France "succeeds in becoming master and acquiring possession of the island of Newfoundland, the subjects of his Catholic Majesty [Spain] are to be admitted to the fisheries." Sympathy for the French point of view on the fisheries is found in Orville T. Murphy, "The Comte de Vergennes, the Newfoundland Fisheries, and the Peace Negotiations of 1783: A Reconsideration," *Canadian Historical Review*, XLVI (1965), 32–46.

8. Ford, ed., *Journals of Congress*, XX, 651–652.

9. Stourzh, *Benjamin Franklin and American Foreign Policy*, 173, stresses Franklin's independent actions.

10. Wharton, ed., *Revolutionary Diplomatic Correspondence*, VI, 110–111; C. F. Adams, ed., *Works of John Adams*, VIII, 18–20; Morris, *The Peacemakers*, 382, 536 n170.

11. Quoted in *ibid.*, 383.

12. Fitzpatrick, ed., *Writings of Washington*, XXVII, 284–285, 288.

13. Shelburne to Jeremy Bentham, March 29, 1789, J. Bowring, ed., *The Works of Jeremy Bentham* (Edinburgh, 1843), X, 197–198; Smyth, ed., *Writings of Franklin*, VII, 242–243; Mays, ed., *Letters and Papers of Pendleton*, II, 478.

14. *Autobiography of Thomas Jefferson* (New York, 1959), 75.

15. Ford, ed., *Journals of Congress*, XXIV, 394.

16. Vincent T. Harlow, *The Founding of the Second British Empire* (London, 1952–1959), I, 4. See generally W. R. Brock, "The Effect of the Loss of the American Colonies upon British Policy," in *Causes and Consequences of the American Revolution* (Chicago, 1966), ed. Esmond Wright, 305–316. The best

study of the Earl of Shelburne is John Norris, *Shelburne and Reform* (London, 1963), which deals extensively with his role in events surrounding the American Revolution.

17. The conclusions presented in the last two paragraphs are a reflection of current British historical works on the subject. The literature is conveniently summarized in Jack P. Greene, "The Plunge of Lemmings: A Consideration of Recent Writings on British Politics and the American Revolution," *South Atlantic Quarterly*, LXVII (1968), 141–175.

18. Alden, *American Revolution*, 212; Peckham, *War for Independence*, 202; Wright, *Fabric of Freedom*, 121–136; Robson, *American Revolution*, 93–174, *passim*; Mackesy, *War for America*, xiv; Richard B. Morris, *The American Revolution Reconsidered* (New York, 1967), 98–105.

19. Palmer, *Age of Democratic Revolution*, I, 210.

20. Mackesy, *War for America*, 517.

21. Paret, "Colonial Experience and European Military Reform at the End of the Eighteenth Century," 55.

22. Charlotte S. J. Epping, trans., *Journal of Du Roi the Elder* (New York, 1911), 107.

23. O'Callaghan, *Burgoyne's Orderly Book*, 113; Higginbotham, *Morgan*, 134; Fortescue, *History of the British Army*, III, chap. xxvi.

24. Fitzpatrick, ed., *Writings of Washington*, XXIV, 487–488. Later the decoration was allowed to lapse, but it was restored in 1933 as the Purple Heart.

25. Jefferson quoted in Louis Gottschalk, "The Place of the American Revolution in the Casual Pattern of the French Revolution," in *Causes and Consequences of the American Revolution*, ed. Wright, 303–304.

26. *Ibid.*, 300. It is contended that French enlisted men, many of whom were peasants, returned to France from freeholding America with a great appreciation of "unfettered private property at its glorious best . . . something that would truly stir a peasant's soul." Moreover, it is claimed that "these veterans formed the dynamic element" in the destruction of economic feudalism in a number of the provinces." Forrest McDonald, "The Relation of the French Peasant Veterans of the American Revolution to the Fall of Feudalism in France, 1789–1792," *Agricultural History*, XXV (1951), 151–161. See also Durand Echeverria, *Mirage in the West: A History of the French Image of American Society to 1815* (Princeton, 1957), 114–115.

# 17. The Revolutionary Impact: America

A revolution must not only be won; it must be held and consolidated after the initial victory. And in fact it always is held by some sort of armed force.

—KATHERINE CHORLEY

. . . no other national institution so symbolizes independence, sovereignty, or equality with other peoples as a country's armed forces. The first thing a new nation creates is a national army. The army symbolizes as well as makes effective, its distinctive identity.[1]

—S. E. FINER

THE AMERICAN EXPERIENCE ran counter to trends found elsewhere in the past and present. The end of the Revolutionary War and the end of the army were virtually synonymous. For the armed forces dissolved back into the populace from whence they came. Thus the military as a separate entity did not help to shape American foreign and domestic policy in the 1780's. Yet many of the officers were profoundly influenced by their years of service. In witnessing the inadequacies of the Confederation in waging war, they became sharply critical of limited government, parochial concerns, and states' rights. Increasingly during the decade Washington, Knox, Hamilton, Greene,[2] and other veterans spoke out in favor of overhauling the central political structure, of bolstering national efficiency in various areas. They were joined by still other men—including the Morrises, James Wilson, James Madison, John Adams, and John Jay—who had been intimately involved in the Continental wartime effort. The war had indeed been a memorable experience that directed the outlook of more than a few thoughtful Americans toward the future needs of the fledgling nation.

As Washington wrote after the adoption of the Federal Constitution: "a century in the ordinary intercourse" would not have accomplished for national unity "what the Seven years' association in Arms did."[3]


## Postwar Military Policy

Though America was born in war—the eagle on the Great Seal of the United States clasps a sheaf of arrows in one talon[4]—it paid scant attention to its military posture in the initial aftermath of the War of Independence. New threats from abroad seemed highly remote in 1783, and Congress was financially exhausted. It was almost wholly dependent for funds upon the states, which in the year 1782 had turned over to Continental receivers only $400,000 of the $8,000,000 requested by the general government. The perennial Anglo-American fear of standing armies, even present in the midst of a war of survival, was once again trundled out by opponents of a peacetime establishment. The recent controversies with the army over half pay and the Newburgh Addresses played into the hands of the anti-army elements, as did the uproar over the Society of the Cincinnati.

Founded shortly before the Continental army disbanded, the society accepted as members all officers who had served three years or were in the army at the cessation of hostilities. The Society of the Cincinnati in its choice of name revealed the neo-classical spirit of the new nation that frequently compared itself with the republic of ancient Rome. The officers saw themselves as not unlike Cincinnatus who had dropped his plough to defend his country and had afterward returned to his own soil.

The order's constitution, the "Institution," contained provisions repugnant to Americans of such diverse social and political views as John and Samuel Adams, John Jay, and Thomas Jefferson. Its hereditary membership, passed only to the oldest male descendant of each Continental officer, appeared at variance with the ideal of no hereditary aristocracy, and many foresaw this as a step toward an American nobility. A class set apart, with the ostentation and glamour that might attend it, was offensive to the Revolution's decidedly moral tone, which, for example, mirrored itself in countless wartime sermons urging a return to the virtues of simplicity and frugality. Franklin stigmatized the members as having "been too much struck with the Ribbands and Crosses they have seen . . . hanging to the buttonholes of Foreign Officers" during the war. Worried citizens also pointed to a statement that each state society keep in touch with others by means of circular letters devoted not only to its own affairs but to "the general union of the states" as well. This supposedly political note indicated that the officers might exert their influence to alter or abolish the present order of government. The provision that each member was to contribute one month's pay to a permanent charitable fund suggested to critics the creation of a treasury to finance any diabolical scheme the association might undertake.[5]

Though Henry Knox, the society's principal founder, described the organization's purpose as "pure and uncorrupted by any sinister design," and though Washington himself agreed to serve as its first president-general, opposition to the society mounted steadily. The most widely published attack came from Judge Aedanus Burke of South Carolina, an eccentric and articulate Irishman, whose *Considerations on the Society or Order of Cincinnati*—castigating the members for actually showing no desire to return to obscure citizenship like Cincinnatus—was praised by democrats and small-government men in New England as well as the South. In fact, it was Judge Burke, said James Warren, who first "roused and alarmed" Yankees to the danger of the "Cincinnati Club." A committee of the Massachusetts legislature branded the society "unjustifiable, and if not properly discountenanced, may be dangerous to the peace, liberty and safety of the United States in General, and this Commonwealth in particular." The North Carolina assembly seriously considered a bill to keep any member of the order from ever holding a seat in that body. Certain Rhode Islanders would have gone so far as to deny the suffrage to any who joined such an antirepublican organization.[6]

Perhaps some officers, albeit not always consciously, did have misgivings about returning to a seamless republican society—to what former Congressman William Duer of New York described to Rufus King of Massachusetts as "a prospect of obscurity if not of actual misery." Conceivably the veterans feared, as King maintained, that their "respectability wd be lost by separation and their pretensions derided." "[W]ithout wealth or family influence," they found the excitement and pageantry of things military "more inviting and pleasant" than the drabness of civilian life. Yet the fact is, they vented their feelings not in a grab for personal power or in an effort to establish a monarchy, although a few at least—including Colonel Lewis Nicola and Brigadier General Benjamin Tupper—were of a royalist bent; they turned instead to the creation of a ceremonial organization. Two additional projects also occupied the energies of various ex-Continental officers: one, an association to settle and speculate in Western lands, eventually known as the Ohio Company, the brain-child of Brigadier General Rufus Putnam of Massachusetts; the other, lodges of Free and Accepted Masonry. By 1784 ten Masonic lodges—"the officers' clubs of the Revolutionary War"— had been founded by Washington's subordinates.[7]

In time the outcry against the Cincinnati began to subside, partly because Washington proposed altering or eliminating the most objectionable features of the "Institution": hereditary descent, honorary membership, and correspondence among societies. (Contrary to public thinking, such amendments were never enacted.) The extent to which some members of the Cincinnati wished to function as a pressure group is unclear. In Massachusetts there were definitely sentiments on the part of members in favor of working in behalf of sound public credit and law and order at the time of Shays' Rebellion. Even in the Bay state, however, there was less criticism. The fickle public had all but forgotten the organization's "Insolent Attempt at distinction" and was selecting the members for high civil and military offices, so James Warren informed John Adams in 1787. Everywhere the group's meetings became principally social in character as they are today. All the same, this fresh outburst of anti-militarism, coming when Congress took up the peacetime army question, further dampened the prospect of a rational solution to problems of defense and preparedness.[8]

As early as April, 1783, Congress appointed a committee composed of Hamilton, Madison, Samuel Osgood, James Wilson, and Oliver Ellsworth to consider future military requirements. At the request of chairman Hamilton, Washington—after consulting with his general officers —gave the politicians his "Sentiments on a Peace Establishment."[9] It is an even-handed document, mindful of the country's deeply ingrained suspicions of men in uniform. "Altho' a *large* standing Army in time of Peace hath ever been considered dangerous to the liberties of a Country," he wrote, "yet a few Troops, under certain circumstances, are not only safe, but indispensably necessary. Fortunately for us our relative situation requires but few." Of prime importance was America's "*distance* from the European States," which "in a great degree frees us of apprehension. . . ." The country could suffice with a permanent force of four infantry and one artillery regiments—a total of 2,631 "Continental Troops"—whose primary duties would be to hold the Indians in check, police the frontiers, and "keep a watch" upon our "Neighbours" in Canada and the Floridas.

Even in the event of imminent foreign danger, America was "too poor to maintain a standing Army"; that "could not be done without great oppression to the people." Should the Revolutionary War debts be paid at some later time, then our more logical course would be in "building and equipping a Navy, without which, in case of War we could neither protect our Commerce, nor yield that Assistance to each other, which, on such an extent of Sea-Coast, our mutual Safety would require."

More unusual, even surprising, were Washington's comments on the militia, a military arm which had performed very unevenly during the Revolution, and which Washington had so frequently berated. Now, however, he spoke of the militia as "this great Bulwark of our Liberties and independence." Owing to the economic and political realities militating against a standing army, only a well-organized militia could save the country in the event of a full-scale invasion. General John McAuley Palmer, the soldier-historian who first called serious attention to this letter to Hamilton, has explained the apparent paradox: Washington in 1783 had in mind a plan quite at variance from the loose, uncoordinated militia systems of the thirteen states.

But Washington's own words leave no doubt as to his desires. He began with the premise—revolutionary by European standards—"that every Citizen who enjoys the protection of a free Government, owes not only a proportion of his property, but even of his personal services to the defence of it. . . ." Here was an explanation that has supported conscription from revolutionary France to twentieth-century America. It was, furthermore, "the idea which historically has tied democratic political revolution to military revolution culminating in total war," observes Russell Weigley.[10]

The Virginian's advocacy of a near-universal obligation perhaps fell within the tradition of the colonial period when theoretically almost all men were included in the militia. After making this point, Washington's proposals were striking. The new militia arrangement was to rest "upon a Plan that will pervade all the States, and introduce similarity in their Establishment, Maneuvres, Exercise and Arms." Even with allowances for this improvement, Washington acknowledged that many men would be ill-suited for a variety of reasons to the task of immediately taking the field against European regulars. Consequently, he proposed the formation of a ready reserve; here too there were precedents in the Massachusetts Minute Men and other special units of the younger and better-trained members of the colonial militia. Washington's special force should be recruited from able-bodied men between eighteen and twenty-five. They were to be exercised as many as twenty-five days a year, partly in their own companies but partly also in battalions and brigades. As a result, "their Discipline would be greatly promoted, and their Ideas raised, as near as possible, to real service." The officers were to be commissioned by the central government, and the entire volunteer establishment was to be subject to the control of the United States.

Washington's "Sentiments" have been praised by John McAuley Palmer and other twentieth-century advocates of compulsory military training. Supposedly, according to their argument, the country had two alternatives following the Revolution, and we chose the wrong one. Instead of building a small but effective standing army buttressed by a large, well-trained reserve of citizen-soldiers, as advocated by Washington, we virtually disbanded the army after each war and never developed a satisfactory reserve system, with the result that every subsequent conflict has found the United States sorely unprepared at the outset. Washington—and Palmer between the World Wars of this century—was interested in bridging the conflicting practices of the Revolution, one relying on professionals or long-term Continental enlistments, the other stressing militia and other irregulars. Washington's plan seemed to be a way of dealing with his own strictures against the amateur soldiers of the Revolution (just as Palmer's related ideas after 1918 were designed to show that Emory Upton's criticisms of the citizens in arms were exaggerated).[11]

Given the temper of the country, neither Washington nor Hamilton's committee seemed overly optimistic concerning the creation of a sound military system. Hamilton's group, though favorably disposed toward Washington's "Sentiments" as well as a similar scheme drafted by Baron von Steuben, recognized that there were those who doubted the constitutionality of maintaining regular forces after the peace treaty. James Madison, himself an ardent nationalist, nevertheless conceded privately that the Articles of Confederation were worded vaguely on this point. Even so, the Congressional committee began its report by expressing the belief that a "Constitutional power in the United States [existed] for that purpose." There were compelling security reasons for action by the general government. Otherwise, "when the forces of the Union should become necessary to defend its rights and repel any attacks upon them, the United States would be obliged to *begin to create*, at the very moment they would have occasion to *employ* a fleet and army." In their specific recommendations, Hamilton and his collaborators pursued closely the Washington-Steuben line, although the committee's sketch of "a well-regulated militia" embraced not two but three classes of militia, the additional one to be a blue-ribbon reserve that received almost the full training of regulars.[12]

Hamilton's report met a chilly reception in the legislative halls of the Confederation. Some doubted the altruism of those favoring a peacetime establishment. "Their professed view," snapped Stephen Higginson of Massachusetts, "is to strengthen the hands of government, to make us respectable in Europe, and I believe, they might add to divide among themselves and their friends, every place of Honour and of profit." A common complaint was that Congress had no legal right to create standing forces in an era of peace. Besides, if such an interpretation of the Articles were conceded, that body could extend its power "indefinitely both as to the number of men and term of inlistment." There was substantial sentiment among New Englanders in favor of relying almost solely upon the militia, not as reorganized according to the thinking of Washington and Hamilton but under complete control of the states. Elbridge Gerry, who was to be the most vocal opponent of centralized military authority in the Constitutional Convention, had already staked out his position: "If we have no standing Army, the Militia, which has ever been the dernier Resort of Libery, may become respectable, and adequate to our Defence . . . but if a regular Army is admitted, will not the Militia be neglected, and gradually dwindle into Contempt? and where are we to look for Defence of our Rights and Liberties?"[13]

Among Southerners a distaste for Spartanism was expressed by Jefferson, Edmund Pendelton, James Monroe, and Richard Henry Lee. "A land army would be useless for offence," declared Jefferson in his *Notes on Virginia*, "and not the best nor safest instrument of defence." The cost of armies was oppressive: it "makes the European laborer go supperless to bed, and moistens his bread with the sweat of his brows." Thanks to the ocean barrier, he believed a small naval arm sufficient to guard the nation from European aggression. As he wrote still later in the Confederation period, "a naval force can never endanger our liberties, nor occasion bloodshed; a land force would do both." Pendleton, a prominent Virginia lawyer and jurist, felt federal military appropriations unncessary short of war. Even the militia had little need to train: "I never discovered other fruits from . . . [their] meetings, than calling the Industrious from their Labour to their great disgust and [to] the Injury of the community, and affording the idle an opportunity of dissipation." James Monroe advised Richard Henry Lee that the continuation of a Continental military apparatus might lead "to the ingrafting a principle in our constitution which may in its consequences, as it ever has done with other powers, terminate in the loss of our liberty." Lee agreed that standing armies destroyed freedom, and "from the construction of human nature . . . it will always *be so*." These Virginians—all but Pendleton—were in the mid-1780's members of the Confederation Congress, Lee himself becoming its president in 1785.[14]

The composition of the federal legislature was changing, as was the higher personnel of the Confederation government generally, from a nationalist to a state-oriented outlook. Madison, completing the three consecutive years in Congress allowed by the Articles, soon retired, as did Hamilton, who resumed his law practice in New York. Gouverneur Morris stepped down as assistant superintendent of finance, followed into private life by his chief, Robert Morris, a year later in 1784.[15]

The central agency of the Confederation did well to meet at all as the states took their responsibilities to the union less seriously after the war. For example, Congress convened at Annapolis on November 26, 1783, but could not conduct official business owing to the absence of a quorum of nine states. Consequently, it had to delay ratification of the definitive treaty of peace, which, according to the terms, was to be completed and formally exchanged with Britain within six months of the signing date. In desperation the lawmakers contemplated a descent upon the sickbed of South Carolina delegate Richard Beresford in Philadelphia, to obtain his state's representation. Finally, a quorum was obtained on January 14, 1784, but the formal notice of American acceptance reached London weeks after the expiration of the time limit. Fortunately, the English made no issue of Congress' tardiness.[16]

Quite predictably, Congress scuttled the Hamilton report. If it did not renounce altogether the idea of maintaining some military complement, if it failed to consider a Massachusetts-suggested constitutional amendment restricting peacetime military activity to garrisoning Western forts and guarding federal magazines, it came perilously close to turning over all military responsibilities to the states. (After a resolution of June 2, 1784, the United States army consisted of eighty caretakers, fifty-five at West Point and twenty-five at Fort Pitt.) If it did not abolish the Department of War, it nonetheless kept the office of secretary at war unoccupied between 1783 and 1785, between the resignation of Benjamin Lincoln and the appointment of Henry Knox. It did, however, regress in the area of finance, replacing Robert Morris with a three-man treasury board directly under Congress.[17]

## Military Fortunes of the Confederation

Congress, for all its inadequacies, had been the vital center of the Revolutionary effort, but now in the military area as elsewhere it leaned heavily upon the states, calling for 700 men—from Pennsylvania, New Jersey, New York, and Connecticut—to establish order in the Northwest,[18] which had recently been ceded to the Confederation. The Indians between the Ohio and the Mississippi were restless, fearing white encroachments on their lands and facing generally an uncertain future after the British recognized trans-Appalachia as part of the United States in 1783. The British, however, continued to make their presence felt among the savages. They sought to maintain their domination of the fur trade and to cement alliances with the Crown's former subjects. They clung to Detroit, Niagara, and other forts south of the Great Lakes in violation of the Treaty of Paris. John Jay, secretary of foreign affairs, conceded that the King's government had a valid excuse: the waywardness of the individual states in fulfilling the peace terms concerning debts and loyalists.

Although there is no graver problem for a nation than the presence of uninvited foreign troops on its own soil, the British-Indian menace failed to arouse the states. Although Congress had asked that the 700 recruits serve only twelve months (and be free of "fits, rupture, and other diseases"), Pennsylvania alone met its quota of men, and Congress suppressed any intention of dislodging the British from the Northern border. The next year, in 1785, Congress endeavored to replace the one-year enlistees with a new body of 700 drawn from the same four states for a period of three years. To facilitate the task, the delegates chose Henry Knox to fill the long-vacant post of secretary at war. When Knox in mid-1786 completed his first assignment, he then tried unavailingly to persuade Congress to raise another 800 soldiers to "awe and curb the British garrisons, and cover effectually the territory of the United States." Instead, Congress took a different approach to neutralize the British influence by instructing the Secretary at War to conciliate the tribesmen. Subsequently, the troops spent much of their time evicting squatters from Indian lands in the Ohio country.[19]

But Indian resentment continued to grow—to the point that the old American nemesis, Mohawk chieftain Joseph Brant, hoped to unite the tribes of the Northwest and to secure open British support. Denouncing a series of recent American-Indian land treaties as detrimental to the red men, Brant led representatives of ten nations, assembled at Detroit in December, 1786, in issuing a series of demands to Congress, one of which said that surveyors be stopped from laying off the so-called "Seven Ranges" in Ohio until a new and more equitable settlement of boundaries was concluded. If their proposals were rejected, the tribesmen announced they would have no alternative but to take up the hatchet and scalping knife. Shortly thereafter, Secretary Knox bluntly told Congress that, with neither sufficient funds nor an adequate army, he could not fight an Indian war. Or as Indian Superintendent Richard Butler stated the matter, "It is certain that the British do . . . stimulate the Indians to mischief"; "until the United States have a respectable force on the frontiers, neither trade, surveyings, or the settlement of lands can be carried on to advantage."[20]

In the South, Confederation forces did not police the interior, for the states below Virginia had not yet ceded their Western lands to the central government. Though relations with the Southern tribes were delicate—both the British and Spaniards afforded succor to the aborigines—Congress could intervene only upon application from the states. Especially alarming was the situation in Georgia, where Alexander McGillivray, the half-breed Creek leader, seemed bent upon unleashing his warriors. Congress declared Georgia "in danger of an invasion," but Knox, pointing to the Articles of Confederation, reminded the delegates of their lack of authority within the state's "legislative jurisdiction."[21]

At times the states openly displayed their contempt of Congressional jurisdiction. In 1786 Virginia sent out a raiding expedition into the country around Vincennes which increased the likelihood of a general outbreak of hostilities. Henry Knox exploded angrily after learning of Governor Patrick Henry's ordering Colonel Josiah Harmar, the ranking officer in the army, to cooperate with the state's militia operations. Afterward, warned Knox, Harmar should obey only "direct orders . . . from the Secretary at War, or Congress itself."[22]

By 1787 the situation on both frontiers was precarious. Because of constitutional limitations, financial difficulties, and state attitudes—the three were interrelated—the Confederation had dealt ineffectually with pressing military problems in the West. As a frontier constabulary, Congress' tiny army had proved inadequate in the Northwest, and it had been legally prohibited from acting on the Southern frontier.

The second martial concern of the Confederation was protecting the Congressional arsenals at West Point and Springfield, Massachusetts: Shays' Rebellion demonstrated, as had frontier defense, the central government's failings in the military sphere.

The year 1786 was one of violence in America, with the possibility of more to come. Hard money was scarce and growing scarcer. Seven states turned to issuing paper currency, a popular means of paying debts and taxes, but also a bitterly controversial issue separating debtors from creditors, the "lower orders" from their "betters." In New Hampshire and Massachusetts paper money advocates sought redress of financial grievances by coercive means. Two hundred men armed themselves, elected leaders, and invaded the chambers of the New Hampshire legislature at Exeter. When the assembly refused their demands for fiat money and the cancellation of all debts, reported clergyman-historian Jeremy Belknap, "the drum beat to arms; as many as had guns were ordered to load them with balls, sentries were placed at the doors, and the whole Legislature were held prisoners; the mob threatening to death any person who should attempt to escape." Only the fear that Exeter's citizens would "bring up the artillery" dispersed the mob, whose leaders were seized by the militia but then released without punishment.[23]

The hard-pressed rural debtors of western Massachusetts posed a more formidable threat to law and order. They held impromptu conventions, refused to pay taxes and fees, prevented county courts from conducting business, and—nearly 2,000 of them—took to arms as they marched hither and yon seeking additional recruits, weapons, and redress of grievances. Their leader, forty-year-old Daniel Shays, was an ex-Continental captain, a veteran of Bunker Hill, Saratoga, and Stony Point, a man of modest talent but genuinely convinced of the righteousness of his cause.

The Springfield arsenal presented an inviting target for the rebellious farmers. The several federal buildings included a foundry for casting brass cannon and a brick magazine containing 1,300 barrels of powder, 7,000 muskets, and 200 tons of shot and shell. Although the Articles of Confederation failed to invest Congress with authority to cope with disorders within a state, the protection of federal stores would provide the lawmakers with grounds for intervening. "Were there a respectable body of troops in the service of the United States, so situated as to be ordered immediately to Springfield, the propriety of the measure could not be doubted," advised Henry Knox. "Or were the finances of the United States in such order, as to enable Congress to raise an additional body of four or five hundred men, and station them at respective arsenals, the spirit of the times would highly justify the measure."[24]

Congress, sharing Knox's concern, voted to increase the army to 2,040 men, but it publicly attributed the expansion to the needs of frontier defense for fear of hastening a Shaysites' attack on the still unprotected arsenal.[25] Unfortunately for Knox, only two companies of artillery could be raised on short notice. The state of Massachusetts obstructed the Secretary's efforts, refusing to allow Continental recruits raised there to take the field lest the state's own attempt to suppress the uprising be weakened. When Major General William Shepherd of the state militia sought permission to equip his men with federal arms at Springfield, Knox felt compelled to decline the request since Congress, lacking a quorum, could not provide him with an answer. Shepherd nevertheless took the government's weapons and used them in repulsing a Shaysites' stab at the Springfield post.

Jeremy Belknap, who seemed to be moving in the wake of rebellions, having left his twenty-year pastorate in New Hampshire for another in Massachusetts in 1787, inquired thusly: "Is not their attack on the Arsenal a declaration of war against the United States? and ought not Congress take them in hand . . .?" Knox, while agreeing, hesitated to act unilaterally; he knew the sensitivity of the states on matters involving their sovereignty: "it might be deemed an interference of Congress in the internal government of the state." Knox did dispatch 125 federal troops (raised in Connecticut) to Springfield, but only after the arsenal was safe and Shepherd and General Benjamin Lincoln were completing the job of routing the insurgents.

Once again the Confederation had experienced humiliation in the conduct of military affairs. Unable to defend its own war stores, it also had been snubbed by state authority. In fact, the Massachusetts legislature, endeavoring to round up the scattered remnants of Shays' followers, empowered Lincoln to send his militiamen into any United States territory whatsoever "for the sole purpose of apprehending the leaders and others concerned in the insurrection and rebellion and bringing them to justice."[26]

## The Movement for Constitutional Reform

The question of the location of military power in the community was only one of the vital considerations that led fifty-five men to Philadelphia in the spring of 1787. But, as Walter Millis reminds us, it was an exceedingly vital one; and the end product, the Federal Constitution, "was as much a military as a political and economic charter."[27] If few Americans feared a foreign invasion in that year, the country faced an uncertain future in its relations with England and Spain, powers openly hostile to the United States, to say nothing of matters concerning the Indian tribes and the maintenance of domestic tranquility in the individual states.

By 1787 the three men most immediately conversant with the military posture of the nation were of one mind that Congress as constituted could not deal satisfactorily with problems of security. Arthur St. Clair, president of Congress, and Colonel Josiah Harmar, the army's commanding officer, shared Secretary at War Knox's belief that a wholesale overhauling of the Confederacy was absolutely essential.[28]

Countless former officers of the Continental army supported the movement for constitutional reform. In fact, historian Charles A. Beard wrote that "had the movement for forming a new Constitution by peaceful measures failed, there is no doubt in my mind that the men of the sword would have made a desperate effort to set up a dictatorship by arms."[29]

Beard's sentiments, though undocumented, could be found here and there in the literature of the period. New England's Noah Webster, the great publicist of cultural independence, later recalled that in 1785 "certain military characters" had resolved "in case of civil convulsion to rally the officers and soldiers of the late army . . . to give a government to this country by force." The future historian of the Revolution, Mercy Warren, sister of James Otis and wife of James Warren, voiced similar fears and directed an accusing finger at the Society of the Cincinnati. Dr. Benjamin Rush predicted in June of 1787 that if the country rejected the offering of the delegates at Philadelphia, then "*force* will not be wanting to carry it into execution, for not only all the wealth but all the military men of our country (associated in the Society of the Cincinnati) are in favor of a wise and efficient government."[30]

If some advocates of states' rights and decentralized government suffered from the specter of a military takeover by ex-Continentals, it is no less true (and insufficiently stressed) that the so-called nationalists and others dedicated to a vigorous restructuring of the United States had nightmares of government by fire and sword; of the establishment of "an armed tyranny . . . on the ruins of the present constitutions." Small

wonder they did when violence climaxing in armed rebellion had occurred in Massachusetts, the one state where the people themselves
had drawn up their own constitution by specially chosen representatives and where the citizens had subsequently given their approval in
town meetings. The insurrection in supposedly politically sophisticated
Massachusetts was all the more likely to be repeated in other states
with less satisfactory instruments of government. The establishment of
petty despotisms, of military tyrannies under demagogues who played
upon the passions of the lower orders, was an all too familiar pattern in
the history of republics in classical times.

Would the same be true of the history of America? Would the rich
and poor in each state engage in civil conflicts? Would these be followed by still different wars in which one state would annex another?
And would a foreign monarchy then step in and gobble up both? In the
spring of 1787 the unenviable record of many ancient sovereignties lay
open to American readers of John Adams' newly published *Defence of
the Constitutions of the United States*, a 300-page study composed in
time taken from the author's duties as United States minister to Great
Britain. Keenly alive to the urgency of political reform at home, Adams
felt that the counsel of history—his anatomy of fifty constitutions—if
properly heeded—would light up the pathway to a more perfect American union by showing the dangers and potentialities of republicanism
and the vices of overly weak, democratically oriented confederacies
such as the one in his own country. The final sentence of Adams'
*Defence* seemed unusually poignant to Americans who had just weath-
ered Shays' Rebellion and who feared similar outbreaks elsewhere:
"Where the people have a voice, and there is no balance [e.g., constitutional checks or restraints upon their actions], there will be everlasting fluctations, revolutions, and horrors, until a standing army, with
a general at its head, commands the peace, or the necessity of an equilibrium is made appear to all, and is adopted by all."[31]

Did nationalists such as Adams exaggerate the ills of America in the
1780's? Were not some of the country's troubles merely growing pains
characteristic of most emerging nations? Assuredly one may debate
whether, in historian John Fiske's phrase, this was "the critical period"
of American history, just as one may find examples of solid achievement during the decade in the chapters of Merrill Jensen's *The New
Nation*. All the same, there were few far-sighted Americans who would
deny that the government of the United States was at present inadequate to perform effectively its assigned tasks. And there were others
who were convinced that a completely new political fabric must be
tailored to replace the Articles of Confederation. Franklin, hardly a
Cassandra, reminded his fellow delegates to the Constitutional Con-

vention of the widely held belief that "our States are on the point of separation, only to meet hereafter for the purpose of cutting one another's throats." The English scientist Joseph Priestley, a warm friend of America, voiced the same idea: "It was taken for granted that the moment America had thrown off the yoke of Great Britain, the different states would go to war among themselves."[32]

Already in America, before Shays took to arms and before the arrival of Adams' *Defence*, there were wheels in motion to create an equilibrium between liberty and order. "The American War is over," declared an anonymous citizen of New Jersey, "but this is far from being the case with the American Revolution. . . . It remains yet to establish and perfect our new forms of government." In various quarters talk increasingly centered on the calling of a grand convention instead of relying on the amending process to revamp the Articles of Confederation, a process that had repeatedly failed owing to the necessity of securing ratification by all the states. "As the present constitution is so defective," wrote Knox to Gouverneur Morris in 1783, "why do not you great men call the people together, and tell them so? That is, to have a convention of the States to form a better constitution? This appears . . . to be the most efficacious remedy." In Knox's own Massachusetts considerable sentiment existed in favor of holding a convention. But when in 1785 the legislature endorsed a proposal to convene representatives from all the states to determine the general powers needed by Congress, that body was embarrassed to learn that its own Congressional delegation refused to introduce the resolution, fearing its implementation might result in the creation of a standing army.[33]

This was only a temporary setback for the ever-strengthening nationalist breezes of the 1780's. Prodded by Madison and Hamilton, the sparsely-attended Annapolis commercial convention—meeting in the late summer of 1786—ended with a call for a general convention to assemble "at Philadelphia on the second Monday in May next," to seek a constitutional solution to the ills of the United States.[34] Shays' Rebellion dramatized the urgency for action, and no one did more to spread the alarm than Henry Knox, whose awareness of the defects of the Confederation was probably unsurpassed among his contemporaries. The Secretary at War directed much of his drumfire at George Washington, who, at age fifty-five, was again living the life of a country squire at his beloved Mount Vernon.

Washington was a good listener; he always had been. During the Revolutionary War he had profited from his exposure to some of the finest young minds in America, men whom he had gathered around him as aides and other subordinates. He now gave an attentive ear to some of these same voices, particularly those of Knox and David

Humphreys. He also listened to his "particular friend" James Madison, who commented darkly on the state of public affairs. Washington had in fact long been the leading critic of the Articles of Confederation, dating from the war years. From the outset, he had doubted their ability to enable Congress to manage effectively matters of continental dimensions. Early in 1781 he acknowledged to Lieutenant Colonel John Laurens the inadequacy of the Articles, suggesting in their place "another [system] more consonant with the spirit of the nation, and more capable of activity and energy in public measures. . . ." Two years later he made the same point more emphatically to Hamilton: "unless Congress have powers competent to all general purposes . . . the distresses we have encountered, the expence we have encurred, and the blood we have spilt in the course of an Eight year war, will avail us nothing."[35]

In 1787 his opinion had not changed but was confirmed and sharpened by recent developments. While agreeing with other critics as to the Confederation's failures in the areas of commercial, fiscal, and foreign policy, he laid stress upon the need for the central government to prevent internal disorders. Likewise, he feared that the existing tensions with Great Britain would increase; America should prepare for any threat from the former mother country. "We ought not therefore to sleep nor to slumber. Vigilance in watching, and vigour in acting, is, in my opinion, become indispensably necessary."[36] Although reluctant to come out of retirement for an assortment of reasons, Washington finally agreed, at the urging of Knox, Humphreys, and Madison, to attend the Philadelphia Convention. They convinced him that news of his favorable decision would encourage other states to send their most distinguished sons and would add luster to the proceedings.

## The Constitutional Convention

The delegates to the Convention were conversant with the military problems of the Revolution and the Confederation. Although Washington was the only one in attendance to have held an important army command, he was joined at Philadelphia by four of his staff officers, thirteen other Continental officers, and another dozen or more officers of the militia. And over half the men who took their seats in the Pennsylvania State House had gained invaluable experience in the art of politics while serving in the Continental Congress.

As the deputies took to their task of nation-building, they were, broadly speaking, in agreement that the military authority of the United States was in need of strengthening. Governor Edmund Randolph of Virginia commenced the deliberations with a "long and elaborate" speech on the proper objectives of the union and the present inadequacies of the federal system. The first "defect" was "that the confederation produced no security agai[nst] foreign invasion; congress not being permitted to prevent a war nor to support it by th[eir] own authority." Madison, the unofficial secretary of the Convention, recorded that Randolph then proceeded to cite "many examples." Most of them "tended to show, that they could not cause infractions of treaties or of the law of nations, to be punished: that particular states might by their conduct provoke war without control; and that neither militia nor draughts being fit for defence on such occasions, enlistments only could be successful, and these could not be executed without money."[37]

From the outset the initiative lay with the nationalists, who succeeded in making the Virginia Plan the principal subject of debate leading to an entirely new constitution, one more compound and less confederated than under the Articles. Even the small-state representatives could not be termed diehards on the question of expanding authority at the center. Their New Jersey Plan, offered by William Paterson and other advocates of retaining the old federal principle, provided for "the federal Executive" to "direct all military operations." More amazing—even to such an ardent nationalist as Madison—was the provision empowering Congress to use force if necessary against any state that failed to comply with laws, treaties, and requisitions of the United States.[38]

After the defeat of the New Jersey Plan, the delegates completed their examination of the Virginia Plan and then instructed the committee of detail to transform "general principles" into explicit language. The committee report (August 6) contained a clause giving Congress authority to raise and, as amended (August 18), support armies. Here, stated simply, were two significant extensions of Congressional power. Similar provisions as expressed in the Articles of Confederation reflected the notion of the sovereignty of the states: Congress was "to agree upon the number of land forces, and to make requisitions from each state for its quota, in proportion to the number of white inhabitants in such state." It was likewise the states that were to "cloathe, arm, and equip" these soldiers "at the expence of the United States." The inadequacies of this system were common knowledge to the men at Philadelphia. With state sovereignty no longer a fact, the United States could now act directly upon the citizens by enlisting them in the army and by taxing them for needed revenue.[39]

Elbridge Gerry, consistent with his earlier fear of militarism, noted that the committee's draft failed to prohibit Congress from maintaining a large army in peacetime: "great opposition to the plan would spring from such an omission." Backed by Luther Martin of Maryland, he moved that the support-of-the-armies clause be altered to include a statement limiting the size of the land forces to no more than 3,000 men except when the country was actually at war. It may well be an apocryphal story that Washington responded to a nearby delegate in an audible whisper that the Convention should also declare it unconstitutional for an enemy to invade the country with more than 3,000 men; but it is beyond doubt that the overwhelming majority were as exasperated as his reputed sarcasm implies. Both Charles Cotesworth Pinckney of South Carolina and Jonathan Dayton of New Jersey were quick to reply, pointing out a degree of preparedness was essential at all times. Without further debate, the Gerry motion was decisively defeated.[40]

The outcome of the brief, one-sided standing army scuffle can probably be explained in the words of the moderate nationalist John Langdon of New Hampshire: he could see "no room for Mr. Gerry's distrust of the Representatives of the people." The delegates felt that they were taking sure-footed steps to guarantee civil supremacy in the forthcoming constitution. For this reason they deemed it unnecessary to consider the proposed clause by the younger Charles Pinckney that "the military shall always be subordinate to the Civil power"; it merely stated the obvious. The commander in chief of the armed forces was to be a civilian, the President of the United States. It was he who would appoint the officers of the army and the navy, subject to confirmation by the Senate. But if the sword was placed in the hands of the executive, the purse remained in the hands of Congress, the representatives of the people. Here too there were safeguards; the Framers restricted the authority of Congress to raise and support armies with the stipulation that "no appropriation of money to that use shall be for a longer term than two years."[41] (No such restriction affected the maintenance of a navy.)

Although the militia provisions of the Constitution provoked heated controversy, the debates show a kind of consensus that the land forces of the individual states should to some degree be under the jurisdiction of the United States. No one opposed the part of the committee of detail's report empowering the national legislature "to call forth the aid of the militia, in order to execute the laws of the Union, . . . suppress insurrections, and repel invasions." This in itself marked a radical departure from the colonial and Revolutionary past when each colony had maintained its own militia virtually independent of effective British jurisdiction, and when, later, each state's forces were free from Congressional direction.

Friction erupted after Virginia's George Mason, himself one of the more state-minded delegates, introduced the subject of regulating the militia, which could scarcely be effective in the "public defence" without overall coordination. He therefore moved that Congress have the "additional power" of making "laws for the regulation and discipline of the Militia of the Several States, reserving to the States the appointment of the Officers." Charles Cotesworth Pinckney sprang to his feet to second Mason's motion. As a former Continental officer, he had witnessed the frailties of the militia during the British invasion of the lower South, where the "dissimilarity" of the irregulars had "produced the most serious mischiefs."[42]

Judge Oliver Ellsworth of Connecticut led off for the opposition. Mason went too far in his opinion. "The whole authority over the militia ought by no means to be taken away from the states, whose consequence would pine away to nothing after such a sacrifice of power." Ellsworth's Connecticut colleague Roger Sherman agreed, as did the respected John Dickinson of Delaware; he declared that "the States never would nor ought to give up all authority over the Militia." Predictably, an even harder states' rights position was taken by Gerry, who in the succeeding debates trundled out the timeworn arguments against entrusting remote authority with controls that might be used to subvert the liberties of the people. Should the delegates continue in their present vein, they would imprint upon the Constitution "as black a mark as was set on Cain." He for one had "no such confidence in the Genl. Govt. as some Gentlemen possessed, and believed it would be found that the States have not."[43]

Mason retreated, fearing he was "creating insuperable objections to the plan." Perhaps the delegates would accept the idea of only "a select militia" under the general government. He called for "a power to make laws for regulating and disciplining the militia, not exceeding one-tenth part in any one year. . . ." Ellsworth remained unconvinced that the states would ever acquiesce to the same militia regulations. His next remark must have brought wry smiles from the Southern delegates. "Three or four shillings as a penalty," he said, "will enforce obedience better in New England, than forty lashes in some other places." The Southern nabobs could always enjoy a joke at the expense of their "Eastern" friends who were reputed to pinch their pennies.[44]

The nationalists were also unwilling, but for different reasons, to accept Mason's watered-down substitute. It was imperative, warned Pierce Butler of South Carolina, to submit the entire militia to Congressional jurisdiction since the states were not responsible for the safety of the country. Or as General Pinckney expressed it, divided authority would be "an incurable evil." "If the States would trust the Genl. Government with a power over the public treasure," argued Madison, then surely "they would from the same consideration of necessity grant it the direction of the public force."[45]

The Convention referred the matter to the committee of eleven—

assigned to clear up various pieces of unfinished business—which subsequently reported a militia clause in almost the same form that appears in the completed document: Congress was "to make laws for organizing, arming and disciplining the Militia, and for governing such part of them as may be employed in the service of the U—S, reserving to the States respectively the appointment of the officers, and the authority of training the Militia according to the discipline prescribed by the U. States."[46]

The language was a distinct victory for the nationalists, who beat off efforts to alter significantly the committee's phraseology. The states, grumbled Gerry, were reduced to little more than "drill-sergeants" and would assuredly regard themselves victims of "a system of Despotism." Madison gave the New Englander even more cause for alarm by seeking to amend the clause so that the states would be confined to making militia appointments *"under the rank of General officers."* At this point Gerry made no bones about his bitterness. To be consistent, he exclaimed, one might as well go on and abolish the state governments, appoint an hereditary executive, and elect the Senate for life. By pushing for an excess of centralization, the people "of a more democratic cast" would oppose it with every resource at their command: "a civil war may be produced by the conflict." On this small point Gerry had his way, and the Madison motion failed to carry.[47]

Perhaps because he saw the need to muster support for the ratification of the Constitution, Madison endeavored to appease his adversary when Gerry sought to preface the militia clause with these words: "that the liberties of the people may be better secured against the danger of standing armies in time of peace." Although, as Madison said, this did not restrain Congress from maintaining forces in peacetime, Gerry's proposal was opposed by Gouverneur Morris, Charles Cotesworth Pinckney, and Gunning Bedford of Delaware—Morris denouncing it for placing "a dishonorable mark of distinction on the military class of citizens." By a vote of nine to two the Convention turned thumbs down on the Gerry amendment. Gerry, along with Randolph and Mason of Virginia, were the only members present who failed to sign the Constitution on September 17. But Gerry alone specifically gave "the general power of the Legislature . . . to raise armies and money without limit" as a reason for his not signing.[48]

The Founding Fathers (excluding an occasional crabbed particularist) believed they had provided well for the defense of the country against foreign enemies or domestic upheavals, without sacrificing the liberties of the people or the welfare of the states. Military authority in the central government was divided between the President and Congress, and at a different level it was divided between the central government and the states. Specialists have regularly pointed to the militia provisions as characteristic of the federal nature of the American Constitution. Indeed, the Framers divided control over the militia in more specific detail than they separated any other authority. "And in the course of American history," writes Theodore Riker, "there can be no doubt that the militia has been the most significant of the jointly administered functions."[49] The Constitution, in summary, provided for a dual military system consistent in outline but not in detail with America's historic traditions: the state militias, rooted in the colonial past; and the United States army, corresponding roughly to the Continental army of the Revolution.

## Ratification

The Antifederalists adhered to a different view. They believed that the new document provided for too much consolidation in the central government. They expressed a profound distrust of political power and the intoxicating influence it had upon those who held it. The natural and inevitable tendency was for men in authority to seek to increase and abuse the power at their disposal. The Framers themselves shared a common political heritage with the Antifederalists, an awareness of the frailties of human nature. But whereas the Federalists saw sufficient safeguards in the Constitution, their adversaries did not.

Here we come to the very core of the Antifederalists' intellectual argument. Adequate restraints were impossible when the form of government for America was to be a republic in place of a confederation of states that retained all or most of their sovereignty. Both history and contemporary political theory were on the side of the Antifederalists, who pointed out that republics had never been successfully attempted for such a huge, sprawling country as the United States, whose people were diverse and heterogeneous. The very idea of a "republick, on an average one thousand miles in length, and eight hundred in breadth, and containing six millions of white inhabitants all reduced to the same standard of morals, of habits, and of laws, is in itself an absurdity, and contrary to the whole experience of mankind," exclaimed James Winthrop of Massachusetts. "You might as well attempt to rule Hell by Prayer," exploded Thomas Wait of Maine, as to consolidate "the vast Continent of America . . . into one Government." Such a political system could be maintained only by "military coercion." And "a military execution" of the laws, warned Richard Henry Lee, would "very soon destroy all elective governments in the country, produce anarchy, or establish despotism."[50]

It would be impossible, for example, for Congress to propose direct internal taxes that would not prove harmful to some states or interest groups. Invariably the army would be the means of collecting unpopular and unjust revenues, complained Antifederalists in Massachusetts and Pennsylvania. Melancthon Smith, an influential Antifederalist, informed New Yorkers assembled at Poughkeepsie to pass on the Constitution that the instrument which "has all power and both purse and Sword has the absolute Gov't of all other Bodies and they must exist at the will and pleasure of the Superior."[51]

Undoubtedly, these particular fears of the army were heightened by the fact that the Antifederalists saw no legitimate need for a standing force. It was claimed that the instigators of such a grant of power were members of the Society of the Cincinnati, who desired to monopolize the offices of high rank in what would become a European-type army. "The military profession will then be respectable," shrilled Eleazer Oswald's Philadelphia *Independent Gazetteer*, "and the Floridas may be conquered in a campaign—The Spoils of the West-Indies and South America may enrich the next generation of the Cincinnati."[52]

In any case, the country faced no threat from abroad; and if ever one occurred, the methods of the Revolution would again suffice, predicted a contributor to the *Pennsylvania Packet*:

Had we a standing army when the British invaded our peaceful shores? Was it a standing army that gained the battles of Lexington and Bunker Hill, and took the ill-fated Burgoyne? Is not a well regulated militia sufficient for every purpose of internal defense? And which of you, my fellow citizens, is afraid of any invasion from foreign powers that our brave militia would not be able immediately to repel?"[53]

To preserve the militia, the Antifederalists felt it imperative to reject or modify the Constitution. The national government would fail to arm and organize the militia—the chief protector of American liberties—so that it might resort to a standing army with impunity. Patrick Henry's "great objection" to the new government was that "it does not leave us the means of defending our rights or of waging war against tyrants. . . . Have we the means of resisting disciplined armies when our only defence, the militia, is put into the hands of Congress?"[54]

Other critics perceived a more subtle threat to the health of the states' militia systems, a more devious means of subverting freedom by means of a standing army. It was that Congress might indeed build up the militia and, by rigid disciplining, turn its citizen-soldiers into professionals of the European mold: "mere machines as Prussian soldiers," devoid of sentiments of freedom and dignity and divorced from the great mass of the body politic. The militia, in short, would become a standing army, which might be marched up and down the American continent, an instrument of oppression directed against the states and their inhabitants. The Pennsylvania Antifederalists warned that the militia of their state might "be marched to New England or Virginia to quell an insurrection occasioned by the most galling oppression. . . ." Thus the militia would rivet "the chains of despotism on their fellow-citizens and on one another."[55]

The Antifederalists proposed numerous additions and amendments regarding the Constitution's military sections:

1. That the people have a right to keep and bear arms. . . .
2. That a well-regulated militia, composed of the body of the people trained to arms, is the proper, natural, and safe defence of a free state. . . .
3. That each state respectively shall have the power to provide for organizing, arming, and disciplining its own militia, whensoever Congress shall omit or neglect to provide for the same. That the militia shall not be subject to martial law, except when in actual service, in time of war, invasion, or rebellion; and when not in actual service of the United States, shall be subject only to such fines, penalities, and punishments, as shall be directed or inflicted by the laws of its own state.
4. That the militia of any state shall not be marched out of such state without the consent of the executive thereof, nor be continued in service out of state, without the consent of the legislature thereof, for a longer term than six weeks.
5. That no standing army or regular troops shall be raised, or kept up, in time of peace, without the consent of two thirds of the senators and representatives present in each house.
6. That the President shall not command the army in person without the consent of Congress.
7. That no soldier be enlisted for a longer time than four years except in time of war, and then only during the war.
8. That, in time of peace, no soldier ought to be quartered in any house without the consent of the owner, and in time of war only by the civil magistrates, in such manner as the law directs.
9. That any person religiously scrupulous of bearing arms ought to be exempted upon payment of an equivalent to employ another to bear arms in his stead.[56]

From the Antifederalists' list of particulars, one can see why they considered themselves to have a monopoly on the Anglo-American military heritage. In speaking of the dangers of standing armies and the necessity of local control of the militia they repeated phrases uttered by opponents of the Stuarts, by the commonwealthmen in the reign of William III, by the authors of *Cato's Letters*; and, on the western side of the Atlantic, by "Massacre Day" orators, by Jefferson's Declaration of Independence, by the makers of the state constitutions and the Articles of Confederation. There was a degree of rigidity in Revolutionary thought, much of it the preserve of the Antifederalists. They were more ideologically oriented, more doctrinaire, in their outlook. The long controversy with Britain had accustomed many Americans to think beyond practices and policies which at the present might seem satisfactory: to look instead to the principle involved and the unfortunate precedent that could be the result.

The Federalists, of course, could reply that they themselves were not stepchildren of the eighteenth century; the Constitution, including its military features, borrowed substantially from colonial and Revolutionary antecedents. But they could not deny that in combining various aspects of their own experience their political engineering was highly innovative, providing as it did for a vigorous restructuring of power favorable to the national government.

In countering their opponents' arguments, the Federalists advanced practical explanations to show that the Constitution posed no threat to liberty and that it was essential to the safety of the country. James Madison penned the best justification for a republican form of government for an area as expansive and diverse as the United States. He could see small chance of Congressional legislation that would be so unpopular as to necessitate the mustering of troops to compel enforcement. In a large republic, he explained in the tenth *Federalist*, "you take in a greater variety of parties and interests; you make it less probable that a majority of the whole will have a common motive to invade the rights of other citizens."[57]

Still, the government would insist on upholding the laws of the union: "That force must be used, if necessary, can not be denied. Can any government be established that will answer any purpose whatever unless force be provided for executing its laws?" But muscle, however vital in theory, was to be a last resort in actuality. Here, as elsewhere, the Federalists accused their adversaries of pushing their arguments to the most extreme possibilities. "It is supposed," complained Edmund Randolph (now back in Virginia championing the handiwork he could not bring himself to sign in Philadelphia), "that, instead of using civil force in the first instance, the militia are to be called forth to arrest petty offenders against the laws. Ought not common sense to be the rule in interpreting this Constitution? Is there an exclusion of the civil power? Does it provide that the laws are to be enforced by military coercion in all cases? No, sir. All that we are to infer is that when the civil power is not sufficient the militia must be drawn out."[58]

When the militia was called out, whether to enforce the laws, or to suppress insurrections, or to repel invasions, "common sense" would prevail. Madison, Randolph, and Thomas McKean of Pennsylvania considered it ridiculous to assume that Georgia militia would be dispatched to New Hampshire or vice versa. All the same, whatever part of the militia that was in the service of the United States must be coordinated and directed by the central authority to achieve maximum effectiveness. But in a war against an enemy with a professional army, the militia could not shoulder the greatest part of the burden. "War, like most other things," noted Hamilton, "is a science to be acquired and perfected by diligence, by perseverance, by time, and by practice."[59]

Just as the Federalists discounted any threat from a federalized militia, so they also maintained that apprehensions of a regular army were groundless. As Hamilton patiently explained in the twenty-sixth *Federalist*, the much-revered English Bill of Rights had been aimed primarily at the executive (the Crown) rather than the legislature (Parliament), which was not forbidden from sustaining a peacetime military force. America under the Constitution was equally safe, for the Congress was not "*at liberty* to vest in the executive permanent funds for the support of an army." The national legislative body itself was the surest guardian of the people's rights against an excess of militarism. Since Congress could not appropriate funds for any longer than two years at a time, the lawmakers, at the end of each such period, would be compelled to review the whole question of "keeping a military force on foot . . . and to declare their sense of the matter, by a formal vote in the face of their constituents." It would "always be a favourable topic for declamation. As often as the question comes forward, the public attention will be roused and attracted to the subject. . . ." With money bills originating in the House of Representatives, there could be no provision for a standing army, said Edmund Randolph, "without the consent of the democratic branch." Finally, as Archibald Maclaine of North Carolina remarked, a measure of faith was called for. He doubted that "the representatives of our general government" would "be worse men than the members of our state government. Will we be such fools as to send our greatest rascals to the general government? We must be both fools and villains to do so."[60]

The nationalists of 1787, to quote James Wilson, sought to convince their fellow citizens that "the *power* of raising and keeping up an army in time of peace is essential to every government." The authors of the *Federalist* depicted nations, like men, as ambitious and grasping. "It is true," sighed John Jay, "however it may be to human nature, that nations in general will make war whenever they have a prospect of getting anything by it." Even when their people would gain no advantage, monarchs were often disposed to disturb the peace "for purposes and objectives merely personal, such as, a thirst for military glory, revenge for personal affronts; ambition, or private compacts to aggrandize or support their particular families or partizans."[61]

Although, as Hamilton conceded, a wide ocean separated the United States from Europe, various factors warned against undue confidence in the country's security. America's frontiers, weak and undefended, bordered the possessions of England and Spain, both of them also powers in the nearby Caribbean area. Furthermore, since Americans were a commercial people, they must have a navy, with appropriate dockyards and arsenals; and while the American fleet was in its infancy, coastal installations would be imperative to protect the navy from destruction.[62]

A strong union would cause a potential aggressor to give pause before acting, while it would also lessen the chances of a war in which this country was the wrongful instigator. Several issues of the *Federalist* demonstrated that throughout history weak leagues and confederacies had been sucked into wars—or fought among themselves—owing to the caprices of their individual members. So it was that Jay, still serving as secretary of foreign affairs, could speak authoritatively in the third *Federalist* of a number of the *sovereign* states bringing the Confederation perilously close to hostilities with Britain because of their failure to honor the provisions of the peace of 1783 regarding the loyalists and the collection of debts owed to English merchants. According to the Constitution, however, the national government would not be "affected by . . . local circumstances" and would "neither be induced to commit the wrong themselves, nor want power or inclination to prevent or punish its commission by others."[63]

The test of time favors the judgments of the Framers. The military establishment in the next century was no threat to the republic. Congress in the Militia Act of 1792 (the basic legislation on the subject before 1903) refused to follow the various plans of Washington and others for meaningful federal supervision and support of the militia. The irregulars, therefore, were exclusively state forces except when in the actual service of the United States. All the while the peacetime regular army was invariably small; its duties were only tangentially related to the national defense as it policed, explored, and developed the public domain.[64] It proved scarcely necessary, save from the point of political expediency, for the pro-Constitution elements to promise amendments to the new charter: Articles II and III of the Bill of Rights:

A well regulated Militia, being necessary to the security of a free State, the right of the people to keep and bear Arms, shall not be infringed.

No Soldier shall, in time of peace, be quartered in any house, without the consent of the Owner, nor in time of war, but in a manner to be prescribed by law.

There were to be future wars in keeping with the prediction of the Founding Fathers, who had astutely delineated the causes of international discord. For as James Wilson observed, the world was not ready to enter "the millennium."[65] If the country would stumble unprepared into most of its later conflicts, the fault lay not in the Constitution but in the manner in which Congress utilized its authority to raise and support armies and navies. Congress, of course, merely mirrored the attitudes of the American people, who had not changed fundamentally in their distrust of militarism, and who continued to believe that the Atlantic Ocean was—despite the contrary experience of the War of 1812—the great safeguard of the nation. More than a century after 1787, President Charles W. Eliot of Harvard spoke in the spirit of the anti-militarists of the eighteenth century: "The building of a navy and the presence of a large standing army mean the abandonment of what is characteristically American. . . ." Even the "building of a navy . . . [was] English and French policy. It should never be ours."[66]

The civilian coloration to military affairs continued in the nineteenth century to reflect patterns of the colonial and Revolutionary era. Units would be raised from scratch, often by influential citizens. The political generals of the Revolution, such as Schuyler and Putnam, would have their counterparts in Benjamin F. Butler and Nathaniel Banks in the Civil War. Congressional tampering with Washington's legitimate functions as commander in chief was at least roughly analogous to Lincoln's frustrations at the hands of the Committee on the Conduct of the War. Nor did friction between the states and the central government completely disappear. In 1812 and again in 1898 militia regiments refused to serve outside the United States. The mutual antipathy between Continentals and militia in the War of Independence was to be repeated in subsequent hostility between the regular army troops on the one hand and volunteers and other nonprofessionals on the other.[67]

This is not to say that the men who won American freedom in the Revolution and then put that freedom on a firmer foundation in the Constitution should have been able to solve all these and other future difficulties. It is not the lot of men to be so gifted. They did, however, provide an instrument through which the country could respond to its military needs without losing freedom of civil control. In an age of immense military spending, with a blurring of the previously identifiable divisions between the scientific and industrial sectors and the defense establishment, our heritage from the Revolutionary generation is one to be guarded jealously and adjusted to modern needs and conditions.

## NOTES

1. Chorley, *Armies and the Art of Revolution*, 13; Finer, *The Man on Horseback*, 33.
2. Greene died in 1786.
3. Fitzpatrick, ed., *Writings of Washington*, XXXV, 199–200.

4. It took Congress nearly six years to agree on a satisfactory design for the Great Seal. Ford, ed., *Journals of Congress*, XXII, 338–339.
5. Franklin to Sarah Bache, Jan. 26, 1784, Smyth, ed., *Writings of Franklin*, IX, 161. The "Institution" is printed in William S. Thomas, *The Society of the Cincinnati, 1783–1935* (New York and London, 1935).
6. Knox to Benjamin Lincoln, May 21, 1783, quoted in Wallace E. Davies, *Patriotism on Parade: The Story of Veterans' and Hereditary Organizations in America, 1783–1900* (Cambridge, Mass., 1955), 5; *Warren-Adams Letters*, II, 237; Edgar E. Hume, "Early Opposition to the Cincinnati," *Americana*, XXX (1936), 597–638; Warren, *History of the Rise, Progress and Termination of the American Revolution*, III, 359; Nathanael Greene to Joseph Reed, May 14, 1784, W. B. Reed, *Life and Correspondence of Joseph Reed*, II, 409.
7. C. R. King, *Life and Correspondence of Rufus King*, I, 621; Sidney Kaplan, "Veteran Officers and Politics in Massachusetts," *William and Mary Quarterly*, 3d ser., IX (1952), 29–57; Louise B. Dunbar, *A Study of Monarchial Tendencies in the United States, from 1776 to 1801* (Urbana, Ill., 1922), 40–53.
8. Warren to Adams, May 18, 1787, *Warren-Adams Letters*, II, 291–292.
9. Hamilton to Washington, April 9, 1783, Syrett, ed., *Papers of Hamilton*, III, 322–323. The officers submitted written replies, which are in the Washington Papers, Library of Congress: Steuben to Washington, April 15, 21, 1783; Samuel Huntington to Washington, April 16, 1783; Knox to Washington, April 17, 1783; William Heath to Washington, April 17, 1783; Timothy Pickering to Washington, April 22, 1783; Rufus Putnam to Washington, April 25, 1783. The commander in chief's "Sentiments on a Peace Establishment" are in Fitzpatrick, ed., *Writings of Washington*, XXVI, 374–398.
10. John McAuley Palmer, *Washington, Lincoln, Wilson: Three War Statesmen* (New York, 1930), 3–5, 146–148, 375–396; Russell F. Weigley, *Towards an American Army: Military Thought from Washington to Marshall* (New York, 1962), 11.
11. Among Palmer's prolific writings, consult especially *Washington, Lincoln, Wilson*; also *America in Arms* (New Haven, 1941), Weigley, *Towards an American Army*, chap. xiii, evaluates Palmer's place in American military thought.
12. Baron von Steuben, *Letter on the Subject of an Established Militia and Military Arrangements Addressed to the Inhabitants of the United States* (New York, 1784); Fitzpatrick, ed., *Writings of Washington*, XXVII, 360; Brant, *Madison*, II, 291–293; Gaillard Hunt, ed., *Writings of James Madison* (New York, 1900–1910), I, 478 n–479 n; Ford, ed., *Journals of Congress*, XXV, 722–725, 136–141.
13. Stephen Higginson to Samuel Adams, May 20, 1783, Massachusetts delegates to the Massachusetts legislature, June 4, 1784, Elbridge Gerry to the Massachusetts legislature, Oct. 25, 1784, Burnett, ed., *Letters of Congress*, VII, 167, 542–543, 604–605.
14. Jefferson, *Notes on Virginia*, query xxii; Boyd, ed., *Papers of Jefferson*, X, 225; Mays, ed., *Letters and Papers of Pendleton*, II, 473, 493; Monroe to Richard Henry Lee, Dec. 16, 1783, Stanislaus M. Hamilton, ed., *The Writings of James Monroe* (New York, 1898–1903), I, 23; Ballagh, ed., *Letters of Richard Henry Lee*, II, 287.
15. Jensen, *The New Nation*, 82–83.
16. Morris, *The Peacemakers*, 447–448.
17. Burnett, ed., *Letters of Congress*, VII, 542–543; Ward, *Department of War*, 39–48, *passim*. On June 2, 1784, Congress, in reducing the army almost to the vanishing point, denounced a standing army in time of peace as "inconsistent with the principles of republican governments, dangerous to the liberties of a free people, and a potential agent in establishing despotism." Ford, ed., *Journals of Congress*, XXVII, 524.
18. *Ibid.*, 530–531.
19. *Ibid.*, XXVIII, 223–224, 247; John K. Mahon, "Pennsylvania and the Beginnings of the Regular Army," *Pennsylvania History*, XXI (1954), 33–44; James R. Jacobs,

*The Beginning of the U.S. Army, 1783–1813* (Princeton, 1947), chaps. i–ii. See Knox's correspondence with Congress in the Papers of the Continental Congress, No. 150, I–III, No. 151, I, National Archives.

20. Downes, *Council Fires on the Upper Ohio*, chap. xii; Knox to the President of Congress, July 10, 1787, Clarence E. Carter, ed., *The Territorial Papers of the United States* (Washington, 1934—), II, 31–35; Richard Butler to Henry Knox, Dec. 13, 1786, Papers of the Continental Congress, No. 150, II, 117, National Archives.

21. Ford, ed., *Journals of Congress*, XXXIII, 530–531; Mohr, *Federal Indian Relations*, 126–127, 159.

22. Knox to Harmar, June 22, 1787, quoted in Ward, *Department of War*, 67–68.

23. Jeremy Belknap, *History of New Hampshire* . . . (Boston, 1813), II, 360–364.

24. Knox to the President of Congress, Sept. 28, 1786, Papers of the Continental Congress, No. 150, I, 569–570, National Archives.

25. Ford, ed., *Journals of Congress*, XXXI, 891–892.

26. Belknap's observations are in J. P. Warren, ed., "Documents Relating to Shays' Rebellion," *American Historical Review*, II (1897), 693. Knox is quoted in Ward, *Department of War*, 80. Marion L. Starkey, *A Little Rebellion* (New York, 1955), 179, reproduces part of the Massachusetts legislative resolution. See a fresh "Political Interpretation" of Shays' Rebellion in J. R. Pole, *Political Representation in England and the Origins of the American Republic* (New York, 1966), 227–244.

27. Millis, *Arms and Men*, 41.

28. Arthur St. Clair to Samuel Huntington, Aug. 13, 1787, Josiah Harmar to William Irvine, May 25, 1787, cited in William A. Benton, "Pennsylvania Revolutionary Officers and the Federal Convention," *Pennsylvania History*, XXXI (1964), 421, 433.

29. Charles A. Beard, *The Republic: Conversations on Fundamentals* (New York, 1943), 24.

30. Noah Webster, *A Letter to General Hamilton* (1800), 5, quoted in Vagts, *History of Militarism*, 102; Alice Brown, *Mercy Warren* (New York, 1898), 296–297; Butterfield, ed., *Letters of Rush*, I, 418.

31. Knox to President of Congress, Oct. 11, 1786, Papers of the Continental Congress, No. 150, II, 69–70; C. F. Adams, ed., *Works of John Adams*, IV, 588.

32. John Fiske, *The Critical Period of American History, 1781–1789* (Boston and New York, 1888); Jensen, *The New Nation*; Max Farrand, ed., *Records of the Federal Convention of 1787* (New Haven, 1911–1937), II, 642–643; Douglass G. Adair, "Experience Must Be Our Only Guide: History, Democratic Theory, and the United States Constitution," in *The Reinterpretation of Early American History: Essays in Honor of John Edwin Pomfret*, ed. Ray A. Billington (San Marino, Calif., 1966), 138.

33. *New-Jersey Gazette*, Nov. 6, 1786; Knox to Gouverneur Morris, Feb. 21, 1783, Sparks, *Gouverneur Morris*, I, 256; Robert A. East, "The Massachusetts Conservatives in the Critical Period," in *The Era of the American Revolution*, ed. Richard B. Morris (New York, 1939), 369. Even before the final state ratified the Articles of Confederation, Alexander Hamilton made a detailed list of "the defects of our present system" and urged immediately a convention of all the states" to construct a government possessing dignity and authority. Hamilton to James Duane, Sept. 3, 1780, Syrett, ed., *Papers of Hamilton*, II, 400–418. See also *Notes of Debates in the Federal Convention of 1787 Reported by James Madison* (Athens, Ohio, 1966), 11–12.

34. Charles C. Tansill, ed., *Documents Illustrative of the Formation of the American States* (Washington, D.C., 1927), 43.

35. Fitzpatrick, ed., *Writings of Washington*, XXI, 109, XXVI, 188.

36. *Ibid.*, XXIX, 124. See also *ibid.*, 77, 113, 119, 121, 125, 138, 151, 167, 169, 170, 172, 175, 181.

37. Farrand, ed., *Records of the Federal Convention*, I, 18–19.

38. *Ibid.*, 242–245, III, 611–615. As Madison observed earlier in the deliberations, "the more he reflected on the use of force, the more he doubted the practicability, the justice, and the efficacy of it when applied to people collectively and not individually. A Union of the States (containing such an ingredient) seemed to provide for its own destruction. The use of force agst. a State, would look more like a declaration of war, than an infliction of punishment, and would probably be considered by the party attacked as a dissolution of all previous compacts by which it might be bound." *Ibid.*, I, 54.

39. *Ibid.*, II, 102, 329, 323.

40. *Ibid.*, 329–330.

41. *Ibid.*, 330–341.

42. *Ibid.*, 326, 330; Marvin R. Zahniser, *Charles Cotesworth Pinckney: Founding Father* (Chapel Hill, 1967), 94.

43. Farrand, ed., *Records of the Federal Convention*, II, 330–331, 332.

44. *Ibid.*, 331, 332.

45. *Ibid.*, 331, 332.

46. *Ibid.*, 333, 356.

47. *Ibid.*, 385, 388.

48. *Ibid.*, 616–617, 632–633.

49. Theodore H. Riker, *The Soldiers of the States* (New York, 1957), 10. See also John K. Mahon, *The American Militia: Decade of Decision* (Gainesville, Fla., 1960); Jim Dan Hill, *The Minute Men in Peace and War: A History of the National Guard* (Harrisburg, Pa., 1964); Martha Derthick, *The National Guard in Politics* (Cambridge, Mass., 1965).

50. Paul L. Ford, ed., *Essays on the Constitution of the United States* (Brooklyn, 1892), 65; Thomas Wait to George Thatcher, Nov. 22, 1787, *Historical Magazine*, XVI (1869), 258; Jonathan Elliot, comp., *The Debates in the Several State Conventions on the Adoption of the Federal Constitution as Recommended by the General Convention at Philadelphia in 1787* (Philadelphia, 1891), IV, 52; Richard Henry Lee, "Letters from the Federal Farmer," in Cecilia M. Kenyon, ed., *The Antifederalists* (Indianapolis, 1966), 214.

51. Jackson T. Main, *The Antifederalists: Critics of the Constitution, 1781–1788* (Chapel Hill, 1961), 144; [Samuel Bryan?], "The Letters of 'Centinel,'" in Kenyon, ed., *The Antifederalists*, 8–9; "The Pennsylvania Minority," in *ibid.*, 54.

52. Robert A. Rutland, *The Ordeal of the Constitution: The Antifederalists and the Ratification Struggle, 1787–1788* (Norman, Okla., 1966), 47; "Philadelphiensis," in Kenyon, ed., *The Antifederalists*, 77.

53. *Pennsylvania Packet*, Sept. 23, 1787.

54. Elliot, comp., *Debates*, III, 47–48.

55. [Samuel Bryan?], "The Letters of 'Centinel,'" in Kenyon, ed., *The Antifederalists*, 23; Elliot, comp., *Debates*, II, 552, III, 378, 410–412; J. B. McMaster and F. D. Stone, *Pennsylvania and the Federal Constitution* (Lancaster, Pa., 1888), 481.

56. These changes were offered by the Antifederalist minorities in the state ratifying conventions. They are grouped in this note according to the states that proposed them. Two are also from Rhode Island, which initially refused to call a ratifying convention. Nos. 1, 2, 3 (Virginia): Elliot, comp., *Debates*, III, 657, 659, 660; nos. 4, 5 (New York): *ibid.*, I, 330, 331, II, 406; nos. 6, 7 (Maryland): *ibid.*, II, 552; nos. 8, 9 (Rhode Island): *ibid.*, I, 335.

57. Cooke, ed., *The Federalist*, 64.

58. Elliot, comp., *Debates*, III, 410–411, 400–401.

59. Elliot, comp., *Debates*, II, 537, III, 90, 91; Cooke, ed., *The Federalist*, 162.

60. Cooke, ed., *The Federalist*, 165–166; Elliot, comp., *Debates*, III, 600, IV, 63–64.

61. McMaster and Stone, *Pennslyvania and the Federal Constitution*, 409; Cooke, ed., *The Federalist*, 18–19.

62. Cooke, ed., *The Federalist*, 155–156.

63. *Ibid.*, 16.

64. There is a growing literature that deals with the army's role in the internal

development of the nation. Only a few examples may be cited here: Francis P. Prucha, *Broadax and Bayonet: The Role of the U.S. Army in the Development of the Northwest, 1815–1860* (Madison, 1953); Prucha, *The Sword of the Republic: The United States Army on the Frontier, 1783–1846* (New York, 1969); Edward S. Wallace, *The Great Reconnaissance: Soldiers, Artists and Scientists on the Frontier* (Boston, 1955); Robert G. Athearn, *William Tecumseh Sherman and the Settlement of the West* (Norman, 1956); Forest G. Hill, *Roads, Rails and Waterways: The Army Engineers and Early Transportation* (Norman, 1957); William H. Goetzmann, *Army Exploration in the American West, 1803–1863* (New Haven, 1963); William H. Leckie, *The Military Conquest of the Southern Plains* (Norman, 1963); Robert M. Utley, *Frontiersmen in Blue: The United States Army and the Indian, 1848–1865* (New York, 1967).

65. Elliot, comp., *Debates*, II, 520–522.
66. Quoted in Barbara Tuchman, "History by the Ounce," *Harper's*, CCXXXI (1965), 66.
67. Several of these themes are treated in Marcus Cunliffe, *Soldiers and Civilians: The Martial Spirit in America, 1775–1865* (Boston and Toronto, 1968).

# Bibliographical Essay


THE DECADES SINCE the end of World War II have witnessed a vast out-pouring of books and articles dealing with all aspects of the American Revolution. Moreover, the approaching bicentennial of American independence will likely stimulate many new publications on the subject. It is to be hoped that our forthcoming military studies will avoid a reversion to the dry bones of "drum and bugle" history that characterized so much of our earlier historical literature. We should continue the recent trend of regarding military history within the context of society as a whole. As I have pointed out previously, an examination of military factors may help us to resolve certain broad problems about the Revolution: "American Historians and the Military History of the American Revolution," *American Historical Review*, LXX (1964), 18–34.

Because of the staggering quantity of literature on the subject, this discussion of sources and authorities must be highly selective. Some works listed in the footnotes will not be repeated here; but certain useful publications not previously cited will be noted. The reader is entitled to a word of explanation concerning manuscript sources. Although I made no effort to utilize all or even most of the important unpublished papers in various depositories, I did consult a number of collections, especially those at Duke University, the University of North Carolina, and the North Carolina Department of Archives and History in Raleigh—all within easy reach of my home in Chapel Hill. Among the other collections I researched were the Papers of the Continental Congress (National Archives), the George Washington and Nathanael Greene Papers (Library of Congress), the Horatio Gates Papers (New-York Historical Society), the Henry Knox and Artemas Ward Papers (Massachusetts Historical Society), along with scattered items from other depositories that I had used in connection with other research projects or that were placed in my hands through the courtesy of friends.

No student of the period should fail to become acquainted with the published guides to manuscript literature put out by state archival agencies and independent historical societies. They should be employed in conjunction with Philip M. Hamer, ed., *A Guide to Archives and Manuscripts in the United States* (New Haven, 1961), and the Library of Congress' *National Union Catalog of Manuscripts*. Manuscript research has also been greatly facilitated by photocopy editions of numerous valuable collections. Grants from the National Historical Publications Commission have led to microfilm reproduction of the Lee Family Papers, the Thomas Burke Papers, the Lloyd Smith Papers, to mention only three of value for the Revolutionary War.

In two other areas, pamphlets and newspapers, the "microfilm revolution" has been of immense benefit to me in the preparation of this book. I have made extensive use of Clifford K. Shipton's *Early American Imprints, 1639–1800*, a microprint edition of every extant pamphlet, broadside, and book printed in what is now the United States through the year 1800—a project keyed to Charles Evans' *American Bibliography*. Particularly valuable have been the various editions of eighteenth-century newspapers that are now available on film. The American Antiquarian Society, sponsor of *Early American Imprints*, is issuing runs of important papers. The North Carolina Department of Archives and History has made available all of the state's extant newspapers for the eighteenth century, which are described in H. G. Jones and Julius H. Avants, eds., *North Carolina Newspapers on Film* (Raleigh, 1965). The work of the Historical Society of Pennsylvania, to take another example, has been impressive with the publication of such newspapers as the *Pennsylvania Gazette*, *Pennsylvania Journal*, *Pennsylvania Packet*, and *New York Journal*. The indispensable guide to newspapers of the period is Clarence L. Brigham, ed., *History and Bibliography of American Newspapers, 1690–1820* (2 vols., Worcester, Mass., 1947). An inventory of the British side of the Revolution is Ronald I. Crane and F. B. Kaye, *A Census of British Newspapers and Periodicals, 1620–1800* (Chapel Hill, 1927).

The states have published extensively from their public records covering the colonial and Revolutionary years, as one can see from Oscar Handlin *et al.*, *Harvard Guide to American History* (Cambridge, Mass., 1954). Some state records are available through the *Early American Imprints* series or on microfilm as described in William S. Jenkins, ed., *Guide to the Microfilm Collection of Early State Records* (Washington, 1950). An illuminating article is Jack P. Greene, "The Publication of the

Official Records of the Southern Colonies," *William and Mary Quarterly*, 3d ser., XIV (1957), 268–280. A substantial number of colonial laws dealing with military affairs are located in Arthur Vollmer, *Background of Selective Service*, Monograph No. 1, Vol. II, entitled *Military Obligations: The American Tradition* (Washington, 1917).

The military institutions of the colonies have been sadly neglected by scholars. The most valuable studies in print at this time are periodical articles and short essays or chapters in more general histories. See Walter Millis, *Arms and Men* (New York, 1956), chap. i, for a penetrating analysis of the early American military experience. Another thoughtful contribution is Daniel Boorstin, *The Americans: The Colonial Experience* (New York, 1958), 341–372. A highly original piece, stressing the complexity and diversity of the colonial military establishments, is John W. Shy, "A New Look at Colonial Militia, *William and Mary Quarterly*, 3d ser., XX (1963), 175–185. And one should not overlook Louis Morton, "The Origins of American Military Policy," *Military Affairs*, XXII (1958), 75–82; and Allen French, "Arms and Military Training of Our Colonial Ancestors," Massachusetts Historical Society, *Proceedings*, LXVII (1945), 3–21. For comparative purposes, see J. R. Weston, *The English Militia in the Eighteenth Century* (Toronto, 1965).

Francis Parkman has given us our most extensive treatment of the Anglo-French struggle for North America, published in nine volumes between 1865 and 1892: under the general title *France and England in North America*, splendidly written, with an eye for colorful and dramatic events. A corrective to some of Parkman's biases is found in W. J. Eccles, "History of New France According to Francis Parkman," *William and Mary Quarterly*, 3d ser., XVIII (1961), 163–175. Two recent surveys are Edward P. Hamilton, *The French and Indian Wars* (New York, 1962) and Howard H. Peckham, *The Colonial Wars, 1689–1762* (Chicago, 1964). Douglas E. Leach, *The Northern Colonial Frontier, 1607–1763* (New York, 1966), contains several excellent chapters on the wars with France. The French and Indian War, the only Anglo-French conflict to be given more than passing notice in this study, receives detailed treatment in volumes VI–VII of Lawrence H. Gipson, *The British Empire before the American Revolution* (14 vols., Caldwell, Idaho, and New York, 1936–1969). There is an assessment of Gipson's monumental history, which covers the period 1748–1776, by Richard B. Morris, "The Spacious Empire of Lawrence Henry Gipson," *William and Mary Quarterly*, 3d ser., XXIV (1967), 169–189. The tensions between colonial leaders and British army officers are revealed in Stanley Pargellis, *Lord Loudoun in North America* (New Haven, 1933). Eugene I. McCormac, *Colonial Opposition to Imperial Author-*

*ity during the French and Indian War* (Berkeley, 1911), is superficial. The relationship between military affairs and colonial politics is also examined in John F. Burns, *Controversies Between Royal Governors and Their Assemblies in the Northern American Colonies* (Boston, 1923), and Jack P. Greene, *The Quest for Power . . .* (Chapel Hill, 1963).

Among the worthwhile biographies and monographs are Lee McCardell, *Ill-Starred General: Braddock of the Coldstream Guards* (Pittsburgh, 1958); Christopher Hibbert, *Wolfe at Quebec* (London, 1959), sound popular biography; C. P. Stacey, *Quebec, 1759: The Siege and the Battle* (New York, 1959), corrects Parkman on various points; Stanley Pargellis, "Braddock's Defeat," *American Historical Review*, XLI (1936), 251–259; John R. Cueno, *Robert Rogers of the Rangers* (New York, 1959); John A. Schutz, *William Shirley, King's Governor of Massachusetts* (Chapel Hill, 1961). Robert C. Newbold, *The Albany Congress and Plan of Union of 1754* (New York, 1955), provides the best coverage of that subject. On diplomacy and international negotiations, one should turn to Wilbur R. Jacobs, *Diplomacy and Indian Gifts: Anglo-French Rivalry along the Ohio and Northwest Frontiers, 1748–1763* (Stanford, 1950), and Zenob E. Rashed, *The Peace of Paris, 1763* (Liverpool, 1951). For contemporary diaries, letters, and other source material, consult the bibliographies in Gipson, Peckham, and Leach.

American political and anti-military thought is covered by a wide range of books and articles. Two profound studies are by Bernard Bailyn, *The Ideological Origins of the American Revolution* (Cambridge, Mass., 1967), and Gordon S. Wood, *The Creation of the American Republic* (Chapel Hill, 1969). Clinton Rossiter, *Seedtime of the Republic: The Origins of the American Tradition of Political Liberty* (New York, 1953), is a stimulating book, one of the first to draw attention to the impact of radical English thinkers on American thought. These same Englishmen are given detailed treatment in Caroline Robbins, *The Eighteenth-Century Commonwealthman* (Cambridge, Mass., 1959). That the colonists, in opposing standing armies, tended to romanticize the pre-Norman militia is demonstrated in H. Trevor Colbourn, *The Lamp of Experience: Whig History and the Intellectual Origins of the American Revolution* (Chapel Hill, 1965). The beginnings of the standing army controversy in England and its impact on political thought are dealt with in J. G. A. Pocock, "Machiavelli, Harrington, and English Political Ideologies in the Eighteenth Century," *William and Mary Quarterly*, 3d ser., XXII (1965), 549–583, and Lois G. Schwoerer, "The Literature of the Standing Army Controversy, 1697–1699," *Huntington Library Quarterly*, XXVIII (1965),

187–212. Older but still worthwhile are Randolph G. Adams, *Political Ideas of the American Revolution* (Durham, N.C., 1922); Charles H. McIlwain, *The American Revolution: A Constitutional Interpretation* (New York, 1923). A splendid collection of sources is Bernard Bailyn, ed., *Pamphlets of the American Revolution, 1750–1776* (1 vol. to date, Cambridge, Mass., 1965—). Except for the nineteenth-century historian George Bancroft, no one has attempted to produce a multi-volumed history of the era from 1763 to 1789 as James Ford Rhodes did for the Civil War and Reconstruction. Claude H. Van Tyne's projected three volumes on the *History of the Founding of the American Republic* was halted after the second volume (at 1777) because of the author's untimely death. W. E. H. Lecky, *History of England in the Eighteenth Century* (8 vols., London, 1878–1900), and George Otto Trevelyan, *The American Revolution* (4 vols., New York, 1899–1907), are whiggish in orientation, but packed with information—both by Englishmen, as are Henry Belcher, *The First American Civil War* (2 vols., London, 1911), and Eric Robson, *The American Revolution . . .* (London, 1955). From Great Britain has come another account of the period by Esmond Wright, *Fabric of Freedom, 1763–1800* (New York, 1961). Two brief summaries of the entire period are excellent: Edmund S. Morgan, *The Birth of the Republic, 1763–1789* (Chicago, 1956), and Dan Lacey, *The Meaning of the American Revolution* (New York, 1964). More lengthy books have come from John R. Alden, *The Revolution in the South, 1763–1789* (Baton Rouge, La., 1957), and *A History of the American Revolution* (New York, 1969), both splendidly written. Thoughtful efforts to summarize much of the post-World War II literature have been advanced by Richard B. Morris, *The American Revolution Reconsidered* (New York, 1967), and Jack P. Greene, *The Reappraisal of the American Revolution in Recent Historical Literature*, pamphlet no. 68 of the American Historical Association Service Center for Teachers of History (Washington, D.C., 1967).

Of the countless studies that analyze the beginnings and development of Anglo-American discord between 1763 and 1775, the most recent contributions will be emphasized here. Volumes IX–XII of Gipson's *British Empire before the American Revolution* examine the rising storm from a view sympathetic to the mother country. So does Gipson's condensed version: *The Coming of the Revolution, 1763–1775* (New York, 1954). George L. Beer, *British Colonial Policy, 1754–1763* (New York, 1907), retains some value. Beer and Charles M. Andrews, *The Colonial Background of the American Revolution* (New Haven, 1924), are sympathetic to Britain's problems. Whereas it is claimed that Beer and Andrews stood with both feet in London in viewing the imperial scene, Merrill Jensen, *The Founding of a Nation: A History of*

*The American Revolution, 1763–1776* (New York, 1968), traces the Revolutionary movements in the colonies, noting that in each province the patriot party developed its own unique characteristics. Arthur M. Schlesinger, Sr., has written *The Colonial Merchants and the American Revolution* (New York, 1918) and *Prelude to Independence: The Newspaper War on Britain, 1764–1776* (New York, 1958). It is the contention of Oliver M. Dickerson, *The Navigation Acts and the American Revolution* (Philadelphia, 1951), that the merchants were sometimes victimized by British customs collectors. A more favorable estimate of the customs service is advanced in Thomas C. Barrow, *Trade and Empire: The British Customs Service in Colonial America, 1660–1775* (Cambridge, Mass., 1967). The related subject of vice-admiralty courts is carefully explored in Carl Ubbelhode, *The Vice-Admiralty Courts and the American Revolution* (Chapel Hill, 1960). Richard D. Brown, *Revolutionary Politics in Massachusetts: The Boston Committee of Correspondence and the Towns, 1772–1774* (Cambridge, 1970), appeared after my manuscript was in press, as did Hiller B. Zobel, *The Boston Massacre* (New York, 1970). Two brilliant monographs probe the stamp and tea crises: Edmund S. Morgan and Helen M. Morgan, *The Stamp Act Crisis* (Chapel Hill, 1953), and Benjamin W. Labaree, *The Boston Tea Party* (New York, 1964), both stressing the colonists' concern for constitutional principles. The fullest accounts of specific British ministries during these years are John Brooke, *The Chatham Administration, 1776–1768* (New York, 1956), and Bernard Donoughue, *British Politics and the American Revolution: The Path to War, 1773–1775* (New York, 1960). Carl Bridenbaugh, in *Mitre and Sceptre . . . 1689–1775* (New York, 1962), argues that colonial fears of an aggressive Anglican church have been a neglected cause of the Revolution. The whole subject of the religious origins of the Revolution has been surveyed more broadly by Alan Heimert, *Religion and the American Mind: From the Great Awakening to the Revolution* (Cambridge, Mass., 1966), and by Perry Miller, "From the Covenant to the Revival," in *The Shaping of American Religion*, vol. I of *Religion in American Life*, eds. James W. Smith and A. Leland Jamison (3 vols., Princeton, 1961). Michael Kammen, *A Rope of Sand: The Colonial Agents, British Politics and the American Revolution* (Ithaca, 1968), shows the declining influence of the colonial agents following the repeal of the Stamp Act.

The American West and the British army are examined in Beer, *British Colonial Policy*; Alden, *Revolution in the South*; Bernard Knollenberg, *Origin of the American Revolution, 1759–1766* (New York, 1960); and especially John Shy, *Toward Lexington: The Role of the British Army in the Coming of the American Revolution* (Princeton, 1965), which on most points supersedes all previous investigations of the subject. Jack M. Sosin, *Whitehall and the Wilderness* . . . *1763–1775* (Lincoln, Neb., 1961), largely replaces Clarence W. Alvord, *The Mississippi Valley in British Politics* . . . (2 vols., Cleveland, 1917), on British Western policy. Matters relating to the interior are also handled in John R. Alden, *John Stuart and the Southern Colonial Frontier* . . . *1754–1775* (Ann Arbor, 1944); Francis Philbrick, *The Rise of the West, 1754–1830* (New York, 1965); Jack M. Sosin, *The Revolutionary Frontier, 1763–1783* (New York, 1967).

The best general accounts of the Revolutionary War years are John C. Miller, *Triumph of Freedom, 1775–1783* (New York, 1948), and John R. Alden, *The American Revolution, 1775–1783* (New York, 1954). The best military histories are Willard M. Wallace, *Appeal to Arms* . . . (New York, 1951); Christopher Ward, *The War of the Revolution*, ed. John R. Alden (2 vols., New York, 1952); George F. Scheer and Hugh F. Rankin, *Rebels and Redcoats* (Cleveland, 1957); and Howard H. Peckham, *The War for Independence* . . . (Chicago, 1958). A valuable collection of contemporary accounts is Henry Steele Commager and Richard B. Morris, eds., *The Spirit of 'Seventy-Six* . . . (2 vols., Indianapolis and New York, 1958).

Studies of British political behavior in the Revolutionary era almost unfailingly reflect the interpretations of Sir Lewis B. Namier, especially his *The Structure of Politics at the Accession of George III* (2 vols., London, 1929) and *England in the Age of the American Revolution* (London, 1930). Together with John Brooke, Namier edited *The History of Parliament: The House of Commons, 1754–1790* (3 vols., New York, 1964). Namier and his followers, besides showing us the complexity of politics and the absence of party, have brought about a more favorable estimate of George III, most fully developed in Richard Pares, *George III and the Politicians* (Oxford, Eng., 1953). Herbert Butterfield, in *George III and the Historians* (London, 1957), is critical of the Namerian school of history and suggests that principle and the Rockingham alignment may have amounted to more than Sir Lewis admitted. The King himself may be read through his *Correspondence* . . . *1760–1783*, ed. Sir John Fortescue (6 vols., London, 1927–1928), to which one should add Namier's volume of *Additions and Corrections* . . . (London, 1937). The political outsiders are presented in Archibald S. Foord, *His Majesty's Opposition, 1714–1830* (New York, 1964). See also Ian R. Christie, *Wilkes, Wyvill and Reform: The Parliamentary Reform Movement in British Politics, 1760–1785* (New York, 1962), and Eugene C. Black, *The Association: British Extraparliamentary Political Organization, 1769–1793* (Cambridge, Mass., 1963). The English press is discussed in Fred J. Hinkhouse, *The Preliminaries of the American Revolution as Seen in the English Press, 1763–1775* (New

York, 1926), and Solomon Lutnick, *The American Revolution and the British Press, 1775–1783* (Columbia, Mo., 1967). Internal conditions during the final years of the war are described in Herbert Butterfield, *George III, Lord North, and the People, 1779–1780* (London, 1949), and Ian R. Christie, *The End of North's Ministry, 1780–1782* (London, 1958). A general political survey is Charles R. Ritcheson, *British Politics and the American Revolution* (Norman, Okla., 1954); J. Steven Watson, *The Reign of George III, 1760–1815* (Oxford, Eng., 1960), covers all aspects of British life.

Biographies of political leaders and administrators are plentiful, but some men have still escaped scholarly attention and others need more careful analysis. O. A. Sherrard, *Lord Chatham and America* (London, 1958), is useful but not definitive. Lewis B. Namier and John Brooke, *Charles Townshend* (New York, 1964), is scarcely flattering to the subject. Alan Valentine, *Lord North* (2 vols., Norman, Okla., 1967), is disappointing. Burke's relationship to American questions is handled competently in Carl B. Cone, *Burke and the Nature of Politics: The Age of the American Revolution* (Lexington, Ky., 1957); but one should also delve into volume III of *The Correspondence of Edmund Burke*, edited by George Guttridge (Chicago, 1961). See also Guttridge's books on *David Hartley, M. P., An Advocate of Conciliation, 1774–1783* (Berkeley, 1926), and *The Early Career of Lord Rockingham, 1730–1765* (Berkeley and Los Angeles, 1952). In *Lord Dartmouth and the American Revolution* (Columbia, S.C., 1965), B. D. Bargar writes sympathetically of the Colonial Secretary. Although the Earl of Shelburne needs a scholarly biography, John Norris, *Shelburne and Reform* (New York, 1963), is helpful as far as it goes. George A. Martelli, *Jemmy Twitcher: a Life of the Fourth Earl of Sandwich, 1718–1792* (London, 1962), is inadequate. One should go to a publication of the British Naval Records Society: G. R. Barnes and J. H. Owen, eds., *The Private Papers of John, Earl of Sandwich, First Lord of the Admiralty, 1771–1782* (4 vols., London, 1932–1938). While Gerald S. Brown, *The American Secretary: The Colonial Policy of Lord George Germain, 1775–1778* (Ann Arbor, 1963), is a sound and sympathetic study. Alan Valentine, *Lord George Germain* (New York, 1962), is too harsh and is carelessly done.

The fullest account of the British side of the Revolutionary War is Piers Mackesy, *The War for America, 1775–1783* (Cambridge, Mass., 1964), which examines the London war machine and the men who ran it; Mackesy, in the opinion of most American reviewers, is too kind to Germain and Sandwich. Edward E. Curtis, *The Organization of the British Army in the American Revolution* (New Haven, 1926), is valuable. Other worthwhile administrative histories are Mark A. Thomson, *The Secretaries of State, 1681–1782* (Oxford, Eng., 1932); Margaret M.

Spector, *The American Department of the British Government* (New York, 1940); Dora Mae Clark, *The Rise of the British Treasury: Colonial Administration in the Eighteenth Century* (New Haven, 1960); and Franklin B. Wickwire, *British Subministers and Colonial America, 1763–1783* (Princeton, 1966).

A variety of studies cover Britain's military fortunes during the Revolution. Volume III of Sir John Fortescue, *A History of the British Army* (13 vols., London and New York, 1899–1930), is opinionated but worthwhile, revealing the author's tendency to side with the commanders in the field at the expense of civilian authorities in London. Paul H. Smith, *Loyalists and Redcoats: A Study in British Revolutionary Policy* (Chapel Hill, 1964), shows that England consistently made mistakes in dealing with the King's friends. Some of the best work on campaigns may be found in articles by William B. Willcox: "The British Road to Yorktown: A Study in Divided Command," *American Historical Review*, LII (1946), 1–35; "British Strategy in America, 1778," *Journal of Modern History*, XIX (1947), 97–121; "Rhode Island in British Strategy, 1780–1781," *ibid.*, XVII (1945), 304–331; and "Too Many Cooks: British Planning Before Saratoga," *Journal of British Studies*, II (1962), 56–90.

An examination of the role of individual British commanders may profitably begin with George A. Billias, ed., *George Washington's Opponents: British Generals and Admirals in the American Revolution* (New York, 1969), which contains essays on Generals Gage, William Howe, Clinton, Carleton, Burgoyne, and Cornwallis; and Admirals Arbuthnot, Gambier, Graves, Hood, and Rodney. Bellamy Partridge, *Sir Billy Howe* (London, 1932), is a poor attempt at popularization. It is doubtful that materials exist in sufficient quantity for full-scale biographies of the Howe brothers. One of the first significant monographs on the British side of the war is Troyer S. Anderson, *The Command of the Howe Brothers during the American Revolution* (New York, 1936), dealing primarily with the General and throwing new light on the Saratoga campaign. But it may well be superseded by Ira D. Gruber's forthcoming book on the Howes, which draws heavily on manuscript materials. John R. Alden, *General Gage in America* (Baton Rouge, 1948), details the origins of the march to Concord. William B. Willcox, *Portrait of a General: Sir Henry Clinton in the War of Independence* (New York, 1964), a Pulitzer Prize winner, is an example of life-and-times biography at its best. Willcox has also edited *The American Rebellion: Sir Henry Clinton's Narrative of His Campaigns, 1775–1782* (New Haven, 1954). Franklin B. Wickwire and Mary Wickwire, *Cornwallis: The American Adventure* (New York, 1970), see much to admire in the man and are only mildly critical of his generalship. There is no biography of Carleton based on modern scholarship. A. L. Burt, author of several articles on Carleton's Canadian career, has penned a brief assessment that may be too harsh: *Guy Carleton, Lord Dorchester, 1727–1808* (Ottawa, 1964). Burgoyne is equally in need of further investigation; Francis J. Hudleston, *Gentleman Johnny Burgoyne* (Indianapolis, 1927), is romantic and anecdotal. Robert D. Bass discovered the Tarleton papers, previously missing since 1833, and wrote *The Green Dragoon: The Lives of Banastre Tarleton and Mary Robinson* (New York, 1957).

As in other wars, the military men on the losing side rushed into print to defend their conduct. Burgoyne and Howe did so before the conflict was over: John Burgoyne, *A State of the Expedition from Canada as Laid Before the House of Commons . . .* (London, 1780), and Sir William Howe, *The Narrative of Lt. Gen. Sir William Howe in a Committee of the House of Commons . . .* (London, 1780). Tarleton, equally defensive, was not far behind: *A History of the Campaigns of 1780 and 1781 in the Southern Provinces of North America* (Dublin, 1787). Roderick MacKenzie, wounded at Cowpens, reduces Tarleton's reputation in *Strictures on Lt. Col. Tarleton's History . . .* (London, 1787). For the pamphlet war between Clinton and Cornwallis, see Benjamin F. Stevens, ed., *The Campaign in Virginia, 1781: an Exact Reprint of Six Rare Pamphlets on the Clinton-Cornwallis Controversy* (2 vols., London, 1888). Charles Stedman, a Pennsylvania loyalist who served Cornwallis as a commissary officer, wrote *The History of the Origin, Progress, and Termination of the American War* (2 vols., Dublin, 1794), which gives a good picture of British logistical problems in the South. But Stedman must be used with caution, declares R. Kent Newmyer, "Charles Stedman's *History of the American War*," *American Historical Review*, LXIII (1958), 924–934. See also Roger Lamb's *An Original and Authentic Journal . . .* (Dublin, 1809) and *Memoirs of His Own Life* (Dublin, 1811); *The Diary of Frederick Mackenzie* (2 vols., Cambridge, Mass., 1930); E. H. Tatum, ed., *The American Journal of Ambrose Serle, Secretary to Lord Howe, 1776–1778* (San Marino, 1940); E. A. Benians, ed., *A Journal of Thomas Hughes, 1777–1789* (Cambridge, Mass., 1947); Mrs. E. Stuart Wortley, *A Prime Minister and His Son* (London, 1925); Eric Robson, ed., *Letters from America, 1773–1780* (London, 1950); Roy W. Pettengill, ed., *Letters from America, 1776–1779* (Boston, 1924); Margaret W. Willard, ed., *Letters on the American Revolution, 1774–1776* (Boston, 1925). Bernhard Uhlendorf has edited two compilations of German accounts: *The Siege of Charleston . . . Diaries and Letters of Hessian Officers from the Von Jungkenn Papers in the William L. Clements Library* (Ann Arbor, 1938) and *Revolution in America: Confidential Letters and Journals 1776–1784 of Adjutant General Major Baurmeister of the Hessian*

*Forces* (New Brunswick, N.J., 1957). The lively young wife of Burgoyne's German commander has left us with a fascinating account of the Saratoga campaign. Marvin L. Brown, ed., *Baroness von Riedesel and the American Revolution: Journal and Correspondence of a Tour of Duty, 1776–1783* (Chapel Hill, 1965).

Of the published papers of prominent British figures, in addition to those already noted, see Clarence E. Carter, ed., *The Correspondence of General Thomas Gage* (2 vols., New Haven, 1931–1933); Charles Ross, ed., *The Correspondence of Charles, First Marquis Cornwallis* (3 vols., London, 1859); Charles K. Bolton, ed., *Letters of Hugh, Earl Percy, from Boston and New York, 1774–1776* (Boston, 1902); George C. Rogers, Jr., "Letters of Charles O'Hara to the Duke of Grafton," *South Carolina Historical Magazine*, LXV (1964), 158–180, shows Cornwallis' army coming apart at the seams in the spring and summer of 1781. A number of volumes published by the Historical Manuscripts Commission are invaluable for British aspects of the Revolution, including the Carlisle, Dartmouth, Hastings, Knox, and Lothian manuscripts. The *Report on Manuscripts in Various Collections* (8 vols., London, 1901–1914), VI, contains some Cornwallis material, although the bulk of the Cornwallis manuscripts is in the British Public Record Office, the most important depository in Great Britain for research on the American Revolution. I used primarily Lord Germain's correspondence in the *Report on the Manuscripts of Mrs. Stopford-Sackville, of Drayton House, Northamptonshire* (2 vols., London, 1904–1910).

Although they disagree at times, the best assessments of British naval strategy are in the above-mentioned studies by Willcox and Mackesy. There are also several general naval histories available. William M. James, *The British Navy in Adversity: A Study of the War of Independence* (New York, 1926), retains little value. More helpful are Michael Lewis, *The Navy of Britain* (London, 1948), and G. J. Marcus, *A Naval History of Britain: The Formative Years* (Boston and Toronto, 1961). Christopher Lloyd and Jack L. S. Coulter, *Medicine in the Navy, 1714–1815* (Edinburgh and London, 1961), is a fine work. M. J. Williams' unpublished Oxford doctoral dissertation (1962) is revisionist in its favorable attitude toward "The Naval Administration of the Fourth Earl of Sandwich, 1771–1782." The naval war is seen in perspective by Gerald S. Graham, *Empire of the North Atlantic: The Maritime Struggle for North America* (Toronto, 1950), and A. T. Mahan, *The Major Operations of the Navies in the War of American Independence* (Boston, 1913). None of the British admirals involved in the American war has had adequate biographical treatment; the reader is referred to the essays (and their bibliographies) in Billias, ed., *George Washington's Opponents*. The Naval Records Society in

London has brought out, along with the *Sandwich Papers*, editions of various other source materials, such as the *Hood Papers*, ed. David Hannay (1895); the *Barham Papers*, ed. J. K. Laughton (3 vols., 1907–1911); the *Barrington Papers*, ed. C. K. Bonner (2 vols., 1937–1941). The Naval History Society issued the *Graves Papers*, ed. French E. Chadwick (New York, 1916).

A wide assortment of printed public documents and published works of American civilian and military leaders is available. Worthington C. Ford, ed., *The Journals of the Continental Congress* (34 vols., Washington, 1904–1937), is basic. So is Edmund C. Burnett, ed., *Letters of Members of the Continental Congress* (8 vols., Washington, 1921–1936), which, unfortunately, omits parts of letters dealing with local politics and military affairs. Francis Wharton, ed., *Revolutionary Diplomatic Correspondence of the United States* (6 vols., Washington, 1889), should be superseded. Benjamin Franklin Stevens, ed., *Facsimiles of Manuscripts in European Archives Relating to America, 1773–1783* (26 vols., London, 1889–1895), is a miscellany of military and diplomatic documents. Peter Force, ed., *American Archives . . .*, 4th series (6 vols., Washington, 1837–1846) and 5th series (3 vols., Washington, 1848–1853), was never completed; but the nine volumes brought to fruition contain a mountain of information on military affairs during 1774–1777. Smaller documentary collections include Hezekiah Niles, ed., *Principles and Acts of the Revolution in America* (Baltimore, 1823); R. W. Gibbes, ed., *Documentary History of the American Revolution . . . Chiefly in South Carolina . . .* (3 vols., New York, 1853–1857); Frank Moore, ed., *Diary of the American Revolution from Newspapers and Original Documents* (2 vols., New York, 1860); John J. Meng, ed., *Dispatches and Instructions of Conrad Alexandre Gérard, 1778–1780 . . .* (Baltimore, 1939).

Since World War II the editing of the papers of prominent Revolutionary leaders has passed to a new and advanced level of comprehensiveness and sophistication. The editors have not only included incoming correspondence, but they have also, in many cases, printed collateral documents and penned essays on the significance of their materials. The following are in a class by themselves: Julian P. Boyd, ed., *The Papers of Thomas Jefferson* (Princeton, 1950—); Leonard W. Labaree, ed., *The Papers of Benjamin Franklin* (New Haven, 1959—); Harold C. Syrett, ed., *The Papers of Alexander Hamilton* (New York, 1961—); William T. Hutchinson and William M. E. Rachal, eds., *The Papers of James Madison* (Chicago, 1962—); Lyman H. Butterfield, ed., *The Adams Papers: Diary and Autobiography of John Adams* (4 vols., Cambridge, Mass., 1961), and *Adams Family Correspondence, 1761–1778* (2 vols., Cambridge, Mass., 1963); Robert A. Rutland, ed.,

*The Papers of George Mason* (3 vols., Chapel Hill, 1970). Because these projects are in various stages of progress, the researcher must still on occasion use older and less satisfactory editions. A new edition of Washington's papers is being planned, although John C. Fitzpatrick, ed., *The Writings of George Washington* . . . (39 vols., Washington, 1931–1944), is trustworthy; but the Fitzpatrick edition does not include letters to Washington. Some of these may be found in Jared Sparks, ed., *Correspondence of the American Revolution: Being Letters of Eminent Men to George Washington* (4 vols., Washington, 1853), and Stanislaus M. Hamilton, ed., *Letters to Washington and Accompanying Papers* (5 vols., Boston and New York, 1896–1902). Moreover, Sparks' own edition of *The Writings of George Washington* (12 vols., Boston, 1834–1837), contains documents of such related interest as those bearing on the Conway Cabal.

The following works are among those of the period that are in some ways valuable for military affairs: Charles Francis Adams, ed., *The Works of John Adams* . . . (10 vols., Boston, 1850–1856); Harry A. Cushing, ed., *The Writings of Samuel Adams* (4 vols., New York, 1904–1908); Charles Campbell, ed., *The Bland Papers* (2 vols., Petersburg, Va., 1840–1843); James A. James, ed., *George Rogers Clark Papers, 1771–1784* (Illinois State Historical Library, *Collections*, vols. 8, 19 [Springfield, 1912, 1926]); Hugh Hastings, ed., *The Public Papers of George Clinton* . . . (10 vols., Albany, 1899–1914); Charles Isham, ed., *The Dean Papers* (New-York Historical Society, *Collections*, vols. 19–23 [New York, 1887–1890]); Albert Bates, ed., *The Deane Papers* (Connecticut Historical Society, *Collections*, vol. 23 [Hartford, 1930]); Albert H. Smyth, ed., *The Writings of Benjamin Franklin* (10 vols., New York, 1905–1907); Verner W. Crane, ed., *Franklin's Letters to the Press, 1758–1775* (Chapel Hill, 1950); Charles F. Heartman, ed., *Letters Written by Ebenezer Huntington during the American Revolution* (New York, 1914); *The Correspondence of Mr. Ralph Izard of South Carolina* . . . (New York, 1844); Henry P. Johnston, ed., *The Correspondence and Public Papers of John Jay* (4 vols., New York, 1890–1893); Worthington C. Ford, ed., *The Letters of Joseph Jones of Virginia, 1777–1787* (Washington, 1889); Louis Gottschalk, ed., *The Letters of Washington and Lafayette, 1777–1779* (New York, 1944); William G. Simms, ed., *Army Correspondence of Colonel John Laurens in the Years 1777–1778* (New York, 1867); Richard Henry Lee, *Life of Arthur Lee* (2 vols., Boston, 1829); *The Lee Papers* (New-York Historical Society, *Collections*, vols. 4–7 [New York, 1872–1875]); James C. Ballagh, ed., *The Letters of Richard Henry Lee* (2 vols., New York, 1911–1914); Worthington C. Ford, ed., *The Letters of William Lee* (3 vols., Brooklyn, 1891); James Graham, *The Life of General Daniel*

*Morgan* . . . (New York, 1856); Jared Sparks, *The Life of Gouverneur Morris with Selections From His Correspondence and Miscellaneous Papers* (3 vols., Boston, 1832); Philip S. Foner, ed., *The Complete Writings of Thomas Paine* (2 vols., New York, 1945); William B. Reed, *The Life and Correspondence of Joseph Reed* (2 vols., Philadelphia, 1847); George H. Ryden, ed., *Letters to and from Caesar Rodney, 1756–1784* (Philadelphia, 1933); Lyman H. Butterfield, ed., *Letters of Benjamin Rush* (2 vols., Princeton, 1951); Otis G. Hammond, ed., *Letters and Papers of Major-General John Sullivan* . . . (New Hampshire Historical Society, *Collections*, vols. 13–15 [Concord, 1930–1939]); William H. Smith, ed., *The St. Clair Papers* (2 vols., Cincinnati, 1882); *The Warren-Adams Letters* (Massachusetts Historical Society, *Collections*, vols. 72–73 [Boston, 1917–1925]); C. Harvey Gardner, ed., *A Study in Dissent: The Warren-Gerry Correspondence, 1776–1792* (Carbondale, Ill., 1968); Elizabeth Kite, ed., *Correspondence of Washington and de Grasse* (Washington, 1931); Worthington C. Ford, ed., *Correspondence and Journals of Samuel Blachley Webb* (3 vols., New York, 1893).

American diaries, journals, and memoirs are numerous. Unfortunately, few of the prominent American military leaders left personal accounts of their service. William Heath's *Memoirs* . . . (Boston, 1798), are generally impersonal and unenlightening. Henry Lee, *Memoirs of the War in the Southern Department of the United States* (2 vols., Philadelphia, 1812), and James Wilkinson, *Memoirs of My Own Time* (3 vols., Philadelphia, 1816), are highly partisan narratives, but Lee's is of real value. Lafayette's *Mémoires, Correspondances et Manuscrits du Général Lafayette* . . . (2 vols., Brussels, 1837–1838), must be used with caution, which is also true of *The Narrative of Colonel Ethan Allen*, introd. Brooke Hindle (New York, 1961). William Moultrie, *Memoirs of the American Revolution* . . . (2 vols., New York, 1802), is valuable. The literary quality of the contributions of enlisted men scarcely equals that of the Civil War's Johnny Reb or Billy Yank, who seems to have found more time for keeping a diary or notebook. A fascinating *Autobiography of a Revolutionary Soldier* (Clinton, La., 1859) is by James Collins. Perhaps the best soldier's memoir is Joseph P. Martin *Private Yankee Doodle* . . ., ed. George F. Scheer (Boston, 1962). The trials and tribulations of junior officers are the theme of Herbert T. Wade and Robert A. Lively, *This Glorious Cause: The Adventures of Two Company Officers in Washington's Army* (Princeton, 1958).

The following are no more than a wide sampling of additional personal accounts by civilians and soldiers: Enoch Anderson, *Personal Recollections* . . . (Historical Society of Delaware, *Papers*, vol. 16

[Wilmington, 1896]); Elias Boudinot, *Historical Recollections of American Events during the Revolutionary War* (Philadelphia, 1894); Jack P. Greene, ed., *The Diary of Colonel Landon Carter . . .* (2 vols., Charlottesville, 1965); Howard H. Peckham and Lloyd A. Brown, eds., *Revolutionary War Journals of Henry Dearborn, 1775–1783* (Chicago, 1939); *Elijah Fisher's Journal While in the War for Independence . . .* (Augusta, Me., 1880); R. G. Albion and L. Dodson, eds., *Journal of Philip Vickers Fithian, 1775–1776* (Princeton, 1924); Alexander Garden, *Anecdotes of the American Revolution* (3 vols., Brooklyn, 1865); Alexander Graydon, *Memoirs of His Own Time . . .* (Philadelphia, 1846); William A. Graham, ed., *General Joseph Graham and His Papers on North Carolina Revolutionary History* (Raleigh, 1904); Jacob C. Parsons, ed., *Extracts from the Diary of Jacob Hiltzheimer* (Philadelphia, 1893); A. S. Sally, ed., *Colonel William Hill's Memoirs of the Revolution* (Columbia, S.C., 1921); William Duane, ed., *Extracts from the Diary of Christopher Marshall . . ., 1774–1781* (Albany, 1877); *Diary of Thomas Rodney* (Historical Society of Delaware, *Papers*, vol. 1 [Wilmington, 1879]); George W. Corner, ed., *Autobiography of Benjamin Rush* (Philadelphia, 1948); Josiah Quincy, ed., *The Journals of Major Samuel Shaw . . .* (Boston, 1847); Franklin B. Dexter, ed., *The Literary Diary of Ezra Stiles . . .* (3 vols., New York, 1901); Henry P. Johnston, ed., *Memoir of Col. Tench Tilghman . . .* (Albany, 1876); *Autobiography, Reminiscences and Letters of John Trumbull from 1756 to 1841* (New York, 1841); James Thatcher, *A Military Journal During the Revolutionary War . . .* (Boston, 1823); John C. Fitzpatrick, ed., *The Diaries of George Washington, 1748–1799* (4 vols., Boston, 1925); Caroline Gilman, *Letters of Eliza Wilkinson During the Invasion and Possession of Charleston, S.C. by the British During the Revolutionary War* (New York, 1839); Otho Holland Williams, "Narrative of the Campaign of 1780," in William Johnson, *Sketches of the Life and Correspondence of Nathanael Greene* (2 vols., Charleston, S.C., 1822), I, appendix B. There are fine modern editions of two French accounts: Evelyn M. Acomb, ed., *The Revolutionary Journal of Baron Ludwig Von Closen, 1780–1783* (Chapel Hill, 1958); Marquis de Chastellux, *Travels in North America, in the Years 1780, 1781 and 1782*, ed. Howard C. Rice, Jr. (2 vols., Chapel Hill, 1963). To these may be added an assortment of sources. Thomas Balch, ed., *Papers Relating Chiefly to the Maryland Line* (Philadelphia, 1855). Two compilations were edited by Franklin B. Hough, *The Siege of Savannah . . .* (Albany, 1866), and *The Siege of Charleston . . .* (Albany, 1867). Kenneth Roberts, *March to Quebec* (New York, 1937), reprints the major journals of the Arnold expedition. Countless historical periodicals shelter diaries and journals. *The Historical Magazine,*

*The Magazine of American History*, *The Pennsylvania Magazine of History and Biography*, and *The South Carolina Historical Magazine* are especially rewarding. A useful tool to research in Virginia periodicals is Earl G. Swem, comp., *Virginia Historical Index* (2 vols., Roanoke, 1934–1936). One should not miss the impressive bibliographies in Commager and Morris, eds., *Spirit of 'Seventy-Six*; Scheer and Rankin, *Rebels and Redcoats*; and Hugh F. Rankin, *The American Revolution* (New York, 1964).

As Wesley Frank Craven has remarked, the weight of recent Revolutionary studies, "whether viewed quantitatively or qualitatively, falls in the general category of biography." Craven, "The Revolutionary Era," in *The Reconstruction of American History*, ed. John Higham (New York, 1962). For the military leaders, one may begin with George A. Billias, ed., *George Washington's Generals* (New York, 1964), which contains interpretive sketches of Washington, Lee, Schuyler, Gates, Greene, Sullivan, Arnold, Lafayette, Lincoln, Knox, Wayne, and Morgan. Charles A. Jellison, *Ethan Allen: Frontier Rebel* (Syracuse, 1969), is the best of the Allen biographies. Willard M. Wallace, *Traitorous Hero: The Life and Fortunes of Benedict Arnold* (New York, 1954), is splendid; so is James T. Flexner, *The Traitor and the Spy: Benedict Arnold and John André* (New York, 1953). Other fresh biographies include John Bakeless, *Background to Glory: The Life of George Rogers Clark* (Philadelphia, 1957); John D. Barnhart, *Henry Hamilton and George Rogers Clark in the American Revolution . . .* (Crawfordsville, Ind., 1951); Chalmers G. Davidson, *Piedmont Partisan: The Life and Times of Brigadier General William Lee Davidson* (Davidson, N.C., 1951); Blackwell P. Robinson, *William R. Davie* (Chapel Hill, 1957); George A. Billias, ed., *General John Glover and His Marblehead Mariners* (New York, 1960); Theodore Thayer, *Nathanael Greene: Strategist of the American Revolution* (New York, 1960); Broadus Mitchell, *Alexander Hamilton: Youth to Maturity, 1755–1788* (New York, 1957); North Callahan, *Henry Knox, Washington's General* (New York, 1958); Louis Gottschalk, *Lafayette Comes to America* (Chicago, 1935); Gottschalk, *Lafayette Joins the American Army* (Chicago, 1937); Gottschalk, *Lafayette and the Close of the American Revolution* (Chicago, 1942); John R. Alden, *General Charles Lee . . .* (Baton Rouge, 1951); Kenneth Rossman, *Thomas Mifflin and the Politics of the American Revolution* (Chapel Hill, 1952); Don Higginbotham, *Daniel Morgan: Revolutionary Rifleman* (Chapel Hill, 1961); North Callahan, *Daniel Morgan: Ranger of the Revolution* (New York, 1961); John F. Foche, *Joseph Reed: A Moderate in the American Revolution* (New York, 1957); Don R. Gerlach, *Philip Schuyler and the American Revolution in New York, 1733–1777* (Lincoln, Neb., 1964); Martin H. Bush, *Revolutionary Enigma: A Re-*

*appraisal of General Philip Schuyler of New York* (Port Washington, N.Y., 1969); Charles P. Whittemore, *A General of the Revolution: John Sullivan of New Hampshire* (New York, 1961); Alan Valentine, *Lord Stirling* (New York, 1969). The fullest life of Washington is Douglas S. Freeman, *George Washington: A Biography* (7 vols., New York, 1948–1957). Also commanding serious attention is James T. Flexner, *George Washington* (3 vols. to date, Boston, 1965—). Marcus Cunliffe, *George Washington: Man and Monument* (Boston, 1958), is brief but perceptive. Bernhard Knollenberg sheds light on the young Washington in *George Washington: The Virginia Period, 1732–1775* (Durham, N.C., 1964). In *Washington and the Revolution* (New York, 1940), Knollenberg writes somewhat critically of Washington and sympathetically of Gates during the Conway Cabal. Curtis Nettels, *George Washington and American Independence* (New York, 1951), contends that the Virginian pushed his countrymen toward a total break with Britain in 1776.

Certain other biographies should be mentioned: John Pell, *Ethan Allen* (Boston and New York, 1929); Stuart H. Holbrook, *Ethan Allen* (New York, 1940); Samuel W. Patterson, *Horatio Gates . . .* (New York, 1941); George W. Greene, *Life of Nathanael Greene* (3 vols., New York, 1867–1871); Friedrich Kapp, *Life of John Kalb* (New York, 1870); M. Haiman, *Kosciuszko in the American Revolution* (New York, 1943); Paul A. W. Wallace, *The Muhlenbergs of Pennsylvania* (Philadelphia, 1950); John M. Palmer, *General von Steuben* (New Haven, 1937); Anne K. Gregorie, *Thomas Sumter* (Columbia, S.C., 1931); Charles Martyn, *Life of Artemas Ward* (New York, 1921); Harry E. Wildes, *Anthony Wayne* (New York, 1941).

Among the best of the biographies of civilian leaders are Page Smith, *John Adams* (2 vols., Garden City, 1962), probably the most rewarding Adams biography but more descriptive than analytical; E. W. Spaulding, *His Excellency George Clinton* (New York, 1938); Edward P. Alexander, *James Duane . . .* (New York, 1938); Aubrey C. Land, *The Dulanys of Maryland* (Baltimore, 1955); Carl Van Doren, *Benjamin Franklin* (New York, 1938); Gerald Stourzh, *Benjamin Franklin and American Foreign Policy* (Chicago, 1954); Herbert S. Allen, *John Hancock, Patriot in Purple* (New York, 1948); Frank Monahan, *John Jay* (New York, 1935); Merrill D. Peterson, *Thomas Jefferson and the New Nation* (New York, 1970); Marie Kimball, *Jefferson . . .* (3 vols., New York, 1943–1950); Dumas Malone, *Jefferson . . .* (4 vols. to date, New York, 1948—); Robert Ernst, *Rufus King: American Federalist* (Chapel Hill, 1968); David D. Wallace, *Life of Henry Laurens . . .* (New York, 1915), needs to be replaced; George Dangerfield, *Chancellor Robert R. Livingston of New York, 1746–1813* (New York, 1960); Irving Brant,

*James Madison* . . . (6 vols., Indianapolis, 1941–1961); Robert A. Rutland, *George Mason: Reluctant Statesman* (Williamsburg, 1961); Clarence L. Ver Steeg, *Robert Morris: Revolutionary Financier* . . . (Philadelphia, 1954); David J. Mays, *Edmund Pendleton* (2 vols., Cambridge, Mass., 1952); Alfred O. Aldridge, *Man of Reason: The Life of Thomas Paine* (Philadelphia, 1959); Marvin R. Zahniser, *Charles Cotesworth Pinckney* . . . (Chapel Hill, 1967); Brooke Hindle, *David Rittenhouse* (Princeton, 1964); Nathan G. Goodman, *Benjamin Rush* . . . (Philadelphia, 1934); John Cary, *Joseph Warren* . . . (Urbana, 1961); Page Smith, *James Wilson* (Chapel Hill, 1956).

Although our best studies of the American aspects of the war have appeared in the last few decades, a number of earlier contributions may still be examined with profit, such as Richard Frothingham, *History of the Siege of Boston* (Boston, 1851); Henry P. Johnston, *Campaign of 1776 around New York* . . . (Brooklyn, 1878); Lyman C. Draper, *King's Mountain* . . . (Cincinnati, 1881); David Schenck, *North Carolina, 1780–1781* (Raleigh, 1889); William S. Stryker, *The Battles of Trenton and Princeton* (Boston and New York, 1898), and (with William S. Myers) *The Battle of Monmouth* (Princeton, 1927).

In the early twentieth century, the seminar-trained historians largely turned away from military history, considering it too narrow and chauvinistic. Consequently, we have only a handful of military studies from that era. Mention may be made of Charles K. Bolton, *The Private Soldier under Washington* (New York, 1902); Louis C. Hatch, *The Administration of the American Revolutionary Army* (New York, 1904); Justin H. Smith, *Our Struggle for the Fourteenth Colony* (2 vols., New York, 1907); Hoffman Nickerson, *Turning Point of the Revolution* . . . (Boston, 1928). Allen French, a talented patrician historian, contributed excellent books on the early days of the war: *The Day of Concord and Lexington* . . . (Boston, 1925); *The Taking of Ticonderoga* . . . (Cambridge, Mass., 1928); *General Gage's Informers* . . . (Ann Arbor, 1932); and *The First Year of the American Revolution* (Boston, 1934). More recent studies are Arthur B. Tourtellot, *William Diamond's Drum* . . . (New York, 1959), a good descriptive account of Lexington and Concord; Bruce Bliven, Jr., *Battle for Manhattan* (New York, 1956); Alfred H. Bill, *Campaign of Princeton, 1776–1777* (Princeton, 1948), and *Valley Forge: the Making of an Army* (New York, 1952); Leonard H. Lundin, *Cockpit of the Revolution* . . . (Princeton, 1940), covers the war in New Jersey; John J. Stoudt, *Ordeal of Valley Forge* . . . (Philadelphia, 1963); Randolph G. Downes, *Council Fires on the Upper Ohio* (Pittsburgh, 1940); James H. O'Donnell, "The Southern Indians in the War of Independence, 1775–1783" (Unpubl. Ph.D. diss., Duke University, 1963); Dale Van Every, *A Company of Heroes: The*

*American Frontier, 1775–1783* (New York, 1962), thoughtful and readable, for the layman; Alexander A. Lawrence, *Storm over Savannah . . .* (Athens, Ga., 1951), is excellent for the Franco-American siege; Burke Davis, *The Cowpens-Guilford Courthouse Campaign* (Philadelphia, 1962); M. F. Treacy, *Prelude to Yorktown: The Southern Campaign of Nathanael Greene, 1780–1781* (Chapel Hill, 1963); Harold A. Larrabee, *Decision at the Chesapeake* (New York, 1964); Carl Van Doren, *The Secret History of the American Revolution* (New York, 1941), the best work on spies and conspiracies, was the first major investigation of Arnold's treason; Allen Bowman, *Morale of the American Revolutionary Army* (Washington, 1943); Walter Blumenthal, *Camp Followers of the American Revolution* (Rutland, Vt., 1952); Victor L. Johnson, *Administration of the American Commissariat during the Revolutionary War* (Philadelphia, 1941); Carl Van Doren, *Mutiny in January* (New York, 1943); Christopher Ward, *The Delaware Continentals, 1776–1783* (Wilmington, Del., 1941).

The Revolutionary navy has been neglected. Hopefully William Bell Clark's edition of the *Naval Documents of the American Revolution* (5 vols. to date, Washington, 1964–) will lead to new endeavors in this field. Gardner W. Allen, *A Naval History of the American Revolution* (2 vols., Boston, 1913), remains the standard work, but it should be replaced. The best naval biography is Samuel E. Morison, *John Paul Jones: A Sailor's Biography* (Boston and Toronto, 1959). See also the notes to chap. xiii for other biographies, especially those by William Bell Clark.

Political, social, and economic developments are treated in a multitude of studies. These are particularly helpful for the home front: Edmund C. Burnett, *The Continental Congress* (New York, 1941); Margaret B. Macmillan, *The War Governors in the American Revolution* (New York, 1943); E. James Ferguson, *The Power of the Purse: A History of American Public Finance, 1776–1790* (Chapel Hill, 1961); Anne Bezanson, *Prices and Inflation during the American Revolution: Pennsylvania, 1770–1790* (Philadelphia, 1951); Robert A. East, *Business Enterprise in the American Revolutionary Era* (New York, 1938); Curtis P. Nettels, *The Emergence of a National Economy, 1775–1815* (New York, 1962); Jackson T. Main, *The Social Structure of Revolutionary America* (Princeton, 1965); Evarts B. Greene, *The Revolutionary Generation, 1763–1790* (New York, 1943); Richard B. Morris, *Government and Labor in Early America* (New York, 1946); Brooke Hindle, *The Pursuit of Science in Revolutionary America, 1735–1789* (Chapel Hill, 1956); J. F. Jameson, *The American Revolution Considered as a Social Movement* (Princeton, 1926); Winthrop D. Jordan, *White over Black: American Attitudes toward the Negro, 1550–1812*

(Chapel Hill, 1968); Arthur Silversmit, *The First Emancipation: The Abolition of Slavery in the North* (Chicago, 1967); Carl L. Becker, *The Declaration of Independence* . . . (New York, 1922); Julian P. Boyd, *The Declaration of Independence* (Princeton, 1945); David Hawke, *A Transaction of Free Men* (New York, 1964). For examples of useful state and local studies, see H. J. Eckenrode, *The Revolution in Virginia* (Boston, 1916); Richard F. Upton, *Revolutionary New Hampshire* (Hanover, 1936); Bernard Mason, *The Road to Independence: The Revolutionary Movement in New York, 1773–1777* (Lexington, Ky., 1966); Oscar T. Barck, *New York City during the War for Independence* (New York, 1931); Thomas J. Wertenbaker, *Father Knickerbocker Rebels: New York City during the Revolution* (New York, 1948); Lee N. Newcomer, *The Embattled Farmers: The Massachusetts Countryside in the American Revolution* (New York, 1953); Robert J. Taylor, *Western Massachusetts in the Revolution* (Providence, R.I., 1954); Kenneth Coleman, *The American Revolution in Georgia, 1763–1789* (Athens, Ga., 1958); Adrian C. Leiby, *The Revolutionary War in the Hackensack Valley* . . . (New Brunswick, N.J., 1962); Oscar and Mary F. Handlin, "Revolutionary Economic Policy in Massachusetts," *William and Mary Quarterly*, IV (1947), 3–26.

The first comprehensive history of the opponents of the Revolution is Claude H. Van Tyne, *The Loyalists in the American Revolution* (New York, 1902). William H. Nelson, *The American Tory* (New York, 1961), looks at the composition of the loyalist party and the philosophical viewpoint of the Crown's adherents; Wallace Brown has contributed *The King's Friends* . . . (Providence, R.I., 1966), an examination of the loyalists' postwar claims for compensation, and *The Good Americans* . . . (New York, 1970), a popular history of the tories; Leonard W. Labaree, "Nature of American Loyalism," American Antiquarian Society, *Proceedings*, LIV (1944), 15–58, stresses the conservative aspects of tory thought. See also William Benton, *Whig-Loyalism: An Aspect of Political Ideology in the American Revolution* (Rutherford, N.J., 1969), a study of those tories who found the choice of independence versus loyalty to the Crown the most difficult. There are numerous studies of individual loyalists, of which the best include Julian P. Boyd, *Anglo-American Union: Joseph Galloway's Plans to Preserve the British Empire, 1774–1788* (Philadelphia, 1941); L. F. S. Upton, *The Loyal Whig: William Smith* . . . (Toronto, 1969); W. J. Sparrow, *Knight of the White Eagle: Sir Benjamin Thompson, Count Rumford of Woburn, Massachusetts* (New York, 1966); Jules D. Prown, *John Singleton Copley: In America, 1738–1774* (Cambridge, Eng., 1966). Lorenzo Sabine, *Biographical Sketches of Loyalists of the American Revolution* (2 vols., Boston, 1864), is a useful reference work. For the loyalists' own story, see the autobiography of Jonathan Boucher, *Reminiscences of an American Loyalist, 1738–1789* (Boston, 1925); Peter Oliver, *The Origin and Progress of the American Rebellion* . . ., eds. Douglass Adair and John A. Schutz (San Marino, 1961); L. F. S. Upton, ed., *The Diary and Selected Papers of Chief Justice William Smith, 1784–1793* (2 vols., Toronto, 1965). State studies of loyalism are mostly narrow and somewhat dated, but the following are among those of continuing worth: Alexander C. Flick, *Loyalism in New York during the American Revolution* (New York, 1901); Harold B. Hancock, *Delaware Loyalists* (Historical Society of Delaware, *Papers*, new ser., vol. 3 [Wilmington, 1940]); Isaac S. Harrell, *Loyalism in Virginia* . . . (Durham, N.C., 1926); Robert O. DeMond, *Loyalists in North Carolina during the Revolution* (Durham, N.C., 1940); Wilbur H. Siebert, *Loyalists of Pennsylvania* (Columbus, Ohio, 1920) and *Loyalists in East Florida, 1774–1785* (Deland, Fla., 1929); J. H. Stark, *Loyalists of Massachusetts* (Boston, 1910); O. G. Hammond, *Tories of New Hampshire* (Hanover, 1917); Robert W. Barnwell, Jr., "Loyalism in South Carolina" (unpubl. Ph.D. diss., Duke University, 1941); Harry B. Yoshpe, *Disposition of Loyalist Estates in the Southern District of the State of New York* (New York, 1939). Generalizations about the social and economic effects of the confiscation of loyalist estates are difficult to make, for the pattern varied from county to county and from state to state. There are good articles on the subject in the *William and Mary Quarterly*, 3d ser., XVIII (1961), 558–576, XX (1963), 80–94, XXI (1964), 534–550, and XXII (1965), 433–456; and there are pieces dealing with individual loyalists in VI (1949), 361–382, XVI (1959), 61–72, and XXII (1965), 105–118.

Many books cover the diplomatic history of the Revolution. Colonial thinking on the balance of power and other matters related to foreign affairs is examined in Max Savelle, *The Origins of American Diplomacy* . . . (New York, 1967). The shift away from mercantilism and entangling alliances in American thinking is the theme of Felix Gilbert, *To the Farewell Address: Ideas of Early American Foreign Policy* (Princeton, 1961); it also is stressed in Paul A. Varg, *Foreign Policies of the Founding Fathers* (East Lansing, 1965). For the French background, see John F. Ramsay, *Anglo-French Relations, 1763–1770* (Berkeley, 1939), and Carl L. Locke, *France and the Colonial Question: A Study in Contemporary French Opinion, 1763–1801* (New York, 1932). Edward S. Corwin's pioneer *French Policy and the American Alliance of 1778* (Princeton, 1916), has been replaced by a more comprehensive study: William C. Stinchcombe, *The American Revolution and the French Alliance* (Syracuse, 1969). The standard French and Spanish histories, though dated, contain valuable documents: Henri Doniol, *Histoire de la participation de la France à l'établissement des États-Unis d'Amérique* (6 vols., Paris, 1884–1892); J. F. Yela Utrilla, *España ante la independencia de los Estados Unidos* (2 vols., Lérida, 1925). Specialized monographs and articles are also helpful: Bernard Fäy, *The Revolutionary Spirit in France and America* . . . (New York, 1927); Frances Acomb, *Anglophobia in France, 1763–1789* . . . (Durham, N.C., 1950); Marvin L. Brown, ed. and trans., *American Independence Through Prussian Eyes* (Durham, N.C., 1959); Isabel de Madariaga, *Russia, Britain and the Armed Neutrality of 1780* . . . (New Haven, 1962); Julian P. Boyd, "Silas Deane: Death by a Kindly Teacher of Treason," *William and Mary Quarterly*, 3d ser., XVI (1959), 165–187, 319–342, 515–550; Weldon A. Brown, *Empire or Independence* . . . *1774–1783* (Baton Rouge, 1941); Alan S. Brown, "The British Peace Offer of 1778," Michigan Academy of Science, Arts, and Letters, *Papers*, XL (1955), 249–260; Elizabeth S. Kite, *Beaumarchais and the War Of Independence* (2 vols., Boston, 1918); Claude-Ann Lopez, *Mon Cher Papa: Franklin and the Ladies of Paris* (New Haven, 1966); Kathryn Sullivan, *Maryland and France, 1774–1789* (Philadelphia, 1936); H. James Henderson, "Congressional Factionalism and the Attempt to Recall Benjamin Franklin," *William and Mary Quarterly*, 3d ser., XXVII (1970), 246–267; Samuel F. Bemis, *Hussey-Cumberland Negotiation and American Independence* (Princeton, 1931). The Treaty of Paris of 1783 is the focus of Richard B. Morris, *The Peacemakers: The Great Powers and American Independence* (New York, 1965).

The Confederation period requires much additional study. For too long historians have held extreme views of the 1780's and the movement for constitutional reform—polarized by such writers as John Fiske as opposed to the followers of Charles Beard. Since we are beginning to recognize the complexity of the decade, it is particularly unfortunate that the new projects to publish source materials leave a gap between the Revolutionary War and the creation of the Federal government in 1787. Still of value is Charles C. Tansill, ed., *Documents Illustrative of the Formation of the American States* (Washington, 1927). Max Farrand, ed., *Records of the Federal Convention of 1787* (4 vols., New Haven, 1911–1937), is basic. Jonathan Elliot, comp., *The Debates in the Several State Conventions on the Adoption of the Federal Constitution as Recommended by the General Convention at Philadelphia* (5 vols., Philadelphia, 1891; and various other printings), will be replaced on completion of the National Historical Publications Commission's Documentary History of the Ratification of the Constitution and the First Ten Amendments. The Documentary History will include such writings as those in Paul L. Ford, ed., *Pamphlets on the Constitution of the United States* . . . (Brooklyn, 1888), and *Essays on the Constitution of the United States* (Brooklyn, 1892). A thoughtful selection of Antifederalist writings is Cecelia M. Kenyon, ed., The *Antifederalists* (Indianapolis, 1966). The positive aspects of the Confederation are detailed in Merrill Jensen, *The Articles of Confederation . . .* (Madison, Wis., 1940) and *The New Nation: A History of the United States During the Confederation, 1781–1789* (New York, 1950). Forrest McDonald, *E Pluribus Unum: The Formation of the American Republic* (New York, 1965), is a popular survey. For attacks on Charles A. Beard's *An Economic Interpretation of the Constitution* (New York, 1913), see Robert E. Brown, *Charles Beard and the Constitution . . .* (Princeton, 1956), and Forrest McDonald, *We the People: The Economic Origins of the Constitution* (Chicago, 1958). The best books on the work of the Constitutional Convention are Max Farrand, *The Framing of the Constitution of the United States* (New Haven, 1913); Charles Warren, *The Making of the Constitution* (Cambridge, Mass., 1947); Carl Van Doren, *The Great Rehearsal . . .* (New York, 1948); and Clinton Rossiter, *1787: The Grand Convention* (New York, 1966). Nationalist sentiment in the 1780's is scrutinized in E. S. Corwin, "The Progress of Constitutional Theory between the Declaration of Independence and the Meeting of the Philadelphia Convention," *American Historical Review*, XXX (1925), 511–536; Merrill Jensen, "The Idea of a National Government during the American Revolution," *Political Science Quarterly*, LVIII (1943), 356–379; E. James Ferguson, "The Nationalists of 1781–1783," *Journal of American History*, LVI (1969), 241–261; Richard H. Kohn, "The Inside History of the Newburgh Conspiracy: America and the Coup d'Etat," *William and Mary Quarterly*, 3d ser., XXVII (1970), 187–220. The only comprehensive investigation of the Constitution's opponents is Jackson T. Main, *The Antifederalists . . .* (Chapel Hill, 1961). The best overall view of the ratification fight is Robert A. Rutland, *The Ordeal of the Constitution: The Antifederalists and the Ratification Struggle, 1787–1788* (Norman, Okla., 1966). The negative aspects of Antifederalist thought are developed in Cecelia M. Kenyon, "The Antifederalists and the Nature of Representative Government," *William and Mary Quarterly*, 3d ser., XII (1955), 3–43. Specialized studies of value to me in looking at military matters were Jennings B. Sanders, *Evolution of the Executive Departments of the Continental Congress, 1774–1789* (Chapel Hill, 1935); Marion L. Starkey, *A Little Rebellion* (New York, 1955), the Shays uprising; and Harry M. Ward, *The Department of War, 1781–1795* (Pittsburgh, 1962). A brilliant overview of the period is Robert R. Palmer, *The Age of Democratic Revolution* (2 vols., Princeton, 1959–1964).

*Index*

Acland, Christian Henrietta, 188
Acland, Maj. John, 188
Adams, Abigail, 83
Adams, John, 13, 25, 26, 27, 82, 83, 93,
  95, 96, 97, 108, 117, 146, 159, 190, 205,
  215, 243, 252, 270, 275, 289, 299, 305,
  315, 332, 336, 341, 348, 438, 439, 441,
  450; describes Revolution, 1; favors
  Washington, 8, 84, 85; fear of milita-
  rism, 207, 208, 211, 390; foreign aid,
  228, 229, 234; author of navy regula-
  tions, 334; in peace negotiations, 421,
  424, 425
Adams, Samuel, 37, 44, 45, 58, 66, 70, 77,
  95, 96, 107, 205, 207, 218, 353, 408, 439
Adams, Zabdiel, 266
Albany, N.Y., 177, 178
Albany Plan of Union, 7, 8
Alden, John R., 146
Allen, Ethan, 3, 66–67, 403
Amboy, N.J., 163, 170
American Philosophical Society, 305
Ames, Fisher, 414
Amherst, Jeffery, 21, 22, 52, 107, 140
Anderson, M. S., 423

Anhalt-Zerbst, 130–133 *passim*
Annapolis Convention, 451
*Annual Register*, 122, 128
Anson, Adm. George, Lord, 129
Anspach-Bayreuth, 130–133 *passim*
Antifederalists, the, 457–460
Aranda, Conde de, 425, 428
Arbuthnot, Adm. Marriot, 356, 357, 377,
  379, 381
Armstrong, Col. John, 300
Armstrong, Maj. John, Jr., 408, 409, 410
Army, American, beginnings of, 82–85
  *passim*; first general officers, 89–91;
  Articles of War, 92–93; Washington
  takes command, 92–106 *passim;* enlistments, 390–393, 416; Negro troops,
  394–397; camp followers, 397–398; discontent and desertion, 398–403, 405–
  411; mutinies, 403–405; federal pensions, 412; patriotism, 412–414; influence on European practice, 433–435; in
  the Confederation period, 445–448 *passim*
Army, British, in America before 1763,
  10, 16, 19, 20, 21, 22, 23; before 1775,

Army, British (*cont.*)
  29–48 *passim*, 51, 52; colonial opinion
  of, 14, 16, 19, 20, 29, 34, 35, 42, 43,
  44, 45, 47, 48; common soldier,
  123–124; caliber of officers, 68, 69, 76,
  124–125; treatment of loyalists, 137–
  139; machinery in London, 139–143
Arnold, Gen. Benedict, 121, 162, 167, 176,
  189, 202, 278, 376, 377; at Ticonderoga,
  66–67; leadership qualities, 69, 102;
  Quebec expedition, 109, 110, 111, 112,
  113, 114, 115; campaign of 1777, 193,
  194, 195, 196, 197; treason of, 402–403
Arnold, Peggy Shippen, 402, 417
Articles of Confederation, 81, 294, 298,
  299, 303, 459; military provisions of,
  206, 443, 446
Asbury, Francis, 276
Augusta, Ga., 373
Austria, 236, 238, 239, 424

Bailyn, Bernard, 12
Ballendine, John, 308
Bancroft, George, 410
Banyar, Goldsbrow, 281
Barbados, 25, 106, 251
Barclay, David, 54
Barker, Lt. John, 61, 63
Barnhart, John D., 321
Barras, Comte de, 380, 381, 382
Barrett, Col. James, 62
Barrington, William Wildman, Lord, 40,
  41, 140
Barrington, Adm. Samuel, 250, 251
Barry, Capt. John, 335
Barton, Joseph, 119
Bathurst, Henry, Lord Chancellor, 197
Baum, Lt. Col. Frederick, 192
Beard, Charles A., 449
Beaumarchais, Caron de, 233
Beford, Gunning, 456
Beer, George L., 30, 53
Belknap, Jeremy, 3, 447, 448
Bemis Heights, 194, 196
Bennington, Vt., 191, 263
Beresford, Richard, 445
Berkeley County, Va., 89
Bermuda, 106
Berniere, Ensign Henry de, 63

Biddle, Capt. Nicholas, 339, 347
Bill of Rights (English), 15, 19, 143, 461
Bill of Rights (U.S.), 259, 462
Billias, George A., 161
Black Horse, N.J., 168
Blackstone, Sir William, 44
Bland, Humphrey, 2, 47
Blane, Sir George, 129
Board of Trade, 31
Board of War, 218
Bolton, C. K., 101
*Bon Homme Richard*, 338, 341, 342, 344,
  345
Boone, Daniel, 325
Boone, Gov. Thomas, 27
Bordentown, N.J., 164, 166
Boston, 5, 24, 42, 43, 45, 46, 49, 50, 65, 67,
  68, 70, 74, 86, 98, 99, 105, 108, 121, 150,
  152, 242, 248, 251, 263, 303, 339
Boston Massacre, 43–44
Boston Port Bill, 58, 86
Boston Tea Party, 46
Bowman, Allen, 414
Bowman, Thaddeus, 60
Boyd, Julian, 117, 377
Brackenridge, Hugh H., 261, 319
Braddock, Gen. Edward, 3
Brandywine, Pa., 88, 185, 186, 209, 210,
  220, 263
Brant, Irving, 296
Brant, Joseph, 325, 446
Breymann, Lt. Col. Heinrich von, 192
Breed's Hill, 70, 71, 72, 73, 75, 77
Brinton, Crane, 49
Brodhead, Gen. Daniel, 329
Broglie, Charles François, Comte de, 215
Brooklyn, N.Y., 153, 154, 155, 158, 167,
  169
Brooks, Col. John, 406, 408
Brown, John, 6, 307
Brown, Nicholas, 6, 307
Brunswick, 131–134 *passim*
Bryan, George, 210
Bryan's Station, Ky., 325
Buford, Col. Abraham, 361
Bunker Hill, 57, 70, 75, 76, 79, 123, 189
Burgesses, House of, 19
Burgh, James, 16, 25
Burgoyne, Gen. John, 74, 75, 124, 125,

Burgoyne, Gen. John (*cont.*)
    150, 162, 179, 180, 181, 182, 183, 184,
    185, 187, 200, 203, 359; character of, 69;
    plans for 1777, 175, 176, 177, 178; ad-
    vances from Canada, 188, 189, 190, 191,
    192; defeated by Gates, 193, 194, 195,
    196, 197, 198
Burke, Aedanus, 440
Burke, Edmund, 52, 122, 132, 240, 421
Burke, Dr. Thomas, 208, 213, 273, 298
Burlington, N.J., 164
Bushnell, David, 311
Butler, Maj. John, 325, 327, 328
Butler, Pierce, 455
Butler, Capt. Walter, 325, 327, 328
Butler, Richard, 446
Butler, Col. Zebulon, 325, 327
Butterfield, Lyman, 225
Byng, Adm. John, 255
Byron, Adm. John, 245, 250, 251
Bute, Earl of (John Stuart), 30, 34, 124

Cadwalader, Gen. John, 166, 168, 220
Cahokia, 320, 322, 323
Calcraft, John, 53
Calvert, Cecilius, 33
Cambridge, Mass., 50, 65, 70, 97, 98, 100,
    103, 109, 111
Camden, Earl of (Charles Pratt), 52
Camden, N.J., 163
Camden, S.C., 357, 359, 360, 363, 364, 365,
    367, 371, 372, 373, 422
Campbell, Lt. Col. Archibald, 354, 355
Campbell, Lt. Col. Daniel, 113
Campbell, Col. John, 327
Campbell, William, 135, 364
Canada, 10, 22, 30, 98, 120, 171, 180, 191,
    220, 232, 249, 425; American invasion
    of, 106–115
Canada Act of 1791, 430
Canso, 340
Cape François, 303
Cape Verde Islands, 305
Carleton, Gen. Guy, 107, 110, 111, 112,
    113, 114, 150, 151, 162, 176, 179, 181,
    189, 193, 198, 255, 321, 428
Carlisle Commission, 240
Carnot, Lazare, 310
Carr, Capt. Patrick, 362

Carroll, Charles, 108, 413
Carroll, John, 108
Cartagena, 10
Carter, Charles, 307
Carter, William, 103
Castle, William, 5, 17
Caswell, Richard, 359
Catherine the Great (Russia), 130, 236,
    237, 243, 424
Cavendish, Frederick, Lord, 125
Catholics, 107, 108, 134
*Cato's Letters*, 16, 459
Cayuga Indians, 320, 329
Chapelle, Howard, 339
Chapin, Bradley, 279
Charles I (England), 93, 265
Charles II (England), 14
Charles III (Spain), 235, 423
Charlestown, Mass., 63, 67, 74
Charleston, S.C., 5, 50, 120, 136, 137, 150,
    152, 242, 345, 356, 357, 360, 371, 373,
    374, 422
Charlotte, N.C., 364, 365, 367, 374
Chase, Samuel, 292, 332
Chatham, Earl of. *See* William Pitt
Chauncy, Charles, 293
Cherokee Indians, 8, 25, 321
Cherry Valley, N.Y., 327, 328
Cheraw, S.C., 357, 365
Chew, Benjamin, 186
Child, James, 271
Choiseul, Duc de, 226, 230, 238, 245
Chorley, Katherine, 438
Church, Col. Benjamin, 10–11
Church, Dr. Benjamin, 58, 100, 268, 278,
    312
Clark, Abraham, 214, 220
Clark, Col. George R., 319, 322, 323, 324,
    325, 330
Clarke, Col. Elijah; 11, 373
Clarke, Jonas, 61, 64
Clausewitz, Karl von, 87
Clemenceau, Georges, 204
Clergy, 264–268
Cleveland, Col. William, 351, 364
Clinton, Gov. George, 219, 273, 296
Clinton, Gen. Henry, 79, 124, 151, 163,
    175, 183, 248, 250, 251, 273, 278, 331,
    345, 404; qualities of, 68–69; at Boston,

Clinton, Gen. Henry (*cont.*)
  69, 71, 74, 75, 76; attacks Charleston,
  135–137; at Long Island, 155; on the
  Hudson, 195, 196, 197; succeeds Wil-
  liam Howe, 243–244; Monmouth cam-
  paign, 245, 246, 247; in Southern cam-
  paign, 353, 354, 355, 356, 357, 360, 362,
  363, 366; Yorktown, 378, 379, 380, 382,
  386
Clinton, Gen. James, 328
Closen, Baron Ludwig von, 413
Cochran, Dr. John, 312
Coercive Acts, 46, 51, 60, 271
Colden, Lt. Gov. Cadwallader, 50
Collier, Sir George, 172
*Common Sense*, 116, 221, 331
Commonwealthmen, 15
Concord, Mass., 4, 17, 29, 50, 57, 58, 59,
  61, 62, 63, 64, 65, 70, 77, 78, 79, 123
Congress, Continental, 9, 66, 77, 81, 86,
  98, 100, 101, 104, 110, 114, 120, 153,
  181, 182, 193, 197, 205, 232, 247, 248,
  251, 252, 259, 261, 263, 266, 267, **268**,
  278, 288, 289, 290, 291, 292, 294, 304,
  305, 320, 332, 364, 365, 389, 399, 401,
  402, 414, 424, 426, 428, 429, 446, 447,
  464; First Continental, 46, 49, 51; adopts
  army, 82–85; early military preparations, 89–95; desires Canada, 106, 107,
  108; declares independence, 115, 116,
  117, 118; military powers, 206; friction
  with army, 207, 208, 211, 213–215, 406–
  412; Conway Cabal, 216–222; seeks
  foreign aid, 227, 229, 230; relations with
  Spain, 235–236; loyalty tests, 269, 270;
  nationalist sentiment in, 297–303; creates navy, 333–335; postwar military
  policy, 439–445
Connally, John, 135
Connecticut, 7, 8, 9, 20, 37, 48, 66, 70, 84,
  90, 206, 268, 269, 274, 306, 397, 445
Constitution of 1787, movement for, 449–
  452; making of, 452–457; ratification
  of, 457–461; retrospect, 462–463
Continental Association, 49, 93, 271
Continental currency, 5, 93, 288, 289–
  292, 293, 303, 316; state issues, 293, 294,
  295; loan office certificates, 290, 313;
  counterfeiting, 314; lotteries, 314

Conway Cabal, 216–222, 224, 225, 402
Conway, Gen. Henry, 125
Conway, Gen. Thomas, 216, 217, 219, 222
Conyngham, Capt. Gustavus, 340
Cook, Capt. James, 129, 429
Cook, Samuel, 265
Corbin, Margaret, 398
Cornwallis, Charles, Earl, 186, 243, 273,
  406; campaign of 1776, 161, 162, 163,
  170; in South Carolina, 357, 359, 362,
  363, 364; opposes Greene, 367, 370,
  371; Yorktown campaign, 375, 376, 377,
  378, 379, 380, 382, 385, 386
Corsica, 229
Coudray, Col. Philippe du, 215
*Countess of Scarborough*, 342
Cowpens, S.C., 11, 366, 387, 434
Craig, Gordon, 135
Craik, Dr. James, 219
Cramahé, Hector, 112
Cresap, Daniel, 3
Cresap, Michael, 102
Cresap, Thomas, 3
Cromwell, Oliver, 14, 93, 204
Crown Point, N.Y., 9, 29, 67, 83, 150
Cruzat, Gov. Francisco, 423
Cumberland, Richard, 423
Cunliffe, Marcus, 88
Cunningham, Patrick, 275
Cushing, Thomas, 6

Dana, Francis, 237
Danvers, Mass., 63
Dartmouth, Earl of (William Legge),
  52, 58, 105, 143, 150, 321, 343
Davie, Col. William R., 363
Davidson, Gen. William L., 363, 385
Dawes, William, 58, 59
Dayton, Jonathan, 454
Deane, Silas, 26, 116, 214, 215, 229, 230,
  231, 232, 233, 300, 335, 436
De Berdt, Dennys, 45
Declaration of Independence, 115–119,
  459
Delaware, 92, 95, 268
Delaware Indians, 322, 329, 330
Denmark, 15
Detroit, 29, 320, 325, 331, 445, 446
Diamond, William, 60–61

Dickerson, O. M., 42
Dickinson, John, 26, 34, 455
Donop, Col. von, 168
Dorchester Heights, 105, 120
Dorn, Walter, 2
Douglass, Elisha P., 131
Draper, Lyman C., 362
Drayton, William H., 261, 262, 275
Duane, James, 83, 90, 297
Duer, William, 216, 440
Dulany, Daniel, 34–35, 228, 277, 279
Dunmore, Earl of (John Murray), 9, 115, 135, 321
Duportail, Louis, 214, 310
Dwight, Timothy, 383
Dyer, Eliphalet, 34, 85, 220, 221

East India Co., 46
Eden, William, 149
Edenton, N.C., 271, 278
Edes, John, 258
Effingham, Earl of, 125
Eliot, Charles W., 463
Ellery, William, 338
Elliott, Bernard, 392
Ellis, Gov. Henry, 27
Ellsworth, Oliver, 441, 455
Emerson, William, 62, 64, 78, 101
Enlightenment, 4, 46, 266
Essex County, Mass., 99
Estabrook, Prince, 60
Estaing, Charles Hector, Comte d', 244, 245, 246, 248, 249, 250, 251, 354, 356, 381
Ewing, Gen. James, 166
Eutaw Springs, S.C., 373, 374

Falmouth, Maine, 332
Fanning, David, 273
Farragut, Adm. David G., 345
Faucitt, Col. William, 132
*Federalist* Papers, 461, 462
Ferguson, Maj. Patrick, 357, 364
Finer, S. E., 438
Fiske, John, 450
Fiske, Nathan, 420
Flamborough Head, 342
Fleming, John, 100
Fletcher, Andrew, 15, 45

Flexner, James T., 120
Floridablanca, José de Moñino y Rodondo, Comte de, 231, 235, 236, 344, 423
Floridas, 246, 342, 422, 425, 427
Forbes, Gen. John, 21
Forman, David, 186
Fort Chambly, 109, 110, 111, 112
Fort Clinton, 195
Fort Duquesne. *See* Fort Pitt
Fort Edward, 190, 191
Fort George, 35
Fort Granby, 371, 373
Fort Laurens, 328
Fort Lee, 162, 308
Fort McIntosh, 328
Fort Mercer, 187
Fort Miller, 190
Fort Montgomery, 195
Fort Motte, 371, 373
Fort Pitt, 29, 320, 327, 329, 445
Fort St. George, 5, 50
Fort St. Johns, 67, 109, 110, 111, 112
Fort Stanwix, 193
Fort Ticonderoga, 29, 57, 66, 67, 83, 105, 108, 109, 111, 150, 167, 189, 190, 193, 321, 402
Fort Washington, 161, 308
Fort Watson, 371
Fort William and Mary, 50
Fortesque, Sir John, 434
Fox, Charles James, 52, 122, 139, 240, 427
France, 5, 14, 19, 22, 23, 33, 49, 52, 116, 123, 126, 139, 174, 181, 197, 211, 225, 226, 238, 240, 252, 253, 290, 340, 379, 420, 422, 423, 424, 425, 426, 427, 430; attitude of, 230–232; French aid, 232–237; evaluation of French contribution, 431–432
Franklin, Benjamin, 30, 39, 51, 53, 54, 82, 83, 95, 117, 133, 159, 226, 290, 305, 307, 311, 330, 340, 389, 429, 436, 439, 450, 451; works for French alliance, 228, 230, 231, 232, 233, 234, 236, 237; as peace commissioner, 424, 425, 426, 427
Fraser, Gen. Simon, 194, 195, 196
Frederick County, Va., 10
Frederick the Great (Prussia), 433
Fredericksburg, Va., 9

Freeman, Douglas, 87, 172
Freeman's Farm, 194, 196
French, Allen, 77
French and Indian War, 5, 6, 7, 17, 19,
    30, 37, 52, 65, 82, 89
Freneau, Philip, 261, 374

Gadsden, Christopher, 26, 37, 353
Gage, Gen. Thomas, 24, 35, 36, 38, 40,
    41, 42, 46, 50, 51, 52, 58, 63, 65, 68, 69,
    72, 77, 78, 84, 99, 100, 124, 130, 150,
    198, 279, 346
Gainsborough, Thomas, 368
Galloway, Joseph, 135, 277
Gálvez, Gov. Bernardo de, 423
Gansevoort, Col. Peter, 193
Gardoqui brothers, 235
Gaspée, 227
Gates, Gen. Horatio, 89, 91, 116, 187,
    189, 202, 203, 207, 209, 210, 211, 218,
    219, 222, 224, 241, 357, 359, 360, 362,
    365, 409, 410, 411; background of, 89;
    commands Northern Department, 189,
    194; defeats Burgoyne, 195, 196, 197
Gay, Ebenezer, 4
George III (England), 34, 50, 100, 101,
    116, 130, 132, 134, 138, 140, 143, 144,
    226, 232, 238, 242, 255, 267, 269, 270,
    323, 422, 425, 431; on quartering troops,
    36, 43; advocates force, 51, 52; attacked
    by Jefferson, 117–119; political role of,
    118–119, 139
Georgetown, S.C., 357, 371, 373
Georgia, 16, 21, 25, 35, 37, 235, 307, 353,
    354, 355, 395, 396, 446
Germain, Lord George, 43, 68, 148, 149,
    150, 153, 154, 171, 184, 185, 191, 198,
    200, 226, 238, 241, 242, 255, 346, 353,
    354, 356, 377, 421, 422, 423, 431; evalua-
    tion of, 143; great effort in 1776, 151;
    fails to coordinate campaign of 1777,
    175, 176, 177, 178, 179, 180, 181
German Flats, N.Y., 327
Germantown, Pa., 88, 186, 187, 188, 209,
    210, 221
Gerry, Elbridge, 96, 216, 220, 401, 444,
    453, 454, 455, 456
Gibraltar, 130, 232, 245, 424
Gibault, Pierre, 323

Gilbert, Felix, 229, 252
Gilbert Town, N.C., 364
Gipson, Lawrence H., 22
Glorious Revolution, 15, 18
Glover, Gen. John, 99, 160, 166, 167, 187,
    213, 401
Gnadenhütten, 322
Gneisenau, Count Neithardt von, 87
Goddard, William, 259, 260, 261, 279
Goethe, Johan Wolfgang von, 131
Gordon Riots, 422
Gordon, Thomas, 16
Gordon, William, 78, 219, 284
Gottschalk, Louis, 215, 216, 435
Grant, Gen. James, 21, 155, 164, 165
Grasse, Adm. François Joseph Paul,
    Comte de, 376, 380, 381, 382, 422, 423
Graves, Adm. Samuel, 336, 382
Graves, Adm. Thomas, 379, 381
Great Awakening, 265
Green Mountain Boys, 67
Green Spring, Va., 378
Greene, Gen. Nathanael, 2, 7, 66, 90, 91,
    119, 155, 158, 160, 162, 166, 167, 173,
    182, 184, 185, 186, 189, 190, 209, 215,
    268, 301, 351, 372, 373, 376, 385, 407,
    408, 438; favors French aid, 116; on
    burning New York City, 159; on
    dominating Washington, 211, 212; as
    quartermaster general, 364; North
    Carolina campaign, 365, 366, 368, 369,
    370; South Carolina campaign, 374;
    evaluation of, 374, 375
Grenville, George, 34, 35, 36, 40, 41, 124,
    239
Gridley, Col. Richard, 70
Griffiths, David, 224
Grimaldi, Jeronimó, Marquis de, 231
Guibert, Comte de, 13
Guilford Courthouse, N.C., 368, 369, 370,
    374
Gunby, Col. John, 372

Halifax, 40, 41, 43, 105, 151, 244, 250
Hamilton, Alexander, 170, 199, 218, 219,
    255, 279, 292, 294–295, 297, 298, 308,
    313, 396, 401, 407, 408, 409, 411, 438,
    441, 442, 444, 445, 458, 461
Hamilton, Henry, 322, 323, 324, 330, 331

Hamond, Andrew S., 183, 184, 200
Hancock, John, 26, 44, 58, 59, 66, 70, 77, 120, 182
Hancock, Thomas, 6
Hand, Gen. Edward, 327, 330
Hanger, Maj. George, 120
Hanover, 30, 129, 238
Harcourt, Col. William, 170
Hardy, Capt. Seth, 339, 349
Harlem Heights, 160
Harley, Robert, 15, 33
Harlow, Ralph V., 290, 293
Harlow, Vincent T., 430
Harmar, Col. Josiah, 447, 449
Harris, James, 237
Hartley, David, 240
Harvey, Adj. Gen., 149
Haslet, Col. John, 20
Havana, 10, 308
Hawes, Col. Samuel, 372
Hawke, Adm. Edward, Lord, 128, 129
Hawley, Joseph, 263
Hayne, Col. Isaac, 362
Head of Elk, Md., 183, 184
Heath, Gen. William, 45, 47, 77, 90, 91, 162, 168
Heister, Gen. Philip von, 155
Henry, Patrick, 48, 218, 225, 291, 324, 447, 458
Herder, Johann Gottfried von, 13
Herkimer, Gen. Nicholas, 11, 193
Hesse-Cassel, 131–134 passim
Hesse-Hanau, 131–134 passim
Hewes, Joseph, 6, 84, 266, 334
Higginson, Stephen, 443
Hill, Whitmill, 362
Hill, William, 361
Hillsborough, Earl of (Wills Hill), 41, 42, 43
Hillsborough, N.C., 273, 363
Hobkirk's Hill, S.C., 372, 374
Hodgkins, Lt. Col., 400, 413
Holt, John, 258, 292
Honeyman, John, 168
Hood, Adm. Samuel, 129, 381
Hopkins, Esek, 332, 335, 345
Hopkins, Stephen, 335
Hopkinson, Francis, 261
Hotham, Commo. William, 171, 250

Houstoun, Gov. John, 354
Howard, Col. John E., 366, 367
Howe, George Augustus, 148
Howe, Lady (wife of Lord Howe), 197
Howe, Adm. Richard, Lord, 51, 52, 129, 145, 150, 151, 161, 162, 163, 164, 172, 187, 245, 246, 248, 251, 339; as peace commissioner, 149, 153, 154, 159; violates spirit of instructions, 171; campaign of 1777, . 183, 184; failure to blockade, 242; resigns, 197, 198
Howe, Gen. Robert, 354, 355, 356
Howe, Gen. Sir William, 70, 79, 100, 124, 125, 135, 148, 150, 151, 153, 175, 176, 188, 189, 193, 200, 245, 246, 271, 272, 276, 308, 331, 339, 371, 390, 400, 405; background of, 68; at Bunker Hill, 71, 72, 73, 74, 75, 76, 77; evacuates Boston, 105; at Long Island, 154, 155, 158, 159; takes New York City, 160, 161, 162; occupies New Jersey, 163, 164; failure to crush Washington, 171; several plans for 1777, 178, 179, 180, 181; sails from New York City, 182, 183, 184; Brandywine and Germantown, 185, 186, 187; resigns, 197, 198
Hubbardtown, N.Y., 190
Hudson River, 66, 84, 108, 115, 153, 177, 178, 179, 180, 183, 190, 191, 193, 195, 196
Huger, Gen. Isaac, 368, 370
Hughes, Sir William, 423
Humphreys, David, 261, 451–452
Hunt, John, 165
Huntington, Lt. Col. Ebenezer, 398, 401
Huntington, Gen. Jedediah, 400
Huntington, Samuel, 365
Hutchinson, Thomas, 3, 43

Ile aux Noix, 111
Ile Madame, 340
India, 423
Indians, 1, 3, 4, 12, 25, 31, 32, 33, 40, 64, 192. See also various tribes
Intolerable Acts. See Coercive Acts
Iredell, James, 261, 272–273
Iron production, 5
Iroquois, 3, 328, 329
Irvine, Gen. William, 330
Izard, Ralph, 236

*Jägers,* 2, 192, 433

Jamaica, 106, 120

James II (England), 14

James, Maj. Thomas, 35

Jay, John, 81, 159, 235, 236, 407, 424, 425, 426, 438, 439, 445, 461, 462

Jefferson, Thomas, 4, 18, 26, 82, 98, 133, 205, 265, 280, 306, 318, 324, 369, 378, 424, 425, 429, 435, 439, 444; Declaration of Independence, 115–119

Jenkinson, Charles, 140, 353

Jensen, Merrill, 450

Jervis, Capt. John, 129, 145

Jews, 134

Johnson, Guy, 325

Johnson, Capt. Henry, 340

Johnson, John, 325

Johnson, Dr. Samuel, 221, 412

Johnson, Sir William, 30, 31, 89, 90, 325

Johnston, Samuel, 263, 297

Jones, David, 266

Jones, Capt. John Paul, 319, 332, 335, 337, 338, 340, 341, 342, 344, 345, 348

Jones, Joseph, 219, 297

Jones, Thomas, 384

Kalb, Baron Johann de, 209, 211, 357, 359, 360, 399

Kaskaskia, 320, 322, 323

Kaunitz, Prince, 424

Kemble, Peter, 279

Kemble, Stephen, 164

Kennebec River, 110

Kentucky, 322, 323, 324, 325

Keppel, Adm. Augustus, Lord, 128, 129, 145, 244, 255, 344

Kettle Creek, S.C., 362

King George's War, 17, 82

King, Rufus, 440

King's Bench Prison, 42

King's Mountain, S.C., 11, 364, 434

Kingston, N.Y., 259

Kirkland, Moses, 275

Kirkwood, Capt. Robert, 373

Knollenberg, Bernard, 221

Knowles, Capt. Charles, 339

Knox, Gen. Henry, 93, 105, 160, 186, 189, 211, 212, 214, 218, 308, 382, 389, 438, 440; student of warfare, 2; favors

artillery school, 93; acquires Ticonderoga ordnance, 105; at Trenton, 167, 168; at Newburgh, 407, 408, 411; Secretary at War, 445, 446, 447, 448; on constitutional reform, 449, 451, 452

Knox, William, 43

Knyphausen, Gen. Wilhelm von, 133, 185

Loyalists, 9, 268, 271, 272, 273, 275, 355, 356, 357, 369, 371, 375, 384; nature of loyalism, 135–139; against patriot militia, 273, 274, 275; British planning in the South, 353–354; numbers inflated, 361, 367

Lafayette, Marie Joseph, Marquis de, 115, 215, 218, 220, 249, 378, 380, 428, 435

Lake Champlain, 66, 67, 84, 109, 162, 177, 180, 188

Lake George, 66, 105, 190, 191

Lamb, Sgt. Roger, 195, 197, 368

Lancaster, Pa., 102, 120, 306, 308, 419

Landis, Capt. Pierre, 341, 342, 344

Langdon, John, 454

Langdon, Samuel, 70

Laurens, Henry, 208, 211, 214, 218, 221, 395, 402, 413, 424, 425

Laurens, Col. John, 220, 221, 395, 413, 452

Laws, Capt., 114

Lawson, Gen. John, 369

League of Armed Neutrality, 236, 237

Lecky, W. E. H., 122

Lee, Arthur, 228, 230, 231, 235, 236, 345, 436

Lee, Charles, 4, 46, 47, 89, 99, 101, 106, 116, 120, 136, 137, 152, 164, 207, 211, 246, 247, 255, 261

Lee, Francis Lightfoot, 216

Lee, Henry, 250, 352, 369, 372, 373

Lee, Jesse, 276–277

Lee, Richard Henry, 34, 38, 117, 120, 216, 228, 248, 377, 444, 457

Lee, Gov. Thomas, 392

Lee, William, 228, 236

Le Havre, 344

Leith, Scotland, 342

L'Enfant, Pierre Charles, 310

Leslie, Gen. Alexander, 144, 366

Leutze, Emmanuel, 167

Levering, Jeremiah, 391

Levy, Leonard, 259
Lewis, Andrew, 11, 208
Lewis, Michael, 126
Lexington, Mass., 4, 29, 50, 57, 58, 59, 60, 61, 62, 63, 64, 65, 77, 79
Lincoln, Gen. Benjamin, 192, 208, 299, 354, 356, 357, 445, 448
Lipset, Seymour, 204
Livingston, Dr. Edward, 239
Livingston, Robert R., 297, 299, 427
Livingston, Gov. William, 188, 261, 284, 296, 405
Lloyd, William, 6, 87
Locke, John, 16, 46, 257, 375
Long Island, N.Y., 88, 153, 154, 155, 159, 166
Lord Dunmore's War, 8
Loring, Betsy, 164
Loring, Joshua, 164
Loudoun, Earl of (John Campbell), 19, 20, 22
Louis XIV (France), 33
Louis XV (France), 227
Louis XVI (France), 230, 231, 232, 233, 379
Louisbourg, 6, 9, 10, 21, 68
Lovell, James, 44, 205, 210, 211, 216, 217, 219, 221, 377
Loyalty oaths, 269–270
Luttrell, John, 52, 145
Luzerne, César Anne, Chevalier de la, 299, 372
Lynch, Thomas, 97

Macaulay, Catherine, 14, 205
Mackenzie, Col. Frederick, 125
Mackenzie, Maj. Roderick, 362
Mackesy, Piers, 122, 241, 433
Maclaine, Archibald, 461
Maclean, Col. Allen, 112, 114, 135, 138
Macmillan, Margaret B., 295
McCarthy, Sen. Joseph, 220
McCrea, Jane, 191, 201
McDougall, Gen. Alexander, 164, 186, 406, 407, 408
McGillivray, Alexander, 446
McIntosh, Gen. Lachlan, 327, 328
McKean, Thomas, 460
McWilliams, Maj., 217

Madison, James, 79, 120, 408, 438; in Congress, 294, 296, 297, 298; on the Constitution, 451, 452, 453, 455, 456, 460, 466
Magaw, Col. Robert, 162
Mahan, Alfred, 244, 345
Main, Jackson T., 292
Malden, Mass., 389
Malouine Islands, 229
Manufacturers, 303–308
Marion, Gen. Francis, 351, 352, 362, 365, 372, 373
Marshall, Christopher, 210
Martin, Joseph Plumb, 392, 399
Martin, Gov. Josiah, 115, 135
Martin, Luther, 453
Martinique, 303
Marine Corps, 335
Maryland, 92, 108, 135, 263, 274, 307, 394, 395
Mason, George, 206, 454, 455, 456
Massachusetts, 8, 9, 20, 22, 37, 42, 43, 45, 46, 47, 48, 50, 51, 63, 69, 70, 77, 82, 83, 85, 103, 206, 263, 266, 389, 394, 395, 397, 402, 447, 448, 450, 451
Massachusetts Provincial Congress, 47, 59, 65, 66, 77, 82, 95
Mathews, John, 297, 298, 360
Maudit, Israel, 238
Mawhood, Col. Charles, 169, 171
Mayhew, Jonathan, 107
Mecklenburg County, N.C., 262, 359, 363
Menatomy, Mass., 59
Mercer, Gen. Hugh, 169
Methodists, 276–277
Miami Indians, 320
Michilimackinac, 29, 320
Middleton, Col. Henry, 21
Mifflin, Gen. Thomas, 46, 168, 207, 208, 212, 216, 218, 222
Militia, 94, 104–105, 192, 385; colonial, 7–13; engages loyalists, 273–275; postwar reorganization proposals, 441–445; and Federal Constitution, 454, 455, 456, 457, 458, 459, 460, 461, 462, 463
Militia Act of 1792, 462
Miller, Perry, 267
Millis, Walter, 11, 93, 449
Minorca, 130, 232, 255, 422, 427

Miquelon, 427
Mob activity, 48–51. *See also* Stamp Act Crisis; Militia; Loyalists
Mobile, 232, 320
Mohawk Indians, 320
Molasses Act, 31
Molesworth, Robert, 15, 33
Monge, Gaspard, 310
Monmouth, N.J., 88, 246, 255
Monmouth's Rebellion, 15
Monroe, Lt. James, 168, 444
Montagu, Edward, 15
Montgomery, Gen. Richard, 90, 91, 109, 110, 111, 112, 113, 114, 167
Montreal, 9, 21, 111, 112
Moore, Charles, 96
Moore's Creek Bridge, 9, 135, 137, 275
Morgan, Gen. Daniel, 3, 182, 218, 220, 246; raises riflemen, 102; Quebec campaign, 110, 113, 114; opposes Burgoyne, 189, 194, 196, 197; in the South, 352, 365, 366, 367, 368, 378, 383, 384, 385, 401, 403, 434
Morgan, Edmund S., 37
Morgan, Dr. John, 312
Morison, S. E., 335
Morris, David H., 391
Morris, Gouverneur, 407, 408, 438, 451, 456
Morris, Lt. Col. Lewis, 413
Morris, Richard B., 432
Morris, Robert, 299, 300, 301, 302, 303, 313, 335, 348, 390, 407, 408, 410, 411, 438, 444, 445
Morristown, N.J., 165, 170, 182, 399, 403
Mount Holly, N.J., 168
Mount Vernon, 86, 87, 428, 451
Moyle, Walter, 15
Muhlenberg, Gen. Peter H., 267
Murray, Capt. James, 64
Mutiny Act, 15, 18, 19, 20, 36, 44
Mystic River, 73, 74, 76, 98

Namier, Sir Lewis, 118
Navy, American, 331–346, 349, 441, 462
Navy, British, 125–129; machinery in London, 139–144; strategy for, 242–243
Needham, Mass., 63
Nef, John U., 310

Negroes, 12, 25, 61, 123, 389, 394–397, 401, 416
Nelson, Gen. Thomas, 378
Nettels, Curtis, 288
Nevins, Allan, 221
Nevis, 421
New Bedford, Conn., 250
New Bern, N.C., 263
New Brunswick, N.J., 163, 166, 170, 182
New England. *See* the various colony-states
New Hampshire, 9, 21, 48, 50, 104, 306
New Ipswich, N.H., 390
New Jersey, 35, 37, 92, 163–171 *passim*, 178, 179, 183, 206, 210, 268, 272, 273, 305, 307, 406, 445
New Orleans, 320, 324
New Providence expedition, 106
New York, 16, 20, 21, 35, 37, 38, 83, 85, 90, 92, 135, 150, 176, 177, 178, 242, 244, 248, 249, 250, 251, 259, 268, 279, 280, 292, 395, 445
New York City, 5, 66, 115, 151, 154, 159, 160, 171, 176, 177, 179, 183, 271, 274, 339, 376, 377, 379, 380, 381, 390, 428
New York Restraining Act, 38, 39
Newburgh Addresses, 405–411, 439
Newfoundland fisheries, 424, 426
Newport, R.I., 5, 50, 150, 161, 178, 242, 244, 248, 376, 379
Newspapers, 258–260
Niagara, 21, 29, 320, 325, 328, 331, 445
Nicholas, Samuel, 338
Nicholson, Capt. James, 340, 345
Nicola, Col. Lewis, 440
Ninety-Six, S.C., 357, 371, 373
North Carolina, 135, 136, 268, 271, 272–273, 285, 292
North, Frederick, Lord North (courtesy title), 52, 126, 134, 144, 145, 148, 240, 241, 242, 353, 383; as cabinet leader, 139, 143; fall of, 421, 422
Nova Scotia, 9, 121, 135, 340

Ogden, Col. Matthias, 406, 408
O'Hara, Gen. Charles, 144, 367, 368, 372
Olive Branch Petition, 118
Oliver, Peter, 73, 75
Oneida Indians, 320

Onondaga Indians, 320, 339
Orangeburg, S.C., 372, 373
Ordinance of 1785, 412
Oriskany, N.Y., 193
Orvilliers, Adm. d', 244, 344
Osgood, Samuel, 441
Oswald, Eleazer, 458
Oswald, Richard, 423, 425, 426
Otis, James, 16, 34, 66, 285, 449
Otis, Samuel A., 6
Ottawa Indians, 320

Paine, Thomas, 116, 165, 229, 252, 261, 262, 265, 268, 275, 277, 289, 293, 307, 331, 357
Palmer, John McAuley, 433, 443
Palmer, Robert R., 382, 432
Pares, Richard, 238
Paret, Peter, 433
Parker, Capt. John, 59, 60, 61
Parker, Jonas, 61
Parker, Sir Peter, 129, 135, 136
Parkman, Francis, 22
Parliament, 14, 15, 18, 19, 20, 33, 34, 35, 36, 39, 42, 44, 49, 51, 93, 124, 129, 132, 148, 155, 240, 383, 414, 421, 425, 430, 431
*Parliamentary History*, 122
Parsons, Gen. Samuel H., 403
Paterson, John, 187
Paterson, William, 272, 273, 453
Peale, Charles W., 96
Pearson, Capt. Richard, 342, 344
Peckham, Howard H., 389
Peekskill, N.Y., 186
Pelham Bay, N.Y., 161, 166
Pells Point, N.Y., 161
Pemberton, James, 276
Pendleton, Edmund, 444
Pennington, N.J., 164
Pennsylvania, 27, 95, 99, 108, 135, 188, 206, 210, 263, 268, 272, 279, 280, 285, 291, 292, 301, 307, 397, 445
Pensacola, 29, 244, 320
Pepperrell, William, 6
Percy, Gen. Hugh, Earl, 63, 161
Peters, Richard, 220
Petersburg, Va., 377
Philadelphia, 46, 49, 82, 83, 84, 92, 94, 95, 98, 99, 119, 176, 178, 179, 180, 181, 182, 183, 184, 185, 186, 209, 242, 245, 251, 262, 266, 306, 339
Phillips, Gen. William, 144, 370, 376, 377
Pickens, Gen. Andrew, 11, 362, 366, 367
Pickering, Timothy, 4, 12-13, 47 48, 211, 218
Pigot, Gen. Robert, 73, 74, 79, 248
Pinckney, Charles, 454
Pinckney, Charles Cotesworth, 454, 455, 456
Pitcairn, Maj. John, 59, 61, 62, 63, 73, 78
Pitkin, Gov. William, 41, 42
Pitt, William, 20, 38, 51, 52, 122, 145, 238, 240, 241, 242, 253
Pittsburgh. *See* Fort Pitt
Pointe aux Trembles, 113
Poland, 239
Pollok, Cullen, 277, 278
Pollock, Oliver, 324
Pomeroy, Gen. Seth, 90, 103
Pontiac's Rebellion, 30
Poniatowski, Stanislas, 46
Poor, Gen. Enoch, 196, 329
Port au Prince, 305
Port Royal, 6, 9
Portsmouth, N.H., 50, 339
Portugal, 30, 69
Poughkeepsie, N.Y., 259
Preble, Jedediah, 47
Prescott, Dr. Samuel, 59
Prescott, Col. William, 67, 70, 71, 72, 73, 75, 79
Preston, Maj. Charles, 111
Prevost, Gen. Augustine, 354, 355, 356
Price, Dr. Richard, 435
Priestly, Joseph, 451
Prince Edward Island, 106
Princeton, N.J., 88, 164, 169, 170
Privateering, 99, 337–338, 340
Privy Council, 38, 50
Proclamation of 1763, 31, 40
Prussia, 236, 238, 239
Pugh, Evan, 357
Pulaski, Count Casimir, 214
Putnam, Gen. Israel, 66, 67, 71, 74, 79, 90, 103, 105, 154, 155, 403, 463
Putnam, Gen. Rufus, 440

Quakers, 134, 261, 275, 276, 397

Quarles, Benjamin, 396
Quartering Act, 36–39, 55
Quebec, 6, 9, 10, 12, 21, 40, 41, 73, 107, 112, 113, 114, 115, 121, 135, 162, 167, 263
Quebec Act, 107, 121
Queen Anne's War, 47
Quesnay, François, 13
Quincy, Josiah, Jr., 14, 16, 34, 44

Rall, Col. Johann Gottlieb, 166, 167, 168, 171
Ramsay, David, 264, 294, 307, 357, 395
Ramsour's Mill, N.C., 368, 370
Randolph, Edmund, 96, 290, 452, 453, 456, 460, 461
Rankin, Col. William, 378, 379
Rapin, Paul, 14
Rawdon, Francis, Lord, 75, 124, 152, 372, 373, 374, 375
Ray, Martha, 126
Rayneval, M. de, 425, 426
Read, Capt. Thomas, 345
Reed, Joseph, 101, 159, 211, 222, 404
Reveley, John, 308
Revere, Paul, 58, 59, 60, 77
Rhode Island, 48, 66, 90, 171, 248, 249, 269, 307, 356, 394, 397, 407
Richardson, Richard, 11, 275
Richmond, Duke of (Charles Lennox), 24
Richmond, Va., 48
Riedesel, Baron von, 188, 191, 194, 195, 196
Riedesel, Baroness Frederika, 188, 191, 196, 197
Riflemen, 5, 102–103, 104, 120. See also Daniel Morgan
Riker, Theodore, 457
Rittenhouse, David, 307, 311
Rivington, James, 274, 280
Robbins, Carolyn, 15
Robertson, Lt. Col. James, 36
Robinson-Morris, Matthew, 24
Robson, Eric, 367
Rochambeau, Jean Baptiste Donatier, Comte de, 379, 381, 388
Rockingham, Marquis of (Charles Wat-son-Wentworth), 36, 122, 240, 421, 422, 423, 425
Rocky Mount, S.C., 357
Roderique Hortalez and Co., 233, 234
Rodney, Adm. George, 129, 316, 379, 381
Rossiter, Clinton, 107
Rousseau, Jean Jacques, 13, 46
Rowan County, N.C., 363
Rowlandson, Mary, 3
Roxbury, Mass., 63, 105
Rozenthal, Gustav, 224
Rush, Dr. Benjamin, 89, 205, 209, 210, 211, 216, 217, 219, 221, 224, 225, 307, 311, 411, 449; medical contributions of, 312
Russia, 49, 130, 236, 239. See also League of Armed Neutrality
Rutledge, Edward, 159
Rutledge, John, 273, 356, 361

Sackville, George. See Lord George Germain
Sail, John, 393
St. Augustine, 29, 40, 42, 244
St. Clair, Gen. Arthur, 189, 190, 207
St. Croix, 303
St. Eustatius, 303, 316
St. Lawrence River, 9, 108, 110, 112, 114
St. Leger, Lt. Col. Barry, 193, 395
St. Lucia, 244, 249, 353
St. Malo, 344
St. Pierre, 427
Saints, Battle of, 422, 423
Salem, Mass., 4, 50
Saltonstall, Dudley, 335, 338
Sampson, Deborah, 398
Sandwich, Earl of (John Montagu), 143, 145, 244, 255; optimism of, 52; management of the Admiralty, 125, 126, 127, 129; resigns, 422
Saratoga, N.Y., 196, 197
Savannah, Ga., 150, 249, 354, 371, 373, 374
Saxe, Marshall, 69, 76
Scharnhorst, Gerhard von, 87, 433
Schlesinger, Arthur M., 259
Schubart, Christian, 131
Schuyler, Gen. Philip, 182, 206, 208, 218, 274, 395, 403; political influence of, 90,

Schuyler, Gen. Philip (*cont.*) 443; Canadian campaign, 109, 110, 111, 112; upper New York, 189, 190, 192, 193, 195, 203, 204

Scientific activity, 309–313

Seume, Johann G., 132

Secker, Thomas, 283

Seneca Indians, 320, 329, 330

Senegal, 427

*Serapis*, 34

Sergeant, Jonathan D., 210, 211

Serle, Ambrose, 165, 258, 276

Seven Years' War, 10, 18, 19, 22, 23, 29, 30, 31, 34, 69, 126, 127, 151, 394, 433

Sevier, Col. John, 67, 351, 364

Shaftesbury, Earl of (Sir Anthony Ashley Cooper), 14

Sharpe, Gov. Horatio, 33

Shawnee Indians, 330

Shays, Daniel, 447

Shays' Rebellion, 447–448

Shelburne, Earl of (William Petty), 38, 39, 422, 423, 425, 426, 427, 429, 430

Shelby, Col. Isaac, 351, 364

Shepherd, Gen. William, 448

Shepherdstown, Va., 102

Sherman, Roger, 91, 455

Sherwood, Joseph, 54

Shippen, Dr. William, 312

Shirley, Gov. William, 17

Shurtleff, Robert, 398

Shy, John, 93

Sidney, Algernon, 14

Simpson, Lt. Thomas, 337

Six Nations, 31

Skene, Philip, 190

Smallwood, Gen. William, 186

Smith, Adam, 229, 234

Smith, Lt. Col. Francis, 50, 58, 59, 62, 63

Smith, Jonathan B., 220, 221

Smith, Melancthon, 458

Smith, Paul, 379

Society of the Cincinnati, 439–441, 449, 458

Sons of Liberty, 35

Sorel River, 68, 109, 110, 111

South Carolina, 4, 16, 20, 35, 37, 50, 136, 235, 266, 353, 355, 394, 395, 396

Spain, 5, 14, 52, 116, 123, 126, 197, 225, 226, 228, 235, 236, 239, 240, 253, 420, 422, 423, 424, 425, 426, 427

Sparks, Jared, 221

Spencer, Gen. Joseph, 66, 90, 103

Springfield, Mass., 447, 448

Stamp Act Crisis, 17, 34–36

Stanwix, Gen. John, 31

Stark, John, 11, 66, 73, 74, 192, 193, 263

Stedman, Charles, 158, 361, 368

Stephen, Gen. Adam, 186, 208

Steuben, Friedrich Wilhelm von, 214, 222, 246, 247, 255, 378, 413, 443

Stevens, Gen. Edward, 208, 359

Stewart, Lt. Col. Alexander, 373, 374

Stewart, Col. Walter, 410

Stiles, Ezra, 45, 50, 283

Stirling, Lord (William Alexander), 155, 208, 216, 217, 218, 224

Stockbridge Indians, 321

Stuart, Col. Charles, 124, 125, 175, 183, 412

Stuart, John, 321

Suffren, Balli de, 423

Sugar Act, 34

Sullivan, Gen. John, 90, 91, 115, 167, 168, 186, 187, 189, 207, 208, 215, 248, 297; at Long Island, 155; at Brandywine, 185; Indian campaign, 328, 329, 330; in Congress, 405

Sullivan's Island, 136

Sumter, Gen. Thomas, 67, 352, 361, 362, 373, 385

Sutherland, Lt. William, 63

Talmadge, Benjamin, 158

Tarleton, Lt. Col. Banastre, 361, 363, 366

Ternay, Charles Louis, Chevalier de, 379

Terrell, Anne, 262

Thatcher, Dr. James, 312

Thomas, Gen. John, 90, 91, 103, 115

Thompson, Benjamin, 277

Thurlow, Edward, Attorney General, 51–52

Tilghman, Tench, 218

Timothy, Peter, 258

Tobago, 427

Todd, Col. John, 325

Townshend, Charles, 40–41

Trenchard, John, 15, 33, 44

Trenton, N.J., 88, 163, 165–170, 308

Trevelyan, G. O., 122
Trumbull, Gov. Jonathan, 306
Tryon, Gov. William, 152, 179
Tryon County, N.Y., 274
Tucker, Samuel, 164
Tupper, Gen. Benjamin, 440
Turgot, Anne Robert Jacques, 13
Turkey, 130, 249
Tuscany, 236
Tuscarora Indians, 320

Upton, Gen. Emory, 6, 39, 443

Valley Forge, Pa., 187, 212, 215, 219,
    221, 246, 247, 294, 297, 305, 306, 399
Van Rensselaer, Gen. Robert, 329
Van Schaack, Peter, 277
Van Tyne, Claude H., 277, 294
Varnum, Gen. James, 218, 220, 297, 399
Vaughan, Gen. John, 195
Vergennes, Charles Gravier, Comte de,
    226, 230, 232, 233, 239, 344, 424, 426,
    427, 436
Vetch, Samuel, 6
Vincennes, 320, 324
Virginia, 8, 21, 48, 85, 87, 99, 136, 266,
    269, 274, 340, 376, 377, 378, 380, 386,
    394, 396
Voltaire, 13

Wabash, 320
Wadsworth, Benjamin, 3
Wait, Thomas, 457
Waldeck, 130–133 passim
Waldo, Dr. Albigense, 399
Walker, Adm. Hovenden, 10
Wallingford, Conn., 35
Walpole, Horace, 238
Walton, Col. George, 354
War of the League of Augsburg, 15, 33
War of the Regulation, 8
Ward, Artemas, 47, 65, 66, 70, 80, 85, 89,
    98
Ward, Christopher, 62, 76
Warner, Seth, 11, 67, 192
Warren, James, 84, 106, 108, 205, 440, 441,
    449

Warren, Dr. Joseph, 16, 44, 45, 58, 66, 72,
    75, 79, 82, 95
Warren, Mercy, 55, 104, 449
Washington, Gen. George, 26, 46, 69, 76,
    96, 97, 115, 116, 120, 121, 122, 133, 207,
    212, 213, 215, 223, 224, 266, 267, 268,
    269, 277, 294, 298, 307, 332, 353, 379,
    388, 390, 392, 399, 400, 405, 413, 414,
    415, 428, 438; in French and Indian
    War, 2, 3, 19; appointed commander in
    chief, 8, 65, 85; qualification of, 85–88,
    106, 171; at Boston, 98, 99, 100, 103, 104,
    106; at New York City, 152, 158, 160,
    161, 162; evacuates New Jersey, 163,
    164, 165; at Trenton and Princeton,
    165, 166, 167, 168, 169, 170, 171; in cam-
    paign of 1777, 181, 182, 183, 184, 187,
    189, 193, 194, 202; critics of, 209, 210,
    211; Conway Cabal, 216–222; campaign
    of 1778, 246, 247, 248, 249; assists Sulli-
    van's expedition, 328; Yorktown cam-
    paign, 379, 380, 381, 382, 383; at New-
    burgh, 406–412 passim; inspires troops,
    413, 415; as a disciplinarian, 414–415;
    on a peacetime establishment, 441–443,
    444; supports constitutional reform,
    452; symbol of nationalism, 264
Washington, John A., 164
Washington, Lt. Col. William, 168, 366,
    369
Watertown, Mass., 63, 65
Wayne, Gen. Anthony, 187, 211, 378,
    403, 404, 405
Weathersfield, Conn., 380
Webster, Lt. Col. James, 370
Webster, Noah, 459
Wedderburn, Alexander, 52
Weems, Mason L., 88, 209, 361
Wentworth, Gov. Benning, 17, 42
Wentworth, Gov. John, 145
Wentworth, Paul, 239
Wesley, John, 123, 276
West Indies, 16, 116, 128, 249, 250, 251,
    252, 303, 305, 380, 381, 382, 422, 423, 429
West Point, N.Y., 403, 445, 447
Westborough, Mass, 311
Wheeling, 320

Wheelock, Eleazer, 279
White Plains, N.Y., 161, 248
Whitehaven, Scotland, 341
Whitemarsh, N.Y., 188
Whitney, Eli, 311, 318
Wickes, Capt. Lambert, 339
Wilkes, John, 42, 431
Wilkinson, James, 217, 224
Willcox, William, 243, 376
William III (England), 15, 33, 459
Williams, Col. Otho H., 360, 369
Williamsburg, Va., 9, 50, 324
Williamson, Gen. Andrew, 275, 357
Williamson, Col. David, 322
Willing, Thomas, 6
Wilmington, Del., 183
Wilson, James, 26, 213, 438, 441, 461, 462
Winchester, Va., 102

Winslow, Edward, 137
Winthrop, James, 104, 457
Winthrop, John, 307
Wolfe, Gen. James, 6, 21, 69, 73, 76, 107, 112
Women, 262–263, 397–398
Wooster, Gen. David, 90, 114
Worcester, Mass., 258
Wormley, Ralph, 279
Wright, Gov. James, 27
Wyandot Indians, 320
Wyoming Massacre, 325, 327, 328
Wythe, George, 334

Yorkshire Association, 421, 430
Yorktown, Va., 86, 299, 301, 345, 351, 379, 380, 381, 382, 383
Young, Capt. James, 339